To Doug Lenat,
for being more th
this attempt to launch me
upper ontology

Bertrand du Castel
50 Pascal dr
Ros Roy
ducastel@pls.com

# Computer
# Theology

# Computer Theology

*Intelligent Design*
*of the World Wide Web*

**Bertrand du Castel**

**Timothy M. Jurgensen**

Midori Press

Austin, Texas

# COMPUTER THEOLOGY

## Intelligent Design of the World Wide Web

By: Bertrand du Castel and Timothy M. Jurgensen

## Published by:

Midori Press LLC
2720 Mt. Laurel Lane
Austin, TX 78703 USA

http://midoripress.com

First edition, 2008
Printed in the United States of America

ISBN-13: 978-0-9801821-1-8
ISBN-10: 0-9801821-1-5
Library of Congress SR 1-33735636 (Review Edition, 2007)

## Warning and Disclaimer

## Trademark Acknowledgments

Blackberry is a trademark of Research In Motion. CATIA is a trademark of Dassault Systems. IBM 650, IBM 1620, IBM 407, IBM1401, IBM1410, IBM 360, IBM 370, OS/360, OS/370 and OS/2, are trademarks of IBM. iPod, Lisa and Macintosh are trademarks of Apple. Java and Java Card are trademarks of Sun Microsystems. LINUX is a trademark of Linus Torvalds. Multos is a trademark of Maosco Ltd. MS-DOS, Word and Windows are trademarks of Microsoft. Skype is a trademark of Skype Ltd. UNIX is a trademark of The Open Group. All other products or services mentioned in this book are the trademarks or service marks of their respective companies or organizations.

**Cover**: Rock art at Cueva de las Manos, Patagonia, Argentina, UNESCO World Heritage

# Dedications

Bertrand du Castel:

## To Christine, Clémente, Julien-Marie and Léonard

Timothy M. Jurgensen:

## To Becky, Miriam, Sarah and Kevin

# Acknowledgments

This book has been a work in progress for longer than we might like to admit. During the course of this work, we have been privy to countless discussions with our friends and colleagues. We gratefully acknowledge the contribution that these discussion have made to the form and content of this work and we express our heartfelt thanks to all those who so participated. There is always a risk when extending thanks to specific people that some may be overlooked, and to anyone so offended we offer our sincere apologies. However, we feel compelled to make special note of a few people who have been especially generous with their time and thoughts on our rather arcane endeavor.

The authors would like to thank two precursors in the field of computer theology, Anne Foerst in *God in the Machine* and Donald Knuth in *Things a Computer Scientist Rarely Talks About*. They opened the door to us.

Bertrand thanks Reid Smith and the directors of the Association for the Advancement of Artificial Intelligence for inviting him at the 2000 AAAI meeting to make a presentation which would become the forerunner for this work. Then the students at the University of Maryland at Baltimore County, Massachusetts Institute of Technology, University of Texas at Austin, Purdue University, Peking University, Tsinghua University, University of Hannover, University of Grenoble and University of Paris, commented on subsequent versions of the presentation that eventually led to this project, when Tim offered that it was possible to transform this set of tentative ideas into a comprehensive work of religion and science. I would like to thank the computer security community that participated for so many years in several organizations that I had the honor to found and participate in as chairman or president, in particular the Java Card Forum, where Tim and I had the opportunity to not only discuss the topics at hand, but also to launch this book in Berlin, Germany, in 2005. Finally I thank my former colleagues at Axalto, now Gemalto; and foremost the management and the employees of Schlumberger, for their promotion of fundamental values of scientific integrity that are as good for the business as they are for the human adventure. I have a particular debt towards Schlumberger Fellows Fikri Kuchuk and Mike Sheppard for penetrating critique. Eric Abecassis, Guillermo Arango, Danièle Cuzin, Richard Dollet, Tim Finin, Thomas Fisher, Zhian Hedayati, Philippe Lacour-Gayet, Mark Leveno, Robert Leydier, Mathias Lorieux, Yi Mao, Yogi Mehta, Fiona Pattinson, Elena and Jean-Claude Perrin, Guy Pujolle, Alain Rhelimi and Alain Sigaud contributed erudite insights during discussions that, one way or another, shaped my thoughts. After the long evenings and week-ends and all my ratiocinations, I owe so much for my family support, which extended to helping elaborate parts of the book, including cover design by Léonard, and picture by Clémente. Moreover, my wife Christine suggested that Computer Theology is about Intelligent Design of the World Wide Web.

Tim would like to acknowledge the seminal discussions about the broader aspects of privacy and identity with Ken Binion and Marilyn Binion. Discussions regarding religion and technology with Mike Montgomery and with Ksheerabdhi Krishna were of great benefit. Gerry Smith was an excellent sounding board for some of our early ideas, with the sidewalk cafés of Paris providing an incredible backdrop. Scott Guthery and Mary Cronin were invaluable sources of technical expertise along with a wealth of encouragement. Ann Daniel has been a marvelous source of publishing guidance and general encouragement. Sarah Bremer offered a number of extremely relevant observations on art, art history and legal scholarship. Miriam Jurgensen offered a wealth of information regarding presentation and artistic interpretation. Theresa Schwarzhoff and Jeffrey Cua provided a number of interesting insights on concepts of political discourse. Mike Neumann has offered many discussions on the relationship between secure computing and religious interpretation.

Through the course of this writing, Bill Carlson has often lent a friendly ear and offered many useful suggestions. Ed Dolph has always been there to offer his support. Last and most, I must recognize the incredible patience and support from my wife, Becky.

## Thanks to Our Reviewers

In order to help us in our interdisciplinary enterprise, we published in November, 2007, a limited edition of this book (ISBN 0-9801821-0-7) that we submitted to a panel of reviewers of various backgrounds and expertise. While we do not construe their review and subsequent comments as an endorsement of the assertions and conclusions that we draw nor as an endorsement by the organizations with which they are affiliated, we definitely owe them a debt of gratitude in their helping us in our attempts to build a better argument and in their correcting many of our miscomprehensions.

That said, the deficiencies that remain in the book are ours alone.

The following are an integral part of our effort:

| | |
|---|---|
| Saad Bargach, M.S. | Managing Director, Lime Rock Partners |
| Harry Barrow, Ph.D. | Fellow of the Association for the Advancement of Artificial Intelligence, Scientific Advisor at Schlumberger |
| Ken Binion | Assistant VP - Commercial Credit Reviewer, Sterling Savings Bank |
| Marilyn Binion, Esq., J.D. | Semi-retired attorney and author |
| Kevin Bremer, M.B.A. | Server and Workstation Market Analyst, Advanced Micro Devices |
| Jerome Denis, Ph.D. | Marketing Director at Gemalto |
| Yi Mao, Ph.D. | Principal Consultant, atsec |
| Mike Montgomery, M.S. | Scientific Advisor at Schlumberger |
| Fiona Pattinson, M.S. | Director Business Development & Strategy at atsec |
| Elena Perrin, M.D. | Eli Lilly Fellow, Director European Medical Team at Eli Lilly |
| Mireille Piot, Ph.D. | Professor of General Linguistics, University of Grenoble |
| Leonard Pojunas, Esq. | General Counsel, North America, Gemalto |
| Guy Pujolle, Ph.D. | Professor of Computer Science at the University of Paris, Professor Honoris Causa at Beijing University of Posts and Telecommunications |
| Bob Schwartzhoff, Ph.D. | Defense Intelligence Agency |
| Mike Sheppard DPhil | Schlumberger Fellow, Honorary Fellow of Darwin College, Cambridge |
| Edward L. Shirley, Ph.D. | Professor of Religious Studies, St. Edward's University |
| Gerald Smith, B.S. | Senior Consultant at Identification Technology Partners |
| Claire Vishik, Ph.D. | Security & Privacy Standards & Policy Manager at Intel Corporation |

Once again, we want to warmly thank our reviewers and the numerous others who helped us along the way, for the honor they granted us in participating in our journey.

# About the authors

Bertrand du Castel is a Schlumberger Fellow, with publications in artificial intelligence, linguistics, logic and software engineering. As chairman of several computer organizations, he won in 2005 the coveted Visionary Award from Card Technology magazine. Bertrand has an Engineer Diploma from École Polytechnique and a PhD in Theoretical Computer Science from the University of Paris-Sorbonne.

Timothy M. Jurgensen has authored two acclaimed books on computer security as well as publications in communications and physics. As a consultant to government and industry, Tim is a key contributor to the evolution of the network infrastructure of the United States. He has taught in the Graduate School of the University of Hong Kong and at the University of Texas at Austin. He has a BS from Oklahoma State University, an MA from Rice University and a PhD in Nuclear Physics from Rice University.

# Contents

# 8 In Search of Enlightenment 249

# 9 Mutation 293

# 10 Power of Prayer 341

# Dieu et mon droit

*Begin at the beginning and go on till you come to the end: then stop.*

The King in *Alice in Wonderland*
by Lewis Carroll

---

We hold these truths to be self-evident, that all men are created equal, that they are endowed by their Creator with certain unalienable Rights, that among these are Life, Liberty and the pursuit of Happiness. — That to secure these rights, Governments are instituted among Men, deriving their just powers from the consent of the governed, — That whenever any Form of Government becomes destructive of these ends, it is the Right of the People to alter or to abolish it, and to institute new Government, laying its foundation on such principles and organizing its powers in such form, as to them shall seem most likely to effect their Safety and Happiness.

From the *Declaration of Independence*

---

These seminal words of the social order of the United States of America provide a rare direct illustration of an evolutionary event known as *speciation*; the creation of new species from old. From these words, we can begin to draw parallels between biological processes and social order. The Declaration of Independence is grounded in the metaphorical understanding from which is derived context sensitive communication. Consider that a mere 15 years after it was published, a subsequent defining document of the social order, the Constitution of the United States of America prescribed that men were significantly superior to women and that black men or women were distinctly less than equal to either white men or women. Women of any hue were not allowed to participate in the governance so divined and black people of any gender were declared worth three fifths of a person for purposes of establishing participatory power within this governance structure. Otherwise, they could be property owned and traded as chattel goods. The words "equal" and "Rights" were metaphors meshed in the social interactions of the time. That one could look upon these words and derive from them something other than gender independent suffrage, and in particular could draw from them an acceptance of human slavery, is critically foreign to our current mores. Such is the double-edged sword instilled in metaphorical understanding. As the 42nd President of the United States suggested to us, "It depends on what the definition of 'is' is." Despite its somewhat self-serving nature, this was in fact a prescient observation.

Computers are complex tools of the human species. To make them work well for us, we have to specify their actions in very great detail. When properly instructed, networks of computers take on the trappings of human social orders derived from the physiological characteristics and capabilities of our species. To create a social order, we engage in grouping mechanisms through which the actions of the individuals within the group are influenced. From a technical perspective, such grouping mechanisms form the trust environments within which we can effect policy. Historically, the most comprehensive such environments have been formed by religions. Within a specific religion, the policy framework is established by a statement of theology. So, if we connect all the dots, when we want to tell our computers how to act in a manner paralleling human social orders, we must define for them a theology. Thus, we come to the beginning of the path on which we'll journey during the course of this book. As the epigram above suggests, we plan to go on until we come to the end. Then, we'll stop.

Our beginning is the assertion that trust and policy are salient features of human social organizations and in particular of their iconic form that we know as religion. Hence, the title of this prologue seems pertinent; *Dieu et mon droit*. Literally translated, "God and my right" is emblazoned on the Official Coat of Arms of Great Britain and Northern Ireland and displayed throughout the world. It is the motto of the Sovereign, forming an integral element of the Royal Coat of Arms as well. This motto addresses the most basic features of what we will come to describe as a social ecosystem. The British Monarchy comprises such a social ecosystem, characterized first by a trust infrastructure, in this case derived from God. Encompassed by this trust infrastructure is then found a policy infrastructure, in this case based on the divinely granted rights of man. Continuing down the path that we've started, *Computer Theology* then is a book about *trust*, specifically encompassing the manner in which trust is establish and projected as the basis for adhering to policy. It is equally a book about *policy*, including its definition, implementation and application. Its ongoing theme is the development of a highly nuanced understanding of these rather commonly used concepts.

In its most basic guise, policy is the establishment of the rules of interactions. It can be simple; a door with a sign marked PULL for example. This illustrates the concept of an almost intuitive policy aimed at establishing the rules of interaction between a person and a door. Pull on the door and it will open; at least, that's the promise of the sign. Push on the door and it remains closed. So, how is this policy implemented? Well, the door is constructed such that the hinges allow it to open in only one direction, so the implementation of the policy is built into the door. What's the consequence for the application of this policy? If one adheres to the policy then the door opens; if not, the door stays closed. Not exactly rocket science, but if you run full tilt into a door marked PULL rather than PUSH, it's likely to hurt no matter how smart you are.

With only a bit of extrapolation, policy can become significantly more complex. Consider that you'd like to visit a friend in her apartment on the upper east side of New York City. The street level front door of her restricted apartment building might display a sign beside an intercom transceiver that states the simple instruction, "Call the apartment you are visiting for admittance." When contacted through the intercom, your friend in her apartment presses a button to disable the front door lock; the door lock buzzes, thus letting you know when to pull the door. This policy for getting through a door now encompasses a *protocol* for the conduct of the interaction.

A protocol is a method comprised of a series of well-defined steps. Through this method we can implement policy. Consider the following statement of policy, one of the first rules that we teach our children: "Never talk to strangers!" This imperative forms a rather succinct admonition that belies a potentially complex set of steps, in other words a protocol that we want children to perform as they engage in conversation with another person. First, we need for the child to recognize the start of the conversation. An infant will communicate with those around it, but it speaks when it wants to speak, such as when it's hungry. It listens when it wants to listen, such as when it's bored and wants to be entertained. The concept of a formal conversation, with a beginning, middle and end has yet to be learned. So, we seek to teach the toddler to develop the process in steps, and the first step is to recognize the start. At the start of a conversation, it is important to consider who is being spoken to or listened to. Part of the start is to ascertain whether that person is a threat. Is it someone that it's all right to talk to? If the person, once recognized, is assessed to not be a stranger, then the conversation can begin. Otherwise, an alternative course of action is called for. We might tell the child to "Be aware!" or we might suggest a stronger reaction; "Run away!"

Thus far, our defined steps aren't too difficult, except for the points that we haven't thus far considered. We haven't yet defined what it means to recognize someone. Nor have we said how we determine that they're not a threat. Well, good grief! These seemingly simple concepts called trust and policy, along with an equally simple concept called a protocol for implementing trusted policy, suddenly offers the prospect of getting a bit out of hand. Trust us, it gets worse! For example, we certainly need to more fully consider what trust really means. When we ask for trust, as we've just done, how does that relate to subsequent interactions that are driven by policy? For an answer, it will help if we first delve a bit deeper into policy itself.

Let's consider in some detail the implementation of policy that lets us visit a friend in her apartment. It should now go without saying, but the point is so central to this particular protocol that we have to say it again, "Don't talk to strangers!" Thus, our friend in the apartment must, or at least really should, establish some degree of confidence that entry of the visitor is desired, or at least benign, before opening the door. Few will open the door for a person they perceive to be a threat; that's the whole point of the door, the lock and the intercom system. Through these mechanisms, the friend is offered the opportunity to divine the identity of a visitor, at least to such a level as to ascribe some degree of assurance that the visitor is not a threat. Now, the simple policy conveyed by a sign that was marked PULL has rather quickly encompassed many of the characteristics of a *social ecosystem*, a concept that we'll get into in some detail within this book. The characteristics that we're particularly interested in comprise the infrastructure for general interactions, and how they enable a very specific form of interaction which we'll term a *transaction*. This is an interaction for which we can uniquely define and apply policy, from a well defined beginning to a well defined end.

The moderately complex protocol we've just considered is rather ubiquitous in most urban environments. Consequently, the policy and its subsumed protocol are disseminated through social convention. We might also consider another example, the policy for opening the door of a tenant safe in a hotel room. This procedure is probably unusual enough for the common traveler, who might well see lots of different variants of room safes in hotels around the world that it's useful to have the protocol written down on an instruction sheet. Generally the instructions are presented in several languages in order to accommodate the widest variety of travelers. For most such safes, the protocol begins with the instructions to reset the safe to a known starting state and to allow the guest to enter a code that only she knows. Once the door is closed and locked, the safe will open only when that code is entered.

So, thus far through our examples we've discerned two distinct mechanisms for establishing trust within an interaction. In the first, the friend hears the voice of a visitor at the door and, based on purely subjective means of identification, decides whether a state of sufficient trust has been established so as to warrant opening the door. In the second, the safe door sees the appropriate code entered such that it can also determine that a state of sufficient trust has been established, based on the purely objective decision rules built into its control circuitry, so as to warrant opening the door. In either case, the protocol was an element of a system through which trust could be established in order to support the occurrence of a transaction. Trust is our measure of confidence in the validity, consistency and probable consequences of the specification and application of policy. To elaborate slightly, we can say that within an environment in which an acceptable degree of trust can be established, a protocol can be enacted between multiple parties through which a transaction can take place, enabling the parties to negotiate to an agreed upon conclusion; to wit, in this case getting the door open.

"Well," one might be considering at this point, "how does this consideration of trust and policy impact either on the reality presented by computers and computer networks or the social reality of religions and their guiding theologies? If there's any substance to the book's title then there ought to be some relationship, correct?" We respond that "Indeed, there is!" Correspondingly, this book is an attempt to relate the development and evolution of computer technology to the development and evolution of humans and their social environments, particularly as these environments are impacted on or defined by religious systems. Our review of the literature presented in the bibliography suggests to us that religions are paragons of human social organizations. Such organizations have their foundations in human physiology, including the genetically determined characteristics of the human brain. However, social organization, very specifically including religion, has impact beyond the physiological level through facilities derived from the evolution of the species. This evolution has given rise to means by which to satisfy an ascending hierarchy of needs. Based on a consideration of needs fulfillment versus social grouping, we will express a model for human social organizations that maps readily into the world of computers and computer networks.

Illustrating our methods for examining these relationships, the book presents an anthropomorphic view of computer systems *vis-à-vis* a consideration of human interactions, and observes a number of parallels in the development and use of computers. Based on these parallels, we suggest the emergence of a new species of truly personal, portable, trusted computers that forms a cognitive tool intimately associated with its bearer. Further, based on the current literature of evolutionary biology, psychology and sociology, as well as contemporary works of anthropology and cognitive science, we adopt the view that religion is an integral aspect of human evolution through the formulation of goals, social mores and mechanisms of self-actualization, transcendence and their derivative social interactions. In essence, we recognize that religion supports a multi-level selection facility within the general evolutionary framework of the human species. Religion comprises the archetypical template of social ecosystems through which all higher-order human interactions occur. We observe that a number of similar traits have arisen in the development of computer technology. These parallels are not grounded merely in the physical aspects of certain computer platforms. They are also based on the traits of trusted, portable and personalized computers akin to the human states of ecstasy and the rituals that underlie the essence of trust imbued by religious systems that form the foundation of our model of social organization. These traits, seemingly wrought from mysticism much like that which forms the basis of religious frameworks, differentiate the model from simple rule-based computational infrastructures.

We suggest that this emergent species of personal electronic devices will, through further evolution, be positioned as the dominant, portable individual computers. Encompassing cellular phones, digital assistants, electronic payment cards, key fobs, game and multimedia players, as well as all sorts of intelligent tags, they are not just computers that the person can use, but computers that embody the trust and policy formulation and utilization characteristics through which individuals can engage in the physical and electronic interactions of their daily lives. Specifically, these trusted computers are a means of injecting the person much more intimately into the increasingly complex interactions that characterize current society. They are destined to become, in fact, the personal deictic centers of the electronic world. Based on the parallels that we see between the current mechanisms of information technology and societal (centrally religious) development through history, we qualitatively project the future evolutionary developments that enhance the ability of such computers to further fulfill their analogous potential to emulate and facilitate human interactions.

We were initially drawn down this path by the observation that images passed to us from prehistory to the modern era characterize mechanisms that are readily found in the design and implementation strategies of personalized computers. This suggested a continuum in concepts on which human cognition is grounded; a continuum that stretches from the emergence of modern man to the current incarnation of mankind's most intimate tools. This elicited a curiosity on our part in the human evolutionary process from both an individual and a group viewpoint. Since much of pre- and proto-historical imagery and ongoing cultural development is synonymous with religious environment and practice, this appeared to be an interesting model through which to try to understand general and specific computer developments.

If one starts with a rudimentary view of living organisms, we recognize that they evolve in a manner guided by changes over time in their basic chemical language defined structure. Today, we know this basic chemical language as DNA. The DNA molecule found in the cells of organisms comprises a book that details the design and operational characteristics of the organism. Changes to the design are effected through adaptation and mutation of the book and their efficacy is judged through natural selection. Natural selection, in turn, functions through individual and multi-level mechanisms, religion being a non-trivial example of the latter. Over time, religious communities have grown and interacted, internally and among each other. Within the context of these communities, the individual members interact through special protocols. On a grander scale, entire religious communities interact among themselves through special protocols as well. Driven by theologically inspired stimuli, religions respond individually and collectively to internal and external threats. We see in these processes great parallels to the desired behavior of computer networks in which the facility for human involvement across the full range of needs based stimuli extends from networked personal electronic devices.

Computers have evolved, just as have the distinct individuals of other species, as well as the species themselves and the environments in which they interact; they all continue to evolve. Computers were born as successful entities in and of themselves through a series of mutations that found fertile ground among a variety of concepts that, while certainly interesting in a mechanical world, actually thrive in the electronic world. They have continued to evolve through invention and the application of market pressures. Individual and multi-level selection is effected in the marketplace, both economic and ideological, through a variety of protocols reminiscent of religious practices. Devices with built-in security substrates have recently emerged as a distinct strain of computer, the harbingers of the new species we've suggested. In today's highly networked environment, these devices, be they labeled as, say, smart mobile phones or personal assistants, are computer analogues of people. They attempt to address the complex policy considerations of individual interactions throughout extended technical and social communities. Within the electronic world, they become people. Moreover, their operational capabilities require them to ponder their position and orientation in the world in which they periodically find themselves, and from this contemplation they must derive, in total isolation, the manner in which they will choose to interact with their current surroundings. It is this deeply contemplative state, coupled with the derivation of trust in policy from it, that strikes us as growingly analogous to an early stage of ecstasy that is a recurring theme in the religious experience, expressed in meditation, and reflected in art and ritual.

Lest our discussions appear too opaque, let us reiterate that the policy we're talking about involves us as individuals from the time we wake up in the morning until we go to bed at night. Much of it is mundane, for example, what time to set the alarm clock to ring. Some of it is moderately complex, such as remembering all the details emanating from the early flight on Thursday. In the extreme, it transcends banality and portends rationale bordering on the sublime. Consider, for example, our personal involvement with the law. Among our earliest childhood admonitions is this, "Ignorance of the law is no excuse." This edict offers a lot of surface area where policy rubs against us, across the full range of the sensori-motor experience. Moreover, this area is increasing at an accelerating rate. As a consequence, lest we be totally overwhelmed, we seek more and better support in dealing with it. We currently call it lots of things; personal profiles, individual preferences or perhaps rules of engagement. We find it subject to withering cross-currents of conflicting context, influenced by concerns for personal security and bounded by various rights of privacy. It finally culminates in the uneasy framework of social compacts. It seems clear to us that the need for an emergent computer theology is grounded in the ambiguities of this technology-enhanced social infrastructure.

We suggest that the evolution of individual computers has tended to match the early evolution of people and their societal interactions. We anticipate a variety of opportunities for future evolutionary pathways in which truly private, portable trusted computers parallel the evolution of more complex human social systems.

The book is not a rigorous book as it pertains to religious doctrine and mechanisms, nor is it an exhaustive study of evolutionary mechanisms. However, the book is significantly grounded in the literature of both fields. The book is a moderately thorough review of computer evolution and is rather detailed in its treatment of the emergence and development of trusted computer technology and its interaction with the World Wide Web. We find quite striking the parallels between the way people react, both individually and within groups, to personal and societal challenges, and the way computers, obviously as developed by people, behave in the increasingly complex and interconnected world wrought by modern technology. We feel these parallels to be an interesting culmination of this writing. Of course, it leaves us wondering: in regards to technology, are the new species of trusted computers destined to be among the lower primates or are they the direct precursors of *Homo sapiens sapiens*, the sub-species designation that we also know as *modern man*? In regards to religious orders, are they precursors of computer ecosystems, or their very constitution?

# 1 Tat Tvam Asi

*Om!*
*May my speech be based on the mind; may my mind be*
*based on speech.*
*O Self-effulgent One, reveal Thyself to me.*
*May you both be the carriers of the Veda to me.*
*May not all that I have heard depart from me.*
*I shall join together day and night through this study.*
*I shall utter what is verbally true;*
*I shall utter what is mentally true.*
*May That protect me; may That protect the speaker;*
*may That protect me; may That protect the speaker,*
*may That protect the teacher!*
*Om! Peace! Peace! Peace!*

Nada-Bindu Upanishad

## In The Beginning

Humans are social animals. As members of the species, we are embedded within social systems from the time of our birth to the time of our death. It has always been so. We cannot survive our infancy without the support of a social order. Our natural condition as adults is to engage in social interaction. If we're ever incarcerated, solitary confinement is the penultimate sanction for abrogation of the rules of the social order, exceeded only by execution. Should we seek to do so, our abilities to lead solitary lives devoid of social contact are characteristics more tolerated than endorsed by the social systems in which we exist. Personal isolation is not our normal posture. In the XVII[th] Century, John Donne expressed this social state of being in his Meditation XVII (published in the *Works of John Donne* by Henri Alford):

> No man is an island, entire of itself; every man is a piece of the continent, a part of the main; if a clod be washed away by the sea, Europe is the less, as well as if a promontory were, as well as if a manor of thy friend's or of thine own were: any man's death diminishes me, because I am involved in mankind, and therefore never send to know for whom the bells tolls; it tolls for thee.

A social existence is not the result of a lifestyle selection on our parts. We are driven to seek social acceptance and social structure by our physiological makeup. Our perception of the world around us is defined by our sensory system and the stimuli for our response to that world are driven by needs that have common form across all members of the species. Hence, Donne's reflection addresses not a personal choice, but rather a physiological condition of the biophysical person. At least since the emergence of proto-historical records and artifacts of modern humans more than 30,000 years ago, social structures have extended beyond those based purely on familial connections. The dominant forms of these larger grouping mechanisms have long been grounded in religion.

Religion, theology and policy are three concepts that are intertwined and together provide the focus of the collectives that form much of the basis of human evolutionary success. These collectives derived initially from the basic family unit and evolved into ever increasing ensembles of individuals, culminating in religious congregations that have been foundational in their provision of social structure that has been so essential in the ascent of mankind. We use the term *religion* to identify a system of beliefs generally shared by its adherents, including the basis in trust for that sharing. *Theology* in turn refers to the specific framework for those beliefs including how they are to be applied and the potential consequences of that application. Finally, we evoke the realm of *policy* in specific regards to the beliefs themselves, essentially defining for the individual those actions selected from among various choices whose objectives are both the furtherance of the religion on which are based the actions and the benefits to the individual suppliants of the religion.

Religions are grounded in the facilities of the human mind. They draw their strength from emotions and their behaviors from cognitive processes. By exploiting these physiological characteristics, religion provides the framework for commonly held belief systems through which the actions of groups of people are focused and directed. Through the affirmation of moral and ethical values that are shared by the group, codes of conduct that guide the behavior of individuals within the group can be defined. These moral and ethical values posit a justification for actions aimed at the well being of the many, even at the expense of sacrifice on the part of the one. Thus is formed a basis for personal altruistic behavior; a behavior that is often asymmetric in its application and effect. Consider for example the soldier who throws himself upon the grenade thereby accepting certain death for himself in return for the possibility of saving his comrades. In a like manner, the mother in a poor and starving family might forego food for herself thereby accepting the ravages of continuing hunger in order to provide a little more sustenance for her children. Closer to religion, a similar stimulus drives a pilot to crash his aircraft into a ship of war or a building of commerce to placate his perceived responsibility to the prevailing social order. These are all illustrative of a policy system grounded in profound trust that evokes an action presumably beneficial to others at the expense of self as being the preferred response to threats of a given type. While such acts are not the exclusive domain of religion, we suggest that altruism is a characteristic of a general model of social organization for which religion is an iconic example. Acts of altruism or of its harsher sibling, sacrifice, are harbingers of uncertainty within the biological concepts of evolution and natural selection. Indeed, altruistic behavior is generally viewed as counter intuitive from the perspective of natural selection. It is, however, an undeniable, recurring theme of social organization, and it is through social organization that mankind achieves its evolutionary eminence.

We can readily discern through its repetitive occurrence over the ages that religion provides its groups of believers with sets of common values. Further, we can also observe that the stimulation of actions based on such values is the central aspect of the concept of policy. To fully understand this connection between values and actions, it is necessary to consider the complete environment within which policy is defined and implemented; an environment we term a *trust and policy infrastructure*. The establishment of effective policy infrastructures elevates the trust infrastructures of religion and religious systems to the forefront of human social order. Religion is not a mere perturbation of the human cognitive system; it is a natural product of that system. The long ages of natural selection have wrought theologically guided religious practice just as they've culminated in the opposing thumb. Within the implementations of distinct religions are found the varied theologies that form the architecture for each one's definition and conveyance of policy. It is this elaboration of policy mechanisms that makes religion the premiere manifestation of social orders from human cognition.

The common basis for the group-wide sharing of religious theology and practice derives from the concept of *faith*, a term we might not normally attach to the definition or implementation of policy. Rather, we tend to steep the concepts of policy in terms of *trust*. While both terms, faith and trust, are very close, we will ascribe a definition to trust that allows it to subsume that of faith. Thus, we say that *trust is an expectation of an outcome with some degree of assurance*. More succinctly stated trust is a probability of an anticipated outcome. Hence, we see gradations in the degree of assurance associated with trust: "I trust him with my life." versus "I don't trust him as far as I can throw him!" Interestingly enough, both statements indicate high levels of trust under our definition. Given either statement, we can form a probability of outcome for various policy affectations that we might undertake. When presented with a choice, we follow the path that we anticipate will lead to the outcome we desire; the certainty of our anticipation reflects our level of trust in the path. If we don't have a choice, then our trust level still allows us to anticipate the outcome whether it might be good or bad. At the most physiologically primitive level, trust determines whether our response to stress stimuli is fight or flight. At a more sublime level, trust is the basis for our actions of self-actualization and transcendence; terms of some ambiguity at this point, but which we will consider in some detail in subsequent chapters. Faith then is a guidepost on the road to trust.

When we consider the grouping mechanisms that we assume have been present since the time of emergence of the species, we readily identify families, clans, tribes and ever larger congregations of individuals seeking the benefits of group associations. Groups enhance the collective prospects for their constituent individuals to survive and thrive. Indeed, the action of humans through groups is such a recurrent theme that it exhibits all the properties of an evolutionary trait, forged by competition, with humans banding together as they have always done against the threats posed by an unyielding, physical world. So, one can pose the question, "What is the difference between religion and other social structures?" From our perspective, the difference lies almost exclusively with the sources of trust and with the mechanisms through which policy is derived based on this trust.

Let us postulate first the form of trust. With appropriate stimuli, the brain can create through chemical means at a cellular level an altered state of consciousness within its cognition enabling structures. For some, with appropriate training, virtually the same state can be created purely through cognitive activity. Likewise, this altered state can be created through ritual activities aided by appropriate external stimuli. It can also be evoked through external chemical means, and through combinations of all of the above. From within this altered state of consciousness, the mind establishes a high level of confidence in the cognitive processes encountered or evoked. This confidence forms the basis for our subsequent interactions. We call trust the expectation that we can essentially predict with some level of expected certainty the outcome of interactions.

At its strongest, the altered state of consciousness may be identified with being in touch with God. In milder form, a feeling of euphoria can be experienced and at its most benign, it might elicit simple acceptance. Anecdotal experience suggests that this emotional state varies in intensity among different individuals or even within a single individual. Hence, trust can present as a spectrum to which an arbitrary normalization can be applied. If we call the less intense state faith and the more intense state rapture, then we start to see a connection to religious belief. On the other hand, one can ascribe different normalization terms. For example, if we use allegiance as one extreme and duty as the other, then we can draw a parallel to other social orders. If we consider the extreme spectrum of apprehension ranging to terror we find the basis of trust in despotic regimes. In any case, it is the level of this state of altered consciousness that determines our degree of trust in the cognitive concepts associated with it. The secret of religion's success as a social structure is in simultaneously evoking a similar feeling of trust in all the members of a group. While it may not be a feeling of the same intensity, it can be a distribution of uniformly directed trust among all individuals in the group toward a common policy. What then is the source of this trust?

Religion seeks to draw a common foundation of trust for its adherents from a source outside the realm of physical experience. This forms the primary differentiation between religions and other social structures. As we will consider in greater detail in subsequent chapters, with specific emphasis in Chapter 7, trust can derive from causality. Religions, particularly theistic religions, establish basic causality from beyond natural sources; by *supernatural* means. Causality validation is in turn based on perceived results, a statement that we will expand on in Chapter 9. Did the believed causality lead to an ostensibly better understood outcome than might otherwise have been anticipated? Can successful predictions of perceived future outcomes be based on this causality? If trust derived from a supernatural source can thus be reasonably established, then a second order question to be addressed is, "How does policy derive within the infrastructure of trust that springs from this source?" With religion, the answer is virtually always through the same mechanism; from a *shaman* who acts as the intermediary between the source of trust and the specification of policy. In this manner, policy is established that determines the basis for subsequent interactions. The source and mechanisms of trust on which policy depends typically include the establishment of identity for the individuals who are subject to these policy specifications, including the rules governing interactions and the consequences of these interactions. The shaman, often acting under the guise of *prophet* or *lawgiver*, becomes the source of policy under the auspices of the source of trust. Simply stated, God dictates the laws to the prophets and the prophets convey the law to the believers. From this point on, all social structures behave in essentially the same manner. Trust and policy infrastructure may elicit different effects, but the mechanisms are much the same.

Illustrative of our contention that theology is, in fact, about trust and policy are the circumstances of at least one of the great *schisms* of the Western Church. A schism in reference to social orders is a process for change within social frameworks that foments as a product of diminished trust due to the effects of prescribed policy based on this trust.

This diminution often results in a subsequent reformulation of policy or perhaps in the creation of a whole new basis of trust. We view a schism as essentially an evolutionary process periodically encountered in social structures of all forms. In the Western World, the Protestant Reformation was such a schism and was most certainly about trust and policy. It was formulated by arguably one of the great policy wonks of any age, the erstwhile priest Martin Luther. Working from within the most powerful policy infrastructure of the day, the clergy of the Roman Catholic Church, he challenged the very precepts of that infrastructure. He questioned how both trust and policy were established, how trust was conveyed, how policy was implemented, the consequences of adherence or abrogation of policy, and the very boundaries of the trust and policy infrastructures. Consequently, he brought into question the details of the Church's policy predicated upon the basis of trust originally established by the Church, and in so doing he incited a stark repudiation of that policy.

Martin Luther was a German monk described by Will and Ariel Durant in *The Story of Civilization*, from which we derive much of the following discussion, as an earthy man. He was also a scholar, holding a Doctor of Theology degree from the University of Wittenberg. After a life of contemplation of his relationship with his God, Luther finally reached a point in which his trust in the teachings of the Roman Catholic Church did not match his perceptions of this relationship. While in his writings Luther noted many concerns, the central focus of his preemptive challenge to the Church dealt with the sale of indulgences, particularly by a Dominican priest by the name of Johann Tetzel. In 1517, Tetzel, under authority granted by Rome, was charged with raising money through the sale of indulgences for the continued construction of St. Peter's Basilica. An indulgence was a credential that, for the bearer diminished the prospect of temporal punishment for sins, for some arbitrary period of time, while not completely removing all consequences of such sins in the afterlife. Tetzel's marketing approach might not have been quite so nuanced, leading the buyer to perhaps expect full remission of sins. Luther's precipitous act was to nail a list of 95 Theses, that is, questions and assertions regarding both claims and nuance, on the door of Wittenberg Cathedral on All Saints Day in the year 1517. The document comprised a point-by-point appraisal of the concepts of sin and its consequences resulting in a wholesale condemnation of the policy defined and implemented by the Church through its collective interpretation of the *Christian Bible*.

Consider the 8th of his 95 Theses; roughly translated it tells us "The penitential canons apply only to men who are still alive, and, according to the canons themselves, none applies to the dead." This is a rather radical re-definition of the boundaries of the theological infrastructure of the Roman Catholic Church of the XVIth Century. It asserts that the directions of the Church, as applied to the actions of man, extend only to the boundary between life and death, not beyond. Beyond death was strictly the purview of God, not worldly constructs such as the Church. For the Church of that era, this was not merely intellectual dogma; this was the economic livelihood of the papal organization itself. Being specifically aimed at the sale of *indulgences*, those "get out of purgatory free" cards so popular with the ecclesiastical community of the time, Luther's challenge, if not thwarted, would result in the loss of significant financial prowess, and hence power, of the Church within this worldly domain. Adding emphasis to the point, the Church of Rome truly needed any financial assistance it could get. Pope Leo X, from the House of Medici in Florence, was something of a suspect steward of the Church's treasury. Within two years of his ascendance to the Throne of St. Peter in 1513, his profligate spending had almost totally depleted the ample treasury of the Church that had been accumulated under the tutelage of his predecessor, Pope Julius II. Consequently, indulgences, or at least their sale, were among the few equity resources remaining. Hence Luther's machinations were of the highest importance to the Church.

The 20th of the 95 Theses is equally profound, "Therefore, the Pope, in speaking of the plenary remission of all penalties, does not mean 'all' in the strict sense, but only those imposed by him." Not only are the boundaries of the policy infrastructure revised, but also the administrative authority of the primary policy arbiter of the infrastructure is restricted. In fact, as prefaced in the 6th Thesis, "The Pope himself cannot remit guilt, but only declare and confirm that it has been remitted by God..." As we will see in more detail later in this book, the success of this challenge constitutes a change in the policies of the Roman Catholic Church as well as in the very boundaries of influence and control of the Church itself. This is policy definition or redefinition of the first order. Such an analysis and proposal would today certainly be a worthy subject of the Harvard Business Review. Given the limitations on printed material, the cathedral doors of the Castle Church of Wittenberg on All Saints Day was a more appropriate method of that era. In any case, it certainly made for good marketing of his ideas.

Because of his policy machinations, Luther put himself into direct conflict with Pope Leo X, earning the considerable enmity of the papal establishment in the process. Of course, as sometimes happens, a confluence of minutiae turned Luther's actions from an evolutionary trial balloon into an actual societal mutation. In particular, his actions occurred within an environment of personality types intertwined with technology and social upheavals so as to create not just a theological schism but a social one as well. The technological aspect of this mix was the invention and subsequent widespread availability of the printing press. The social aspect was the translation of the Bible into German, English and other popular common languages. This meant that the discussion of Luther's ideas wasn't confined to the *literati* and conducted in Latin. Rather, it meant that the common man, or at least the societal elite outside the power structure of the Church, could follow the discussion and ponder and participate in the potential outcomes. Thus, Luther was able to bring what might have been a purely religious turmoil into the world of main street politics; in essence, he was able to redirect the orientation of the policy infrastructure within the trust infrastructure. He did not challenge the trust of believers in God, but rather the projection of policy based on that trust.

It was this facet of the event, its more purely social side, or perhaps we should say secular side, that ultimately amplified the profound nature of the situation. Besides Luther himself, the two dominant personalities involved were Pope Leo X, whom the Durants describe thus, "His morals were good in an immoral milieu…" but "All his faults were superficial except his superficiality." On the more secular side was found Frederick the Wise, "…a pious and provident ruler." These personality characteristics strongly influenced the sequence of events and the ultimate outcome; essentially, Pope Leo didn't perceive the problem quickly enough and Frederick offered political and physical cover to Luther long enough for the paradigm shift to take hold. The end result was a dislocation between the trust infrastructure, the Christian God in this case, and the policy infrastructure. The question was, "If policy isn't defined by the Roman Catholic clergy then by whom is it defined?" The ramifications had long legs indeed.

What, then, were some of these ramifications? First, it is important to note that the Protestant Reformation resulted in a new policy infrastructure within the same trust infrastructure. That is, protestant believers view themselves as adherents to essentially the same God as do Roman Catholics. Of course, the policies of one church derived within this trust infrastructure are sometimes viewed as heretical from the perspective of other churches. So, in fact the multiple churches that trust in the same God were, after the schism, competitors. The original church continued; the new churches developed. This is exactly the same situation that exists with the emergence of new organic species; competition and coexistence until such time as a winner emerges or benign coexistence stabilizes. Such is the case with modern Christianity; we're in an environment where different denominations are in subtle, or not so subtle, conflict with one another.

So, we interpret one perturbation in the major social system that is Western Christianity in terms of a great schism in existing policy infrastructures. Many other societal mutation events followed from it, but perhaps the most profound is recognized in another great schism; that resulting in an iconic example of Western Democracy. It began in the late XVIII[th] Century when Thirteen Colonies of Great Britain, located among the eastern reaches of the continent of North America, began the steps to remove themselves from the trust and policy infrastructures defined by the British monarchy. The Declaration of Independence, which we first considered in this light in our Prologue, is very similar to Luther's 95 Theses from the standpoint that it was a defining moment in the continuum of social structures at which a significant change of direction arose. The declaration very clearly established both a new trust infrastructure and the seminal policy infrastructure that would allow development of a more comprehensive social structure, although the seminal policy infrastructure very clearly did not define what this comprehensive structure would be. By removing the Thirteen Colonies from the existing trust infrastructure, and creating a new trust infrastructure, the relationship between the two trust infrastructures resolved to interactions within the physical environment where both existed. The only constraining trust that encompassed the two was the trust that derives from causality based on the understanding and application of physical laws. The consequences of policy within this trust infrastructure are potentially mortal interactions in which the fitter adversary prevails.

Bear in mind at this point that our goal is to establish a consistent model through which to understand the interactions among and within social structures. In dealing with the most profound aspects of such interactions, it might well go without saying that when push comes to shove, the interaction resolves to pure, physical conflict. Physical aggression and conflict is pretty much the natural environment within which organic species evolved. The purpose of social structures is to alter this natural environment in favor of social interactions that are ultimately beneficial to the group, not just the individual. Consider in the case of the emergence of the Thirteen Colonies, while both sides of the conflict would profess to be nations and military establishments of gentlemen, each possessing codes of civil conduct, once the interaction between entities reverted to pure physical conflict then the resulting war was conducted, as wars generally are, in an extreme fashion. In an absolute sense, one would be hard put to portray the fledgling colonies on a par militarily with the British Empire. However, when the specific environment was defined in which the conflict would play out, the new proved superior, or at least more resilient than the old within this environment. As we will consider in the next chapter, when one seeks to gauge the survival of the fittest it is necessary to determine the fittest on a case-by-case basis.

The pronouncement of the Declaration of Independence began a period of warfare and uncertainty that lasted a full 15 years before some semblance of stable trust and policy infrastructures were established within the former colonies through the adoption of the Constitution of the United States. In fact, the first significant policy infrastructure that was developed following the war, the Articles of Confederation, proved insufficient to bind the Thirteen Colonies into a viable social structure. It was not until the formulation of the trust infrastructure of the Constitution that stable seminal policy infrastructures were derived. From the Constitution, springs the trust infrastructure from which popular adherence to the policy infrastructure that it creates is established; a trust infrastructure that emanates, as the Declaration of Independence said it must, with government drawing its authority from the consent of the governed. This culmination in the Constitution represented more than a mere schism. It was a social mutation of the first order.

In the resulting United States, a central tenet of government is the separation of church and state. While this separation ostensibly guarantees the freedom of both church and state from the interference of the other, the Constitution establishes a hierarchy of policy control which guarantees the superiority of state over church. The very definition of church is the purview of the state. As Chief Justice Marshal noted in the Supreme Court opinion in the case of McCullock v. Maryland:

> ... the constitution and the laws made in pursuance thereof are supreme; that they control the constitution and laws of the respective States, and cannot be controlled by them. From this, which may be almost termed an axiom, other propositions are deduced as corollaries, on the truth or error of which, and on their application to this case, the cause has been supposed to depend. These are, 1st. That a power to create implies a power to preserve. 2nd. That a power to destroy, if wielded by a different hand, is hostile to, and incompatible with these powers to create and to preserve. 3d. That where this repugnancy exists, that authority which is supreme must control, not yield to that over which it is supreme . . .

Thus, in being able to define what constitutes a church the position of the state effectively becomes supreme. Since the state can create a church it can take steps to preserve it, but it can also take steps to destroy it; at least as a recognized subordinate trust infrastructure. It then becomes of interest to understand how the state is different from the church? It would seem that the defining control of government over religion constitutes a social organization that is, at best, only mildly distinct from the religions over which it exerts control. Indeed, for many religious devotees the characteristics of this control constitute a new religion in its own right; secular humanism is a term sometimes used for this perceived quasi-religious social structure. Certainly government within the United States has many of the trappings of religious organizations, with defining documents that establish a core set of beliefs or dogma along with the rationale for their application and the consequences of their action; in other words, a theology. It effects a governing organizational structure, and a means of enforcing adherence to dogma. Moreover, it establishes the equivalent of a clergy to act as arbiters of policy and to help adherents to understand the paths to righteousness.

While we proudly proclaim that we are a nation of laws, we also consider the Constitution, our primary source of dogma, a living document subject to evolving interpretation according to the prevalent social environment of the time. As we noted in the Prologue, this is an artifact of language based on metaphorical understanding adapted to context. As we also observed in the Prologue, the resulting interpretation and re-interpretation can result in huge swings in applicable policy. Our understanding of the physical world suggests a characteristic of immutability for laws that minimizes subjectivity. However, social systems are predicated upon the subjective interpretation and application of policy. Thus, while our societal laws are there to ostensibly guide the actions of everyone, should a problem of interpretation arise we must resort to some form of consequence resolution. Our mechanism for such resolution, the judicial system, is so complex and arcane as to require representation from a "clergy" for guidance in navigating its treacherous shoals. Moreover, we are admonished that "one who represents himself in legal proceedings has a fool for a client."

The assumption is that the actions of attorneys, through the protocols of the judicial system, are in fact required to render the final interpretation of applicable policy. Even in these situations, it seems that most litigating attorneys will assert that they can never predict what a given jury will decide. The end result is that one might well anticipate more assurance in handicapping a horse race than in predicting how a particular social law will be interpreted and applied. While the interpretation and application of socially derived policy might not be quite as arbitrary as our words have implied, in fact virtually no company would think of issuing a public proclamation without running it by the lawyers first. The fact that we must all rise when the judge enters the courtroom seems as clear an act of contrition and supplication as genuflecting upon entering the sanctuary or making a cross of ashes on our foreheads on a certain Wednesday of each year. However, there are perhaps no more revealing illustrations of the parallels between religious and secular systems, at least within the United States, than are found in the concept of *sovereign immunity* and in the act of *apostasy*. Sovereign immunity refers to the principle that the sovereign, which within the United States refers primarily to the federal government, cannot be the target of criminal or civil prosecution or action. In essence, the state can do no wrong. Apostasy on the other hand is defined in *A Church dictionary*, by Walter Farquhar Hook, as "A forsaking or renouncing of our religion, either formally, by an open declaration in words, or virtually, by our actions." As defined by the Constitution, the comparable act with regard to the United States is termed treason.

Treason is a crime specified by the Constitution. From the perspective of the model that we are pursuing, treason entails an act of apostasy against the trust infrastructure that forms the basis of governance within the United State. While Congress can establish the punishment for treason, the specifics of the criminal act itself are defined in Article III, Section 3 of the Constitution. There, we find that "Treason against the United States, shall consist only in levying War against them, or in adhering to their Enemies, giving them Aid and Comfort." The fact that the crime of treason is rarely prosecuted, whether during times of war or peace, is a testament to the power of metaphorical understanding. In normal situations, adherence to a person or a person's ideas is a well defined concept. Similarly, the concepts of providing aid and comfort are relatively straightforward as well. Given the spectrum of political thought within the United States, this would seem to constitute a rather low bar that an overt act must clear in order to be rendered treason. In fact, however, the bar is viewed by the courts as being quite high indeed. Nonetheless, the crime is there; established within the primary trust infrastructure of the social order. Consider then its corollary within more purely religious orders.

The first of the Ten Commandments found in both Christianity and Judaism includes the admonition, "Thou shall have no other gods before me." In either religion, to renounce the primacy of God is to commit an act of apostasy. Within a theistic religion, the specification of policy is typically perceived to come directly from the deity. Hence, the admonition is one grounded within the trust infrastructure of the social ecosystem. Under both Christianity and Judaism, the punishment for leaving the faith is a judgment to be ultimately rendered by God. Under Roman Catholicism, the limit of earthly punishment is typically excommunication; in essence, a direct recognition by the social order of the act of the apostate. Under Islam, the crime of apostasy is treated much more severely; particularly within theocratic states. There, the punishment can be death.

With respect to the concept of sovereign immunity, the major theistic religions indicate that the actions of God are without limit and without suppliant recourse. We will consider this concept in a bit more detail in Chapter 10. For the moment, we note that within these theistic religions, God is perceived to work in mysterious ways and for reasons not to be questioned by man. The net result is that one can sue neither God nor government.

Just as ostensibly secular governance often takes on the trappings of religious ritual, religious dogma in turn insinuates itself into secular government through the establishment of community morals and tenets of ethical conduct. Within the *Christian Bible*, Jesus establishes a demarcation between church and state through the admonition "Render unto Caesar the things which are Caesar's, and unto God the things that are God's." Although Western Democracy as typified by the United States federal government extols this philosophy, it is often realized only with significant strings attached. For example, while the separation of church and state is prominently mandated, the ostensibly secular state involves itself with the concept of marriage, which is most typically associated with religious dogma. It does this by blending the concept of marriage with the concepts of common ownership and conveyance of property, particularly through inheritance, which all derive from legal dogma. This intertwining is melded into a single, state defined condition, but a condition that has become associated with questions of morality and ethical conduct more typically engaged by religious orthodoxy. As this obviously reflects an attempt to make law that is steeped in religion-inspired moral values, the result is often less than accommodating to divergent views of morality. The admonition found in the *Christian Bible, Matthew 6:24* is perhaps applicable, "No one can serve two masters; for either he will hate the one and love the other, or he will be devoted to one and despise the other. You cannot serve God and mammon." We do understand that the word mammon refers directly to wealth. However, in Chapter 5 we will offer for consideration the concept that the establishment of a system of commerce, and hence a framework for wealth, is an evolved characteristic of religious social orders.

A significant aspect of the commonality between government and religion is that of identification. Religion has historically involved itself with the identification of its suppliants. Indeed, in times of physical conflict among religious and secular social structures, knowing who is a believer and who is not can be a life-or-death consideration. Some of the earliest identification mechanisms were cultural and biometric. Consider the admonition from the *Christian Bible, Judges 12:6 "Then said they unto him, Say now Shibboleth: and he said Sibboleth: for he could not frame to pronounce it right. Then they took him, and slew him at the passages of Jordan: and there fell at that time of the Ephraimites forty and two thousand."* As the passage suggests, the social group called the Ephraimites used a spoken language in which the "sh" sound was not normally present. So, members of this group could not naturally pronounce the word shibboleth. Hence, it provided a socially enabled biometric facility. This precursor leads rather inexorably to the similar, but more cognitively demanding mechanism used by American soldiers during the Battle of the Bulge in World War II. There, when approached by other ostensibly American soldiers who were in reality German agents, they asked a very context sensitive question such as, "Who won the World Series in 1939?" With both mechanisms, cultural conditioning provided the establishment of context through which an effective identification process could be enacted.

The basic family has naturally been a seminal concern of religious groupings. As a consequence, religions have a strong inclination to establish identity through the family's progression. The acts of procreation, familial bonding and death form significant social events within the religious domain. As technology enabled it, record keeping of births, marriages and deaths became commonplace within religious frameworks. The fact that such records were established within the relatively high trust environment of religious structure also meant that such records were, and still are, highly trusted throughout the social environment. If we then consider the emergence of government within the United States under the auspices of the Constitution, we see that a seminal activity of the prescribed policy infrastructure was to count, and hence to identify, the peoples from which subsequent governance authority would derive. As this policy infrastructure became more thoroughly defined, Bureaus of Vital Statistics were formed, often using the registries of churches as the starting points for their records.

Such blurring of the distinction between governmental organizations and religious organizations is common, whether in dictatorships, theocracies or democracies. All of these are of interest to us in that they are all concerned with the establishment of policy environments. One of the earliest impacts that we will see of this is in the application of policy adjudication mechanisms. The United States judicial system uses, as do many such systems, a venue of adversarial interaction moderated by a trusted third party in the determination and application of consequences to policy based interactions. Decisions of fact are made by a randomly selected group called a *jury* while decisions of law are established by a clergy that we've previously recognized as the judiciary. It is the task of these arbiters to interpret policy specifications and to apply sanctions when the specifications are in some way abrogated. While this system is designed to preferentially guarantee resolution as opposed to accuracy, in fact subsequent revisions of the system to enhance accuracy have had rather apparent deleterious impacts on resolution in the form of lengthy appellate processes.

At the present time, the primary policy environment in which we live our lives derives ostensibly from government policy, not from religious dogma; however, sometimes it's hard to tell them apart. In the course of our nation's history, the two have often been even more intertwined than they are today. In perhaps homage to those earlier social structures, today most U.S. politicians seeking to assume the mantle of governance do so under the guise of seeking to engage in public service. The term invites the somewhat facetious comparison to the Damon Knight science fiction short story in which the alien book with a title translated as "To Serve Man," rather than being a tutorial on constructive coexistence between species, is actually found to be a cookbook (Knight's story is also entitled *To Serve Man*).

In any case, those who aspire to public service typically present themselves as religious individuals with the implication that a subsequent basis of their public actions may be keyed to their private religious beliefs or at least to the morality and ethical codes of conduct that they derived from those beliefs. The bottom line is that social structures encompass grouping mechanisms that are in competition with one another. They encompass aspects of divergent social environments in which the process of natural selection is still at play on multiple levels. This existing tension is reflected in our consideration of the extension of social systems through the use of tools such as computers and computer networks.

As humans require social structure from which to derive evolutionary benefit, they also require tools. If completely devoid of tools, a naked human would have a difficult time merely functioning as a predator. Simply dismembering the slain prey for food can be a difficult if not impossible task without at least a sharp stone to use as a cutting tool. While today's vegans might heartily approve, it's not clear that the ascendance of the species would have been as pronounced on a diet of nuts and berries as on the high-protein meals provided by meat. During this evolution of the species, as our physiological facilities encompassed the higher level cognitive functions of our expanded brains, our tools were required to keep pace. We have learned, through our tool systems, to derive high-protein foods from vegetable sources. So, today our knives perhaps don't have to be quite as sharp. On the other hand, over the last few decades, electronic stored program computers have emerged as the most complex and cognition enabling tools ever devised by the species. Computers and their networks have great impact on the social systems that we are driven to exploit. Consequently, the mechanisms we use in our natural grouping systems should have parallels in the mechanisms used by our tool systems. Hence, we would expect to see some reflection of religion and religious mechanisms in computers and computer networks.

# A Theme

*Computer Theology* presents computers and computer networks as both concrete technological elements and as abstract components of modern society. It details their historical and prospective development and compares their evolution to today's most advanced personal machines, that is, to human beings. Throughout our presentation we will follow the guiding principle of the actions of individuals and of individuals acting within groups, which is to say evolution and evolutionary mechanisms. As the reader might infer from the title, we consider religion to be a significant recurring mechanism of evolution; certainly as it pertains to multi-level natural selection, a subject we'll discuss in depth in Chapter 2.

The concept of evolution has been around for a long time. However, while some might suggest that cursory discussions of what today we think of as evolutionary mechanisms can be found among the writings of the ancient Greeks, for our purposes, we will view the seminal establishment of the principles of evolution to be the products of the XVIII[th] and XIX[th] Centuries in the form of pioneering research and writings by Jean-Baptiste Lamarck, Charles Darwin and Gregor Mendel. While there were other players in the game, these particular innovators were instrumental in forming the context for thought and discussions about evolution in the form that we know it today. Darwin and Mendel were actually contemporaries, with Mendel very aware of Darwin's works. As it happened, however, Mendel's work was not well known outside his immediate vicinity. So, in all likelihood Darwin was never aware of his work. Larmarck predated them both by a few decades and both were well aware of the writings of Lamarck.

Jean-Baptiste Larmarck first gave significant impetus to the concept that members of species inherited characteristics from their progenitors. He proposed a model for the evolutionary process. A summary of his basic views is found in his work *Philosophie zoologique*. There he offers the following assessment (our translation):

> So, any change acquired in an organ through a habit of sufficient usage for having effected it, conserves itself through generation, if it is common to the individuals who, in fecundation, concur together to the reproduction of their species. Finally, this change propagates itself, and so passes into all succeeding individuals subject to the same circumstances, without them having to acquire it the way it was really created.

Thus, Lamarck formalized the idea that change that occurs within an organism can be propagated into succeeding generations. Such change, even if it occurs in minute steps, could have a cumulative effect over time. In his view, the impetus for change was an organism's need to adapt to its specific environment. In other words, the environment was the agent that stimulated change within the organism. Charles Darwin modified the proposition as follows in *The Origin of Species*:

> How much of the acclimatisation of species to any peculiar climate is due to mere habit, and how much to the natural selection of varieties having different innate constitutions, and how much to both means combined, is a very obscure question. That habit or custom has some influence I must believe, both from analogy, and from the incessant advice given in agricultural works, even in the ancient Encylopaedias of China, to be very cautious in transposing animals from one district to another; for it is not likely that man should have succeeded in selecting so many breeds and sub-breeds with constitutions specially fitted for their own districts: the result must, I think, be due to habit. On the other hand, I can see no reason to doubt that natural selection will continually tend to preserve those individuals which are born with constitutions best adapted to their native countries.

As we see, Charles Darwin, without obliterating Larmarck's view, added *natural selection*, the proposition that within the evolutionary process the environment may judge the efficacy of change rather than cause it. This presupposes that change itself can take on a rather arbitrary guise that may or may not be directly applicable to a given environment. One change mechanism springs from reproduction, for which Gregor Mendel established a model of two laws related to the propagation, or inheritance, of characteristics. One is called the law of segregation, which formulates the concept of dominant and recessive properties as the mechanism for variance in the progeny of a single set of parents. The other is called the law of independent assortment, which suggests that there are in fact characteristics of a species that may be inherited independently; for example, a human's hair and eye colors. Other change mechanisms such as mutation (with environment as a judge) and epigenetic inheritance (with environment as a cause) would in time add to the picture.

Thus was established a conceptual model for the evolutionary progression of organic species. What was missing was a detailed understanding of the mechanisms involved in this progression. In particular, missing was knowledge of the DNA molecule and the manner in which its facilities for replication form a basis for passing characteristics of the entities of a species from one generation to the next. The discovery of this facility awaited the work of Francis Crick, Rosalind Franklin, James Watson and others, in the middle of the XX$^{th}$ Century. The DNA molecule provides both history and blueprint, but mostly blueprint that provides a statement of design and construction for living cells. DNA possesses the elements of language, and of documents written in that language, that we will later view as central to the creation of social order. Thus, we begin to perceive a possible parallel between biological and social systems. We'll delve into a discussion of the biology involved in all this in the next chapter, as certain characteristics of the DNA molecule itself and of its process for replication bring some clarity to such a parallel.

From our consideration of Charles Darwin's formulation of the theory of evolution in the XIX$^{th}$ Century, we gained some of the impetus to write this book. Whereas Darwin observed nature and questioned its purposes and procedures, we so question technology. Through our quest we recognize the need to question nature again. Our goal has been to understand the evolution of computer systems within the context of their use by and interaction with the human population, both collectively and as individuals, as well as within the context of their own interactions. Our observation is that religion more than any other characteristic trait specifically mirrors this goal. So, this quest has led us to consider the evolutionary roots of religion and then, starting from these roots go to the core of the most intimate computers to find the spiritual in the silicon.

By the year 2000, the career progression of both of this book's authors had reached those esoteric nether regions that seem to exist in every industry where a small circle of specialists from an ostensibly common business domain are able to debate the future and to consider the path best followed for that domain to flourish. The discussions flourished in a variety of venues such as collaborative system development efforts, technical specification consortia and standards making bodies. Sometimes such consideration is effective in providing guidance, but sometimes not. In any case, a common understanding of the challenges ahead sets a landscape where, hopefully, future directions will be compatible enough such that the domain itself will not vanish under useless internecine strife that doesn't produce any material benefits to the industry collective. Often, the most interesting discussions center on defining what the industry is really about. In our particular situation, during the mid-to-late 1990's, it became increasingly apparent that an emergent species of the computer family, a variant we term the personal electronic device, was becoming the ultimate carrier of personal identity in the digital world. Each device has the ability to contain the critical, private personal information that was needed to access any service with flexibility, such that the secure core of the device can actually control what is, for all practical purposes, how the rest of the world sees the person through the prism of electronic networks. Our consideration of the intimate relationship of trust and policy, together with their derivative requirement for the establishment of identity, illuminates the systemic requirements of these devices such that individuals are able to more forcefully project the roles that they play within every social infrastructure that they participate in.

To relate computers to people, we need to understand groups and grouping mechanisms. For the human species, anticipating the development of group mechanisms was the development of basic communication among individuals. Within the domain of computers, personal electronic devices, like people, find their expression in communication and through this expression they find their persona; their identity. In the context of network access, be it for telecommunications, financial transactions, transport or the Internet, personal electronic devices exchange credentials, warrant the authority and enable the privacy required in the age of digital society. Moreover, while identity is a central and recurring theme of an individual personalized computer, their true utility extends into the conveyance and application of policy that controls actions in specific, though variable situations.

By the end of the XX$^{th}$ century, the market for personal electronic devices had expanded enough that we could see their efficacy in several policy domains. For example, we can specifically note the role of such devices in the field of international telecommunications with cellular phones with or without digital capabilities of all sorts, in the flow of financial interchange with chip-enabled bank cards, in the development of digital entertainment on the Internet with music players enforcing digital rights and in the establishment of secure international networks by companies and organizations spanning the planet with instantaneous links through the auspices of identities protected by secure tokens. These devices have a common ingredient that we refer to as a secure core, commonly an embedded computer chip that is used for the secret, private and highly trusted parts of their operations.

While personal electronic devices were instrumental in the earliest efforts to facilitate access to and control of complex policy environments, we have come to recognize that a larger theological perspective is necessary for the shaping of our understanding of the relationship between real human beings and their network personae expressed by their secure cores. This recognition further suggested a need for us to better understand the role of the more intimate aspect of religious frameworks, particularly the mystic experience that is found at the base of every religion. Such an intriguing prospect stimulated our consideration and accompanied us in the extended journey of this writing.

Our perspective is that truly portable, private personal computing devices, like religions, are ultimately about trust and policy. They embody the current man-machine interface at the level of establishment, conveyance, implementation and boundary definition of our complex, often bewildering maze of competing and conflicting trust and policy infrastructures. They provide for the recognition of trust authorities and for the identification of the individual within the spheres of influence of those authorities. Furthermore, they are trusted conveyors of the policy environment itself, encompassing both *authority* and individual *identity*. A central characteristic of capability and utility is their ability to act as trusted arbiters of an individual's policy choices within that environment. We might think of them in a certain guise as filling the role of *shaman*, a bridge between the divine source of trust and the earthly reality of policy.

As we have lived through and subsequently studied the explosive evolution of computer technology and social mores of the last half-century, we have drawn parallels between the development of religion and religious practice through the ages and the manner in which computers have emerged as at least one evolutionary pathway of mankind's migration from the purely physical world to the cyber-world that frames our current society. The secure cores of personal electronic devices are now the most prevalent computers in the world. They are the central element of the wireless revolution. They are the mind of a two billion mobile phones and the heart of hundreds of millions of credit cards. They're the keys to uncountable doors and the identities of faceless, nameless and oftentimes anonymous users of computer systems and networks around the world. They encompass the most advanced hardware and software to bring personal, private computing to the world population in the most egalitarian spread of advanced technology seen in many generations. Rest assured we chose the concepts of faceless, nameless and anonymous most judiciously; they all are critical roles enabled by personal electronic devices.

# Variations on the Theme

Policy is a construct that is sensitive to context. Consider the admonition from our Prologue, "Don't talk to strangers!" If we consider the implementation of this rule, we're first struck with the need to establish the context for the transaction to which, or within which this rule applies. Moreover, the potential consequences governed by the outcome of the transaction have tremendous bearing on the trust levels that will be necessary or acceptable in the conduct of the transaction. If the policy is being applied by one's five-year-old daughter approached by a man in an automobile, then extreme caution is obviously required. If it's being applied by an adult answering the telephone at the office, then a different level of required trust is appropriate. Consider the image that is conjured in our minds by the statement: "He's a scrooge." If we're thinking of Ebenezer Scrooge as he appears early in the telling of Charles Dickens' *A Christmas Carol*, then we think of a bitter, miserly old man. On the other hand, at the end of the story we know that Scrooge "...was as good a man as the good old city knew..." The context is the defining ingredient. This suggests to us then the potential use of trusted computers in the establishment of context prior to, or as part of the application of policy. This is an area in which the best of our computer systems are just beginning to show promise of utility. To see how far we have to go, it is interesting to consider the range of the human mind in its use of context for the act of communication. Perhaps nowhere do we see the subtleties of context sensitive communication as well as through the arts.

Art is a process that can evoke transitional changes in the state of consciousness of the beholder. In various guises, different art forms address the complete sensory experience of human physiology. Through this sensory experience, the emotional as well as cognitive responses may be impacted. The result is that what might be thought of as the normal state of consciousness of the beholder is induced into an altered state. Within this state, an enhanced level of trust is attributed to the message conveyed by the art. That trust then allows the brain to record the message as part of its trust infrastructure. Once the message is recorded the brain can return to its initial state, albeit with a modified trust infrastructure which may later have consequences on its cognitive functions. We will consider these mechanisms in more detail in Chapters 4 and 5. The net consequence is that art tends to represent a direct conveyance of trust from the purveyor to the beholder.

From an historical perspective, if we consider art in all its various forms that has been passed down since the dawn of civilization, it is clear that religion has been an organizing principle. Indeed, religion takes the facility of art to stimulate a common state of consciousness among a body of participants. This brings us to the initial connection that we perceived between religion and computer networks; a foundation in the concepts of trust and subsequently derived policy through which is achieved coordinated activity among a group of individuals. From the earliest religious activities, art has been intimately linked with the expression of mystical states and the marriage of spirit and social behavior. We suggest that art shows us the path that relates the theology that forms the framework of policy with the trust that derives of ecstasy in the ultimate revelation of our inner selves. If computers allow us to mesh in the digital world of policy effectuation, can computers be so foreign to our real identity that our theology would stop at the edge of society, and not, in any way, reflect through them some image of higher religious states?

Art and religion at many times and in many aspects are virtually indistinguishable. This holds true for art in its various guises and is just as applicable to religion in its many forms. It is in the artistic impressions from antiquity to the present that we find much of the foundation for the future evolution of personal electronic devices. Religious significance is fairly easy to come by in museums filled with artistic endeavors. It is also found in the parietal art of cave paintings and perhaps even in the modern renditions of Campbell Soup cans. Consider some examples.

The Louvre Museum's Mesopotamia section presents the bullae of the fourth millennium B.C. They were first simple clay receptacles, the size of an egg with tokens inside, illustrating the number of, say, sheep to be brought to market. The herdsman would receive the bulla from his master and would bring the herd to destination, giving the clay pot to the buyer who could check that the sheep have all arrived. As time passed by and counterfeiting became a recurring threat, bullae became beautiful objects patterned with intricately decorated seals that were the holograms of the time. Such patterns were difficult to replicate and thus were a deterrent to fraud, but the counterfeiters eventually overcame this obstacle. When gods were finally represented on the bullae to insure that nobody would dare to duplicate the seals lest they would endure divine punition, the bulla had ascended to become the conveyor of commerce, a summit of ancient art and the religion endowed carrier of the policies of the time. Naturally, such mechanisms would offer little impediment to non-believers.

In part through various artistic media, human beings have evolved ever more powerful means of communication that have yet to find a match in the computer world. They are an affectation of policy through subtle means rooted in the ecstasy of the mind that we do not yet know how to describe, let alone implement within computer systems; but we can start. We ascribe substance to these mechanisms through the art and art forms that parallel mankind's ascendancy among species that function as individuals within a collective. The problem is one of context-sensitive conveyance of policy; of policy specification as applied to a given set of participants, at a given time, in a given place and with an agreed upon purpose.

In the XVIII$^{th}$ Century, an ukiyoe print from the shogunate era of Japan (the XVII$^{th}$ – XIX$^{th}$ Centuries) entitled The Cat's Claw expressed for us the power of such communication in one picture. The print is by Utagawa Kuniyoshi and is representative of an age of repression on the forms of art. To defy authorities, Kuniyoshi painted in a form of graffiti that diminished the appearance of his message of theatrical exchange while keeping its content intact. (We are indebted to Maki Hirotani, a student of Japanese cultural periods whom we had the pleasure to encounter when researching this print, for helping us seek references. Any error of interpretation, naturally, is ours.)

This meaning within a meaning relevance of art permeates many, if not all of our endeavors. Consider the paintings of Giuseppe Arcimboldo. Here was a XVI$^{th}$ Century painter at the court of Rudolf II (of the Hapsburg dynasty) who painted in vegetables. A number of his paintings hang in the Louvre. From a distance, they appear to be portraits of the patrons of the time. On closer

1  Tat Tvam Asi

inspection however, one sees that a face is really a collection of various forms of flora. A nose might actually be a pickle and an ear a leaf of lettuce. To a modern observer such presentation suggests merely early experiments with form and technique. However, in fact in the context of the era the paintings offer a deeper significance. Certainly no other artist of the era exhibited more creativity in symbolizing the desired balance between nature and personal harmony that was ostensibly achieved by Rudolf's reign.

Whether there is any direct connection, it is interesting to note that where Arcimboldo painted "in vegetables," a couple of centuries later Kuniyoshi painted "in people." In some of his works, the details of the faces of geisha are comprised of silhouettes of people. We suggest that in both instances, the sub-text offered by the innovative forms was instrumental in establishing the appropriate context for full appreciation of the art. While the vegetables expressed the power of nature, the silhouettes expressed the nature of power.

Like many artisans of that era, Arcimboldo's interests ranged into other areas as well. He experimented with new forms of musical notation using colors, an earlier intuition of an actual brain phenomenon called *synesthesia*. Today we experiment with the use of different fonts to convey semantic meaning in written material. Musical notation in color is perhaps even more intriguing in that later, in examining the ability to decompose analytical problems into computational segments that can be pursued in parallel, it is interesting to consider the abilities of the musical composer, who understands the language of chords, as a similar facility. Parallel processing has much in common with musical composition in chords; the melody is important but the harmony makes the music.

Subtle communication through context is obviously not constrained to the visual arts. Many of us remember the coming of the dawn as we read, or even better, listened to Marc Antony extol, "Friends, Romans, countrymen; lend me your ears. I come to bury Caesar, not to praise him." The feelings evoked by the soliloquy, as intended by Shakespeare, were indeed ones of praise for Caesar and condemnation for Brutus and the other conspirators. The message within the message was clear to the most opaque of us. Indeed, we have come to realize that theatre as an art form perhaps most closely parallels the consideration of social ecosystems that are the focus of this book. We will be drawn back to the genre in the discussions of our final chapter.

As additional examples, we note that from Picasso's *Guernica* to Jonathan Swift's *Gulliver's Travels*, we are taken from the visual shot in the mouth to the literary *double entendre*. Too many artists have researched alternate states of consciousness in order to stimulate and preserve their creative endeavors to render it possible to ignore the spiritual élan behind art communication as the premier form of context sensitive communication. If computers would ever represent us in the ornate details of bouncing policies, will they not have to take the route through art school?

Context sensitive communication can be extremely efficient. Through established context, a message can impact not only the cognitive functions of the mind of the receiver but the emotional centers as well. The result can be a strong stimulus to action on the part of the receiver. Consider for example the story of Jonah in the *Christian Bible*. We generally remember the part about Jonah being swallowed by a great fish during his flight to avoid God's mandate to take a message of impending condemnation to the people of the City of Nineveh. Jonah really didn't want to be the messenger because he knew too well the manner in which his God acted. He was likely to show mercy and forgiveness to the intended receivers of the message and yet, not necessarily with a particularly good immediate outcome for the messenger. Finally succumbing to the will of God, Jonah travels to Nineveh. Arriving at the bordering walls, he then treks for three days to reach the center of the city. There, he utters his entire message: "Yet forty days and Nineveh shall be overthrown." At which point, the citizens of Nineveh got religion! They quickly comprehended the context within which the message was sent. This was pretty much their last chance. They should best perceive the consequences of ignoring the policy that the message suggested. In due fashion, they repented of their evil ways. They donned sackcloth and they accepted the redemption opportunity that God had offered them. Such is power of context. A message, though succinct, can move mountains.

As is always the case, examples that demonstrate the negative are as interesting as the positive. Our theme is that religion has been instrumental in reinforcing the evolutionary survival of its groups of believers. We can consider three religious social groups that, to varying degrees, demonstrate that such groups are in fact engaged in an evolutionary struggle and that not always do they win. Let us consider the Shakers, the Incas and the Mayas as object lessons; certainly there are others, but these give us a flavor of the threats that must be engaged and overcome if the group is to survive.

Formed as an offshoot of the Quakers, the Shaking Quakers and hence the Shakers were, for a time, a thriving religious community. Their beliefs, however, were perceived to be at significant odds with more dominant religious affiliations and as a consequence they suffered severe discrimination at the hands of other religions' followers; a demonstration that competition among religious communities can sometimes be a contact sport.

Religious persecution notwithstanding, the Shakers made a number of extremely innovative contributions to the art and technology of the day. These included highly functional and utilitarian architecture, beautiful albeit simple furniture and a highly organized lifestyle. For a time, they thrived. Unfortunately, their religious dogma suffered from two rather debilitating deficiencies. First, they had a very strong moral stance that endorsed the practice of celibacy. Interestingly enough, this had the very positive benefit of diminishing the social distinctions between men and women. Probably more than any other social or religious grouping, the Shakers were truly gender neutral with respect to their everyday environment. Unfortunately, total celibacy runs at cross currents with the biological evolutionary process; continuation of the species becomes problematic. Moreover, as we'll consider in some detail in Chapter 8, a necessary capability of social structure is the proper provisioning of the young to carry on the existing social order.

A deficiency of Shaker dogma was the source and interpretation of the dogma itself. Shakerism was not heavily grounded in either written words or long-held traditions. Consequently, the philosophy and direction of the church tended to vary as the old leaders died and new leaders came to the fore. As a warrantor of trust, the continuity of a belief system over long periods is a source of strength for a religious organization. If long-term stability over many generations of believers is not achieved, then the group may well find itself at a societal disadvantage relative to other groups. In this case, the end result seemed to be that the Shaker faithful either died off or drifted away from the faith. The end result was the virtually total decline of the religion itself. Thus, we would suggest that from an evolutionary standpoint, the Shaker variant of Protestant Christianity sprung up as a point mutation. While its characteristics were laudable in certain instances, this variant was not judged worthy by the process of natural selection and hence became extinct.

Another example on a significantly larger scale is that of the Incas. In their emergent times, the Incas formed a thriving culture in the mid-Andes of South America. Over the ages, they developed a comprehensive, complex social order. They built cities, they developed commerce and technology and they demonstrated superior capabilities of defending themselves against their neighboring social groups. Then, the Spanish showed up on their doorstep.

The Spanish social order, grounded in Roman Catholicism, was extremely adept at the game of national and international interaction. Under the auspices of the Church, the Spaniards pursued the business of extending the reach of their society around the world through exploration, conquest and colonization in order to enhance their position on the world's stage. One might argue that this is as much a function of social systems as finding new techniques for killing wooly mammoths was a function of the early hunting parties of *Neanderthals*. When the Spanish conquistadors encountered the Incas they had an ace in the hole that even they didn't realize. Existing on the gigantic land mass of Europe and Asia, with easy lines of communication to Africa, the basic physiology of Spanish humans had encountered a myriad of diseases. As a consequence, they had developed some ability to ameliorate the impact and spread of such diseases. At least they weren't totally surprised when large numbers of people dropped dead. The Incas were not so fortunate.

When the first explorers from the old world arrived, they brought with them many instances of old world diseases. From this source various epidemics decimated the Incan society, killing perhaps as many as two thirds of the population. This had two effects. First, it diminished the ability of the Incan social order to respond to the physical threat of the Spaniards. But, perhaps even more insidious, the appearance of death in the form of completely unknown diseases struck at the very basis of trust of Incan society. The end result was the virtual capitulation of Incan governance, although many vestiges of Incan religious symbolism continue to this day. Thus, while providing superior characteristics in a closed environment, the Incan social order proved insufficient to meet the threats posed by exposure to an environment that included other social structures.

A third example is that of the Mayan civilization. Spanning a much longer time period than the Incas, the Mayas dominated a region centered on today's south-eastern Mexico and Guatemala, They built cities, they developed commerce and technology and they demonstrated superior capabilities of defending themselves against their neighboring social orders. However, while today we still see vestiges of Mayan culture and symbolism, the grandiose social structure disappeared in an almost mysterious fashion several hundred years ago. While some of the last remnants of the society were conquered by the Spanish, much as had been the case with the Incas, the heart of the extended civilization was long dead by that time. There are a number of suggested causes for the decline and demise. For example, Jared Diamond in his book *Collapse* considers several possible causes for such a social downfall: excessive damage to their natural environment, climate change, internecine struggle, deficiencies of the social order itself and interruption of trade, and commerce with other social orders.

In the case of the Mayas, the most common perception is that climate change coupled with severe deforestation of the local ecosystem in order to support their style of agriculture was among the leading causes of decline. In essence, the social system could not affect sufficient control over the physical ecosystem in order to adequately support the population. The empty shells of the great cities of the Mayas reflect depopulation, not external conquest or internal struggle. Hence, we surmise that the social order encountered a threat for which it had no adequate response. Being unable to adapt, the trust infrastructure of the social order collapsed and the suppliants vanished, or changed their sustenance to meet their social needs.

In any case, through such examples, we are led to recognize that behind the richness and complexity of human social interactions laid interrelated mechanisms that allowed the building and destroying of societies in their constant renewal.

# The Technical Realm

Computers and computer networks extend across a broad plane of cost and capability. Some work for us, the individual users, while others often treat us as resources under their purview. We have observed that personal electronic devices are iconic examples of systems that work on our behalf. The implication is that such systems are small and inexpensive enough to allow their ubiquitous deployment; essentially every person can have at least one, but perhaps several. Be they called e-mail communicator, mobile phone, personal assistant, ultra-portable computer, key fob or credit card with a chip, they are meant to always be on the person of their bearer. They contain bearer-related information of importance whose protection is assumed by both the person owning the device and the institutions in communication with the device. For example, the account information in the mobile phone is private and is used to appropriately charge communications. Another example is the personal information allowing employees to link to their company network. Certainly the employee and the company count on it to be protected. Finally, yet another example is the information on the chip of a credit card. It actually represents money, always a target for theft. Most important, however, is the ability of the computer to establish and vouch for the unique identity of the computer bearer. It is through this ability to establish and convey identity in a highly trusted fashion that such computers truly become the conveyors of policy in the modern world.

What we plan to explore in this book is a required set of characteristics of personal electronic devices that allow them to function as our representatives within the cyber-world. From our perspective, the optimal such computer does not yet exist. However, personal devices that deal with important private information have at their core a security system. The actual security varies considerably from device to device. The core security mechanisms range from barely protected software keys to specialized hardware called a *trusted module* whose purpose is to encompass dedicated security circuitry or even specialized processors. If the optimal private computer is the culmination stepping stone of the evolution of private, personal, secure computational facilities, then the trusted module is perhaps the emergent species of this family. The size of a match head, a trusted module is oriented from its design onward toward being a secure token for the individual being. As such, it is an excellent kicking off point as we consider the connection between computer systems in general and the social structure of human groups.

Personal electronic devices are at the forefront of an emerging technological infrastructure within which people live and work. The infrastructure offers us every increasing levels of service and yet we find ourselves at an increasing disadvantage as we try to exist comfortably within it because of its extent, speed and complexity. We desire it, or are required to make use of it, but we often do so at our peril because of these factors. Certainly, few among us are completely comfortable in engaging in complex transactions with faceless, nameless and anonymous entities that exist in the amorphous cyberspace that defines much of our current world. Our physical environment is similarly suspect. Often we find ourselves quite uncomfortable with the presence of strangers in certain venues of our lives. Yet, we must interact with the ill known and the unseen; it is the way of our existence.

Within the various computers on the network, the spread of viruses, worms, Trojan Horse and other malevolent diseases threaten the health of the entire infrastructure. If one has an e-mail address that's been around for a decade or so, it is likely that it is on so many spam lists as to render it incapable of conveying useful information. When one out of a hundred messages is actually good, the channel is of little use. Of almost equal concern is the economic paradigm of the infrastructure, driven largely by advertising. Trying to read a body of information while seeing brightly colored bouncing balls on one side of the screen and falling raindrops on the other is a tough way to gather and act on information. It is, of course the economic model of the Web. The admonition is no longer, "Lend me your ears." but rather, "How about I rent them for a while?" We exchange our time and our attention for the daily sports scores or a timely weather report. At some point, this becomes a bad bargain. Personal electronic devices are an emergent technology that needs to show us a way out of this morass.

In their biggest numbers, personal electronic device cores are just computers. They contain a screen, a keyboard, a microphone and a speaker phone, a central processing unit, some forms of memory and a bunch of glue-works that hold them together, both literally and figuratively. They function within the social infrastructure of the day; today's infrastructure being the world of ubiquitous computers, worldwide networks, complex transactions and interactions and a social, legal and economic framework that has not quite caught up to the technology. The characteristics that make personal electronic devices distinct from earlier computer technology are rooted in the manner in which they are constructed and their intended use.

Personal electronic devices aim to be unyielding, yet affordable computing platforms; their very being is grounded in the concept of trust as we have previously described it. They are cheap enough to achieve ubiquity yet they are capable enough to establish a trusted platform that can launch at least our identity, but more important our personality into the cyber-world as well as into the physical world. They become part of our person in a physical sense and they subsume our person in an electronic sense. They provide a place for us to store personal information that really belongs only to us.

While not provably immune from the problems that plague other technologies that seek to fill many of the same functional niches, they possess characteristics that make them arguably more appropriate to the domain than other technologies. Their secure core is built around principles that foster the security necessary for trust to be established in their capability to safeguard privacy. For example, the connection of the secure core to the outside world is simple at its base but capable of conveying complex concepts, much like the artistic channels that we mentioned previously. This simplicity offers the prospect of defense against, if not immunity from the diseases that infect other technologies.

The most defining characteristic of the secure core of personal electronic devices is their apparent monolithic structure, as compared with other computer systems. They are quite small relative to other computers; about the size of a match-head. At the extreme, a personal electronic device can be made of just a private, secure core. In this case, it is typically called a *chip card*, or a *smart card*, or an *RFID* (Radio-Frequency Identification) tag. Consider for example the chip card that is used for payment in many countries of the world; such devices number in the hundreds of millions. The plastic case in which they are mounted, the form that we all think of as a credit card, is a convenient vehicle for transporting them and using them; but, it is a peripheral characteristic to the genre. In this case, the form-factor of the card pre-dates the existence of the computer that we put inside. The existence of the surrounding environment that could deal with that plastic card form-factor made for a convenient entry point for this most elementary personal electronic device.

The credit card form-factor found its early footing in the arena of financial transactions, as an enabler of cash-less vending in the world of multi-national and multi-cultural economics. The size of the card is heavily based on personal ergonomics and fashion. One of the earliest, if not the first incarnation was the Diners' Club card, circa 1950. The card was of a size that nicely fit into a shirt or coat pocket, or could be more securely carried within a wallet. The working man's wallet, the billfold suggested a size about half that of a dollar-bill if you didn't want it to get creased when you put your wallet in your back pocket and sat on it. The earliest card provided its trust conveyance through its printed body. It provided a token that established the financial integrity of the bearer to the vendor, at least to the extent that local restaurants would let you charge dinner if you had a card. The card worked in a relatively small locale where everyone knew everyone or, at least most everyone that needed to know knew of the card and what it meant.

Of course, where there's money there are people that want it, without necessarily deserving it. Less obvious than the appearance of the first credit card was the appearance of the first counterfeit credit card. But, it did occur, and thus began the attack and countermeasures cycle of the use of the card. The early cards migrated from a generically printed card to one that had a name and perhaps an account number of some type on it. This initial usage was followed by the desire to employ the card as a means of commerce beyond the local neighborhood. That required greater infrastructure: a citywide, statewide, nation-wide and then worldwide infrastructure. In order to both level the playing field, and make it something of a trustworthy playing field at that, standards had to be established. This is the way of technology.

Lest you think we're moving rather far a field from our starting point, bear in mind that standardization in the world of computing infrastructures is something of an amalgam of Mecca connected to Jerusalem via the Ganges and protected by the fortress of Machu Picchu. It is a nexus of divine guidance within a world of chaos.

Today, one can, while waiting for a plane at the Austin, Texas airport, pay for lunch with a credit card. Then, boarding the plane, leave the confines of Austin, fly to Hong Kong, walk into a hotel, and pay for a room with the same credit card. That's something of a *tour de force* of standardization. This was the goal as the earliest credit cards began their journey through the standards making maze.

First, the size of the card was fixed; then some of the numbers and words; account numbers, not just the numbers, but also their internal structure. Who issued them, who stood behind them and were they accurately represented on the card. Notice that we're now getting into the realm of conveying information; and, not just any information, but information that we, as the card bearer, really do want the hotel clerk in Hong Kong to believe and accept as payment for our room. So, more and more information content was affixed onto the surface of the card.

The issuer's logo conveyed an idea of who stood behind the financial transactions involved. In Hong Kong, they don't know us from Cain and Abel (to lapse back into the whirlpool of the metaphoric build-up of religious expression) but they do seem to understand Visa, MasterCard or American Express. Unfortunately, the people that all this information needed to be conveyed to, the people that really needed to trust it, are the short-order cook at the Austin airport and the night-clerk at the hotel in Hong Kong. Today, a listing of all of the identity-type cards issued by *trust authorities* in the United States alone comes to about one hundred small-print pages. A listing to include all the passport documents in the world, with details of how to tell that each one is valid, adds two or three hundred more pages. If one is really going to trust a card presented by a stranger, then one needs to be able to apply the rules of authentication for the specific card. This is a very complex transaction to be performed and we're still just at the point of wanting to understand and believe the information on the face of the card. The world we've evolved into in just a half-century is already too complex for the Secretary of the Department of Homeland Security, let alone the hotel night-clerk to individually apply all the necessary rules; and rest assured, to show understanding, we could just as correctly reverse the order of that comparison.

The complexity arises because, when it's just printed plastic, it doesn't take a national mint to build a fraudulent card. All the pure printing mechanisms can be attacked through ever evolving printing technology, and at ever decreasing prices. So, as a way to address counterfeit printing, additional information conveyance mechanisms were added to the card; embossed characters, holograms and magnetic stripes. Each step an increment towards a more secure token and, interestingly enough, often a step toward machine readability as a way to automate the authentication process. So, we've now advanced beyond just conveying information and have entered the world of interpretation of that information. Thus, the current incarnation of the banking chip card is a regular banking card with a small computer inside

As we will consider in some greater detail later, communication is an ever more increasingly complex problem. Conveying more and more information is a tough problem, but the intelligent use of that information is even more daunting.

The basic banking chip card physically looks like a credit card with a small metal faceplate on the front of it. That faceplate allows for electrical connectivity between the outside world and the computer embedded in the plastic card. This electrical connectivity is one means of effecting basic information flow between the card's computer and the outside world, as represented by another computer. First, electrical power can flow across this metal faceplate so that the outside world can provide the power to run the computer in the card. An interesting point, when the card is in your pocket it's not powered. So, it's not operating, thus keeping it away from a class of electronic attacks.

Also, across the metal faceplate on the card can flow bits of data, strings of electrical ones and zeros that convey information from the computer in the card to the computer in the outside world. This information flow allows the two computers (the outside world and the card) to cooperate on deciding what to do in certain situations and perhaps even how to do it; that is, they can negotiate and implement policy.

Relate this back to the conveyance of information through various artistic media that we mentioned earlier. There we saw that the true information transfer was often submerged somewhat below the surface of what we initially or easily perceived. Such is the case with trusted computer communications. The early transactions between the outside world and the embedded computer were simple indeed. "Tell me where you come from: Visa, MasterCard or American Express?" But, then cards began to be counterfeited and the questions became, "After you tell me where you came from, tell me your 'account number'." Implicit in the question was the fact that the questioner had a way to check on the account number through some mechanism external to the card. But, it was awkward to always have this alternative mechanism.

So, the trusted core evolved to only give up its information if it really trusted the computer it was talking to. "Show me yours and I'll show you mine." became a way of doing business, as it perhaps has always been. With such enhanced trust conveyance, more detailed information could be conveyed to and from the core and more involved, and perhaps sensitive and/or valuable transactions pursued. This is the evolutionary pathway that we're going down; it will be interesting to see where it leads. Whether we use a mobile phone, a personal digital assistant or an ultra-mobile computer, we trust them to represent us faithfully on the network. And that is a real topic for the remainder of the book.

# Some Method in the Madness

It is hopefully clear, but never too late for us to clarify the fact that we see parallels between many aspects of the application of religion and similar aspects in the use, or potential use of computers. We do not consider computers in general, or their trusted core, as religious objects in their own right or as elements of overt religious practice. The parallel that we've drawn to the evolution and use of computers is the recurring presence of religion and its mechanisms during the evolution of mankind. We do this with the utmost respect for religious practice. We do not perceive our considerations as demeaning the concepts of religion, but rather of elevating the concepts of technical evolution in general and computers specifically. That said, we do recognize somewhat tongue in cheek that a properly laminated variant of one's American Express Platinum Card would make a good tombstone in that it says a lot about how we spent our lives as well as our money.

It is anecdotally appropriate to mention that we were drawn to the idea that religion is a recurring theme in societal evolution from the viewpoint of how we've seen technology, particularly computers, evolve. It was only after this slow dawning that we perceived that religion as an evolutionary mechanism was a mature field in its own right as studied from the viewpoint of evolutionary biology. Building on this realization, we subsequently found many interesting and diverse chains of discovery within the literature of fields of study centered on cognitive science and developmental psychology. We have drawn from some of the seminal works of the genre a number of areas that seem to offer striking insights into the technology realm of computers.

Perhaps one of the more profound aspects to us has been the concept of multi-level selection derived from grouping mechanisms, as well as individual natural selection, as evolutionary principle of species. Specifically in the case of humans, it has been illuminating to note the credibility of religion as a general mechanism in the multi-level selection process. While our digital identity plunges into the networked crowds and their subtle, reflexive, ever bouncing interactions, where does the trusted computer take its inspiration? Or does it need to? Does it belong?

For millennia, the justification for governance in China derived from the Mandate of Heaven. For cycle upon cycle of dynasties of Chinese emperors, the right to govern was derived from this precept; those who come to power must discern among paths they follow and select those that provide for the welfare of the people. For those dynasties that depart from the correct way, Heaven withdraws its mandate and a new regime is obligated to revolt and assume control. While China is today ostensibly one of the most a-religious countries in the world, in fact it is difficult to see much difference in governance from the days of the emperors. The Cultural Revolution of the second half of the XX$^{th}$ Century has most of the characteristics of a theocratic schism. Such characteristics include a vision from a charismatic leader, a shaman by any other name, that guided the actions of multitudes of the faithful to effect justice and vengeance on those not sufficiently fervent in the faith. A fertile field, it would seem, in which to sow the seeds of the trusted computer variety of complex policy.

The largest market for personal technology today is China. A powerful country where the fragile equilibrium between independence and centralization has endured millennia of conflicts, this was a country where historical happenstance would widely open the gates for various technical venues, personal computers included. Bypassing the establishment of pre-digital infrastructures found in old industrial countries, the expansion of China has been fueled by the deployment of extremely advanced telecommunications and banking infrastructures; all based on the possibility to locally secure and rule personal expansion through technology. We will consider in a later chapter the evolutionary characteristics that this leap-frogging of technology represents, but we can introduce the concept here.

The evolutionary principles that one can see within religious organizations are often found within business infrastructures as well. There are well-defined life cycles within the business community in general, and within its technological components specifically, that often manifest themselves through the widespread adoption of new technologies in favor of incremental evolution of older technologies. If a technological mutation falls on particularly fertile grounds, perhaps from a sociological point of view, the results can be a very strong reinforcement of the specific mutation through group selection mechanisms. We consider this model as particularly appropriate for viewing private computing as a technological mutation with its acceptance in China.

Found within the archeological record of China are early examples of abstractions of the human identity; visualizations of that aspect of the human condition that attempts to distinguish us from the other animals and portray us as permanent, supernatural beings in our own right. Jinsha village is a suburb of the capital city of Sichuan Province. In 2001, ruins were discovered that dated back 3,000 years. Unearthed from the ruins were artifacts covering a wide range of media as well as very diverse segments of the society of ancient China. The artifacts were replete with intricate detail and made use of materials and art-form expressions that are relevant even in today's world. They represent to us the fact that human expression has evolved less over the last few thousand years than has the technology that we can use to extend that expression.

The use of individual devices in China cuts across all aspects of Chinese society, from cultural to economic to political. In the Special Administrative Regions (SARs) of the former British colony of Hong Kong and the former Portuguese colony of Macau, chip cards have been strongly adopted in two distinct realms. Found in the financial venue, the Octopus Card in Hong Kong is a contactless card, i.e. a card communicating with radio waves, which is used as a bearer's electronic purse. At specific kiosks throughout the city cash can be loaded onto the card. The card can then be used for a wide variety of cash-oriented transactions, ranging from paying for a subway or train ride to purchasing groceries at a convenience food market. The transactions are fast, which benefits the consumer and they are cashless, which benefits the vendor.

On the legal front, electronic identity cards are being introduced to speed the movement of people between the special administration regions and mainland China. Effecting the philosophy of "one country, two systems," the legal framework of mainland China is significantly different from that in the Special Administration Regions. As a consequence, the movement of citizens between the regions is monitored and controlled, much as the movement of people among different sovereign states is monitored and controlled throughout the rest of the world. Electronic identity cards are being used in large-scale pilot programs to facilitate the movement across borders. This is quite analogous to the extension of *Machine-Readable Travel Documents* (MRTD) used by member countries of the *Visa Waiver Program*, of which the United States is a prime mover. These electronic credentials, when fully deployed, offer the possibility to speed travelers through passport checkpoints with enhanced identity authentication and yet ostensibly minimal inconvenience to the traveler. The goal, of course being enhanced authentication of the identities of the travelers for the states involved.

If China represents the opportunities of the marketplace, contributions to the fountain of technological innovation come from many societies, both cultural and economic. While cellular telephony derived its early pilot deployments within the United States, it was really the

Scandinavian countries that fully exploited the technology. It was a rather interesting confluence of geography, culture, economics, as well as technical and manufacturing capabilities that came to create the focal point for deployment of cellular technology. More people on a per capita basis have cellular phones in Scandinavia than anywhere else in the world.

Cellular telephony is very interesting in that it represents the joining of two significant technologies (cheap, personal mobile telephony and secure core computers) related to complex human interaction. We remember hearing Douglas Adams, author of *The Hitchhiker's Guide to the Galaxy*, recount in a humorous lunchtime presentation at the 1998 CardTech/SecurTech conference in Washington D.C. how he watched his children and their friends adopt as their own, as the young have a tendency to do, the new, ubiquitous communication technology. Based on his observations of their use of cellular phones, he concluded that such phones provide excellent mechanisms for establishing the size, extent, and current activities of the herd.

Also, from Scandinavia, the firm Ericsson was the first major company to introduce a headset powered by Bluetooth, a means for small devices to communicate seamlessly over short distances. When we first saw this device around 1999, we realized that computers were getting very personal indeed. To that date, cellular phones, digital assistants and other personal electronic devices had been manipulated by hand. Suddenly, they found a host much closer to the human person. In a sense, they were just one step closer to becoming somehow, a part of human nature. As an extension of the brain, or perhaps more accurately, a new part of the brain, isn't it to be expected that they be permeated by the spirituality that pervades humanity itself?

# Onward through the Fog

A Chinese proverb suggests that "A journey of a thousand miles begins with a single step." As with all metaphorical references, fully appreciating this maxim requires context. Consider a child, exhausted from an active day of play but setting out for an evening stroll at the behest of her parents. Viewed within this context, the proverb might engender a feeling of futility and dread on the part of the child, "I'm tired! I don't want to go for a walk! When are we going to get back home?" However, to a young solder, beginning physical therapy in order to learn to use a prosthetic device after losing a leg in battle, the proverb might engender apprehension toward the impending struggle with perhaps a bit of eager anticipation of regaining a degree of mobility that suggests a return in some small way to a world of normalcy. For Forest Gump, from the movie of the same name, it might pass as an unnoticed afterthought as he sets out to run, just because he felt like running: to the end of the lane, across town, across Greenbow County, across the Great State of Alabama and on to the ocean. Thus we recognize allusion to both the journey and to the traveler. Based on this opening chapter, we're ready to begin our trip. We know something of the destination but the path to get there is still shrouded in the fog. A map, or at least some guideposts, might help us keep to the trail, arcane though it may be. By establishing context for the journey, when we look up and realize "we're not in Kansas anymore!" we might still know that we're on the yellow brick road that leads to the Emerald City.

Our fellow travelers appear to us as well-read and formally educated. Given that one doesn't necessarily imply the other, in fact either alone will probably suffice to assure a good understanding of the material we'll present. Much of the journey that we're embarking on relates to language; its foundation and its use. This leads us to try to use words rather carefully. In many instances, this has required us to stretch our own vocabularies a bit and as a consequence we might enlist an expansion on the part of our readers. Language is an enabling facility for the formation and operation of groups. Grouping mechanisms, or perhaps a bit more formally stated, social orders form a central theme of this book. We will observe that the evolutionary progression of social order is very much an application of the process of metaphor development and subsequent redefinition. This is how our Prologue started. Later in the book we will further consider the premise that a salient feature of modern humans is that of metaphoric comprehension. Hence, the reader must also be a bit wary of the commonly held definitions of the metaphors we address. We will attempt to make our specific understanding clear and in some instances we may deviate a bit from convention.

Our trip is of necessity interdisciplinary. Traveling from Chicago to Los Angeles on old Route 66 involved traversing a great variety of terrain. So it is with our journey. The prairies of the upper Midwest are far removed from the rugged vistas of Death Valley. Likewise, human physiology and computer programming are similarly displaced along our route of travel. In due course, we will introduce our perceptions of the many disciplines that we will encounter. For those with reading tastes and experiences consistent with our own, some of this detail may seem a bit redundant. However, for those more comfortable in only certain of the domains, which we expect to be the greater number, the detail is necessary. Where the trail meanders into slog, we'll suggest an appropriate detour over the high ground. Our intent is to provide context and nuance. Our goal is a work that provides a prism through which is displayed the rainbow hidden in the light emanating from the fog.

Our first step is the assertion that human social orders are a direct manifestation of the species. They derive as much from explicit anatomical and physiological characteristics as from cognitive impulse. In fact, we suggest that the cognitive impulses aimed at establishing social order are themselves anatomical and physiological manifestations. Anatomy establishes our means and model of thought. Physiology guides how we think and what we think about. Subsequently, we observe that computers are tools of the species. Interconnections of these tools form computer networks that are best exemplified as direct extensions of social orders. Thus, based on an assumption that we may be traveling to common destinations from similar points of departure, we anticipate a parallel between organic evolutionary mechanisms and the mechanisms of technological design of complex systems. Starting from the physical world that establishes the foundation of the metaphors through which we express and understand the social world, we will attempt to use the well known characteristics of each domain to better understand the lesser known characteristics of the other. Prayer is a well investigated subject in theology, whereas trust is a well formalized concept of computer networks. The reverse is not yet true, which we will see creates the opportunity to better appreciate each of theology and computers from a new perspective.

Our plan for proceeding is somewhat historical, somewhat physiological and somewhat sociological in nature. First, we want to draw parallels of the evolution of computers and computer systems over the last half-century to the evolution of major biological species. The comparisons that we will make are not always intended to be literal. Often, they are simply indicative that similar evolutionary processes are at work. The overarching framework for selection within the computer world is akin to the biological selection mechanisms of living organisms. Species of computers and computer systems are successful in adapting to the changing world around them, or not; but, the framework within which adaptation must occur is formed by processes of virtually biological qualities.

We begin our journey by considering the means of design, construction, change and evaluation within the domains of social orders and computer networks. This illustration of the foundational concepts of evolution is the subject of Chapter 2, entitled *Mechanics of Evolution*. Here we will note that DNA encompasses a design language as well as the blueprint-level design of life itself. Change in this design can be precipitated by mutation and genetic adaptation. The design of computer systems is similarly established through languages and blueprints, although in this case we observe that they are significantly more arcane, more verbose and yet less powerful. Change wrought in technical design is largely a result of human research; itself an adaptive or mutational mechanism of serendipitous effect. As far as evaluating the design and its ongoing modifications is concerned, the mechanisms are similar for the two domains; natural selection for organic life and the marketplace for computer systems. While the progression of organic life is fairly commonly understood, in an effort to illustrate to the reader the parallels we'll conclude this chapter with a survey of distinct evolutionary epochs drawn from the historical record of computer progression.

While mutation, genetic adaptation and natural selection are central features of evolution, the environment in which they operate actually determines their efficacy. Thus Chapter 3, entitled *Environment*, begins with an overview of the concept of an ecosystem as the melding of organic life with its supporting infrastructure. We then use this concept as a means to introduce a derivative specialization termed a social ecosystem as an organizing medium of trust and policy in the formation and functioning of human groups. We characterize the progression of human grouping mechanisms through reference to family, clan, tribe, religious congregation and an emerging group associated with the nation-state that we term égalité. Within the containing environment of these various collections of humans, among-group and within-group interactions emanate from the definition, application and consequences of policy. We observe a connection between the human needs hierarchy as expressed by Abraham Maslow and the impetus of human interactions that occur as a consequence of, and according to this policy construct. Throughout the remainder of the book, this rationale for interaction stimuli forms a central feature of our considerations of human grouping mechanics and their relationship to computer networks. The basis for this consideration is the recognition of a foundation for social structure that is grounded within human physiology, which is the topic of the next chapter.

Within Chapter 4, entitled *Physiology of the Individual*, we begin with a cursory overview of human anatomy that provides the structure within which the mind exists and operates. Centered in the brain, the mind establishes its understanding of the world through stimuli from a collection of senses and it in turn effects responses through the body's motor system. These are the means through which a person functions within the surrounding environment. The needs hierarchy manifests as distinct appetites that stimulate the acquisition of sustenance of various forms, forming a feedback loop maintained through a command and control facility centered on the mind, and distributed across the full sensori-motor system through the form and actions of the central and peripheral nervous systems. We then draw significant parallels between human anatomy and physiology with similar facilities found in computer systems. The anatomical structure of computers is established according to the specifications of a self-replicating machine suggested by John von Neumann; in essence, a specification of an automaton that functions much like organic life. The physiological processes of computers follow the model of computation known as a Turing Machine. From these facilities are derived much of the architecture of modern computer systems. We follow the progression of such architectures to a culmination in the personal electronic device; computer-like mechanisms that relate to individual people on a one-to-one basis.

To summarize just a bit, through the first four chapters we peruse the parallel perspectives of evolutionary progression of organic life and of computer technology during its emergent half century. This brings us then to a consideration of the establishment of higher-level groupings and the mechanisms that guide their formation and enable their successful operation. Continuing the corollary between human and computer based systems requires that we extend the parallels beyond physiological characteristics and include organizational and behavioral characteristics as well. This entails a somewhat detailed consideration of multi-level, among-group selection issues and the appearance of mechanisms of complex policy that we see as the most fertile ground for the explosive expansion of personal electronic devices. These topics are the focus of our next four chapters.

Chapter 5, *Fabric of Society*, centers on the description of a general model for social systems. A distinguishing characteristic of multi-entity constructs versus the individual entities themselves is the emergence of altruistic behavior. Natural selection applied to individual entities would seem to minimize if not eliminate behavior that is detrimental to the individual. Nonetheless, within social orders, altruistic behavior on the part of individuals forms a basic manifestation of successful systems. The model suggests that the overarching characteristic of social order is a trust infrastructure that enables group-wide correlation of effective policy application. We suggest that this model of social grouping has evolved from the development of the human species that has subsequently been reflected in the progression of successive grouping mechanisms. Within this model, the most basic articulation between religious social orders and secular social orders is the source of trust on which the social system is based. We note that theistic religions are grounded in supernatural causality while secular governments are subsequently grounded in trusted processes derived from foundational policy specifications. This leads us then to consider in the next three chapters the primary aspects of interactions within social orders: content, causality and process.

Human interactions serve to satisfy appetites through the acquisition of or access to content. In Chapter 6, *The Shrine of Content*, we take a detailed look at the concept of content as it ranges across the full spectrum of the needs hierarchy. Content can be as basic as the air we breathe and the food we eat or it can be as complex as the drive to excel at a particular task. Following the needs hierarchy, content builds in a recursive fashion so as to sate higher order appetites through successive fulfillment of those of the lower orders. Within this chapter, we take a rather detailed look at both content and the projection of content within computer systems and computer networks. We extend the social ecosystem model introduced in the previous chapter into the cyberspace world of the Internet and the World Wide Web. This requires that we consider not only content *per se*, but also associated characteristics such as ownership and value. Central to this extension is the derivation of trust inherent in content aimed at various needs. This then provides the impetus for a much more detailed look at the establishment and conveyance of trust; the subjects of the next two chapters.

Chapter 7, *In His Own Image*, considers causality as a seminal source of trust. Here, we present the iconic example of the establishment of trust within the human mind through the ecstatic affirmation of supernatural sources. We perceive this ecstatic state as the culmination of the progression of causality chains that is foundational to the establishment and conveyance of trust within the scientific world. We consider that the primary distinction between religion-based and science-secular oriented social systems is found in the terminus of the causality chains of their respective trust infrastructures. Within this chapter, we expose the establishment of trust within computer networks which then leads us to the consideration of trust based on recursive processes. This is the topic of the next chapter.

In Chapter 8, *In Search of Enlightenment*, we consider the establishment and conveyance of trust through the inevitability of process. This approach is foundational to science-oriented systems such as the Internet or the World Wide Web, but it is also central to non-theistic religions such as Buddhism. We return to the anatomical and physiological basis of human interactions by considering a conceptual interpretation of intelligent systems derived from the works of Paul MacLean, Merlin Donald and Jean Piaget. Through this conceptualization, we suggest a parallel between the structure, operational characteristics and psychological development of the human mind and the architecture, software and provisioning characteristics of computer systems and computer networks. We observe that the highest order needs of the human mind are grounded in the facilities of metaphorical understanding. Moreover, we draw the parallel to the organization of knowledge in today's most advanced computer systems. With this conceptualization in hand, we are fully positioned to attempt our own bit of prophecy toward the future development of computer systems and their networks, particularly as they apply to the cyberspace extension of human social systems.

In the first four chapters of the book, we considered the mechanisms through which organic and technical systems evolve. In the final three chapters we look forward as we anticipate that the development of the Internet and the World Wide Web will evoke requirements for new capabilities in order to respond to emerging appetites stimulated by the human needs hierarchy. From a technical progression standpoint, we anticipate that meeting these needs will involve a mutational leap in the capabilities of personal electronic devices as they seek to connect people to the network.

In Chapter 9, *Mutation*, we will suggest the emergence of the transcendent personal device as a major component of this mutational leap. We will consider the distinct levels of the needs hierarchy and extract from each the required capabilities of the transcendent personal device. In some cases, the requirement impact goes beyond the device itself and impinges on the environment in which the device operates. In the end, we suggest that the overarching facility required of the evolving network is an ability to support the same interaction mechanisms found in the inter-personal interactions of human social orders. Central to such interactions is the ability to establish trust through support for the concepts of identity and reputation. These are among the more profound capabilities of the transcendent personal device. The interaction environment is the subject of our penultimate chapter.

Chapter 10, *Power of Prayer*, suggests an environment derived from the facets of prayer, an interaction model that is applicable across the complete spectrum of a trust-policy infrastructure. Prayer forms a template for interactions grounded in deictic discourse. To be effective in the digital world, it requires the needs hierarchy derived capabilities of computer systems. The recursive nature of prayer-like interactions is based on the existence of an encompassing covenant relationship. From an interaction perspective, prayer allows redress of interaction consequences directly by the purveyor of trust in the social system. This essentially forms the basis of interactions that are ultimately subject to law. Distinct prayer-like interactions cover the full range of the needs hierarchy.

The title of this first chapter comes from the Chandogya Upanishad and is literally translated as "Thou art that!" This prayer expresses the goal of establishment of identity of the supplicant within the context of Brahmin ("that") as an aspect of each person in the form of "Atman." In essence, one achieves identity within the context of one's deities. While we most likely do not comprehend the full nuanced meaning of this prayer, it voices a desire for truth and clarity which we most certainly seek to attain. What really attracted our attention, however, was the fact that it has elements that suggest intuitive insight into the physiological mechanisms in which from our perspective much religious thought is grounded. At its most basic level, this prayer is an application of a policy mechanism; an interaction seeking affirmation from a trusted third party. Prayer in general, and this one in particular, seeks the intercession of the ultimate trust authority within the specific religion. It seeks assistance in defining and conveying the ideas of the supplicant (the one expressing the prayer) to the reader. Through this prayer, the supplicant also seeks to establish an identity within the trust infrastructure such that the reader might ascribe some positive degree of trust to the ideas presented.

Perhaps, the most intuitive aspect of this prayer is contained in its opening line: "*May my speech be based on the mind; may my mind be based on speech.*" The complementary concepts of speech and mind engender an appreciation for the physiological processes that have been discovered in the electro-chemical workings of the human brain, areas that we'll consider in some detail in Chapters 4 and 8. As preface to those discussions, it is timely to suggest that speech is indeed a remarkable mechanism derived from the cognitive facilities of the brain of modern humans. It is possible that an extension of the brain made it able to support language and marked a milestone in the emergence of modern man from the precursor hominids. Similarly, it is reasonable to conjecture that the ability of speech to extend influence at both a cognitive as well as emotional level from one person to another forms the foundation of large grouping systems. Principal among such systems are religions.

The *Book of Revelation* found in the *Christian Bible* is an icon of apocalyptic prophesies and as such it suggests a fitting approach through which to establish the context for Chapter 11, correspondingly entitled *Revelation*. Following from the *Book of Revelation*, the final chapter expresses the evolutionary pathway that encompasses the blending of the Internet, the World Wide Web and human social systems. Earlier in this first chapter, we suggested that art in general is a mechanism through which trust can be directly conveyed via the purveyor to the receiver. In the last chapter, we will build upon this concept by using distinct forms of the art of theatre as expressions of three distinct stages of this pathway. Through allusion to the scripted play, we will examine the role of the transcendent personal device as it might function in today's world of extremely constrained interaction protocols. In the near future, the device might be expected to exhibit a bit more creativity in the conduct of relatively standardized interactions, a process that we will examine through the form of Commedia dell'Arte. Finally, in the longer term, we anticipate that the device will be required to engage in inductive activity; essentially to learn how to establish a trusted interaction environment or, perhaps as important, how to recognize and avoid an untrusted environment. This future process we find startlingly revealed by the art form of improvisational theatre. These three stages of evolutionary melding of human social orders and computer networks lead us finally to a recognition of the continuity of the development of human social order from the emergence of the species to some future day; a continuum that we discuss in our final section *Laying-on of Hands*.

So our theme is set. Our first step has now been taken. In the end, we should see a justification of the observations and assertions that we've made in this initial chapter. Of course, in religion and technology, as in most endeavors, the devil, quite literally as well as metaphorically, is in the details. As we wind our way through the technological progression of the last few decades we see the recurrent application of evolutionary principles. Some technologies were quickly obsolete and became effectively extinct. Others prevailed and may find their way, through evolutionary principles, well into the future. The modern technical archaeologist has an interesting problem in that much technology has gone from the primeval ooze to the dustbin of history within a few short years. Consequently, we sometimes have difficulty extracting the details because the era went by too fast. Perhaps we can contribute a bit of perspective on the last few decades based on our experience in the trenches, where the details often stand out in stark relief. The relationship between technical systems and social systems is a bit more subjective on our part. We hope you'll enjoy this book and find in it a unique personal adventure; just deserving of its foray into the theological realm. Perhaps you'll find with us the inner spirit of our digital selves, our own "soul of the machine." Together we embark on our journey across the landscape to be explored behind the facade that bounds the realm of the computer gods.

# 2 Mechanics of Evolution

*Events of sufficiently small probability,*
*when they actually occur,*
*are indistinguishable from miracles.*

## That Which Doesn't Kill Us Makes Us Stronger

Computer systems mirror the structures and mechanisms of people. Not too surprising an assessment, but it does provide justification for suggesting that just as with people who are physiologically inclined to form and maintain complex social organizations, the evolutionary progression of computers has embraced the concepts of trust and policy within widespread collections of devices. Indeed, these collections form social organizations in their own right. Within human social structures, policy environments, including the means of policy implementation, arose as a collection of mechanisms through which humans were better able to coordinate their activities and to establish shared patterns of behavior for their collective benefit. Thus, we observe that social policy is a natural result of the human evolutionary process. Consequently, we might anticipate that the evolution of computer systems, and more to the point, the mechanisms that are enabled by those systems, will mimic the behaviors found in the human species. We would then further suggest that the personal electronic device, currently the most intimately personal variant of computer, represents an emergent species within the larger domain of computer systems; a species that offers the prospect of bubbling to the top of the evolutionary froth, just as did its organic forbearers.

Few would question modern mankind as the current pinnacle of the biological evolutionary process. However, a suggestion that a new, currently minimalist variant of computer might be associated with some future apex of computer evolution is perhaps less obvious. Certainly, we would expect more general agreement that current incarnations of basic personal electronic devices are still far from reaching their full potential. Consequently, suggesting that they portend the emergence of a paradigm that could significantly impact the state of computer technology as an extension of personal social interaction and personality characteristics requires a bit more justification. An interesting question is, of course, is it plausible that achieving their full potential will entail significant extension through the evolutionary process? Further, can we anticipate the direction of this evolution based on comparisons to the processes that resulted in current social orders? These are among the questions we seek to explore, if not answer.

As a guide to consideration of these rather tenuous concerns, it is instructive to look at the foundations, first of organic life and then of computer systems, in order to better consider their similarities, as well, perhaps, as some of their differences. While of course we recognize the chasm between the biological and mechanical nature of the individuals of the respective species, we do see significant similarities in the basic evolutionary directions that define the development of each as collections of cooperative entities.

A common theme, often found in various bodies of literature, is to equate computer hardware to the body and computer software to the mind; or, more specifically, the brain to hardware and the mind to software. We find this theme to be incomplete and perhaps just a bit misleading. As the distinction between the brain and the mind is ambiguous at best, that between hardware and software is similarly obtuse, based as it is on convenience and efficiency. Some of the most profound contemporary thinkers outside of computer science, when they venture into comparing human and computer capabilities, eschew the world of recursive concept elaboration to be found in computer science. There is indeed a tendency to observe a reducing perspective on computers, and particularly on computer systems. For example, Roger Penrose seems to suggest as much when he bases his analyses on an equation of computing with Turing machines in *The Emperor's New Mind*, even considering the extreme example of a Turing machine with infinite memory, infinite state variables and unlimited computing time; there is more to computing than theoretical equivalence. Gerald Edelman denies the expression of degeneracy in computers in *Wider than the Sky*. He suggests that degeneracy, which is very generally speaking the facility of achieving similar function through different mechanisms, is a natural characteristic of organisms derived through evolutionary processes guided by natural selection. It is a means by which these same organisms achieve resiliency in the face of effected threats. We would observe that we are very early in the evolutionary progression of computers and that degeneracy is only beginning to emerge as an aspect of high availability, fault tolerant systems. In reality, computer science is extremely rich in conceptualizations, at ever increasing levels of complexity. This said, as we venture into domains outside our core expertise, we are very aware that it is the nature of inter-disciplinary studies to expose their students to criticism from the experts in the fields that they are yearning to learn from.

When we consider the result of evolutionary processes acting on people living in and interacting through groups, we see significant similarity with the facilities provided by computer networks. Even greater similarity becomes evident if potential mutational extensions of the individual computer elements are taken into account. Finally, when we consider the group activities of people directed within various organizational structures, including religious orders and their enabling mechanisms, we see an organizing principle that helps us understand the current incarnation of computer systems in general. We suggest that this principle can provide guidance in understanding the evolutionary progression of personal electronic devices, or their derivative species, well into the future. So, we'd like to understand something of the evolutionary processes of organic life. Then we seek to compare and contrast them with the processes through which computer systems have developed.

Considering the basic mechanisms of organic life and computer systems, we understand each as being subject to a continuing process of change and evaluation. The evaluation process validates the effectiveness of the change through the results of the replication process by which the numbers of the entities either increase or decrease, depending on whether the change is effective, ineffective or worse. This process is the most basic variant of policy, distilling its application and its consequences to the most primal criteria. It requires that a policy framework be in place to enable the interactions of the entities and to provide a means of effecting and evaluating consequences for these interactions. From an anthropomorphic viewpoint, we'd like to be able to assess the consequences as either good or bad. In the case of organic life, these policy machinations are an embodiment of the natural world in which life exists. In the case of computer systems, policy definitions and processes are artifacts of the societal extensions of the natural world introduced by the human species. Policy in this environment is defined by and applied by social systems and their intersection with the physical world. If one views computers from the purely materialistic perspective, then the primary area of this intersection is through the social structure termed the marketplace. Thus, as we seek to establish an understanding of this area of intersection, we need to have at least cursory knowledge of how the distinct environments of the relevant species actually work. To that end, we will consider first the mechanisms applicable to the distinct species; that is the topic of this chapter. In the next chapter, we will consider the environments themselves within which the individuals of the species interact.

Evolutionary progression comes to organic species through two distinct collections of processes. One set allows change and evaluation to occur within the biophysical makeup of the individual entity within any species. Studies and references to the origin of an individual from its seminal existence as a germ cell through its maturation as an adult member of a species are termed *ontogeny*. A second set of processes allows for change to individual members of a species, or groups of these members through the interaction of the entities with their containing environment across generations. The origin and development of a set of entities within a species or even collections of such sets is termed *phylogeny*. A concept we'll revisit from time to time is that ontogeny, in some instances and in some limited fashion, reflects phylogeny. The growth sequence of a specific animal may reflect some characteristics of the sequence that led to that animal's species appearance on earth over millions of years. Similarly, the organization of a network management structure in a modern computer reflects the sequence of network technology improvements that led to that computer species' appearance over the past decades.

In order for the evaluation process to have any bearing on future development directions, either of organic life or of computer systems, there must be a means of defining the structure of each that can be influenced by the evaluation process. In essence, there must be a language through which the policy, that is the means and mechanisms of existence, can be codified over time; perhaps over a very long time. In the case of living organisms, the most basic language of policy is that found within the DNA molecule, and the resultant evaluation method is the application of physical processes to the resultant living entities. This constitutes the process or collection of processes generally referred to as *natural selection*. For computer systems, the language of policy is perhaps more arcane. It certainly is more ambiguous and nuanced. It is actually an amalgam of the languages of design and manufacture, along with the languages of interaction, including interactions among people, among people and machines, and among machines. For the computer, the basic policy evaluation environment is the market within which and for which computer systems are developed and deployed. This is an environment purely defined by people as it encompasses their interactions with each other and their interactions with computers. It would seem that for group associations of both the human species and of computer systems, the languages of policy are largely products of cognitive development. This is an assessment that we will explore at some depth during the course of this book.

Let us then consider very briefly the mechanisms and mechanics of the evolution of living organisms. As we noted in the last chapter, this will entail a rather simplistic lesson in biology. It is useful for us to highlight certain characteristics central to the processes of change evocation that present during the act of cellular replication Based on this cursory view of organic processes, we will then consider the basic mechanisms that have thus far guided the progression of computer systems. We must point out that any of these processes or mechanisms must operate within an environment or framework comprised of both living and non-living components; a concept that is generally termed an *ecosystem*. We'll consider the definition and characteristics of an ecosystem in more detail in the following chapter, but for the moment we'll simply assume a definition of the term to be *a constrained environment of living and non-living elements that facilitates interactions among its various components*. So, as a start, let's delve just a bit into the processes of living things.

# Organic Design and Development

We make a seminal assumption that the repetitive production of some entity, be it organic or mechanical, requires a *design* and a subsequent means to apply *policy* through which the operational existence of the entities proceed. The words we've selected might be viewed as slightly provocative, but we will try very hard to use them carefully. To suggest or even to consider a design does not require consideration of a designer, either for organic systems or for electrical and mechanical systems. We suggest that a design is required because it is difficult, if not impossible, to explain systematic replication without one. Bear in mind of course, we view it as completely consistent with this assumption that a design can encompass randomly derived components. A snowflake is the result of a very well defined design. However, the design includes a random component inherent in the crystallization of water that renders every snowflake unique. Taken *en masse*, they readily form a blizzard or an avalanche. In a similar vein, as we suggested in our Prologue, policy is the way we explain or define how things work. A rock, sitting on a hillside, effects policy. At the very least, it is subject to the policy established by the basic physical forces. In some cases, the rock is stationary for a geological age. Then, an earthquake impacts the rock's policy infrastructure and it rolls down the hill. So, based on these assumptions, let us first examine the landscape for living organisms.

Based on *deoxyribonucleic acid* or DNA, life has evolved on the earth through a process that an electronic circuit designer might recognize as a general feedback loop. In the April, 1953 edition of the journal Nature, James Watson and Francis Crick published a paper entitled *A Structure for Deoxyribose Nucleic Acid* that provided the first definitive description of DNA's form. Their model development was apparently enhanced by the x-ray crystallography of Rosalind Franklin, although she did not participate in authoring the seminal paper. Crick and Watson found that the molecular structure of DNA is that of a polymer whose resultant shape resembles a spiraling railroad track; the famous shape termed a *double helix*. The rails of a strand of DNA are comprised of alternating sugar (deoxyribose) and phosphate molecular components. Much like the cross-ties of a railroad track, attached to these rails in a perpendicular fashion and at periodic connection points are pairs from a set of four nucleotide bases: adenine, cytosine, guanine and thymine. Adenine can only be paired with thymine, and cytosine can only be paired with guanine. Each such cross-tie is termed a *base pair*. One can readily see from this basic architecture that there is a high degree of systematic chemical as well as mechanical structure in the DNA molecule.

Drawing for example from *Understanding DNA* by Chris Calladine, Horace Drew, Ben Luisi and Andrew Travers, we learn that the total DNA complement within a single human cell, typically referred to as the genome, amounts to approximately three billion base pairs distributed among 46 chromosomes. A single base, when combined with the sugar and the phosphate radicals, forms a structure termed a *nucleotide*. Hence, one can view a DNA molecule as a long sequence of paired nucleotides. At this point, it might be interesting to draw attention to the metaphor that we have selected to represent the DNA molecule; that of a railroad track. Most texts use a ladder metaphor. Our selected theme has some relevance if we consider the following.

Each of the 46 DNA molecules in a human cell is approximately two nanometers in diameter and if added together would be approximately two meters in length when stretched out like a taut string. Scaling these dimensions up by a factor of one billion, the resulting structure resembles a railroad track that is two meters wide by two million km long with cross ties positioned about every two-thirds of a meter along the track. This rather closely approximates a true railroad track. Consider that there is a total of around 375,000 km of railroad track in the United States and we see that our metaphoric expression of the human genome is perhaps five times as large; a truly huge structure. Moreover, it is a characteristic of the railroad track infrastructure within the United States that we can perceive it as a long, linear structure, but of course, it is comprised of many discrete segments. DNA is similar in this regard as it is subdivided into the well formed, discrete sections called chromosomes that we mentioned above. Moreover, when we look ever so generically at how DNA processes actually work, we see that they most generally make use of only small sections of the entire genome. This bears significant similarity to the structure of computer memories. We'll come back to this point when we consider computer memory in subsequent chapters.

What is most appropriate about this metaphorical representation of DNA is that it illustrates some sense of the volume of information that can be conveyed by a single molecule of DNA. For example, three nucleotides convey sufficient information for a cell to specify one distinct amino acid from a set of 20 such amino acids. Amino acids in turn are the building blocks of proteins, and proteins are the building material for living cells of all types. The human genome must convey sufficient information to construct all of the material that comprises the human body as well as provide instructions for how much of each material is to be produced and how it all fits together. The metaphorical illustration offers at least some plausibility that this requirement is well met. Well actually, if it is not met, then there must be some other design or policy mechanism besides DNA involved in the replication of organic life. For the moment, we choose not to pursue that path.

DNA is replicated according to basic interactions among constituent components that are driven by properties of the electromagnetic force between elementary particles modulated by the conservation of energy. To leap ahead just a bit, such interactions are an effectuation of policy established by the electromagnetic force. In the case of DNA, the process is a marvelous dance of recursive interactions of nucleotides with a large dose of parallel processing thrown in. It is through the replication process that characteristics and capabilities of organic structures based on DNA are remembered and subsequently passed on to the descendent organism's DNA; and hence, to the next generation individuals of the species. Following replication, through which DNA acts as an historical archive of the construction of the generation that went before, DNA then acts as the construction blueprint for the building of the next generation.

In the lifecycle of living things, new generations of organic material are created from time to time; this is what living things do. It is the essential, unique characteristic of life. It is the derivation of the lifecycle metaphor itself. The DNA molecule participates in this creation process through division and replication of itself. Within a cell, a chemical compound called adenosine triphosphate provides a source of energy for the formation of new chemical compounds, including the DNA replication process itself. The cell also contains a reservoir of nucleic acids and other constituent components of DNA. When sufficient energy is available, the two rails of the DNA molecule separate into single strands with a single base of each cross-tie remaining connected to each rail. This process is interesting to us in that it provides a point, actually a multitude of discrete points, within the processing of living material at which very small changes, changes perhaps at a single molecule level, can have very profound subsequent effects because the change can essentially be magnified by the downstream processing. We will look ever so slightly deeper into this set of mechanisms just a bit later.

At this point, we need to note that within higher organisms, including *Homo sapiens sapiens*, there are two very different classes of cells that go through the replication process: germ cells and somatic cells. The seminal cells of a new organism, the cells that participate in the sexual reproduction process, are termed *germ cells*. For a single individual within the human species, the point of conception involves the fusion of two germ cells, one from the female and one from the male. These two cells combine to form the first cell of what will become a new person; a zygote. From this cell, which contains a DNA sequence that completely defines how to construct this new person, a series of new cells will derive. So, changes within the DNA sequence of a germ cell, either during the replication process or within the completed zygote prior to further replication, can ultimately be reflected in the construction process of the trillions of newly created cells that directly derive from the zygote in order to form the next generation person. Hence, a change in the initial state of a germ cell or the zygote can result in profound changes in the resulting person. With the completion of germ cell combination, the cell structure transforms into a *somatic* cell. With the formation of the first somatic cell begins the person construction phase of human replication. From this point, changes to the DNA molecule in any subsequent cell will very likely be constrained to make modifications only in that cell and its descendents; that is, the DNA changes probably won't be directly conveyed into changes throughout the person.

The DNA replication process of unraveling and reconstruction occurs in discrete sections of the DNA molecule simultaneously. Specific protein molecules attach to the DNA strands at select points in the base pair sequences and become markers that define the sections, while other proteins later remove these markers from the replicated strands when the process is completed. Just as we'll find later on with computer systems, this parallel processing in the replication mechanism is necessary in order to complete the operation within a time period consistent with other, large-scale operations of the organism. Of course, the evolutionary process actually derived the connection in the inverse order. That is, the timing of larger scale operations, which we can observe externally, followed the timing of the replication process of cells which ultimately enabled all that follows.

As the double helix unwinds, a complementary rail and base structure that is constructed from raw materials found in the cellular interior anneals itself onto each strand from the original DNA molecule. When reconstruction of the individual sections is completed, a final finishing process essentially checks the accuracy of the replication operation. The base error rate for the initial recombination is found to be in the range of one base pair error in approximately every 10,000 base pairs replicated. Subsequent error-correcting mechanisms applied following the initial recombination process serve to lower the effective error rate for the full replication operation to one error in each billion base pairs. With the subsequent fault tolerance of the cell construction from the new and old DNA strands, this low error rate guarantees that cell duplication is a highly reliable process. In the end, two complete DNA molecules are formed, with one going into each of two new cells. Each of these new DNA molecules is a replica of the original DNA molecule, so each new cell now has the same DNA blueprint that was contained in the parent cell. This blueprint determines the function and form of the new cell in (very roughly) the following manner.

The sequence of base pairs found in the DNA molecule determines a code that is translated through cellular chemistry into the construction of highly specialized proteins at various points within a cell. Essentially, a monorail molecule analogous to DNA, termed RNA (*Ribonucleic*

*Acid*) copies segments of the DNA; that is, it makes a copy of the base pair sequences through a process called *transcription*. This messenger RNA then physically conveys this template from a cell nucleus to cellular structures called *ribosomes*. Ribosomes attach to the end of the messenger RNA molecule and travel down the template, translating the information encoded in its base sequence and incorporating specified amino acids into a growing protein molecule. Multiple ribosomes will attach to a single messenger RNA molecule, simultaneously translating the information contained in the template into multiple growing protein molecules, all of which have an identical amino acid sequence that defines its form and function. The ultimate result is the physical construction of cell components according to the DNA blueprint.

Our consideration of the DNA replication process is not nearly of sufficient detail to provide a significant insight into the molecular chemistry involved; and, that is not our intent. Rather, what is interesting is how modifications to just the right molecules at just the right times within the replication process can have pronounced effects on the resultant, replicated DNA. A change in a single base pair can perhaps have an effect in the cell construction and operation that derives from the DNA. More likely, however, such a change will be compensated for by the fact that only relatively small sections of the DNA are actually utilized for these processes in a typical cell. That is, within the cell the higher probability is that a random DNA change will impact a neutral segment of the DNA molecule. However, if for example the change results in a modification of the attachment point for the protein molecule that delimits a section of the DNA being replicated, then the resultant DNA contains a much more significant change.

The individual members of *Homo sapiens sapiens* emerge from a single cell; the result of the initial *conception* of the individual. Historically, there have been at least two central questions that revolve around this point; one philosophical and one technical. The philosophical question is, "Does a person come into being at the point of conception, or does the person emerge at some later point in the development process?" Fully understanding the metaphorical reference to person is obviously central to answering this question. This is, of course, a central point of intersection and conflict among social systems today. While we might contribute some technical information around the edges, we are certainly unable to offer an answer to this question. The second question is related, but can be couched as a technical rather than philosophical consideration. Specifically, "Is the entity that derives from conception complete from the point of conception, or is there a development process that essentially builds up a new, complete human over time?" This latter concept was given the designation of *epigenesis* and more accurately reflects the biological development process of a person. The result is the specialization of cells to form the many constituent components of a living organism and to facilitate the special services provided by these various components; germ cells, then specialized differentiated cells, then organs and then the complete organism.

Our extremely elementary rendition of how DNA replicates and guides the specialization of form and function of cells is aimed at a couple of basic points. First, at its most basic, life appears to be about mass. To replicate or reproduce is to increase the mass of comparable life; this defines *good* within the policy process evoked by the basic physical processes of life. Failure to reproduce does not increase mass and, in the extreme results in the total absence of *comparable life*. This defines *bad*. The terms good and bad apply an anthropomorphic and more specifically *moral* view to essentially mechanical and chemical functions, but they at least give us a sense of direction in the consideration of evolutionary mechanisms. They provide the guidelines and goalposts of a process called natural selection. If sufficient new constituent components are available, if sufficient energy is available to drive the alignment and recombination mechanisms and if the processes themselves are allowed to proceed unhindered, then life continues. If either sufficient energy or new components are missing, or if the processes themselves are interrupted in some fashion, then life ceases. For the very simplest life-forms, the replication process may well be the ultimate end in itself. Thus, their fullest *meaning of life* is to exist, and through that existence to cause more of their kind to exist. We're hard pressed to say that this is not also the basic meaning of life for more complex species as well. The question of whether a meaning of life should be attached to the grown organism or to its origin is examined in depth by Richard Dawkins in *The Selfish Gene*. Actually, the question can be extended to any aspect of the organism during its development. Beyond the basics, a meaning of life will have to be found elsewhere than, for example, in the need for the individual to exist and reproduce through a hosting organism.

Through DNA's blueprint facility, a construction pattern is passed from one generation to the next. If the pattern is changed, then the new generation is different from the old generation. This feature can be used to extract a history of sorts regarding the changes among different generations of a species or between one species and its precursor species. Specifically, relatively minute changes within certain sections of the genome of a species when compared to similar sections in the genome of a precursor species can give an indication of the time lapse since the divergence of the two species. With an assignment of a value of *good* to the quantity of a specific living entity (or collection of similar entities) then it is indeed good for a particular common genome to propagate and bad if it terminates. Continued propagation translates into more living material and termination of propagation translates into less. This could be innocently rendered as the *purpose of living entities* at its most basic level.

Once we move beyond the simplest forms of life, purpose becomes a more abstract concept to apply and to interpret. To some extent, the more simplistic purpose still applies; we see at least the tinge of this logic applied in the highest and most esoteric levels of sentient life. Through complex groups of people, for example, evolutionary principles to a large extent play out just as they do with simpler life forms. With such groups, however, the mechanisms of change and selection are also more complex than those found for simple and/or single organisms. But similarly, the social structures that are effected through the grouping of individuals are largely about ensuring that they propagate to the superiority of other similar structures at best, and at the very least survive in the face of these other structures. However, it seems likely that this isn't the complete story of the interaction of complex groups, as we'll consider a little later on.

# Mutation and Genetics

The principle of evolution involves two distinct phases: first, the introduction of an organism with new characteristics into an environment and second, the process of natural selection through which the efficacy of the new organism, or, perhaps more appropriately, its new characteristics within the environment are judged to be *beneficial*. Just what constitutes beneficial will be considered in the following section. For the moment, in considering the first of these phases, that is, the introduction of a new organism into an environment, we find two generally accepted mechanisms for change. Living organisms can be significantly altered in form through a change process call *mutation*. A mutation is a change in the base-pair sequencing within a DNA molecule. Any such change can impact the subsequent production of proteins. This might result in the production of altered proteins or changes in the operational instructions regarding the amount, location and functional purpose of the proteins produced. If the change occurs in the germ cells or zygote that are so central in the earliest stages of reproduction and the mutation is not lethal, then the resultant change will be propagated throughout the entire new individual. Genetic variability is also introduced into organisms as a result of *genetic recombination*, also called *chromosomal crossover*, that occurs during the formation of germ cells. Genetic recombination involves exchanges of parts of homologous chromosomes (matching pairs) and results in genetic mixing between the chromosomes derived from the original parents. Together, mutation and genetic recombination provide ample opportunity for wide variance in the form and capabilities of living organisms. That said, let us first consider the concept of mutation in a bit more detail.

As we considered in the previous section, there are many physical locations within the constituent elements of cell replication of the DNA molecule in which molecular level changes can result in relatively large-scale changes in the resultant cell structure. If these changes occur within a differentiated cell, that is one of those cells that comprise the resultant organism, the changes are typically limited to that cell and its descendents. In the vast majority of cases, a change will have no effect, or it will cause the cell to die. And in most cases, the loss of a single cell will not significantly affect the full organism. However, if the change alters cell replication it can sometimes turn the cell into a virulent enemy of the full organism. Specifically, it can become a *cancer*. We might also consider the available mechanisms through which simple changes at a molecular level can be induced.

Probably the most prevalent form of molecular level mutations occurs spontaneously as point error in the replication process that we've just considered. The frequency of such mutations can be increased by exposure of the replication process to various *mutagens*. The most common variants of mutagens are ionizing radiation and chemicals. Thus, there is always enhanced concern with any exposure of cells during the reproductive process to sources of radioactivity or to a wide variety of mutagenic chemicals. The greatest potential for impacting succeeding generations of a species lies in modifications induced in germ cells; that is, at the very earliest stage of the construction of a new entity. If changes occur at this time, they have the potential to be conveyed into virtually every cell of the new individual. Consequently, they may, by default, be included within the germ cells for the next generation. Thus, if a change can be induced, for example in a particular base pair sequence in a germ cell DNA segment, then it will affect the resulting new organism; a mutation at the entity level rather than purely restricted to a single cell level. As we've noted, while certain chemicals and radiation are known to induce mutations, probably the greatest source of mutational change comes from errors in the DNA replication process itself. Although this process is moderately fault tolerant it is not guaranteed to be error free. These are concepts that we consider in relation to mechanical and cognitive processes in subsequent chapters.

However effected, the vast majority of mutations are either totally harmless or ineffective, meaning that they induce no noticeable change in the next generation, or the induced change results in catastrophic modifications of the next generation organism, rendering it unable to continue life at all. Thus, we can see that the typical evolutionary feedback to such a change is that it is bad; life in the specific form of the original generation does not continue, at least in this one offspring. If subsequent reproductive episodes of the original organism are not subject to a mutation at the germ cell level, then the succeeding generation offspring will more likely be successfully constructed. In general, it is difficult for an analysis to determine if the whole series of reproductive episodes with a specific individual have a net positive or net negative impact on continuation of the species. Rather, it is typically only by looking at the resulting population increase or decline, within a relatively stable environment over a long period of time relative to the reproductive lifetime of the species, that a determination can be made as to whether a particular mutational change is good or bad.

As was noted in the previous section's cursory description of the DNA replication process, there are points within the replication process of somatic cells and more importantly in germ cells specifically, where a modification to a single molecule can actually have a significant impact on the descendant generation. One specific instance would be a change to the molecular structure of the protein molecules that serve as markers for the replication process for a relatively long segment of the DNA molecule. In this case, it would seem that the induced change in the marker protein, or in its point of connection to the DNA molecule, could result in shifting the length of the DNA segment that is replicated, or perhaps impacting whether the segment is even replicated at all. In any case, the resulting change in the new generation might well be a major change in the new DNA molecule, rather than just a highly localized change. As with point mutations, such a major systemic mutation is likely to have a catastrophic impact on the construction of the new individual, probably rendering it non-viable. However, in very rare occurrences, this type of change might significantly affect the new individual, perhaps giving it some new characteristic that renders it better able to survive and reproduce within its environment. Since the mutation would be passed along to successive generations of this particular individual, the net impact over time might well be positive relative to continuation of the species. ·

In our first chapter, we briefly considered the work of Gregor Mendel in establishing the field of genetics. Through the processes described by genetics, the act of procreation provides a well defined approach for effecting changes among the resulting progeny. Individual characteristics of an organism derive from the set of genes that make up its genome. The gene for a specific characteristic can encompass some spectrum of allowed values for that characteristic. The spectrum of allowed values is termed *genetic variability*. It may be broad, meaning that a characteristic can present many different states or values. In other cases, the genetic variability that results from this process may be quite narrow and present only a very few states or values. Specific states of a characteristic are selected when DNA material from two parent individuals is contributed to the descendent generation individual. In the case of the human species, this is the result of the creation of the original zygote of an individual which requires a pair of each chromosome, with one chromosome of each pair derived from each parent. Chromosomes are differentiated DNA molecules in the cell: humans have 22 pairs of similar chromosomes, and one additional pair of chromosomes, similar in women (XX), and dissimilar in men (XY). The result is that replication of the zygote is then driven by a completely new DNA sequence relative to either parent. In some instances, an environment in which an organism exists can preferentially select for certain states or values. The resulting organisms so selected are said to benefit from *genetic adaptation* to that environment. To reiterate, this is a normal characteristic of sexual reproduction of a species.

Many of the traits found in individuals can vary in the extent to which they are represented in a new generation, depending on the characteristics of this new combination. This means that variances in different traits may have an impact on the relative reproductive success for the descendent generation. This essentially provides variations that can then be subsequently judged through natural selection. If natural body mass could have an impact on the survival of the individual, then natural selection might enhance the generational numbers of either larger mass individuals, or smaller mass individuals depending on the characteristics of the environment in which the individuals are found. It is probably obvious, but it should be noted that the greater the genetic variability found in a species, the greater is that species capacity to adapt to a changing environment through the process of genetic adaptation. Species with little genetic variability essentially don't have the option of making as many changes to adapt, so there are fewer chances to make a *good* change when a change is necessitated by a new environment.

While we have obviously only skimmed the subject, we hope to have conveyed at this point some appreciation of the intricacies of the biological substrate of evolution in sufficient details to support our further discussions. A more complete presentation would include considerations of the neuron and the role played by evolutionary mechanisms in the construction of the brain (Gerald Edelman's *Neural Darwinism*). We will bravely assume that we've transmitted enough of the message that we can now turn to looking at computer systems, weaving their description with that of biological systems, even at the risk of touching material that we have not properly introduced.

# Technological Design and Development

Evolutionary processes for organic life can derive from mutational events coupled to a form of feedback process control effected through the modulation of genetic adaptation by natural selection; in essence, a crap shoot coupled to a positive feedback loop. Note that we mention a positive feedback loop. Such a feedback mechanism has the tendency to reinforce the change that caused it. Within an electrical circuit, such a feedback mechanism will tend to force a circuit into unstable saturation; within living organisms, it will tend to enhance the propagation of newly developed traits.

Certainly all of this discussion has an a-religious ring to it; but again, the devil is in the details. As was observed in the previous section, the vast majority of mutations prove to be either innocuous or fatal to the resulting individual organism. Certainly, the probability of a chance mutation becoming a contributing facet of the evolutionary design of a species is very low indeed. On the other hand, low probabilities applied over a sufficiently long time period can yield non-zero results. So, perhaps it is useful to consider our epigraph for this chapter. If an event of exceedingly low probably actually does occur, it is difficult to name its true origin; was it chance, or was it due to very subtle design selections? Or more radically, is chance simply an abdication of design? For example, Stephen Wolfram in *A New Science* has shown that a sequence of numbers fulfilling all known tests for randomness could be generated from a deterministic automaton. The concept of *causality* arises as a point of interest because of its subsequent impact on the mechanics of policy. From a policy consideration standpoint, causality is important because it can be related to trust; and trust, we will contend, is the basis of all policy mechanisms, including social organizations.

So, now let us consider the progression of computer systems. Does a change mechanism similar to the mutation of DNA structure exist for computer systems? In fact it does. It can be characterized as directed or serendipitous *basic research*. Subsequent fine tuning of new characteristics first introduced through such mutational change occur through an analogue to genetic selection that is generally termed *applied research*. As with organic design and feedback loops through the DNA molecule, research based mutation and refinement are completely grounded in physical law. These two forms of fundamental change show characteristics more like a roulette wheel than of the pair of dice in a crap game. That is, they may result in a profound, beneficial development along the lines of hitting *en plein* (a straight bet on the ball landing on a specific number which pays 35 to 1 odds); but, a more modest enhancement may result, corresponding perhaps to hitting a *dozen bet* (a wager that the ball will land on one of twelve selected numbers which pays 2 to 1 odds).

Basic research is best characterized as an undirected search for answers to previously unknown questions, while applied research is aimed at finding new approaches (e.g. new technologies) to solve known problems in more effective ways. As we said, one might at least qualitatively compare basic research to a mutation and applied research to genetic adaptation. Indeed, just as the typical organic mutation results in either a benign variant or in a catastrophe, so is the result of basic research most often a dead-end, if not a catastrophe in its own right when evaluated by the actions or reactions of the market. The useful discoveries of basic research tend to be serendipitous; in many instances the long-term value of the result of basic research is not known immediately. To truly achieve utility, there usually must be a fortuitous confluence of environmental factors, which in the case of most technological advances we would term an accommodating market potential. Consider the invention of the transistor; a device illustrative of mechanisms so profound that there was virtually no environment that could immediately exploit them or that could not ultimately be totally transformed by them. Were Shockley, Brittain and Bardeen searching for a better way to make computers when they began their research on semiconductors? No, they were searching for a better amplifier for long-line telephony signals when they created the first transistor. Of course, transistors make good signal amplifiers, but that barely scratches the surface of their ultimate utility. Whether driven by altruistic recognition of this fact or ignorance of the serendipity, AT&T, a telephony monopoly at the time, in agreeing to license this technology to all interested parties performed what was perhaps the transforming marketplace driven event of the XX$^{th}$ Century.

Applied research on the other hand, is typically well directed to identify incremental enhancements of technological components. Basic research gives us the transistor while applied research gives us the integrated circuit. Together, they provide either new technology or technology enhancements that make things faster, smaller, more robust, cheaper, and perhaps all of the above. The situation is that for essentially all research, direction is provided by a confluence of the interests of researchers who possess the ability to derive new technologies and funding agents who possess the resources to support the work of the researchers. When the two are aligned, a viable research environment is enabled. Today, the primary difference between basic and applied research is whether the research environment intersects in any strong way with a specific market. In essence, basic research is aimed at areas with no currently known commercial application. Of course, at this point it seems reasonable to pose the question, "Why do we want to differentiate between basic and applied research?" Our reasoning is that to extract the relevant understanding of truly mutation class discoveries from basic research, one has to be subject to a religious type epiphany, whereas discoveries from applied research entail application of well-known mechanisms for their interpretation. We'll consider this in more detail in Chapter 7.

Our comparison of natural change mechanisms with *man-made* change mechanisms is yet somewhat disjoint. The discontinuity derives from the differences in the languages or at least the language mechanisms that are used to convey the results of research based change versus the mutation or genetic change found in organic systems. For living material, the DNA molecule is the center of all change as well as the conveyance of all change. For computer systems, change can occur within a myriad of sub-systems that comprise the total computer and computer network. However, the utility with which such changes can be fed back into the product development cycle is heavily dependent on the design and manufacturing technology used in the current product generation.

As we consider the parallel of mutation and genetic adaptation with basic and applied research, we find it interesting to expand our speculation to encompass a parallel between biological and computer species. Consider the introduction of the earliest forms of the electronic, stored-program computers. The first large-scale computer, both in size and in terms of market potential and realization was the IBM 650. It was a drum memory machine. Drum memory was a forerunner of today's disk drives, using a rotating drum-like surface of magnetic material onto which magnetic patterns could be imprinted and then read by a read/write head floating over the surface. IBM was first to market with its machine, and it sold perhaps a couple of thousand units for a price in the range of $200,000 to $400,000 of that era's dollars. IBM's primary competitor at the time was Sperry Univac and they had a similar drum memory computer that they placed on the market shortly after IBM's offering. Univac, however, also had a newer variant of computer that made use of a new memory mechanism: core memory. This constituted what we would call a significant mutation event; not quite comparable to the invention of the transistor, but certainly a new technology enabling smaller, faster and more reliable computers.

The marketing decision by Univac was to defer introduction of the core memory based machine in the United States; releasing it instead in Europe. In the United States, they concentrated on selling the drum memory machine, in direct competition with the IBM 650. The result was that the Univac drum machine was nowhere near the success of the IBM 650, but the core memory machine was a big hit in Europe. By the time that U.S. customers enticed Univac to market their core memory machine in the United States, IBM had a very competitive core memory variant ready for the market. The bottom line is that the core memory upgrade to the earlier, drum memory oriented computers was more than an enhancement; it was a new species. Consequently, it made obsolete the earlier machine and replaced it in the marketplace rather than building upon its success.

# Natural Selection

Through natural selection, the characteristics of living organisms are judged to be beneficial or not. As specified by their DNA, the succeeding generations of an organism contain both an extensive history of their ancestors as well as the blueprint for their own construction and that of their progeny. Through a variety of mechanisms, the characteristics of an organism can change, either within a generation or between generations. As we noted above, these changes may be due to genetic variability, to mutations in germ cell DNA during the propagation from parent to child or, in very special cases, to changes in the current generation of a specific cell. In any of these cases, the dominant factor that determines whether characteristics are passed to succeeding generations is the degree to which they prove useful in allowing the current generation to live and procreate. As a consequence, if characteristics in general are passed from one generation to the next, then beneficial characteristics tend to be more plentiful in succeeding generations. Essentially, this defines the fact of their being beneficial.

The characteristics of an organism that are continually judged or evaluated for every member of every generation of a species fall into two main categories: first are the characteristics of each entity that impacts its interactions with the physical environment in which it exists, and second are the characteristics of each entity that impacts its interactions with the members of other species found within the physical environment, or with other members of its own species. If a characteristic or a combination of characteristics help the entity survive within the environment, then that characteristic may be termed good. Below, we will consider much simpler characteristics or at least much simpler thought experiments in order to better understand the concept of natural selection. Our goal is simply to illustrate the basic concepts of natural selection and to attempt to convey the tenuous, statistical nature of the evolution process.

For humans, the characteristics that impact interactions with the environment are much wider in scope than for other species, due to the fact that people have proven more adept at modifying the terms of their interactions with the environment than members of other species. This is not to say that other species do not alter the context of their interactions with the environment. Many species migrate within or between ecosystems to obtain more favorable conditions for certain periods of their lifecycles. Termites build mounds for protection from the natural elements as well as predators, and birds of many species build an incredible variety of domiciles (nests) to further their respective mechanisms of procreation. Of course, adaptation to the environment is a trait that evolution preferentially selected for over the long history of the human species. It is a trait that benefits the human species relative to other species existent within the same environment. At some point in their existence, people began to make clothing to protect them from the weather. They made shelters to allow them to accommodate great climatic variations and they made tools through which they could extend their impact on their environment, including on other species. In a similar fashion, humans would appear to have superior facilities to effect interactions with other species. That is not to ignore the fact that sometimes the shark wins, but in the preponderance of interactions with other species, humans can pretty well stack the deck in their favor. At the present time, the greatest threat to humans from other living species probably derives from the microscopic varieties: microbes and viruses. Why is this? Perhaps, it is because these organisms operate at the very boundaries of our cognitive understanding. They constitute an extremely asymmetric threat environment (more about such asymmetries a bit later). Consequently, in a conflict we may find ourselves much in the same situation as the Incas at the arrival of the Spanish; our social order may simply not be capable of dealing with this particular threat.

In the simplest environment, individual organisms attempt to exist within the world solely through their own actions and interactions with the environment or with other organisms. Each organism must find or produce its own food from which it derives energy to search for, consume or produce more food, and to replicate itself. The better able an organism is to achieve the goals of finding sustenance and of fending off threats, perhaps threats of it becoming food itself, then the more likely it is to have the opportunity to replicate or reproduce additional organisms of a like kind. Consequently, one way to perceive the principle of natural selection is to couch it in terms of an ability to ameliorate threats. For the purpose of this book, we will define individual natural selection as:

*For individuals under threat, transmissible individual traits that minimize that threat preferentially propagate relative to traits that don't.*

To illustrate this principle, let's perform a simple thought experiment. Consider a group of red and yellow fish subject to the threat of a special cat that likes to eat primarily yellow fish (our cat is special in that it is definitely not color blind). If a population of fish, equally distributed between red and yellow color, are subject to this cat, then the yellow fish will be preferentially eaten. Note that the cat doesn't necessarily eat only yellow fish. It might consume a red fish every once in a while; hence, the statistical nature of the selection process. Over time, however, it is expected that more yellow fish be eaten than are red fish. One can then reasonably infer from this that red fish have a longer average life span than yellow fish, and hence have a greater opportunity to produce offspring. If red fish begat red fish, and yellow fish begat yellow fish, then, if the cat eats enough fish, over time the yellow fish will be no more.

The more likely scenario is not, however, that red fish begat red fish and yellow fish begat yellow fish. Rather, we might expect that the genetic variability of the fish species allows for both red and yellow colored fish. And, an even more likely situation is one in which the colors of the parents influence the distribution of colors among the offspring; for example, the case of a red mother fish and red father fish produces a distribution of baby fish that are preferentially red. The case of a yellow mother fish and a yellow father fish in a similar fashion produces a distribution of baby fish that are preferentially yellow. If the mother fish and the father fish are of different colors then the distribution of offspring might be equally weighted between red and yellow baby fish. We can see that in this modification of the scenario, the fact that the cat still prefers yellow fish says that over time we will see the color red predominate. If the balance of the environment is such that the cat can eat fish very slightly faster than they can reproduce, then ultimately the cat will have eaten all the yellow fish and only red fish will remain. It then becomes an interesting question whether the cat can live on an exclusive diet of red fish?

While this thought experiment is extremely simple, it does present a metaphorical description of the situation in which rapid, perhaps instantaneous change occurs within a stable environment. The yellow fish and the red fish might well have existed in their little pool over the course of many generations, stabilizing in a population nearly equally split between the red and the yellow. Now, a perturbation is introduced into the environment; a cat whose taste buds appear directly connected to his eyes wanders by. The ability of the species within the environment to react to this new, until now unknown threat, determines the future course of the species within the pool. If the fish population did not already exhibit the genetic variability to generate progeny of different colors, then none of the fish in the pool would realize any preferential situation, at least related strictly to coloring, relative to the other fish.

Now, however, suppose that a mutation event occurred within the fertilized egg of one of the fish, such that the offspring was colored red. Now, even through there is only one red fish, it has a very slightly enhanced probability that it will live long enough to generate offspring. After all, among all the threats to its existence, which are common with all the other fish in the pool, at least this one fish has a smaller chance of being eaten by the cat than the others. The chance of such a random mutational event occurring is very small; however, the impact can be quite significant.

Of course, the amelioration of threats is usually not simple. As it happens, in some instances if one threat is diminished, its diminution might actually enhance the prospects for a different threat. Let us consider a characteristic of the human species whose impact is less obvious. For example, if a specific person has the characteristic of preferentially storing excess food in the form of body fat, then that particular person might well derive a benefit in an environment where food sources are somewhat unreliable. The ability to store food when it's available and then use that body fat (in effect, to sacrifice the body fat) to live off of when food becomes scarce has some obvious benefits. Of course, these benefits might be offset by certain liabilities that accrue as well. A layer of body fat might help preserve core body temperature if the environment in which the person lives is a cold climate. On the other hand, this characteristic might present a severe liability in a warm or hot climate. We recognize today that this characteristic, or actually this collection of characteristics, forms the basis for an extremely complex interaction impact analysis. In fact, this example brings to the fore many issues involved in evaluating natural selection processes. This more complex situation is termed *multi-level selection*.

Stored body fat has the near term effect of staving off starvation when food is not supplied to the body on a timely basis. In the early periods of mankind's emergence as a species, when pure physical interactions with the surrounding environment were the dominant natural selection processes, having a metabolism that used food energy efficiently was a beneficial trait. However, as the species excelled in its ability to compete with other species and to mitigate the impact of environment, the life span of an average human increased significantly. This has brought into play more complex mechanisms and interactions. For instance, on an anecdotal basis we recognize the liability of excess stored body fat, both physiologically as well as socially. Obesity is a well recognized precursor to cardiovascular disease and diabetes. Within social systems, being overweight is a liability in the ascent to the corporate boardroom or in simply getting a date for that matter. Many counter examples suggest this was not always true, showing the impact of changing social standards over relatively short periods of time. So, this particular characteristic becomes one of many whose evolutionary impact might vary significantly depending on the prevailing environmental conditions over a long period of time. We would be hard pressed to determine through a cursory analysis the natural selection benefit or liability of such characteristics.

Natural selection, as initially proposed by Darwin, is a process that involves interactions among individuals. Almost since its inception, there has been heated discussion about whether natural selection extends to mechanisms and processes involving not just individuals, but groups of individuals. For many species, termed *social species*, their individual members tend to live and operate within groups. The point of controversy relates to whether the groupings within social species contribute to the evolutionary success or failure of these species. The debate centers specifically on whether any evolutionary benefit accrues to the groups themselves or just to the individual members of the group; or, do groups have any evolutionary significance at all? Do groups evolve relative to each other, hence implying there is some evolutionary feedback loop within the individual members that pertains to group organization and operational dynamics; or, does a group simply provide an enhanced environment in which individuals within the group benefit in the natural selection process versus other individuals?

Certainly, from their membership in a group the individual members of a species may well receive a benefit relative to individual selection since propagation of the species is a product of individual propagation. However, it also appears relatively assured that groups are beneficial in that they extend the natural selection process from a simple gauge of individuals (a single level selection process) to a more complex gauge of individuals, first as members of a group and then as individuals, thus resulting in a multi-level natural selection process. We can therefore encompass the concept of multi-level selection within our working definition of natural selection by defining the concept of multi-level selection as:

*In a group under threat, transmissible traits of the individuals within the group that minimize that threat grow at the expense of traits that don't.*

For the moment, this definition certainly begs the question of what the transmission mechanism might be. For the individual organism, DNA provides such a mechanism. We will defer until a later chapter a consideration of a potential mechanism for groups. Indeed, what we do see at this point is that evolution applies to all venues of life, and within the human species, various grouping mechanisms are certainly consistently recurrent venues. A recurring theme within these venues is that of sacrifice. Sacrifice is a concept that is counter-intuitive when considering the process of natural selection. Sacrifice, by its very definition, suggests that an individual performs some act, either consciously and subconsciously, that may well be detrimental to that individual and yet beneficial to another. Should the act result in the death of the individual, then there is no opportunity for that trait, the trait of sacrifice itself, to be further propagated to a new generation. Hence, it would seem that natural selection, over time, would remove the concept of sacrifice from the vernacular; but this would not appear to be the case, with many species.

In Africa, wildebeest are documented to cross a river full of crocodiles, letting some die while the majority makes it safely to the other side. The threat stems from the initial situation that there is not enough food for the herd. One might speculate that there would be enough food for any one wildebeest, if all the others were gone. So, no wildebeest would seem to have an incentive to cross the river. In fact, it would seem that the paramount incentive would be to let the other wildebeest cross. Apparently, however, wildebeest do not like to live alone. Hence, the recurring scenario that plays out with every cycle of the wet season turning to dry finds the herd moving to new grazing grounds. When the herd encounters the river, the individual members plunge into the water in an egalitarian display of terminal dodge ball. The crocodiles lying in wait under the water can't tell if the wildebeest they are about to drag beneath the surface in a death roll are healthy, weak, a mother or among the newborn young. So, our conceptions of the laws of nature resulting in the culling of the old or the weak from the herd fall by the wayside. In fact, some arbitrary few are sacrificed and the herd benefits.

How does this fit into the framework of selection? Well, we have to consider the possibility that a threat can be global to the group as well as to an individual. The sacrificial trait can grow in order to minimize the global threat. By developing the sacrificial trait, wildebeest are able to survive as a group. Of course, we haven't yet explained why the wildebeest want to be in a group. Nevertheless, the group by surviving, in turn allows many of them to survive individually. This is the core and the enabler of multi-level selection. Thus, we suggest that multi-level selection might well be observed when applied to groups of individuals. Under threat, the groups are under pressure, as well as the individuals in each group. Individuals will be faced with the conflicting demands made on them by both group and individual threats. Of course, we must remember that in some instances the impetus for grouping fails. The Mayans we considered in the first chapter apparently crossed this boundary; the wildebeest didn't.

As another example, let's consider a military anecdote; a company constituted of four platoons, facing an overwhelming enemy. The company commander may decide that the only way to save most of the force is to sacrifice one platoon to fix the enemy in place, thereby limiting the enemy's mobility while the other friendly platoons withdraw. One might think that the soldiers of the platoon left behind would have different personal preferences. However, some mechanism causes them to orient their actions toward the group's benefit rather than their own. Interaction between the selective pressures will define the situation, all under the prism of evolution. The interesting question remains; in the case of selection favoring a group, what is the feedback mechanism that speaks to the continuation of the group? We'll consider this in greater detail in Chapter 5.

Perhaps one of the more difficult aspects of evolutionary processes for us to assimilate is the statistical nature of their being. It is the classical situation of forests and trees. When we're immersed in the individual characteristics of a tree, it requires some rather careful analysis to perceive the statistical nature of the forest. Our rather natural inclination is to attempt to see and appreciate the dynamics of evolutionary change in terms of our everyday experience; through anecdotal example if you will. Indeed, we've already suggested that very low probability events are indistinguishable from miracles. Seen in this light, it is difficult to fathom the prospect of evolutionary change that leads from the most simple, single cell life to the magnificent logical complexity of the human mind or the subtle mechanical complexity of the human eye. To make this leap through a single mutational event seems too fantastic to believe, and, in fact, it is. On the other hand, if we can accept the results of statistical processes involving very large numbers confronted with lots of opportunity for small changes in an incredibly large number of instances spread over an incomprehensible amount of time, then evolutionary change seems much more palatable.

# Selection by Markets

At the beginning of this chapter, we set out to consider the area of overlap of the mechanisms of evolutionary change of first, organic life and then, of computers. At this point, we've made our overview examination of the mechanisms of life; now let's look at the mechanisms of computers.

The tools created by people, including computers and their networks, are subject to their own evaluation processes, but of a type that appears more subjective than the natural selection that we've discussed relative to individual and multi-level appraisal of living organisms. The success or failure of computers is directly influenced by their efficacy for a specific purpose or collection of purposes as judged by the human users of these systems. However, this efficacy is certainly not the only parameter used in the judgment. Or, perhaps we should say that "Efficacy, like beauty, is in the eye of the beholder." The rules against which goods or services are judged are fluid and extremely context sensitive. For example, a highly portable, ubiquitous audio and visual telecommunication device seemed like an excellent idea in the 1930's when it was introduced in the Dick Tracy cartoon strip as a wristwatch TV. In those days, the technology to realize such a device was but a pipe dream at best. In fact, basic television technology was first introduced in a public market capacity during the 1934 World's Fair in Chicago. In the 1960's and 1970's, a fixed line variant of a personal video transmit and receive device seemed like a close approximation when the videophone was introduced by Ma Bell. At that time, the market gave it a "Thumbs down!"

At the dawn of the XXI[st] Century, when ubiquitous cellular telephony connectivity, digital photography and an incredibly mobile population has fomented a new market, the concept comes alive almost naturally as coexisting capabilities converge to provide new functions, such as image transmission, which could establish themselves in an evolutionary manner in the global telecommunication network. Observe a major news event, particularly one presenting a dramatic visual image and what do you see? You see a lot of observers, people who just happen to be in the area, holding up their cellular phones to capture still or video images of the event. In the current environment, not only does everyone have their 15 minutes of fame, as suggested by Andy Warhol, but everyone has a similar shot at distributing the images of a major newsworthy event; perhaps providing someone else with their 15 minutes of fame.

So, what is this decision-making mechanism that we term a market? We view it as a special characteristic of a social ecosystem, which we'll consider in some detail in the next chapter. We can get a bit ahead of ourselves, and using language that we'll more fully develop in the next chapter, suggest that markets assess the value derived from the sating of appetites. At the moment, this description sounds a bit like the policy arbiters of religions, who we might paraphrase as saying in effect that markets work in mysterious ways. Nonetheless, let's proceed by considering that a major goal of a market is actually a simplification of the interaction process. In the abstract, the function of a market is to provide for the competition among congruent products and services such that only cost or price versus performance is the determining factor by which one or the other product or service wins or loses. In this guise, cost or price functions in a similar capacity to trust as we consider it within more general policy infrastructures. If a computer system is accepted by a particular market, that is, if it is judged to be good within that market, then it succeeds. If a computer system is not accepted within a market, then the system fails and, over time, it will cease to exist within that market. If a market functioned in a "pure" fashion, then computer systems would be judged solely on price versus performance. Markets are, however, social environments for the exchange of goods and services and as such they are subject to the same subjective evaluations as are other aspects of social systems.

The concept of a market likely grew out of the increased relevance of groups beyond the basic nuclear family. In the distant past, but just as relevant as if it happened just last week, when a family group found food, it was distributed to the members of the group according to the group's organizational structure. This distribution was, and is, a significant factor in the efficacy of one group versus another. As groups became larger and more diverse, extending across larger areas, they found themselves in direct competition within ecosystems. However, at some point the groups began to stretch the envelope of the ecosystem, perhaps migrating into significantly disjoint ecosystems. This led to specialization in the acquisition of food or other materials necessary to allow the group, and the individuals within the group to better adapt to their own specific ecosystem. The development of the market occurred apace.

Initially, the market was probably a physical location that simply provided a place of food distribution. When a variety of foodstuffs became available from different members of the extended group, then the market perhaps became a place to exchange foodstuffs from different members or subgroups. The hunters brought game to the table, the farmers brought wheat and the foragers brought berries and honey. With a healthy dose of self-interest thrown into the mix, it likely became obvious that the effort to acquire these various goods differed greatly, as did the value or desirability of the goods to the rest of the population. While it might have been a relatively frequent occurrence for a hunter to be trampled by a wooly mammoth, or a forager to suffer a number of bee stings during the capture of a comb of honey, the farmer likely didn't often get attacked by a shock of rampaging wheat. So, the effort to acquire the goods, their basic cost if you will, was significantly different. Likewise, while grain begets bread and hence daily nourishment, a handful of honey now and then was probably an incredible treat and much to be desired; more so than the wheat, at least from time to time. How then to exchange these various materials?

At the extremes of possibility would be confiscation by the strong and powerful at one end of the spectrum and confiscation by the group at the other end of the spectrum. In either case, the middle-man would become the arbiter of goods and services. This, unfortunately, leads to less than desirable results for both the actual providers as well as the consumers of goods and services. Another answer, perhaps somewhere between the extremes, would be to enable a negotiated exchange governed by the concepts of supply and demand, but perhaps restricted by certain governing principles of the group. These principles might well have been determined collectively by the group, or by the governing power elite within the group; the purveyors of policy. The changing environment would likely feed into the situation regarding the bartering of the various products. Through the market, the value of different items could be established through agreement by the supplier and consumer, depending on the availability and desirability of the various materials. Thus, we see the introduction of the concepts of free market supply and demand. How do you establish the value of salt versus the value of grain; the value of oil versus the value of a spice? It all derives from the actual or perceived cost versus the relative worth of the items as determined by interactions between the provider and the consumer.

As markets became even larger, involving more people and more types and sources of goods, the whole concept of barter perhaps became too inefficient to allow the effective interchange of necessary products or services. A common technique through which to address this problem was the creation of, or definition of, a single exchange currency for the market. This required the ability of abstract thought in order to equate tangible goods to the much more intangible concept of currency. The idea was to establish a currency to represent value and then to establish the value of various goods and services in terms of this currency. Once this was done, it became possible to directly compare the values of different goods and also to consider the value of goods in terms of the amount of services necessary for one to provide in order to earn currency with which to buy goods.

Within present day social systems, the foremost grouping mechanism of the abstract market is the *company*. Companies are made of individual employees, to whom the natural selection principle applies. Here, threat entails employees potentially losing their jobs, and the rectifying trait involved is their capability to provide business value to the company. A specific company can acquire this trait, essentially producing it by hiring the right persons. However, what happens when we have a group of companies under market threat; meaning that they're not earning sufficient profits to justify their existence? These companies are threatened just as well as their employees, who risk losing their jobs due to poor financial results that might not be of their own making. Before formalizing what happens, we need to return to the concept of sacrifice.

If we consider a group of companies faced with the threat of marketing obsolescence, the trait we consider is that of developing new business processes in accordance to new market needs. Some companies will create offspring, as General Motors did by creating its Saturn division to compete with Japanese imports. Some companies will develop the competence internally (Ford and its "worldwide" cars), and some will be absorbed (Chrysler). Alternatively, a variety of techniques are used to manipulate the definition of, and hence the applicability of, markets. One technique that is often used to effect this manipulation is the definition of a *standard* that governs all, or part of the relevant market. Through standards, the innovation (and hence potential divergence) within a particular market can be at least regulated, if not minimized, thus benefiting those who can most efficiently bring standard products to the market. Standardization has the beneficial effect of protecting the consumers' investment in products; for high volume consumers that buy large numbers of various products, this can be an important benefit. This, of course has the result of creating a market for standards, driven by the typically large entities that thrive in a standards regulated marketplace. And this, in fact, is a prevalent trait of computer markets.

The first evolutionary trait exemplified by the short history of computers that one can directly observe involves the price of a mix of computing power, memory and storage. Each time a new technology has broken that price by a factor of one hundred, a new wave of products has emerged with each deploying perhaps a hundred times more abundantly. This is on par with the observation made by Clay Christensen in *The Inventor's Dilemma*, which illustrated graphically by considering storage subsystems, how new waves of products first come in under the previous technology in capabilities, then improve until replacing it if their price is significantly lower and eventually boost the storage capabilities by a correspondingly order of magnitude. Following Christensen's lead, we'll term such technologies which drastically change the rules of the game, *disruptive technologies*.

The struggle around this first evolutionary trait of exploding computer capabilities played out in both synchrony (within one generation) and diachrony (across generations). From computer history, it appears that the synchronous rule is that one vendor dominates as long as the rule is not countered in anticipation. The diachronic rule is that a disruptive technology puts so much in question the functioning of the market participants, that no one company manages to dominate the new market as it dominated the previous ones. As the first dominant computer market innovator, IBM was eclipsed by Digital Equipment, so was it subsequently eclipsed by Intel and Microsoft. Now, when personal computers and later personal electronic devices came into play, the natural selection lessons around the first evolutionary trait had been learned. In particular, the synchronous rule of player domination had been well understood, and that rule in itself became a threat.

Therefore, the second evolutionary trait is related to sacrificial behavior as we described it earlier. Companies that are aware of the risk of dominance have to ponder carefully their chance to be that dominant player. In particular, should they attempt to go alone into the new disruptive technology? If enough players decide that they don't stand a chance, they may all accept a lesser competitive position, and therefore their interests will be in having as level as possible a field of competition, less they can tilt it in their favor. That's exactly what happened with personal computers, where several PC companies ended up in strong positions. However, they didn't manage to avoid the first rule altogether as the standards they relied on took the names of Intel and Microsoft, now dominating as much as their predecessors, but in a new field.

This allows one to recognize the second evolutionary trait as the emergence of standards. Standards are agreements across some domain that levels the competitive field. In essence, companies agree to sacrifice some of their margin of maneuver so that the entire market progresses in a way beneficial to them individually. They either do this of their own volition, to avoid having one of them eliminate the others, or they do it under pressure from their customers, who want to avoid depending on a single source. In any case, they give up on the capability to accumulate superior profits that only a dominant position can provide in the long term.

Standards can be *de facto* (emerging), or *de jure* (the result of committee work). In the case of personal computers, the microprocessors and software standards ended up being set by two companies. The computer manufacturers had successfully avoided a dominating computer manufacturer. However, they had created Intel and Microsoft in the process. These companies became dominant in their own areas and took with them most of the profit of that industry. This lesson would not be lost on personal electronic devices manufacturers, who would carry computer history to multi-level selection.

# Epochs of Computer Evolution

Over the last century, the evolution of computer technology can be assessed through four epochs following a prologue period in which the computer species actually emerged in a recognizable lineage. This prologue period is concerned with the development of the basic technologies of electronic components, circuits and memory systems that allowed the realization of stored-program computing systems. We suggest that this progression is best presented as a series of mutation events relative to the mechanical computing devices that had gone before.

The first real epoch of computers is the mainframe era. This involved the construction of large machines with large price tags. Moreover, the mainframe era entailed the first division of labor between the hardware that comprises the anatomical entities that are computers and the software that actually effects their physiological manifestations. Interestingly enough, during the mainframe era the development of software outpaced the development of hardware such that the general cognitive abilities of large mainframes was extremely advanced, even by current standards that are well along the computers' evolutionary ascent. The software capabilities of early mainframes, if mapped into current hardware architectures, make one consider what the evolutionary outcome might have been if dinosaurs, in addition to evolving into extremely large organisms, had similarly developed enhanced brain sizes as well; perhaps to the relative brain size of humans. Extremely large, powerful individuals with well developed cognitive abilities; they might have given *Homo sapiens* a run for their money. Certainly, they would have made for truly industrial strength National Football League franchises.

The second epoch is the mini-computer era. This period was induced with the miniaturization of large sections of mainframe computers through the use of integrated circuits. This transition from the mainframe to the mini-computer is viewed as an adaptation transition rather than a true mutational event. With this transition, the mainframe did not lapse into extinction, largely because certain of its software characteristics (which might be presented as wrapped in the concepts of complex policy) have yet to be supplanted. In fact, the transition from mainframes to mini-computers involved something of a retrograde advance for software systems.

The third epoch is the personal computer era. Wrought from another adaptation event, personal computers were based upon the high volume production of basic processor units which, while significantly less capable than the processors of mainframes or mini-computers, were nonetheless able to address many of the basic issues faced by the office worker as well as peoples' private activities as well. From a software standpoint, if mini-computers entailed a retrograde advance then personal computers turned that into a rout. Certainly the mainframe developers could have considered the early personal computers as evolutionary throwbacks; a reversion from vertebrates to insects if you will. As Darrel Royal, legendary football coach at the University of Texas so eloquently commented in equating a decided underdog victor over the Longhorns to cockroaches, "It's not what they eat that's the problem, it's what they get into and mess up!" In any case, limited in scope and capability though they may have been, personal computers certainly brought the species out of the pure workplace and into the home, giving us computers that travel with us and that provide us services on a 24x7 basis.

The fourth epoch is the personal electronic devices era. Traditionally well represented by cellular phones and their Subscriber Identity Modules (SIM), they are used in the billions as of this writing. Newer forms have developed, such as personal digital assistants, e-mail communicators (such as the much used Blackberry e-mail manager) and Radio-Frequency Identification (RFID) tags (such as the tags used to pay toll on the highway). Based on the adaptation event comprised of a small assembly of computer processor and memory, we entered this era in the early 1990's and at the present time we are still in an environment involving competition among the relevant technologies. The competition is constructive at the moment, perhaps indicating a time of sufficient resources for nature to experiment. However, the competition is turning into a dog-eat-dog contest.

In considering each epoch, we will consider not just the technology, but also the dominant companies involved in each. The evolutionary process in this case involves the organizational environment as well as the technical. Financial considerations will be discussed rather tersely at best. The transition between epochs generally finds an inflation-adjusted cost of raw computing power to vary inversely with the numbers of computers or their power.

# Vacuum Tubes and Dinosaurs

Mathematical computation has always invited the invention of performance enhancing tools. In early days, marks or pebbles of different sizes were used to represent different numbers of items; in essence, objects were used as metaphorical representations of collections of other objects. The abacus was one of the earliest mechanisms that facilitated relatively simple mathematical operations. In more recent centuries, more complex mechanical assemblies were constructed to perform complex, repetitive operations. In any specific era, the nature of these tools was limited by the construction technologies currently available. It required a true mutational discovery in 1879 to provide the seminal event in the development of the computer; an invention by the icon of modern invention, Thomas Alva Edison. His invention was, of course a commercially viable, integrated system for electric lighting, exemplified by the incandescent electric light bulb. The light bulb went on; a new idea for the ages was the result. The symbolism is almost staggering.

Edison was primarily searching for a source of light that could derive from electricity rather than hydrocarbon gas or liquids. However, he arrived at something that provided a great deal more than just light. The serendipitous concept that flowed from Edison's light bulb was the discovery that when heating is induced in a filament in a vacuum by passing an electric current through the filament, a stream of free electrons was sent emanating from it. If a metal plate was placed in the same vacuum, in proximity to the filament, then an electric current could be detected passing from the filament to this plate; a configuration that came to be known as a *diode*. John Fleming, who patented the diode tube only to see the patent invalidated by the United States Supreme court, subsequently discovered that various configurations of vacuum tubes could be used to detect radio waves in the *aether*; that is, radio waves passing through the vacuum of the tube would actually imprint themselves upon (i.e. modulate) the electric current passing through the vacuum of the tube. Lee de Forest then found that by placing a third element into the same vacuum, a grid placed between the filament and the plate, he could create the first amplifier *vacuum tube*; the triode. The triode had the ability to modulate an electric current flowing between the filament and the plate, amplify that same signal and form a switch allowing the signal (current) to be turned on and off. He found that by attaching an antenna to the grid, he could systematically modulate the electric current with radio waves, thus forming the first true radio. In any case, among these various facilities are found the basic operations needed to build an electronic computer.

Through the applied research efforts of many scientists, the period up through the late 1940's resulted in the development of a number of computer-like devices, culminating in what is generally recognized as the first electronic, store-program computer; the Eniac machine constructed at the University of Pennsylvania. Of course, we must observe, albeit just a bit early in our considerations, the impingement of a superior social organization in the form of the United States District Court for Minnesota that found, in the civil case of Honeywell Inc. versus Sperry Rand Corporation and Illinois Scientific Developments, Inc. that John Vincent Atanasoff at Iowa State University developed and built an automatic digital computer.

# Mainframes

The first great epoch of the computer age is the era of the *mainframe*. One can derive much of the architecture of such machines purely from the name: mainframe. Such computers made use of large electrical components as building blocks; vacuum tubes, discrete electronic components (resistors, capacitors and the like) and even some mechanical elements. Much of what went into the computer was simply connection material that held the more involved pieces together and that allowed electrical signals to flow among them. As a consequence, the various pieces of the computer were assembled on standard size frames or racks that provided mechanical regularity for these pieces, including the provision of electrical power and cooling. Indeed, these large machines generated tremendous amounts of excess heat from their incredibly inefficient (by today's standards) operations. Mainframes encompassed a wide variety of computer characteristics. Their large size brought with them a large price tag, both for acquisition and for operations. This, in turn, placed a number of requirements on the software that brought the mainframes to life. These include the concepts of high availability, high security and very high computing and storage capacity, yielding a high trust environment for the users of such systems. Moreover, a high trust environment that can address the full range of problems amenable to computer activity.

Mainframes appeared in the early-to-mid-1950's, led by the IBM 650 as a transitional machine that extended the species from the one-of-a-kind systems that arose at the initial emergence of electronic computers into a significant number of machines of a common design that established a market for the genre. Somewhere in the range of 200 to 400 of these machines were sold at a price of around $400,000 each. The IBM 650 was vacuum tube based and it made use of a mechanical drum for its main memory. This memory was comprised of a metal drum approximately 6 inches in diameter and 16 inches long that rotated at something greater than 10,000 revolutions per minute. A series of read and write heads were positioned along the rotational axis of the drum, allowing them to magnetically record signals on the surface of the drum that represented numbers encoded in a digital form and then to subsequently read them back from the surface.

During the mainframe epoch, the problems to be addressed by computers were typically divided into two categories: business problems and scientific problems. Keeping the books for a multi-billion dollar corporation is a pretty clear example of a business problem. Providing local forecasts of severe weather is obviously a scientific problem, along with simulating the physical results of a large-scale chain reaction such as that produced by a thermonuclear device. In the early days, these problems were addressed by somewhat different sets of equipment. Business problems required lots of data storage capacity and the ability to stream input and output data to and from this storage. Magnetic tapes were the preeminent mechanisms providing this facility in the earliest systems. Scientific problems required lots of main memory and a significant amount of intermediate capacity for fast input/output storage. The main memory demanded direct access by the central processing unit of the computer; such memory was extremely expensive at the time. Fast intermediate storage was provided by disk drives; they were higher speed and higher capacity derivatives of the drum memory used for the earliest mainframes.

In the business world, such as in banking, or insurance, the necessity of linking computers together to exchange information came early; ad hoc computer-to-computer links started to develop that in time would give birth to the first private networks. Some of those networks are still active today, for example for inter-bank transactions.

Mainframe computers were big and expensive. They required specially prepared environments, giving rise to the term and concept of a *computer room*. Such facilities had raised floors, allowing cabling among the many boxes comprising the computer to be run as necessary. Raised flooring also allowed for air handling such that chilled air, or water, to be directed through the various racks of electronic gear in order to dissipate the large amounts of heat given off as a byproduct of the inefficient circuitry of the age. Because of their expense, mainframes were of necessity multi-user. Of course, this had the beneficial effect of causing computer designers to be cognizant of the probability that all of these users were going to offer the possibility of creating problems for all the other users. Consequently, computer architectures had to provide mechanisms for keeping the work done by the computer for each user separate from all other work. Also driven by size, power and expense constraints, the problems to be addressed by mainframe computers tended to require strong economic justification. As a result, the problems addressed tended to be big and complex.

As we'll see in some later chapters, a central feature of cognitive abilities, whether it is of people or of computers, is connection of the sensori-motor experience to the computing mechanism. The successive epochs of computer evolution can be characterized by the sensori-motor linkage between the computer and the person. Indeed, it is clear that a significant aspect of computer evolution has been to more closely mimic the direct sensori-motor experience of the human species. Consider the manner in which the earliest computers, the mainframes, were connected to their human users, both for control (input) and results presentation (output).

At the beginning of the mainframe era, the dominant mechanism for control input was the punched paper card, and in some instances the punched paper tape. A punch card was made of moderately stiff paper approximately 3 ¼ inches by 7 3/8 inches. The card presented 80 columns of 12 rows each. One or more positions in a column could be punched, leaving holes in the card that represented characters. Such cards could be used to enter programs, that is, instructions defining the operations that the computer was to perform, or data, that is, the information that the operations were to use in their processing. The communication protocol between the person and the computer was, by today's standards, cumbersome and non-intuitive. This is a bit more understandable given the fact that punched card use in computer technology derived from their use in the Jacquard looms of the early 1800's. Computers tended to be viewed as extensions of mechanical devices, so this form of input fit well with the paradigm.

Output from mainframe computers, that is the output that was used directly by people, tended to be either printed documentation, produced by a *line printer* device, or graphic displays produced by *pen-plotter* devices. Interactions between a person and a computer tended to involve a cyclic protocol. Instructions for processing operations were punched into cards, as was input data that was to be the fodder for those operations. The computer read, interpreted and acted upon the instructions and data from the punched cards (a rather graphic illustration of the term *number crunching*) and then printed the results of the processing to a line printer or pen-plotter. Variants on this protocol might entail the creation of intermediate result data on other cards punched by the computer, or the storage of data on magnetic tape or early disk drive units, and then the protocol would start anew.

The first family of truly high production volume mainframes was the IBM 360 series. These started making their appearance in corporations in the 1960's before subsequently maturing in the 1970's in the form of the IBM 370. Total production of these machines ran into the *tens of thousands* around the world to perform business tasks of all sorts. The cost of those computers and the environment they required ran in the *tens of millions* of dollars.

IBM started as a small company that emerged at the time of mainframe developments as the undisputed leader of a pack of companies whose names included Burroughs, Control Data, General Electric, Honeywell, RCA, Sperry and Univac.

It is historically interesting to remember that the United States space endeavors that first placed a man on the moon in 1969, Project Mercury, Project Gemini and finally Project Apollo, were all products of the computer mainframe epoch. But, to put things in scale, the entire computational capability of the National Aeronautics and Space Administration (NASA) in 1969, including processing power, main computer memory and on-line disk storage, was probably less than what is today available on one fully configured personal computer system. More to the point, certainly a very significant, if not the primary contributor, of computing resources came in the form of bamboo and plastic; that is, the *slide rules* that hung from the belts of most NASA engineers.

# The Semiconductor Mutation

The mutational event that truly launched the age of the computer was the 1948 invention by William Bradford Schockley (with John Bardeen and William H. Brittain) of the transistor. The transistor is a device that makes use of the properties of a class of materials known as semiconductors. These characteristics offer very different operating mechanisms than vacuum tubes, but they can be used to effect much the same capabilities as various vacuum tube configurations. Through these configurations, the operations necessary to construct stored-program computers were possible in much smaller physical configurations than those constructed using vacuum tubes. An important characteristic that derived directly from the smaller physical size of components was the fact that transistors required significantly less power to achieve the same operations than would be the case with vacuum tubes. The net result was a capability to build computers that were orders of magnitude smaller in size and required proportionally less power for their operation. In addition, because of the small size of components, they could be physically situated much closer to each other; consequently electrical signals from one component had a shorter distance to travel to another component. The end result was that operations could be performed faster with transistor-based components versus vacuum tube based components.

As a corollary to components using less power, the same semiconductor based components operated at much lower temperatures compared to vacuum tubes. Thus, the computer itself dissipated much less heat when built with transistors. This had the added benefit of decreasing the requirement for air conditioning systems to keep the computer in a temperature range that was safe for all the components as well as for the human operators of the machines.

In essence, the semiconductor mutation brought with it a whole series of characteristics that both allowed the computer to perform better and to operate within the bounds of an entirely different environment compared to vacuum tube systems. The mainframe epoch of computers began with vacuum tube based systems. However, the advent of transistor based circuitry rose to the fore during expansion of mainframe technology. Thus, over the course of the epoch, we see the size of individual computers compressed from the size of large rooms to the size of closets. We see power dissipation decline from a level that required chilled water circulated through the computer circuitry in order to extract the large amounts of heat generated to a level that could be handled by chilled air based systems.

# Minicomputers

The second epoch of computers arrived with the introduction of mini-computers, of which the Digital Equipment Corporation VAX series is most famous. This started with the development of small, real-time oriented computers, culminating with the PDP 16 bit series which showed up first in consistent volumes in the 1970's. The more powerful VAX 32 bit computers replaced the PDP machines and developed in volume in the 1980's, actually replacing mainframes in many functions. They also extended the range of computer applications thanks to their reduced costs. Mini-computers deployed in *millions* (a hundred times more than mainframes) and were priced in the *hundreds of thousands* of dollars (a hundred times less than mainframes).

Mini-computers brought new advances in the area of real-time operations. Multiple tasks could be executed concurrently serving connected devices to acquire data from them, and control them accordingly in the laboratory as well as in the field. Also, mini-computers started the era of wide-scale networks, with Digital Equipment leading the charge in creating the first homogeneous networks based on its own standard called DECnet.

Mini-computers were used intensively for scientific and technical purposes. Digital Equipment started as a small company that emerged during the time of mini-computer developments as the undisputed leader of a pack of companies whose names included Data General, Gould, Harris, Perkin-Elmer and Prime Computers. When mini-computers started to be used also for business, IBM, seeing the threat to its business, reacted by developing its own line of mini-computers (the AS/400), which proved enough to keep its customers from bolting.

Although introduced with mainframe machines, the mini-computer epoch saw a complete migration of the human to computer interface away from punched cards and toward text and modest graphic mechanisms. These were first introduced through teletype terminals, which formed the earliest variants of non-voice, network communications. These terminals became the primary source of input to and then output from mini-computers. Rapid advances in the technology migrated from the mechanical teletype terminals to cathode ray tube devices that used typewriter *qwerty* keyboards for input and electron display tubes for output. The end result of this was a much tighter linkage between the human and the computer. Developing computer software and using the resultant software products became much more of an interactive activity.

# Integrated Circuits as Genetic Selection

In 1958, Jack Kilby with Texas Instruments constructed the first integrated circuit. This device allowed for the construction and interconnection of many transistors and other semi-conductor devices on a single substrate of material. This provided yet another order of magnitude decrease in both physical size as well as electrical power consumption in order to achieve comparable computer operations. Smaller size again meant faster operation. While incredibly profound, we tend to characterize this development as comparable to genetic selection as opposed to mutation. In fact, the goal of the research and development work from which this event resulted was generally aimed toward this end.

Prior to this selection event, electrical circuits were comprised of discrete components: transistors of various sorts along with resistors, capacitors and induction coils connected by highly conducting material such as copper or gold wire. The connections between components and their conducting links were generally effected by soldering the materials together. A significant innovation that occurred across the boundary between mainframe computers and minicomputers was the *wire-wrap* connection. This form of interconnection involved attaching components to a mounting board that had, on its reverse side, short peg-like extensions at the connection points of the components. Then a very flexible conducting wire could be wrapped around one of these extensions for a connection point of a component and then extended to and wrapped around a different extension for a connection point of a different component. This approach had the benefit of not requiring the use of high temperature tools around potentially sensitive components.

# Personal Computers

The third epoch of computers is comprised of personal computers, whose history is different from that of mainframes and mini-computers, although the trend is similar. Personal computers showed up in volume in the 1980's, to become prevalent as mini-computer replacements in the 1990's, until they started to also replace mainframes in some functions in the 2000's. Personal computers sold in the *hundreds of millions*, a hundred times more than mini-computers, in prices around a *thousand* dollars, a hundred times less than mini-computers.

Personal computers brought a new type of applications into being. The best example was VisiCalc, the first spreadsheet of widespread use. A personal application, VisiCalc by itself would be enough to justify the purchase of a computer. Over time, personal computers would end up being used not only by individuals, but also in the back office as powerful *servers* doing tasks previously performed by mainframe or mini-computers. Coincident with the development of the personal computer was the development of the graphic display terminal as the primary form of human to computer interaction. The paradigm for such interaction evolved through a number of government funded, university enacted projects. From a chain of development at MIT, the Stanford Research Laboratory and Xerox's PARC finally emerged the Apple Lisa computer with a highly intuitive graphical user interface.

The Lisa is probably more appropriately viewed as representative of an intermediate step between mini-computers and personal computers, the *scientific workstation*. Such machines were, in general, mini-computers packaged with a high-definition screen. However, they were priced in the same range as a mini-computer, and couldn't compete with personal computers. They nevertheless served a useful purpose, as many concepts found in personal computers, such as windowing interfaces, were first developed and experimented with on scientific workstations. In fact, the Apple Macintosh did emerge from this path as a true personal computer.

One innovation of scientific workstations was networking. Local networking (Ethernet) was developed at Xerox and would prove to be so forward thinking that it is still at the base of today's local networks, not only wired, as they were at the time, but also wireless, such as Wi-Fi. Local networks would assemble into the Internet, a worldwide standard with the most successful network protocol in history, TCP/IP, the Transmission Control Protocol/Internet Protocol.

With personal computers, history played differently than with mainframe and mini-computers because by the time personal computers appeared, the market players had learned from past experience and would not let one company dominate the hardware supply. So Compaq, Dell, Gateway, IBM and others shared the market. However, two companies, each in its field, ended up dominating personal computers. In microprocessors, Intel took the same overwhelming lead that had been previously taken by IBM with mainframes and by Digital Equipment with mini-computers. In software, Microsoft did the same with operating systems and key applications. In passing, let's note that unlike IBM, which survived both the mini-computer and personal computer attacks on their business, Digital Equipment died spectacularly for having ignored the personal computer capability to replace mini-computers. Its death knell was marked by the supposed utterance of Ken Olsen, founder and CEO of Digital in 1977 that there is no reason for people to have a computer at home. When he realized his mistake, he tried to launch his own line of personal computers along the same proprietary lines as his mini-computers. It was too late; the game had changed.

# Personal Electronic Devices

The fourth epoch of computers is comprised of machines that most people don't even think of as computers. We might even say that they don't think of them as belonging to any particular category. They are just useful day-to-day tools that have clear functions and make life easier. They are our personal electronic devices. They number in the *billions*, and some of them are already priced in the $20 dollar range or less (some are free), in this case *100 times* cheaper than personal computers in time-adjusted dollars.

They are *trusted*, in that they are assumed to be always available when needed and to perform the functions they are used for flawlessly, and they are *personal*, in that they are portable, belong to one person, and may be secured against forbidden usage by others. As we'll see, they have also started to expand beyond the person, as there are new forms of trusted personal devices which now are attached to an object, in a personal way, if we allow ourselves to be overly anthropomorphic.

Personal electronic devices are split in two related categories. The first one is that of hand-held devices, the second one is that of chip centered devices. The first category encompasses cellular phones, personal digital assistants, music players, portable game consoles, global positioning satellites navigators and other such objects of everyday use. The second category encompasses chip cards (bank cards with embedded chips), Subscriber Identity Modules (SIM: the removable chip-bearing card inside most cellular phones next to the battery), Radio-Frequency Identification tags (RFID: the chip-bearing tags used to pay the highway toll, or to identify products at the supermarket), personal storage key fobs and other such objects directed at identifying, authenticating, authorizing and carrying private information.

All those devices are networked, or on their way to being networked, because their function is to involve the user in participatory activities, with institutions (such as banks, government, phone operators) and with others with similar devices (such as communicating via voice and messaging, or gaming). Hand-held devices have screens, and speakers, and other means of communication with their owner; chip-centered devices have built-in security mechanisms at their core. Hand-held devices and chip-centered devices are related in that chip-centered devices are often found inside hand-held devices, where their function is to take charge of the most private and secure function of the combination. However, one can find hand-held devices that do not contain a chip-centered device, as they handle security functions on their own, like the current generation of music players (they handle digital rights protection), and chip-centered devices that are autonomous, like the bank chip cards (when needed, they hook up to specialized computers, called *readers*, for power and communication with the world).

Personal electronic devices use both the networks born of the telecommunication industry and those born of the computer industry. An example of a telecommunication network is GSM (Global System Mobile), the ubiquitous standard of billions of cellular telephones. An example of computer network is of course the Internet. At the time of writing, network technologies are merging in a phenomenon called *convergence*.

Whereas the personal electronic devices manufacturers wouldn't let the IBM mainframe and the Digital Equipment mini-computer hardware stories replay, they also were wiser from having seen the Microsoft and Intel stories unfold in software and microprocessors. At the present time, no single player dominates the personal electronic devices market, be it in hardware, microprocessors or software. We'll expand later on the fundamentals of that story, but in the meanwhile, we observe that personal electronic devices should play toward personal computers the same role as personal computers played to mini-computers and mini-computers to mainframes in their time. It is with such devices that we suggest the human to computer interface has entered the world of complex policy considerations. More than simply reflect our individual commands, we seek computer assistance in projecting our cognitive needs into the cyber-world.

Before coming to the end of this chapter on the mechanics of human and computer evolution, we would like to devote some quality time to smart cards. Smart card is a generic name for most forms of chip-centered devices. They are used daily by the billions, as they are the heart of most cellular phones in the world. Anyone owning a GSM cellular phone, which means most everyone around the world now (more than two billion at the time of this writing) can open the back of the phone, remove the battery, and find next to it a removable smart card the size of a thumbnail. At the center is a metallic module and at the center of the module is a chip the size of a teardrop. This is the same chip that is found in the credit cards used in much of the world outside the United States. It is the same chip that is carried by every soldier of the United States armed forces, and it is the same chip found in every satellite-television home equipment set. Since most hand-held devices contain a smart card, we thought that we could present computer evolution in action, and tell a smart card story, a good example of how computer history actually unfolds under evolutionary market pressures.

# Odyssey

Smart cards were born in the 1970's from concurrent French, German and Japanese development. Early patents in the area were also developed in the United States, but European efforts predominated. By the end of the 1970's, a French journalist named Roland Moreno had accumulated a series of patents for placing microcircuits on a card, which would first take the shape and form of credit cards. He sold patent rights to two French-originated companies, Groupe Bull and Schlumberger, and this started the smart card industry. By the mid-1990's, Bull had invented the microprocessor card (an invention of Michel Ugon), and the market established itself in the 1990's along evolutionary lines of the first order.

The main card manufacturers were Bull CP8, De La Rue, Gemplus, Giesecke and Devrient, Philips, Oberthur, Orga and Schlumberger. The integrated circuit chips themselves were built by Motorola, Philips, Siemens and SGS Thomson. Philips deserves a special mention as in the mid-1990's they tried to get into the smart card manufacturing business, only to abandon the effort later in a good example of evolutionary struggle. Later on, Motorola tried a similar move and ended up divesting both their smart card chip business and their smart card business. The lines of responsibility were drawn; meaning a workable food chain was established. Chip manufacturers designed and manufactured integrated circuit chips while card manufacturers merged the card and chip, installed operating system and application software and personalized the cards for mass usage. To adopt language from later in the book, the card manufacturers *provisioned* the smart cards.

The fact that there were no dominant players either among the chip manufacturers or the card manufacturers was not due to chance. Card manufacturers had been kept in check by French governmental direction, which allowed Gemplus to emerge as a competitor to first-dominant Schlumberger by giving them a forced part of the phone card market share. We'll recount this particular episode in Chapter 6. In any case, this created a second sourcing culture in the smart card business which, to this day, dictates that most card buyers insist on respecting standards that allow them to obtain second sources for their card supplies. In turn, card manufacturers made sure that their own source of chip supply would be diversified by creating a competitive culture among the chip manufacturers.

However, in the mid-1990's, the smart card business was ready for a mutational event. Every card manufacturer had a well diversified line of products with all imaginable combinations of operating systems. However, by that time Intel and Microsoft had become the dominant players in personal computers, and most advanced thinkers in the respective segments of the computer business wanted to become Intel, for the chip manufacturers, or Microsoft, for the software makers. The smart card domain, something of a backwater of the computer world, was no exception. Research teams had been created in all participating companies to that effect. One such research team was Schlumberger's Austin team.

At Austin, Texas, the site of Schlumberger's general computer system research and development facility, based on a proposal by the Paris-based smart card marketing group, the chairman of Schlumberger elected to create a team charged with creating a new smart card system. Thanks to the center's privileged position as the main system development group within the global corporate structure, the team could draw on some of the senior and prominent computer scientists gathered in Austin in 1996.

This assembled team knew next to nothing about smart cards, but they had considerable experience in operating systems. Moreover, they were very well versed in the concepts, mechanisms and history of computing in general, and computing in the face of highly constrained resources specifically. Since the specific development effort dealt with operating systems, it seemed clear (as it would to virtually anyone in the computer world) that if it was a success, then the long-term competitive threat would likely come from Microsoft, not the other smart card companies. It was also clear that in this realm, Schlumberger, for all its *gravitas* in the oil patch, had no chance to combat such a threat alone. The food chain danger in this case was to follow the commoditization fate of computer manufacturers, or rather, a much worse fate, since cards don't have the myriad of peripherals which allow computer manufacturers to innovate in various ways. From the business perspective, a considerable part of smart card value comes from operating systems and applications. Leaving that to others was unthinkable.

Therefore, it was clear to the team that they'd better design an operating system that other card manufacturers would agree with, so that a level field would be created allowing them to compete for excellence. The system requirement was provision of a secure smart card facility that would allow faster deployment of new applications, and specifically the deployment of these applications after the smart card was already in the hands of the end consumer. The concept was termed *post-issuance programmability*. At the time, there was but one obvious choice. This was to make use of Java from Sun Microsystems. Unfortunately, at the time Java was relatively big and smart cards were absolutely little. The only way to shoehorn Java into a smart card at the time was to lop off a couple of toes; that is, to subset Java.

So, in June 1996, the Schlumberger team went to Cupertino, California to propose to Sun to subset Java in order to make it run on a smart card. Sun was less than enthusiastic, as was reasonably to be expected. The credo of Java was "Write once, run everywhere!" If the language were subsetted, a smart card Java application could be made to run on a mainframe, but a mainframe Java application probably couldn't be made to run on a smart card. While philosophically this is a compelling argument, from a business standpoint it rather missed the point. Smart cards offered a potential market of billions of units. That is also quite compelling, even in the world of the Internet. So, in September, the team managed to go visit Sun again, this time through new contacts within Sun's more business-computing oriented groups. The idea of subsetting Java was then more amicably received by Sun, even by the spiritual leaders of the Java effort within Sun. In fact, the subsetting had already been done by the Schlumberger team, which was able to present a working Java subset implementation on a smart card as a *fait accompli*.

Once Sun accepted the philosophical concept, the next step was to insure common acceptance of a new operating system standard within the smart card industry. Java is an interesting thing from a standards perspective, because it is the intellectual property of Sun Microsystems. In order to attract a sufficient user community, all of whom were skeptical of adopting single source (essentially proprietary) mechanisms, Sun adopted a moderately open process for the care and feeding of the Java Specifications. The smart card industry, being similarly skeptical of the single source nature of Java, chose to create a consortium called the Java Card Forum to act as specification development body, along the lines served by the European Telecommunications Standards Institute (ETSI) in the telecommunications world. The Java Card Forum worked closely with Sun (and actually still does) to evolve the specification for Java Card, the smart card specific version of Java. In what we might refer to in later chapters as a symbiotic relationship, the Java Card Forum is central to developing specifications for smart card aware facilities within the Java world. Forming the other half of the symbiotic relationship, Sun takes these specifications and blends them with the Java for the rest of the computer world and disseminates formal specifications and conformance tests. The success of the approach is signaled by Java Card based smart cards now comprising a majority of the SIMs of cellular phones and expanding into other arenas of smart card activity in the Internet world.

While this story presents as a rather smoothly perceived and followed plan, there were indeed a number of internecine struggles along the way. Natural selection in the market world is like that. Indeed, there are competitive species seeking their toe-hold in this business domain as we write. Schlumberger begat Axalto, which later merged with Gemplus to form Gemalto, henceforth the largest current smart card company. However, there are other competitors on the veldt; from Gemalto's .NET card and Multos in the technical domain to competitive threats from completely different industry segments in the business domain.

While the battle was raging in the technical arena in establishing the new era of open systems in smart cards, the business action was equally active. Several markets developed among the early adopters of Java Card technology, bringing smart cards solidly on the playing field of computer evolution. Since 2004, they have become the most prevalent form of computer in the world. If personal computers were the cockroaches of evolutionary progression, smart cards seek to be the *Jeholodens*. This early emergent form of mammal, which was an insectivore by the way, perhaps counts among its descendent lineage the human species. A recurring theme for the remainder of this book will be considering what directions this evolutionary path might take. As we have seen, and will continue to see, it is very much a context sensitive process.

For example, when Java Card was invented, Mobile Communications marketing teams within card manufacturers operations thought that the market was most interested in developing applications in an easy way on smart cards. Remember, before Java Card, all smart cards were programmed in different ways; mostly in assembly language, one of the hardest ways of programming a computer. Java could directly address this problem. So, marketing teams went to mobile phone operators touting this new capability. Interestingly enough, what seduced operators was not that feature, but the capability to download applications to the card over the air. The lesson here is that it is hard to predict which features of a new product will stick, when developing new technology. The ultimate irony of the Java Card story is that the application programming business really didn't actually pick up. Rather, mobile companies just asked the card manufacturers to do the programming for them. But certainly, the story doesn't stop here. As we will consider in some detail in the following chapters, the development of new species happens around the edges of the main body of the existent species.

An emerging market for smart cards is in Information Technology. By the mid-1990's, there was a nascent market for smart cards to authenticate users on secure networks; for example, military networks or corporate networks in businesses where data are most highly valued. As with telecommunications and banking, Java Card introduced the capability to easily add functionality to smart cards after issuance. For example, on a ship, the card could be used to access the computer network as well as to pay for goods at the ship's gift shop. By 2003, led by organizations like the Department of Defense of the United States and corporations like Shell Oil, millions of smart cards were used around the world in Information Technology. This forms the opening salvo in the extension of computer networks to fully accommodate human social systems. This, we suggest, is the path out of the primeval swamps of current chip centered incarnations of personal devices.

In this chapter, we have examined some of the basic mechanisms on which the evolutionary progression of living things, and computers, is based. Quite obviously, of course, mechanisms often coalesce into systems. Systems in turn impact, and are impacted by, the environments in which they function. Such environments essentially form context for the systems. We are on the path to understanding that context sensitive, metaphorical comprehension is the basis of the human mind from which social systems have emerged. So, we now need to delve into these environmental considerations; the topic of our next chapter.

2  Mechanics of Evolution

# 3 Environment

All *life* is biology.

All biology is physiology.
All physiology is chemistry.
All chemistry is physics.
All physics is ***mathematics***.

*Life Is: Mathematics*

Dr. Stephen Marquardt
Lecture to the American Academy of Cosmetic Dentistry
April 29, 2004

# It's All Relative(s)

Evolutionary processes occur within an environment through which their effectiveness is judged, an environment termed an *ecosystem*. The name ecosystem brings into focus the fact that living things require a number of conditions to support life and that when many different species are present, these conditions and species all form an interrelated *system*. Within such a system, the elements often exhibit the characteristics of one or more mechanisms, and each of the various mechanisms in a system can impact the others' operations. Hence, the constituent elements of an ecosystem impact one another, perhaps simply through their existence or perhaps through the operations of their mechanisms. The boundary of an ecosystem is formed by the set of characteristics that makes it distinct from other ecosystems, and it provides a relatively closed space to constrain the conditions and mechanisms of the living species contained. Within this space, that is, within the boundaries of an ecosystem, the efficacy of each mechanism, relative to its supporting conditions and to all other mechanisms, is judged.

A popular term for the judgment or evaluation process is *survival of the fittest*. While this expression might be apt if one delves sufficiently into the meaning of the word fittest, we will prefer the appellation *natural selection*. Survival of the fittest may be construed as meaning that the bigger and more powerful the entity, the more fit it is to survive (an extreme abuse of the term has been found in the XIX[th] Century with the Social Darwinism movement, that took exactly this understanding to promote supremacist ideas that would foster some of the worst events of the XX[th] Century). If that were the case, then one rightly ponders, "Where are the dinosaurs today?" An atypical, perhaps even cataclysmic event, can always take a species or a collection of species to the brink of extinction; perhaps even take them over the brink. In such a case, one might surmise that if the infrastructure for life itself survived the event, then why would not the same dominant species re-emerge, albeit slowly, through the same evolutionary processes that proved to their benefit in ages past? The answer is found by noting that fittest is a relative term that must be derived on a case-by-case basis. Its situational definition is constrained within the scope of an environment or ecosystem through which its meaning is actually determined. Consequently, the definition of the phrase can only be determined within the context of a specific ecosystem. Much like the universe at large, as Einstein showed us, it's all relative. Consider a couple of examples.

The boundary between the Permian and the Triassic periods of the geologic calendar marks the demarcation between the Paleozoic and Mesozoic eras. This boundary corresponds to perhaps the greatest of the extinction events that appear to have occurred from time to time throughout the earth's history. During this boundary period, which lasted for perhaps a million years or so, some 90 percent of all marine species of life and 70 percent of terrestrial vertebrate species became extinct. For a time, at the beginning of the Triassic period the dominant terrestrial species were actually various forms of fungi. The era subsequently gave rise to dinosaurs as the dominant family of species. Throughout the Mesozoic era, mammals and bird species also lived and evolved. However, the environment in which these species found themselves as they came into being perhaps was most hospitable to the characteristics of the dinosaurs. In this era, that is, in this ecosystem, the concept of fittest was well characterized by the traits exhibited by the dinosaurs.

A couple of hundred million years later a new extinction event occurred. At the boundary between the Cretaceous and the Tertiary periods came the rapid downfall of the dinosaurs. In the new ecosystem that characterized the Tertiary period, mammals and birds flourished. While there is considerable speculation about what caused these two major extinction events, the point of most significant interest to us is that the concept of fittest changed significantly at the boundary in each case. Specifically, if we consider the dinosaur population comprised of big individuals, then the post-dinosaur era to current times would seem to be comprised of small individuals. While we don't necessarily understand which characteristics of the environment led to this dramatic shift in what constitutes the fittest, it seems clear that the shift did occur. Thus, the details of the ecosystem define the evaluation criteria that pass judgment on the evolutionary processes that occur within that ecosystem.

Natural selection is generally recognized by evolutionary biologists as a well-defined principle describing the basic interactions among individual entities of all species in their quest to simply live and propagate. Much more ambiguous is the role played by collections of entities, *social groups*, in the propagation of individuals and their respective species. What is ambiguous is whether groups, particularly with respect to the human species, constitute evolutionary entities in their own right. That is, do human groups compete in an evolutionary manner with other groups, and consequently is there a natural selection process in play among such groups? History is replete with examples of the human species functioning within social groups. Do such groups simply impact the evolutionary ecosystems of individual humans, or do they represent entities with their own ecosystem-based interactions? When we discussed the mechanics of evolutionary processes in the previous chapter, we suggested that natural selection required a language mechanism through which could be conveyed the design of the species. Human groups are not obviously constructed from a blueprint mechanism with anywhere near the apparent efficacy of DNA as it pertains to individual entities of the species. Perhaps, however, there are higher order, and hence much more subtle design mechanisms in play with groups. It seems obvious that the most basic human social group, that is the *family*, constitutes a response mechanism to the physiological constraints or requirements of the human infant. Beyond the basic family however, it becomes more uncertain as to what makes the formation of human groups such a recurrent mechanism and what holds such groups together once they are formed. Our conjecture is that the feedback mechanism for such groups encompasses the higher cognitive functions of the mind. However, since we do not seem to have a grouping instruction manual that has been passed down to succeeding generations through the ages, the physical manifestation of grouping design has yet to be well defined.

We assume that since the human species' earliest days of emergence, when all its members lived in the wild with all other species, the physiological needs and capabilities of the human infant have not changed significantly. That is, since the beginning of the species, the human infant has been not only totally helpless, it has always constituted a burden upon its mother or any other humans that felt compelled to sustain its life. An infant today cannot protect itself from the simplest of dangers and our assumption is that it has always been thus. For example, any number of other species, ranging from ants or other insects on the ground or in the bushes, to the major predators of the day (lions and tigers and bears; oh my!) are all threats to the human infant. The infant has virtually no defensive capabilities beyond the fact that, in most cases, its mother and father feel a natural compulsion to provide for their infant. While this results in a realization of the infant's need to be carried and protected by larger humans, it also results in the inhibition of these humans' ability to hunt for or gather food. The species has evolved mechanisms of grouping together for the enhanced protection and support of these individuals; very specifically the infants. However, the manner in which the design for these mechanisms is conveyed from generation to generation is still unclear. It does seem more than plausible that the conveyance mechanism does exist. Through the evolutionary process, the basic human group (the family) developed around the enhanced ability to protect the individual members of the group, beyond their individual capabilities to protect themselves, and to garner sufficient food for all the members of the group beyond what they were able to garner individually.

It seems most plausible that this earliest grouping formed around what today we know as the basic *nuclear family*; a man and a woman with a child or children. Of course, there is also documented evidence, for example in Australia's outback, of larger family units in prehistoric settings. There, as the children grow, mate and have additional children, the family itself grows, perhaps with the result that it becomes multi-generational and perhaps even multi-familial. Similar social structures are still found preferentially in rural America, although their prevalence has diminished since the middle of the XX$^{th}$ Century. While the basic family unit is arguably grounded in physiological principles derived from established evolutionary processes, large groupings involve enhanced communication and social skills on the part of members of the human species. This leads to the establishment of larger and more complex groups. We identify these larger groups as first, *clans*, then *tribes* and then very large-scale groups. We refer to the largest human groups as *congregations* and then as *égalité*. While we don't have a firm history of this development, the existence of all such groups throughout recorded history is a strong indication that each revealed a successful evolutionary mechanism. That is, the emergence of groups certainly enhanced the survival characteristics of the individual; they enhanced the individual's natural selection chances. Moreover, according to some researchers, such as David Sloan Wilson in *Darwin's Cathedral*, a variety of indicators suggest that among-group selection is at work as well; that groups compete and that certain group characteristics enhance the natural selection chances of specific groups beyond that simply of the individuals within the groups.

In this case, the principles of natural selection are applied in a recursive fashion, thus giving rise to group-selection as well as individual-selection processes. With multi-level selection processes as the backdrop, our consideration of ecosystems must keep apace. Thus, we would like to consider the structure of ecosystems in which complex selection mechanisms for humans can function and then consider comparable ecosystems for computers and computer infrastructure, including an amalgam of the two. We characterize this extension of the basic concepts of an ecosystem as a *social ecosystem*. From time to time, throughout the remainder of this book, we may refer to the original concept of an ecosystem as a *physical ecosystem* in order to unambiguously differentiate it from a social ecosystem. If we use the word ecosystem alone, we are generally referring to a physical ecosystem.

Social ecosystems offer an environment for complex modes of interaction among its inhabitants, while ultimately supporting the basic mechanics of natural selection. A social ecosystem is always contained within a physical ecosystem. These complex modes require considerably more mechanisms of interaction, including the means to support interactions at a distance. As we expand our considerations into these areas, we will see more and more similarity between the operation of complex group mechanisms such as religion and the complex computer environments in which personal electronic devices come to the fore.

# Ecosystems

The word ecosystem is a *portmanteau*, a word derived from the combination of other words that evokes a blending of their meanings. Ecology refers to the relationships among living things and their environment. System refers to a mechanism or collection of mechanisms with a unified purpose. Hence, an ecosystem refers to an environmental framework through which, or within which the interactions involving the species found therein can occur and through which these interactions can by analyzed and understood; more specifically, interactions among species and between species and their containing environments. Thus, an ecosystem comprises a complex space with a complex set of boundaries for the various systems that derive from or support the existence of the living things found within the space.

It is important to understand the use of the plural form in referencing the concept of boundaries relative to an ecosystem. In fact, an ecosystem is a multidimensional construct, not just a simply defined physical area; it may well owe its delineation to other dimensions besides location or extent.

The concept of an ecosystem arises from evolutionary biology's consideration of the framework within which natural selection of species operates. In such an examination of the evolution of species, it may be assumed that both single as well as multi-level selection processes are at work. Consequently, it is necessary to allow the concept of ecosystem to encompass the framework within which simple and complex interactions occur. For social species, for example with the human species, this brings into play a variety of modes of interaction in both individual as well as in group form.

So, we can consider what forms the boundaries of ecosystems, and to what purpose. We are particularly interested in the behavior of humans and computer systems within the ecosystems that they inhabit, either individually or collectively. We would like to understand the establishment of boundaries because they will play into the definition of the bounds of policy infrastructures when we start to examine the behavior of human group organizations and interactions. The boundaries are not always formidable, physical barriers. Sometimes they are relatively tenuous, in the wild as among organizational groupings. Let us consider an extremely simplistic example.

Suppose that we find an island that contains a fresh water spring, a wild lettuce patch and rabbits. This will constitute our example ecosystem. The climate supports periodic rain that nurtures the lettuce. The rabbits have little rabbits and they all eat the lettuce and drink the water. If they have too many babies, then the overpopulation of rabbits eats up all the lettuce; when the lettuce is gone, they all die. If the lettuce is infected with blight and dies, then the rabbits either learn to become cannibals, or else they all die. If the spring dries up, then all the rabbits die of thirst. If the climate changes and the rains don't provide adequate sustenance for the lettuce, then it dies. There seem to be lots of opportunities for bad news for the rabbits. Of course, if everything goes along in an unchanging manner then the rains fall, the lettuce grows and the rabbits create little rabbits in numbers that exactly match the food value of the growing lettuce.

In the small this illustrates that the extent of an ecosystem can be established along a number of axes. In our little hypothetical ecosystem, there are a number of boundary characteristics; for example, the amount of land suitable for growing lettuce, climatic conditions including rainfall rates, propagation rate of rabbits, total number of rabbits, total amount of lettuce, and the amount of water produced by the spring. We can probably identify quite a number more, but these certainly provide a good start. Thus, we see that by identifying various attributes of a specific ecosystem, that ecosystem can be characterized and thereby allow analysis, and some understanding of the interactions that occur within. Consequently, we consider that such attributes constitute the effective boundaries of the ecosystem.

Extrapolating from our very simple ecosystem to a more complex realistic one, we see that a boundary can be simple and straightforward in identification and understanding, or it may be quite abstract. In some instances, a purely physical boundary may delineate an ecosystem, or at least some aspect of an ecosystem, while in others a virtual boundary formed by a strong gradient of change in a critical characteristic may occur. The boundaries of an ecosystem might form a complex container of interactions; one part perhaps providing a barrier to passage of certain species while a different characteristic (that is, a different boundary) effects a barrier for other species.

We view an ecosystem as a piecewise closed environment, recognizing that it is unusual to be able to characterize a completely closed environment for the full range of species found within, unless, of course, one simply considers the single ecosystem of the earth and the nearby celestial environment that bears directly upon it. Looking at ecosystems in the small, it is rather typical to find some species that can cross the boundaries of ecosystems and move rather freely among many ecosystems. While diverse ecosystems can perhaps be characterized without significant regard to such migratory species, in fact the migratory species depend on a variety of ecosystems for various aspects of their lifecycle. This constitutes a hybrid variant of an ecosystem; one that can be compartmentalized into significantly different subsections. Consider some of the unique wetlands ecosystems that exist along the coastlines of landmasses throughout the world, and specifically those of the Pacific Northwest and the Gulf Coast regions of the United States.

In the wetlands of the Columbia River basin, and among the estuaries of the Columbia River system, anadromous species such as the Pacific Salmon are born and spend their adolescent lives in the fresh waters of the wetlands. Passing adolescence, they migrate to the deep oceans where they reach sexual maturity and from which they subsequently return to the wetlands from whence they came. Here, they can spawn and create the next generation of the species. Thus, two very different environments can be viewed as merged into a single super-ecosystem within which the Pacific Salmon goes through its complete lifecycle. In a similar vein, but a very different manner, the whooping crane is hatched and nurtured in the wetlands along the upper Gulf coast of Texas. The wetlands there provide the fertile feeding grounds and refuge from many predators that allow the nesting, hatching and early development of the next generation of the species. Year after year, more than half of the entire whooping crane population of the earth makes its trek to the Texas coast and winters there. In the spring, they migrate to their summer feeding grounds in northwestern Canada. So, the whooping cranes have adapted to one ecosystem for a part of their lifecycle and a different ecosystem for a different part of their lifecycle. While at the present time, whooping cranes are so rare that they don't provide a significant drain on the resources of either ecosystem, their adaptation lessens their drain on each ecosystem, and affects their relationship to predators.

The boundaries of an ecosystem determine the extent of the various processes occurring within the ecosystem. Note that we say *processes* (plural); in fact, there are many processes operating in parallel as contributors to the effective natural selection result. Also, there are actually boundaries (plural) to be found within an ecosystem. Several boundaries may result in a single function, or one boundary may achieve several functions.

Consequently, we will also speak of the *parameters* that define an ecosystem's functions rather than its boundaries. A well specified set of ecosystem parameters allows the characteristics of the species it contains to be assessed by the applicable selection processes at work. Certain parameters of distinct ecosystems are geographic in nature and are perhaps easiest to understand when they present themselves this way. Darwin observed that the Galapagos Islands formed a closed ecosystem for many of the terrestrial animals found on it. His epiphany was that some of the species he observed actually existed because they had characteristics that particularly suited them to this ecosystem. They had evolved as variants of species that he had observed elsewhere, but based on their needs for survival in this ecosystem, they exhibited different characteristics than had been the case elsewhere. So, the geographical boundary of the Galapagos Island ecosystem is the water of the Pacific Ocean that surrounds the island. At least, the ocean waters form the boundary for the land based species and the amphibious species that are unable to bridge the waters to the mainland by swimming. For avian species, however, the ocean doesn't necessarily provide a fixed barrier. Here, we see that the concept of parameters of an ecosystem is more adequate than a boundary. It is the parameter that allows the boundary to be hard for some species and yet soft for others. The function of the boundary varies with the parameter. This allows the ecosystem definition to be tailored to each species.

As we noted earlier, many wetlands areas provide ecosystems that are distinct from surrounding areas, but ecosystems where a boundary is formed, not by a lack of water, but by a change in the water characteristics of the area. That is, a wetlands area typically features standing or at least slowly moving water with some consistent water source and drainage area. The standing water may well be home to varieties of vegetation that thrive in the constant water source, but by the water being constantly recirculated, it contains the necessary nutrients and gases to support many species of plants and animals. In such an ecosystem, for many species a parameter might be established by the presence or absence of water, or by water with particular characteristics; for example, a specific oxygen content range, a particular salinity or a particular temperature range.

In high altitude areas, the temperature and air pressure which vary with altitude may form parameters of an ecosystem for some species. This is particularly true for many species of trees, with the average temperature gradient parameter forming the *timberline* boundary above which trees don't grow. In coastal bays and inlets, ecosystems may be established by the parameter showing the salinity of the water, with certain species of fish and shrimp migrating in rainy seasons to track the high saline areas as the rivers pour fresh water into the bays.

The common characteristic of any specific parameter of an ecosystem is that it delimits some aspect of the natural selection process. In the case of pure geography, an island for example, the physical land area affects the ability of the various species contained within it to either enhance or diminish their potential for interaction with other species. The rabbits are constrained with the foxes if you will. At its most basic, this geographic boundary mandates that the rabbits will compete with each other for the available vegetation and the foxes will compete with each other for the available rabbits. If the rabbits eat all the available vegetation then they will become extinct and thereby remove the food source for the foxes, rendering them extinct as well. We can also consider the abilities of various species to modify the effects of a parameter. Consider birds. In some ecosystems, birds lay and hatch their eggs directly on the ground. In other areas, various species will build nests of sticks, straw and other material high in the canopy of the tallest trees. In the former situation, grounded species with a taste for bird eggs would seem to have easy pickings; hence, the probability is that there are no such predators in the ecosystem. Or, if there are, then the ability of the bird population to lay eggs and hatch the next generation of the species is superior to the predators' ability to find and eat the eggs.

# Appetite and Sustenance

In our very simple example ecosystem comprised primarily of lettuce and rabbits, two of the basic boundary parameters of the ecosystem insofar as the rabbits are concerned, are lettuce and water. Of course, implicit in this ecosystem is air, thus establishing the three primary ingredients for sustenance of life: food, water and air. We've alluded to the fact that in a more realistic, complex ecosystem the processes through which life presents itself gain impetus from a variety of sources. A most basic process is that of cell operation and reproduction and the impetus for this process is energy in the form of chemical bonds that can be made available to the DNA replication process and to the synthesizing of proteins within the cell under the direction of instructions from the DNA; more about this in the next chapter.

Central to any physical ecosystem is the existence of one or more food chains that support the species of plants and animals found within it. From the perspective of the ultimate energy source, there are two distinct variants of food chains within earth ecosystems: solar-based chains and chemical-based chains. Interestingly enough, one derives ultimately from the strong nuclear force while the other is enabled largely by the weak force. For most food chains, the ultimate source of energy is the sun which runs on nuclear fusion derived from the strong force. Energy is conveyed from the sun to the earth through the electromagnetic force, with the basic energy of the food chain then being derived from sunlight. In the typical solar food chain ecosystem, a variety of plant species are able to directly convert solar energy into chemical sugars that form the foodstuff of other plant and animal species. Among the animal species, herbivores feed on plants and predator animals feed on the herbivores and other predators. Some omnivorous species, such as humans, can be opportunistic with respect to their food sources; for example, they can pretty well make do on a purely vegetarian diet.

Recently, we have also become aware of ecosystems surrounding sub-ocean volcanic vents that derive their basic energy source from minerals dissolved in the super-heated water emerging from them. In areas where magma from the lower mantle makes its way relatively close to the surface, ground water is heated and then expelled through vents in the ocean floor. This hot water dissolves large amounts of minerals from the surrounding formations, particularly large amounts of sulfurous compounds. In these areas, the food chains are grounded in bacteria species called chemosynthetic autotrophs that can convert these various minerals into the chemical sugars that can feed other species. Since the minerals themselves and the primary source of heat that produces the molten magma that dissolves the minerals derives from the initial creation of the planet, augmented by tidal force heating (from the deformation of earth under the same gravitational forces that deform the sea) and weak-force based radioactive decay within the earth, this truly does constitute a food chain that does not ultimately derive from solar fusion. Well, technically all the higher mass elements, beyond hydrogen and helium, are the by-products of solar fusion released through nova and supernova explosions, but that's kind of pushing a point.

In any case, the ultimate effect of the food chains within an ecosystem is to provide basic life with a means to obtain energy in order to replicate or reproduce. Some organisms derive energy from basic physical processes such as light or chemical reactions based on inorganic material. Other organisms derive energy from other organisms. This leads us down the path to predators and prey, the top of the food chain that culminates in the human species. But, as the *Christian Bible* tells us, "Man does not live by bread alone."

Modern humans bring into play a more complex requirement for sustenance. As a purely biological organism, the species requires an energy source to support replication and propagation. However, as we'll consider just a bit later, human requirements for life can extend beyond simple energy requirements and encompass higher order needs as well. Very specifically, the human *mind* requires sustenance in its own right. The mind can drive the body to seek this additional sustenance in a complex dance of needs and fulfillment. So, how and more to the point, *why* are these various aspects of sustenance in play?

The acquisition of sustenance in all its varied forms is typically driven by action stimuli that are associated with the particular sustenance needed. We will ascribe the term *appetite* to this stimulus for action. In essence, appetite provides the feedback to a loop mechanism; when a particular sustenance is missing or is in short supply, then an appetite is created that stimulates action to gain a new supply of the sustenance. Another instance of asymmetry is sometimes found when the feedback loop involves an indirect connection between appetite and sustenance. Consider the appetite for oxygen and the physiological urge to breath that forms the feedback loop to sate that particular appetite. The body senses carbon dioxide levels in determining whether to autonomically stimulate breathing; so a high carbon dioxide level translates into an urge to breath. Sometimes underwater divers, or novice swimmers, will take several deep breaths before setting off to swim some distance underwater. Their perception is that these deep breaths will increase the oxygen in their systems and they can consequently hold their breath longer. In fact, what the deep breaths do is to lower the carbon dioxide levels in the blood. Now, when the diver is underwater and depletes the available oxygen, the carbon dioxide level may still be so low as to not stimulate the urge to breath. The result is that the diver may actually lose consciousness due to a lack of oxygen. This is definitely not a good thing when it happens while a person is under water.

We tend to apply a lot of names to this concept of appetite: a shortage of water creates a *thirst*, a lack of food creates a *hunger*, a deficiency of salt creates a *craving*, and so on. We've all alluded to the cravings of a pregnant woman for pickles and ice cream; in fact, the demands of gestation do present extreme demands on certain forms of sustenance and the appetites that are generated as a result can present as relatively innovative stimuli. The feedback mechanisms that we can observe are certainly not limited to humans, or to *animalia* for that matter. Consider that the need for water stimulates the growth of taproots in many plants, and the sunflower changes the orientation of its bloom during the day in order to track the movement of the sun and thereby gain more light. So, the recurring theme that is far-reaching in its consequence is the feedback loop as a means of stimulus and control of the actions of living things. The lack of sustenance creates an appetite which stimulates action to alleviate the deficiency of sustenance. Another way of saying this is that the need for sustenance effects policies to alleviate the need.

The needs that we've considered thus far are basic physiological needs. As we're going to consider a couple of sections hence, humans exhibit needs at much higher (cognitive) levels. Each need, in turn, has its own appetite signaling when a need is going unfulfilled. For example, we have a need for safety and security. When this need is unfulfilled, we feel apprehension and fear; feelings that provide impetus to stimulate actions to alleviate this need.

# Foundations of Policy

The universe is an all encompassing, dynamic physical system. It is comprised of matter and energy, all of which interacts through four basic forces. Within this physical system, life exists. The piece of this universe within which any particular variant of life can be found, we've called an *ecosystem*. Thus, within any ecosystem, as we have thus far discussed them, the four basic forces apply. This is why we have referred to ecosystems as *physical ecosystems*. We do this in order to be able to unambiguously introduce an analogue extension to such ecosystems that we have termed a *social ecosystem* in which, in addition to basic physical interactions, extended rules exist that allow for the initiation and control of more varied interactions.

We will find, when we examine them in more detail, that the rules of the social ecosystem can change among the various systems; it is not a given that the same rules apply everywhere as they do for physical ecosystems. Whether we are discussing the basic laws governing the forces in a physical ecosystem or the rules that govern a social ecosystem, these laws or rules form the central elements of policy within the respective ecosystem. While we tend to think of policy as being a mutable set of rules, in fact the pairing of variable social rules with the immutable laws of nature show us the full range of characteristics that we want to model in the form of a policy infrastructure.

Any two or more physical entities can interact by way of the four basic forces: the strong nuclear force, the weak force, electro-magnetic force and gravity. The range of these forces is infinite, but their magnitude as a function of distance varies such that each tends to dominate interactions within vastly different domains of separation of the interacting entities. The strong force dominates at separation distances on the order of the size of an atomic nucleus while the weak force dominates at much smaller than nuclear distances. Electro-magnetic forces dominate over distances that are familiar to humans in their everyday lives. Gravity dominates over the range of distances from everyday life to inter-galactic interactions. At every level, there are characteristics of the various forces that lend variability to the result of interactions; specifically, quantum mechanical effects in the basic forces and variability in the initial conditions of interactions. That is, because of our lack of precision on the initial states of the interacting entities and because quantum mechanical effects are modeled with a statistical distribution of outcomes, it is impossible for us to predict exactly the result of any specific interaction. Hence, the old homily that says "Doing the same thing over and over again and expecting a different outcome each time is the definition of insanity." might be taken with a grain of salt. Not only can repetition of interactions lead to different results, quantum mechanics grounds this uncertainty into the very fabric of nature. On the macroscopic scale of human interactions, repeatability of observable results is considerable, but billiards is still a game requiring great skill and they continue to play best four out of seven games to determine the winner of the World Series in baseball each year. As we noted at the beginning of this chapter, what the same thing is (that we do over and over again) requires case-by-case definition with extreme precision of the initial conditions, with acknowledgement that even then we can't know the outcome for sure.

Interactions within a physical ecosystem involve only basic physical laws and the characteristics and capabilities of resident species to exploit the mechanisms of physical systems. For example, the most elementary interaction between two entities within a physical ecosystem is bringing them into physical contact. Among the basic forces, the force of gravity is infinite in extent, meaning that an attractive force is constantly at work to bring various entities into physical contact. The initial conditions of motion of the entities determine whether they ever actually touch. Going a bit further afield, we might consider the situation of living entities brought into close physical proximity or contact. There is obviously something more than gravity at work in making this happen. If the entities are from divergent species, a lamb and a lion for instance, then the ultimate interaction may well consist of the lion eating the lamb; in some circumstances, the lion may lie down with the lamb, but that would be a low probability event.

The act of bringing two individual entities in close proximity such as to allow physical interaction will typically involve sensory capabilities of one or the other of the individuals to detect the presence of the other at a distance. Moreover, it will likely entail the motor functions of one or both of the entities to propel them together. Predators may use keen eyesight, sensitive hearing or a comprehensive sense of smell to detect the presence of prey through their forensic wakes in the physical world. Conversely, species that comprise typical prey may display physical characteristics or capabilities that make them difficult to detect or to directly attack. In essence, they learn to camouflage their forensic wakes. The arctic hare, which changes color between the summer and the winter, is a good example. Once a predator does locate its prey, it may use a variety of motor skills to achieve physical contact; motor skills that range from stealth to speed. Once in physical contact, the offensive and defensive facilities of the entities determine the end game of the interaction. The western coyote consumes the lamb, but retreats in pain from the defensive spray of a skunk.

For between-species interactions, extensions to purely physical system interactions fall into five major categories: coexistence, competitive coexistence, symbiotic, parasitic and predatory. These categories provide classification of the basic ground rules of interactions, specifically indicating how different species share the physical ecosystem in which they exist. The most benign form of sharing an ecosystem is coexistence. Through this style of interaction, inter-species contact is typically casual with little or no aggressive behavior exhibited by either species. In essence, coexistence defines the sharing of an ecosystem with no offensive or defensive interactions specifically initiated between species. In the most independent of cases, different species would be members of entirely different food chains. If one considered a highly constrained ecosystem of a lettuce patch populated by rabbits and earthworms, then the rabbits and the earthworms very probably live in a totally coexistent relationship. Their continuance as species is only tenuously related through the lettuce plants and excretion of body waste by the rabbits (and the earthworms and the lettuce for that matter), and it is quite plausible that either species could be removed without significantly impacting the other.

Perhaps, a more common variant of ecosystem sharing would be one in which species live in a state of competitive coexistence. Being contained or confined within the same ecosystem indicates that limitations imposed by the boundaries of the ecosystem are shared among the species it contains. For example, if two or more herbivore species share an ecosystem in which all members subsist on the vegetation within the ecosystem, then the ecosystem's ability to support vegetation serves as a cumulative limit on the populations of all the herbivores. If food or water becomes in shorter supply due to the abundance of herbivores, whatever their species, then the numbers of each species will likely be limited. However, in this situation, if one species can preferentially consume the food supply, then that species may well have a natural selection advantage within that ecosystem. Consider a system of vegetation that both rabbits and cattle might consume. Rabbits reproduce more rapidly than cattle, but one cow eats more food than many rabbits. Following a period of competitive coexistence, it is quite plausible that the number of rabbits will increase to a level that can consume enough of the food supply to leave the cattle insufficient food for continued propagation. After that, the number of rabbits might well vary in some equilibrium determined by the growth rate of the lettuce.

Symbiotic relationships among species are a bit rarer. That is, a truly symbiotic relationship in which two species have adapted their interaction behavior such that both benefit from the relationship is not terribly common. Certain species of ants, for example, will maintain farms of aphids. The ants provide food and protection for the aphids, and the aphids in turn produce an excess of sugar laced honeydew that the ants gather for food. In this relationship, both species derive a direct benefit from the others' behavior; one species is not a direct predator of the other.

Parasitic interactions connect different species through relationships in which one species derives some essential benefit from the other species without providing a reciprocal benefit in return. In many instances, a parasite may well be detrimental to its host species, but perhaps not to the extent of causing the death of the host. Thus, the relationship can last over multiple generations of the two species. Large vertebrate species carry invertebrate parasites within their digestive or cardiac circulatory systems.

Finally, we come to the predatory relationships that define much of our conceptualization of nature. Many ecosystems have evolved complex food chains that encompass the interaction types that we are discussing. Throughout such food chains we might well observe a variety of predatory relationships and their subsequent interaction types. We're well aware of the predatory nature of large carnivores given the innate fear that most members of the human species have for them; "Lions and tigers and bears; Oh my!" But, predators and prey exist at all levels within ecosystems, as the poem, usually attributed to Jonathan Swift, says:

> Big bugs have little bugs
> Upon their backs to bit'em.
> And little bugs have littler bugs,
> And so ad infinitum.

Within a physical ecosystem, success of a species may be measured by the number of members of that species found. To achieve that number, there are no *a priori* limits on the actions or behavior of members of any specific species in their interactions with members of other species. *Eat or be eaten* is probably a pretty good catch phrase for operating within such an ecosystem. However, the interactions among species and within species are replete with examples of sacrifice and behavior that we view as altruistic when we give it an anthropomorphic guise.

A mother bear will challenge much larger male bears if she feels they are threatening her cubs. Male penguins sit for months without eating in order to incubate an egg in the frozen reaches of Antarctica. And birds, both mothers and fathers, will work incessantly to forage for food to feed their nestlings. However, such higher-order behaviors are subject to the satisfaction of lower-order needs. A mother gazelle may abandon her young if it is unable, perhaps due to injury or illness, to keep up with the movement of the herd from which the mother derives protection and support. Many other counter examples to apparent altruistic behavior exist as well. Some species will actually eat their young if they encounter them following their birth. Male bears are known to attack cubs in some instances. And, sometimes birds will abandon their nests for yet unknown reasons. Such examples serve to illustrate that full understanding of inter- and intra-species interactions is not warranted; however, a variety of models have been suggested for various species. Since the primary objects of our interest are humans, computers, their groupings and their interactions, we will concentrate our discussion in these areas.

# Distributions and Anecdotes

We observed in the last chapter that keeping score in the game of natural selection involved the use of statistical analysis of populations. Correspondingly, we have suggested that it's mostly about mass; the greater the accumulated mass of a particular species, the better off it is faring in the game. Scoring the selection mechanism presented by social ecosystems is not nearly so objective. Indeed, the rules are more arbitrary and the scorekeeping is largely subjective. Within social ecosystems, there is often significant asymmetry, if not total indirection, in the cause and effect feedback loops that impact the evaluation. We can contrast the evaluation processes for physical versus social ecosystems through a metaphorical representation of the two processes: statistics and anecdotes.

Statistics comprise an objective evaluation mechanism. While. we may cast statistics in a pejorative light (a quotation attributed to Mark Twain suggests "…there are lies, damn lies and statistics!"), they provide a measure of the effects of processes, and in the case of processes applied to large populations, they are really the only objective way to effect such a measure. Anecdotes, on the other hand, attempt to evaluate the effects of processes through metaphorical understanding. As we'll hopefully understand in better detail through the next couple of chapters, this approach is well attuned to the cognitive and emotional facilities of the human mind. Consider some (dare we say it) anecdotal assessments.

Up to the early 1800's, the passenger pigeon (*Ectopistes migratorius*) was one of the more prevalent species of bird in the United States. The size of the native flocks was estimated at somewhere between 5 and 15 billion birds. Yet, by just after the turn of the century, the passenger pigeon species was extinct. In a somewhat perverse twist, we actually have an attribution of the last member of the species; its name was "…Martha and it died alone at the Cincinnati Zoo at about 1:00 pm on September 1, 1914," as noted on the Chipper Woods Bird Observatory Web page. It would appear that the species fell victim to the appetites for food of the emerging cities along the eastern reaches of the United States in the last half of the XIX[th] century. While some stories relate that the birds were hunted to extinction, in fact they were apparently harvested to extinction. Hunting might evoke an image of a hunter and a gun, but passenger pigeons were harvested with gigantic strings of nets to catch the birds in flight and through picking the chicks up off the ground before they had achieved flight. The birds were packed in barrels by the millions and shipped off to feed the populations in the growing industrial centers. The decline and demise of the passenger pigeon is a story told rather plainly and simply through statistics.

Birds in the wild are elements of an ecosystem. The sustenance for them to survive within the ecosystem is a function of their numbers. Their propagation as a species requires a density of members that allow them to procreate; a density that obviously has a threshold below which the continuation of the species becomes problematic. In the case of the passenger pigeons, by depleting their nesting areas, depriving them of their natural foods and diminishing their numbers in an incredible fashion (millions of birds per day were harvested). it finally became statistically unlikely that they could continue; and, in fact they didn't.

We might compare this to the whooping crane (*Grus americana*). From flocks of perhaps 1500 birds in the mid-1800's, the species had declined to only 20 birds by the early 1900's. Statistically, the whooping crane was destined to go the way of the passenger pigeon, but in this case the story took a different twist. Actions by humans to protect them, to modify their ecosystem if you will, by denying their hunting by humans and by preserving their natural habitat has brought them back from the edge. The story isn't over by any means; an out of season hurricane along the Gulf Coast of Texas or a major prairie fire along their migration pathway could still take them over the brink. However, through the subjective evaluation of humans it was determined that one species should be saved while such a commitment was lacking on behalf of the other. Thus, we have very different outcomes; an objectively defined outcome in one case and a subjectively defined outcome in the other. Statistics provide a good measure of the one, while the other is best represented by anecdote. Obviously, the two mechanisms demonstrate a significant asymmetry in evaluation processes.

Anecdotal assessments tie directly to our facilities for metaphorical understanding. Consider another situation. Amber Alert is a national program aimed at quickly disseminating alerts when a child has been abducted. As described on the Amber Alert Web site presented by the United States Department of Justice: "AMBER stands for America's Missing: Broadcast Emergency Response and was created as a legacy to 9-year-old Amber Hagerman, who was kidnapped while riding her bicycle in Arlington, Texas, and then brutally murdered." This particular episode became so illustrative of an innate fear within the basic family unit, which is, having a child abducted and killed, that it engendered a national response. Given that orders of magnitude more children are killed each year in traffic accidents than through abduction, the response might be viewed as disproportionate. However, the rationale is rooted in the subjective assessment of the human emotional system, not in objective, dispassionate statistics.

# Social Ecosystems

All life, certainly including members of Homo sapiens, exists within physical ecosystems. While we might not typically think of it as such, in fact a physical ecosystem provides an environment through which policy derived from physical laws is implemented. We'll get in to this in much more detail a bit later, but consider for the moment that aspect of policy which entails the rules that govern interactions. We often view rules as arbitrary concepts. However, consider that rules which take on an immutable property we call *laws* and we can perhaps understand the policy of a physical ecosystem as one in which the *laws of nature* prevail. When living entities are considered within a physical ecosystem, particularly entities that are capable of voluntary action driven by their cognitive facilities, then the concept of rules does take on the more arbitrary character that occurred to us in the first place. The greater the cognitive abilities of the species, the richer are the rules of policy governing the interactions of that species. It would seem that when we get to the complex, and, in many instances, almost perversely arbitrary nature of human interactions, we need to establish a different characterization of an ecosystem through which to analyze and understand these interactions. Hence our characterization of a social ecosystem, viewed here from a new angle.

Social ecosystems extend beyond the physical, and in so doing they allow for policy considerations of human interactions whose impetus derives from beyond purely physical initial conditions and proceeds according to other than physical laws. These policy considerations allow for significantly more complex and seemingly arbitrary rules governing the conduct for interactions, but of course, which may ultimately resolve to the physical as well.

As we discussed in the last chapter, there is evidence that the human species has evolved not only through natural selection at an individual level, but also through natural selection within and among groups. While the whole concept of among-group selection as a natural evolutionary mechanism is still a subject of active discussion and research, what is not ambiguous is that throughout the entire breadth of the recorded existence of the human species, there have been obvious grouping mechanisms. Further, for the last several millennia, there is overwhelming historical evidence that various groups have cooperated with and competed against each other; often for the survival of a group's identity or its very existence for that matter. One need only search for current descendants of the Carthaginian Empire to understand the implications of among-group competition during recorded history. When Rome ultimately defeated Carthage on the battlefield, it took the extreme step of wiping all evidence of its once great adversary from the face of the earth and forcing its remnant survivors to scatter across the Roman Empire. While the physical representation of those survivors still exists within the collective gene pool, their representation in a social context no longer exists; it is extinct. So, since there appears to be solid evidence for among-group selection during recorded history, it also seems quite plausible that such mechanisms can be identified with the human species from the time that it emerged as unique, where surviving direct evidence of the competition is far less obvious.

The grouping mechanisms of humans seem to follow an evolutionary track comparable to that of the capabilities of the individual members of the species. Most basic is the social grouping necessary to allow the development of the person from infancy to adulthood. The infant child is incapable of supporting itself and, in isolation, the infant places extreme demands on its mother, or to any adult the child bonds to for elemental life support. In fact, it is highly likely that the species could not have survived without social mechanisms in place to support the mother and infant child, at least until the child is well past infancy. The basic social grouping that is readily identifiable is the nuclear family; mother, father, siblings and the extended family that can grow up around this core through multi-generational association.

At some point in its development, the family (or perhaps an extended family) reaches a threshold of size due to the sustenance limitations within the ecosystem that the family inhabits. That is, the physical interaction characteristics of the individuals with each other and with the ecosystem can only support groups of a given size. The makeup of the physical ecosystem obviously has a very significant impact on the family, and the evolutionary environment presented to the establishment of more complex groups. So, let's look in a bit more detail at the groups that we recognize within the human species.

# Individuals and the Family

The African Wild Dog (*Lycaon pictus*) pup is born after a gestation period of 70 days. The pup is weaned from its mother's milk at about 10 weeks. At three months, the mother and pups abandon the den and the pups begin to run with the pack. At 10 months of age, pups can kill easy prey and by 14 months they are fully capable of fending for themselves. They can join the rest of the pack in bringing down prey many times their own size. In comparison, during its first month, a human baby can not support its own head and it can only see objects a few inches in front of its face. It can mimic certain behaviors of another individual, usually its mother, if they are observable. At three months it can roll from its back to its side and it finally discovers its hands and feet. The skull of the infant is segmented and loosely connected at birth, enabling the head to deform as necessary in order to fit through the birth canal of the mother. After birth, the skull segments become rigidly connected in place, and the brain continues to grow. Its growth provides for a geometric expansion of synaptic connections, a process that lasts until about 30 months. At this point, the human infant has established a preponderance of the physical and mental characteristics of the human species. The pup is an adult at one and a half years while the infant is a fairly fully functional human at three years. However, it will take another three to five years before the young human can effectively care for itself within the wider world. It will be 14 to 18 years or so before the infant becomes an adult person. Obviously, relative to the wild dog, the human requires some type of intensive support infrastructure for a long period of time, many years in fact. Small wonder, then, that the social environments of humans, from which this long-term support derives, are quite distinct from the lower animals.

The infant bonobo (*Pan paniscus*) has quite similar development characteristics to the human, with the exception that from birth it possesses the physical dexterity to grasp its mother's fur in order to be carried about the arboreal environment in which these close relatives of the human species live. They are considered close relatives in that they shared a common ancestor species about 6 million years ago. Beyond this earlier (relative to humans) ability to attach itself to its mother and hence travel about, the infant bonobo develops in a manner and time frame that bears significant similarities to that of an infant human. Frans de Waal has shown in *Chimpanzee Politics* and *Bonobo* (with Frans Lanting) that the base family groupings of bonobo and chimpanzees bear similarity to that for humans. It is an obvious divergence of their respective evolutionary paths that humans went beyond the basic extended family in developing the mechanisms to support more complex groupings while these apes did not.

As the human species emerged, the basic family group provided the support infrastructure in which the young could survive and develop. The most basic requirements for this survival were safety and protection from the elements and from predators along with the provision of food and water. In a hunter gatherer environment, a reasonable assessment of the value of the group in any form is the ability to focus effort and resources to the most pressing problem at any point in time, and the ability to share the results of the attempt to solve these problems across the entire group. A mother or some other caretaker could remain with an infant while others in the group searched for food. On finding food, it could then be shared with the rest of the group. If the group could adapt to the physical ecosystem, then it could optimize its prospects for finding food, or shelter or safety, perhaps by subdividing the group. If one hunting party found game, then the entire group might eat. If one hunting party failed, then perhaps the entire group did not have to starve. If a hunting party was out on the hunt, then others might remain with the young as protection. The grouping mechanism of the extended family unit was beneficial as long as the physical ecosystem could support it.

In a hunter-gatherer system, the physical ecosystem almost certainly places a limit on the size of group that can be supported in the basic mode; that is, in the mode of searching for sustenance and protection. Individual members of the group, or other small units, might tend to split off to form other groups or to integrate themselves into other existing groups. In any case, many groups would likely find themselves derived from a single, or small number of base family units and hence might offer some semblance of multi-group cohesion; essentially providing ground for a larger scale grouping mechanism in the form of a *clan*.

# Clans

During the human species emergent period, as the extended family unit exceeded the nominal size that can be supported by its geographic extent within the physical ecosystem, the group may have tended to become less advantageous, and rather began to pay something of a price for its excessive size, and may have divided into multiple units in order for each smaller, derivative group to retain the competitive advantage offered by the family grouping mechanism. Over evolutionary time, it may well have transpired that multi-level selection benefits could accrue to even larger, multiple related family units if some new means of coordination of group activities could be brought into play; that is, if an entirely new group dynamic could be established. For example, under the auspices of the larger grouping entity, smaller groups may well have entered into non-competition agreements with respect to the available feeding and hunting territories. Through such accommodations, each smaller group had primarily to deal with other species within the ecosystem and less with direct conflict with other human groups.

Clans exist in the current world as social groupings that encompass multiple extended families, all of which tend to have significant genetic commonality. So, a clan is typically viewed as a super family grouping, but one that relies upon different traits of the individual humans within it to effect its grouping mechanisms. The establishment and maintenance of clans requires greater facilities on the part of the individual human, than does the establishment and maintenance of the basic, nuclear family. A necessary such trait that offers enhanced capabilities for building a larger group is the ability to recognize and pass along the successful behaviors of the individual and the group. This facility is presented as mimetic learning on the part of the individual human by Merlin Donald in *A Mind So Rare*. We'll consider this mechanism in more detail in Chapter 8. Mimetic learning is the ability to recognize in others the successful application of complex behaviors and to disperse that learning through a process of repetitive imitation of the original behavior. This ability would, for example, be extremely valuable in the development and propagation of tools that allow humans to exert a stronger influence on their physical ecosystem than they could accomplish through their purely physical body based facilities.

A clan, based on closely associated families, represents a more concentrated gene pool than is present in large grouping mechanisms. As a consequence, groupings of this size will suffer the misfortunes of a lack of genetic diversity. They have a more restricted facility for genetic adaptation than might be the case for larger groups; negative characteristics are more likely to present and thereby prove detrimental to the group. So, there are, or were, very likely multi-level selection mechanisms at work in this regards.

# Tribes

The tribe is the next extension of the grouping mechanisms of the human species and is, like the clan relative to a single family, largely characterized as a larger group, or collection of groups, that can still present coordinated activities that benefit both the group and the individual members of the group.

A hypothesis formulated in particular by Steven Mithen in *The Prehistory of the Mind* is that the need for a larger group might have come from the entry of man into the savannah at a time when the forest receded. The larger group was more capable to fight the new predators of vast expanded spaces. A theory that many may find extravagant at the first mention by Terence McKenna, in *Food of the Gods*, is that the new social order was facilitated by the discovery of new intoxicant mushrooms, a point we'll come back to in Chapter 5. Within the human species one would consider that a new group or a new grouping mechanism evolved from the old, perhaps to replace the old or perhaps to subsume the old.

As the species evolved further, tribes emerged as a larger, more effective grouping mechanism. It was perhaps in this environment that the individual physiology extended beyond mimetic capabilities to symbolic capabilities, as presented by Terrence W. Deacon in *The Symbolic Species*. Within a tribal social order, the group is sufficiently extended such that to communicate across its full geographic dispersal required the full capabilities of language; that's a step that we will discuss later, together with the flourishing of the common attributes of modern man.

# Congregations

From an extension perspective, the clan is probably the largest human grouping mechanism that derives primarily from the human family grouping facilities. That is, most of the group-reinforced mechanisms of the clan find their beginnings in the primitive activities that the family brings to the preferential behaviors of the species. It would seem that to achieve beneficial grouping at a larger scale than the clan requires a synthesis of many individual characteristics, giving rise to the concepts and mechanisms that we recognize as religion.

The emergence of religion as the dominant grouping mechanism likely evolved as an exploitation of the more profound developments of the human mind, specifically the experience of ecstasy that transcends the basic consciousness. When coupled with rituals as a means of coordinating activities and information among diverse populations, the ability of religion to bring concerted action to bear on the issue of group survival and predominance began to be truly realized. While the tribe is the first form of congregation enabled by religion, higher-order groups can use the same mechanism of congregation to form in ever increasing size. In parallel with the more advanced group coordination and control that has been brought by religion, humans could use many of the same mechanisms to effect control over the physical ecosystems in which they exist. That is, through the development of trade and commerce, mankind has insulated itself from many of the direct manifestations of the physical ecosystem. Trade and commerce allow a more efficient exploitation of natural resources and provide for greater protection against relatively unusual excursions of the natural environment that might normally tax people in spite of the greater protections offered by their grouping mechanisms.

A common theme that runs through all of these grouping mechanisms is the propensity of the group to establish the rules of interaction among members of the group and, in some cases, between members of different groups. Family units within a clan were likely subject to the same social mores; separate villages within a tribe likely evoked similar customs of behavior. We suggest the characterization of this arbitrarily defined environment of rules and the interactions that follow as a *policy infrastructure*.

# Elements of a Policy Infrastructure

For the moment, drawing from standard dictionary definitions of the word, we define the concept of *policy* as *a definite course or method of action selected from among alternatives and in light of given conditions to guide and determine present and future decisions; a plan of action adopted by an individual or social group*. To fully consider the manner in which social ecosystems address policy, we must consider the full infrastructure through which policy is effected. The environment within which interactions occur is essentially the boundary of the policy infrastructure. Note that we do not characterize the policy infrastructure as being equivalent to a social ecosystem. There's a characteristic that the application of policy requires, the characteristic of trust that we will describe in much more detail starting in Chapter 5 when we delve deeper into social ecosystems. For the moment, let's concentrate on the various aspects of policy.

Within a policy infrastructure, a set of rules governing interactions can be established. Remember, these are now rules derived from human cognitive processes. In some infrastructures, the rules are referred to as *law*; in others, as *codes of conduct*. Along with the rules generally comes a definition of the characteristics of the interaction process, including how is an interaction initiated, how is it terminated and what goes on in between. A central necessity of having rules is knowing whom the rules apply to. As a consequence, a policy infrastructure must either provide, or have access to, a means of identification of the members of the social ecosystem. At the termination of an interaction, there typically is a result. In some instances, the existence of an interaction generates forensic evidence that it has occurred; in fact, this may actually be formalized in an interaction record that makes an historical artifact of all the aspects of what went on. Finally, there are typically consequences to interactions. These consequences may simply be the result of the interaction, or they may comprise collateral attributes that naturally follow from the transaction. In some instances, the consequences may involve sanctions in the event that the results of the transaction don't follow the rules.

The function of the policy infrastructure is to facilitate interactions. The structure of interactions is interesting in its own right.

# Interactions

The mechanism through which one entity influences another is termed an *interaction*. All interactions ultimately are effected through the four elemental forces of nature that we alluded to earlier. Within a physical ecosystem, these forces are the root enablers of all interactions. We note that these elemental forces are infinite in scope; that is, they are continuously in effect. This infinite extent is ameliorated in many instances by virtue of the fact that the influence of the various forces can be infinitesimally small over large interaction distances, where large varies from force to force. Within social ecosystems, however, we can identify more complex forms of interactions. Of greatest interest to us are the interactions among people, between people and members of other species and between people and specific aspects of the ecosystem in which they exist. Because computers and their subsequent combinations through networks are in many functions the mechanical extensions of people, we view them as natural elements of interactions.

If, for the moment, we limit our consideration to interactions between people that do not make use of any type of mechanical means to extend their presence or effect within the ecosystem, then these interactions must occur between entities in relatively close proximity to each other; close being determined by the specific physical mechanisms through which the interaction occurs. People can see each other at significant distances and can interact through visibility mechanisms at such distances; think hand gestures and signals. Interactions based on sound will typically have a somewhat lesser extent than visibility mechanisms. In many environments, people can see further than they can hear, and their abilities to interact are correspondingly limited; think plains and deserts. Of course, in other environments sight may be limited and sound the longer distance mechanism; think jungles or a dark night. Interactions based on tastes or smells can be of even shorter range. These two senses are highly interrelated and allow for very subtle characteristics to be addressed during interactions.

Sight and hearing will typically offer some directionality. "I see a large animal over there" or "I hear a threatening sound from that direction." The sense of touch offers a very close range tactile appraisal of the physical world nearby. The body is replete with sensors that register a variety of sensations, from the coolness of a breath of wind on one's face to the warmth of the sun on one's back; or, perhaps the sharp pain of a predator's claw to the throat. In a world devoid of mechanical aids, all that we know is what our senses tell us of that world close by.

The complementary facilities to our senses are the motor mechanisms through which we initiate and sustain interactions ourselves. These are comprised of the skeleton supported muscle systems that allow us to push and shove, to walk and run, to jump, to grasp, to rip apart flesh with our teeth; the list is limited pretty much by the lengths or heights that we are driven to in any particular instance by our overarching needs. Our ability to extend our actions or the effect of our actions, beyond the limits of our immediate reach, rests with our motor abilities to impact our physical environment. Our vocal system allows us to make directed sounds that project our presence for some moderate distance; we can shout a warning or a plea for help. We know that our scent betrays us to many predators or prey, so we approach the deer from down wind.

These two sets of facilities together form our sensori-motor system; the means through which we interact with our physical ecosystem.

# Impetus of Interactions

Through our sensori-motor system, we learn about threats and we react to those threats. If our ability to react to threats were strictly limited to our innate, physical abilities then we might be in some serious trouble as a species. There are a lot of big predators that are stronger and better equipped at hand-to-hand combat than are we. As one crocodile, laying contentedly sated on the sunny riverbank, surrounded by a pith helmet and other accouterments of an explorer on safari, is seen commenting to another crocodile in a Far Side cartoon, "That was great! Just warm and pink; no horns, or scales, or fur, or claws, or teeth!" So, at least some of our dominance as a species has derived from an ability to shape the ecosystem to our advantage; to shelter ourselves from the heat and cold, to cloth our bodies from the ice and snow; and to create tools to magnify our abilities to protect ourselves and to extract food from other species. The ability to accomplish these ends quite successfully has allowed humans to rise to dominance. Collectively, we have little to fear from our natural predators, although an errant camper still gets attacked by a bear from time to time and swimmers have unsuccessful encounters with sharks with some regularity. Rather, it is microbes at one extreme and cataclysmic physical force at the other that remain perhaps the most serious threats to our existence. These are things that interact at the very boundaries of our understanding and ability to manipulate our environments. Collectively, we're still all situated in too small a volume of space to get too smug about our long-term survival chances.

So, we might consider, is there some guide or impetus to human activities that bridges the expanse from physical ecosystem to social ecosystem? If, as appears to be the case, the acquisition of food and physical sustenance is only part of what drives the individual human, then what other stimuli might there be to drive people to interact? As it happens, Abraham Maslow suggested in *Toward a Psychology of Being* just such drivers in the form of a set of behavioral stimuli that he presented as a *hierarchy of human needs*. He proposed that people are motivated by a collection of physical and social stimuli that are hierarchically related; that is, if a lower level stimulus is satisfied then a higher-level stimulus may come to the fore. If a lower level need is not satisfied, then it may overwhelm a correspondingly strong need at a higher level of the hierarchy. We will conceive of the hierarchy as layers in which each subsequent need is stacked on the previous one as follows:

- Transcendence – Connect To Something Beyond The Ego

- Self-actualization - Find Self-Fulfillment and Reach One's Potential

- Aesthetic – Symmetry, Order and Beauty

- Cognitive - Need to Know and Understand

- Esteem – To Achieve, Be Competent, Gain Approval

- Belonging – Affiliate with Others, Be Accepted

- Safety and Security – Out of Danger

- Physiological Needs – Hunger, Thirst, Bodily Needs

Maslow introduced this set of human needs with a specific eye toward the individual. He classifies them into two categories: *deficiency needs* and *growth needs*. Deficiency needs relate to basic requirements to support life while growth needs relate to the enhancement of the person, and they provide something of a roadmap of just what *enhancement* means. This needs hierarchy gives some clarity to the concept of multi-level selection. In essence, by invoking stimuli according to the drive afforded by the individual levels, the efficacy of response is in direct association with multi-level selection.

On an ongoing basis, an individual person is subject to this set of needs at all times. Within our conceptualization, we would posit that these needs are considered, either directly or indirectly, consciously or subconsciously, with every interaction entered into by the individual, and further, these needs, collectively, are also to be found in the impetus for group oriented interactions as well. This leads to rephrase a question that we discussed earlier, and ask: "Is there a hierarchy of needs of the group?" In Chapter 1, we suggested perhaps the opening gambit in forming such a list when we noted the rather common admonition in both religious and secular groups, "Thou shall have no other gods before me!" This leads us to also pose a subsequent question, "Can the group impose its needs upon the individual such that individual needs can be superseded by group needs?"

Of course, the needs hierarchy also brings to mind the conveyance mechanism that we talked about earlier as a parallel to the DNA of biological selection. Perhaps the hierarchy of needs points us to a higher cognitive evaluation of the brain, a vector for individual selection. Furthermore, we should now reformulate the debate on multi-level selection, asking if a hierarchy of needs exists for the group, or if group selection is based on the combination of individual hierarchies of needs, and their complex interactions. Additionally, we note that even if a group hierarchy of needs would be formed, it would still remain necessary to investigate how it aggregates from individual needs. So perhaps for the moment we should stay with the individual hierarchy of needs as the primary guide of selection.

The lowest level in the hierarchy, physiological needs comprise the basic requirements for human life to continue. These constitute the primary *deficiency needs* of a person. Air to breath, water to drink and food to eat are at the very core of this set of requirements, and essentially in that order. Failure to satisfy any of these needs can lead to death, with the urgency of satisfying each being generally relative to the human body's physiological needs. A lack of air kills within seconds or minutes. A lack of water kills in days and a lack of food kills within weeks, if not sooner. Consequently, when a person is placed within the limits of vulnerability for these basic, life-sustaining elements then the stimuli from these needs is likely to overwhelm any other basis for action or interaction. On the other hand, if these absolutely essential needs are met, then a person might be able to concentrate on slightly more mundane issues, like avoiding being eaten by a bear.

Subordinate to physiological needs is the need for personal safety of the individual and, by extension, the group that the individual is a part of. Obviously we can envision situations in which safety and physiological perquisites are somewhat interrelated. It is certainly one of the major characteristics of group associations that a successful group can influence the individual's assessment of safety needs. For a group that truly commands the allegiance of its individuals, the safety of the group can be made paramount, subordinating personal safety as a result. The mechanisms used to elicit such desired behavior from group adherents have evolved over time, much as individual capabilities have evolved. They in fact form the basis of social orders.

The deficiency needs of Maslow's hierarchy are the most directly relevant to the individual as an isolated being. While subsequent association with a group may impact these needs, perhaps making them easier or harder to attain, they represent the greatest testimony of humankind's membership in the general animal kingdom. It is upon these levels that the group can exert its greatest influence in order to force the individual toward some forms of altruistic behavior that are detrimental to self while beneficial to the group.

The remaining six levels constitute the *growth needs* of Maslow's Hierarchy. It seems interesting to us that the higher level needs seem to *a priori* consider stimuli for the individual within a larger group context. A personal sense of belonging implies the presence of a group to which the individual can belong. Self-esteem is obviously an important driver of the individual, but the esteem held for an individual by a group of peers is of significant importance as well. In this light, we note that Michael Tomasello in *The Cultural Origins of Human Cognition* raised the point that the compatibility of the needs hierarchy among individuals can be a strong factor for driving a set of individuals to seek out and become part of grouping mechanisms in order to cooperatively satisfy their collective needs. The six higher levels of Maslow's hierarchy, Belonging, Esteem, Cognitive, Aesthetic, Self-actualization and Transcendence bring the individual person into a social environment. These levels may not dictate a person's membership in a group, but they are more likely to involve interactions with other people in order to satisfy.

# Mechanics of Interactions

Assuming sufficient impetus to foster an interaction, be it between people or between computers or with things that go bump in the night, we are left to consider the mechanics which facilitate the interaction itself. The problem of establishing an environment for interaction is already difficult when two or more parties agree in advance as to the efficacy of interactions and further agree upon mechanisms through which interactions will occur. The problem faced by the parties when no such agreed upon set of protocols exists becomes daunting indeed. Of course, in the extreme, the parties simply revert to the mechanisms of the physical ecosystem; essentially, the law of the jungle. It is interesting to note how much of literature, particularly of the genre known as science fiction, deals with just this issue. Consider four rather recent classic works of science fiction that have been presented as movies: *Close Encounters of the Third Kind, Independence Day, Star Trek: First Contact* and *Contact*. These four movies present perhaps the broadest spectrum of potential protocols for the initial establishment of an interaction environment between two dissimilar yet sentient species.

The 1984 movie entitled *Close Encounters of the Third Kind* presents one of the more involved and protracted interaction protocols for initial contact between intelligent species of greatly differing technological capabilities. In this presentation, a species external to the earth is offered as the more technologically advanced and the instigator of the interaction. The protocol of first contact presented here involves the alien species extracting a number of members of the human species; ostensibly to learn from them and about them. Subsequently, the alien species initiates a series of events, all pointing toward a major interaction to occur at The Devils Tower geological formation in the northwest United States. When this interaction actually occurs, the two species go through a very basic establishment of an interaction language, culminating in the exchange of ambassadors between the two species to participate in a long-term cultural introduction exercise. The bottom line presented here is one of mutual interest in establishing an interaction environment through non-belligerent means. The procedure is long, laborious and requires significant involvement from both parties. More to the point, the procedure assumes a significant parallel between the two species, derived from their distinct approaches to dealing with common physical ecosystems. In essence, the derived interaction protocol assumes that the sensori-motor experiences of the two species would arrive at similar mechanisms (that is, a common metaphorical basis) under which the interaction could occur.

A second movie, the 1996 rendition of *Independence Day* takes a much more primal approach. The movie adopts a very similar theme to H.G. Well's *The War of the Worlds*. Specifically, an alien species which has a modest, but significant technological advantage over the human species, approaches the earth with the most basic of purposes; the invasion of earth and eradication of the human species in order to obtain unfettered access to the natural resources necessary for their subsistence. This approach requires total control of the basic physical ecosystem. If the alien species can eliminate the human species then they will have that control. There is no thought given to benign contact or cooperative involvement; the initial contact is aimed simply at the identification and eradication of the human species.

This particular movie employs a rather interesting anthropogenic assumption at a critical juncture of the interaction. In a desperate attempt to thwart the invasion by the alien species, a computer virus is planted within the control systems of the aliens' mother ship. By crippling the computational capabilities, and thus the command and control facilities of the alien craft, the humans are finally able to bring their air borne military capability to bear on the invasion craft. Simultaneously, a large thermonuclear device is detonated within the alien mother ship. It should be noted that this movie was created during the period when computer viruses aimed at Windows operating system platforms and at the central Internet switching system were gaining widespread notoriety within the public at large. This coincided with the very significant market penetration of personal computers and of routine Internet connectivity by these personal computing platforms. The concept of malicious computer viruses gaining popular awareness notwithstanding, if one considers the rather far flung development of computer systems for the past fifty years, the idea that a laptop computer (and an Apple Mac at that!) would be similar enough to a completely alien computer system so as to allow, first of all a direct communication link between different computers to be established, and then a set of instructions (the virus) to be transferred from one to the other, the result is one of those very low probability events that are indistinguishable from a miracle.

Of course, this points to the fact that because the blueprint of all known living organisms is similar, disease mechanisms can sometimes cross species boundaries; for example armadillos can carry human leprosy, a fact perhaps not well known outside of Texas. Computers at this point do not have a single blueprint, which make viruses quite dependent on specific architectures, and punctuates the parallels between biological and computer evolution.

Another 1996 movie, *Star Trek: First Contact* took a somewhat different approach in considering the interactions among alien species. It posed the rationale that a species essentially signals its readiness to engage in off-world contact by enabling faster-than-light travel. In the parlance of the book, they create a *warp drive*. In this movie environment, while powering a spacecraft to an effective speed beyond that of light, a warp drive also creates a signature detectable through appropriate instrumentation. The movie centers on the seminal event, termed *First Contact*, when *Homo sapiens sapiens* first encountered beings from another world. In this case people from Vulcan, home of Mr. Spock, made a visit to Earth. Such a scenario is not without merit. It says, essentially, one only needs to worry about interactions when the two parties are in close proximity within a common physical ecosystem. Close proximity, as we've suggested previously, is a function of the use of the four primary forces to facilitate an interaction. It is also perhaps interesting to consider our current situation in light of such an admission test. We have not yet created a warp drive, and despite the popularity of the concept among various entertainment venues, apparently no alien species have approached us yet. Of course, this is reminiscent of the peddler in old Oklahoma offering an aerosol spray to repel wild elephants. "But," the potential buyer observed, "there aren't any wild elephants in western Oklahoma." "It works well, doesn't it?" was the peddler's reply. More seriously, this discussion plays into our consideration of various approaches for seeking causality in the world around us; a topic of Chapter 7.

The final movie that we'll consider in this regard is the 1997 release of *Contact*. We must note that the book on which this movie is based was written by Carl Sagan, a noted astronomer. However, more than his technical contributions to astronomy, probably Sagan's greatest contribution, and memorial, was his ability to communicate. Through a variety of efforts, he presented a thoughtful and well-understood commentary on the relationship of science and humanity. What is perhaps interesting in this regard is that this movie, derived from Sagan's book, presents the issue of contact between intelligent species from as much a religious perspective, as from a scientific one.

Incidentally, the book *Contact* posits something of a different ending from that in the movie. Sagan seemed to care very deeply about the interrelationships between religion and science. In his book, essentially as a post-script, he presents a scenario in which researchers who are working to establish the value of *Pi* to an arbitrary level of accuracy find something very interesting a few million binary digits into it. There, they find a very long sequence of bits whose sequence length is the product of two prime numbers. When they displayed this sequence as a two-dimensional picture using one prime number to define the x-axis and the other to define the y-axis, the resulting display of ones and zeros produced a picture of a circle. Such an occurrence would constitute an excellent, celestial "Kilroy was here" sign.

The movie paints a picture of the human side of the initial contact with extra-terrestrials from the viewpoint of a SETI group (SETI – Search for Extra-Terrestrial Intelligence) that, through their diligent monitoring of radio-frequency transmissions from non-earth sources, detects a signal from the vicinity of the star Vega. As it happens, the extra-terrestrials, who are never actually identified in the movie, apparently had their own version of SETI, triggered by their reception of our earliest high-power television transmissions. As it happens, the aliens only had a listening post in the vicinity of Vega; their home world was not in this neighborhood.

On receiving the initial earth TV transmissions, rather perversely a broadcast featuring Adolf Hitler opening the Olympic Games of Berlin, twenty-seven years after their transmission (Vega is located twenty seven light-years from earth), the aliens begin broadcasting a response message back toward the earth. So, about 54 years after the Berlin Olympics, when it is detected and deciphered by the SETI team, the alien message comprises a set of construction plans for an inter-galactic conveyance system. It will carry one person there and back, wherever "there" is. Of course, this approach smacks of the technology test that we observed in the *Star Trek: First Contact* movie. In any case, when the central character of the movie returns from her journey through the conveyance device, it is found that no record of what transpired was retained. In essence, it then becomes a question of faith as to whether the contact actually occurred. "It has always been done this way" was the message from the alien race.

So, we see a variety of visualizations of how interactions *might* occur within an environment where everyone is not on the same page with respect to how interactions *should* occur. We can summarize these visualizations by noting that when this situation occurs, the possibilities are either to get everyone to the same page or to revert back to the page that we are all born with; the physical ecosystem. For earthly species, when we revert to the physical ecosystem we essentially view the interaction as proceeding from a face-to-face encounter. Without putting a vertebrate guise on the illustration, with off-world aliens we would have to assume a "face-to-something" posture.

Our perspective is that, as least at it pertains to people and to computers, there are some preferable ways. We observe that interactions among computers are virtually a direct analogue to interactions among people, or even groups of people for that matter. The primary distinction arises from the fact that both the physical as well as social infrastructures within which computers and computer systems operate are based on a variety of mechanisms not available to exclusively human interactions. One might think of it as a case where computers have a different set of physical senses that connect them to their environment, which includes both people as well as other computers. To provide a way to support complex interactions, we suggest that the approach taken is to define a comprehensive policy infrastructure.

Now, before we continue, we must make slight amends for our selection of movie examples. In homage to probably the greatest movie of this genre, we must make note of Stanley Kubrick's movie rendition of Arthur Clarke's story, *2001 – A Space Odyssey*. This movie is simply too broad in scope to use in illustrating the more mundane point that we wanted to make. Clarke's masterpiece is itself a foundational telling of the story of human evolution. It is an epic, mythic tale such as we will later observe formed a critical phase of human evolutionary progression. From our perspective, mythic comprehension forms a seminal facility in the formulation of religion. Thus, we suggest that *2001 – A Space Odyssey* is better studied as religious allegory as opposed to simply illustrating concepts of communication protocols.

# Computer Interactions

Interactions among computer systems exhibit all of the characteristics of person to person physical interactions, with the additional dimensions of expanded scope in both physical proximity and temporal extension. Thus, interactions can take place at varying distances between the involved computers and they can take place over an extended period of time as opposed to a more tightly constrained interval that is typical for most purely physical interactions that involve people. The first concept on which the computer interaction model is based is that of a protocol. As we have noted previously, a protocol is a well-defined sequence of actions that are entered into as a way for two or more parties to arrive at a mutually agreed upon state. A protocol is involved in virtually any interaction, whether between people, between computers or between people and computers. Quite obviously, there can be effective protocols and ineffective protocols; protocols that solve problems and protocols that cause problems. We'll try to stick to protocols that have been found effective in addressing real-world problems.

A seminal facet of protocol is that of establishing *contact*. Humans do it by looking each other in the eye, touching, picking up a phone and calling, flashing a signal, sending a messenger, sending a letter and so on. In each case, the existence of a potential physical conduit of communication is established. A second facet is that of establishing *readiness* to engage in an interaction. Humans do it by shaking hands, embracing, saying "Hi," flashing a signal back, answering e-mail and more. A third facet is that of *conversing*, which follows rules, such as how to talk in turn, what subjects are approached, how they are developed; in short, all the conventions that have to be followed for the interaction to proceed. This leads to the concept of a *protocol stack*. A stack is a set of protocols related to each other and dependent upon one another. For example, in France when two persons want to talk, they may first establish eye contact, then say "Bonjour" and then converse. Here we have three protocols, each dependent on the previous one. We say that the three protocols are *stacked*, as they each lay upon the foundation created by the other.

Staying in France, another way for two persons to talk is for them to pick up a phone and first dial a number, then say "Allo" and then converse. In this case, contact is established through the phone line connection instead of through the eyes, readiness is signaled with "allo" instead of "bonjour" and conversation on the phone follows slightly different rules than face-to-face conversation. Actually, the pattern contact-readiness-conversation is a general pattern of interactions, a fact that has not escaped the attention of the pioneers that were tasked with making computers talk to each other. Accordingly, in the early stages of the evolution of the computer (within the modern era), the International Standards Organization, based in Switzerland, undertook an effort to better understand the mechanics of computer-to-computer interactions within an infrastructure of widespread connectivity among computer systems; that is, interactions through networks of computers. This effort resulted in the development of a computer interaction model known as the Open Systems Interconnection (OSI) Reference Model.

The Open Systems Interconnection reference model decomposes the general problem of two entities communicating with each other into seven layers, stacked on top of each other; specifically:

- Application Layer
- Presentation Layer
- Session Layer
- Transport Layer
- Network Layer
- Link Layer
- Physical Layer

The physical layer is the way computers establish a conduit for communication. Such conduits may be a wire, or may be radio waves. In the later case, the communication is said to be *wireless*. Wired communication can use, for example twisted pairs, coaxial cable or optical fibers. Wireless communication can be done through various radio technologies like cellular telephony, Wi-Fi, or via other means such as optical lasers.

The next four layers are about establishing readiness to talk. The link layer allows two computers directly connected physically to recognize each other. The network layer allows two computers not directly linked physically to still recognize each other, using intermediate computers to which they are physically linked, thus establishing a chain of physical connections yielding the desired result. The transport layer allows two computers linked either directly or in a network fashion to define the way they acknowledge messages to each other in order to avoid losing information. Finally, the session layer allows the two computers to recognize when messages belong to the same stream of conversation, allowing them to exchange information back and forth in a sustained fashion.

The next two layers are about making sure that the computers actually understand each other. Just as two humans can't communicate if they speak different languages unknown to each other, computers need to make sure that they speak the same language. That's the function of the presentation layer. Finally, even if they speak the same language, humans speak differently, depending on circumstances. Each situation is a particular application of our communication capabilities. Similarly, computers speak about different topics and with different rules depending on the circumstances. That's what the application layer does; it establishes context.

All together, we see that computers interact in pretty much the same way as humans. They need to find a communication medium, they need to establish readiness to talk and then they need various conventions to converse effectively. The physical characteristics of humans and computers dictate different techniques and technologies, but the general order of operations, as well as their nature, is similar. In many cases, it's just a matter of nuances. While it is customary for computers to talk through other intermediate computers, it is a less usual situation with humans. However, there are indeed cases where humans communicate through intermediaries; for example, through messengers. Conversely, humans actually establish several channels of communication at once in face-to-face conversation. Hand gestures, body signals and facial expressions are all part of communication that accompany the mouth-to-ear channel. Computers are typically more reserved, using only one channel at a time. In fact, they use one channel at once like people do when they talk by phone.

The reference communication model of computers actually expresses a hierarchy of needs. To communicate, two computers require electricity for a physical link, they need to associate with each other reliably, and they need to exchange meaningful information. In the same way, humans need food and links to each other, they need to be accepted by others and gain their approval, and then they need to engage in meaningful and fulfilling exchanges. While at this point we will not claim an immediate parallel between the two models of behavior, we can see that Maslow, as a psychologist, and the Open Systems Interconnection committee, as computer scientists, chose to model humans and computers with similar means. The very commonality of approach will allow us to examine in turn each level of the human and computer protocols and examine in depth where they converge and where they differ. In the end, we will suggest that in fact the needs hierarchy of humans has a parallel adjunct in the application layer of computers. Similarities and dissimilarities will be equally revealing, and will be the ferment for subsequent inquiries.

# Characteristics of the Infrastructure

Beginning with the Open Systems Interconnection reference model as a starting point, a rather general model of interactions can be constructed that encompasses general human interactions as well as human to computer and computer-to-computer interactions. This model of *interaction infrastructures* results from merging the connection facilities of the Open Systems Interconnection reference model, an interaction impetus model based on Maslow's hierarchy of needs, and a trust model derived from the physiological basis of human interactions. At this point, we're only going to go part of the way towards this model. Specifically, we're going to consider the model as based on the security characteristics of computer networks. We'll defer the inclusion of a human trust model until we've had an opportunity to review some basic physiological characteristics in the next chapter. So, what's the difference?

Well, when we look at the historical emergence of computer networks, we find that the very concept of trust was totally submerged within a number of characteristics of an interaction environment that was (and is) termed *security*. As we will see, the characteristics of security are typically considered individually. The degree to which any particular characteristic is provided is often not considered relatively to other characteristics. Consequently, there is typically not a characterization of the overall level of trust with which a particular interaction environment should be imbued. We will address the concept of a cumulative level of trust in Chapter 5. For the moment, let us consider the foundations of computer networks and their various *security characteristics*.

Early computer networks were typically provided by a single vendor, the vendor of the computer systems involved in the network. Such configurations were termed *proprietary networks*. The characteristics of security provided on such networks were typically defined by the characteristics of the computer systems themselves. The idea of heterogeneous networks, enabling the connection of a wide variety of different computers, was somewhere off in the future. It was with the advent of such networks that the idea of computer and network security finally came to the fore. So, let us consider the mechanisms of computer networks as typified by the initiative which ultimately culminated in today's Internet. This seminal development activity was started within the United States Department of Defense in 1969, at the height of the Cold War exacerbated by the war in Vietnam. The primary networks in use at the time were those of terrestrial wired telephony; telephone networks based on fixed circuit switches. Such switched systems were susceptible to disruption through attacks on the switches themselves. In an effort to guard against a total loss of network connectivity from a highly directed attack, a project to consider the development of adaptable routing networks was started within the Defense Advanced Research Projects Agency (DARPA); the project ultimately developed the ARPANET, forerunner to the Internet.

Paradoxically in view of its origin, within the emergent world of the Internet, security in any guise was not a highly prized design characteristic. The network took form within a rather cloistered environment. Physical access to the communication pathways was restricted, meaning that many intervening personnel and physical access policies of organizations that had access to the fledgling network greatly restricted the presence of malevolent users. The early design requirements of the network were resilience and utility. It needed to survive a nuclear attack and it needed to facilitate useful information interchange and processing. As a consequence, the network was imbued with a significant level of trust by its highly restricted set of users. Only when it was opened to the general public did the deficiencies become obvious.

At the time of introduction of the general network to the public at large, physical connectivity of networks was still mostly through terrestrial wires, the end-points of which were typically in the offices of the telephone company. Thus, they were perceived to be moderately safe from eavesdropping. Indeed, covert surveillance of telephone conversations was usually done at the end points of the circuits; by using bugs in the phone or in the room, as all fans of James Bond movies clearly recognize. However, other techniques such as inductive coupling allow intercepting signals over, say, sub sea cables. Such clandestine technologies were not widely appreciated with the early inception of computer networks in general, and with the Internet specifically. Rather, in those early days, the concern regarding networks was with uptime and ubiquity, not with security. When the threats posed to network traffic were fully recognized, remedial action was the order of the day, not redesign of the basic networks to encompass security characteristics. Consider it an example of *evolution in action*, a term first introduced in 1981 by Larry Niven and Jerry Pournelle in their science fiction book *Oath of Fealty*. It suggests a characteristic of certain situations to anecdotally illustrate the evolutionary process itself.

So, as something of an afterthought, within widespread, heterogeneous computer networks, the consideration of the environment for interactions was ultimately focused on the concept of *security*. As it is typically used, the word or concept of security is a rather nebulous thing. Too often this ambiguity in meaning is by design rather than through imprecise usage of language. The word is intended to suggest the presence of characteristics that may not, in fact, be provided. We would suggest that a better way to refer to the cumulative set of security characteristics is through the concept of trust, but as we said, we'll get to that down the road a bit.

So, from this beginning, the discussion in deployment circles tended to focus on security as add-on capability that needed to be somehow attached to the network, rather than a basic physiological requirement. In essence, the trust that should ensue from a high degree of security became a higher level need to be fulfilled somewhere in the protocol stack. So, at this point, we should consider the various characteristics that comprise the amalgam called security.

Within the general field of physics, in the study of interactions among particles, whether it be in the macroscopic world of classical mechanics or in the sub-atomic world of particle physics, dealing with two particles at a time is a more readily solved problem than is the situation when more than two particles are involved. In general, the equations of motion for two-body interactions offer exact solutions whereas three-body or higher groupings allow only for approximate solutions. Consequently, one approach to the classical many-body problem has been, historically, to break the problem down into a multitude of two-body interactions. A very similar situation holds in the interactions among people, which was the first guide to the behavior of computer interactions.

Our model for the interactions among people is to view them as being composed of *transactions*; specifically, of two party transactions. We suggest that this definition can be further refined to enumerate two very specific characterizations of a transaction. First, a transaction is time limited and second, or perhaps the corollary, a transaction has a well-defined beginning and a well-defined conclusion or outcome. Within the world of computer systems and computer networks, we tend to think in terms of a preferred environment in which we can conduct transactions. Operating within some known *security infrastructure*, the preferred transaction environment provides some degree of the following characteristics:

- Privacy
- Authentication
- Authorization
- Information Integrity
- Transaction history providing non-repudiation

These five areas, encompassed as they must be by some means of establishing their respective characteristics, form the metric by which we judge the efficacy of the security of computer systems and computer networks. It is in this playground that personal electronic devices become the big kid players. So, what do these characteristics really mean in the computer world? Well, they mean much the same thing as they do in our everyday world, since these are also characteristics that we must establish to some degree for any type of interaction among people.

The term *privacy* has at least two distinct connotations. First, the term is applied to the concept of freedom of action. Within the purview of United States law, the historic Roe versus Wade decision by the United States Supreme Court brought this concept of privacy into focus. Defined through the *penumbra* of more specifically stated rights within the Constitution of the United States, the *right to privacy* illuminated by this decision bears directly on the power of the individual to completely control certain aspects of personal interactions that they may engage in, devoid of any control by the state or other individuals. The right of a woman to terminate a pregnancy, specifically early in the pregnancy, is held to be inviolate. However, as the terminus of the gestation period approaches, the decision finds that there may be compelling state interests that would serve to limit the afore-mentioned right to privacy. Consequently, the result is a right with a fuzzy boundary.

A second aspect of the concept of privacy is control over the possession or dissemination of information. Within the provision of an environment for transactions, we tend to reference this latter definition more often. That is, privacy most often refers to the limitation of the details of a transaction, or even to the conduct of a transaction itself, to specific, denominated entities privy to the information. As we will discuss in significantly more detail in Chapter 6, this brings into perspective the actual ownership, and hence control of, information.

For the moment, we will focus on the idea that privacy implies a limitation on the visibility of information or processes involved in a transaction.

In the military, "Who are you?" can be a death or life question. This is why soldiers wear uniforms, also why they don't completely trust uniforms and try to complement them with specific signals, or other means to make sure that the person really is whomever he or she claims to be, for example by providing a password.

By definition, transactions involve the participation of various entities. Some entities might be inanimate, and some might be humans. Transactions effected between two or more entities are constrained by specifications of policy that are directly linked to the identity of entities that participate in the transactions. For the moment, we will ascribe a definition to the term *identity* as being the unique differentiation of one entity from all others. If we are able to establish the identity of an entity from time to time and/or from place to place we say that we can *authenticate* the identity of the entity.

Knowing that the soldier is one of your own is usually not enough. Some are authorized to give orders, some to take them and a very few to ignore them. In the military, one way to signal authorization is by patching grades on the uniform. Some officers are authorized to transmit messages on the radio of a certain importance, and only them.

Once the identity of various entities involved in a transaction has been authenticated, another policy characteristic of a transaction that can then be effected is to allow various capabilities to be ascribed to the authenticated identity. This allowance of capability is termed *authorization*. The two most common processes required within any policy infrastructure are the authentication of identities and the authorization of capabilities to those authenticated identities.

We all know the game in which a chain of children pass a message to each other from one end of the chain to the other, to discover to their astonishment that the message is totally garbled as it reaches its destination. Avoiding this is the purpose of integrity techniques. For example, we can use two chains of children and compare the messages at the end, or ask each child to repeat the message for confirmation before forwarding it. With computers, there are much more powerful techniques, but we'll be satisfied with those examples for the time being.

Certainly, central to the concept of policy and a seminal aspect of the concept of trust is the ability to ascertain the *integrity* of information involved in a transaction, less we can trust that information.

The ultimate goal of transactions is the attainment of a consequence. Within some policy infrastructures, we sometimes don't address the consequences, or at least certain aspects of the consequences, until the transaction is over. Thus, we typically need a *history* of what went on during the transaction. In the military, messages must be traceable. If something goes wrong, we want to know what happened, to avoid the same problem in the future. So we want to keep a good record of the message. More generally, the more we know about past interactions and their outcome, the better we may be in the future in the face of adversity.

Trust requires verification. So it is necessary to track at least some elements of the transactions. Thus, we recognize the concept of a feedback loop through which reputation in the form of history is used to modify the trust infrastructure for future interactions. In this way, we see the emergence of recursion within the mechanisms of the trust and policy infrastructure. This will be a developing concept through the remainder of the book.

3  Environment

# 4 Physiology of the Individual

$$\nabla \bullet B = 0$$
$$\nabla \times E + \partial B/\partial t = 0$$
$$\nabla \bullet D = \rho$$
$$\nabla \times H - \partial D/\partial t = J$$

.James Clerk Maxwell

## Turtles Ad Infinitum

"We are all made of stars," so says the song by Moby. Indeed, theoretical physicists suggest that hydrogen and helium were constituent results of the original big bang. They further suggest that all of the heavier elements could only have been made within the thermonuclear furnaces of stars. Carbon based organisms that require oxygen to support their life-processes owe their elemental existence to the violent end of stars as nova or supernova explosions. In the distant past, these cataclysmic events discharged from stellar interiors the heavy elements that were the detritus of the fusion reactions from which stars derive their energy. These castoff remnants then found new purpose as they formed the foundation of planetary development, which in turn supported the emergence of life, in at least one case. This causal history of the development of the universe appears as a progression of well-understood physical events. It is at the juncture of causality punctuated by the emergence of life that physical ecosystems impinge upon the creation legends of religions.

Stories of creation and existence are found in most religions; descriptions of how people came into and upon the world, while offering an understanding of how their existence melds with that of their physical and spiritual universes. These seminal events of mankind's existence are the focus of the curiosity of virtually every person as they grow from infancy to adulthood. The stories that have been passed down through the generations are based on imagery, metaphor and allegory, just as are the languages used to recite them. Hearing these stories from our earliest recollections of consciousness, they form within us the foundation of our perception and understanding of the world. It is from this foundation that we derive trust. Trust is then a salient feature of the platforms from which the levers of our collective minds can move the universe. Through the ages, the great philosophers and scientists have given rigorous voice to the imagery and allegory recited to us by the storytellers and historians.

The epigraph for this chapter is a perfectly reasonable translation of an act of creation, although theoretical physicists tell us that we haven't quite got the full text available yet, so our translation is currently incomplete, if not incorrect. That notwithstanding, we generally recognize Maxwell's equations, a detailed specification of electromagnetism, as a sentence of creation. For the devoutly secular, the existence of the sentence is sufficient; a speaker of the sentence is not required. For the religiously devout, the speaker is central. When the two views bump into each other the amalgam can be interesting. As an old joke goes, a little old lady recounted to a young student the certain fact that the world was indeed sitting on an elephant that was riding the back of a gigantic turtle. "But," questioned the young man, learned in the ways of science, "What holds up the turtle?" "Well, it rides on a larger turtle," replied the lady. "And then," queried the young student, "What about that turtle?" "Sitting on another turtle," said the woman, who then concluded the conversation. "I know where you're going with this young man, and you should know that it's turtles, all the way down!"

Well, in fact we really do need to understand where the world ends and the turtles begin. Perhaps more important, we need to know where the turtles end; and, what do we find in their ending? Through the ages, as a species we have developed a more rigorous understanding of the world around us. From that understanding, we establish the causality through which we derive trust in the mechanisms around us and in the processes that we engage in. When we reach the boundary of that understanding, we enter the realm of mythical understanding. We will consider the relationship among trust, causality and process in much greater detail in Chapters 7 and 8. In this chapter, we seek to provide a rather succinct appraisal of a bit of what we understand about living organisms and their inherent processes compared and contrasted with what we understand about computers and their processes.

We are all made of star stuff and DNA is the blueprint of our construction. DNA can help us understand something of the history of our journey, albeit without telling us if we found our consciousness in primeval ooze or in celestial grace; "dust thou art to dust returneth," just add water. Research is beginning to unlock detailed interpretations of DNA sentences and how these sentences are subsequently translated into biophysical entities. Across a very large range of species, the commonality of DNA is startling. There is considerable overlap among seemingly divergent species with respect to their physiological makeup. So, perhaps its not turtles all the way down, but it certainly appears to be turtle parts at least a good part of the way. That brings us to our more specific goal for this chapter, to understand something of the detailed physiology of the human species. It is from this physiology that humankind establishes the metaphorical basis through which the complex interactions of people, including the recurrent appearance of religion throughout history, are made part of the cognizance of the species. Perhaps then we can draw parallels between such occurrences and the development and evolution of computer architectures, thereby providing some insight into what the future evolution of that family of species holds.

Human information processing has evolved over millions of years, whereas computers have evolved over only a few decades. Comparing the human brain, which has been stable in its current form for tens of thousand of years, to the computer, which has existed in something like its current form for about half a century, is bound to be a meaningless exercise unless one is very careful with the details of the comparison. For example, it is quite common to see comparisons between computers and people expressed in terms of software and hardware. Software, it is said, is like the mind, and hardware like the brain. In actuality, this is hardly illustrative, or conducive to elaboration, because the brain and its implementation details and mechanisms are in general only qualitatively understood and their relationship to the mind is still an area of fundamental research. Perhaps more surprising is that the distinction between hardware and software in the computer domain is not clear either, or at least it is becoming less clear. For example, the number of processing elements found in a large scale computer, or in a washing machine for that matter, makes the delineation between hardware and software almost a matter of faith; perhaps an odd juxtaposition of theological bent. The parallels are there; we just need to start at the correct beginning and measure at the correct way posts.

Humans, like computers, can be considered either in isolation or in groups in terms of information architecture. A single person, interacting with the surrounding environment, processes information derived through sensori-motor channels, just as an isolated computer at home might process input and output information to produce, say, a printed memo from a document typed at the keyboard. In either case, the interaction of the individual with the external world through sensori-motor channels forms the basis for all subsequent ability to abstract the myriad components of the world, thus not only comprehending the actions of the various components, but from that abstraction being able to project an understanding of a well known situation to a less familiar one. Sensori-motor channels, by virtue of their gathering of information and their projection of action, provide the foundation of metaphorical extension that feeds thought and consciousness. A group of persons, or of computers, performs a particular type of information processing characterized by the exchange in parity of data and commands between the participants, following rules of engagement that permit the information to actually be meaningful. This characterization, along with the rules of engagement, forms a significant piece of what we have termed policy.

So, we seek to compare humans and computers, first as individuals, and then as participants in groups. For isolated persons, we consider their foundational impetus for interactions to be well characterized in the hierarchy of needs of Maslow, which starts by considering the physiological requirements of individuals, such as food, air and water. This more primitive impetus for interactions then evolves to successive hierarchical levels encompassing security, interpersonal relationships, and so on. Ostensibly, a higher order stimulus for human interaction is found in the concepts of self-actualization and then transcendence, the ultimate realization of one's given potential and the projection of the environment that facilitates that realization. For an individual computer, there is not yet such a formal model related to the reason (stimulus) for a specific computer interaction; that's part of what we're about with this book. So, we'll start out by establishing a parallel between Maslow's scale and a computer's needs beginning with the requirement for electricity (food), integrity of processing (being able to process instructions without crashing, which is related to security), the capability to establish communication channels with other computers (relationships), and on including self-actualization, which we would characterize as the use of applications maximizing the capabilities of the computers, be they in terms of processing unit, memory or input/output channels.

Concerning group interactions, we'll consider first computers. As we noted in the previous chapter, computer interactions can be characterized by a rather formal consideration of interaction protocols through the Open Systems Interconnection (OSI) model of data interchange. This model views interactions as occurring through a stack of protocols at the bottom of which we find the medium of communication, for example a cable, or radio waves. Building on this physical basis, the model suggests we then proceed to establish a link between two computers by mutual recognition. Given a pair-wise connection, we can then extend the interaction environment to more than two computers, and so on, until a multitude of computers are able to communicate information in a reliable, ubiquitous manner.

Our observation is that humans follow similar conventions, starting with the physical means of exchange (say using voice or signals), ways to start a conversation (e.g., greetings), the possibility to introduce more than two persons, methods of coordination, and so on, until people around a table can, for example, conduct a meeting with some meaningful results. Or, at the other end of the interaction spectrum, they can engage in a ferocious war to the death!

To finish this rapid overview of human and computer information processing capabilities, we need to consider that in a group, humans and computers express their individualities. We can say that in effect, the information architecture of humans and computers is built out of two components, the individual one and the group one, each building its capabilities on top of the other. This is to say that, for a group to operate, individual capabilities have to be adjusted to permit establishment of the proper protocols. For example, the computer must be able to process the input of the other computers using first its appropriate specialized input/output modules, and then the applications that know how to process the information at hand. Correspondingly, a person needs to hear the voice of another person and interpret it, using voice recognition modules and more general capabilities of language understanding.

Once a group is established, within the group each person can use an interaction or collection of interactions to promote the business at hand. For example, a person may read a document to the group, using document processing skills (reading and modulation of content) as well as communication skills (converting the content into spoken sentences processed by the voice output module). Similarly, the computer may, for instance, be scanning a photo, converting it into the proper bits of information via the scanner interaction module, and then, say use a compression application, and then the transmission module, to send the image to another computer. In this way, the computer and personal applications can effect their desired end.

So, we have something of a cursory overview of the interaction environment that we'd like to better understand. Let's now delve into an overview of the inner workings of people and then computers in order to see if we can find some similarities in the basis for the policy environments in each case.

# Human Structures and Processes

The abstract, systematic study of the human body includes a number of discrete disciplines. Two basic and interrelated such disciplines are anatomy and physiology. Anatomy comprises the study of the static characteristics of the body. It encompasses the consideration of the body's structure and makeup: skeleton, linkage tissues, muscles, nerves, fluid systems, organs and the like. The study of the general dynamic systems of the body is termed physiology. Physiology concerns itself with the physical processes through which a person's body supports its continued living as facilitated by both its internal interactions as well as its interactions with the physical world in which it exists. As a prelude to consideration of the human body's operational processes, it is perhaps useful to observe that most such processes make use of active control of systems that operate from positions of unstable equilibrium. Thus, generally opposing mechanisms are used to effect motor control through positive impulses from the body's control systems, the central and peripheral nervous systems. To move an arm requires the coordination of opposing muscles and to transmit an impulse across a nerve requires coordination of opposing chemical components. Such an approach to command and control of the body relies heavily on a highly structured and hence hierarchically capable cognitive system that is the centerpiece of the human sensori-motor experience. In turn, the sensori-motor experience provides conceptual framework for human cognition. Consider the following.

As we discussed previously, the physical ecosystem within which living organisms exist effects interactions through the four basic forces: gravity, the electromagnetic force, the weak force and the strong force. Virtually all interactions that human physiology supports are based on electromagnetic and gravity based processes. Many of the electromagnetic based processes are presented to the human body through secondary or indirect mechanisms. These indirect mechanisms establish the metaphors through which cognitive system perceives the physical world around us. We *see* things. We *hear* things. We *feel* things. We *touch* things. We *smell* things. We *taste* things. These are all manifestations of the electromagnetic force. Establishing context through which metaphorical understanding becomes a significant basis of human cognition would certainly be more limiting if we referenced all of these effects simply as electromagnetism at work.

We want to consider just a bit more about these various sensory manifestations. For example, how does the electromagnetic force relate to acoustic compression (sound) waves or to chemical reactions? It is non-intuitive to recognize that the vast majority of physical interactions that we're aware of in our everyday lives are in fact due to the electromagnetic force. When we lay a book upon a table, no atoms of the book ever touch the atoms in the table; or, in fact, do they? What do we actually mean by touch anyway? Well, at the atomic level, touch means that the electron cloud of the surface atoms of the book repels the electron cloud of the surface atoms of the table. So, at a very primary level, touch indicates an action at a distance, albeit a very small distance. So, the metaphor is quite accurate when we say, "I was touched by her portrayal of Juliet."

Sound, on the other hand, is a pressure wave in which a group of molecules in a material, when set in motion by having their electron clouds repulsed by the electron clouds of some other material, proceed to move until their electron clouds bump into the electron clouds of other molecules in the material. Energy is transferred from one molecule to the next molecule, and the compression wave propagates through the material.

We know that at a macroscopic level, matter tends to be perceived as gaseous, liquid or solid. It is interesting to consider the characteristics of the electromagnetic force that enable this differentiation. Electrons that occur as constituent components of atoms are attracted to atomic nuclei by the electromagnetic force. As the number of electrons increases in concert with an increased number of protons within the atomic nucleus, the strength of the binding between a specific electron and the nucleus becomes greater. In certain configurations of adjacent atoms, one or more electrons may actually be shared between different atoms; perhaps even atoms of different elements. This results in a binding of the two atoms together; the sharing of electrons forming what is called a *chemical bond*. Such binding of atoms results in molecules of various types. Molecules in turn form aggregations based on similar electron sharing. This can range from the tenuous collections of molecules that we know as gases, to the more tightly bound, yet highly malleable collections we know as liquids. Finally, extremely tight bonds can form solids; ranging from highly symmetrical formations of atoms in crystals to more seemingly random formations found in less structurally integrated materials.

Electromagnetic based interactions involving the transfer of energy among the various participants in an interaction also come in several macroscopically observable flavors: conduction, convection and radiation. Conduction involves the movement of energy within a material, perhaps through the diffusion of internal kinetic energy (heat) or the propagation of electrons (electrical current). Convection refers to the transfer of energy through a material by moving the material itself; this is typically observed as a movement of fluids. Radiation is the presentation of the internal kinetic energy of a material as quanta of electromagnetic energy. Relative to the human body, this most often refers to low frequency variants of electromagnetic energy that we typically perceive as heat. An interaction based on conduction mechanisms involves the transfer of energy from one mass to another through direct interaction of the electron clouds of the surface components of the two masses. Such mechanisms may also actually entail the transfer of mass. Convection based interactions are typically associated with fluids and denote the transfer of energy from a static mass to a fluid mass and the subsequent dissipation of energy within the fluid mass. This fluid mass might be brought in contact with another static mass, resulting in a further transfer of energy from the fluid to the second mass. Finally, radiation involves the transfer of energy through the emission and absorption of electromagnetic bundles of energy, termed photons when the involved energies are close to the visible spectrum wavelengths.

Because of these various mechanisms, it can be viewed that human physiology comprises a complex set of electro-chemical and electro-mechanical processes derived through evolutionary mechanisms applied to living organisms over very long periods of time. These processes define the very *concepts* of life in that they encompass, in the case of the human species, the full range of human experience; from sensory input to the action stimuli represented by Maslow's needs hierarchy. In *The Brain's Concepts: The Role of the Sensory-Motor System in Reason and Language*, published in 2005 in *Cognitive Neurophysiology*, Vittorio Gallese and George Lakoff offered the insight that concepts, rather than coming from cognitive processes centered outside the human sensori-motor system, are actually abstractions derived directly from the human sensori-motor system. In effect, the relationship of a person to the external world, and the way in which that person *thinks* about this relationship in abstract terms, is established by input from the sensory systems, and cognition based output through the body's motor systems. Hence, one should recognize the sensori-motor experience as the primary basis for humans' understanding of the world and their interactions with it. From this understanding comes a metaphorical basis for comprehending aspects of the physical environment that are totally independent of the body and its experiences.

Within the human body, sensory stimuli are first conveyed from discrete sensors at the body to external world interface, through the peripheral nervous system until they are ultimately absorbed by the human cognitive system. The brain, comprising the primary component of the central nervous system, is the focal point of cognitive functions, although certain reflexive responses to sensory input may be handled by outlying nervous control pathways. Given the various forms of sensory input, the cognitive and reflexive systems of the body effect response actions to the sensory stimuli. We characterize the process that the human body goes through in developing the ability to associate actions with, and derive actions from, sensory inputs as *learning* or *training*. In Chapter 8, we will suggest that this process is perhaps more expansively described by the term *provisioning*. This will draw a strong parallel with the basic operational processes through which computer systems are readied to function in the real world.

If an action response to sensory input requires conscious cognitive consideration, implying that there may actually be a variety of possible actions in response to common sensory inputs, then we tend to call the process for associating response to sensory input, *learning*. The implication is that, over time, we develop an ability, that is we learn, to select a response action that gives us the most desired effect. If, on the other hand, an action is pursued as a near reflexive response to sensory input, we tend to call the process *training*. It has been found that through repetitive stimulation and response cycles one can actually enhance the body's reflexive response to certain stimuli. The sprinter can be trained to leap out of the starting blocks more quickly at the beginning of the race while the body of the long distance runner can be trained, at the biophysical level, to more efficiently convert the stored energy in body fat into propulsion.

As we noted just a bit earlier, the motor mechanisms that the human body utilizes in dealing with its encompassing physical environment tend to be positive, antagonistic control mechanisms. For each mechanism, there exist component elements that drive the mechanism in opposing directions. This counter-force approach seems to exist all the way from the microscopic, biochemical level to the macroscopic, mechanical level. The interesting characteristic of such an approach to control facilities is that it allows the continual modification of *default actions* as the body learns to accentuate one force versus the other based on learned or trained feedback. We'll try to make note of such characteristics as we briefly review the various structural and procedural aspects of the human body. As an initial observation on the derivation of abstractions from the sensori-motor experience, we note that one of the oldest metaphysical concepts of the operation of the world is that of *yin* and *yang*; the complementary but opposing forces that ancient Chinese philosophy tells us are constituent ingredients of all things in the universe. They would seem to start within our most basic interactions with our physical ecosystems.

# Smart Bricks and Mortar

The human body is comprised of a number of distinct but highly interrelated systems, such as the digestive, respiratory, cardiovascular, musculoskeletal, endocrine and nervous systems. For such a complex array of operational components to support and preserve the living condition of the individual, we may look for some coordinating means. Indeed, a command and control facility for the human body is found in the body's nervous system augmented by the endocrine system. There are two main components of the nervous system, the central nervous system and the peripheral nervous system. The central nervous system is comprised of the brain and the spinal cord, while the peripheral nervous system is comprised of a number of nerve bundles that connect the central nervous system to all parts of the body, largely through interconnections with the spinal cord. In a complementary fashion, the endocrine system provides an associated communication pathway interconnected to the nervous system at selected points that functions in the control of longer term behaviors of the human body.

At various points along the spinal cord, a total of 31 pairs of nerve bundles branch off and connect to various sensory and motor elements scattered throughout the body. In each pair, one nerve branch collects sensory input destined for the spinal cord and possibly the brain, while the other nerve branch can carry signals away from the brain and to the motor facilities, also scattered throughout the body.

While other organs and their contained processes are better understood, we recognize that the brain is the seat of the true uniqueness of the human species. The adaptation and accommodation facilities that the brain enables, and that the body supports through physical actions, provide *Homo sapiens* with a unique ability to adapt to and to thrive within the physical ecosystems in which the species exists. The study of the brain is the domain of disciplines such as neuroanatomy and neurology, which deal with study of the static and dynamic properties of the brain. The study of information processing by the brain is the domain of many other disciplines, but we'll follow the current practice of organizing around the concept of cognitive science, wherein disciplines like anthropology, ethology, linguistics, psychology, its sub-discipline developmental psychology, and others bring their various, specific illustrations to the subject.

The seminal building blocks of the brain, and of the nerves that course throughout the body, are two specialized cell types called *neurons* and *glia*. From a computer science perspective, it's interesting to draw the very general parallel that these elements allow the construction of an organic analogue with many of the characteristics of electronic computers. The glial cells form the structural and environmental support, while a variety of neuron cells form the various elements of the actual computer of the brain. We won't consider the glial cells in much detail, other than to observe that they provide not only for the structural and environmental support of neurons, but they also provide for the electro-chemical isolation of neurons. This is accomplished through the creation of myelin sheaths, which serve to enhance the electrical conductivity of neurons and also to separate the neuron components so that instances of organic short circuits are minimized.

The active components of the nervous system are the neurons. Neurons allow for the conveyance and processing of information; information derived from the body's various senses, with corresponding control responses derived from this information being formulated by collections of neurons either in the spinal cord or in the brain, and then directed outward towards the body's motor and other support systems. The mechanisms effected by neurons form an organic equivalent to an extremely complex electrical circuit. Taking a very simplistic view, it can be observed that specifically, they roughly correspond to an analogue circuit that provides the operations of a diode, an amplifier and a band-pass filter; along with a wealth of processing and memory capacity. One uses such components in the purely mechanical world to form an analog computer. Further, from a digital computer standpoint, these are necessary elements for gates and switches, which are essential to the logic operations of such computers. As a basic characteristic of its physical makeup, an individual neuron allows for the conveyance of electro-chemical representations of information in only one direction through the cell. In a more general computer network configuration, we would refer to this as a simplex communication channel. So, how is this generally useful facility realized?

In a most simple overview, a neuron cell is comprised of three main components enclosed within a common membrane: a cell body called the *soma*, a collection of appendages called *dendrites* and another appendage termed an *axon*. There is, in general, only one axon per neuron cell, while there may be many dendrites. The dendrites are the input channels for information into the cell while the axon is the output channel. In its steady state, a neuron builds up a net electrical charge across the membrane which defines the boundary of the cell. This membrane is an insulator, composed of lipid molecules with modulated ion channels that pass through it. Through these channels, the neuron pumps sodium ions out of the cell and potassium ions into the cell resulting in a small negative potential when measured on the inside of the membrane relative to the outside of the membrane. Given a chemical stimulus through the dendrites, the neuron can evoke an electrical discharge that is termed an *action potential*; a process very similar to an electrical capacitor's discharge. The discharge originates at the *axon hillock* where the axon meets the soma. This action potential is then propagated along the axon of the cell. At the axon's terminus, the electrical impulse can be conveyed to a different neuron through a very interesting chemical, not electrical, mechanism termed a *synapse*.

Two neurons can be physically connected when an axon extension from one neuron, the pre-synaptic neuron, becomes permanently attached to a different neuron, the post-synaptic neuron. The connection point can occur at any location on the post-synaptic neuron: on its dendrites to form an axodendritic synapse, on its soma forming an axosomatic synapse or on its axon forming an axo-axonal synapse. The axon from one neuron can make many connections to a single post-synaptic neuron and it can make connections to many different post-synaptic neurons. The attachment point of one of these axon connection points, called a *terminal button*, to a post-synaptic neuron is a synapse and the space between the pre-synaptic and post-synaptic boundaries is called the *synaptic cleft*. So, for any collection of neurons, the number of synapses can be much larger than the total number of neurons. The total information handling capacity, a characteristic directly related to the cognitive capacity of the brain, appears to be related to the number of active synapses in the brain.

At a synapse connection, some rather complex operations are activated through which information is passed from one neuron to another. An action potential within a neuron, when it reaches the terminal button of the axon, causes the release of one or more of a variety of chemicals termed *neurotransmitters*. Neurotransmitters are able to cross the synaptic boundary to the post-synaptic neuron. As regulated by this post-synaptic neuron, the neurotransmitter material may tend to stimulate, or in some cases to inhibit, the post-synaptic neuron in the evocation of an action potential of its own. We use the term "tend" to call attention to the fact that a threshold level of stimulation may be required by the post-synaptic neuron; that is, the chemical stimulation may need to exceed some minimum level before the second neuron is caused to discharge. From a computer programming perspective, this is an extremely interesting aspect of the activation process because the stimulation can be cumulative across all the synapses connected to the post-synaptic neuron; if enough synapses are stimulated, the second neuron may be caused to discharge, even though the level of stimulation from any single synapse may not be sufficient to exceed the threshold. Again, from a computer programming viewpoint, this activity characterizes a decision making process; that is, it forms a gated switch. Consequently, not only can the information represented by the electrical discharge be propagated throughout a collection of neurons, but it can be propagated in an intelligent way because of the effects of many collections of neurons.

Paralleling the nervous system in most parts of the body is the endocrine system, which uses a similar communication channel to connect ductless glands with various cells of the body. When stimulated through their interconnections with the nervous system, these glands secrete distinct chemical molecules called hormones into the interstitial fluid surrounding cells relatively close to the glands, and from there into the blood stream where they are carried to specific receptor molecules found in various cells that may be far removed from the secreting gland. A hormone supplies a very similar function to a neurotransmitter, albeit within a different communication channel. In fact, a number of hormones are also neurotransmitters.

Within the endocrine system, each type of hormone effects what amounts to a logical communication channel through a physical fluid pathway. Each such pathway can carry different hormones and each hormone provides an information conveyance from the secreting gland to the receiving cells of that specific hormone. In a manner similar to synapses, the effect of a particular hormone may be reversed by a different hormone functioning in an antagonistic pair combination. When considering the secretion of hormones stimulated by control signals from the nervous system, the endocrine system appears as a distinct transport protocol layer (including a degenerative mode) if we view it in the guise of the communication reference model that we considered in Chapter 3. Through this layer, discrete sessions can be established to provide control of distributed cells over time via a feedback loop. We mention this point to illustrate the rather general interpretation that can be applied to interactions through a layered protocol model. We will make significant use of this approach in considering social systems in subsequent sections and chapters.

A particularly pertinent molecule for us to mention is one that functions both as a neurotransmitter as well as a hormone; the polypeptide, oxytocin. Known for its dual function in neural networks as well as within the endocrine system since the early XXth Century, the chemical structure and properties of oxytocin were studied and subsequently synthesized by Vincent du Vigneaud; work for which he was awarded the Nobel Prize in Chemistry in 1955. Functioning as a hormone, oxytocin is known to induce labor in pregnant women. Closer to our subject, more recent work suggests that functioning as a neurotransmitter, oxytocin is involved in the establishment and application of "trust" in human interactions. We present the term in quotes because it's a bit unclear whether the use of the term in reported research exactly matches the definition we have adopted in this book. That slight ambiguity noted, it is most interesting to consider the report of experiments performed by Michael Kosfeld et al. in Nature in 2005 in an article entitled Oxytocin increases trust in humans. A subsequent article was published in the June, 2008 issue of Scientific American by Paul J. Zak, a member of the research team making the previous report in Nature.

The Scientific American article is entitled The Neurobiology of Trust. In both cases, the studies reported indicate that by applying oxytocin in the form of a nasal spray the level of "trust" displayed by people engaged in specially orchestrated, financially oriented social interactions can be increased by a statistically significant amount. Whether these experiments illustrate a manipulation of a personal trust infrastructure, or a manipulation of the anticipated interaction outcome assessment within such a personal trust infrastructure, we find this to be a most interesting illustration of the physiological basis of social systems. We will delve into this concept in much more detail in the coming sections and in subsequent chapters.

The human brain is the unique feature of the species that has enabled its dominance in the physical ecosystem of the earth. About the size of a grapefruit with a cranial capacity of approximately 1500 cc, the brain sits at the anterior end of the spinal cord. It is encased in an exoskeleton component call the *skull*. While the human body is based on an endoskeleton, the skull and the vertebrae of the spine exhibit the excellent support and protection characteristics of exoskeletal structures. Our typical visual image of the brain is that of the partially bifurcated, semi-globular form whose surface is marked by deep fissures giving something of the appearance of a tightly coiled mass of rope. This visible, outer area of the brain is composed almost completely of neurons, with their soma, which are naturally gray in color, visible at the outer surface. This gives rise to the image of the brain as gray matter.

The brain structure encased in a bony skull is an evolutionary feature that developed early in the emergence of the vertebrates. The human species is notable for its brain size, relative to its body size, although some of the larger primates have almost comparable relative sizes. While the cranial capacity of the skull is relatively larger in humans that in other primates, the brain size is really enhanced through the development of folding of the mass of neurons into ridges and grooves, termed *gyri* and *sulci* respectively. This mechanical orientation of neurons allows for increased surface area of the brain, which, in turn, allows for more neurons to be supported by the same arrangement of glial cells. Moreover, the amount of white matter, that is the number of neuron axons, appears to be the really distinguishing feature of the human brain. This would effect a larger number of synapses, reinforcing the idea that these are the determining factor of cognitive power.

If one visualizes one's own brain as existing as a mass above and behind the eyes, then a number of common features of all human brains can be identified. First, the visible outer area, that area of gray matter, is termed the *cerebrum* and it is divided into two hemispheres by a deep fissure that completely divides the left half of the brain from the right half, save for a connecting bundle of fibers called the *corpus callosum* located midway between the front and back extremes of the hemispheres. A number of general *lobes* or areas of the brain provide location coordinates for specific functional sections that have been identified through various forms of research. The front portion of each hemisphere is termed, appropriately enough, the *frontal lobe*. The rear portion of each hemisphere is termed the *occipital lobe*, and a rather narrow section of each hemisphere between these two lobes is termed the *parietal lobe*. On each side of the brain, looking a bit like earmuffs, are the *temporal lobes*. Functional areas of the brain are then located through references to these lobes. For example, in the lower, rear portion of the left hemisphere's frontal lobe is found Broca's area; a neural network that is in particular heavily involved in language processing.

The spinal cord connects in to the bottom of the brain through a structure called the *brain stem*. A region between the brain stem and the cerebrum is termed the *diencephalon*. It is in turn comprised of the *hypothalamus*, the *thalamus* and the *epithalamus*. These sections are largely responsible for maintaining a stable internal environment within the human body. For example, they regulate body temperature, heart rate, respiration rate and the like. Finally, behind the brain stem, and still underneath the cerebrum, lies the *cerebellum*. This is the control area for the body's balance, posture and coordination.

While the basic components that form the various processing elements of the brain, that is the vast number of neurons, are very similar, the brain is not a single, generic neural network that develops functionality as the body grows and matures. However, the neocortex of the brain establishes distinct areas of auditory, visual, somatic, frontal, motor and other facilities that result in the same functionality showing up in the same areas of the brain for virtually every person. Moreover, each of these areas presents a remarkably similar, sophisticated local architecture. This functional orientation is an evolutionary artifact based on the DNA blueprint that has evolved through the ages. It likely derives from two distinct mechanisms, one structural and one chemical. First, the growth of every brain proceeds in the same general order. This results in neuron-to-neuron connections that follow a very similar pattern in all individuals. Not every neuron can connect to every other neuron; nor can every sensory input be directly connected to every neuron. Consequently, the various areas are predestined through construction to be associated with certain functionality. The other mechanism, the chemical one, derives from the specific neurotransmitters that are active within various neurons. It is through the neurotransmitters that different neural networks, the organic analog to electrical circuits, can develop from a single physical layout.

Within the human mind, memories are the stored results of sensory input received from throughout the body, along with the analysis and actions undertaken by the body in response to that input. Given the appropriate stimulus, stored memories can be accessed and information gleaned from them to some level of detail of the original input stimuli, analysis and response. The processing of these memory stimuli by various areas of the brain and nervous system can proceed, and resulting control or other cognitive actions can be taken as a result of the stimuli. When we recall memories, they tend to present themselves as reproductions of our original sensory input, generally with a degraded level of specificity. If a given activity induces stress, either through reflexive reactions to events or due to cognition induced profundity, then a memory might be enhanced. Consider that most of us can remember detailed aspects of our physical situation when Neil Armstrong first stepped onto the moon or when we first heard that John Lennon had been shot; or perhaps "the day the music died." For Generation X, the death of Kurt Cobain evoked a similar emphasis; even our contextual exclamation points are context sensitive.

The concept of memory is well established in the brain, through experiments matching the intuition that we all have that there are different domains of memories with variable capabilities of retention. Identifying the memory of a person with that of a computer seems reasonable from a general perspective, although it is clear that some constructs of human memories are much more efficient than any computer memory ever devised for certain operations, such as recognition. This apparently derives from structural properties such as neuron channels which offer significant parallel processing facilities that computers have yet to exploit with anywhere near the same level of efficiency.

Memory is a collection of mechanisms and processes through which sensori-motor experiences can be stored for subsequent retrieval. The parallels between human memory and computer memory are significant. Thomas K. Landauer, a research scientist at Bell Communications Research in the 1980's, suggested that human memory is a "novel telephone channel that conveys information from the past to the future." Memory is a central feature of cognition. The chain of causality that connects the two facilities is not well understood at the present time. However, it would not be unexpected if they are both different facets of the same thing. We will consider some parallels with computer based memory in Chapter 8 that might lead one down that particular bunny trail.

*Cognition* is the term applied to the acquisition and interpretation of knowledge. Not just the reception of and reflexive reaction to various physical stimuli, but the integration and correlation of various sensory inputs to derive an understanding of the cause of the physical stimuli and the synthesis of a response appropriate to this comprehensive understanding. In considering Maslow's hierarchy of needs in the previous chapter, one might in general view that the deficiency needs primarily drive reflexive responses to stimuli, while the growth needs drive cognitive responses.

It is the cognitive systems of the brain that truly set modern man apart from his hominid precursors. The cognitive ability to think about the world observed through the sensory system in an abstract way, and then to influence or control the motor system's response through this abstract thought, offers humans the capability to not just be reactive to the world, but proactive as well.

Structures and mechanisms made available by the brain and the complementary nervous systems facilitate the cognitive processes of the mind. Many areas of the brain are pre-ordained from the time of their construction to fulfill certain functions in the cognitive process.

In the early 1990's, a research team at the University of Parma in Parma, Italy, headed by Giocomo Rizzolatti, discovered a class of neurons and neuron structures that would appear to provide a hard, physical basis for the brain's ability to deal with contextual situations of complex stimuli along with the induced actions or reactions taken in response. While the exact sequence of events leading to their discovery may actually be more mundane, the urban legend tale of the discovery of mirror neurons is illustrative of one of those serendipitous occurrences of research. In an experiment designed to observe the behavior of a primate during various acts of stimulation, for example the stimulation of certain areas of a monkey's brain while eating an ice cream cone, it was subsequently discovered that these subject areas of the brain of the test animal also exhibited the same stimulation when observing a lab technician eating an ice cream cone. The conjecture was that specific neurons or more likely collections of neurons forming specific neural networks within the brain are trained to represent a specific activity context. These neurons or neuron collectives then present an expression and understanding of the stimuli and the expected response actions when this activity, associated with this context, is observed in oneself or other individuals. In essence, our sensori-motor experiences build a contextual representation of activity in such a way as to allow us to internalize our understanding of the actions and reactions within the context of that activity when we perceive it in ourselves or in other individuals.

Subsequent studies by the University of Parma team, and by other researchers, such as discussed in the November, 2006, Scientific American article *Mirrors in the Mind* by Giacomo Rizzolatti, Leonardo Fogassi and Vittorio Gallese, have shown that mirror neuron comprehension extends to emotional as well as physical responses when stimulated by various, sometimes subtle sensory input. They observed that seeing a look of disgust on another's face as they smell a distasteful odor evoked a similar feeling of disgust within us. As suggested in the article, a man, upon seeing a fleeting smile on the face of his lady friend as she picks a flower, enables him to quickly surmise that the flower will be given to him. The very powerful result from this particular wiring in our brains allows us to quickly, almost effortlessly, establish a context for sensory stimuli based on our individual experiences, and from that context determine a likely and appropriate response when we observe activities within this context in others, and, naturally, vice-versa. To link this back to the central theme of this book, this would appear to be a biophysical mechanism through which our minds can quickly establish trust in the interpretation of an interaction onset and the subsequent determination and application of policy to effect this interaction. In particular, by understanding the levels of trust derived from our own experiences we can project that trust to interactions involving others.

We observe an interesting parallel between mirror neurons and the basic concepts of a technology found within the computing world called *object-oriented programming*. During the earliest days of computers, there existed something of a dichotomy between data (information) and procedural processing. The two concepts were viewed independently and consequently required a significant amount of attention within computing systems to establish a coherent context that related data to the appropriate processing. In the early 1960's, two Norwegians, Ole-Johan Dahl and Kristen Nygaard developed a programming language called Simula that is today considered the first example of an object-oriented language. One of the most basic characteristics of an object-oriented programming language is that data and appropriate actions on that data are combined within a context called an *object* by a process called *encapsulation*. By stimulating an object through an appropriate *action*, sometimes called a *method*, a context appropriate response can be evoked from the object. This is very similar to the apparent operation of mirror neuron structures and, as with object-oriented programming, this allows for rather quick connections of cause and effect of ostensibly generic and tenuously related stimuli.

For example, coming back to the mirror neuron experience of watching someone eating ice cream firing the same neurons that are activated when we eat ice cream ourselves, here is how the computer would perform a similar action. Let's consider the operation of displaying a file on a screen or on a printer. The two actions have in common the part that consists in reading the file and understanding the kind of data it contains. Where they differ is in formatting the data differently for each output device. So we can consider the part of the program that reads and understands files as the mirror neuron part of the operation, just as the sequencing of seizing the ice cream and bringing it to one's mouth is common to both watching and eating the ice cream. The sensori-motor domain is where the experience differs. The computer directs the data to either the screen or the printer, activating those mechanisms. Similarly, in the case of watching the ice cream, we activate our visual mechanisms. In eating the ice cream, we activate our maxillofacial apparatus. The way the computer represents the mirror neuron part of displaying the file is by defining an object encapsulating the actions of reading and understanding the files. The sensori-motor part is made of two different methods on that object, one that directs the result of the actions of reading and understanding a file to a screen, and the other that directs them to a printer.

Earlier, we considered the differences between analog and digital computer systems. The mechanisms pertaining to the dynamic processes of the brain that we've reviewed in this chapter are most likely illustrative of analog processes, i.e. processes that directly reflect the physical phenomena they interpret. On the other hand, digital processes pertaining to computer systems are virtually always time based. The binary bits that form the atomic units of computation of digital computers are generally established by sampling a particular quantity according to some repetitive time interval. In such a mechanism, the amplitude of the quantity is unimportant, as long as two distinct levels can be unambiguously determined. Thus, by sampling the quantity at a systematic time interval, the value of the quantity can be determined and mapped to a value of zero or one; thus, establishing a binary value. We have noted that with neuron functions, the state of the neuron can behave somewhat digitally in that once a neuron fires, at some future time the neuron will be reset back to a stable state, waiting for another stimulus to cause it to fire again. However, unlike a purely digital system, the various reset functions found within the nervous and other systems fire and reset on varying time intervals; in the computer world we would say asynchronously. In fact, within the brain time *per se* is not the independent variable in most cases.

Rather, the intervals are generally determined by levels of various chemical factors, which may increase or diminish at varying rates, so they are only qualitatively based on time. Thus, in order to identify true digital mechanisms within the body, it would seem necessary to identify pure time based processes. In fact, are there any such processes?

Well, the cognitive ability of the mind to perceive the passage of time derives almost completely from the sensori-motor experience, not from some well regulated clock circuit as it is in a digital computer. That is, the mind understands the passage of time through relating the temporal extent of previous, particularly repeated, episodes. The passage of five minutes is how long it took to accomplish a particular activity. The sensori-motor experience can be extremely subtle, like the sensitivity to fine clues in the environment that make us wake up the day of the exam just one minute ahead of the alarm clock. If presented with an environment in which external stimuli are greatly reduced, then one's ability to accurately comprehend the passage of time, at least at a fine-grained level, is severely diminished. For example, when placed in a state of severe sensory deprivation, a person's cognitive perceptions of reality can be greatly altered. This effect can be so extreme as to actually be considered *torture* in certain situations.

Depriving a person of sleep for a long period of time has been used to extract confessions to crimes, sometimes totally fabricated confessions. Removing routine temporal markers such as light and dark or manipulating environmental factors are techniques that have also been used to induce stress in prisoners. The bottom line is that there are few direct relationships between cognitive processes and an abstract determination of time. Rather, most actions and reactions of the body derive for indirect associations with time. At a very basic sub-cognitive level, there are recognized, repetitive sequences that drive many processes within the body; one such mechanism being the *circadian rhythm*, a term that derives from the Latin and means around a day. However, the study of the association of basic biological processes with an abstract concept of time (*chronobiology*) has not established associations that would offer the quantitative periodicity of digital biological processes, at least at a fine grained level.

Finally, in our cursory review of the facilities of the mind, we turn our attention to *emotion*. Emotions are a reflection in the mind of the cumulative effects of sensory inputs; in essence, the emotions provide a value judgment of the net effect of the contextual integration of sensory input. Klaus Scherer, in *The Nature of Emotions* (edited by Paul Ekman and Richard Davidson), suggests that emotions lay between sensory input and response output. In effect, emotions present an assessment of the timeframe within which a person's motor system must respond to sensory input. If one hears a loud noise nearby, we may jump if our emotions tell us we have to respond quickly. If we stand beside the road and hear the distant sound of an approaching car then we cognitively formulate the more leisurely response of moving a bit further off the road and turning to watch the car as it passes, because our emotions did not put a stamp of urgency on the response. We interpret this line of reasoning to suggest that emotions can be related to the needs hierarchy; and, through this relationship, they can affect action stimuli ranging from the near reflexive to the cognitively derived. At the most basic, emotions seem directly tied to the appetites that form the stimuli related to needs. Thus, emotion is a moderator to the impetus provided by the brain to enable action by the body. The stimuli provided by emotions range from just beyond instinctive reflex responses to conscious, premeditated action. Scherer also observes that in a situation that is so urgent there is little time for what he terms ego-involvement. The mind is forced to resort to what he calls the *wisdom of the body* to effect a response stimulus. It would seem to us that the mirror neuron structures that we reviewed a bit earlier, with their facility for context-based metaphorical comprehension encompassing both emotional assessment and cognition-based action response stimulation, suggest an appropriate mechanism for effecting this *wisdom of the body*. We certainly can not demonstrate such a connection. We're simply observing that the description of the mirror neuron facility from the literature seems to match well with the noted function.

At the instinctive end of the emotion spectrum are the appetites for air, water and food. Given the varying time frames that drive these basic, physiological needs, the emotions derived from each range in intensity. When deprived of air for a few seconds, or at most tens of seconds, a strong emotional response ensues; if an individual does not directly control a release of the deprivation, then it will likely reach a panic state in a very short order. When faced with the lack of water, being driven by a longer time-frame need, the mind will instill an emotion of mild desire which, if unfulfilled for many hours, or extending into a day or two, will reach a state of near irrationality, again a state made stronger if a person does not directly control the means to quench the thirst. The need for food, based on an even longer time frame, evokes a range of emotions that begins with a mild hunger after a few hours and that progresses to ever-stronger desires after days have passed. Of course, literally not knowing where your next meal is coming from induces a very different emotional response from suffering hunger pangs from being on a restricted diet. At all levels, the stimulus of emotions is subject to progressive learning by the higher cognitive functions of the mind. A point to keep in mind, of course, is that the emotions, derived to a large extent from cognitive processes, provide a degree of controlled access to the autonomic nervous system. At this level, the body actually can't tell the difference between a lack of food due to starvation and being on a restricted diet.

If one is deprived of air unexpectedly, then an irrational response may ensue. People who are trained to act in high stress situations, however, can learn to override their instinctive emotional stimuli and proceed through various, ordered alternative approaches to rectifying the situation. For example, military training may entail going into a closed room filled with tear gas and being ordered to remove a gas mask. The goal of the training is to instill an appreciation for how long one can act rationally in the face of the debilitating gas and the benefit of acting in a rational manner to relieve the situation. Similar training is used for other stress inducing environments: sleep deprivation, cold or hot environments, and the like.

Emotions derive from the limbic system of the human midbrain. As we will see in a bit more detail in Chapter 8, this particular system of the vertebrate brain has evolved in the progression of reptiles to mammals. Various levels of emotional response are an evolutionary enhancement of mammals particularly suited to the development of a strong bond between parent and infant in order to insure care for the infant while it is at its most vulnerable stage.

# Sustenance for the Body

The provision of energy to drive the life engine of living material has evolved to keep pace with the complexity of the organisms that have resulted from the interplay of the earth's physical ecosystem. At the most basic level, in order to support the replication of the DNA molecule, sufficient excess energy must be present in the material that surrounds the initial parent DNA. This energy exists in the form of chemical compounds in a state suitable for extraction to support first the cell replication process and then the sensory and motor functions that each cell performs.

Human physiology supports two distinct macroscopically observable systems through which cells can obtain the necessary energy to procreate and to operate. These are termed the aerobic and the anaerobic systems and they work very much in concert with the body's response system to threats. Specifically, the anaerobic system provides a very rapidly metabolized energy source that can support a high rate of physical activity for a relatively short period of time, perhaps 30-45 seconds or so. The aerobic system, on the other hand, provides a much longer term energy supply for the body's activities, but one that requires a longer time to bring up to peak performance. Subsequently, its peak performance level is then suited to keeping the body operating at an elevated, but not peak, performance level for a much longer period of time. The aerobic system is the energy system that drives the body during routine activities. It is a highly throttleable system. In sports terms, the anaerobic system is for sprinters while the aerobic system is for long distance runners. There's an interesting anecdote that well illustrates the distinct characteristics and value of these two energy systems.

The sport of competitive swimming is very much about building the body's energy systems to peak performance levels and then optimizing the actual swimming of races to make the best use of all the energy available to the swimmer. At the 1988 Summer Olympics in Seoul, Korea, the swimmers Daichi Suzuki (Japan) and David Berkoff (USA) made use of a startling new starting technique in the 100 M backstroke event. Berkoff swam 33 meters of the first 50-meter lap completely underwater using only a dolphin kick, surfacing just before the turn, far ahead of his competition. Suzuki, who actually won the race, used the underwater kick for only a slightly shorter distance at the start of the race and following each turn. This technique was very effective in improving the times of both swimmers due to two effects: (a) an underwater kick of this length makes use almost exclusively of the body's anaerobic energy system while during the remainder of the race they utilized their aerobic energy systems, meaning that by the end of the race, the swimmers had expended the maximum amount of their bodies' available energy; they didn't bring anything back to the wall with them, and (b) the underwater dolphin kick is much more powerful than the often used flutter kick at the start and turns of a backstroke race, so the longer it can be maintained, the faster the swimmer goes and the greater time advantage the swimmer has. This tactical approach to the race was termed the Berkoff Blastoff after its originator. However, the approach made such a dramatic change in the appearance and times of the backstroke event that the rules for the stroke were changed shortly after the Olympic Games to limit the swimmers to a 10 meters distance at the start, and at each turn, before they are required to surface and actually swim the backstroke. This distance was increased to 15 meters in later years.

The basic energy store found within every cell is comprised of molecules of adenosine triphosphate, or ATP. ATP functions like a battery, storing energy in the form of phosphate radicals when surplus energy is available and releasing energy in the form of these same phosphate radicals when the cell requires energy. The trigger for the release of energy within the cell is the enzyme ATP synthase. The ATP molecule itself is comprised of a sugar molecule (ribose), a nucleic acid base (adenine) and three phosphate groups. The energy required for cell processes is actually derived from the phosphate groups. Under control of the ATP synthase enzyme, one or more of the phosphate groups are stripped from the ATP molecule in a reaction that leaves adenosine diphosphate. If there is not an immediate energy requirement signaled by the enzyme, then any available food such as phosphate-creatine and muscle glycogen, or sunlight in the case of plants, is used to manufacture ATP from the adenosine diphosphate available in the cell. Photophosphorylation is the process used by plants and oxidative phosphorylation is used within animal cells. This is all part of the chemiosmotic theory of cellular energy process, with Peter Mitchell receiving a Nobel Prize in 1978 for his original formulation. The discovery of the detailed workings of the ATP molecule subsequently earned the Nobel Prize in 1997 for three researchers: John Walker from Cambridge University in the United Kingdom, Paul Boyer from the University of California at Los Angeles in the United States and Jens Skou from Aarhus University in Denmark.

Under stress, the base ATP store can supply the cell with energy for up to perhaps 10 seconds. After that time, the primary anaerobic system kicks in deriving more energy from muscle-stored glycogen. This process lags by a few seconds because it requires inter-cell transfer of glycogen. The muscles can store enough glycogen to meet the body's cellular requirements for several tens of seconds. This anaerobic system creates significant byproducts in the form of lactate and hydrogen ions. Saturation of the tissue with hydrogen ions then limits the continuation of the operation of the anaerobic system. Depending on the capabilities of the circulatory system, the hydrogen ions and lactate will either be removed from the muscle or will be stored within the muscle in the form of lactic acid; this latter mechanism being what causes the muscles to be sore after an unusual amount of strenuous activity.

Of course, physical activity of the body generally requires an energy system that will function continuously over a much longer time period than a minute or two. This is the domain of the aerobic system. At the base cellular level, this system still works through the short term storage and retrieval of energy using the ATP molecule. However, the aerobic system draws fatty acids from adipose tissue found beneath the skin and around internal organs within the body. When excess food is taken in to the body, the amount beyond what is needed for current organic processes can be stored as fat within this tissue. When operational demands of the body exceed that found in local stores within individual cells and muscle tissue, the aerobic system responds by conveying the fatty acids to the cells where it is used to continually replenish the supply of ATP. The aerobic system is limited by the amount of stored body fat, but in most instances it can support the body's operations for days and longer.

The body requires a continuing supply of several materials in order for it to continue operating (living). The most urgently required such materials are air, food and water. Food encompasses a significant range of materials in its own right due to the many systems within the body, many of which require very specific materials for their continued operation. For most of the required materials, there is a sensory feedback mechanism through the brain that indicates deficiencies whenever there is a shortage. The dominant of these indicators are hunger, thirst and a feeling of suffocation, indicating respectively, of course, a lack of sufficient food, water or air. If we consider these indicators in terms of the needs hierarchy, then these needs reflect physiological requirements of the body. At this level, it is difficult to differentiate the specific indicator from an emotional state on the part of the person. Beyond these primary indicators, the mind will sometimes evoke cravings, specifically regarding food, that indicate mounting deficiencies in very specific substances needed by the body. Such cravings for things sweet, sour, salty or bitter are indicators of deficiencies of various minerals that are needed by the body.

The central gut gives rise to the alimentary canal, the basis of the digestive tract that provides for the processing of raw food materials into a form suitable for storage and use within the body. Much like the reduction of base ore into finished metal, the digestive process involves first mechanical deconstruction of raw foodstuffs through mastication (chewing) and preliminary chemical breakdown by saliva within the mouth. Then, the food is transported to the stomach and the intestines where further chemical breakdown reduces all foods to a variety of chemical components, primarily sugars and lipids that can be directly used by the body or stored for later use. As we noted in the brief consideration of the aerobic and anaerobic energy systems, the human body makes use of several distinct energy provision systems in order to meet its requirements for the necessary materials. As have many other species, humans have developed an ability to store excess food internally within the body in the form of fat. This capability allows for significant decoupling of the acquisition and subsequent use of the various forms of sustenance needed by the body. As we alluded in Chapter 2, variations on this storage and retrieval facility are likely the subjects of an ongoing appraisal through multi-level natural selection.

In the physical environment, a significant premium is due to individuals of the primate species that can react well to real and perceived threats. For the hominids, which do not have a lot of inherent passive defensive or offensive mechanisms at their disposal, the ability to respond quickly and decisively to stressful situations is quite beneficial. Consequently, a foundational characteristic of the species was recognized by Hans Selye as the *fight or flight response* to stress. He published a 1946 paper describing the *general adaptation syndrome*, of which the fight or flight response is essentially the first stage, in the *Journal of Clinical Endocrinology*. When presented with what may become a life or death situation, the human body undergoes an almost instantaneous set of physiological changes that prepare it either for battle or for a mad dash away from danger. In parallel with these physiological responses, the mind forms an emotion modulated cognitive response based on a contextual appraisal of the specific sensory stimuli, which answers the rather profound question, "Do I run or do I fight?" The answer can well determine the continuation of the person. Winston Churchill's famous remark comes to mind, "There's nothing quite so exhilarating as to be shot at without effect!" To engage the fight or flight response is to place a number of exclamation points after the need to determine an action stimulus based on sensory input.

In response, many of the body's physiological changes are internal. Blood vessels constrict in certain areas in order to essentially shut down non-essential organs such as the kidneys and the digestive tract. Sensory awareness is heightened, the heart and lungs kick into high gear, ready to support extremely increased physical activity. Glucose stored in the liver is released into the blood stream to provide an intermediate term energy boost, while epinephrine and endorphins are released to first stimulate immediate physical capability and second to diminish the body's reaction to pain that may result from ongoing combat.

These latter two materials are actually neurotransmitters. They function at the synaptic chemistry level of the body's nervous system. In essence, they change the impedance and amplification characteristics of the many different neuron circuits through which sensory stimuli are received, the cognitive facilities through which they are analyzed and the motor system through which the body's response is channeled. In situations of severe stress, we see and hear better, we think faster and we become stronger and faster. We also tend to wet our pants, a reaction that lightens us up a bit and might also, in our native condition, surprise a predator that attacks us. In more modern combat, it's a small price to pay if bullets are evaded.

In order to acquire the necessary sustenance, evolution has molded the body to enhance the process based on the environment. Within the *animalia* kingdom, only two phyla possess articulated skeletons that provide shape and structural support for the individual members of their various species: *arthropoda*, including insects and lobsters, and *chordata*, which includes all the vertebrate species. Articulation of the skeleton indicates that the various structural components of the individual skeleton meet at various points called joints. Joints allow different parts of the skeleton to move relative to other points. This structure establishes a common form for all the members of a specific species and it also provides for mobility of the entities.

Arthropods possess an exoskeleton. That is, the skeleton is comprised of a strong shell that forms the outer boundary of the individual. Muscles, or other mechanisms that induce movement, are present within this skeletal boundary. Typically, an exoskeleton provides protection along with the other characteristics provided by skeletons. From an evolutionary standpoint, exoskeletons tend to limit the size of individuals that can develop within the typical physical ecosystem. Conversely, the endoskeletal form of the vertebrates tends to facilitate a number of the physical characteristics that enhance the evolutionary prospects of all species within the phylum in general, and Homo sapiens specifically.

An internal skeleton is one of the hallmarks of the vertebrates. An internal skeleton, specifically of all mammalians, is composed of bones, which are, in turn, comprised of an organic and an inorganic component. The inorganic component is primarily calcium phosphate. Bone provides an excellent structural component for the body. Its internal structure provides a superior strength per mass ratio, meaning that bone provides support for the body without increasing its weight too much. Bone provides the mechanical component of the body which, when coupled with musculature, provides mobility or motor facilities. Structurally, endoskeletons offer superior support characteristics compared to exoskeletons, allowing the body of the individual to grow bigger without incurring as many liabilities due to increased weight. Exoskeletons, on the other hand, provide significant safety and security benefits by providing protection to sensitive organic material contained within the external skeleton and thus shielded from predatory or other physical threats. The internal skeleton of the human body provides support for the full sensori-motor systems that are suspended from it as well as enhanced mobility that improves the survival characteristics of the species.

While noting that the defining feature of the vertebrates is the internal skeletal structure, it is also interesting to observe that two of the skeleton's primary features, the skull and the spinal column, actually function in an exoskeletal manner: the skull protects the brain and the spinal column protects and supports the primary central nerve that traverses the body of all species within the phylum *chordata*. These structures certainly manifest themselves within the primates. First, let us consider the spine.

The spinal column is composed of thirty-three short segments of bone called vertebrae, which are tied together in a stable, but highly flexible structure. Between each pair of adjoining vertebrae is an intervertebral disc made of cartilaginous material that serves both to hold the vertebrae together and to provide a flexible joint that allows the two vertebrae to move relative to each other, albeit in a highly constrained manner. The spinal column contains within it the main nerve, the *spinal cord* that emanates from the brainstem within the skull of the individual and descends through the abdomen. It terminates in the bony structure called the *coccyx*, which is a vestige in humans of the prehensile tail that exists in the lower primates and in other vertebrate species.

Vertebrate species generally derive a facility for independent movement from their four appendages tipped with phalangeal mechanisms and from the tip of the vertebrae skeletal feature; that is, from the development in many species of the feature called the *tail*. The motor (or muscular) sub-system of the body provides the propulsive force that allows the individual the freedom to move relative to its surrounding environment. Such movement enhances the ability of the individual to obtain sustenance. The range and speed of movement varies tremendously across the vertebrate species; from the slow crawling turtles and sloths to the highflying eagles and condors.

Mobility of the human body certainly has a significant impact on the ability of the species to both control its environment and to compete with other species. Mobility allows humans to escape from the heat or the cold by migrating to more moderate climes, and it allows people to avoid predators and to conquer prey. Mobility also translates into an extremely expanded set of metaphorical contexts for the human cognitive systems to understand and portray through actions and language. The motor system of the body is driven by muscles.

Muscles are comprised of cells that are able to contract when stimulated by the nervous system. There are three general types of muscle found in the human body: heart muscle, smooth muscle and striated muscle. Heart muscle is unique to the heart and smooth muscles form the various involuntary muscles of most organs. Striated muscles form the voluntary muscles that provide mobility to the skeleton. These muscles are linked to bones by tissues called *tendons*. Most of the movable portions of the skeletal arrangement have muscles arranged in opposition to each other across a joint; a configuration termed an antagonistic muscle pair. Consider for example that the arm can flex back and forth at the elbow joint. One muscle called the *biceps* connects the bones in the shoulder with the small bone in the forearm, the *radius*. A separate muscle, the *triceps*, located on what we typically view as the backside or underside of the arm connects the large bone in the upper arm, the *humerus*, with the large bone in the forearm, the *ulna*. Thus, the biceps and the triceps form an antagonistic pair. Muscles only exert force when they contract, so when the triceps contracts, the lower arm is extended away from the body. When the biceps muscle contracts it moves the forearm back toward the body. Similar muscle arrangements are found in virtually all moveable sections of the body.

It's interesting to consider why expansion muscle tissue hasn't developed through evolutionary processes. Perhaps it is for the same reason that it is hard to work with a rope by pushing on it. Highly directional extension processes typically require hydraulic operations which in turn tend to require rigid, yet extensible structures. Short of organic growth through cell division, it is difficult to identify any such processes in nature.

The control pathway for muscles consists of a direct motor neuron to muscle connection through a specialized variant of a synapse termed a *neuromuscular junction*. The motor neuron that comprises the pre-synaptic neuron of this junction, when its action potential is stimulated, emits the neurotransmitter *acetylcholine*. This neurotransmitter causes the muscle cells to contract. Following the contraction, the junction is reset when the enzyme *acetylcholinesterase* breaks down the acetylcholine. Without this resetting operation, the muscle would continue to contract. Repetitive activation of a stiated muscle tends to stimulate the growth of muscle mass and to enhance the efficiency of the contraction and reset mechanisms. Thus, an illustration of the concept of training or conditioning. Metaphorically similar is the concept of programming and teaching; an athlete programs her muscles in practice to move in a strict manner when swimming the butterfly stroke in competition during a swim meet. When the race starts, the body must function on learned behaviors.

The ability to walk erect on two legs is viewed as one of the major evolutionary changes that differentiate the human species from its more primitive primate ancestors. Using only two limbs for mobility leaves the arms and hands free for the creation and use of tools; particularly, ever more complex tools. In essence, by walking erect the human body is able to devote much more of the upper appendages to tool making and use.

The use of only two legs for mobility also offers the significant benefit of allowing the head, with its all important eyes, ears and brain to be positioned higher off the ground. The eyes and ears are obviously positioned so that they provide a superior longer-range sensory capability, and the brain is positioned in such a manner that it allows the rest of the body to protect it.

As we noted earlier, virtually all motor processes within the human body make use of opposing actuators that drive the particular movable element in opposite directions. The element, whatever it might be, arm, hand, finger, thumb, foot, etc. is essentially in a position of unstable equilibrium such that it requires a positive driving force to maintain a stable position. Otherwise, when any type of force is applied to the element, the element moves at the whim of the external force.

Coupled with antagonistic control mechanisms, the body's motor control also benefits from the sense of touch in providing tactile feedback to operations with the movable portions of the body. This allows a person to firmly grasp a tool or weapon in order to wield it with force and to also handle delicate objects or structures like infants or eggs.

Most joints in the human body consist of bones held in a fixed but flexible position by strong connective tissue. When coupled with the antagonistic muscle arrangements described above, a great deal of flexibility of position is achieved. Various appendages can bend and, to a certain extent, rotate about various axes. The spine provides the ability for the trunk of the body to bend and to rotate, which allows the upper torso to be positioned at a variety of angles relative to the legs. The same flexibility in the neck allows the head to rotate relative to the rest of the upper body. This particular capability allows the two main long distance sensors of the body, the eyes and ears, to be easily positioned to different attitudes, which in turn enhances the ability of a person to locate and track various threats. Moreover, this ability to reposition the body's sensors offers the prospect of enhanced cognitive processing of the basic sensor data, and through this processing to develop a better sense of depth perception for visual input and directionality for auditory input. A perhaps more significant facility enabled by the flexibility of the skeletal form is the ability for detailed manipulation of objects.

The arm and wrist can rotate, allowing the hand to manipulate things away from the body as well as things on or of the body. One of the more intriguing anatomical features of the primates is the construction of the hand; specifically, the profound roles of the opposing thumb. No other mechanism in the animal kingdom can offer the same agility in holding and positioning objects. With metaphors building upon the sensori-motor experiences, advanced manipulation capabilities lead to high capacities of abstraction. Geometry, kinematics and topology come to mind; this subject has been extensively studied by George Lakoff and Rafael Núñez in *Where Mathematics Come From*.

# Sustenance for the Mind

Organic life exists within a domain where a collection of physical rules or laws applies. All interactions among members of different species adhere to these physical rules. The human species, like many others, has evolved a variety of mechanisms through which it interacts with the physical world; a collection of mechanisms termed the senses. Within the mechanical world, the senses would generally be characterized as transducers whose purpose is to take purely physical stimuli and convert these impulses into an energy form that can be processed by the central processing unit. Perhaps more appropriately stated for the human body, the stimulus of physical interactions is converted through various senses into impulses that can be transmitted through the nervous system to the brain, where they become the fodder for subconscious and conscious thought processes. Computer systems can have analogues to the senses possessed by humans, and then some.

The parallels between sensory input to the brain and input channels to computers offer some insight into the means that each processing system has for establishing its physical and logical position within the world around it; its context if you will. In general, each system must make use of this input as foundation information that it can use for the subsequent formulation and application of relevant policy in various situations. Ostensibly, it is through this information that each system can perceive the evidence of information applicable to its respective hierarchy of needs.

Over the period of the evolutionary development of life on the earth, the principle sources of light have been direct sunlight, reflected sunlight (moonlight) and fire. In certain instances, photoluminescent sources might have provided small amounts of light, but probably not sufficient to impact the development of *sight* in the form of light sensory organs in land based, surface organisms. That portion of the electromagnetic spectrum that comprises visible light is a small frequency band for which sensors have evolved in a number of species. These light sensors vary in the intensity levels that they can detect and in the specific frequencies that they can resolve. Bordering the band of visible light frequencies are infrared (lower frequencies than visible light) and ultraviolet (higher frequencies than visible light). In fact, certain species can see better at the lower frequencies; essentially they are able to discern the heat radiated by other living creatures. This is a particularly useful trait for creatures that interact with their world nocturnally.

The first prototypical eyes in the vertebrate lineage may have emerged over 500 millions years ago. This form of eye was the first capable of rendering an actual image of the field of vision. This capability, at virtually any level of acuity, would have presented a serious mutational event in the balance between predators and prey. The survival of members of a species in the respective food chains likely depended on their developing comparable or superior visual function, unless the entire area of such detection was rendered far less important by other characteristics such as natural camouflage, perhaps through color variations.

The eyes comprise an optical sensor that is able to take light within the wavelength range of 4,000 to 8,000 angstrom units and convert it into a continuous signal stream through the optic nerve directly into the brain. This is an extremely high bandwidth channel and the brain has highly developed sections that can receive and interpret the information from this channel, and subsequently make use of it in the form of image perceptions within the brain. Each eye has a series of mechanical elements used for collection of light and focusing it on a plane of receptor sensors within the retina. These sensors, a collection of differentiated cells termed rods and cones, translate light into stimuli applied directly to the optic nerve. A single rod can detect a single photon, and fire an impulse upon reception that is conveyed to the brain.

Eyes to the front of the head improve depth and motion perception over a limited field of view, oriented toward the front of the individual. This is superior eye placement for animal predators. On the other hand, eye placement for species that rather naturally form the prey for such predators is usually to the side of the head, offering the widest area of vision to both the front and back of the animal.

The physical ecosystem in which the human species finds itself includes a mechanism for interaction at a distance through a process of induced pressure waves in our surrounding medium; a mechanism that we call sound. Sound is a mechanical process. It is generated by a mechanism capable of creating a sharp gradient in the density of a material. A membrane vibrating in air can render a sinusoidally repeating pattern of pressure waves, a constant frequency wave train: a middle C on an oboe for instance. Instantaneously raising the temperature of some medium by a large amount can create an impulse wave train that moderates through the propagation of an expanding, spherical wave front in the atmosphere; hence the thunder follows the lightning. We can postulate an answer to the age-old question, "If a tree falls in the forest with no one around to hear it, does it make a sound?" The answer is, "Yes, because people have ears." The sound existed before the ears did; the ears exist because the sound already did.

Human *hearing* is a rather complex example of a mechanical to electro-chemical transducer; complex at least with respect to other mechanical assemblies found within the human body. The sense of hearing encompasses the three divisions of the ear system: the outer ear, the middle ear and the inner ear. Sound waves are first detected and collected by the mechanical assembly of the outer ear. This assembly includes the fleshy, external ear (the auricle) located on the side of the head. The assembly acts as an acoustic wave-guide to focus externally generated sound waves (i.e. pressure waves in the atmosphere) into the ear canal where they encounter the tympanic membrane, more commonly called the eardrum that forms the boundary of the middle ear. The eardrum is connected via a fluid filled channel to an assembly of very small bones whose movement is modulated by the membrane's movements. Deep within the inner ear, the vibrations propagated through a fluid filled passage finally encounter a collection of hair cells that convert the mechanical vibration into a nerve impulse that is then conveyed to the brain.

The sense of *touch* is a very short-range facility; to be activated there must be physical contact between the impinging object and the human body. In our previous considerations of the basic forces through which physical entities interact, we alluded to the fact that physical contact in fact derives from the electromagnetic force. Two entities never actually achieve contact in the sense that a part of an atom from one physical entity directly coincides in space with a part of an atom from a different entity. Rather, the atoms which make up the different entities come in close enough proximity that the electromagnetic forces derived from the electron cloud of the atoms of one entity strongly interacts with, and actually repel, the electron cloud of the atoms of the other entity. If one entity is driven by its skeletal motor system toward a different entity, then the strength of this electromagnetic repulsion is converted through nerve endings into impulses that make their way to the brain. The result, insofar as the brain is concerned, is the recognition of a sensation of touch.

Earlier in this chapter we commented briefly on the three macroscopically observable mechanisms for physical interactions based on the electromagnetic force: conduction, convection and radiation. Two of the basic human senses, those of *smell* and of *taste*, make use of chemical reactions in their respective sensors. Consequently, these senses actually make use of the conduction mechanism. The odor of some object derives from the emission of particles from the object that are conveyed to the olfactory sensory organs within the nasal passages of a person. These particles are typically molecular emissions from the source object. Once conveyed into the nasal passages, these molecular components encounter organic olfactory sensors with a material on their surface into which the components dissolve.

The sense of smell is important to the human species, but is a bit less developed than is the case for other mammals. For example, the human nose contains approximately 40 million olfactory sensors, compared to approximately 100 million for rabbits and 1 billion for dogs. As one might expect from these numbers, the sense of smell is far more important to dogs as they cope with their physical environment than is the case for humans. It's interesting to note the comparison between rabbits and dogs, since one might assume the rabbit to be prey for the dog. Were it not for hearing, as reflected in the relative size of the ears, rabbits might be at a distinct disadvantage. Actually, they probably are; it is just that rabbits compensate by reproducing like, well, rabbits.

Taste, like smell, is another sense based on a chemical analysis of material carried from the thing we taste to the taste sensors, small entities found primarily on the tongue. In general, the taste material is comprised of food that has been placed in the mouth, physically broken into smaller components through chewing with the teeth and partially dissolved in saliva. The taste sensors are termed taste buds and are on the order of 10 microns in diameter. The tongue holds approximately 90% of the 10,000 or so taste buds found within the mouth of a normal human.

The sense of taste is rather comparable to the sense of smell and, in fact, the two work in concert. More specifically, the sense of smell has a strong influence on the sense of taste. How something smells is reflected in how it tastes. While the sense of smell can help in the recognition of things at a distance, when coupled with the sense of taste the goal would seem to be the determination of whether something should actually be ingested. Things that our digestive system is going to find impossible to handle, such as decaying material, can generally be detected sufficiently in advance to avoid actually swallowing them. While they may leave a bad taste in our mouths, we at least have the opportunity to dispel them from our mouths and avoid becoming ill, or worse.

An extremely important sense for humans, especially for their mobility, is the detection of *balance*. It derives from sensory input from the inner ear, from the eyes and perhaps other senses as well. As a composite of these various sensory inputs, it provides to the brain an indicator of orientation of the body. Based on this input, the brain can discern whether the body is positioned upright or is perhaps in a prone position, or somewhere in between. This sense is extremely important to the human sensori-motor experience that establishes the metaphorical basis of our understanding of the world around us. We prefer an up market and we don't like to feel down.

Other human senses that are sometimes identified reflect in fact the disconnection that can occur between certain aspects of our cognitive functions and our sensori-motor system. Specifically, when we encounter certain mental states, we seek causality for those states outside of our sensori-motor system. One such aspect of this is termed *extra-sensory perception*. Some people will insist that they have a facility for anticipating the occurrence of physical events, sometimes referred to as pre-cognition. Others claim the ability to cause movement of disconnected objects, termed *telekinesis*. Such events, while seeming to lack physical cause, fit within the foundations of religious systems that we will begin to consider in the next chapter.

Throughout the course of its evolutionary progression, *Homo sapiens* has continually benefited from a capability for its constituent members to act in concert. The search for sustenance for the mind and body is a significant impetus for such collective action. While this capability exists within other social species, it is more limited in size and scope. One can speculate that the reason for this limitation is due to the mechanisms through which members of the species interact with one another. As the members of any species become more dispersed, physically, the means of interaction become problematic at best. The basic facility that enables humans to thrive in the face of physical diaspora is the multi-faceted means of *communication* that the species has evolved.

Humans communicate with others of their kind through all of the sensory channels that we've considered above. In their most basic forms, these various channels are used in low bandwidth modes; that is, they convey information at a much lower rate than the respective channels are actually capable of handling. For example, communication via sight consists primarily of signaling and observation of actions or events, until more sophisticated mechanisms like, say, hand gestures, are instituted using the sight input/output channel.

Language is the critical element in the establishment of extended groups of humans, providing as it does a mechanism through which individuals within the group can communicate in complex concepts and can communicate across time and space. Language is a means of communication, between people, machines, and between people and machines. Languages are traditionally split in two categories: natural languages, which are typically learned by all children early in life, and formal languages, which are learned later, typically at school and university, for many purposes such as mathematics and computer programming. Natural language is by no means the only natural way of communication between people. Babies communicate via gestures and mimicking long before their first word, and they absorb interpersonal communication in various forms of play and representations, such as dancing, long after their first word.

All forms of communication involve sensori-motor activities. For language, sound is the first medium of transmission, later followed by writing in many societies. Even there, language is not' unique; music is a communication mechanism based on sound, and painting is a communication mechanism based on graphical representation.

As presented for example by Michael Tomasello in *Constructing a Language*, hearing children learn language by associating social situations with sequences of sound that progressively allow them to designate objects, and actions on these objects, in ways that affect the situations in directions of their choice ("Mamma, bring bear!"). As presented by David McNeill in *Hand and Mind*, deaf children do the same with sequences of signs. As children grow up, situations become more involved, and so does their use of language, building up from sensori-motor actuations to abstract considerations (from "I see the bear" to "I see your point").

Technically, the description of spoken languages starts with sounds (phonetics). From sounds are built individual units, called phonemes, that coalesce, for example, all "r" sounds, however they are pronounced, into a single category. One level up in the construction of language, phonemes allow assembly of sounds into morphemes (say "eat" and "-ing"), which in turn are constituents of words ("eating"). Words are built up into sentences according to rules of syntax ("I love eating." is good syntax; "I love eated." is not). Then sentences are assembled into discourse, completing an overall construction of representational logic where all elements contribute their part, together with context interpretation. Meaning eventually refers to the sensori-motor experience. As presented by George Lakoff and Mark Johnson in their seminal *Metaphors We Live By*, "I see the bear!" provides a direct reflection of observable facts, while "I see your point of view." maps back to the sensori-motor experience by building an abstract landscape modeled after a concrete one. The point you see may not exist in the sensori-motor reality, but it follows nevertheless the same construction ("Your points of view are all very close.") via the set process called *metaphor*. Abstract constructs can themselves be assembled into higher meaning by mixing disparate elements into coherent wholes ("Pythagoras retorts to your point via his theorem."). Experiences from different domains can be therefore be elaborated into new information by set mechanisms defining how the mixing operates. This operation, called *blending*, is described in details by Gilles Fauconnier and Mark Turner in *The Way We Think*. From such narratives are established complete stories that can in turn be brought back to the sensori-motor level by inversing the blending and metaphor processes, which is essentially the derivation of mythology.

A formal language is much simpler than a natural language. Whereas the latter has to contend with sounds, phonemes, morphemes, words, sentences and discourses, we can say, rather generally speaking, that formal languages make do with words, sentences and discourses. Whereas an educated person may have a vocabulary of 50,000 words in natural language, a formal language will contain perhaps tens of them. An example of formal language is that of arithmetic. In this language, "2 + 2 = 4" is a sentence, where "2", "+", "=", "4" are words. In fact, this is read as "Two plus two equals four," which we see maps very well with its natural language equivalent.

Another formal language is that of computers. "If x = 2 then stop" is a sentence, where "If", "x", "=", "2", "then", "stop" are words. This reads, "If the variable x equals 2 then stop," again a natural sentence. Now, the main difference of formal languages compared to natural languages is that whereas the latter map to the entire sensori-motor experience of humans, the former maps to a much more restricted domain, reflected in part by the restricted vocabulary, and in part by the restricted set of rules applied when assembling sentences together, that is, the grammar of the language. However, this restricted nature doesn't make formal languages easier to understand than natural ones. Remember, as we've seen, formal languages can actually be made into equivalent subsets of natural language. If the sentence "The integral of x is half the square of x plus a constant" sounds complex to you, it won't make the statement simpler to understand if it is written in a formal way. However, when formal languages are used by computers, instead of humans, the story is different. To a computer, the sensori-motor mapping of the formal language, limited as it is in vocabulary and rules, is, in fact, natural to it, just as our primary sensations are natural to us as humans. For us, those primary sensations don't need explanation since they are just what we are. So what's formal to us, referring to a particular metaphoric mapping of our sensori-motor experience, is, in fact, natural to the computer, referring directly to the computer's sensori-motor capability. Conversely, natural language, which refers to our basic sensori-motor experience, is foreign to computers as long as they have not evolved a sensori-motor apparatus, or a simulation thereof, comparable to ours. But then, that is what this book is all about.

The precursor species to modern man could communicate long before the ability of speech as we know it today evolved. The brain of the archaic Homo erectus may be considered, based on cranial capacity, as possessing the semantic capabilities to support language, but the *vocal* facilities of this particular species may not have been advanced enough mechanically to allow for the nuances of natural language. Perhaps, not until some time before the emergence of Neanderthals did the mechanical configuration of larynx, tongue and throat evolve to support the full range of sounds that allowed natural languages to be spoken. In fact, three distinct systems are required for humans to realize the vocal facilities they currently possess.

First is the mechanism for compressing air and expelling it in a manner capable of vibrating a membrane that can produce sound. Second is the vibrating membrane itself; that is the larynx, a mechanism that sits in the throat of a person in a manner so as to allow air expelled from the lungs to pass over a membrane, the vocal cords, so as to produce a sound. Finally, a throat, mouth and tongue mechanism that can modulate the sounds emitted from the larynx. These mechanisms, in concert, allow the production of sounds that can express the structure of natural languages.

The culmination of natural language came with the advent of *writing*, the facility to express language through symbols which could be imprinted on material and subsequently read back from that material. This brings us to the earliest forms of recorded history of the species, a facility that separates humans from all other species. That is, mankind appears to be the only species that has prepared a permanent visual image of complex thought that can be passed to other members of the species over long distances or over long periods of time.

Finally, we draw your attention to the communication facilities provided through *art*. In our first chapter, we alluded to the use of art as an efficient means of context sensitive communication. Please note that in referring to art, we're referring to the full variety of art forms. Indeed, there are various types that impact on all of the human senses, both individually and collectively. Consider the art of theatre. Certainly, William Shakespeare is generally perceived to be among the greatest artists of this genre. Now, let us look within his play *Henry V* and consider the soliloquy of King Henry to his troops prior to the Battle of Agincourt; a recitation sometimes referred to as the St. Crispin's Day Speech. Through this speech, King Henry instills a higher purpose in his tired and beleaguered army on the eve of battle. His words evoke the loyalty of comradeship on the battlefield even today: "For he today that sheds his blood with me shall be my brother!" This is the conveyance of trust at its most sublime.

Consider it further in a recursive fashion. The words in the script of the play convey one level of trust to the reader. However, a superb actor can use these words to instill in his audience a semblance of the trust that a King, in a further level of recursion, would actually seek to instill in his troops on the eve of battle. This form of communication is at the heart of human groups. This is one of the mechanisms through which the group can instill a moral code within the individual that will engender sacrifice of the one for the benefit of the many. This level of information conveyance is achieved because artistic communication encompasses not only sensory input, but the emotional and cognitive analysis and response to that input. Consequently, we view art as the means by which the artist can convey not only information to the receiver, but trust as well. If we consider this in concert with the needs hierarchy, then the conveyance of trust is perhaps a different facet of the need of aesthetics. It is a need that encompasses cognition and subsequently forms the basis of self-actualization and transcendence.

# Computer Architecture

The early precursors of the computers that we know today were mechanical calculating machines. Adding machines and typewriters are perhaps the most recent examples of such machines, actually co-existing for some period of time with the computing systems that form their superior descendants. Well, superior unless you happen to be on a deserted island with no electricity and you want to write home. In that case, a typewriter, a piece of paper and a bottle might still be superior to a word processing computer. As we've noted before, it is all relative. Anyway, in the early XIX[th] century, Charles Babbage developed the concept of a mechanical calculating machine he termed his *difference engine*. The device was an ingenious assembly of levers and gears of various sizes and connections. Through the selection of the correct gears and their couplings, a sequence of arithmetic operations could be performed with precision and speed relative to the same operations being performed by a person or a group of people. While the concept was intriguing, it really did not represent a mutational leap of performance from arithmetic by hand. He never actually completed work on this device, due a shortage of funds. However, it was completed in the late XX[th] century by a group of scholars interested in confirming that the design was sound. It was.

Babbage's machine is an example of what we might term a very simple algorithmic computer. In this type of machine, variables are somehow entered into or imprinted on the machine and the processing is started. In its functioning, the machine implements a very specific sequence of manipulations, called an *algorithm*, on these initial variables. The algorithm itself is implemented as a sequenced connection of mechanical components, primarily intermeshed gears that have the result of amplifying, diminishing or recombining the initial state information. The device is perhaps more closely the distant ancestor of an automobile's automatic transmission than that of a laptop computer. Nonetheless, it represents a relatively recent foray into automatic computing machines, prior to the mutations necessary to allow the new species of computers to be competitive in a new evolutionary fray.

The concepts of what computers could become pre-dated the evolution of the mutational technologies that actually made computers feasible. These concepts arose as ideas in the minds of prescient thinkers and provided nourishment to the tenuous social ecosystems into which the computers emerged, quite similar to the Christian concept of the word made flesh. The philosophical underpinnings were conceivable even though the means to effect the concepts had not yet arrived. Perhaps the first stone of the foundation was found in the concepts of mathematics.

Recent research, in particular by George Lakoff and Rafael Núñez, in *Where Mathematics Come From*, has revealed the interesting probability that the human capability to deal with mathematics, starting with our ability to distinguish and manipulate numbers, actually derives from our physical motor skills. The theory holds that the capability of the human brain to manipulate numbers follows from our ability to manipulate objects with our hands and feet. From this facility for manipulation of objects, the human brain subsequently extended the ability to also deal with the manipulation of numbers and then with more abstract concepts. This metaphorical capability is also closely aligned with language.

A refinement on the concept of the mechanical computing machine that pushed it more in the direction of today's computers was the definition of the *Turing machine*. In 1936, Alan Turing published a paper, *On computable numbers, with an application to the Entscheidungsproblem*, in which he described a computation process that was directly applicable to what would become stored program computers. Specifically, Turing described a model of computing that was built on the conception of a moving tape divided into cells. Each cell contained the parameters that completely specified a state of the machine. By moving to successive cells, the machine could be made to move from one state to the next state. The tape, in turn, could be written on and moved in both forward and reverse directions. The end result was a completely constrained computational sequence, an incarnation of a finite state machine. As we have noted, the Turing machine pre-dates the computer as we know it today. Its importance was in establishing a model of a computing process. The true precursor to the modern computer was conceptualized by John von Neumann.

John von Neumann was something of a modern renaissance man. He was responsible for world-shaping developments in a number of fields, most notably in mathematics. However, perhaps his most memorable discovery, certainly as far as this book is concerned, was his work in automaton theory and specifically his specification of a self-replicating machine. This machine has an eerie similarity to the operational characteristics of the DNA molecule, together with its supporting infrastructure found in the living cell. What's intriguing about this is the timing; von Neumann's architecture was published almost a decade before Crick and Watson published their discovery of the DNA molecule and its double helix structure. Moreover, after the presentation of the structure of DNA, it was another several decades before the interaction of the molecule with the various protein interactions through which it works became fairly well understood. Only recently has it become moderately well understood how DNA functions as a self-replicating machine in a manner well characterized by von Neumann's specifications.

Von Neumann's self-replicating machine was defined with two parts, each a distinct machine in its own right. The two machines were termed a universal computer and a universal constructor. The purpose of the constructor was to follow a sequence of commands from the computer and, using raw materials at its disposal, construct a perfect replica of itself and of the universal computer. The program from the universal computer (parent) was then loaded into the new computer (child). Thus, the new machine would be instilled with the goal of replicating itself via its program instruction set. Von Neumann enhanced the general definition of the universal computing machine by showing an architecture for such a machine; an architecture that has become a common feature of virtually all computers that we know today.

The von Neumann computer is comprised of a number of discrete elements; a list, if you will, of the simple machines of the computer age. These elements are the *central processing unit*, the *main memory*, the *bulk extended memory* and *input/output units*. All of these are found in virtually all computers today, from supercomputers to the smallest personal electronic devices.

The cognitive center of the electronic computer is the *central processing unit*, often referred to through its acronym of CPU. Most computer programmers tend to anthropomorphize the central processing unit as the center of consciousness of the computer; it is the point where instantaneous thought occurs. Procedurally, the central processing unit is the point within a computer where computing actually takes place. It is the place where the language understood by the specific computer is transformed into action. Unlike the human brain, however, the computer central processing unit is essentially only a single state transition machine. A central processing unit interprets a single instruction that views a known state comprised of specific parameters, coupled to a specification of a process to evoke a new state from this known state. This instruction is stored within a mechanism that allows for storage and retrieval over time of these state transition specifications; a mechanism termed *computer memory*. If this mechanism, that is computer memory, allows for the storage of only one state transition specification then it may not be particularly useful as a general computing facility. In order to effect and manipulate a more complex state machine, a computer must have many such storage locations and the ability to draw from them a series of processing steps to allow transition from all known states to new states. We'll consider this in more detail in the following section.

The central processing unit provides us with a clear illustration of how the sensori-motor system of an entity ultimately defines the metaphorical basis for that entity's cognitive functions. The basic form of the world to which the sensori-motor system of a central processing unit reacts is a series of containers, each filled with a string of two-position switches. We tend to call the containers *words* or *bytes*, depending on their size, and each is comprised of some number of switches that can be turned on or off. The sensory systems of a central processing unit can detect words and the state of the switches within the various words that are detected. The motor system of a central processing unit can select the specific word to be impacted through motor actions that comprise the subsequent alteration of the state of the switches in the word.

If we create a computational model that assumes an on switch corresponds to a one and an off switch corresponds to a zero, then our container appears as a string of binary *bits*, a bit being a switch set either to 1 or to 0. A string of 8 bits may be referred to as a byte or an *octet*. Typically today, a word may be made up of 32 bits. We're a little ambiguous about the concept of a word relative to computer systems because over the historical age of computers, say a few decades at most, many different computers have used word sizes that range from 8 bits to 64 bits; perhaps even larger for some rather specialized machines. So, perhaps we can say that a central processing unit is completely organized around an ordered collection of words, each comprised of a set of constituent bits.

A central processing unit implements a series of operations based on this concept of a word comprised of bits; the ability of general computation comes with the added provision that there exists many of these words. Moreover, a central processing unit assumes a structure to these many words and makes use of an ability to uniquely identify each word through an address. Thus, the operations that a central processing unit can perform comprises a language based on the sensori-motor environment that defines its existence; that is, through an ordered set of words comprised of bits. The motor operations performed by a central processing unit are directly related to this model. One operation might test to see if a particular bit in a word is a one or a zero and then switch to perform some different operation based on the value detected. Another operation might shift the bits in a word, essentially giving an order to the arrangement of bits within a word. If we view word addresses as an ordered stack of words and bit positioning as an ordered string of bits then the sensori-motor environment of the central processing unit assumes the properties of extent and directionality. Thus, at its most basic, a central processing unit exists within a two dimensional world.

The point we're trying to derive in this description of the metaphorical environment of the central processing unit of a computer is that it intrinsically deals with a very limited set of objects: words and bits. As the most powerful tool yet developed by *Homo sapiens sapiens*, this provides a very limited basis through which computers can contemplate the full range of sensori-motor experiences of the individual human. The way in which a more expansive view of the world is achieved is through the development of computer languages that more closely match the human experience. Through the form of sets of processing instructions, which we will call *programs* or *codes*, computer cognitive tools known as interpreters and compilers can be built through which human sensori-motor experiences can be translated back to the pure computer sensori-motor world of words and bits.

So, the central processing unit doesn't accomplish much without some additional computer elements, most specifically, memory, which we will consider in more detail next. For the moment, let us just consider that memory provides a means of storing strings of ones and zeros; that is, strings of binary symbols. Any specific central processing unit is designed to respond to its own set of definitions of such binary symbols. In essence, the specific set of symbols form a language which the central processing unit can interpret and effect.

As with human memory, *computer memory* is a recording mechanism for sensori-motor experience. Human memory reflects the storage of the continuous sensori-motor experiences of a person. An adjunct to memory as a storage mechanism is a complementary retrieval mechanism that provides a means through which a series of experiences, once experienced and stored, can later be retrieved and re-experienced. Computer related memory derives from a similar concept, but with the added wrinkle that it is the computer sensori-motor experience being saved. Thus, with computer systems it is basically a collection of words comprised of bits that can be saved and subsequently retrieved. Somewhat distinct from human memory systems, at least to the extent that they are currently understood, is the recognition that computer memory is extremely context insensitive. That is, the basic content of memory is a string of words comprised of bits, independent of the context in which sensory mechanisms obtained the information that is ultimately stored in memory. Thus, the higher-level interpretation of those words and bits, when retrieved from memory, is dependent on re-establishing the context from which the information was obtained in the first place. This then requires the storage of contextual information as well as the derived sensor data. So, let us be sure we understand the concept of *context* in this regards.

As our first consideration of context, let us refer back to our cursory discussion about human DNA in Chapter 2. At that time, we noted that the DNA molecule, as metaphorically illustrated by the railroad track system of the United States, could be viewed as either a single linear structure or as a collection of interconnected segments. We further noted that DNA based processes most generally make use of small sections of the molecule. Indeed, the term *gene* references a very short section of molecule that is generally perceived to be related to the production of a specific protein. If we think of these distinct segments as illustrative of contexts, then there is a very strong parallel to computer memory. While at its most basic, computer memory appears as a string of individually addressable words filled with bits, in fact we can layer a much more complex information organization on top of this. For example, by designating a section of memory to the task of defining further subsections, where they start, their extent and some general way to refer to them, then we can create a *file system* on top of a linear memory structure. The files give us the first level of decomposition into discrete contexts. We can make the various contexts even more specific by not only organizing the way that we reference memory, but by assigning specific procedures in the form of distinct sets of computer code to interpret specific segments of memory. Consider, for example the recording of music within the domain of a computer.

Music is a complex rendition of sounds that are conveyed from source to destination by way of acoustic waves that propagate through various materials. The sensori-motor experience of a computer central processing unit does not encompass sound; it encompasses words containing bits. Consequently, to remember music, a computer needs to detect the acoustic wave form and to translate this into the sensori-motor representation form of a central processing unit by digitally sampling the acoustic waveforms of music, and by doing this, create a stream of words and bits that can be stored in a mechanical device through an electromagnetic based process. When these words and bits are retrieved, the context of the original music must also be retrieved and reestablished, thus allowing, through translation, the bit streams to be re-cast as acoustic waveforms emanating from a speaker. Now, we hear once again the original music. In a similar fashion, a series of words and bits can be recorded that derive from visual images.

The mechanisms through which computers store information, including sets of instructions that tell the central processing unit of the computer what to do with that information, are termed memories. We use plural of the term advisedly in that there are several memory technologies, which offer different characteristics to the overall computer architecture. From an historical perspective, memory has been a major area of evolution of electronic computer systems since their inception in the 1940's. Variants for computer memory that we can introduce now, but which we'll explore in more detail in later sections, are, among others: read-only memory, random access memory and bulk memory such as disk drives and magnetic tape.

We have noted that just about all computers today have a so-called Von Neumann architecture, where instructions and data are contained in memory, and a processing unit reads the instructions and executes them on the data. Computers also have *input/output channels* that give them access to the outside world. Each channel typically has its own processing capabilities, dedicated to the management of the flow of information in and out of the computer through that channel. Let us consider three examples.

A print channel allows sending information from the computer to a printer. It is essentially an output channel, since the main flow of data goes from the computer to the external device. However, it is also an input channel because the printer may send data back to the computer, for example a signal indicating that it doesn't have any more paper. A small unit of processing capability links the computer and the printer and manages the flow of data and signals, moving information between the memory of the computer and the memory of the printer when the signals show readiness. One equivalent of the printing example by computers might be singing by humans. In singing, the main flow of information within the singer goes from the brain to the buccal system, which itself governs the various anatomical maneuvers that lead to the expression of the song. A feedback system is capable of signaling, for example, an echo, or other acoustic phenomena possibly requiring alterations of the song delivery. Here we have in action a singing module that renders whichever songs are concerned, just as the printing module rendered documents on paper for the computer.

On the other hand, a recording channel allows one to record information. For example, a microphone can be used to record a voice and store it in the computer. This is essentially an input channel because the main flow of information goes from the external device to the computer. It most likely is also an output channel since the computer may need to send signals to the microphone, for example to turn it off or change its parameters. A small unit of processing links the computer and the microphone and manages the flow of data and signals, moving information between the memory of the computer and the memory associated with the microphone when the signals show readiness. The equivalent of the voice-recording example by computers might be scene recognition by humans. In this case, the main flow of information goes to the brain through an elaborate hierarchical system of sensors, starting with the eyes, decomposing the scene into various elements of processing. A feedback mechanism exists to command, for example, the eyes to look in a different direction. We see again a specialized module processing input conditions, much like the electronics converted audio information and placed it in the memory of the computer.

A modern printer, or microphone, can actually comprise a specialized computer. However, a communication channel between two generic, less specialized computers is more symmetric, as the data may typically flow both ways in similar fashion. The interaction between the two computers is governed by sophisticated rules allowing, for example, the computers to not talk at the same time, to exchange information in an orderly fashion, and to understand each other in the various contexts involved. Because communication between computers on the grand scale of a worldwide network requires a considerable number of rules to be made explicit, the communication between generic computers is a very well formalized domain, which has already reached a maturity that makes it a prime target for comparison with similar functions in humans. Indeed, corresponding to computer-computer interaction, we have human-human interaction, with language as a most obvious example of an enabling mechanism. The flow of information is essentially symmetrical, with elaborate mechanisms of synchronization and recovery at several levels. Much as computers cannot keep interrupting each other, humans need protocols allowing one person to talk and the other to listen at appropriate moments. Also required are systems of understanding based on shared contexts. Just as computer-computer interactions are very sophisticated theoretical constructions of computer science for fundamental reasons of pragmatic success in communication, language and its realizations have been the object of deep empirical and formal studies.

The stroke of genius in the earliest electronic computers was the recognition that the control of actions taken by the computer needed to be extremely malleable; or, perhaps the more important realization was that they *could* be malleable. Babbage's mechanical computer had a process control that was largely cast in stone in the form of the interconnection of gears of fixed size and with fixed ratios of size relative to other gears. Consequently, the device was fairly adept at repeating a series of well-defined algorithmic steps, but it was difficult to impossible to take the machine very far afield from the problem for which it was constructed.

*Software* is the instruction set that, through interpretation by a central processing unit, effects a series of computational operations by a computer. If you wish, software allows one to change the size and ratios of the gears of the machine. Software is the script that controls the actions of a computer, much like the script of a play controls the actors in the play. We will come back to this comparison in our final chapter. Software is written in a language that can be understood by the computer. The ever-changing landscape in the computer world is the attempt to construct languages that bridge the gap between the sensori-motor environments of the computer with the sensor-motor environments addressed by the programmers that create the software. A good programmer can think like a computer; a good computer language sounds like a person talking to another person. Software expresses the computer, and as such, is the mechanism that translates the concepts of this book into practice.

At the high-level at which we're looking at computers, we need to add the concept of an *application framework*. Such a framework specifies how the software needed for a particular task is installed in the memory of the computer. In a very large sense, this is how computers acquire new skills, or, actually lose them if the application is removed. Applications are programmed to build on the innate capabilities of the computer to introduce new processing of input and output information. Here we are using the word programmed in exactly the same way that we referred to the establishment of acceptable stimulus-action responses within the human brain. We view the programming or training as coming from an external source and, through some type of positive action, imprinted upon the controlling, cognitive elements within the computer.

We noted in the second chapter that the early decades of computer development and deployment saw reciprocal effects in the size and number of computers. Early computers were big, bulky and relatively few in number. Over time, the computers became smaller and subsequently much greater in number. The connection between the two effects illustrates the variability of the ecosystems in which computers operate. With larger systems, their sources of food, that is the energy to run them, and the amount of it needed, formed a distinct limitation on where such machines could be located. They required considerable logistical support for their operation as well; air conditioning systems to keep the systems from melting themselves and, perhaps more important, from cooking the people required to operate them and to keep them in a proper state of repair.

A rather typical computer circa 1965 would require a room of a few hundred or a few thousand square feet in area and a staff of perhaps ten to twenty people to keep it running around the clock. Such machines were expensive to own and to operate. The net result of this large, logistical infrastructure certainly limited the mobility of the computer (once they were put in place, one simply did not move them without exceptional cause) and consequently limited the types of problems to which they could be applied. With the advent of the transistor and subsequently the invention of the integrated circuit, the size of computers began to decrease and with each diminution came a new realm of use for the machines.

The evolutionary process of natural selection applied itself quite well to the emerging, smaller computer systems. Each design iteration provided systems that could be housed in more varied locations, required fewer and less specialized operators and were subsequently applicable to a much broader range of problems. The noises of the dinosaurs as they became extinct were noteworthy in their lack of comprehension; "Why would anyone want a computer in their home?" Ken Olsen, founder and chairman of Digital Equipment Corporation, reportedly questioned before his company folded with the advent of the very personal computer he decried.

In 1959, future Nobel laureate Richard Feynman made a classic presentation entitled *There's Plenty of Room at the Bottom* in which he suggested the possibilities inherent in making all of our machines smaller. In contemplating the usefulness of miniaturized computers, he noted a lack of understanding of how to accomplish the miniaturization in a cost effective manner at that time, but interestingly enough he selected a marvelous example of its usefulness. He suggested that a machine that could recognize a face would be of immense value; not just recognize a picture, but recognize a face as seen from all angles and from varying distances. The human mind, he noted, was fully capable of seeing a face in these various guises and still recognizing the person. How useful it would be if we had a machine that could accomplish the same thing. But, it needed to be a machine of a small size, not something the size of a large building, if its full utility was to be realized. It was a presentation that lit the way for computer systems to become truly ubiquitous extensions of the human species.

# Personal Electronic Devices

Personal electronic devices are computers that have all the characteristics described above. They have a central processing unit, various input/output devices, and different forms of memories. Your cellular phone has a small keyboard, a microphone, speakers, most likely a screen and a camera. All this is just like your laptop computer, only smaller. The keyboard connects to your fingers, the microphone to your mouth, the speakers to your ears, and the screen and camera are for your eyes. A big difference today between your phone and your laptop, however, is that inside your cellular phone there is another computer, one that contains your private information, that which makes the cellular phone truly yours. That computer is typically located in a small encasing under the battery, from which it can be removed. That computer inside the computer is called the *Subscriber Identity Module* or SIM. If you take your SIM out, your phone doesn't work anymore because it can no longer be recognized by the cellular phone network as yours. If you take your SIM out and transfer it to another cellular phone, then that new phone becomes yours and can be used to make calls just like the older one could. This is because the SIM contains all the information pertaining to you, which the phone consults before connecting you to someone else.

At the time of this writing, there are more than two billion cellular phones containing a Subscriber Identity Module operating in the world. What differentiates the Subscriber Identity Module from other computers is defined by its role. Since the information it contains must be, and remain, confidential, this computer must be protected from outside intrusion of all sorts. Therefore, it is a very special kind of computer, with many specific features, all oriented toward protecting your information inside. Physically, it presents itself in the form a plastic substrate into which a small chip is embedded.

The most salient feature of the Subscriber Identity Module is the *monolithic computer architecture* it presents. By monolithic, we mean that the complete computer is constructed as a single integrated circuit chip. This includes the central processing unit, memories and means of communicating with the world outside this computer. By virtue of a single integrated circuit chip structure, the interconnections between the components of the computer are embedded within the chip. Consequently, it is very difficult for these interconnections to be accessed by external monitoring equipment, which is a desired property for a computer whose main function is to protect its content against unauthorized access of all kinds. As a result, the chip provides a computing platform in which information can be stored, while the only means of accessing that information is through the input/output facilities provided by the chip itself. If the computer within the chip can adequately safeguard this input/output channel, then we can achieve a secure information storage platform as well as a secure processing platform.

Also embedded within the integrated circuitry of the Subscriber Identity Module are several types of *memory*. One type, termed *read-only memory*, is actually populated with binary information at the time of construction of the chip. Once constructed, the bit patterns stored in read-only memory cannot be altered. So, if the stored program that provides the instructions that the processor can execute is stored in that memory, then that program cannot be altered after the construction of the integrated circuit. With proper techniques, this form of construction allows to render the program stored in read-only memory at least very difficult to read and essentially impossible to modify without destroying the electronic module itself. From this property, the Subscriber Identity Module derives the intrinsic characteristics of tamper-resistant and tamper-evident. Taken together, these characteristics ensure a significant degree of trust in the code embedded in the SIM. So, from this position of trust, the SIM gains credence as a secure information storage platform and a secure computation platform. The operations that it provides are strongly protected from modification by forces external or internal to the electronic module. These two characteristics, secure information and secure program, give us what we can term a *trusted computer platform*. It is this characterization from which we will draw the direct connection of personal electronic devices to religion; both are seminally grounded in the concept and realization of trust. The subsequent implementation of a policy infrastructure, whether it is for a religion, or for a personal electronic device, is totally grounded in trust. The trust conveyed to the personal electronic device by the Subscriber Identity Module derives from: (a) a monolithic structure of processor and memory, (b) immutable code, (c) personal possession by the phone owner, and (d) a simple, well defined and highly constrained input/output channel. It should be a useful exercise to consider further these physiological features.

Since it is the trusted core of more than two billion cellular phones, the Subscriber Identity Module is designed for deployment in high volumes at low cost. It is intended to be placed inside the cellular phone and used to facilitate secure transactions as required and desired by the person and by the telephone system operator. It is a token that can, through a variety of identity authentication protocols, establish a strong likelihood that it is acting on behalf of the person using it. From these rather straightforward requirements, one can derive an applicable manufacturing technology for the construction of Subscriber Identity Modules: specifically, small size, low cost and high reliability. Meeting these requirements translates into using established computer technology whenever possible. Correspondingly, the central processing units used in Subscriber Identity Modules have tended to be technologies that are less powerful than the best central processing units at any specific point in time. However, for some specific functions, like special arithmetic operations needed for the most secure transactions, they are often more advanced than those central processing units. At the present time, high performance Subscriber Identity Module central processing units make use of internal bus structures that can address binary addresses that are 32-bits in length. They operate at very high clock speeds and consequently can obtain very high execution speed for programs that they run.

Computers require electrical power to function. The evolution of the computer in the electronic age has given us different schemes for providing power to the processor. These schemes bridge the expanse from large scale, fixed location computers to personal computers and then personal electronic devices.

The current incarnations of the Subscriber Identity Modules do not incorporate an on-card power source. Consequently, the power to run the electronic module of the SIM must be supplied by the phone. This obviously impacts the derived level of trust of the SIM.

If you look at the Subscriber Identity Module in your phone, you'll find that there are 8 contacts showing on its surface. Two of these contacts are used by the phone to provide power to the chip; the others can be used for several functions, of which one is communication between the phone and its trusted core. This provides a communication pathway for the transfer of information in the form of bit-strings between the phone and the SIM. As the communication pathway allows for communication only in one direction at a time, it is called *half-duplex* in the trade. This channel supports data transfer speeds of up to several hundred thousand bits per second. This input/output channel is the only means for a Subscriber Identity Module computer to communicate with the outside world. The primary mechanism for protecting this channel as it supports communication with the outside is *cryptography*, the science of making data impenetrable to the unauthorized.

The Subscriber Identity Module contains three types of memories; actually, sometimes four. The first one is called read-only memory. This is memory containing the program that controls the operations of the module. It is written at the factory and cannot be changed without destroying the module, therefore guaranteeing that the module does what it's supposed to do without alteration. The second one is called random access memory. It is very fast memory used by the central processing unit for its immediate operations. This memory enters into action when the module is powered up, and stops functioning when the computer is powered down. Therefore, all information in it is transient. Information that must be kept alive is stored in permanent memory, of which there are various forms. Like all memories, permanent memory is actually always encrypted to add a layer of information security to the other physical means of protecting the SIM against possible attacks.

Trust is the primary feature of personal electronic devices. Trust must emanate from the operational characteristics of the devices and, consequently, trust must be a salient feature of the device derived from its original manufacture. The Subscriber Identity Module manufacturing process provides an interesting illustration of certain features of a distributed manufacturing process that help to instill trust and trustworthiness into personal electronic devices.

As we've noted above, the central feature of the personal electronic device secure processing element is a single, monolithic computer platform constructed as a single integrated circuit chip. While not completely tamper-proof; because that's impossible, such an element is tamper-resistant because of the difficulty of non-destructive analysis of the chip. Moreover, destructive decomposition of a secure module, which may yield access to the information it contains, is impossible to accomplish without physical possession of the chip. Once the decomposition is completed, it is virtually impossible to make the chip operable again. Consequently, the device offers excellent characteristics of tamper-evident behavior, which in turns allows an integrated system an opportunity to detect the attack on a specific unit and to operationally segregate it from the rest of the system. It can be amputated if you will.

# Foundations of Consciousness

*Ontogeny* (the development of an individual over one generation) recapitulates *phylogeny* (the development of subsequent individuals across generations). This is the crux of what Ernst Haeckel first suggested in 1866 as the *biogenetic law*. His thesis was that the embryonic development of an individual passed through the phases of the evolutionary stages of its species. While shown to not be accurate in details, it still offers insight to the complex processes that have emerged through evolutionary development. Actually, the new science of evolutionary developmental psychology, presented by Sean B. Carroll in *Endless Forms Most Beautiful*, is precisely dedicated to the study of these processes. If one examines the evolution of the social systems of *Homo sapiens*, a progression can be identified in which the various stages would seem to derive from specific plateaus in the evolutionary development of the species.

Human social structures are based on the cognitive abilities of the human brain. The salient aspect of cognition that gives rise to social structure is the ability within the brain to form contextual frameworks that allow the individual to project through metaphorical processes an internal understanding of the sensori-motor experience to the external world at large; then, based on this metaphorical understanding, to reflect upon and act upon the external world based on processes internal to the individual. It seems to us that mirror neuron systems, with integration of emotion, provide the basis of consciousness through which this metaphorical basis of action through interaction is achieved.

Just as we showed earlier how computer constructs elaborated in the context of object-oriented programming are parallel to mirror neuron systems, we can understand, with the example of either watching an ice cream being eaten or eating it ourselves, how a computer effects consciousness. For this, we'll consider the sentence "I don't remember eating the ice cream; I did it unconsciously." Here, we clearly associate memory with consciousness. Similarly, we all have had the experience of driving unconsciously, where we can't remember how we went through a long stretch of a familiar road. In order for this to work, the brain must have circuitry that can detail and store the many steps of a process. What this circuitry does is look at the whole process as well as its constituting parts. Some time just the whole process is remembered, and sometime the constituting parts are remembered as well, creating the conscious part of the process that we've discussed in the examples above. For a computer, that property is called *reflexivity*. When we described earlier how an object that contains generic instructions on how to read and understand a file, reflexivity allows the computer to inquire the object as to how it sequences those instructions. Whether the computer then records a process in memory or both the process and its sequence of instructions is up to higher evaluations, just as it is for humans. Certainly emotion represents a higher evaluation system of this kind in humans. Why should we remember things we're not interested in?

Mirror neuron systems establish contextual envelopes for an individual's sensori-motor experience. They encompass the formation of emotional responses to this sensori-motor experience and they reflect the actions that can or may be taken in response. When the sensori-motor experience is observed in others, that is in the external world, then the mirror neuron systems may formulate sympathetic emotional responses within the observed context. However, they will not have access to the actions encompassed by the mirror neuron context because this observed context is beyond the individual's motor system. One individual's mind cannot control another individual's actions directly through the mirror neuron complex. This, it would seem, recognition and contemplation, but without a direct ability for action, is a reasonable definition of consciousness. In that perspective, consciousness is the capability to relate to oneself as one relates to others.

Through relatively recent evolutionary development, the human species has evolved this ability for metaphorical projection. Further, in concert with this mechanism for consciousness, the species has developed the means of communication that can represent this complex, metaphorical projection. Specifically, the species evolved the means of language, which in its spoken and written form, allow the individual the indirect means to effect actions on the part of others based on our internal sensori-motor experience. This, it would seem, forms the foundation of social ecosystems. We will explore this in much more detail in the next chapter.

4  Physiology of the Individual

# 5 Fabric of Society

*The brain may devise laws for the blood;*
*but a hot temper leaps over a cold decree...*

William Shakespeare
*The Merchant of Venice*

## Democracy: Sharia of Christianity?

People, as practicing vertebrates, are in and of the world. Within the purely physical world, all interactions are grounded in the basic laws of nature. No matter how ethereal is our perspective when we start, we ultimately play by the rules of our physical ecosystem. Here, interactions are physical in the purest sense; they're face-to-face, claw-to-claw, *mano-a-mano*. This is a place where being knee deep in alligators has a very real and pragmatic connotation; particularly, if you're a wildebeest crossing a river made shallow by the dry season and yet containing the entire crocodile population, all competing for food. Wildebeest is particularly tasty this time of year!

From the physical ecosystem come the metaphors for our being and behavior. "We *fight* for the things we believe in!" "We *thirst* for knowledge." "We *struggle* to lose weight." "We can't quite *grasp* the solution to Fermat's Last Theorem." In the fullness of time, evolutionary processes have provided a path away from the pure, objective nature of the physical ecosystem. Collectively, and in collectives, we sort of left, but we carried our metaphors with us. We say "sort of" because it should be clear by now that we really can't completely divorce ourselves from the physical ecosystem. However, with the emergence of living organisms a variety of levels of cognitive capability were brought into play. A more subjective interaction process was the result. Thus, while the lion usually has the prowess to catch and eat the antelope, if it is somewhat sated from a prior feast and not driven by pending hunger, it might choose not to engage in the hunt. "The lion sleeps tonight!" and we extend our metaphorical concepts into the realm of allegory.

So evolution, through the mechanisms that it saw prevail, availed to the human species an ostensibly better opportunity. When we, as a species, became physiologically capable of it, we found that we could create an artificial environment that mitigated many of the threats posed to us by the physical world. These artificial environments we term *social ecosystems*. When we enter this more subjective world, interactions can take on more extended and complex forms; perhaps profound, perhaps whimsical. As Willy Wonka tells us, "We are the music makers; we are the dreamers of dreams."

Individual organisms have distinct and complex physiologies that govern their capabilities within the realms in which they exist. As we noted in the previous chapter, there are parallels to these capabilities found in the architecture of computer systems. As we explore extending these parallels to encompass human social structures, of course, we must consider multi-entity constructs. This is what gives meaning to the concept of *social*. For humans, this facility is expressed through subjective, complex interaction-enabling structures that have evolved since the emergence of the species. A current culmination of such structures is found in the religious organizations through which humans effect the complex policies that have allowed them to ascend to the top rung of the evolutionary ladder. For computer systems, the social analogue is grounded in computer networks; but, not just simple networks. Rather, we find the more profound illustration in the interconnection of networks; that is, within the all-encompassing network construct that we know as the *Internet*.

To be clear, networks provide the framework for a complex organization of computers, and hence in our view they suggest significant parallels with social structures that culminate in religious organizations. However, they do not constitute the religious analogue in and of themselves. Rather, they support an electronic (*cyber*) extension of the fabric of society that encompasses the physical and social ecosystems in which humans exist. As with religion, they still do not solely constitute the fabric themselves. To adopt a weaving metaphor, orthogonal mechanisms form the *warp and the woof* of social systems much like the warp and woof foundations of a fabric on which the weaver creates the finished cloth. So, what forms the fabric of our social systems? To answer this question, we suggest that one should start from the result and try to reverse engineer the cause. The authors, being computer guys in general, and software guys specifically, deem it appropriate to approach the problem by considering the environment that has facilitated the computer world as we know it within the United States.

The question we ask is, "Why has the United States been the preeminent nurturer of the software business or of the computer business in general for that matter?" Indeed, we observe that the vast majority of computer and software product companies are based in the United States. This situation emerged with the appearance of the first operational computers in the 1940's and has now been true for many generations. If we can at least qualitatively understand this, we should be able to discern a patterned framework through which to interpret the architecture of successful software systems and their evolutionary progression. Amazon, Dell, Digital Equipment, eBay, Google, Hewlett-Packard, IBM, Intel, Microsoft, Oracle; these are only a few of the past or present most familiar names that have almost no equivalent anywhere else in the world. If computers and computer networks, as we have suggested, truly reflect the social orders of the species, then we should see at least something of a cause and effect relationship.

As an added wrinkle, we ponder that while the companies that we mentioned all started in the United States, a recent lynchpin of the operational form of complex computer networks has been the emergence of trusted computers, as basic elements of families of personal electronic devices. These devices comprise major components of extensive service networks themselves, and they facilitate an entry of the individual into larger and more comprehensive computer networks. In fact, they form an intimate reflection of the very architecture of such networks. Moreover, these trusted core components of personal electronic devices were developed in Europe. Ah yes, but the software systems into which they are embedded, converging to the Internet, derived from the United States. Other recent examples of a similar kind are Linux, Skype and the World Wide Web. All are inventions made in Europe that migrated to the United States when they turned into businesses. So, again the question, "What, from an historical perspective, made the United States a superior incubator of the computer business?"

One way to look at an answer is to assume the hypothesis that somehow this situation would be reflective of the social ecosystem within which those businesses flourish. From that perspective, within the United States the Constitution forms the basis of social structure on which all else depends. Within the context of the weaving metaphor that we mentioned earlier, the Constitution actually provides the loom. The subsequent set of laws that derive from it form one axis of social interaction, while a moderately regulated and very strongly supported enterprise market system provides the orthogonal axis. It seems reasonable to consider whether these foundational properties are related to a fertile environment for the innovation of computer systems, particularly computer software. So, we have suggested the metaphorical image of the loom, of the warp strands and of the woof strands; but, for the moment, we'll defer the question just who the weaver is. Suffice it to recognize that from this seminal cloth has sprung a cyber-extension to the social fabric in the form of the Internet. In turn, the ubiquitous network has been further enhanced by its cognitive big brother, the World Wide Web. The Web reiterates a European invention that bloomed in the technology business environment set by the United States. More succinctly stated, we put forth the hypothesis that the two main components of the success within the United States of computer systems in general, and software systems specifically are a particular form of democracy and capitalism. If this is correct, it is natural to extend our hypothesis to the local development of protestant Christianity, the common thread to both social systems. It is important to understand that these harbingers to successful software are not based in genetic differences; to the extent of current research, there are no software genes; software jeans, perhaps. Many of the software companies created and flourishing in the United States are in fact developed by recent immigrants, who find in the country the ferment they need. Innovation and development derives from the social substrate of the society, and religion in all its guises is a principal characterization of this substrate.

One might rightly ask, "How can this be the case, when democracy is also subscribed to in other countries, which in many cases are under other than significant protestant Christianity influence?" For example, Japan adopted the concept of democracy from the West explicitly after the Meiji restoration, and extended it to a constitutionally based system during the Allied occupation following World War II. Certainly, Christianity was not and is not a dominant religious influence in Japan. And, we would note, while Japan has reached an eminent position in design, engineering and manufacturing of hardware systems, in particular, high quality hardware systems, it was not successful at taking the step to software dominance with its Fifth Generation endeavor in the eighties. Japan's software prowess has been limited to games and aspects of robotics, with local development the norm. Another counter example that one might suggest is India. It is currently the world's largest democracy; and, it is certainly noteworthy that India has an emerging position of significant strength in the computer software development world. However, at the present time, this strength builds largely upon services to the computer world of the United States, and not in the emergence of major computer and software product companies. The only two major software companies based outside the United States that have excelled in the past 40 years are French Dassault Systèmes (with their CATIA design program) and German SAP (with their business software). Even so, CATIA found its original expansion through IBM marketing in the seventies. This compares to hundreds of dominant computer and software companies in the United States during the same 40 years period. Finally, we need to mention the United Kingdom. A number of advances in computer science came from the UK, in particular in the theoretical realm, for example the seminal work of Alan Turing. Why is it that the UK didn't develop a sizeable computer and software business? Is it in the name: Kingdom? If we observe that the Church of England is still under the ultimate direction of the Queen, and we compare it to the myriad of competing churches in the United States, might we understand how the equally competing situation of software businesses flourished in the market of ideas?

So, we wonder whether the convergence of a constitutional social union and an opportunistic business melee is the ferment on which computer systems and software products could optimally build. Reiterating that many computer-related ideas and innovative concepts, for example, universal mobile technology and the architecture of the World Wide Web, have come from Europe or other parts of the world, their optimal business realization in software product form seems to have happened in the United States. Our central case in point is the propagation of Internet technology, which has been in recent years the major evolutionary factor in the percolation of new system architectures, following the general Darwinian rules that were themselves at the core of American democracy and capitalism. In fact, at about the same time that the Internet was emerging from its formative cocoon within DARPA and a select university culture within the United States, France introduced the Minitel network. It offered many of the same characteristics as the Internet. However, based as it was in the strict discipline of government control reflective of the Catholic heritage of France, it lacked the propagation impetus necessary to compete with the geometric progression of Internet dispersion during the decade of the 1990's.

We see the emergence of democratic systems from a protestant Christian basis as one current boundary of the continuing evolution of group-selection mechanisms. Within the United States, one might speak of the separation of church and state, but conceptually we see democratic institutions as a direct refinement of religious systems and as specifically subsuming these systems. The primary difference is found in the basis of the trust infrastructures that are the natural boundary of state democracy. The religious preeminence found in the Declaration of Independence anticipates the ascendance of democratic control by the Constitution over church in a conscious decision by the founders of the United States. It was a decision that was subscribed to by the resident populations that confirmed the governmental foundation of the United States Constitution. The church exerts influence over policy in the form of the evaluation of moral values, but the authority over the structure of the policy framework lies with representative democracy.

In the context of our evaluation of the evolution of computer technology, we can compare this situation with other relationships between religion, church and state, as with Buddhism and Hinduism in much of central Asia, Confucianism in China and Shinto in Japan, Catholicism in Europe and South America, Judaism in Israel, and the same or other religions in other parts of the world. With Islam, for example, the relationship is typically one in which religion is either ostensibly superior to state or invokes very specific policy definitions within the state construct. In some instances, for example Iran, the state is an institutional theocracy; *sharia* effectively forms the basis for the law of the land. Within this social order, Islam is the superior trust infrastructure with the state being subsumed by it. Pakistan and Turkey are on a democratic spectrum defined in relationship with Islam. Should we then say that *democracy is the sharia of Christianity*, expressing in one formula the conflicting tensions on the trust infrastructure? (We are not alone is this question, as exemplified in *Religion et démocratie*, edited by Patrick Michel.) In all of these example situations, the central point of interest to us is how trust infrastructures are established and how they impact subordinate policy infrastructures. Specifically, how can these mechanisms and relationships be translated into a model for social ecosystems and, through this model, can we better understand the development and utilization of computers, computer systems and networks?

So, let us begin the process of extracting a model of social ecosystems through which we can then qualitatively examine the structure of human grouping mechanisms found within them; and, lest it be forgotten, the primary mechanisms through which group endeavors are effected are those facilities that we've previously termed *trust* and *policy*. To do so, we need to first examine the evolutionary stages of groups, what characteristics influenced their progression and the situation currently manifested by the resulting mechanisms.

5 Fabric of Society

# Evolution of Social Ecosystems

Multi-level selection as an evolutionary process suggests that the ascendance and continuance of various social ecosystems should derive from natural selection preference for the groups and the mechanisms they present, as well as an enhancement of the natural selection preference for the characteristics of the individuals within these groups. At least some of the beneficial characteristics of both groups and individuals are expected to arise from the ontogenetic development, that is the development of one generation, of the individual members of the species, while other of the beneficial characteristics should arise from the phylogenetic processes, that is processes covering several subsequent generations, that emanate as a result of the interaction of individuals within the ecosystems; from the various grouping mechanisms themselves. Based on a survey of current literature in many domains, including archeology, cognitive science, economy, literature, mathematics, psychology and sociology, we have assembled a metaphorical characterization of the processes that have resulted from the evolution of both humans and their social ecosystems. We term this model *pretergenesis*, adopting the term from a group-specific extension of the process called *epigenesis*. While epigenesis characterizes the development of the embryonic individual through a process of successive differentiation, resulting ultimately in the adult individual, pretergenesis illustrates through a series of metaphorical descriptors, the processes that have driven the evolutionary development of the social ecosystems themselves.

The model builds a framework based on the evolutionary progression of the essential characteristics of human multi-level processes. As the species has evolved, people have participated in ever larger and more complex social environments, with their resulting grouping mechanisms, where each successive level draws its strengths from the *within-group* and *among-group* processes of its own and surrounding levels. The full range of the represented social ecosystems is found in the current world, suggesting that these levels can either naturally co-exist, or that the conflict of natural selection is still at play. Most likely, the correct assessment contains a bit of both.

A couple of chapters back, we recognized the model of Maslow's *Hierarchy of Needs* as the basis for interaction stimuli involving humans. The evolutionary progression of species development has given rise to this hierarchy as the foundation of human behavior. Thus, the hierarchy is essentially an illustration of natural selection that resulted in the emergence of a progression of physiological characteristics of the individual person. The following table suggests a series of such characteristics that can be associated with the succession of needs. We should note that the various indicated characteristics always act in a cumulative fashion to meet the body's needs. Successive evolutionary developments may give rise to new needs, but they may also, in parallel, help to satisfy previously expressed needs. The development of an emotional system helped in the struggle to meet physiological needs as well as to express and then satisfy a whole new set of needs, specifically including that of belonging. In fact, it was likely the emergence of the emotional system that formed the springboard for the need of belonging in the first place.

So, we observe that the most basic of needs, *physiological needs*, are a detailed reflection of organic physiology. As we've noted previously, the requirements that the body has for sustenance evoke a variety of appetite indicators that provide a macroscopic signal of the need. Thus, when the body wants for air, a reflexive action to breath is stimulated. When we want for water, thirst stimulates our actions toward finding drink.

The second level of needs, those of *safety and security*, were likely salved by the rise of reflexive facilities that serve to take us more quickly out of harms way. The emergence of the emotional system, a development arising with the mammals, gave solace to the corresponding need for relational *belonging*. Indeed, it was likely the emotional system that allowed for all subsequent facilities that result in social grouping. Emotions represent a characteristic that satisfies more basic needs while giving rise to higher level needs.

*Esteem* could only arise as a basic need whenever humans developed a capability for empathy; we must be able to place ourselves in others situations, to be able to empathize with the world around us, in order to establish our relative position within that world; that is the essence of esteem. As we recounted in the previous chapter, this facility can be appreciated in the context of mirror neuron constructs within the brain. Indeed, these constructs also provide an excellent model for consciousness itself, a fulfillment, it would seem, or a source of the need for *cognitive* satisfaction.

| Needs | Support |
|---|---|
| Transcendence | Religion |
| Self-Actualization | Language |
| Aesthetic | Trust |
| Cognitive | Consciousness |
| Esteem | Metaphoric understanding |
| Belonging | Emotions |
| Safety / Security | Autonomic nervous system |
| Physiological Needs | Appetites |

*Human Needs – A Reflection of Human Ontogeny*

The merging of emotional assessment into mirror neuron constructs offers a very plausible association with the *aesthetic* needs of the mind. This need establishes the foundation of subsequent social grouping in the form of trust, and its conveyance throughout the group. With the facility for metaphorical comprehension and manipulation that is intimately associated with these same facilities, we may hypothesize that the mind was finally geared to thoroughly exploit *language*, and subsequently to concern itself with *self-actualization* as well as having an enhanced capability to meet all the more basic needs.

Finally, the rise of *cognition* and *aesthetics* derived facilities allowed for satisfaction of a need for *transcendence*; a drive to go beyond ourselves and to project our needs and value systems with others, through the establishment of social orders, with religions forming the iconic example.

Human needs, which form the basic stimuli for human interactions, derive from specific physiological developments of the person. Social interactions in turn are derived over generations from the group interaction facilities related to those same needs. Henceforth, we say that social interactions are phylogenetic developments that give rise to the group, enabled by ontogenetic developments of the individual.

Accordingly, we suggest that the following table provides an illustration of the phylogenetically derived facilities that characterize a series of recognized human social ecosystems. Each column in the table, one for each social ecosystem, presents a set of phylogenetically derived capabilities presented by the individual human that, through cumulative aggregation, effects the capabilities, and hence the effectiveness of the respective grouping mechanism. Each row in the table illustrates the ontogenetically derived stimulus for action that corresponds to Maslow's hierarchy. Within the table, the immediacy of interaction stimuli is greatest in the bottom row and diminishes as one goes up any column. Also, within the table time marches from left to right, with earliest developments toward the left-hand side of the table and more recent developments toward the right-hand side of the table. So, let's do a cursory run-through of the table starting at the lower left and considering each successively higher row in a left-to-right fashion.

|  | Family | Clan | Tribe | Congregation | Égalité |  |
|---|---|---|---|---|---|---|
| *Transcendence* | Exploration | Union | Myth | Theology | Governance | *Less Immediate* |
| *Self-Actualization* | Expression | Meaning | Discourse | Ode | Rhetoric |  |
| *Aesthetic* | Adornment | Clothing | Fashion | Grace | Elegance |  |
| *Cognitive* | Purpose | Metaphor | Blending | Induction | Logic | *Immediacy* |
| *Esteem* | Barter | Shell | Bulla | Gold | Commerce |  |
| *Belonging* | Grooming | Gossip | Mimesis | Ritual | Law |  |
| *Security* | Tool | Mechanism | System | Agency | Administration | *More Immediate* |
| *Physiology* | Instinct | Habit | Design | Ecstasy | Eminence |  |
|  | Earlier | | **Time** | | Later |  |

## *Pretergenesis*

The most immediate or urgent needs of an individual are the physiological needs. These needs elicit a stimulus response driven by an appetite when a need is unfulfilled. For the individual, we can characterize the sating of this appetite as occurring through *instinct*. If the oxygen content in the blood is too low then a rise in carbon dioxide levels triggers an autonomic response to breathe; this is true for the newborn infant as well as for the adult. If thirst indicates a strong need for water, or hunger for food, an infant will typically indicate a sense of the deficiency by crying. Correspondingly, if food is placed in the mouth of the infant, particularly when something touches the roof of the mouth, the baby begins a sucking response to ingest the food; infants can really only handle liquid foods. Touch a baby on its cheek and it will turn its head in that direction in anticipation of finding a breast to suckle. Instinctive stimuli will not, of course, allow the infant human to independently make its own way in the world.

Acquiring food and water, staying within breathable air, keeping warm, or at least not freezing, along with all the other behaviors for responding to our various physiological appetites, are activities related to the group. The most basic group, the family, is a direct extension of the human physiological systems. Indeed, within the table we characterize the family according to the characteristics of the individual. An adult must find food and water and must provide this to the infant and the young until such time as they can do it on their own. In situations where it doesn't happen, the young die. When we consider the establishment and operation of groups beyond the family, new phylogenetically derived facilities come into play. For example, in the course of the older meeting the physiological needs of the younger, the methods of their provisioning are behaviors that are learned by the young. Hence the reference to *habit* as the initial grouping mechanism aimed at meeting the most basic of needs. At this level, the necessary behaviors are learned by observation and repetition; they don't necessarily require language, formal training or any other higher-level facilities of the individual human. Moreover, the dispersion of behaviors through habitual response allows mechanisms to be distributed to larger and larger groups.

With increased cognitive facilities, people developed the ability to plan ahead to meet basic physiological needs; to assuage the appetites by proactive *design* rather than reactive response. Animals could be domesticated and thus available on demand, rather than having to resort to the vagaries of the hunt. Such an approach melds well with efforts to meet the physiological needs of a multitude. Consider, for example, the story from the *Christian Bible* of Joseph, who became second only to Egypt's Pharaoh in order to marshal the surplus food during seven years of plentiful harvest and thus be able to provide food for the people during the following seven years of famine. Certainly a religious story, but with a well-defined policy punch line centered on proactive design.

In the story, the conveyance of this policy came to Joseph through Pharaoh's dream; that is, through trust derived from an altered state of consciousness. As an individual person grows and matures, there is a constant learning process that associates emotion and cognition derived response to stimulus input. This response, if evoked simultaneously in multiple individuals, forms a powerful grouping mechanism. In the individual, positive emotions, culminating in *ecstasy*, form a powerful driver for independent action. Mircea Eliade's *Shamanism, Archaic Techniques of Ecstasy* is a pioneering work showing the universality of ecstasy in human dispersion. In the group, a directed emotional response for effecting policy is similarly necessary for early humans to attack a giant, wooly mammoth in order to feed the clan. How they are impelled to overcome their fear is a subject for discussion a bit later.

The continued evolutionary development of the individual, enabling the establishment of larger and more effective groups, has brought humans to a position of *eminence* relative to the satisfaction of their physiological needs. Building upon the previously mentioned facilities, modern individuals, perhaps alone, perhaps through a group, can realize considerable, if not complete, control over the satisfaction of their physiological needs. Correspondingly, current social ecosystems are able to exert considerable, if not complete control, over the physical ecosystem in order to provide for the physiological needs of the multitudes in the group.

Security and safety comprise the next level of the needs hierarchy. For the individual and family, the most basic characterization of attention to and provision for safety is the *tool*. Individual persons are extremely ill suited to survive in the wilderness without some means of enhancing their physical characteristics. This enhancement is accomplished through the preparation and use of tools; implements which can augment the strength and stature deficiencies that humans suffer, for example when compared to the major predators that they face or to the extreme conditions offered by the physical ecosystem.

Building upon the development of individual tools, mankind replaced and augmented the more simple instruments with more complex *mechanisms*. Recently, the wheel and axle formed one of the mechanisms that enhanced the ability to move materials more easily; perhaps to enable living in more defensible locations. Also, as social organization improved, it became plausible to integrate a variety of mechanisms into *systems*; systems to provide offensive capabilities, defensive capabilities or to enhance the provision of food and water both to enhance security and to provide for physiological needs.

Larger and more complex groups gave rise not only to enhanced systems, with their constituent mechanisms, but to sub-groups responsible for their use. The rise of armies and the construction of forts are examples of such *agencies* aimed at the safety and security of the group. Quite obviously, agencies aimed at the meeting of physiological needs offered great benefit to the group as well. Finally, there arose the concept of *administration* of the social and physical environments in order to mitigate threats and to ensure safety and security by proactive measures of provision and prevention, rather than merely through reactive measures.

Next in the ascending hierarchy of stimuli is that of belonging. Metaphorically, we represent the individual or family response to this stimulus with *grooming*. The emphasis is placed on the concept of basic connection between members of the group. This experience has been described by Robin Dunbar in *Grooming, Gossip, and the Evolution of Language*. At the level of family, the connection is physiologically based before subsequently becoming cognitively based. For the larger familial groups, the connection can be represented by *gossip*, a form of grooming that doesn't require immediate physical contact.

At the level of the tribe, a larger group is involved and a more extensive belonging must ensue, that afforded by the propagation of societal links through imitation, or rather *mimesis*, as we want to express the cognitive aspects of the experience. For example, cohesion within the extended group can be enhanced through reenactment of the group's beginning and continuing, as described by René Girard in *Violence and the Sacred*. For even larger groups, this elaboration rigidifies in its structured form; that represented by *ritual*, a process expressed by Victor Turner in *The Anthropology of Performance*. Within the much extended group, the story becomes more formal and, in current societies, has given rise to *law*.

Belonging gives rise to esteem. Esteem is based upon a commonly shared sense of value and a representation of self-worth within that domain. While grooming directs meaning in the context of physical wealth, *barter* represents a progression of the concepts of values as a more abstract characteristic. The *shell* signifies a representation of direct, immediate value. The *bulla* represents an object of exchange, conveying the concept of counting discrete values and propagating them over distance. *Gold* is illustrative of the arriving at an absolute representation indicative of different value systems, with the prospect that some rate of exchange can or could be established among them. Finally, we arrive at the concept of *commerce*, deriving from many domains comprising many value systems in a single infrastructure. Thus, we see the range of esteem: from the basic concepts of just living, for example a good provider, to eminence in the broader reaches of social systems, for example a great statesman.

Beyond the needs of esteem, the cognitive appetite seeks for a more conscious fulfillment. At the most basic level, cognition derives from the display of *purpose,* effected through the individual's sensori-motor system. The ability to develop concepts based on the sensori-motor system and then to extend those concepts through *metaphor* is central to the human cognitive system, as shown by George Lakoff and Mark Johnson in *Metaphors We Live By*. Building upon metaphorical understanding, the cognitive facility is further extended through the mechanism of *blending*; the ability to create even more complex concepts through the melding of multiple metaphors, as presented by Gilles Fauconnier and Mark Turner in *The Way We Think*. The cognitive mechanism of *induction* allows for the creation of new concepts subject to derivations and pragmatic matching with experience. At the apex of cognitive facilities, the full use of *logic* allows for the development of reflexive thought, where thought is its own object.

The aesthetic need is closely related to the cognitive need; perhaps it is best conceived as a blending of cognitive and emotional contexts. We have suggested that this need reflects the emergence of trust as the central ingredient of social order. Conceptually, we would characterize such a blending as art; but in this representation we seek to differentiate among artistic genre. At the individual level, a person may seek aesthetic fulfillment through personal *adornment*. *Clothing* represents the extension of personal adornment to external devices; somewhat like a mechanism that satisfies the aesthetic appetite. In the context of larger groups, *fashion* enters the picture. It elicits an aesthetic response at a social level. For the larger, more structured group grounded in emotional connectivity, *grace* transcends fashion; it instills enhanced emotional bonding to the group. In its current incarnation, we look to art not just to satisfy the emotional aspect of aesthetic fulfillment, but the cognitive aspect as well. This blending we'll represent as *elegance*.

The apex of the cognition-based needs is termed self-actualization. Throughout recorded history, from cave paintings to magnificent social structures, we can trace a trail through the enhanced facilities of the mind. First, people evoked *expressions* derived from their sensori-motor experience. As they developed the capability for metaphoric understanding, expressions gave way to *meaning*; a metaphorical rather than literal interpretation of the world, a concept at the center of Terrence Deacon's *The Symbolic Species*. This was the precursor to *discourses*: a means to record and distribute the subtle nuances of policy throughout a distributed group. It also provides the means to convey this policy across time as well as space. The emotional basis of larger groups derived from the ability to use narratives to manipulate emotional states, as represented by the *ode*, which encompasses poetry and scriptures. And, in the current preeminent characterization of self-actualization, we suggest the use of language in the form of *rhetoric* as its most appropriate illustration.

We share a reading of Abraham Maslow's *A Psychology of Being* and *The Farther Reaches of Human Nature* that establishes a separate, higher need beyond self-actualization; that of transcendence. Transcendence is typically portrayed as the need to extend beyond oneself. We suggest that this description can be refined to encompass the drive to impact the environment so as to allow the subordinate needs to be addressed. The illustration of this need across the variety of grouping mechanisms employed by humans is in fact an expression of the underlying mechanism leading to the respective groups. The individual and family expand through *exploration*. The extension to groups beyond the family is grounded in the concept of *union*, the discovery of mechanisms conducive of expansion through mimesis. Further search leads to the *myth*, stories of creation and existence, looking beyond the observable events of the natural world. Building upon this preternatural causality, people then constructed complex models of social order in the form of religious *theology*. And, finally the species arrived at what we would perceive today to be the frontier of social evolution; the construction of social systems strongly rooted in the physical world and aimed at natural *governance*.

Based on these characteristics of the evolution of social ecosystems, it is interesting to now attempt to devise a model of such systems; a model formulated along the lines of first a qualitative, and perhaps then a quantitative specification that we might use within computer systems as an illustration of the workings of a complex social interaction system. From this model, perhaps we can glean some insight into better understanding the functioning of social ecosystems and where their evolutionary pathway might still be taking them.

We just saw that the hierarchy of needs has both an ontogenic and a phylogenic component. Moreover, the hierarchy correspondingly reflects evolution along both those dimensions, essentially comprising a vector of selection. From that description alone, it suggests the similarity of the hierarchy of needs in social ecosystems and DNA in physical ecosystems. The importance of that observation is that it provides a foundation for a common view of evolution across the two ecosystems. Instead of defining, as Richard Dawkins does in *The Selfish Gene*, on one hand a constituent molecule of DNA with its genes, and on the other hand an equivalent to genes called *memes* that is lacking a constituent organization, we can see a parallel between physical and social ecosystems, with DNA (physical) and the hierarchy of needs (social) as organizational entities, where parts of each carry vectors of evolution. From our perspective, the needs hierarchy itself, with its constituents across the ontogenic and phylogenic dimensions of the pretergenesis table, seems to naturally map to the well-understood function of genes in biology.

# Model of Social Ecosystems

Social ecosystems are the enablers of groups. Groups exist because they comprise effective mechanisms for survival as judged by natural selection. Groups have been essential to the ascendance of the human species; without groups it would be problematic whether individual humans could long survive. A variety of group types are found among the species today. While each type may exhibit different capabilities, they come from a common mold and can be characterized by a high-level model of organization and operation. The capabilities of groups or perhaps more appropriately, of grouping mechanisms, have expanded over time due to a series of evolutionary changes affecting the individual human and through which have arisen enhanced capabilities for the establishment and functioning of increasingly complex multi-person ensembles. These changes presented in the evolutionary development of the individual and then were expressed through groups of individuals.

We propose a model of social ecosystems through which various grouping mechanisms can be represented and compared; a model that offers the prospect of specialization, allowing a characterization of each of the grouping mechanisms that have been identified. With some degree of rigor, we can use this model to consider the mechanisms through which interactions within the groups and among the groups are effected. We observe that this same model provides a means for analyzing the structure and function of computers and computer networks. The model is that of a *trust infrastructure* which subsequently encompasses one or more *policy infrastructures*.

In the physical world that we experience, all activity proceeds through interactions that are grounded in the basic laws of physical processes. The process of interactions effects activity and the laws of physical processes posit a causality of this activity. From the assumption of causality, we derive *trust* in the conduct of interactions. Without interactions, any environment is static and unchanging, which in turn makes the elaboration of causality problematic. As a consequence, we have difficulty in establishing trust within a completely static environment.

We have observed that social ecosystems are more complex than the physical ecosystems we experience. This derives from the fact that a social ecosystem presents a larger number of basic forces than does a physical ecosystem. When the stimulus for interactions comes from people, then the interactions are a function of the needs hierarchy of humans. Consequently, interactions can derive from the full range of human stimuli, from instinctive reflex to cognitive choice. We suggest that the actual evocation of a stimulus for action on the part of a person derives from the characteristic we have termed trust. Consequently, a model for social ecosystems is preferentially oriented towards first a means facilitating the establishment of trust. All other aspects of interactions, indeed the full infrastructure through which interactions in a social ecosystem occur, must be grounded in trust. Moreover, within a functional social group, the trust of the individual members of the group must be congruently based. If the trust of individual members of a group emanates from different sources, then it will be difficult or impossible to subsequently achieve adherence to the mandates of policy. A facility to establish trust, then, is the primary characteristic forming the boundary of a social ecosystem, a concept to which we apply the term trust infrastructure.

The stimulus of human interactions is established by needs and the mechanisms of interactions are governed by policy. So, subordinate to the trust infrastructure is one or more policy infrastructures. A policy infrastructure comprises the environment in which interactions of a particular type can occur. These interactions are defined by a variety of rules that comprise the basic forces that occur within the policy infrastructure. The basic forces within a policy infrastructure can vary by person, or by any other entity that participates in an interaction. Consequently, a necessary facility for a policy infrastructure is a means to establish the identities of potential participants in interactions and a means to allocate authorization of specific characteristics or capabilities to those identities. These facilities make it possible to apply the appropriate rules to the appropriate participants for a specific interaction. The establishment of authenticated identity is so central to the social ecosystem that we view it as very closely aligned with the trust infrastructure, although its constituent mechanisms have the characteristics of policy infrastructure interactions.

Interactions elicit consequences. In fact, the general objective of an interaction is to evoke the desired consequences. The application of policy to interactions anticipates consequences. Policy will certainly anticipate the consequences of a successful interaction; one in which all the participants go away happy. Policy must also anticipate unexpected consequences; what happens when someone is not happy? When an interaction evokes a consequence outside the bounds of the policy infrastructure, the resolution of the consequence may be deferred to the physical ecosystem. In other words, the consequences will no longer be limited to the constructs of the social ecosystem. With this overview of the model in mind, let's now delve a bit more deeply into the characteristics of the component elements of a social ecosystem, beginning with the trust infrastructure.

Trust is a measure of societal metaphoric understanding; it is the basis of all human grouping mechanisms. As we suggested earlier, trust can be defined as *an expectation of an outcome with some degree of assurance*. Trust established within a social ecosystem is the characteristic that determines whether we believe the rules to such a degree that we will abide by them, even if it hurts to do so. This does not mean that within the mind of the individual person, trust is always a consciously considered choice. Rather, it is the application of combined emotional and cognitive evaluation to the potential for stimulation of an action through or by the human motor system. In essence, within the human mind, trust is the characteristic that gates the trigger for an action stimulus. Remembering the association made by Klaus Scherer that we considered in our discussion of emotions in Chapter 4, the level of emotional response forms the clock that determines when we apply this gating function to a potential action stimulus. Moreover, it determines the level of trust required to actually stimulate an action. If we act, then we've achieved this necessary level of trust in our cognitively derived assessment as to whether to stimulate that action or not. Thus, trust is the essential ingredient in the occurrence of interactions in general and is noteworthy in its governance impact on interactions involving people. Specifically, a person must achieve the necessary level of trust in anticipating the outcome of a transaction, or in some contributing factor to a transaction, or else they will choose not to participate in the transaction, or to participate in some different manner or degree. When the mind seeks to stimulate an action, if the level of trust is sufficient then the stimulus is effected, otherwise the stimulus is withheld. This, of course, presupposes that one has a choice relative to participation. Absent such discretion, if an interaction is forced, then people may still try to affect the outcome based on their level of trust in any optional means or characteristic of the interaction at their disposal. It is interesting to note a mental condition known as *abulia* that is symptomatic of the loss of mental capacity to effect independent action. This observation is not intended to draw a direct correlation between the concept of trust that we have suggested and this specific mental condition. Rather, we view the condition simply as indicative of the existence of a governing process for the stimulation of responses.

Trust can be discerned in the interactions with inanimate objects as well as those that include humans or various other organic participants. If we drop a brick, our expectation is that it will fall to the floor; an expectation or trust based on our understanding of the motion of free moving bricks as derived from our previous experience. If we have previously dropped a bucket, but not a brick, our facilities for metaphorical understanding will attempt to apply the correct context to the action of the brick. If we drop a brick directly over our foot, our essentially instinctive assessment that it is going to land on the foot may well be sufficient to trigger a near-reflex action, causing us to quickly move our foot. More generally, our facilities for metaphorical understanding encompass the establishment of trust based on experience. The first time we see someone release a helium filled balloon, we might actually exhibit surprise when the balloon goes up and not down. Should a tree appear near to falling in the forest, with no one around, there might still be a high degree of trust in our expectation that the tree will fall to the ground. Consequently, we might well choose to not park our automobile beside a dead and leaning tree which is next to the campground parking lot.

From a quantitative perspective, trust can be construed as a probability and in some instances can be rigidly specified. A concept with similar characteristics to trust is that of a scattering *cross-section*; that is, the probability of an interaction comprised of one elementary particle bouncing off of another elementary particle in a very specific fashion within a particle accelerator. The unit probability of a cross-section is called a *barn*. The unit derives from early studies on rather simple, high probability interactions. In one such interaction as an example, the probability that a 1/2 MeV electron will interact with a gold atom located in a stationary gold foil is so high that it's like "hitting the side of a barn with a baseball." (You really have to love the sense of humor of those atomic physicists.) The point is that in well-defined interaction environments, a level of trust can sometimes be quantitatively prescribed. Outside the laboratory, when we consciously talk about trust, we don't typically ascribe such a quantitative assessment. We usually refer to it in very general terms: "I trust him," "I don't trust her," "I trust the mortgage company to pay my property taxes on time." All of these statements reflect a cognitively expressed evaluation of a level of trust, but the meaningful expression of trust is the one that results in action or inaction. If I jump out of the plane, I have made a profound evaluation that I trust the parachute to get me safely to the ground. This evaluation is highly dependent on the circumstances surrounding the immediate interaction, including any pertinent emotional response levels incurred within one's mind regarding the pending interaction. One's decision to take a sky dive might well be different if jumping alone is considered versus jumping with one's new potential partner, who is an accomplished parachutist. It will certainly depend on the relative urgency of the needs involved; is the pursuit of sexual gratification the object, or merely esteem? There are those who seek to jump out of airplanes purely in search of aesthetic fulfillment, but to do so, they will have overcome any primal fear through a healthy dose of cognitively derived understanding of the workings of parachutes or through trust derived from well respected third parties.

The evaluation of trust can be highly qualitative and subjective. Under normal driving conditions, my level of trust might allow me to conclude that the car traveling three feet to my left on the freeway, where we're traveling at 70 miles per hour, will not arbitrarily swerve to the right and run us both off the highway. If I perceive some evidence that the driver of that other car is inebriated, then my trust determination may change. I might now conclude that it is desirable to effect an action to slow my car down and let that car to my left pass and get ahead of me. So, where does trust come from? We are born with an instinctive facility for recognizing and expressing emotions, but not necessarily with a pre-defined set of emotional responses keyed to specific sensory input. Rather, our emotional reactions seem to be the result of programming in concert with our cognitive evaluation facilities; in essence, we learn them and we do so at an extremely early age. So, how does this come about? Well, essentially we establish our emotional responses and our cognitive evaluation capabilities based on our experiences. A realized outcome from an interaction will establish our responses to similar potential interactions in the future; and, our cognitive abilities for metaphorical understanding allow such responses to be extrapolated to new experiences based on their similarities to old experiences.

The programming of our responses begins as infants. In his *Handbook of Emotions*, Michael Lewis relates research with infants as young as two and one-half weeks that are able to recognize emotional responses from their mothers and to effect recognizable emotional responses in return. In the best situations, we learn through the interactions with our parents or others around us. We are exposed to interaction situations and we are guided in our responses by the role models around us. A mother blows gently on the stomach of her baby and then she smiles and laughs. The infant perceives an odd sound, a tactile sensation, a facial expression of a role model showing pleasure or happiness and a good sound, and the learned response is one of pleasure and happiness. After a few iterations of this activity, the infant may well start to anticipate the outcome based on the interaction's prelude. So, the trust level of the child is now programmed to perceive the likely outcome of the interaction with positive anticipation. In fact, the infant may well try to indicate to the mother to "Do it again!"

Within a trust infrastructure that forms the basis of a social ecosystem, one should be able to address the question "Where does it start?" Our assertion is that trust begins with, and emanates from, a single, immutable point. Trust may convey from this point through a variety of mechanisms. We suggest that trust ultimately derives from a single point because ascertaining a specific level of trust always resolves to a binary decision; it is either sufficient to allow the stimulation of action, or it isn't. The point is immutable because it cannot be changed within the existing infrastructure without resorting to consideration of an evaluation of trust regarding what would be a policy issue involved in reorienting the trust infrastructure. This would, in essence, require the invocation of a higher trust authority. Rather, if the basis of trust is changed, then a new trust infrastructure is created.

At the physical level, trust emanates from the basic force that effects a particular interaction. Cognitively, our establishment of a particular level of trust emanates from the degree of our understanding of the natural laws involved. In such cases, our level of trust in the various aspects of an interaction is based on an understanding, as presented through our sensori-motor experience, of the characteristics of the physical ecosystem in which this physical interaction occurs. As we each grew up from infancy, long before we more fully comprehended the law of gravity, we understood through our observations of repetitive action that things fall when we drop them. If they're heavy and they fall on our foot, then it is going to hurt. Hence, our experience teaches us that a brick falling toward our foot is worthy of a fast, corrective response. On the other hand, finding a small pellet of plutonium in the back of a cupboard might well not evoke an appropriate response. On finding such a pellet, we will probably be dead shortly, either from chemical or radiation poisoning, since our typical lack of experience with the toxicity of plutonium or with lethal levels of radiation might well create an incorrect assessment of trust. Experience, then, can be viewed as a means for calibrating our trust assessment facilities, if we live through the experience. As we noted in an earlier chapter, "That which doesn't kill us makes us stronger."

Although ultimately grounded in experience, trust can also be viewed to derive from habitual activity. We can be trained to respond "this way" to a given situation. The connection of sensory input to the stimulus for action is programmed to be automatic; an effective means for establishing coordinated responses from members of a group, although sometimes effecting an unfortunate stimulus if the parameters of the situation have changed without our taking sufficient note. Soldiers can respond with appropriate actions in the face of debilitating danger because their training overcomes their fear; that is, the repetitive, ritualistic action on which their training is based essentially recalibrates their trust assessment facilities. Repetition of specific sensory input versus action stimulus in certain situations mitigates what would otherwise be an overwhelming emotional flood for the uninitiated.

One means of establishing a uniform basis for trust within a group is the use of *ritual*, a variant of habitual activity. Various repetitive actions can be used to instill a common emotional state within a group, and from this emotional state, a corresponding state of trust can be derived. Hence, an appeal to emotional anecdotes during the half-time speech by a football coach, followed by a ritual chant and the admonition to win one for the Gipper, is but one example of the use of ritual as a means of instilling confidence, an approximate manifestation of trust within competitive sports teams.

An offshoot to the basing of trust on experience is the redirection of trust through a third party. I place a great deal of trust in John's opinions and John exhibits trust in George, therefore, I have an enhanced level of trust in George also. Obviously this predicates upon my experiential base through which I establish trust in John; but it has the useful effect of expanding my horizons of trust so to speak. This particular mechanism is worth noting, of course, because it has significant impact within social ecosystems, and it will prove very significant when we consider the establishment of trust as a comprehensive determinant of security within computer systems and computer networks.

We've suggested that trust forms the gating parameter for action stimuli. This would, in turn, suggest that there is a gradient to trust, ranging from low to high. We can think of it quantitatively by viewing trust as a measure of the risk inherent in any aspect of a transaction; high risk of something being incorrect or going wrong corresponds to low trust; low risk of something being incorrect or going wrong elicits high levels of trust.

In small groups such as a family, a clan or perhaps a small community, trust is established among the various participants over time and is a primary derivative of the group association. Trust begets confidence in policy and confidence in policy begets altruistic action that may benefit the group at the expense of the individual. Indeed, it is our view that trust is the overarching trait of the evolutionary success of groups. Within a group environment, a person acquires a reputation as a trusted individual through actions or patterns of behavior applied consistently during a significant time period. Perhaps, under the correct circumstances, a single or very few acts of altruistic behavior may be enough to significantly enhance one's credence for trust. Likewise, a single betrayal of this acquired trust may be enough to significantly diminish, perhaps permanently, the credibility so painstakingly acquired. We most often think about trust in terms of individuals; we develop trust in a particular person, perhaps simply through reputation if we don't know the person. Thus, we imbue a person's *identity* with a level of trust relative to some characteristic. This, of course, presupposes that we have processes through which identity can be reliably authenticated across time and space; that is, we must first establish trust in the process through which we determine identity and then it becomes reasonable that we trust some characteristic associated with that person's identity.

If, over time, one is recognized as performing in a trustworthy manner, then one can build a reputation of trust in the eyes of persons not known. Yet another way to build trust is to aspire to the same set of values in our actions as does another person or group of persons. This is a way of establishing a level of trust, although perhaps not trust in a quantitative sense. Being able to say "she's a good woman" is a bit different from being able to say "I'd trust her with my life or the lives of my children." However, the former will facilitate the latter. It is this approach to trust that is embodied in much religious dogma. First, recognize a code of conduct for the group, a *morality*, that can be used to guide and to judge the behavior of individuals. Once a strong correlation is observed, that is, when a person develops a reputation for doing good, then the trust conveys to situations not specifically handled by the moral code.

We must not, of course, forget a source of trust that emanates directly from the physical ecosystem; that is, trust established through force; a form of trust from which comes action based on an overriding fear of doing otherwise. There is, of course, but a subtle distinction between fear of the supernatural versus fear of physical harm in forming the basis of trust. History is replete with social ecosystems based on either, or both. That said, let us continue our consideration of a model for social ecosystems by examining how trust, once established, is conveyed through the ecosystem.

We might surmise that from the earliest emergence of human groupings the ability to convey trust was critical to the success of the group. Conveyance of trust within nuclear family based groups was likely an artifact of normal social interaction coupled to physiological processes. To project trust outside of one's immediate circle of associates was much more difficult; it still is today. As interactions among groups became more widespread, that is as groups became larger and the interaction points became more diverse, the problem of trust conveyance became more acute. And, what is it about group associations that make trust so vital? We noted above that a primary requirement for the group to have competitive advantage over other individuals or other groups is for the group to have well defined policies established for dealing with interactions, both intra- and inter-group. If the group is going to count on adherence by its members in the application of these policies, then the group must have trust in the policies defined as well as in other individuals in the application of those policies. During interactions when policies are applied, it must be possible for individuals involved in the transactions to assess the trust they place in the other interaction participants. So, in order to establish our conceptualization of various groups, we need to be able to understand where the trust is established that is then ascribed to the members and the policies of the group. If viewed in this way, it is clear that trust must subsume policy, or put another way, we have to have trust first and then we'll be able to accept and apply the policies.

Consider the foundational narratives of the Christian religion. One such narrative deals with the mission given to Moses to lead the Children of Israel out of bondage in Egypt. Within this story, when Moses is on the Mountain of God receiving his instructions (policy to be applied), Moses asks of God, "When the people ask, who has sent you? What shall I tell them?" God then responds "I Am that I am. "Tell them that 'I am' has sent you." Now, within a computer security infrastructure, this is a classic example of a self-signed assertion. I am who I say I am; you may accept and trust that or not.

In computer science, an example of a self-signed assertion is called a self-signed *certificate*. A digital certificate is a credential through which a third party can attest to the trustworthiness of two parties that want to enter into a transaction with each other. If both parties individually trust the third party, then they should be able to trust each other. This is the digital equivalent of the Letter of Credence that ambassadors present to a head of state to establish representation. The trusted third party signs one certificate that says "This is Tom." and then a second certificate that says, "This is Sally." Now, the two parties can exchange these certificates and, again, if they trust the signer of the certificate, then Tom trusts that this is Sally and Sally trusts that this is Tom when they meet up somewhere. The question then becomes, how does the trusted third party introduce itself? It does so by signing its own certificate that says, essentially, "I am" and then providing copies of this certificate to both Tom and Sally. If the signature of the self-signed certificate matches that of the signatures on the credentials (certificates) also given to Tom and Sally, then they can each determine that all the certificates came from a party they all trust.

Finally, we must consider again the establishment as well as conveyance of trust that can be accomplished through various degrees of force, ranging from fear for one's physical well being to cognitive intimidation induced by threats and coercion. Trust established in any of these manners propagates directly into the subordinate policy infrastructures in the form of implied or direct consequences of interactions. In such situations, force or fear may be used to shape the form and content of interactions in advance, or to judge the acceptability of the form and content of interactions after the fact. In either case, the fear of the consequences for non-adherence to the rules becomes a guiding principle of the policy infrastructure.

Before addressing the policy infrastructure, we need to emphasize that readers familiar with the literature on trust may find our approach much broader than they are used to. For example, we suggest that interested readers refer to Julian Rotter's seminal paper *A new scale for the measurement of interpersonal trust* for a psychologist's approach to the subject encompassing many elements that will be found in this book. In particular, Rotter studies the relationship of religion to trust in a quantitative manner, the earliest, and as far as we know, the most formal attempt to address the subject in an experimental environment. Obviously, we give trust a much larger importance as we place the trust infrastructure at the center of development of both individuals and groups, and humans and computers. We do not consider trust as an epiphenomenon of human behavior, but rather a central mechanism of human survival. This all shouldn't be too much of a surprise, as the very lack of a global approach to the concept of trust in both human and computer system in the current literature has been a major driver in us writing this book.

The policy infrastructure is that portion of the system that establishes and implements policy at the transaction points of the system. Policy encompasses the following concepts: (a) specification of the rules governing interactions in general, and transactions specifically, (b) processes for negotiating, or otherwise arriving at the rules for a transaction, (c) processes for the application of rules during transactions, and (d) enforcement or consequences of the rules applied during a transaction.

The policy infrastructure is an environment supporting recursion, that is, self-reference in its relevant concepts. Thus, access to the various policy mechanisms is achieved through transactions to which policy is relevant. Identity of the potential participants in a transaction establishes a necessary characteristic for the conveyance of trust, and as such is a central aspect of the application of policy; that is, policy may be ascribed to different identities as well as to transactions. It is worth noting that provision of policy, as an aspect of both parties of a transaction, requiring negotiation between the two prior to a transaction, is absent from most, if not all serious identification systems today. In fact in many, if not most discussions about identity concepts and identification systems, the inference generally made is that the scope of use of identity, that is the policy relative to processes keyed to identity, is the purview of the receiver of identity rather the provider of identity. Consequently, since most identification systems today make use of identifiers through which the identity of people is ostensibly authenticated, the general de facto policy is that if those identifiers are compromised, then they can be used by other people to impersonate the identity of the true target of the identifiers and, through this theft of identity, they can perform any action or make any claim that the impersonated person could perform or make if they were physically present and participating in the transaction in question. This obviously points out an important asymmetry with such identification systems and leads one to at least consider alleviating this situation through another assumption, the provision of user-controlled policy definition mechanisms.

Specifically, neither assumption currently warrants a default status. Rather, to correct the current problem, the policy through which the use of identity is established would have to be expanded in law and then provided for within identification systems. That is, the ultimate source of the policy should either be general law or it should be the result of a negotiation between the provider and the receiver of identity on a transaction-by-transaction basis. There are a wide range of issues from which policy could be defined under the personal control of each individual with the definition of policy itself being the subject of policy definitions related to the strength of the authentication mechanism used to establish the differential identity of a person. Authentication protocols can range from high trust variants, perhaps requiring a person to go to an office equipped with very secure and accurate biometric sensors with smart card access, to low trust variants, perhaps only requiring a person to present a security token, for example a Radio-Frequency Identification tag (an RFID token) at a turnstile. Policy allowing use of varying levels of security for entry of authentication parameters (biometrics, personal identification numbers, etc.) allows for a variety of performance levels when an identity token is presented as well as a variety of trust levels in the resulting authentication.

Through policy definition, it can be specified what trust can the receiver of identity authentication place in materials or services attested to by a specific authenticated identity. For example, a person may want to disavow any trust being placed in casual e-mail messages. Some e-mail messages could be considered akin to a highly trusted, absolutely truthful document to which the signer attests, under pain of liability. Others would be considered part of a highly informal mode of communication, worthy at one extreme of simply passing along gossip. So, it should be possible for a person to establish a policy regarding the trustworthiness of specific messages and allow negotiation and then well defined policy for the sending and receiving of messages. If one side attests only to passing along gossip, and the other side doesn't want to hear any gossip, then no exchange takes place.

The rules governing physical interactions are immutable and they establish a policy infrastructure through which our most basic interactions are effected. Of course, as we noted back in Chapter 3, the initial conditions established at the start of interactions as well as uncertainty in the outcome of physical processes that stem from basic characteristics such as those studied in quantum mechanics provide a significant degree of variability. Consequently, we can learn to work within the constraints of physical laws. We can learn to mitigate their effects in some sense, but we can't change their basic character. As a result, the physical ecosystem is an environment in which the trust infrastructure is congruent to the policy infrastructure. Essentially, within this infrastructure, trust derives from physical laws. While the interplay of many physical interactions creates the concept of chaos, the underlying rules are moderately straightforward. On the other hand, when the concept of social ecosystems is introduced, the rules governing interactions become much more complex, because they are mutable and they appear, in many instances, totally arbitrary.

Within a single trust infrastructure, one or more policy infrastructures can be established. Each policy infrastructure defines a context for interactions that includes the form of interactions and the rules governing those interactions. Within the United States the various governmental entities form a number of hierarchically connected policy infrastructures. From a governance standpoint, all of these policy infrastructures exist within a single trust infrastructure in which the root of trust is established by the Constitution of the United States. This document establishes a social compact through which the interactional relationships among citizens and government are defined. Trust emanates from the Constitution based on personal commitment of the citizens. When a critical mass of the citizenry no longer holds this commitment, then a new trust infrastructure must prevail. If no other social ecosystem is established, then the new, default trust infrastructure will be the physical ecosystem, with its associated immediate violence.

Within the trust infrastructure established by the Constitution, national and state governments have been deemed separate sovereigns, meaning that the laws within each jurisdiction can be independently defined and the procedures for adjudicating those laws can be independently applied. All of these separate jurisdictions are, however, subject to the basic precepts of governance established by the Constitution. As an example of variances among these disparate policy infrastructures, consider that execution under the death penalty, as the extreme consequence of failure to abide by the rules of the infrastructures, is more commonly applied in the State of Texas than in any other state in the United States. This is due largely to the manner in which appellate procedures, a part of the larger scale process for effecting the interaction that is the rule of law, are conducted. In many states, these appellate procedures extend the delay between trial and sentence fulfillment almost indefinitely. In Texas, however, strict rules for the appellate process have been established through law, making the process much more expeditious, resulting in the high number of executions.

Religious organizations within the United States are established under the purview of constitutional government. Such organizations can be deemed as tax exempt, removing them from many of the coercive mechanisms that governments can exert. However, rules adopted within a religion are subject to significant constraints by government, rendering them, in general, subordinate to secular law. For example, certain religions view the reception of blood transfusions as counter to the moral code established by the church. While such rejection of medical treatment is acknowledged by government in many instances, in situations where the subject person is not deemed fully capable of expressing an informed consent to the refusal of treatment, such as minor children or those found to be mentally incompetent, then the state can mandate treatment against the patient's expressed wishes. In general, in the United States, religions cannot exert, as a consequence of interactions within the religious policy infrastructure, rules that have the force of law found within government-established policy infrastructures.

In a physical ecosystem, interactions are essentially infinite in extent. Of course, virtually all interactions have an interval within which the most probable outcome of the interaction becomes known. So, the physical world works through the results of interactions. Human groups form an evolutionary mechanism through their activities and interactions in order to achieve beneficial results with respect to multi-level selection within the physical ecosystems in which the groups exist and operate. The way this should be modeled is debated, with various positions illustrated for example by Scott Atran in *In Gods We Trust* on one hand and David Sloan Wilson in *Darwin's Cathedral*. In one version, it is the groups themselves that compete on a plane comparable to the known individual selection mechanisms that function for all species. The counter argument is not that groups don't exist and have a significant impact on the evolution of the species, but rather that the effects of group activities impact the ecosystems in which individuals exist and that all natural selection is purely dependent on the mechanisms available to the individual. From our perspective, the salient point is that groups do exist and they exert considerable influence on the behavior of their members. As we discussed earlier, the mechanisms that various groups use to establish consistent codes of conduct have evolved in concert with the biological evolution of the species.

It is not our objective in considering a model for social ecosystems to make value judgments regarding the efficacy of particular social structures. Our perception is that such structures are evaluated through the principles of natural selection. That said, it does seem clear within this model that a central point of differentiation among social systems is the manner in which the rules or statements of policy are determined within any particular policy infrastructure. We have used as a representative example of such an infrastructure the system of government that has been established by the United States Constitution. Certainly, other governmental systems can be similarly characterized within the simple constraints of this model. In the following sections we will consider the relationships of religious systems and secular governments. It might be tempting to try to extract subjective value judgments from the considerations; again, it is not our objective to do so. That said, let us look at just a bit more detail in the makeup of the purveyors of policy within various social ecosystems.

The central feature of a policy infrastructure is a compendium of rules that govern interactions within the infrastructure. These rules can derive from a number of sources, each of which typically characterizes a particular type of policy infrastructure. Depending upon the specific infrastructure, we tend to identify these compendia through a variety of names. Most common to us are the laws formulated by various government bodies. The purveyors of the rules in such systems are typically a legislative body of some type. Within the United States, at the state and national levels, the establishment of laws requires concurrence of an executive function: a governor or the president. The fitness of law at all levels is subject to the scrutiny of a judiciary, the arbiters of policy, who interpret the validity of the rules versus the defining dogma of the relevant policy infrastructure.

A computer policy infrastructure concerns itself with the mechanisms of interactions that can be fully characterized through the concepts of the Open Systems Interconnection (OSI) reference model presented in Chapter 3. At the base of the stacked protocols described by the model are the physical interconnections over which or through which interactions occur. A common feature of such mechanisms is networks, general connections among common elements across which one can make an arbitrary association of any two such elements. More generally, roads and highways exist as networks, as do railways. By virtue of our metaphorical connection, one might view the DNA molecule as a network. Indeed, we refer to the social substrate as a *fabric*, an extremely dense network structure. The most common image of networks, at least in current society, is that of our electrical based infrastructures: the power grid, the telephone network and of course, the Internet.

As envisioned by the Open Systems Interconnection model, built upon the constructs of networks are two distinct protocol levels whose direct purpose is to effect interactions between connected elements. The first such protocol level is a *connection*, a moderately short-lived pathway relative to the *circuit* elements that make up the network segments, that can be made to exist during some time interval. Within the Open Systems Interconnection model, *transport* protocols are used to establish connections between specific elements. A *session*, in turn, is an even shorter duration pathway that builds on a connection and whose effectuation is generally well formed as to beginning and ending. A telephone call from one subscriber to another comprises a session. A session allows the higher-level protocols to establish an application level connection between two entities. Of course, in order to establish a session within a network context, it must be possible to establish the *identity* of the entity at each end of the session.

"Everyone knows everyone in a small town." More to the point, as the Cross Canadian Ragweed, a music group that, like one of the authors, made its way to Texas by way of Stillwater, Oklahoma, song tells us, "You're always seventeen in your hometown." Such homilies express a truism of relatively small groups, groups such as small communities, or clans, or perhaps even tribes, that such groups derive a significant strength from the aspect of their very natures that provides for the detailed identification of their members. Only by knowing who is a full-fledged member of a group can it be discerned who is not a member. This demarcation will help to delineate the threat from the ally. Moreover, through such identification it is possible to apply specific rules, or aspects of the rules, to specific individuals, thus establishing the specialization of responsibilities that benefits the group as a whole. Of course, in modern society, which is to say within larger and more complex social ecosystems, the concepts of identity and identification have become quite complex in their own right. In particular, as the size and geographical extent of the group grows, the mechanisms used to establish individual identity must be enhanced beyond those used in small groups.

As a general mechanism, identification means distinguishing one person relative to all other persons within some group. In the most general case, of course, identification means distinguishing one person relative to all other existing persons; and, in the extreme, it means distinguishing one person relative to all other persons who have ever existed. A general system can be established for providing identification services; a system termed an *identity system*. An identity system provides, at a minimum, at least two distinct services: *enrollment* and *authentication*. These two services can also be termed *identification* and *verification*. We will consider the intricacies of an identity system in much more detail in Chapter 9. For the moment, let us consider some of the more basic characteristics involved.

*Enrollment* is the seminal step through which a person is distinguished from all other persons within a group. Two steps, each requiring a specific protocol, are necessary to enroll a person in an identity system. First, it must be ascertained that the person in question is not already contained in the identity system. Second, a unique *marker* must be divined for the person; all persons within the group must have unique markers. The level of trust that can be established in the identity of a person through any particular identity system is dependent on the connection between the marker and the person. The United States Social Security System provides for an enrollment process in which people sort of present themselves to the system for enrollment and, in return they receive a number as their marker within that system. Since no rigorous validation can be made as to whether any particular person is already represented within the system and since the marker issued, that is the Social Security Number, has absolutely no measurable connection with the actual person, the level of trust that can be placed in identification through the Social Security System is negligible to non-existent. As a consequence, the Social Security Number is essentially useless as an identification mechanism. Nevertheless, it represents one of the more prevalent identity systems in use within the United States.

Relative to current technology, the only viable marker for establishing uniqueness for a person is a biometric characteristic of the person. There are a number of characteristics that can be used: DNA, retinal patterns, iris patterns, fingerprints, palm prints and even footprints. Each of these characteristics has many positive features to recommend their use as a marker, but most also have features that argue against their use. For the moment, we will simply assert that from among these characteristics, there are available one or more appropriate markers to be used in an effective identity system. So, what is so important about a biometric characteristic? These are the only features currently available that have an extremely strong association with the person. As a consequence, they are difficult to impossible to counterfeit if the markers are measured with a trusted system. Using a biometric marker, both steps of the enrollment process that we mentioned above are readily accomplished. If a person is already present in an identity system, then a one-to-many comparison of their biometric marker with those already in the system will determine whether they've already been enrolled. Within the vocabulary of identity systems, the term *identify* actually refers to just this type of comparison. The second step of enrollment is accomplished automatically; the marker is essentially provided by the person to the system, not the other way around. Perhaps the strongest feature of biometry based identity systems is that they constitute an extension of the mechanism that humans use for establishing identity within relative small groups.

The biometric comparisons that we utilize through interpersonal identification are daunting when compared to existing technologies for machine-effected identification. We humans use facial recognition, voice recognition, physical response recognition, auditory recognition and cognitive response recognition; and, we do this simultaneously and seemingly effortlessly. As we noted when considering some of the physiological aspects of both humans and computers, Richard Feynman assigned tremendous value to efficient, reliable identification through miniaturized variants of computers that approximate our natural abilities for interpersonal recognition. Indeed, without attributing a moral value to the proposition, we suggest that such identification has been a central aspect of the evolutionary benefits derived from social groups. The identification mechanism alluded to by Feynman is, at its base, simply a biometry based identity system for which, today, the technologies exist so as to allow such a system to be fully implemented on personal electronic devices. Now, once we can establish an identity, how do we attach specific rules to it?

Complementing the concept of identification that flows from social ecosystems is the concept of *authority* that applies to that identity. Both identity and authorization entail not only information, but processes affecting and effecting that information as well. Within an interaction, specific parties (entities) to the interaction can be ascribed the authority, or permission, to participate in various ways. I obtain authority to operate a motor vehicle on public roads by acquiring a driver license, a credential that grants certain authority to my identity. I obtain authority to purchase some item by presenting the necessary form of payment to the satisfaction of the seller.

These examples seek to illustrate the distinction between the character of these two processes, that is between identification and authorization, as well as the mechanisms used to effect them. Identification flows as a unique characteristic of the human body. Authorization flows from a credential from a trusted third party, and that authorization is unambiguously connected to the identity of the person. My iris pattern establishes my identity while a credential (a driver license) from the Department of Motor Vehicles establishes my authorization to legally operate an automobile. What then can we say about the actual interaction process?

Interactions proceed according to the rules defined for a specific policy infrastructure. We alluded to the fact that interactions within the physical ecosystem, deriving as they do from basic forces, are essentially infinite in extent and duration. There are obviously similar interactions that occur within social ecosystems as well, perhaps not infinite in extent and duration, but very wide and long nonetheless. In order to have some chance of understanding the various aspects of interactions, it is useful to define a more constrained process, a well-defined interaction called a *transaction*.

Simply put, a transaction is an interaction of well-defined and constrained scope; the extent of its impact is limited, as is the duration of its conduct. In essence, a transaction occurs in a well-defined place at a well-defined time, and procedurally it has a well-defined beginning, middle and end. The constraints on a transaction are defined as part of the specification of policy within a policy infrastructure. If we think in terms of government-established law, then infractions of the law are generally considered as transactions. The place of their occurrence determines the jurisdiction of law under which they fall. The time of their occurrence determines the degree to which consequences can be affixed to their subversion. In some jurisdictions, certain crimes have a statute of limitations; such a limitation compels the enforcers of laws to prosecute the perpetrator of an infraction within a set amount of time following its occurrence.

In what we would hope would be a more normal case, such as the purchase of some item, a transaction is much more mundane. In a store, we approach a sales agent with an item we want to purchase. The agent determines the total cost of the item and we then offer up some form of payment. When the agent is satisfied that payment has been properly conveyed, the item is put in a bag and we walk out of the store with it. Correspondingly, if we purchase a book from a Web site on the Internet, the transaction model is very similar. We put the book in our "shopping cart" and when we've completed our shopping we "proceed to check-out". Here we proffer our credit card number. The Web site makes a charge against this card and, on this completion of the transaction, schedules our book for delivery by some physical conveyance mechanism; that is, they mail the book to us.

Finally, a transaction has a well-defined end. At the end of the transaction, either appropriate procedures have been enacted to cause the overall state of the infrastructure to change as dictated by the transaction, or the state reverts to exactly that occurring before the start of the transaction. Thus, transactions are generally perceived as atomic events; they either completely occur, or they never happened. Once they occur, of course, we might be concerned with the result; i.e. the consequences.

Transactions are marked by *consequences*; that is their intent. As we alluded above, the purpose of a transaction is to change the state of the infrastructure, perhaps profoundly, perhaps superficially. Under the United States national government and within most state governments, there are at least three distinct forms of law: criminal law, civil law and administrative law. Interactions are governed by a different set of rules within each of these domains, and each incurs its own type of consequences as a result. The laws of the United States, criminal and civil, are established through legislative action, with executive concurrence, and are compiled in written form in the United

States Code. The Code of Federal Regulations is a compendium of rules and regulations issued by the various administrative agencies of the federal government.

The consequences of interactions take rather distinct but general forms within each of the three mentioned domains. Criminal conduct, that is interactions that effect results counter to criminal prohibitions, generally elicit physical sanctions of some form; either fines, a period of incarceration, periods of formal and informal scrutiny of activities or all of the above; that is, sometimes, the consequences might include a combination of all three domains. Interactions under civil law usually take the form of contracts in various guises. Contract law typically requires a specification of consequences within any agreement if that agreement is to be enforceable through further legal action. The consequences of contracts are usually referred to as *consideration*, and to guarantee that a contract, for example between two parties, is enforceable under most law, it is necessary for both parties to receive consideration under the terms of the contract. "I'll scratch your back if you scratch mine." An offer to provide something or to perform some act without provision for receiving consideration in return for it is typically referred to as a gratuitous promise and it may not be enforceable through the legal system. Consideration can take a number of forms: perhaps payment, perhaps a specific service or perhaps a promise to act in a certain way. Both criminal and civil sanctions tend to be backward looking. That is, they are applied after the fact of a transaction, when some party contests the validity of the transaction under the applicable rules.

The consequences of administrative interactions, however, tend to be forward looking. That is, rules and regulations will often require a specific set of actions, perhaps including some type of certification, prior to any governed interactions. A regulation established by the Federal Aviation Agency requires a pilot certification and periodic, acceptable physical examinations before a person is allowed to fly a commercial airliner. A prospective pilot is required to prove adherence to these rules before being allowed to take control of a plane. Failure to demonstrate that these requirements have been fulfilled are sufficient grounds for administrative or police officials to physically prohibit a potential pilot from entering the cockpit of a plane.

# Religion

Religion is a central theme of this book, and we have now finally reached a point of sufficient background to expand upon our concept of religions as instances of social ecosystems; right here in the middle of a chapter; just about in the middle of the book for that matter. Our reasoning has been that religion is a natural result of the evolution of the human species. It is particularly associated with modern man, the term often used to describe the members of the species that have emerged since the last recognizable mutation event of extreme consequences occurred somewhere between 50,000 and more than 100,000 years ago. At the present time, no one is completely sure what the physiological manifestation of this event was, but since it occurred, there has been a steady progression of human development, culminating in the current situation in which *Homo sapiens sapiens* is capable, both intentionally and unintentionally, of overwhelming the physical world to the extent of making it uninhabitable for the human species. Or course, one might readily speculate that, at the point where we collectively proceed over the precipice, the physical world will continue on and some other species will get its shot at the golden ring. But, we'll leave that value judgment, as best we can, for others to consider. Let us, instead, make an attempt to reconcile religion with human physiological characteristics such that we arrive at the current culmination of social ecosystems.

The model of social ecosystems that we have suggested in the previous sections of this chapter is applicable to religious as well as what might be termed *secular* social structures. The distinguishing characteristic of religious systems is the source of trust on which these systems are based. Some religions establish one or more deities as the ultimate source of authority, and hence of trust. Some religions do not postulate the existence of deities, but rather center on a process. The derivative result of either approach is similar; that is, each resolves to a statement of, or a collection of statements of, what we would term policy. In the case of theistic religions, trust in the policy emanates from the deity, or deities, while in non-theistic religions trust emanates from the process. In either situation, the effect is to instill a sufficient level of trust within the minds of the believers such that their actions are properly constrained by the tenets of the respective religion. In this way, the actions of large numbers of believers can be coordinated so as to benefit the group at large, and most of the members individually. So, the interesting concept is how this level of trust is created?

It may have started with a simple fungus.

The human mind is driven by the senses. Widely distributed throughout the human body are sensors for sight, sound, touch, taste and feeling; all wired through the peripheral nervous system into the various lobes of the brain. Forming the input to a multitude of neural network structures, these continuous streams of sensory input become the fodder for information processing. Mirror neurons put sensory input in context, enabling responsive motor actions to be undertaken in an extremely efficient fashion. The integration of emotion into this information processing establishes the basis for action stimulus. The construction of units of manipulation with means to rank and organizing them creates the lego of conceptualization. This is the basis for metaphoric comprehension, a central part of natural language, which, through empathetic understanding of the external world but without a means of reactive motor action, may give rise to consciousness.

An integral aspect of the workings of neural interconnections is derived from the chemical relay of neuron stimulations effected by neurotransmitters at the synaptic connection between neurons. In this relay process, the propagation of sensory input and processing output is modulated by chemical means. It should really come as no particular surprise, then, that if one can impact this chemical modulation, perhaps through other chemicals, the resulting neural processing will be impacted as well; an *altered state of consciousness* results. Such altered states can be experienced by completely normal individuals according to a variety of stimuli that range from emotional stimulation and manipulation to psychotropic drug induced modulation of brain activity. In addition, altered states of consciousness can be experienced as symptoms of a variety of aberrant physical ailments that evoke abnormal mental conditions as a result.

David Lewis-Williams in *The Mind in the Cave* describes a continuum that encompasses a number of stages of altered states. Based on a neuropsychological model, his scale ranges from the mildest level of change which he refer to as alert consciousness to the most severe change that he refers to as deep trance. In continuously changing degrees between the two extremes, are a variety of forms of dreaming, in particular, day-dreaming and lucid-dreaming. He characterizes one of the possible characteristics of the deep trance stage as the occurrence of hallucinations, noting that in particularly deep variants of this state all the senses can be involved. While healthy people can experience altered states of consciousness, Lewis-Williams also notes that several conditions such as schizophrenia trigger hallucinations.

Archeology suggests that early humans discovered hallucinogenic mushrooms. For example, the frescoes of Tassili described by Terence McKenna in *Food of the Gods* show a mushroom-headed goddess. Through the psychotropic drugs contained in these simple fungi, humans found that they could induce an altered state of consciousness approximating, in some instances, that of a deep trance. The most common such mushrooms contain the neurotransmitters *psilocybin* and *psilocin* that act on receptor neurons that are sensitive to *serotonin*. Such neurons are known to be involved in a variety of regulatory processes within the brain, in particular, the regulation of mood and of sensory distribution. One possible effect of the psychotropic drugs derived from mushrooms is to inhibit the reuptake of serotonin by pre-synaptic neurons, essentially enhancing the duration of serotonin induced processes. The net effect is that ingesting hallucinogenic mushrooms can cause significant distortions in the brain's normal processing activities, giving rise to hallucinations. Based on these hallucinations, a person might well perceive effects beyond those of natural sensory stimulation; in other words, they might well induce effects perceived as preternatural. Such effects can present as a state of *ecstasy* within the mind.

The state of ecstasy is largely an emotional state. As such, it would comprise a component of the emotional assessment that lies between sensory input and motor response that we noted in the previous chapter as described by Scherer. If this emotional assessment presents as a component of the contextual compartmentalization and subsequent metaphorical understanding such as might be exhibited by mirror neuron constructs, then ecstasy would have a profound impact on the metaphorical projection of internal sensori-motor experience to the external world. This impact would likely manifest itself as an enhanced degree of trust in the cognitive processes that occur during this altered state of consciousness; a net effect that feels like a connection of the mind to the supernatural, perhaps to God. Thus, it seems quite plausible that the state of ecstasy, including situations where it is induced by psychotropic drugs, is a source of enhanced trust on which a religious framework could be established.

Of course, once recognized, the state of ecstasy became a goal to be sought. It feels good and we derive cosmic understanding from it. "Wouldn't it be great if we could get that feeling without having to find mushrooms?" Indeed the state, or certainly a near approximation of the state, can be induced purely through cognitive processes, augmented by appropriate sensory input. Through meditation, rhythmic chants and sensory manipulation, certain individuals can develop the ability to enter a state of deep trance, and hence of ecstasy, without the need for drugs. Persons particularly adept at this practice can be viewed as special or as weird. If their professions while in a state of altered consciousness coincide well with physical reality, they might well be perceived as chosen ones who could talk with God. If their professions ran counter to others perceptions of the current physical reality, then they might simply be viewed as persons who hear voices in their heads. With one focus they are prophets; with the other they are heretics.

A truly unique and unifying characteristic of all religions, relative to other social ecosystems, is the identity and location of the ultimate purveyor of trust. Specifically, religions seem to establish an ultimate trust purveyor in one of two basic ways: from outside the physical ecosystem in which the social ecosystem resides or as the result of a purely cognitive construct within the mind of the individual. Thus, within a theistic religion based social ecosystem, trust emanates from a *supernatural* source. On the other hand, within a non-theistic religion trust emanates from the processes of the mind. We will look in much more detail at these two approaches in Chapter 7 and Chapter 8 respectively. No matter the specific religion, this ultimate purveyor of trust rarely communicates with humans directly through their sensory system when it is in an unaltered state. Instead, most of those who have heard the source of trust speak to them have accomplished this act through sub-auditory or sub-optical means. It is up to them to subsequently convey the words uttered by the voices to the rest of the people. Thus, we have trust established through group belief that the words of the prophets indeed came from God, or gods, or as a principle of immanent truth, or other establishments of the necessarily immutable terminal source of trust.

Within a theistic religion, policy emanates from the deity or deities that comprise the foundation of the religion. Alternatively, it comes from the same organizing process from which trust derives, in the case of non-theistic religions. In either case, this derivation of policy generally appears to take a very special person to establish the statements of policy under the auspices of the ultimate trust arbiter of the particular social ecosystem. We suggest, then, that this ultimate human policy purveyor is the *shaman*. In various religions, the policy purveyor is known by other names: prophet, lawgiver and the enlightened one. Mircea Eliade has made a seminal review of shamanistic practices in *Shamanism, Archaic Techniques of Ecstasy*. In virtually every case related through anthropology or history, it appears to require the abilities of select, chosen ones to translate the rules given by the deities, or from the ordained process, into the compendium that other believers can access. One explanation would be that only the shaman's ecstasy allows refinement of the trust infrastructure with the necessary detachment from the very policies that are effected by the change. Once the trust infrastructure is in place, its conveyance to policy can take place.

*Ritual* provides a direct connection to human emotions. Consequently, as an aesthetic facility it can bear directly on the conveyance of trust. Few of us have not felt the appeal of certain songs. Often we associate them with particular events or times in our lives, and to hear them over and over again still evokes something of that original feeling. This is, in essence, ritual in the small. Expand upon it a bit and you get the primitive exhilaration of a rock concert or the stirrings of patriotic fervor when the Marine Corps Band (The President's Own) launches into *Semper Fidelis*. This comes closer to ritual in the large. Religion has proven exceedingly innovative in the use of such ritual to evoke a common emotional state among a group of believers. From the great chorales to Gregorian chants, the music of religion can instill a variety of emotional states in its listeners, states that make this audience particularly receptive to trust induced reception and acceptance of messages of many types; from a more abstract view, statements of policy. When properly applied, such emotional programming has similar characteristics to protocols as we have discussed them; protocols through which desired interactions can transpire.

An interaction can be characterized by a collection of protocols, each of which deals with a specific aspect of the interaction. Each protocol involves a series of well-defined steps with decision points interspersed along the way. By following the steps, one is led to the decision points. Each outcome from a decision point then points to a new set of steps which lead to the next decision point. With the outcome of the final decision point of the protocol, the protocol is completed and the interaction is in a known state. A more generic term for this concept of protocol is a *ritual*. Either a ritual or a protocol provides a process through which the parties to an interaction can establish a common state. If the resultant state is one of emotional ecstasy within the human mind, then it becomes an effective means of establishing or reinforcing trust originally derived from that state. As such, ritual becomes a powerful means for establishing or reinforcing trust within a group whose members engage in the ritual in some form of concert. Islam makes use of its Five Pillars that comprise a set of rituals through which the faithful maintain or renew their trust in the faith. Of these, Salah, the daily prayer that must be offered five times each day while bowing toward Mecca, is the most constant reminder of the moral code that should direct the actions of all believers. Meditation, mantras (words or formula), mudras (symbolic hand gestures), are forms of rituals found in eastern religions that are associated with ecstatic stages. In *Maya Cosmos*, David Friedel, Linda Schele and Joy Parker have shown remarkable continuity in the rituals of the Mayas through the dramatic events that their culture has been subjected to in the last millennia.

Perhaps the simplest, yet most dramatic ritual in Christianity is that of *communion*. The taking of bread and the drinking of wine form a powerful reminder to the faithful of the sacrifice made by Jesus when he was crucified; a sacrifice ostensibly made on behalf of all mankind, not just the faithful, whose significance is expressed in the words attributed to Jesus at the Last Supper in suggesting the token, "Do this in remembrance of me." In actuality, the ritual follows good form relative to contract law, which in fact it is intended to be; that is, the establishment of a covenant (contract) with consideration due both parties. The sacrifice made by Jesus in accepting crucifixion as payment for the sins of the people being the consideration due the people; accepting the sacrifice and living as Jesus described being the consideration due to him. Different churches make use of this ritual at various times, but for all it represents a unifying time to remember the basis of the faith; to renew the trust that is the strength of this social grouping.

# Vox Populi, Vox Dei

Social structures based on religious mechanisms were likely the earliest means of large-group coordination. When the collective understanding of physical or social ecosystem is unable to provide explanations, new causality, by definition, can only be initiated through preternatural means, i.e., means perceived to be outside accepted cognition. As new mechanisms such as representative democracy in the early United States, or elsewhere, began to emerge, it was therefore natural to couch the rationalizations for these systems in readily understood religious terms. Thus, it became opportune to imbue the collective wisdom of the people, as expressed through election mechanisms, with religion style trust mechanisms. From this come concepts such as "The voice of the people is the voice of God." Thus, the results of an election can perhaps be better accepted if viewed as the will of God. Of course, as the operation of human stimulus-response mechanisms has become better understood, we are perhaps better able to characterize the results of elections as collective responses to our individual needs hierarchy.

# Social System Ontologies

Through the next few chapters, we will use a construct derived from the field of philosophy as a means to explore a variety of concepts concerning computers and their interactions, a construct called *ontology*. This construct enables language mechanisms to be used to establish metaphorical understanding, in this case, understanding based on the complex, social ecosystems that encompass religious organizations in their various guises. Following Thomas Gruber in *A Translation Approach to Portable Ontology Specifications*, we use as our working definition of ontology, *a specification of a conceptualization*. In the technical world, a specification, particularly a formal specification, carries a relatively well-understood connotation; that is, from a specification one should be able to design an implementation that can be measured to meet the specification. One should be able to describe, in detail, how to build one of the things described by the specification; i.e. convey a message to the architect and builder. So, writing or creating a specification means that one is going to use some language or graphical representation to convey the thoughts in the specification, and the representation one uses must be capable of sufficient detail to pass along instructions for the subsequent architects and builders.

In this case, we want to build an ontology, or at least some salient parts of one, that could serve as a formal specification for a very specific type of social ecosystem, or at least a social ecosystem for which we have a large number of examples. Not only that, we have several well-defined examples of the architects and builders who were deeply involved in building such social ecosystems. So, it will be an interesting exercise to create a conceptualization of sufficient detail that it can be captured in a specification; that is, in our ontology, such that one could perform at least a thought exercise in which the characteristics of these existence proof cases could be derived.

Now, the question becomes what are we going to specify; what is our conceptualization? Well, in the words of Shakespeare, "the play's the thing." The modern addendum then is "You can't tell the players without a program." So, it will be useful later on if we understand the various elements that we ultimately need to consider in our specification.

A central feature of any religion, or any social ecosystem for that matter, is the ability to differentiate the believers from the non-believers: the members of the ecosystem from the non-members. As has been noted more than once, "The benefit to having a club is the ability to exclude people from it." That's a rather cynical view of certain types of groupings, but a relevant concept nonetheless. From our perspective, the greater need is to be able to establish who is in the group, and what special role, if any, various individuals play within the group. Beyond establishing membership, we can anticipate the need for a list of distinct roles within the group that must be played by its members. This implies that the mechanisms that we use to identify the members of the group must be capable of establishing and conveying various attributes associated with that identity.

The premise that we are exploring is the efficacy of social ecosystems as grouping mechanisms in enhancing the competitive advantage of one group relative to other groups. Thus, a group, and hence its general membership, may derive advantage in the natural selection process to which all groups are subject. So, the anticipation is that our conceptualization must provide for the application of rules that the members of the group must or should follow when they interact with other people, with other groups, and with the natural ecosystem in which they exist. Looking forward, we can anticipate that it will prove advantageous to the operation of the group to allow some aspects of the rules to be negotiated among different parties to a transaction. So, our ontology should establish mechanisms through which individual positions relative to the rules can be codified as part of the transaction process.

The rules of the group will encompass a number of variants of interactions. Consequently, it will be necessary to define constraints, modifiers and attributions on the various rules such that the various interactions are recognized and the correct rules applied. We further anticipate that discrete rules, attributed at an individual group member level, may encounter conflicts in at least between-member interactions. The implication of this is that somehow, prior to or during an interaction, the actual rule that applies to the interaction must be discernable. We'll consider this a bit more in a following section.

Finally, some consequence of the application of a rule or set of rules during an interaction will accrue. It seems obvious that different implementations that might follow from the conceptualization will enable different mechanisms for evaluation or enforcement of the rules. So, the conceptualization must allow for a variety of approaches.

The net result of these various requirements for rules within the conceptualization, at least to those of us from the technical computer world, implies that rules will involve both descriptive as well as procedural elements. It further implies that some means to invoke the procedural elements must also be anticipated within the conceptualization.

The thrust of the conceptualization that we want to develop is aimed at explaining interactions: interactions among groups, interactions among individuals, interactions between individuals and groups, and interactions between individuals and other elements of their social ecosystem, including the physical ecosystem that is subsumed by the social ecosystem. To facilitate interactions, it will be necessary to bring the various participants of an interaction into the necessary physical or logical contact so as to facilitate the interaction. This bringing together is the function of a specific role within the ecosystem that is usually termed a *broker*. For the moment, consider a broker as an abstract concept. We'll try to give it more substance in the next chapter.

The goal of the ontology is to fully specify the mechanics of transactions. Once the participants of a transaction are brought into proximity, the rules under which the transaction will occur must be established. This is the function of yet another abstract entity that is usually termed an *arbiter*. The service performed by an arbiter is an abstract concept as well. With regards to the establishment of the rules and consequences of transactions, we will term the functions provided by the *policy arbiters* as those of *arbitration* and *adjudication*.

# Architectures of Computer Interaction

Interactions involving computers can be classified into two main forms: human-computer interactions and computer-computer interactions. As we noted in the second chapter, the main epochs of computer evolution over the last half-century or so can be characterized by a blending of the evolving physiology of computers with the manner in which a person and a computer interact. In a parallel development, the mechanics of computer-computer interaction have arrived at the dawn of fully networked systems; a prospect sometimes characterized as the *grid*. Functioning much like a collection of imprintable neurons within the mind, grid computing assumes an ability to imprint semantic functionality on arbitrary collections of networked computers.

The dominant form of interaction found on the Internet today is one of client-server computing. Through this model, both computer to computer and human to computer interactions can take place, to effect computational activities on behalf of a set process, or of a human user. Within the computer domain, as is often the case within purely human to human interactions, there is often a requirement for formally defined interactions. We have referred to these as transactions.

As we saw, a transaction is the atomic unit of interaction. It is of finite length and can be characterized as to beginning and ending. While a transaction may entail peer-to-peer exchanges, the establishment of the beginning and end of a transaction generally entails a client and server relationship between any two parties to the transaction. By that we mean that in order to proceed through any type of protocol to facilitate a transaction, it is necessary for the two parties to agree which is performing which steps of the protocol. We can define a generic model for such a transaction environment by establishing specific roles for two parties; the roles are that of *supplicant* and *sentinel*. The sentinel is the guardian of the integrity of the transaction while the supplicant is the party that desires to establish an interaction relationship with the sentinel in order to conduct the transaction.

Governance of computer-based interactions derives from policy specification mechanisms that are grounded in trust authorities and mechanisms that can be projected across the network. The detailed architecture of individual computers and the details of their network interconnections is a function of *system administration*. The *administrators*, entities whose role is one of enacting administration functions, derive their authority of control from their identities as established within the trust infrastructure of the network.

The software through which computer based social groupings are effected is generally divided into three component domains: application software, operating system software and middleware. The concepts of application software are based in the language of the problems being addressed at any particular time. Operating system software, on the other hand, is concerned with the sensori-motor environment of the specific computer system in question. Middleware generally comprises some, or all, of the protocols that connect these two domains together.

In the computer world, there is a given with regards to any level of security: a trust infrastructure must be based on a secure computer platform. To draw a parallel to the human mind, a secure platform is one on which it is not possible to establish an altered state of consciousness. This is simply a way of saying that no outside source can be allowed to impinge on the sensori-motor environment of the secure computer. There can be no eavesdroppers to detect and perhaps modify sensitive or secret information, and there can be no substitution or modification of the stored program that controls the sensori-motor environment of the computer. At the present time, the only way to effect any level of security within an unsecured, or dubious platform, is to add yet another platform that is secure and hence trusted.

Given a trusted platform, it is possible to establish a trusted communication channel with another trusted platform across connections that are not, themselves, intrinsically trusted. This can be accomplished through the use or cryptographic processes on the trusted platforms. In the same way, two generals communicate during the battle by sending each other secret messages that cannot be understood by the enemy even if they are intercepted. This allows for creation of a single trust environment within physically disjoint systems where the space separating them is suspect. Thus, it is possible to separate the client element of an application from the server element of an application and still enable them to share a common trust environment, as long as each resides on a trusted platform.

From a trusted platform, it is also possible to measure selected characteristics of another platform in order to imbue some level of trust in that platform. Further, it is possible, again from a trusted platform, to detect changes of certain types and levels in another platform in order to evaluate whether an ostensibly trusted platform has been compromised or not.

Trusted platforms derive their trust from their intrinsic characteristics that make them difficult or impossible to manipulate or modify. The degree to which they are impervious to such manipulation is termed their level of being *tamper-resistant*. Today, essentially no computer platforms are inherently *tamper-proof*; there are mechanisms to subvert virtually all known architectures, albeit at various costs. So, given that no platform is immune from manipulation, a necessary feature of trusted platforms is that of being *tamper-evident*. That is, if a platform is manipulated, then it should exhibit one or more telltale signs that it has been manipulated.

Finally, another given relative to computer systems is that complexity in computer software presents an enhanced threat environment. The problem is that, today, computer programming is still a cognitive process of the human mind. At the highest levels, it requires attention and action from human minds to effect. Such processes are inherently inexact. Consequently, the more complex the environment, the higher is the chance that security holes have been included.

The primary function of an identification system is to contribute to the trust model of the system by supporting the authentication of the identity of the individual persons or other relevant entities registered in, or recognizable by, the system. The document *Special Publication 800-36: Guide to Selecting Information Technology Security Products*, issued by the National Institute for Standards and Technology of the United States Department of Commerce, suggests three ways that authentication can be accomplished: through provision by users of something that they have (e.g. a token), through provision by users of something that they alone know (e.g. a password) or through sampling a personal characteristic of the user (e.g. a fingerprint). Each of these approaches essentially calls for the provision of a marker on the part of the supplicant and the assessment of that marker regarding establishing the identity of the supplicant by the sentinel. Each form of authentication is accomplished by slightly different protocols. However, essentially all of these protocols consist of qualitatively similar procedures. We characterize these procedures as five successive stages.

The first stage we term the *overture*. As with a play, this stage is the prelude to the main action. It entails bringing the supplicant and the sentinel into close proximity such that they both decide that they wish to enter into the authentication protocol proper. The actions that occur during the overture indicate that either side can first take the initiative in the process. The sentinel may first notice the approach of the supplicant and issue a preliminary challenge: "Halt, who goes there?" Alternatively, the supplicant can take the initiative: "Hello the house!" Following this very preliminary exchange, the sentinel can begin the formal authentication procedure; "Advance and be recognized!" The supplicant then responds with an initial assertion; "I'm Jane Doe."

In essence, we've slightly codified an exchange that might occur between two strangers meeting in an isolated location where the intentions of either can range from benign to threatening. In establishing some level of general transaction etiquette, this corresponds to the range of actions from a person's personal electronic device addressing an apparently dormant system and issuing an invitation for the supplicant to "Type your username" or "Insert your token." We've gone a bit overboard in discussing the overture stage because this is an area where operational models of different systems can diverge rather significantly; so, it is useful to model this well such that the two parties can land on their feet no matter how they got started.

The remaining stages are typically understood in a generic sense, but they can vary a great deal in the details. Once a name of the supplicant is asserted during the overture, then the next stage is *marker acquisition* from the supplicant and providing it to the sentinel. The only real new wrinkle here, from a conceptualization viewpoint, is recognizing that these successive stages may be pursued recursively, i.e. at multiple levels, in order to achieve an adequate trust level among all the elements of the two systems; i.e. first recognizing trusted equipment and then establishing trust in the identity of the supplicant. This is particularly important during the marker acquisition stage because, for most current identification systems, this will require the supplicant to trust the sensors of the sentinel through which the marker is acquired.

Once the marker is acquired, the next stage is *marker verification*, a processing step performed by the sentinel to a marker template that was gathered from the supplicant on enrollment into the identification system under whose trust auspices this interaction is taking place.

Following the verification operation of the acquired marker, the sentinel establishes the state of the authentication operation. Once this state is established, the authentication operation is over. The *departure* stage allows for shutting down this particular protocol and gracefully moving to the next one. As we've noted, such protocols can be effected recursively. Indeed, the three approaches to authentication suggested by the NIST document referenced earlier can be applied in repetition; performing any one of them constitutes *single factor* authentication, while using two or all three constitutes *two factor* or *three factor* authentication. Ostensibly, the level of trust established through the authentication operation increases as the number of factors used is increased.

# Networks

Computer networks derive from the mathematical reality of pair-wise interactions; the number of resultant connection pathways goes as the square of the number of end-points. For large numbers of computers, it becomes problematic to provide a dedicated physical connection between each pair. The same problem arises in all manner of interaction environments; the streets within cities, roads between cities, sewer systems among homes and offices, voice telephony, radio telephone and so on. The solution for all of these environments is the same; use shared connection pathways with a single connection for each end point. The shared connection pathways allow for real, logical or pseudo-shared access mechanisms.

When a road is built between two cities, the interactions between the cities take the form of traffic between the two. The traffic may be comprised of a person walking between the two cities or a truck load of goods being hauled from one city to the other. If commerce with a third city is desired then a single road can be built from one of the two initial cities to the third. Thus, three cities can be supported using only two roads. One of the cities now has two roads into and out of it; it has a fashion of redundancy. Regarding interaction capabilities, it is in a superior situation to the two cities with only a single road connecting each to the outside world.

A general network is a totally open network, amenable to all applications. While we really can't list any networks that are purely general, there are several domains which exhibit near-general facilities.

There is for certain one global network at least, the now traditional worldwide network of computers: the Internet. We're going to look a bit at its fundamentals and the relationships among the computers involved, including trusted platform cores. Then we'll use that model as a reference for the very important industrial networks that have otherwise developed.

The original computers of the 1950's were standalone machines, not really thought of as networks of devices by themselves. They had, nevertheless, a central processor unit connected to devices meant to manage the input and output of information to and from the central processing unit. Originally, each link to an input/output device, be it a keyboard, a tape reader, or a printer, was independently conceived. It didn't take long, however, before an organizing component, called a *bus*, came along as a way to connect the central processing unit to output devices in a homogeneous manner.

A precursor to the understanding of a standalone computer as a central processing unit connected in a star network with multiple input/output devices was Control Data, under the guidance of Seymour Cray, who would later become the creator of the famous super-computers of the 1980's bearing his name. In the Control Data model, a standard language of communication (a protocol in parlance that we've adopted) was established between the central unit and the set of input/output devices (called *peripherals* in computer engineering). In this model, which, by the way, is now the dominant model of modern personal computer architectures, the stand-alone computer is a network whose central unit is connected to one or more chains of peripherals, with each peripheral communicating independently, but in a standard way, with the central unit.

As of this writing, the dominant bus protocol is the Universal Serial Bus (USB), which most readers are familiar with since they use it with their notebook computer, their phone handsets, their cameras, and other devices, on a daily basis. As we'll see, the universal serial bus, as it turned out, would be central to an evolutionary event of personal electronic devices, whose trusted cores have been from their inception peripherals.

In the 1960's, transmitting information between computers essentially meant carrying a large, magnetic tape from one computer to the next. Considering the future ramifications, this approach clearly wasn't right. So in the 1970's, computer networking came of age; first, as we would expect, on a local basis, and then on a global one.

Locally, the issue was to link the computers in a computer room, or, to extend the problem a little, in, say, a building. While early solutions were specific to each vendor and would not allow computers from different brands, or often, computers from the same brand but of different models, to communicate, a breakthrough was looming. The local networking revolution was brought by Ethernet, a way to put many computers on a single loop, where computers would interact in exactly the same way as people in a room. In this network architecture, everybody listens to everybody. When silence occurs, somebody can talk. Of course, we all know that what happens then is that two people always seem to start talking at the same time. Well, if that happens, something has to give. So each of the would be talkers pauses, and hopefully, the pauses will be of different lengths, so when the first person starts talking again, the second person will have an opportunity to hear that and will refrain from talking until there is silence again.

Do that real fast and with computers and you have the Ethernet. All computers can now understand each other at a basic level, and nowadays, you're not thinking that this is nothing short of a miracle that you just plug your brand new computer into a network and it tells you immediately that the connection is already ready. If you're using a computer at home or at work, you are using Ethernet to communicate with others in the vicinity.

The concept of a local network based on the Ethernet was so strong that today, about all local networks are Ethernet based, whether wired or wireless, and the increase in speed in the Ethernet network has exceeded all expectations, to the point that each time a new technology tried to position itself beyond the expected limits of Ethernet, it was leapfrogged before having time to establish itself. In time Ethernet would become so important that it would find a place in even the close world of computer to peripheral communications.

While computer rooms and buildings full of computers were being wired for local communications, the next challenge was to interconnect those very buildings and computer rooms, first inside companies or institutions, and then even between those larger conglomerates. This is where the Internet comes into play. As its very name implies, the idea was to interconnect networks. In the local network, all devices know each other by name, just as the family or the tribe can satisfy itself with first names or patronyms. However, when the tribes assemble, last names are introduced. In the same way, interconnection of networks required global naming capabilities so that every computer on the global network could be addressed individually. Additionally, the interconnection had to be robust, that is, not crucially dependent on local failures. While this particular aspect of global network design will not bear directly on the role of personal electronic devices, it's good to remember because it has an effect on security, which is where trusted systems play.

Coming back to naming, and related to what was just said, a hierarchical, distributed naming system was put in place, which we all will certainly be familiar with, having an e-mail address, or entering business names into our Web browsers daily.

The expansion of the *global network* was first geographical, by now expanding to the most remote places in the world. The expansion was also physical, in the sense that all personal electronic devices in the world have been progressively given individual addresses, just like computers were at the beginning. For example, your mobile phone, your camera, your printer, all are getting addresses that will allow anybody on the network to recognize them. To fully enable this level of connectivity, new addressing schemes have been developed that expand tremendously the number of names available for devices. We've rather greatly simplified the story here, but we can summarize the success of the global network in one acronym you may well be familiar with, TCP/IP (Transmission Control Protocol/Internet Protocol), that covers the core essential networking technology that makes it all possible. You don't need to understand the functioning of TCP/IP to read what follows, as it suffices to take it for granted that it is a fundamental means for the network to exchange information, or, if we want to expand on a familiar metaphor, it is the concrete of the Internet highway.

Of course, one device that would benefit for individual naming capability is our trusted analogue for people, the personal electronic devices and their trusted core, now capable to have their own independent presence on the network. But we're walking ahead of ourselves here.

*Industrial networks* are networks of computers and/or other devices that have developed globally to answer specific needs of an industry. We are going to look at three important ones in terms of the computer equivalents of social ecosystems: telecommunications, financial, and television networks.

*Telecommunications* established the first global network in the XIX[th] and XX[th] Centuries. Up to the 1980's, the network was fundamentally a carrier of voice. Wires were used to transmit an analog signal; that is, a signal representing directly the physics of the *transponder* used to record the voice of the user.

To use our general model of networks, the local equipment was that of the phone box and its receiver, the local network was the link between that box and the office of the telecommunication operator, and the global network was the link between that office and other offices throughout the world.

Standard telephony, from the time of Alexander Graham Bell's initial invention, was comprised of a switched circuit architecture based on dedicated terrestrial physical links. A wire was run from one's home to a central switching station, and by entering the address of a desired telephone out there on the network somewhere (e.g. Pennsylvania 6-5000 for Glenn Miller fans) the local switch established a circuit to the local switch for the other telephone, and a dedicated session was brought into being for the time that one remained on the phone. Sometimes, a radio connection was patched into one of the dedicated lines and one could talk to a very remote location, partially through terrestrial line and partially through a radio link. For any telephone call of course, there was a consistent understanding of the end points of the connection; that is, all calls went from one fixed point to another fixed point. This had the great merit, from a business standpoint, of clearly defining who was going to pay the bill for the call time; that is, the caller, unless one reversed the charges by calling collect, in which case the call receiver paid for the call. The terrestrial lines to the local telephone were always available, meaning that the capacity of the system was limited by the number of switch to switch circuits that could be created.

In the 1970's, technology was developed that would provide for a switch to telephone connection made by way of a radio frequency channel that did not require a fixed, terrestrial line; the concept was termed cellular telephony. In the United States, a section of the radio frequency spectrum in the range of 800 MHz was allocated for mobile telephony. Communication in this frequency range is rather limited, with distances between the end-point telephone and the switching station that it talked to being typically in the 10 to 30 kilometer range. Given this range limitation and the rather minimal allocation of total radio frequency spectrum, an architecture was devised that allowed individual switching stations to use a variety of frequencies, with the available spectrum divided up into many carrier channels, each capable of supporting a single voice call. Each switching station was said to support a cell, with adjacent cells alternating frequencies to minimize cross channel interference for telephones equidistant from two or more different receivers. The switch to which the end-point telephones, now termed handsets, would connect was termed a cell base-station. Handsets, as it turns out, would be the first personal electronic devices, and, to this day, the most numerous.

As the network developed, phone companies, and later countries, entered into agreements for charging each other their respective share of the technical consumables associated with each phone call. All these agreements were implemented in central switches which routed the calls to their proper destination while at the same time, accounting for them.

In the 1980's, electronics had gotten to a point where it was possible to put, in a cost effective manner, a mobile phone handset in the hands of the general public. Each handset would communicate by radio to nearby antennas that would be associated with equipment allowing the routing of voice to the telephone operator company office, and from there to the general telephony network.

By far the most successful system is GSM (Global System Mobile), whose users had passed 1 billion in numbers at the turn of the XXI$^{st}$ century, and passed 2 billion a few years later. If you own a mobile phone, it is most likely a GSM phone. As we've seen in Chapter 4, the GSM network was, from the start, designed with a trusted computer component at its heart; a smart card called a *Subscriber Identity Module* (SIM). Every GSM phone has one. The mobile telecommunication network was in fact, the first general network to have addressed straight on the issue of security. This actually became necessary for the simple reason that as long as the telephony network had been relying on a physical cable to the house, hacking into the network would call for tapping into that wire somewhere, something which was not impossible to do, and was actually done, but something that required a physical intervention that could relatively easily be detected and dealt with by the existing legal systems.

When communities were established in a wide manner over the air, the story changed. It would now be possible for somebody to hack into the system by simply communicating via radio with the antenna of the telephone. Henceforth came the idea of associating with the handset the Subscriber Identity Module, i.e. a secure repository of user information. If the mobile phone operator was not presented the secrete data contained on the SIM, communication would not be allowed, and the fraud would be thwarted.

Later on, the presence of the Subscriber Identity Module allowed one further fundamental function, as the deployment of mobile networks brought with it a new need, that of allowing various mobile operators to serve each other's clients. For example, a caller in Chile uses a Chilean operator to speak to someone in China served by a Chinese operator. When an operator serves a client of another operator, that's called *roaming*. Of course, the roaming operator wants the original operator of the client to pay for that service. That's where the Subscriber Identity Module took its second role. As the roaming operator could present to the original operator the secret data of the user, the original operator could not deny paying the roaming operator. What we see here is a fundamental function of the trusted core of personal electronic devices, called non-repudiation, which facilitates electronic commerce, of which mobile telephony was an early form.

The story of the success of the GSM and its smart card architecture must include mentioning that the very portability of the Subscriber Identity Module played a fundamental role, since it allowed the decoupling of the relationship of the mobile phone operator with personal electronic devices produced by the phone handset manufacturers. By moving the SIM from one handset to another, the consumer would get instant service with the same mobile phone operator, keeping the operator more in control of the customer relationship, and less so the handset manufacturer.

The role of computational devices in finance is as old as finance itself. In fact early writing was most often linked with the need to record business information, a fact used by John Chadwick in *The Decipherment of Linear B*, where he made the winning hypothesis that the clay tablets of Knossos in Greece where transactional records. There is then little wonder that some of the early computer networks were associated with inter-bank transfers, which fostered the establishment of networking technology in the banking world. So just like it happened with cellular telephony, with the need of security, cards with embedded trusted electronics, smart cards that the banks called *chip cards*, came into play, enabling consumer usage of the *financial network*. Ironically, when the actual deployment of chip cards started picking up a bit of steam in 1978, a core idea of the inventors was that this was the ideal carrier of electronic money, a form of money akin to banknotes and coins, but in a digital form; however, this vision really didn't end up being central to the early development of chip cards, that took the form of securing banking transactions more similar to a digital form of personal checks.

The extension of the banking system into the realm of networks for consumers required means to recognize the person making the financial transaction. Hence was borne the credit card of today, whose function was initially to carry an identification number that would trigger the various mechanisms needed for the economic exchange to happen.

As we've seen in Chapter 1, in the 1990's, it became apparent that the state of the art to protect banking information, the magnetic stripe of credit cards, was made largely obsolete by the increasing sophistication of the hacker community, and this particularly in countries with an expensive or lacking network infrastructure. Therefore, the most powerful financial card operations, Europay, MasterCard and Visa, defined a standard way, called EMV from their names, to use chip cards to protect individual financial transactions over their private networks. The closed architecture of the network then established the need for a device called a *Point-Of-Sale terminal* (POS), accompanied with a *card-acceptance device*, that allows secure reading of the information of the user's chip card. When you go to the grocery, the point-of-sale terminal is the computer used by the cashier, the successor to cashing machines of yore. Actually, the point-of-sale terminal is also protected by a chip card, called a *Security Access Module* (SAM), which is used by the merchant. The user chip card protects against fraudulent customers, while the merchant chip card protects against fraudulent merchants.

The local architecture of the network is the link between the merchant system (i.e. the point-of-sale terminal) and the office of another participant to the system, called the *acquirer*. The role of the acquirer is to get the information of the chip card and route the proper financial information to the institution that has provided the chip card to the consumer. That institution is called the *issuer* of the chip card.

Original *television networks* were broadcast over the air in such a way that anybody with a television set was able to capture the signal. The revenues of the television broadcaster came from advertising or other resources directly received as the source, so there was no need to secure anything to protect the financial flows. In the 1980's, the idea of providing private television channels caught on, whether through fixed lines ("cable") or over the air. In both cases, the business case for providing the service required that the signal would only be decoded by the person having paid the associated dues. Again, the trusted smart card would become a key component of such systems. However, the case of encrypted signals over the air became a new capability to be provided by the cards, since the communication channel was one-way only, from the emitting station to the television set, with no return signal. No mutual authentication was possible. By this, we mean that it was possible for the user smart card to authenticate that the signal was indeed coming from the right broadcast station, and to use the proper decryption keys, but it was not possible for the broadcast station to know which user was actually viewing the channel. From a technological standpoint, this makes the feat of encrypted programming a very difficult task, because anyone can capture the encrypted signal and then try to decrypt it. This is a process with a good chance of success because the signal was, by necessity, encrypted by general means. This created a race between system implementers and hackers that continues to this day.

Within these television systems, the closed network is comprised of a decoding box and a smart card containing user parameters as well as other information that must be kept secret. If you have cable television or satellite television at home, the smart card is inside the box that your provider delivered at the initiation of the service. The local network is the link between the decoding box and the cable operator, in case of wired communications, or the broadcaster, in case of communication over the air. At the time of this writing, television networks have not evolved to global, roaming agreements like those found in telecommunication and banking. We'll see shortly that this will probably happen in a very different setup.

# Convergence

For as long as a phone was a phone, a merchant terminal a merchant terminal, and a television a television, dedicated industrial networks were perfectly suited to the tasks of their domain. However, things started to change when personal electronic devices started using protocols of general computer networks, like the universal serial bus and, as we saw before, Internet. Mobile handsets added capabilities by connecting to components of general use, for example memory cards, and Internet browsers. Similarly, merchant terminals started to be based on personal computer technology instead of specialized circuitry. And, as cable companies started to provide Internet services on top of their traditional television services so that their customers could browse the Web at home, we began to see companies in turn wanting to provide television services on top of Internet channels. Over time, it appears that all networks will converge to Internet technology, with its central TCP/IP network protocol at the core of all communications.

In *telecommunications*, convergence started when the concept of adding data capabilities to mobile phones emerged. At the beginning, i.e. from the mid-1990 until about 2003, data were added to voice using special protocols specific to the telecommunications industry, as represented by its main body of standardization, the *European Telecommunications Standards Institute* (ETSI). In spite of its name, that institute is now fully international; it just happens that the now prevalent GSM standard in mobile telephony started in Europe. Over time, a pressure started to be felt by mobile telecom operators to give access to Web resources, which are on the Internet. Therefore, standards started to evolve in the direction of providing capabilities like Web browsing to mobile handsets.

During about the same time, new standards emerged from a totally different origin, the US-based *Institute of Electrical and Electronics Engineers* (IEEE). Under the barbaric name of 802.11, those standards specified means to extend the Internet to mobile devices. The public is now familiar with Wi-Fi, one of these radio standards.

Once personal electronic devices where linked by radio to the Internet, something remarkable happened. For a while, the computer industry had been working on carrying voice over the Internet, by chopping voice into pieces that could be sent on the network using TCP/IP and then reconstituted at the end in order to replay the voice at the other side. This is now quite known as *Voice-over-IP* (VoIP). If you are for example a user of Skype or Vonage at home, you're using Voice-over-IP. *Et voila*, a computer, or any device with Wi-Fi, could now play the role of a telephone!

To finish the story for now, we need to come back to the European Telecommunications Standards Institute. When the first mobile telecommunications networks were established, they were dedicated to voice. Voice does not necessitate large network capacity (called *bandwidth*) for each voice channel. So, the original GSM network was good to carry voice, but not good for carrying data. To expand their networks to carry more data, a new generation of networks was developed by the European Telecommunications Standards Institute (in fact, not only them, but we'll keep things simple here) called *third generation*, or *3G* for short. At the same time, the Internet was explosively expanding, and 3G very rapidly took a path to provide Internet services on mobile handset via TCP/IP. *Et voila encore*, a phone handset, or any personal electronic device with 3G, could now play the role of a computer!

All of this is still is being sorted out at the time of this writing, but one conclusion is already forgone. TCP/IP has won the battle of the networks, and the Internet is the worldwide standard for communications, be it for voice or data.

As we've discussed, *financial networks*, for example, as used for inter-bank settlements, are private networks. The same is true for the parts of financial networks that deal with chip card usage by consumers for payment at point-of-sale terminals. Today, payment on the Internet is in fact an expansion of the traditional model of payment on point-of-sale terminals. Simply, the Internet stands as the wire between the card and the point-of-sale terminal situated with the Internet merchant or its agent. As fraud on the Internet expands and chip cards are introduced to palliate it, Europay Mastercard Visa (EMV) smart cards will first be used to talk with remote point-of-sale terminals, and eventually will directly go to the acquirer gateway. Concerning inter-bank networks, they are private to the financial world, which means that they are not connected to the Internet. In fact, they could be connected, since many actually are TCP/IP networks, but it is doubtful that this will be done rapidly due to the depth of established security procedures involved. In fact, this might be a good example of where convergence may not happen for a long time.

In the US, cable television is operated over a private cable company TCP/IP network. In a similarly ubiquitous fashion, in Europe, for example, another technology than cable, Digital Subscriber Line (DSL), allows various companies to deliver to home computers both Internet for their personal computer and video-on-demand services for their television. On personal electronic devices like mobile handsets, television can be served through third generation cellular phone services, or through another path specifically designed to that effect, Digital Video Broadcast for Handsets (DVB-H). We discussed earlier about third generation; digital broadcast allows direct broadcasting to handsets using a part of TCP/IP for the one-way communication typical of television applications, i.e. IP broadcasting. Convergence is at hand between digital subscriber line and third generation technologies, as both are TCP/IP based technologies. Essentially, this will facilitate video access on the general Internet. Digital cable delivery of Internet content together with voice services today means that cable has already converged in the US, and the same can be said of digital subscriber lines in Europe and elsewhere. Broadcast, whether by satellite or DVB-H, may be part of another convergence phenomenon, that of general broadcasting over the Internet, but this may not be actual before the next generation of Internet.

# Current Content Architectures

In the next chapter, we're going to explore the rationale behind an interaction model for computer networks. Essentially, the approach provides client-server access from an individual client to content that is accessible on the network on a server. For the moment, however, we need to lay the groundwork for personal electronic services to support this access to content. In the general network model, we will consider four basic constituents: (a) the trusted core of the client personal electronic device, (b) the client personal electronic device, (c) the content service gateway, which provides access to the content institution, and (d) the content service institution, where the server lies.

From a purely networking perspective, at issue is individual access to an institution, or the work product of the institution, via the network. The trusted core of the personal electronic device represents the identity and credentials of the individual, the personal electronic device provides a means to connect to the network, the gateway provides an entry point, a sentinel if you will, to the network content, and the institution contains the data or processes that the individual needs to access.

Personal electronic devices use a trusted core, whether called a Subscriber Identity Module in telecommunications, a chip card in banking or simply a smart card in other applications like television and government. The personal electronic device provides power to the trusted core, and uses it to communicate to the network. When the personal electronic device establishes a link to an institution on the network, it points to the secure core for the institution to identify whom it is talking with. In order for the secure core to function in a device, it needs to be accessed by a class of software that we earlier termed middleware. *Secure core middleware* in the personal electronic device allows the device to talk with the secure core, and to use specific functions of the secure core that the device is interested in, typically information about you and your preferences.

The most ubiquitous personal electronic device today, the *mobile handset* comes from different manufacturers with very different means of operation, as defined by their operating system. This environment is not like the world of personal computers, where almost all use a version of the Microsoft Windows operating system.

All handset operating systems provide means for the handset to access information in the Subscriber Identity Module. The handset will need to get user information from the SIM to establish a session with the mobile operator gateway and to encrypt the voice for privacy. This is done by software called *middleware*, because it sits in the middle between the handset and the SIM. This part of the handset middleware is defined by a European Telecommunications Standards Institute specification that all handsets in the world must follow, numbered 11.11. Another piece of middleware on the handset is numbered 11.14 and provides means for the SIM to access handset resources. For example, the SIM can use the screen of the handset to display menus for asking users their personal identification number for authorization, or other information like new preferences.

*Point-of-sale terminals* use banking chip cards to perform two basic functions. They talk to the consumer card to establish its validity, and they talk to a commerce gateway to establish the financial transaction. As we've discussed, point-of-sale terminals themselves contain their own trusted core, a chip card called Subscriber Access Module (SAM), which is used to authenticate the merchant owning the point-of-sale terminal. As you can see, the point-of-sale terminal plays the role of the personal electronic device of the merchant here. So just like a mobile handset, a point-of-sale terminal contains middleware that knows how to talk with trusted cores, and that, in turn, knows how to relate information about the transaction to various communication peripherals, be they prompters to confirm the transaction, printers to provide a record or communications to link to the gateway.

When a trusted core, say in the form of a smart card, is inserted into a laptop computer, much middleware software is activated. This is because a computer is a much more general tool than a mobile phone or a point-of-sale terminal. The first layer of software encountered by the smart card is a card service component, which allows the computer to talk with all sorts of cards. It even allows the computer to talk with several cards at once. The second layer allows the computer to use the card for basic operations that are very important to provide a standard set of functions that smart cards perform. This layer is a cryptographic component allowing the cards to serve all sorts of encryption and decryption operations.

Those two layers are found on all Microsoft computers. Then above or next to these layers, other layers can be present that provide various card oriented operations, for example encrypting and decrypting e-mail, or logging on a remote computer to access a corporate gateway to the network.

As we noted earlier, the model for much Internet access today is a client-server model. The users of personal electronic devices are ubiquitously using Web browsers that make use of standard protocols to access a wealth of servers that present content to them. Such a protocol is the HyperText Transfer Protocol (HTTP), a name you would be familiar with as you see it in all those Web site addresses, for example http://www.google.com. The server structure can be quite complex, but the general connection facility, which functions as a *gateway* (or sentinel) to the content is highly standardized. For provision of industry network access (for example, from mobile telephony) to the Internet, the gateway function also provides protocol translation services. For example, it is able to map the over the air protocols between the handset and the base station into TCP/IP to allow connection to arbitrary servers on the Internet.

We will delve much more deeply into the mechanisms and facilities of institutions providing content in the next chapter. For the moment, we merely want to recognize that transaction-specific policy is currently a function specific to each individual server that facilitates access to content, in all its various forms. Based on examples found in other social ecosystems, we suggest a number of evolutionary changes that can be anticipated in this domain.

# Future Architectures

Current content architectures operate successfully due to a lot of faith and a large amount of goodwill on the part of users. The level of malicious users (and faux-content providers) is accelerating, bringing a number of services into serious jeopardy under current usage models. The amount of e-mail spam is rapidly approaching a serious system failure on at least two levels. First, network bandwidth of both telecommunication channels and of content servers is being consumed more rapidly than the current cost models enable increasing capacity. Second, and probably more damaging, the entire trust model of the system is being called into question. If we reach a point where significant amounts of content cannot be trusted, then the utility of the network is in jeopardy.

One of the major evolutionary pressures is toward independent operation of the personal electronic device trusted core. At the present time, the usage models require too much support from non-trusted platforms for their trusted core to operate. Consequently, the trust conveyance by the personal electronic device from its trusted core to the content provider can become suspect.

The major technological enhancements that we see in future content systems derive in two main areas: first, establishing the independence of personal electronic devices, and second, providing enhanced facilities for the specification and implementation of content specific policy. The first of these areas we will consider in detail in Chapter 9 and the second in Chapter 10. For the moment, however, we need to introduce what we see as the underlying foundation of such policy; that is, a universal policy language component. As we know that many readers didn't bargain for a lesson in the technological bases of computing in buying this book, we want to emphasize that they don't need to read the following to understand our book. However, we're trying to make the concepts as easy to grasp as possible, and we trust that most of you will enjoy learning about the fundamentals of the generations of computers to come.

We now need to introduce a *language* that is widely used in the computer world: the Extensible Markup Language, or XML. This language provides us with a way in which plain English can be structured sufficiently to convey details to a computer. It is the central tool of services delivered over the World Wide Web. This language was developed over decades to culminate into a lingua franca of the Web. What makes XML so important is that it is the first self-describing computer language meant to be distributed over the network, and actually the first computer language reaching the expressing capability of natural language. Moreover, as you'll see, it is quite easy to understand.

We will take an example to which anybody can relate, that of an employee whose supervisor changes. Let's see how computers carry this transaction.

To start with, a computer can say in XML:

```
<employee>
    <name> John </name>
    <supervisor> Mary </supervisor>
</employee>
```

In this example, we see a record with an employee's name (John) and the name of his supervisor (Mary). Note that this record is as easy to understand for a person, as it uses everyday words, as it is for a computer, as it has a structure that computers understand.

What makes XML self-describing is that the computer can describe the very structure of the previous record, using the same format. It is done as follows:

```
<record>
    <title> employee </title>
    <element> name </element>
    <element> supervisor </element>
</record>
```

Here again, a person can understand readily how a record called "employee" contains the name and the supervisor of the employee. You can easily match the usage of the words "name" and "supervisor" in both the description and the original record to see how the latter expression describes the former one.

Of course, we have to be fair and mention that we are very much over-simplifying, but this all should evoke the right idea of what XML is. Naturally, the process of self-description can progress ad infinitum, just as it can in natural language, where I can say that John is an employee, that this information is contained in a record, that this record is to be found in a drawer, that this drawer is sitting in a room, and so on.

So far what we've seen is all like an English encyclopedia, except it is an encyclopedia that a computer understands.

Computers can use XML to send *messages* to each other. For example:

```
<message>
    <from> http://www.my-company.com </from>
    <to> http://www.your-company.com </to>
    <content>
        <employee>
            <name> John </name>
            <supervisor> Mary </supervisor>
        </employee>
    </content>
</message>
```

As we can see by reading from top to bottom, the first computer at "my-company.com" has sent to the second computer at "your-company.com" a message whose content is an employee record.

In fact, messages are a little bit richer than we said so far. Instead of what we saw previously, we are more likely to see the following, where we have added one line under the banner "schema":

```
<message>
   <from> http://www.my-company.com </from>
   <to> http://www.your-company.com </to>
   <content>
      <schema> http://www.explanations.com/record </schema>
      <employee>
         <name> John </name>
         <supervisor> Mary </supervisor>
      </employee>
   </content>
</message>
```

What the schema part does is point to an address on the Web, i.e. http://www.explanations.com/record, where the receiving computer will find the definition of what an employee record is. This will help the receiving computer understand the message. In the same way, if your local utility wants to send you an invoice for electricity, it puts in the letter the word "Invoice" so that you know that the numbers in the letter mean that you must pay them. In our case here, the receiving computer just needs to follow the Web link indicated by the schema to understand that the ensuing information is a record.

Indeed, the way the receiving computer figures out that it is receiving an employee record is by going to http://www.explanation.com/record. There, it finds the description of an employee record; actually, the same description that we encountered previously:

```
<record>
   <title> employee </title>
   <element> name </element>
   <element> supervisor </element>
</record>
```

Therefore, the receiving computer now understands how to interpret the message it just received. It now knows that what it received is an employee record made of the name of an employee and the name of the supervisor. Here we see the power of using the network not only to send and receive messages, but also to understand their content.

The fact to remember here is that XML information can be distributed, since the record and its description can be in different parts of the network. That's why we say that XML is the first language allowing one to do totally distributed computing, which is the computer geek's way of saying that we use several computers at once to perform a task. That very property is what makes services delivered over the Web possible on a grand scale.

Let's say now that the computer receiving the message whose content is:

```
<employee>
   <name> John </name>
   <supervisor> Mary </supervisor>
</employee>
```

wants to answer, say, by providing new content:

```
<employee>
   <name> John </name>
   <supervisor> Suzan </supervisor>
</employee>
```

hereby indicating that John now has a new boss, Suzan, in place of Mary.

What the first computer needs is a way to find the supervisor name in the first message, and then to change that supervisor name. Computers do this as follows:

```
<template match="supervisor">
    <replace> Suzan </replace>
</template>
```

What they are doing, as you can see, is following a sort of recipe that says "find where the supervisor name is and replace that name by Suzan." The recipe, like everything we've seen so far, is itself written in XML, which means that the computer can manipulate this template in such the same way as it can manipulate the content of messages. Similarly, we humans can follow recipes (templates) to perform particular actions, and one action we may want to perform is to change a recipe itself.

Well, now, we have really greatly oversimplified, but we hope you get the idea. With XML, computers can understand each other, they can search and interpret information, and they can manipulate data to create new information. And as they can do so, they have a means to express the ontology of social ecosystems that we discussed earlier in this chapter.

So, our considerations thus far have given us a cursory understanding of social ecosystems. We see from our high-level model of such systems the characteristics and mechanisms through which needs based stimuli can give rise to actions aimed at satisfying various appetites. We can now consider the sustenance needed to sate these appetites; sustenance that we will refer to quite generically as *content*. And, that's the topic for the next chapter.

5  Fabric of Society

# 6 The Shrine of Content

*If I had to live my life again
I would have made a rule to read some poetry
and listen to some music at least once a week;
for perhaps the parts of my brain now atrophied
could thus have been kept active through use.*

Charles Darwin

## Satisfying the Cognitive Appetite

We've painted the picture of a social ecosystem as a multi-boundary space that supports the processes derived from the needs of the human species contained therein. Each boundary identifies a constituent element of the ecosystem and subsequently the delineation of a potential contributor through which to satisfy the various appetites that needs evoke. Appetites stimulate interactions to provide sustenance and these interactions can be described by collections of related protocols. Since the emergence of the first groups of humans, this has been a reasonable model of existence. So, in our consideration of computer networks, as typified by the Web, can we use the same model as a means of understanding? In a word, yes.

Interactions are the foci for policy, which elicits the establishment of the players who interact, the rules by which they interact, along with the mechanisms and the consequences of their interaction. This leaves us with the question of why? Why have interactions at all? Our answer has been that interactions serve to satisfy needs. During the course of an interaction, the trust we ascribe to the players and facilities of the containing policy infrastructure provides the final gating of the action stimulus. We either engage in the interaction or we defer. The satisfaction of needs, the sating of our appetites, we suggest, culminates through the ubiquitous interaction objective toward an instance called *content*. From both a real, physical perspective, as well as from this metaphorical perspective, the object of interactions is content. Content is what it's all about.

This definition might be viewed as suggesting a bit of metaphysical sleight of hand. Our general perception of the term *content* suggests a tangible quantity. To the contrary of course, the results of some interactions, particularly those that are stimulated from higher up the needs hierarchy, sometimes seem less than tangible. From the standpoint of a formal or semi-formal description of interaction mechanisms, however, we suggest that the term is appropriate. Perhaps more to the point, it seems necessary. Specifically, the concept of content provides a target for the logic from which we can derive the formal specifications of the policy through which we establish a context for interactions. Essentially content is an object, or perhaps an objective, of the human sensori-motor system and its extensions; it is the means of satisfying the appetites created by the needs as suggested by Maslow.

This definition of content has the effect of consolidating the two aspects of privacy that we discussed earlier. Specifically, we viewed privacy as either freedom of action or control of information. If we now view content as the object of interactions, then control over the interaction can refer to control over both procedure and information; in essence, procedure and information are two facets of the same thing; a concept we'll refer to as *context*, matching the context establishment that mirror neurons provide. This, in turn suggests an intriguing basis for metaphorical understanding; in itself, perhaps a noble goal of content in general. It's certainly not lost on us that this also matches the conceptualization of object-oriented mechanisms in the computer world. So, let's consider a bit about how appetites and content are collectively brought together at the same general table of interactions.

# Content Rituals - Pagans Recapture Their Holiday

Early social groups derived much of their effective policy infrastructure directly from the physical ecosystem. Many of the most productive group activities involved the gathering or creation of food when the time was right to do so, such that the food was made to be available when the time wasn't so right. Particularly for agrarian social groups, this meant that much of the recurring activities such as planting, tending and harvesting crops, or raising animals for consumption as food or provision of other materials, revolved around the annual cycle of the seasons. Solar, lunar and celestial calendars dating back millennia illustrate humans' correlation of observable events with the processes of agriculture and animal husbandry. Try as one might, it really doesn't work to plant crops in what we now know as the fall and reasonably expect to be able to harvest them in the spring. The intervening period of growth and maturation that plants require just doesn't work in the dead of winter, at least not without very significant control over the physical ecosystem. Consequently, it was very useful for early societies, who could not exert this level of control, to know when to anticipate spring and how close was the approaching winter. In the parlance of our social ecosystem model, trust derived from this knowledge; trust grounded in the causality of the seasons and their applicability to the provision of sustenance.

In the dead of winter, it was probably something of an article of significant faith among the people that warm weather was ever going to return. This faith gave assurance that the remaining foodstuffs could be continually consumed in the expectation that a time would come for their replenishment before their ultimate total dissipation. Repeated observation showed that the length of the days got shorter in the fall and early winter. But then, at a specific time in mid-winter, the days began to get longer; a certain predictor of the coming spring. Over the ages, this turning point became an object of celebration, giving rise to a variety of mid-winter festivals. Other such celebrations emerged to mark significant events throughout the climatological year; spring festivals of planting and renewal, summer festivals of rest and enjoyment during the peak of the work season and harvest festivals in the fall to mark the gathering of crops. Many such festivals predated the emergence of what we now think of as the major religions of the world, but they formed the precursors of religious beliefs. Western secular and religious historians have referred to such events as pagan festivals.

When Christianity emerged as a significant religious force, as we observed in the last chapter it made significant use of ritual to establish a common bonding to a shared trust among its adherents. One such ritual was the celebration of the birth of Jesus; the holy day that came to be known as Christmas. While still in its emergent phase, it was certainly useful to the fledgling religion to piggy-back on top of existing celebration events; and particularly on such events that were popular with the common peoples of the time. One class of such celebrations was the mid-winter celebrations of the annual winter solstice, the shortest day of the year. This was a particularly popular celebration in Rome in the early days of the Christian religion. With at most only minor fudging of the dates, it was possible to adapt the celebration anticipating the lengthening of days as the harbinger of the return of spring to the birthday celebration of the Christian Messiah. Hence, the pagan festival aimed at rekindling trust among the people for the return of spring became in addition a ritual celebration to reinvigorate the belief among the faithful in the ascendance of Jesus by recognizing the time and traditions of his birth.

The practice of giving gifts as part of the celebration of Christmas can trace its roots back to the story from the *Christian Bible* about the Magi from the east who followed the star to Bethlehem and there presented gifts of gold, frankincense and myrrh to the baby Jesus. The impact of Christmas on the national economy of the United States is now significant, representing a sizeable fraction of the year's total revenue and an even larger preponderance of the annual profits for consumer merchandising. Given the impetus for separation of church and state, there came increasing pressure in the XX[th] Century to turn the holiday away from its Christian roots and to focus towards a secular ritual, a move facilitated by the fact that so much of a state's economy was at stake in the form of holiday expenditures. The result has been a slow but steady reorientation of the Christian holiday to a secular festival that is built around the giving of gifts and hence provides an annual focus on the Shrine of Content.

This is ritual completely focused on the social grouping that we have termed *égalité*. There is great irony in the coming full circle of a pagan festival, transformed for a couple of millennia into a Christian celebration, and now making its way back toward a secular ritual with as much economic as religious overtone. This is not to say that a significant element of the population, specifically the more devout Christian community, is not struggling to maintain the purely religious focus. But, the existing tension certainly delineates one of the current boundaries in the evolutionary struggle among human grouping mechanisms.

# Content Brokers

When early humans felt thirst, they made their way to the river or spring where they could drink. When they felt hunger, they sought out nuts and berries, or perhaps they hunted for prey that they could kill and eat. Sating an appetite was a matter of individual or small group activities constrained by the physical ecosystem. As social ecosystems evolved, the accepted means for sating an appetite became the purview of subjective policy considerations. If you're hungry, and the first cow you run across happens to belong to your neighbor, it's considered particularly bad form to butcher it for food without first consulting with your neighbor. Instead, the appropriate system of exchange has to be acknowledged. Thus, you might be expected to take your currency, whatever that happens to be, and travel to the marketplace. There you exchange your currency for food.

Beyond questions of ownership, social stigma can also be applied to the search for sustenance. A rather common homily in rural areas is the assertion, "I'm so hungry I could eat a horse!" This is actually a more profound statement than merely specifying an appetite for food. It conveys a sense of urgency that says, generally facetiously, "I'm so hungry I'm willing to overlook social stigma in my search for food!" Indeed, in the days of horse mounted cavalry, it was a terrible admonition of the plight of an army when they had to kill their horses for food in order to survive. So, this may be a colorful description, but what does it have to do with content and the satisfying of appetites?

Well, it says that we have now, and actually have always had, a problem of putting sustenance together with appetites in a socially accepted manner. In fact, social ecosystems are significantly driven by this requirement. With the expansion of social ecosystems beyond the smaller grouping structures, a single marketplace became ineffective as a mechanism through which to bring together *consumers* and *providers* within a specific appetite and sustenance subsystem. More abstractly, we consider these mechanisms under the guise of *market supply* and *market demand* and we recognize that under the constraints of the physical ecosystem these two concepts exist within a state of tension which resists legal (policy) conformance in favor of price elasticity and changes in equilibrium. In such a marketplace, the concept of matching these two ends of a sustenance loop elicits the actions of a *broker*; an entity whose purpose is to match specific needs to available content, hopefully within the constraints of the appropriate policy infrastructure. When policy restrictions place an artificial dislocation on the supply-demand relationship, then new mechanisms may be brought to bear as a means to bring them back into equilibrium: drug dealers, rum-runners, bootleggers, gun runners, and conflict diamond smugglers come immediately to mind. In other words, the space between the legal and illegal supply-demand curves becomes the playground of the illegal broker. When presented in the form of a person, a broker, whether legal or illegal, is one who is typically well known in a particular domain as a trusted third-party. Consumers with needs of a particular type can seek the services of the broker to find a provider to fulfill that specific need. When presented in other forms, a Web portal for example, the same constraints hold true. To be trusted, the broker should be well known in a particular domain.

In a decentralized, market driven economic system, the role of broker is a central feature of the policy infrastructure. Consider a rather simple consideration of what today we would view as retail sales; more specifically, retail food sales. In order to put meals on the table, I need groceries in the pantry. So, I need to locate a store from which to buy the quantities of food that I can reasonably store in my pantry. I don't have a lot of space, and certain foodstuffs won't keep for a long period of time, so I need to be able to purchase them at periodic and predictable intervals in predictably small amounts. Our societal solution to this type of need has been the creation of retail grocery stores. The term retail in this regard refers to the sale of relatively small amounts of various items directly to the consumers of those items. The retail store from which a consumer makes such purchases has a corresponding need to acquire the materials for resale in small quantities. In order to meet the needs of many individual consumers, the retail store seeks to purchase larger quantities of foodstuffs, and in wide enough varieties to satisfy the varying appetites of those different individuals. This entails garnering material from many different producers. To facilitate this level of content acquisition a special type of merchant termed a *wholesaler* came into being. A wholesaler is essentially a broker who serves to connect the wide variety of content producers with the similarly wide variety of food retailers. Producers know about such brokers and retail stores know about such brokers. Hence, one goes to the broker to sell wares in large quantities, while another goes to buy product, also in large quantities, for subsequent resale. In the case of wholesalers, the broker may actually buy from a producer and sell to a retailer. In other sustenance loops, the broker might simply put the buyer together with the seller, thereby enabling a transaction, for a small fee of course.

From what we might view as the more classical perspective of a broker that we've described above, the concept has evolved through a number of significant extensions over the years. A relatively recent example introduces the forerunners of the current secure cores we find in various personal electronic devices; that is, credit cards. The story, fully recounted on the Diner's Club Web site (www. dinersclubus.com), we sketch here:

In 1949, Frank McNamara scheduled a business meal at a New York restaurant called Major's Cabin Grill. Prior to dinner, he changed suits. After dinner, the waiter presented the bill and Frank reached for his wallet . . . and realized that he had left it in his other suit. McNamara finessed the situation, but that night he had a thought, "Why should people be limited to spending what they are carrying in cash, instead of being able to spend what they can afford?" In February, 1950, McNamara and his partner, Ralph Schneider, returned to Major's Cabin Grill and ordered dinner. When the bill came, McNamara presented a small cardboard card, a "Diners Club Card," and signed for the purchase. In the credit card industry, this event is still known as "The First Supper."

While store specific credit cards were a fairly well known quantity at the time, this particular innovation came in two parts. First, the card was very generically associated with currency and hence was useful at a wide variety of stores, restaurants and such. Second, the card introduced the concept of a broker between the card holder (the user of credit) and the bank or other financial institution (the provider of credit). The broker enabled the transaction of lending and borrowing money in relatively small amounts, for a small fee of course. The broker in this case ultimately morphed into the major credit card associations that we know today.

Another evolutionary extension occurred in the concept of a broker with the explosion of the Internet during the 1990's. Consider for the moment that the earliest incarnations of this ubiquitous network enhanced personal communication and the conveyance of information. At the time, the primary examples of brokers in the area of personal communication addressing were the *white pages* and *yellow pages* telephone directories published by AT&T, or the local telephone monopoly of choice; that is, the Baby Bells or various national telecommunications agencies. The primary example of a broker in the area of information availability and interchange was the *card index file* at the library. This file showed a knowledgeable researcher pretty much the entire contents of the library in question, and it was cross-indexed by book title, by subject and by author. Given a monopolistic control over content in both areas, these two mechanisms were fairly useful for accessing resources on a local plane. The Internet, however, just didn't fit this model at all.

Remember that the architecture of the Internet was aimed at avoiding the total loss of resources that would be caused by a nuclear attack on either telephone company switching offices, or the public library for that matter. Consequently, a whole new paradigm evolved for finding both people and information on the Internet; the paradigm of the *video game*. This paradigm, while represented in a myriad of different games, often requires the player to search the abstract space offered up by the game; sometimes to achieve a concrete objective, sometimes just to be able to continue to search. During this search, threats might be encountered, and dealt with, and various objects might be encountered; objects that could be saved for later use in appropriate situations. This concept was instilled into a dynamic index of the Internet effected by *search engines*. Search engines are somewhat analogous to the anatomical feature called ears; their purpose is to scour the forest listening for the sounds of falling trees. Thus, locations on the Internet are addressed through a Universal Resource Locator (URL); for example, http://www.google.com is a universal resource locator, and so is http://www.whitehouse.gov. Search engines spend all of their spare time accessing any universal resource locator that they can come in possession of, and then building a quickly searchable index of the contents derived from the Web pages they come in contact with. Now, when one wants to find some *one* or some *thing* on the Internet, the typical approach is to first enter a set of key words into a search engine and see what universal resource locators it gives in return. The indexing mechanism is dynamic, so as new resources are made available, they generally become known to the various search engines.

The result is that finding a particular bit of sustenance on the Internet that can satisfy a particular appetite is a bit like searching for prey within the primitive physical ecosystem. The tools are different, and the logical capabilities of search engine queries give the effect of configurable senses, but save for the fact that the prey generally wants to be found, the game is much the same. Of significant importance, at least to our considerations, is the fact that the role of broker is a concept of some value; in essence, it represents content in its own right. We would be remiss if we didn't comment on this.

When social ecosystems come into play, the rules concerning interactions become subjective. One of the effects of such subjective judgment is the finding that some appetites shouldn't be sated. In some instances, prohibitions follow arguably sound principles; seemingly appropriate moral judgments if you will. Sanctions against the arbitrary killing of one person by another generally meet with considerable approval of the relevant social groups. Hence, fulfilling the appetite of the sociopath is deemed highly inappropriate. In some instances, of course, satisfying slightly less aberrant appetites meet with considerable, if not overwhelming, approval. An old adage from the New Jersey streets says "Make a law, make a business." The business of broker can have value, even when deleterious consequences incur from its interactions. In essence, there can be great value in providing social middleware. Consider a couple of the examples we alluded to above: illegal alcohol and recreational drugs. We realize, of course, that we're expressing a somewhat parochial attitude by considering alcohol something other than a recreational drug. Our only significant justification is to allow the consideration of two rather distinct environments through anecdotal illustration.

On January 16, 1919 the Constitution of the United States was modified through the ratification of the XVIII[th] Amendment; the prohibition against the "manufacture, sale, or transportation of intoxicating liquors, the importation thereof into, or the exportation thereof from" the United States. By establishing this prohibition within the basic trust infrastructure (the Constitution) rather than simply within the primary policy infrastructure (the United States Code) of the United States social ecosystem, the action took on the overtones of a statement of theology, as it largely was, comparable to what one would find within Islam. The results certainly lent credence to the ostensible New Jersey homily that we noted above; a big, illegal business was created. It was the business of sating the appetites of much of the American public for now illicit alcohol. It resulted in the creation of essentially a parallel social ecosystem; that of organized crime, which adopted a grouping mechanism related to that most basic human social order, the family. The manufacture, sale and transportation of alcohol saw the creation of a generic broker operation, in the form of crime families that, over time, translated operations aimed at the provision of alcohol into derivative business operations in gambling, prostitution and protection. We suggest that this appeared much like a broker arrangement, because a significant aspect of criminal organizations was aimed at connecting legal manufacturers of liquor in foreign countries with otherwise legal entertainment facilities within the United States; e.g. rum runner operations. The efficient operation of this parallel social ecosystem soon resulted in a significant impact on the normal social ecosystem of the country; in essence, the criminal sub-system took on the characteristics of a parasitic relationship with the normal social structure. In time, it seemed that the only way to address this disease was through the repeal of prohibition, which took place through the ratification of the XXI[st] Amendment on December 5, 1933.

A similar situation exists today with the sating of appetites for illegal drugs. Perhaps because many such drugs impact on the basis of human emotional response, that is on the physiological foundation of trust, the struggle, much like the prohibition era in the United States, has religious overtones. A significant aspect of the parallel social ecosystem in this case is controlled by drug cartels that serve as brokers between producers of drugs or drug precursors in foreign countries (and to some degree within the United States) and drug users within the United States. As with alcohol, the economics of this middleman operation are interesting. The actual drug producers, the farmers that grow opium poppies for example, earn a modest living but most don't appear to get rich, while the end users (addicts) are in a position of pricing inelasticity. For them, cost is not of overwhelming importance when one has to have a fix. As a consequence, the middlemen who convey drugs from the producers to the users occupy the position of very high profit margin businesses; buying a product according to its cost of production and selling it according to its value to a captive population with a physiological need for the product. This is, of course, the holy grail of virtually any business; a situation where product pricing is based on value to a consumer with an overwhelming need and the cost of production is determined by a commodity production environment. In the case of illegal drug trafficking, of course, large sums of money and manpower are devoted by law enforcement to interdict the supply chain, rendering the business subject to high risks as well as high rewards. The "credit bubble" of 2007 and 2008 confirmed that normal banking operations are also subject to the proper assessment of risk versus rewards. The bursting of the bubble is an illustration of the consequences of incorrect assessments.

Coming back to the concept of portals on the Internet, a number of specific Web sites have evolved as ubiquitous brokers positioned between producers and consumers of content. We can identify three central genres of such portals: search engines, product portals and service portals. At the time of this writing, the most significant of the search engine portals is Google, the proverbial 800 pound gorilla in this space. Most of their revenue is generated from general and targeted advertising. Hence, the act of providing logical connectivity between producers and consumers of general content has become a content commodity in it own right. This connection content is dependent on a satisfactory experience on the part of the consumer seeking content. In other words, this Web site is able to extract a premium for the trust that consumers derive from its services.

While there are many successful product portals, perhaps the most iconic of the lot is the Amazon.com Web site. With its beginnings grounded as a bookseller, Amazon.com has subsequently expanded into a full range of product offerings. This Web site has very successfully implemented a multi-protocol stack model in its provision of content to the consumer. In particular, Amazon.com was perhaps the first large volume Web site to perfect a two stack interaction mechanism. One stack is purely information and financial transaction oriented. It enables the consumer, through a standard Web browser, to search for a desired book to purchase through a database on the Amazon.com Web site. Once a selection is made, the consumer can pay for the book through a variety of financial services mechanisms, the most common of which is a standard credit card. At the time of order placement, the consumer indicates the address to which the book is to be delivered. Completion of the order placement then triggers the book delivery process that makes use of a different protocol stack.

The deliver stack entails lower level protocols through which the book can be reliably delivered to the consumer's indicated shipping address. The physical layer channel for this protocol stack is a courier service such as UPS. Amazon.com has designed the physical layout of their enterprise such that their book warehouse is adjacent to the hub for the courier service. This means that a book package is delivered to the distribution hub at an airport by surface truck and it is then shipped via air to the destination city. A personal experience of one of the authors had a book order being placed at approximately 10:00 p.m.; the book was picked up by UPS at the Amazon.com warehouse in Louisville, Kentucky at 2:30 a.m. where it was transported to the Louisville hub of UPS. The book package was shipped via air to the airport in Austin, TX where it arrived at 5:30 a.m. and at 7:00 a.m. it left the UPS facility at the Austin airport by truck for delivery to the author's home address. It arrived at approximately 10:00 a.m. A total of approximately 12 hours to purchase a book and have it delivered to a home address. The ubiquitous nature of the overnight courier delivery service, coupled with Web access for shopping and order placement, provides a model through which the full range of the human needs hierarchy can be addressed, in at least many instances.

Service portals cover a wide range of business models, but perhaps one of the most successful is eBay. This Web portal provides a service of connecting consumers to content providers through the mechanism of an auction. A provider can offer specific items for sale through the eBay.com Web site. Consumers interested in any of the items can place a bid. Once the auction period terminates, the highest bidder is allowed to purchase the item. The item is then shipped via some surface delivery system to the purchasers' shipping address. Obviously, this business model requires some special consideration in order to establish a satisfactory level of trust to entice the consumer to pay for an item with confidence that it will then be shipped and will be in satisfactory condition when it arrives. Mechanisms to establish this trust comprise a significant aspect of the service provided by eBay.

So, having glossed through a variety of specific systems, let's step back and delve into some of the basic aspects of the access models used to connect consumers and providers.

# Content Access Models

Brokers allow for consumers and providers to get together, matching appetites to sustenance. Within the physical ecosystem, the interaction mechanisms can vary, depending on whether the access model consists of the consumer going to a marketplace or the provider bringing goods or services directly to the consumer (e.g. a door-to-door salesperson). Within the Internet context, there tend to be two rather distinct access models: a PUSH model and a PULL model. The PUSH model is fairly well characterized by text messaging, facsimile transmission or standard telephony. The PULL model is relatively well characterized by voice-mail and Web pages. Electronic mail is illustrative of a hybrid of the two that we might characterize as a "PUSH me – PULL you" model. In a rather humorous article published in the New York Times Magazine on March 23, 1997, James Gleick reviewed the PULL model as the dominant model of Web access at the time, and he also considered the then emerging PUSH model for Web information. He suggested the quick demise of this latter model because, as he put it "Push implies interruption and salesmanship. Pull implies choice." His characterization, while certainly cogent, does not appropriately assess the financial power derived from the provision of advertising through the PUSH model. As it has thus far transpired, the truly emergent model has been the combination that he expressed in the title of his article, "Push Me, Pull You."

In the PUSH model, the content provider is the originator of the interaction and subsequently causes content to be sent to some receiver or consumer of that content. In text messaging, for example via a cellular telephone, a short string of text is sent from one telephone handset to another telephone handset. The originator of the message pushes the message into the network, using as the destination network address the telephone number of the telephone intended to receive the message. When the receiving telephone gets the message, an indicator is provided to the user to indicate that the message is waiting. It is then up to the user to display the message on the handset.

Facsimile transmissions are handled in a similar fashion. When using a scanning facsimile machine at the input mechanism, the sender enters the network address, which is the telephone number of the destination facsimile machine, and starts the transmission. Depending on the type of receiving equipment being used, the pages of transmitted material may either be printed directly to paper on reception or they may be stored with only an indicator sent on to the intended receiving person. And, of course, standard telephony involves the caller entering an address in the form of a telephone number of the intended recipient of the call. If the receiving unit is not busy, then an indicator lets the person know that a call is waiting; accordingly, the phone rings. Each of these examples illustrates the sender as being the originator of the interaction. Content is either directly delivered to the recipient, or an indicator lets the recipient know that content is pending.

The PUSH model relative to Web services generally involves a Web server providing content to a user at the discretion of the server rather than of the user. In the concept of the model that Gleick discussed, one's interest in certain topics would become known over time, through a public compilation of past transactions that would become available to content providers, and the content providers would then automatically, without expressed invocation on the part of the user, deliver content.

In the PULL model, the recipient of content indicates a needs based stimulus to effect the subsequent provision of content; someone who needs something asks for it to be provided. If we don't want to deal with live telephone calls, then we allow our voice-mail systems to receive the call and queue up messages from the senders. We are then able to listen to our messages at a time of our choosing. In other words, we can pull the waiting messages whenever it is convenient for us.

Probably the more common PULL model example is that which we experience through our Web browsers. The paradigm for this interaction is essentially an imperative, "Show me that!" When we issue this command, we indicate direction to a page that we'd like to look at by specifying a universal resource locator (say http://www.nyt.com for the New York Times) to our Web browser. The browser then proceeds to execute a standard protocol through which the Web server defined by the universal resource locator is contacted and the particular Web page that we demanded to see is displayed on our screen. As the facilities to effect commerce have evolved, as we've become empowered to purchase content on or through the Internet, the paradigm has expanded to include the subsequent command "Provide me that!" or, more succinctly put and appropriate to the consumer role, "Gimme!" This is perhaps the defining characteristic in transforming the more basic Internet into the Web.

# Sustenance *sans* Solace

The Web today can provide content that maps to sustenance in varying degrees across the full range of the human needs hierarchy. However, while the Web is capable of offering this wide range of sustenance, it does not yet facilitate the full range of social ecosystem mechanisms that have proven so necessary to the species in the actual incorporation of such sustenance. Through the Web, our sensory facilities present us the fact or the illusion of sustenance, or perhaps more appropriately stated, they provide us various projections of the existence of sustenance, but we are left lacking the full range of cognition derived facilities to separate fact from illusion. We are bereft the capability to establish an adequate trust infrastructure on which to establish a comprehensive policy infrastructure through which to engage in the necessary interactions to, in fact, obtain the sustenance demanded by our appetites.

When we speak about the projection of the existence of sustenance, in general we are speaking of the availability of information about sustenance; information that, in some cases, comprises sustenance and in others merely points the way. This concept of information is grounded in the cognitive realization of the sensori-motor experience; memories and understanding if you will. The Web comprises an interaction medium through which this information is conveyed from producer to consumer. While the Internet provided for the interconnection of diverse networks first among governments, companies and other entities around the world, these networks merely provided the fabric for the interconnection and interaction of diverse producers and consumers of information. It required the emergence of a common sensori-motor experience across these networks to truly enable an interaction environment that began to merge with the human social ecosystems through which the needs hierarchy is addressed.

The detection and acquisition of information proceeds through interactions that can be modeled with the approaches we discussed in Chapter 3. Specifically, the Open Systems Interconnection reference model describes for us the basic protocol stack necessary to allow two dissimilar entities to interact. The ubiquitous access to information through the Internet derives from a *convergence* in the standardization of two distinct layers within this generic stack. First, in an effort to enable the basic exchange of information, the early development of electronic mail facilities within the context of the original Arpanet incarnation of the Internet stimulated the creation of a family of specifications for representing information to be conveyed. This evoked the development of a series of standards addressing the presentation layer of the general protocol stack. This is the layer where presentation formats are defined. A family picture has a different format than, say, a legal document. However, the actual conveyance of information required the standardization of the next lower protocol level; that of the session layer. Whether I send a family picture or legal document, I can use the same means to get them to the desired addressee. Once a standard way of conveying content is established, I can send all sorts of content besides just family pictures or legal documents. For example, I can send out my Christmas Cards.

Electronic mail evolved according to the paradigm of state provided postal services such as is elaborated as a prerogative of the federal government within the United States Constitution. The concept involves the conveyance of messages across time and space and allows for the pursuance of an extended interaction with another entity across both domains. I write a letter to John. I place it in an envelope on which I write John's address. I put a stamp on the envelope to pay for the conveyance and I enter it into the postal system by dropping it in a mailbox. The postal system then conveys the letter to the destination specified by the address on the envelope where it is then delivered by a person. To receive mail, all one must do is place a qualified mailbox at a standard address, which can be essentially anywhere. Within the United States, the postal service is required by law to deliver mail appropriately addressed and funded with a stamp.

To establish an electronic analog to the postal system, two specifications were developed for use in tandem to transfer messages from the original sender to the final receiver. These were the Simple Mail Transport Protocol (SMTP) and the Post Office Protocol (POP). The first is used to convey messages from the sender to a persistent server that provides a continuously available mail drop for the receiver, while the second is used to allow the receiver to retrieve messages on demand from the mail drop server. Thus, we see e-mail as an implementation of the "Push Me – Pull You" access model that we mentioned previously.

In the millions of years of our development, we humans have established means to convey *information* to each other, and certainly we modern humans have learned to speak without thinking much about it. Through the ages, we talked and made our way through the world. In so doing, our means of expression often became richer depending on our education and other opportunities. However, very few of us had a formal presentation regarding the abstract concepts of what information is really about. On the Web of course, everything was new. Computers could not recreate by themselves millions of years of evolution. They needed someone to tell them how to communicate. Again, since most designers and developers weren't terribly conversant with the abstract concepts of how humans manage information, we had to tip-toe our way through the virgin territory that was the new networks of computers. When we were at last able to e-mail each other messages, we just didn't immediately have a set model of how to send more than elementary text through our computers. In fact, the technology for visual and aural display had not yet progressed to the point where we needed to worry about much beyond simple text. So, we had to make it up as we went along. And, "make it up" we did, improvising to the point that even today there is no well established theory of computer content. It just evolved via cooperating and sometime competing mechanisms. What follows is our best attempt to structure a theoretical model of information exchange between computers, a model which to the best of our knowledge is still to be fully specified.

Information has an organization. This organization encompasses an economic facet and a structural facet. In turn, it is subsumed by a trust infrastructure. We will review these elements, drawing parallels when we can between what was devised for computers and what humans had previously conjured up for their own needs. First, we'll consider organization.

When we send something via the post office, whether it is a letter or a package, it has two distinct parts: an envelope and content. In the same way, a computer mail message has two parts. First, it entails an envelope, which contains facets like the addressee, the title of the message and perhaps some hint of what else the envelope contains. Subsumed within the envelope there is the content, which can be of various forms; for example, a string of text, an image, or, why not, a song.

The envelope of an e-mail message was defined quite precisely in 1982 in a document rather famously known as RFC 822, the standard for the format of ARPA Internet text messages. This document explained how the originator, the destination, the dates, and other useful information were to be conveyed. Anyone who uses e-mail is familiar with the *Date, From, To* and *Subject* fields in computer messages. Well, all of that was specified in the 1982 standard and it has served us well ever since. Actually, we are not typically familiar with all the fields of a message, because some are really for computer usage more than for human consumption. For example, in later developments fields were added that allow the sending computer to specify whether the message has been digitally signed, i.e., whether there are means for the receiving computer to guarantee that the message has not been altered during the transmission. Also, the sending computer can indicate whether the message is encrypted, such that even if interlopers intercept the message they have no means of knowing what it says.

When we deposit mail at the post office next to home, we typically don't write on the envelope whether it contains a letter, a picture or a check. The recipient will open the envelope and is usually smart enough to figure out what is in it. Exceptions must be considered for international letters. For such correspondence, it may be necessary to describe the contents for customs, as it is for packages whose content needs to be specified for special handling. A computer is a little bit different, in that the sending computer cannot assume that the receiving computer will be smart enough to figure out what's inside. This is because humans use varied senses to establish context allowing for the recognition of differences of content. A letter doesn't look like a picture and a check is different from, say, a box of candy. Today, computers use only one sense to see what's inside an electronic message, that's their electric signal detection capability; or, as we have previously expressed it, their basic sensori-motor facility. For computers, everything looks the same until told otherwise. Depending on the context, the same string of electric signals can be that for describing a letter, an image or a check (and no, computers don't eat candy, yet). Computers need to be told how to interpret what is in the envelope.

How content is described for a computer has been specified by an organization called IANA, for Internet Assigned Numbers Authority, under the rather ominous name of Multipurpose Internet Mail Extensions. MIME for short. Such mail extensions describe what is in the e-mail. In other words, they indicate to a computer how to read the content of the e-mail. Another organization, OMA, for Open Mobile Alliance, has further partitioned the MIME types into *discrete media* and *continuous media*. Examples of discrete media are text and images. They are called discrete because they are read at once. Actually, text and images themselves can have different formats. One might be familiar with, for example, *jpeg*. This is a format for images that is used by digital cameras to store picture in an efficient manner. Another example of discrete media is termed *application*. The concept here is that there are so many ways to decide between private parties on specific information formats that it's not worth trying to describe them all. Just let the private parties figure it out within the context of an application. For example, one party may decide in concert with another one to replace all letters by numbers. If that's the way they like it, no one should be able to deny them to do so. However, if they do establish an essentially private standard, they are on their own in terms of decoding the content of the message. Someone not privy to their agreement may not be able to understand what's going on. In fact, that's the basis of private encryption codes where only the two parties in contact know the decoding scheme. A widely used application format that most of us now recognize is *pdf*, a format that computers using software from the Adobe Company can readily understand, making it a ubiquitous presence in most of the world's computers.

Examples of continuous media are audio and video. At the present time, as various business models emerge on the Web, continuous media are particularly interesting because it is easy to attach an advertisement to them. More specifically, continuous media build their context progressively. As a result, we generally need to consume their contained content from beginning to end. This provides an excellent platform for a short commercial that must be viewed before one gets to the content of true interest. Anyway, they are termed continuous because they can be extended in time, perhaps to infinitum. It's important for the receiving computer to understand that the media is continuous, because it's not worth trying to store all the content at once. With, for example, non-stop streaming of music, there will never be enough memory in the receiving computer to store it all. Once the music is played, it can be discarded. Just as discrete media, continuous content can have different formats. Our readers are certainly familiar with the *mp3* format for audio files; that's what their iPod is using to display the music they love to hear. What then of the economics of content?

The value of computer content is sometime as baffling, as, for example, the cost of a painting by Basquiat or Rothko might be to someone not versed in art. However, we can, just as with art or with other forms of sustenance, try to understand the mechanisms that help to establish the value of content. While some people are just gifted and can evaluate art without too much specialized education, the rest of us have to deal with painfully gaining insight into value from what others saw and interpreted for us. However, in most instances, the value of sustenance derives from the balance between the cost of production and the needs of the consumer. As we noted above, the market equation for illicit drugs is an icon for the ideal business model; production costs determined by commodity availability and sales price determined by a consumer who has to have the product.

An important difference between digital content and tangible goods lies in the balance between creation and distribution mechanisms. Typically, digital content may be expensive to produce, but easy to distribute. Certainly, it is much easier to distribute data over the Internet than to send a bicycle from China to the USA on a ship. Even more strikingly, digital content is very easy to duplicate, whereas duplicating tangible goods involves obvious costs of material. Going one step further, digital content can often be modified with little effort and repackaged, while doing so for hard products is often just not economically feasible.

Because it is so easy to alter data, an extensive legal framework has been built around digital content, or, more generally, non-tangible content, under the name of *Intellectual Property* law. Copyright forbids duplication of content without proper authorization, or specific circumstances, patents allow one to create content but not to use it without proper retribution, and trade secrets can be invoked to protect expensive developments. Branding and trademarks also contribute to assessing digital content, by associating a trusted source to the information. The same write-up by the New York Times or by an anonymous blogger will not be given the same weight. Finally, digital content is associated with *privacy*. An evolving body of laws involves the encroachments to privacy afforded by the distribution of information over computer networks. These laws are culturally dependent, as for example France has forbidden for decades the indexing of databases with cross-references allowing gathering a consistent body of personal information about individuals. In the USA, there is no such law, so that social security numbers have been used to index all sorts of databases, with associated privacy encroachment. The cultural aspect of this diversity is grounded in the definition of freedom in the USA, much centered about the freedom of speech, while that of France is more centered around the respect of privacy. Privacy and freedom of speech are in conflict, as they affect each other negatively. For more protection of their privacy, the French have accepted more limitations on their freedom of speech than the Americans afford. Which system is better, of course, is a matter of conventions at least in part originated in religious traditions.

The fact that digital content is most often easy to modify has led to a body of protection practices. Digital signature technology allows evaluating whether information has been modified from its original version, by associating to that information a kind of a summary (the signature) that is synchronized with the content. Thanks to cryptographic techniques, it is not possible, or at least very hard, to change the information and the summary at the same time while keeping them synchronized. But of course, once the information is obtained, it can be modified at will. Therefore, sophisticated processes have been defined for controlling multiple versions and modifications of documents, by several persons if needed. Under the name *life cycle management*, systems can not only track the history of a piece of information, they can also recover the stage of the information at any time in its development. Who contributed, and what they did is logged carefully, and authorization mechanisms are put in place to properly assess further changes. To give an idea of the importance of such precautions, it is just a matter of looking at any Web page. Of course we can read it today, but can we refer it to it to somebody else who will look at it tomorrow? Will it be the same then? There are very few pages on the Web that are versioned today, so that it is very difficult, or impossible, to assert a time-dependent level of confidence in the information.

Now, there is another facet of the story. As it is easy to modify information, can this easiness be turned into a positive attribute? In fact, that's what has happened with the *open source* movement, an approach to the evolution of digital content which maximizes the value of new contributions by providing them a legal framework of much liberty. Contributors as a whole surrender their intellectual property to the community, and in exchange, they receive the right to use the contributions of other participants. This can be done to evolve textual content, as it is done with *Wikipedia*, or, say, software, with developments of entire systems, such as the *Linux* operating system. Naturally, as contributions are voluntary, it is not easy to impart discipline on the participants, and so there is a natural balance established between the open source developments and commercial ones, the former being free and somewhat chaotic, the later being paid and rather disciplined. Of course, there are exceptions in both fields, and we can find open source developments which can be better than commercial equivalents, and commercial developments that beat open source in the capabilities they offer in terms of modifications by eager participants. An example of the former would be certain development tools like those organized around the *Java* language, an example of the later would be the *Amazon* tools for electronic commerce.

The value of digital content is often associated with time. Most news' value vanishes with time. On a light note, the scoring at a game has emotional content when associated with uncertainty about the ultimate result, a feat most easily achieved with simultaneous casting. In the other side of the spectrum in terms of seriousness, the warning of an impeding tornado is only worthy if it is timely. This shows that the value of information is contributed to both by its content and the capabilities of its publication channel. We've already seen that the same content can be differently trusted according to its source. In the same way, content can be differently valued according the efficiency of its publication mechanism. Trust in the publication system conveys to that in the information itself.

The way information is produced, distributed, and valued, also depends on its hosting social ecosystems. Government information, business information, public and private information, all depend on different mechanisms, often formally described in law. And depending on the sphere of activity, the value may take different form. While actual money is by essence the main driver in business information, social effects may be more valued in government information. In all cases, information has a value in term of influence. In business, the very format of digital content can be the object of *standards wars*. The best publicized example of such is the fight between Sony and JVC in the seventies to establish a standard for video cassettes. At the end, VHS beat Betamax, and entire production lines were made obsolete. Obviously, the value of information to government can be measured by the size of the agencies dedicated solely to obtain it from various sources, covert or overt. From a more private, individual perspective, the value of our stock portfolios is just information, numbers. Tell us what stock will be up ten-fold three years from now, and we'll make you rich.

Yet another attribute of digital content is its *transferability*. A song can be transferred, exchanged, reproduced, distributed, with or without commercial terms; that's its function, in most cases. In the opposite, a bank account number and password are closely guarded. In fact, transferability of a bank account is limited by law. For that reason and others, strict means of access to information have to be put in place, by policy and technical means. The policies set in place for the codes to launch the atomic bomb are famous, those surrounding banking information are notoriously secret, and others are a matter of current public debate, like information on the health of individuals. Means of protection belong to the physical and the logical realm. A company like Iron Mountain specializes in storing digital content in places immune to physical breaks. In the logical domain, various mathematical tools have been developed to protect digital content, and they've been progressively surrounded by associated techniques allowing to also communicating how protection mechanisms can be lifted for use.

A different way to partition digital content is to look at it from the perspective of human needs. In modern societies, many physiological needs are fulfilled by the provision of digital content in the form of electronic money. Whether using a credit card at the supermarket or on the Web, all there is to it is a string of numbers flowing from us to some institution. In terms of safety needs, the entry code for our apartment is certainly a good example. More generally, the very protection afforded to data of importance is by itself a type of information related to safety. In terms of the need of belonging, digital content expresses a fabric of society that defines the various institutions that we share with others. The needs for esteem are well expressed by the multiple forms of entertainment, where television takes perhaps a central place. And finally, self-actualization would be reflected by art and other achievement of the higher realm translated into information, be it scientific literature or poetic license.

# Personal Electronic Devices

Now that we have outlined the general attributes affecting the economy of digital content, we can look at personal electronic devices, or rather, at their core, private, secure information part. It is, in some ways, different from other, more general content, as it is difficult to imitate and replicate, thanks to various advanced protection mechanisms, in particular on access methods. This is an indication that the content is highly valued, which is true in the proper sense, as a lot of it has to do with actual money: the rights to phone somebody, the capability to spend money, and other properties associated with fiduciary exchange. In other cases the value is in the privacy, with the quintessential example being health data. But we may want to also think about political information, potentially lethal in certain context, sexual interests, or other elements of our intimate social interactions. Modification of personal electronic devices central content is tightly controlled by the device and the institutions that are allowed to bring change. The device itself links tightly to its owner such that any modification must be properly authorized by the person most concerned about it. Institutions, that grant rights, have an equal interest in tight control, which is why the protocols of modifications are considered as interfacing the person and the institution, the personal electronic device acting as a mediator as well as a digital representative of the owner. A properly configured personal electronic device will keep a log of transactions, and will provide means to administer its content in order to arbitrate between the various demands put on it in the proper manner. For example, if no space is available anymore in the personal electronic device, which comes first: the bank account or the list of contacts? We have presented as an economic attribute of content its timeliness. For example, if I want to see on my personal electronic device the goal scored by my favorite team as it happens, I don't want to be bogged down at that time in a long exchange of messages between my personal electronic device and the broadcaster to make sure that I have acquitted my dues. This function, though necessary, has to be done in microseconds, and that, in turn, will determine how the secure core of my personal electronic device is built, together with all the intervening agents in the chain leading from the personal electronic device to the broadcaster. In terms of the spheres of activities of the personal electronic devices, they cover the full gamut. Government information, as in electronic passports, which are personal electronic devices embedding a radio-frequency identity chip together with extra protection layers to prevent snooping; public information, as in health cards, that limit access to personal data to health care professionals and the individuals concerned; business information, as in banking cards, which allow the personal electronic device to act as a payment broker. And then, we also find non-monetary value in the overall scheme of personal electronic device, as standards battle rage in every corner of that domain of activity, for the various industrial and governmental players to keep their influence and profits. Witness to that are the battlefields of operating systems specifications regarding the functioning of the devices, of governmental practices regarding which country will have less to do in terms of policy changes as the world goes from analog to digital, and in other areas like the format of payment messages and telecommunication operations. Finally, we need to mention that the personal electronic device core content is very controlled in terms of transferability, as much of it is either very private, like health information, or quite expensive to obtain and keep, like bank accounts. In most cases, transferability is in fact not only a matter of personal choice, but also a matter of law. In terms of the satisfaction of needs, personal electronic devices are located at every point of influence, a subject we will develop in Chapter 9.

# Location, location, location

As we see, the economics of information is yet to be written in fullness. However, while our species' pragmatic approach to survival has allowed us to use prose like *Molière*'s Monsieur Jourdain, without even knowing it, computers couldn't do that in the little time of their evolution. They had to be taught, and therefore the partitioning of digital content had to be made explicit for them. Only later, as we'll discuss in subsequent chapters, would they take matter in their own hands, so to speak. For the moment, we need to expand on the very way digital content has been structured and positioned up to now in the computer world. Digital content is located everywhere in computer networks, with means of access in place to produce it, organized in ways that make it palatable, and with the structure of trust that makes it actionable.

Computer data can be found on all sorts of media, so we will concentrate on two attributes of such media for the purpose of our inquiry: *duration* and *security*. The media known longest to mankind are rocks and pots, lasting from thousands to tens of thousand of years. If we were to go for duration based on history, that's probably the media we should chose. Various forms of vegetal products, including paper and tissue, would be next in the list, lasting sometimes up to a few thousand years. And when we reach what is generally considered as a long term medium for computer data, like tapes and diskettes, we already know from experience that they can't last as long as the other inventions we mention. The maximal length of conservation of our computer data counts at best in decades. Now, if we consider lengths in years, our optical disks, hard disks, storage keys, and other flash products can probably do, if we don't mind finding their format forgotten at some point, and having to call costly experts to the rescue. Finally, from microseconds to days, we are talking about transient data, data that will be erased, either on their way from a location to another, or as temporary information allowing some processing to occur. With each form of content, going from the decade to the year to the day, various means of security can be invoked; the first element to be considered is always the physical medium. The security mechanisms are the same as for any physical good, as far as storage media used for decades or years are concerned. For transient storage, circumstances differ, as data can be over the air in case of radio transmission, over or underground in case of wire transmission, in a component of a computer system, or in some part of a personal electronic device. During transmission, data have to be considered unsecured. While over the air snooping is quite easy, the snooping of wires is often more difficult. What's certain is that it can be done, and it has been done often. There is no physical security for data during transmission, in almost all cases (quantum encryption is an exception). Alternative means of protection are needed. For example, in the case of computer systems, they may or may not be in secure enclosures. Again, the security here is similar to that of any physical good, and we have to consider not only the goods themselves (the computers, in one form or another) but also their environment: network links, power supply, temperature control, and the like.

The most interesting case, as far as this book is concerned, is the personal electronic device. Being a small item that accompanies us, it is subject to loss, and therefore its physical security cannot be assumed. As we saw, there are two kinds of personal electronic devices, those with a rich environment surrounding a personal core, like, say, a cellular phone, and those reduced to the personal core, for example chip card for banking. A full-featured personal electronic device is a consumer item, and its cost must be controlled accordingly. For that reason, there are few secured personal electronic devices outside of the military. Typically, the personal electronic device relegates security matters to its trusted core. So, in effect, all personal electronic devices, whether full-featured or bare, end up using similar secure cores. And a secure code must indeed be protected, because it contains the data that are most close to us, whether they are related to our identity, our beliefs, our health or our money. The physical security features of trusted cores are numerous, and we'll expand on them in the next chapter. Simply, we need it to be clearly established that trusted cores are physically protected, and that we can count on that protection when devising applications related to the use of personal data on the network.

Finally, we must acknowledge a limitation of trusted cores in terms of physical attributes. Trusted cores need to be as simple as possible, because with complexity come security gaps, and they need to be inexpensive, so that they can be used everywhere. This necessarily means that they will have limitations in size, in speed, and accordingly in their response time. That's why personal data may actually not be all in the trusted core. In some cases, they will be outside of the trusted core, either on a full-featured personal electronic device, or say, on the network somewhere. As those locations are not necessarily secured, the data themselves need to be protected by cryptographic means, which themselves are enabled by the trusted core. For example, a complete encrypted text can be freely available on the network, but if a trusted core is needed to decode it, it's of no use to steal it; it's protected. In reality, the situation can get very rapidly complex, because in some cases we want to secure in the trusted core only particular pieces of data residing on the network, or some time we just want to use the trusted core as repository for the decoding keys of the data. In the former case, the trusted core may have to be very sophisticated, since we may want it to process the secure part of the data while the full stream of data itself is processed by a general computer. In the latter, we may have a simpler trusted device: that's the case of the Trusted Platform Module, the trusted core found on the circuit board of laptops.

# Access

Wherever they are, if they cannot be accessed physically, data may be accessed logically, i.e., via the network. For that reason, much of the work on computer security is focused on access methods, which are encompassing three domains, named *authentication*, *authorization* and *accounting*. Whereas, as we've said earlier in our discussion of content, there is no full-fledge theory of content that we know of and ours is but a beginning, there is, in comparison, a strong body of work and formalism around access methods and practices. We will then draw on a particular specification of authentication, called SAML (Security Assertion Mockup Language), and on a particular specification of authorization, called XACML (eXtensible Access Control Markup Language), for presenting access concepts and their implementation. Wherever SAML or XACML are lacking, we'll supplement the discussion with input from other, possibly competing specifications. Whereas the theory of access is quite solid by now, there are indeed competing technologies, and therefore there will be variations in any presentation of the subject. Authentication means recognizing that requesters of content are indeed who they claim they are. Authentication relies on two concepts, *identity* and *credentials*. To illustrate the difference, let's consider Marie Doe, who has a daughter, Suzie Doe. There is no doubt on Suzie's identity. However, Suzie may have a passport which is passed limit date. In this case, Suzie has a solid identity, but weak credentials. Reversely, let's consider John Reborn, who has a valid passport, but, who, in fact, is a spy with a false name. The identity of John is false, but his credentials are strong. So we see that identity and credentials are two different concepts. Identity is who the person is; credentials are here to affirm that the person is who he or she claims to be. When presented with credentials, the recipient must first establish trust in the credentials, and then establish how much trust it assigns to the linkage between the credentials and the person they represent.

For a computer to authenticate a person, credentials of the person can be of different forms that we will present in order of increasing confidence. The first credential is the name of the person, then perhaps a password that they can provide, then perhaps an object they carry that they can present to the computer, and further on even a representation of themselves that is associated with their physical presence. If the name of the person is all there is, the trust is minimal, unless the context is such that there is no possibility of mistake. Otherwise, it's easy for anybody to give a false name. Concerning the password, the level of trust can be much higher if the password is complex enough. If the password is, say, four letters long, it's not difficult to try all combinations. Some computers limit the numbers of trials for that reason, but then the odds are high that a password may be compromised when multiple accounts are searched. Long, unwieldy passwords are more secure, although more difficult to remember. In the end, passwords have a major weakness. They are easy to steal.

There are many ways to surreptitiously obtain passwords, and therefore, only limited trust is placed in them. That's why tokens have been introduced, in the form of Radio-Frequency Identification (RFID) tags or smart cards. With these, the user presents physical evidence to the computer. Such tokens can be sophisticated in that they can talk with the recipient computer to make sure that they recognize that computer, and that the computer recognizes them. Moreover, they can be set up such that they are only activated if their owner provides evidence of ownership. Of course, by now you recognize that we can say that the owner *authenticates* to the token, which in turn authenticates on behalf of the owner to the recipient computer. That's two levels of security. The way the owner provides evidence of proof to the token can be through a password or through physical presence, what is called *biometry*. Biometry is the science of associating particular features of humans with their identity. For example, fingerprints, iris scan, hand geometry, DNA, these are all unique identifiers of humans. Biometry can be used in two different ways in the authentication scheme. If this is direct authentication without a token, the user provides, say, the fingerprint, and the recipient computer double checks the fingerprint against a database. With a token, things can be made much more secure, because the user provides the evidence to the token itself, which may double check with its own database, all in the protected environment of the token. The biometric sensor is attached to the token and is therefore much less liable of having been tampered with, and the processing of information happens inside the token. As the token itself is physically protected, the likelihood of interference is very low, and therefore we can say that an authentication system that relies on a token plus biometry is quite strong. In fact, this is how secure governmental facilities are protected, with the additional precaution that not one, but several biometric verifications may be requested at once.

As we've seen, having strong credentials is of little value if all they say is that the person who claims to be John Reborn is actually John Reborn. What if John Reborn has usurped that identity to start with? So we need to know how the credentials have been set up; we say *provisioned* in the trade. For credentials, there are several levels of trust. The first level is when the person establishes a credential, like in "My name is Suzy Doe." Obviously, this has little credibility, even if today it's the most used means of provisioning. One level up is "My name is Suzy Doe, and here is my credit card number." What happens in this case is that the recipient computer can call the institution that has provided the credit card, and check that the bank indeed has issued a credit card of that number to that person. What this says, however, is only that somebody called Suzy Doe has had a credit card, not that the real Suzy Doe is talking. But if we consider that for assuming the name Suzy Doe the person had to also steal her credit card, then we know that the trust is higher in this case than when Suzy just spelled out her name. Now something else may have happen; namely, Suzy may have gone to the bank with a fake identity and got a credit card for her that way. In that case, the initial fraud was in the authentication at the bank. For that reason, there is yet another level of identity proof, which is based on the institution doing the provisioning. What the recipient computers do is inquiring directly with the computers of the company or agency that has identified the person to start with. But now we are entering a field of elaborate mathematics. The way this is done is that a well known institution publishes a number, called a *public key*, very widely, worldwide. That number is found everywhere, and cannot be mistaken. Everybody knows that this is the number corresponding to that institution. Now, using cryptographic techniques, it is possible for a computer to query the institution about the identity of a person. What the computer does is encrypt the query using the public key, in such a way that only the institution can understand the message, using what's called their *private key*, a number that only they know, and which matches the public key. The institution can send back the information about the identity of a person in such a way that the recipient computer is sure that the message comes from the institution. For those interested in the technique, it is the reverse of what we just saw: the institution used its private key to encrypt the message, and the only way to decrypt it is with the public key. Since only the institution knows how to encrypt a message that way, the recipient knows that it comes from there. Now, you're going to say, how can we know that the institution has properly identified the person? That's a valid question, and that's the crux of the matter. In fact, when the institution answers, it also includes information on how the identity was established. Was it based on simply receiving information from the person, or by seeing documents from the person, or by doing interviews with neighbors and such, or by doing an in-depth research such as those associated with military clearance? As we see, there is never a totally full proof way of identifying somebody, but we can reach high levels of trust, and that can be done via computer.

Once somebody is authenticated by a computer, it's time to talk about authorization. What can that person do? In fact, there are many factors involved. The first is to know the *role* of the subject. To give the idea, we can consider the role of persons in a hospital. Obviously, doctor, nurses and administrators have different responsibilities associated with their role. Doctors can prescribe medication that nurses can administer. Most probably, neither doctors nor nurses can sign hospital expense bills, which is what administrators do. So we see that the role of the persons defines what they can do, and therefore it is an important generic element for specifying their authorization limits. Of course, in small hospital, some persons may have combined roles. Depending on the role in which they act, they'll have different authorization levels. Another element to determine right on is whether the authorization is *static* or *dynamic*, which means whether the authorization details are always the same for that person, or whether they may change from one transaction to the next. For example, the nurse may be allowed to administer medication in general (that's a static right), but for some medication, must ask a doctor in each case (that's a dynamic right). Now that the basic authorization rules are understood, it is important to consider the resources which are accessible. They can be of various forms, from documents to specific actions. As far as documents are concerns, some persons may be authorized to read, write, a document, while others are authorized to sign. For actions, some may be able to start them, or stop them, and others may be authorized to carry them. All of this, of course, may be done within specified limits. It can be a time limit, or a number of times, or a period, for example. So as we see, there are many rights that can be set by policy and that are the object of authorization mechanisms. In fact, there is also yet another level, which is the authorization to change the policy itself, yet another level of details using in fact the same authorization mechanisms, but taking as the resource affected the actual policy framework.

Finally, the last leg of access mechanisms is accounting, in a broad sense. Not only are we concerned about particular prices that can be associated with each authorization level and activity, but also about the practices of logging entries, keeping history, and more generally, providing mechanisms to trace, value, and record authorization activities.

Now, the examples we have given were mostly associated with a person accessing a computer, with the computer performing authentication, authorization and accounting. Actually, the mechanisms are exactly the same for a computer accessing a computer. While the computer is not requested to provide biometric iris scans at this point, it has to provide the proof of its identity just like humans do. It's just that this identity is established by different institutions than for humans. All computers in the world access the network through a *network card*. And every network card in the world has a number associated with it at manufacture, a unique number called a *MAC address* (MAC stands for Media Access Control), delivered by the famous Institute of Electrical and Electronics Engineers (IEEE). Here again, we have a trusted institution providing identity to an entity, in this case a computer. However, at this time, there is no mechanism to formally assure that the MAC address given is a bona fide number by questioning the IEEE, just like we described it earlier for human identity. So computer authentication at that level cannot really be trusted, and in fact, secure applications are cognizant of that and use multiple means of authentication to not be dependant on that one alone.

As we said, computers and humans go through the same access mechanisms. This is not surprising, because humans are not directly connected to computers (with some rare exceptions), so they are actually accessing computers via devices and systems that are themselves computer parts or full-computers. So in the end, it's all computers talking to each other, albeit with some representing humans, and some representing just themselves.

# Content model

As we mentioned earlier, we don't know of an existing, widely accepted, encompassing content model theory, so we've attempted to deal with the pieces that exist, and tried to put them together into a coherent whole. If that constitutes an acceptable content theory, then here we have it. Otherwise, we'll have to wait until either we discover that one exists but that we are not aware of it, or some academic constituency will build around the project of writing a better one than ours. Now, whereas in our earlier discussion we had to elaborate a classification of content based on our understanding of the subject from our observation of social practices, here we are going to complement our earlier work by looking at it from an easier perspective, that of the computer. What makes the perspective easier is that with the computer, we can reverse engineer every piece of content, and therefore know exactly how it is built. We don't do that with human brains, or not yet.

Content is in fact organized in repetitive layers, each describing the previous one, and each time in two parts, that of the description, and that of the data themselves. In the computer world, the description of data is called *metadata*. For example, let's consider a music piece registered on a hard disk. What we have here is the first level of content data, that representing the notes of music. What the description associated with those data does is make the format explicit, so that we know how to decode the signal on the disk. For example, the description can say that the music is represented using the familiar MP3 format. Thus we have a first piece of content, the combination of the music and the description of the format used to represent it. Therefore, we will go one step further, by describing that new content, giving it a name, say Like a Virgin, the song by Madonna. Here we go: we have a yet another, more elaborate piece of content, one that is identified by name. Let's go another step up, by combining that song of Madonna with another song, say Material Girl; we can describe the assembly of the two songs, and give that a description, that of the second album of Madonna. What was its title? In fact, it was Like a Virgin; the album had the same name as the song of its first track. But the computer is not confused, because in one case Like a Virgin is associated with a single song, in the other it's associated with an assembly of songs, in this case an album. So here we've seen how content is built up, in an elegant architecture taking simpler elements, structuring each layer into description and content, and then going up from there.

# Network

It is only recently that a model of the world of computer networks has been developed that encompasses all aspects of network development in a single framework. That has come by the meeting of two disciplines of computer science, in the end of the 1990's and the beginning of the 2000's. The first discipline is the Web and its progressive structuring, with the alluring presence of its founder, Tim Berners-Lee. Berners-Lee invented the Web and to this day has been a major influence on its development. The second discipline is Artificial Intelligence, and particularly the part of it which is concerned by the representation of knowledge in computers. You guessed it; the convergence is that of making the network knowledgeable.

Central to the discipline of Web development is Berners-Lee's invention of the *Resource Description Framework*. The idea goes as follows. If I have an album of Madonna on the hard disk of a computer somewhere, how does another computer on the network know about it? Is there any way to devise a universal scheme that allows identifying any resource in the world, anywhere on the network? Because Berners-Lee is such a prescient thinker, he made the question even larger. If a computer wants to designate something that is not in a computer, why shouldn't that be possible also? So here it is: Berners-Lee wanted to have a way to name anything in the world, whether on a computer or not, so that computers could have access to all the knowledge in the world. Of course, since we humans are the ultimate users of the computers, thanks to Berners-Lee's invention, we too can describe any piece of content in the world, be it a song by Madonna, the description of a tree in the Amazon or a black hole far away in the universe. So, Berners-Lee called his invention a *Uniform Resource Identifier* (URI). The genius in the invention is that he had disconnected the naming of things from the description of the things themselves. What he really did is bring to the computer world something that is very natural to humans. We can talk about a bird without speaking about a particular bird, *that* bird. When we talk about a bird in general, with no specific bird in mind, we are using what's known in linguistics as the *connotation* of the word bird. When we talk about a bird in particular, well-designated, we are using the *denotation* of the word bird. Does that sound familiar? Of course it does. A particular bird is the content, just like the music of the song, and the generic bird is the description of that content. What Berners-Lee has done is merge together how humans work with content and how computers work with content. That's the stuff of great progress! Examples of uniform resource identifiers are: "The sun," "http://google.com" and "3.14159." In short, any string of text can be made to describe something.

Now let's get a little bit more specific. You're going to say, fine, Berners-Lee just told me that we can mention Madonna's song "Like a Virgin", and that a computer can also use the terms "Like a Virgin", and that the computer and I can understand each other. I can see that's useful, even though I don't quite see yet what's so revolutionary about it. But that doesn't advance me one bit in finding the song. On which computer can I find it? Where? So Berners-Lee also thought about that. We can associate any uniform resource identifier (say "Like a Virgin", or "bird") with the reference to any particular example of it (say the song on my computer's hard disk, or the bird on my cousin's Web site). And, to make things easier, I can use another invention of Berners-Lee, the *Universal Resource Locator*, to do so. Doesn't that name ring a bell? Of course it does. It's the famous URL: for example http://www.google.com is a universal resource locator, and so is http://mycousinwebsite.com/bird.jpg, a universal resource locator that points to the bird of my cousin's Web site, and so is file:///D:/Songs/track1.jpg, which points to the recording of Madonna's song in my laptop. In short, we now have a means to name everything on a computer, and more. Moreover, when we are talking about something on a computer, we can locate it easily.

The story doesn't stop here. One more advance is needed. Now we can inquire of a computer about a song, such as "Like a Virgin" and about a singer, such as Madonna. We know how to find the song in a computer, and we know how to find the picture of Madonna on a computer; just point to a Web site with that picture. However, how does a computer associate the singer with the song? Can the computer say that "Like a Virgin" is a song by Madonna? In fact it can, and that's where the Resource Description Framework comes into play. It is just a way to associate three universal description identifiers: "Like a Virgin," "Song" and "Madonna."

```
<rdf:RDF>
   <song rdf:about="http://www.example.org/example#song">
      <singer> Madonna </singer>
      <title> Like a Virgin </title>
   </song>
</rdf:RDF>
```

Again, we have to apologize, because computer speak is often not that friendly. However, we hope one can guess by looking at the sequence that we are talking about a song, whose singer is Madonna and whose title is Like a Virgin. If a computer is happy with that, so are we, because we've accomplished a huge feat! Of course, we have simplified somewhat, but not in ways that alter the general idea. Thus, there is a language that is explicit enough for computers and yet general enough for humans. Now, humans and computers can think along similar terms. How similar is what we are going to talk about next.

The second discipline that has affected a general theory of content is Artificial Intelligence. Here is the idea: can a computer contain knowledge and can a computer act on that knowledge in a way similar to humans? We will start by the question of knowledge. Previously, we have described how content can be organized into layers, with each layer containing a description of lower content, together with that content. Now, we will take the question from its more general perspective, and we will recognize that there is a domain of human science that has addressed it; that of *logic*. We've all gone through lengthy sessions at school saying things like x, y, z are numbers; x=y and y=z, therefore x=z. Here, the first layer of content is "x", "y" and "z", which are described as numbers. The second level is made of things like "x=z" and "y=z", which are described as formulae. A third level is made of the full utterance, that we'll describe as a statement. Again, we're simplifying here, but bear with us. We are formally recognizing the layering that we talked about earlier when we were speaking of Madonna. Now, we see that the logic we learned at school allows us to *reason* on content. If we can reason on it, certainly we need to consider that content is knowledge. As a bonus, we now understand how to build more complex content out of elementary content. We know how to increase knowledge. In short, we know how to learn. Logic, of course, doesn't apply only to mathematics. John, Mary and Virginia are children, John is the brother of Mary, Mary is the sister of Virginia, therefore John is the brother of Virginia. As we see, logic is the way we can organize content and build with it more content, whether we talk about numbers, people or anything else that we might be interested in.

In the 1970's, when Artificial Intelligence started to be deeply interested in knowledge and its use, the community of scientists was very innocent, or naïve, if you wish. The pundits were announcing that now that we are masters both of computers and of logic, computers are soon going to perform human feats like law and medicine. Just give us big salaries, and you'll see. Big salaries they got, but nothing was seen. Artificial Intelligence was derided and forgotten, and it took twenty years for the field to recover credibility. What happened? Well in fact, something was forgotten. Incredibly, as we can see in retrospect, because the Greeks had seen the problem and an Austrian called Kurt Gödel had seen it too. More to the point, everyone knew that. So, what happened? What the Greeks had identified is the following paradox: when I say, "This sentence is false." is this sentence true? Well, if it's true, then it is false, isn't it? And if it is false, then it is false that this sentence is false; therefore this sentence is true, isn't it? But then … What we see is that there are expressions of logic for which it is impossible to say whether they are true or false, no matter how long we try. Does that apply to computers? That's what Gödel went out to investigate. Of course he was not thinking about computers at the time, but if you read his famous proof, not an easy reading by the way, you'll see that what he was describing would be called today a computer program. Anyway, Gödel showed that in any form of *rich enough* mathematics, there are statements that are similar to "This sentence is false." and that's unavoidable. Therefore, if a computer uses logic, which it does because that's how computers work, it is bound to have trouble, because some of the situations it will encounter are, as we say in computer science, well, *undecidable*. So, this is how Artificial Intelligence failed at the time. Applying logic in the most general way, computers just couldn't do the job they were asked to.

Well then, "What about humans?" you will say. "They use logic, don't they?" Moreover, "They function, don't they? So, what's the deal with computers, really? In one sentence you just said that all computers use logic, and in the next you said that they can't do the job they're asked to? Isn't that a contradiction?" Well, those are good questions, and it took 20 years to sort them out. Concerning humans, we'll get back to the question later. Concerning computers, the fact is that they use logic and they work most of the time. They work because we design them and then we test them extensively to make sure that they will perform the tasks that they are asked to do. As long as what they do was understood beforehand in the tests, we're in good shape. If not, then we just hope they'll work. That looks strange to the uninitiated, but really, that's how the computer world works. In fact, things are not too bad, because for a long time computers have been asked to do what they know well how to do, that is manipulating numbers, filing data and exchanging messages. These are all operations that are well understood, well tested, and that we therefore are confident in. The problem comes when the computers try to do what humans do, because humans do precisely the introspective things like "This sentence is false." For example, "Did I say what I just said?" or "It's impossible for me to say I'm sorry." However, humans don't stop functioning when that happens, so obviously there is something to understand here.

The first breakthrough in this undertaking was in trying to understand if there were subsets of logic that would be useful while not being prone to the earlier problems found in using logic. Remember, Gödel showed that rich enough mathematics contains problematic statements. Well, he didn't say it exactly like that, but we'll keep it at that because his arguments had to do with a deep understanding of XIX[th] and early XX[th] Centuries mathematics, and we'll spare the reader here. The issue became, was there, in the mathematics not rich enough, something that could be useful after all? Fortunately, the answer to that was positive, because by the end of the XX[th] Century we were interested in new things like a formal description of content, something that was not the purpose of earlier mathematics. So was born a new field of science called *description logic*, which is wonderfully described in *The Description Logic Handbook*, edited by Franz Baader, Diego Calvanese, Deborah McGuinness, Danielle Nardi and Peter Patel-Schneider. Description logic allows the organization of vast amounts of data in such a way that we can reason on them without having to fear falling into inconclusive results. To come back to our previous example, descriptive logic allows us to teach a computer that children of the same parents are brothers and sisters. Now, if the computer learns that John, Mary and Virginia all have the same parents, it can deduce that John is the brother of Mary and Virginia. But, wait a minute? Isn't the word *description* the same word we used earlier, when we saw that the Web community had found a way, the resource description framework, to represent relationships on the network? You got it, thanks to description logic, Artificial Intelligence and the Web would concur. Description logic provides the means to describe complex relationship and the resource description framework allows them to be established on a network of computers. Now, we are ready to have a unified, worldwide, reasoned representation of content.

That's all fine and good, you'll say, but what about the content itself. What's in it? What do we represent? Is it limited to songs by Madonna and family relationships? Well, now computers and humans, for the first time, meet on even territory. Computers can now represent complex, human information. But, we know that even humans have difficulty representing their own information. It takes years of studies to barely master one subject of human knowledge; for instance, music or sociology. To really understand the rules of music that are eventually behind Madonna's success, or to really understand how families flourish in society, clearly these is more than just stating than a song is on an album or that three children are siblings. That's how we get to our next topic, that of *ontology*. This will probably one of the most difficult concepts presented in this book, so we'll make an extra effort here.

Starting in the 1970's, Artificial Intelligence researchers began thinking of a world where computers would collaborate on complex, human-like tasks. In a word, computers would be *agents* interacting to solve a given problem, just like humans do. For example, in a military environment some agents would be weapons specialists, some agents would be planning specialists and other agents would make decisions. This way, the researchers could concentrate on each task independently, working on how computers could fulfill the same tasks as a weapon specialist, a planning specialist or a decision maker. The idea then would be that wherever the computer can fulfill some task of the human, it replaces the human in that task. Wherever it cannot, the human stays in control. In time, that idea would become a tenet of automation, as described in *Humans and Automation*, by Thomas Sheridan. Now, we see that those computer agents, specialized in a domain, must talk to each other. Humans do that naturally, as collaborating on a task is something that language mediates reasonably well. But computers, how would they talk to each other since we don't know yet how to teach them the language of humans? Could we make progress here at all? That's when the idea of defining ontologies came along.

For the weapons specialist, the planning specialist and the decision maker to work together, they needed to agree on common definitions of the data they would exchange, and how those data are articulated. For example, if the decision maker asks the planning specialist on the firepower available, it must be expressed in unequivocal terms. That will then lead the decision maker to ask the weapons specialist to perform actions in a way that also must be without ambiguity. If the decision maker says, "Fire on position 2!" after hearing about it from the planner, there must be some common agreement on what "position 2" means. The build-up of such a terminology, in all its intricacy, is what an ontology is. So, we see that an ontology is a means for computers to share knowledge in a consistent manner. One wonders of course, where does that barbaric term, ontology, come from? Actually, the philosophers, since antiquity, have been themselves puzzled by how humans share information in such an efficient manner, even if some of the time it appears desperately inefficient. They identified the need for ontologies to describe human knowledge, and so we see that the human concept of ontology and the computer concept of ontology are in fact the same thing, except that for the computer to understand humans, the ontology has to be explicit to the smallest details, since the computer lacks the shared sensori-motor experience of humans. The computer is not capable of filling in the gaps in the description. The computer needs the full description logic.

# Thought

Well, now we have a hopefully well-formed theory of content. We know something about how to specify knowledge, we know how to represent it in a computer, and we know how to share it. We should now come back to what people, or agents, do with the content. Clearly, humans do not limit themselves to description logic. They do utter statements like "This sentence is false." without falling down in convulsions with their brains infinitely trying to figure out if the sentence is indeed false, or true, or false, ad infinitum. Humans are just content to say "This sentence is false." and examine the peculiarities it involves, just as they might examine a snail, or a story or anything else. This is just a sentence, and we can think about it. So, what about computers then? Can they limit themselves to a subset of logic, while hoping to do human-like tasks? Clearly they cannot. Computers need to access the full power of logic. If humans do not go into infinite loops when provided with uncertain data, there we need to understand why and give that capability to computers, if we indeed feel that it's worth making computers smarter.

First, let's add to our content apparatus the rules of full logic that are needed for the computer agent to act with full effect. What we will just say is that this is a field still in development. There are several competing kinds of logic and it would be too complex, and not really needed for this book, to go into the details. We would just like to expand on one topic, that of learning. The question is: "Now that we have content, how do we improve it? How do we learn?" For example, let's say that I know that John, Mary and Virginia, are siblings. Let say we learn that there is a new child in the family; Joe. It's easy enough to add Joe to our description. Because none of the rules have changed, the computer knows that Joe is the brother of John, Mary and Virginia. Everything is fine. The computer can learn. But wait a minute, what happens if my initial knowledge was wrong? What if my definition of brother was wrong? Of course, this is not likely to happen, but let's consider a more subtle example. Let's say that we are considering an ontology of ornithology. Sure enough, we'd have in the ornithology ontology the fact that birds can fly. We would be happy working with that in classifying the birds of our village. However, nature sometimes being perverse, one day we are sure to meet a penguin. From the movies, we know they can dance, but can they fly? Well, we now have to change our ontology to say that not all birds fly. So, we have to retract an existing assumption and replace it by a new one. Learning, as we can see, is not only about adding knowledge. It's also about changing or sometime even invalidating previous knowledge. Now we are faced with a new situation; that of realizing that our knowledge is subject to doubt. This leads us once again to *trust*.

# Trust and Content

As we've seen, any content needs to be associated with a level of trust. Whether it is human or computer knowledge, there must be a mechanism to say whether that information is understood such that certain actions can be undertaken with some expectation of the outcome of the action. Alternatively, we need to understand whether the information is not fully understood and that other actions are needed with some alternate expectation of an outcome. Trust is the measure of how well we understand the information such that we can expect a specific outcome from an action with some degree of certainty. Of course, trust as we have defined it is a gradient that ranges from no trust at all to complete trust. Here, we need to make a point; complete trust is a *religious concept*. At this point, we can come back to our famed sentence "This sentence is false." We were observing that humans can process this sentence without difficulty whereas it is seemingly a big problem for a computer. Now, imagine that just as humans have a mechanism to evaluate every piece of knowledge and assign to it a level of trust, before processing, computers would look at every piece of data they have in the same way. When presented with "This sentence is false." the computer would first evaluate its chance of processing it. If it accepts that sentence blindly, it will go in an unending spin. However, if it approaches it with caution, which is with less than complete trust, it may recognize readily that it should be careful and stop processing at once; in case of further uncertainty, it may decide to limit the time it allocates to processing it. That's a small illustration of the concept of trust, and we'll go into it more depth in the next chapter.

The emergence of personal electronic devices centered on secure cores in the commercial marketplace can be illustrated through a number of distinct case studies. In each case, the reason for success or failure can typically be traced to two characteristics of the situation. One characteristic is common across all cases and one characteristic is similar, but just a bit different in each case. The common characteristic is the fact that deployment incurs an infrastructure problem that is generally best solved by a large scale system deployment through which the personal electronic device infrastructure can be added at the ground floor in the development of the full system. The similar, but just a little bit unique characteristic is of course, money.

It is worth noting that these success stories all have the common theme that they illustrate personal electronic devices very much as an emergence species of computer; specifically, taking their secure core as a starting point. None of the stories center on the more significant features of complex social ecosystems that we think are the future of personal electronic devices, or whatever their descendent species offspring might be called. The cases are of interest, however, because they at least give us a view of the concepts, albeit operating at the technical edges of social orders.

The first large scale deployment of a phone card based system was undertaken by France Telecom during the early 1980's. The overarching system of concern was the deployment of pay telephones throughout France. The point of concern was the prospect of fraud in the handling of large amounts of currency in the form of coins. The fraud could take a variety of forms; fraud in the collection and transport of coins from a huge number of pay phones, fraud in the form of theft from the machines and fraud in the form of theft of service by using counterfeit coins. The object of the phone card exercise then was to provide a mechanism to support pay-per-use wireline telephony services at a lower cost than could be accomplished with actual currency.

Now, phone cards always present an infrastructure problem when it comes to their deployment. While their typical physical shape is that of a credit card, their electrical and logical connectivity presents in a very unique form. This was certainly the case at the time of the France Telecom deployment; there were essentially no electrical or logical standards in place to guide the design, production and operation of phone card equipment. In fact, when France Telecom started their considerations for the use of phone card, there weren't even any serious phone card companies in business. To that time, development work had been done by small groups of individuals, or small groups essentially performing applied research within larger, established companies. France Telecom essentially needed to bring a technology, and its supporting industry, into being. To accomplish this, they turned to a worldwide icon of French industry at the time, Schlumberger, then referred to as the IBM of the oil patch; the oil-patch would probably have better understood in these days the reference to IBM as the Schlumberger of the computer world.

Schlumberger was enlisted to bring the fledgling technology of phone cards into commercial reality. This meant, among other things, the development of manufacturing capabilities allowing the production of phone cards in sufficient quantities with sufficient quality and at a low enough cost to enable a nationwide pay telephone network. This situation is a bit unusual among business entities, although it is not that strange in a government to industry relationship; France Telecom, in this case, being a state institution. The situation: well, it could be considered one of a big customer requiring the availability of a product in short (as in, non-existent) supply. This is a situation that forms a positive feedback loop within a market; demand significantly outpaces supply and a customer that is not cost limited by normal market pressures. Recognizing this, France Telecom did what most governments do in a similar situation; they instituted artificial market pressures to augment the normal marketplace. In this case, France Telecom required Schlumberger to support the establishment of a competitor in order to guarantee a second source for phone card technology. Thus, once the technology was in place, Gemplus was founded as the dominant competitor to Schlumberger in the phone card marketplace.

To this time, phone card development consisted largely of companies or individuals identifying characteristics that were well developed in the computer world in general and adapting the concepts for use with phone cards under the recognition that that they were an emergent species from the typical computer of the day. Schlumberger acquired licensing rights for a number of basic patents from the two principal companies that held the salient patents, Groupe Bull and Innovatron, the company established by Roland Moreno to license the patent portfolio that he established during the early 1970's. The end result was that a marketplace for a new technology was brought into being by the force of will of a large entity with deep pockets, and a commercial need for which the phone card was a reasonable, although not unique, match. This is about as close as one gets to a technical rendition of the Big Bang in which a whole new ecosystem, with its own set of physical laws, is brought into being through a single impulse. So, the process managed quite nicely to solve the general infrastructure problem that is a mandatory step in the establishment of phone card systems. But, did it handle the other problem specific to the pay-telephone application for which it was developed?

Well, in fact it did. From a technical standpoint, the phone card certainly filled the bill. It was intuitive to use and it provided adequate security of keep attackers from using the general phone card as a means to essentially print their own money. That means that the value represented by the card could be spent for the purpose intended and there was a very good accounting match between the value sold in the form of cards and the value regained by use of cards in pay-telephones. Moreover, an ingenious match was found between a French social institution, the ubiquitous Tabac stores, and the need to market the phone cards. The cards were simply sold in the stores, which are everywhere in France, and the system ran rather swimmingly. France Telecom could treat the phone card much like any other product sold in the stores; sold at a slight discount that allowed for the store to garner a profit. Payment by the store followed the same path as payment for any other product; a mechanism far simpler than would have been the special arrangements necessary to collect and convey large numbers of coins from all the pay-telephones in the land. It formed a nice success story driven by the need to minimize fraud in a system offering many opportunities for it to occur. Minimizing the logistics of collection, certainly a significant opportunity for minimizing fraud, was icing on the cake.

A second great success story was found in the world of mobile (cellular) telephony. There are some similarities with our first success story; that is, the scenario deals with payment for telephony services. This time, however, the issue at hand which led to the use of secure cores was not so much about fraud as it was about portability of identity and the subsequent ubiquity of service.

The early deployment of cellular mobile telephone systems in the United States and the United Kingdom were analogue based systems. Such systems tend to be inefficient users of radio frequency bandwidth and the voice channel quality is generally low compared to all-digital systems. Further, the international rules for implementation and deployment of such analogue systems tended to lead to disjoint systems in the various countries in which they were deployed. With the emergence of the European Economic Union, there was a recognized need for a pan-European mobile telephone system; a system that would allow many providers and yet span all of Europe with one large or many small but interoperable systems. Enter the Groupe Spécial Mobile (GSM), whose story has been chronicled in *GSM and UMTS: The Creation of Global Mobile Communication*, edited by Friedhelm Hukkebrand.

In the early 1980's, the GSM set out to develop the technical specifications for a digital mobile telephone architecture that could be deployed across Europe and throughout the world. The system they arrived at was given the designation of Global System for Mobile communications, allowing for the efficient reuse of the GSM acronym. God forbid that we should run short of acronym space. One of the more profound aspects of the GSM architecture was the use of a specific trusted component within the telephone handset; a Subscriber Identity Module (SIM).

The SIM, not the handset *per se*, establishes the account to which access charges are billed for the use of the cellular telephone. Because of the trust placed in the identification of the account owner through the Subscriber Identity Module, GSM system operators worldwide have been willing to enter into cross-system usage agreements. Through the trust infrastructure put in place by the SIM, the various operators that might be involved in providing system support on any specific call made through a GSM handset, located perhaps anywhere in the world, are duly compensated through the policy infrastructure that is encompassed by the trust infrastructure.

Because of the GSM architecture and its use of the Subscriber Identity Module, changing handsets is a trivial operation requiring essentially no administrative support to accomplish. Simply take the SIM out of one handset and insert it into another handset and you're off and running with a new, personal telephone (there are some exceptions to that rule in the United States, where operators artificially limit handset capabilities, a remnant of proprietary practices). In a complementary fashion, because of the SIM and the worldwide standardization of GSM systems, one can take the same handset, with the same Subscriber Identity Module, and make calls through distinct GSM local systems around the world. So, we see another success story for secure cores, this time due to the need for worldwide roaming on the part of the cellular telephone user. Today, the overwhelming majority of cellular phones in the world, more than two billion of them actually, contain a SIM, and other phones are converting to the SIM mechanism to provide international and national roaming capabilities.

The third success story can be found in the distribution of direct broadcast television, a system based on satellites placed in geosynchronous orbits that are used to distribute television broadcast signals over a wide area. The *raison d'être* for the use of a secure core in such systems is the need to limit access to the broadcast signal to those who have properly subscribed to the service; that is, to limit access to those who have paid for it.

Direct broadcast television makes use of a concept popularized by science fiction author Arthur Clarke. This is the use of satellites placed in a geosynchronous orbit. This orbit is a well defined path, located directly above the equator of the earth, for satellites to orbit the earth in exactly one day. By making the satellite move from west to east, the satellite revolves around the earth exactly in time with the earth's rotation on its axis. The result is that a satellite in geosynchronous orbit hangs in the sky at a fixed spot directly above the equator. By selecting a satellite location that can be seen from within a specific area, for example by all the area comprising North America, an operational communication system can be implemented with relatively inexpensive equipment. The operational frugality derives from the ease of keeping the earth station antenna pointed at the satellite.

For a satellite in an orbit other than a geosynchronous orbit, an earth station on the ground must track the satellite as it moves through its orbital path if the earth station is to be able to exchange radio signals with the satellite; and, tracking stations are expensive, even for earth stations that use small, one meter diameter antennae. For a satellite in a geosynchronous orbit, however, the satellite sits at a fixed point in the sky. So, one simply has to point the antenna at that point in the sky and the earth station and the satellite can exchange radio transmissions. Now, if a large earth station transmits a strong signal up to a satellite, and the satellite receives that signal and then re-broadcasts it back toward the earth at a slightly different frequency, then any earth station antenna pointed at that location in the sky can receive the signal. Thus, a single television station can now be received by any earth station within the footprint of the transmission antenna on board the satellite. This allows the distribution of a television station across continent sized areas; much larger reception areas than can be achieved with normal transmission towers on the tops of buildings or mountains. From a business planning perspective, this architecture does leave a bit of a problem. If the satellite carries only a single channel, the distribution model is very inefficient relative to cable television distribution. So, another wrinkle is necessary.

The added wrinkle is a channel accessing scheme that allows many discrete sets of information to be carried within a single channel; essentially making a single radio frequency channel carry many simultaneous television channels. To realize this wrinkle requires that a digital data stream be transmitted from a single, large uplink earth station to a satellite which then re-broadcasts this stream back to the earth to be received by small earth station antennas at the home of each subscriber. Now, with a digitized stream carrying many channels, it is technically feasible to encrypt the stream and to lease the decryption mechanism to each subscriber. In this way, a revenue stream can be generated for the provider of the satellite system. This is where secure cores come into play.

All that is technically required on a subscriber's reception station is a digital decryption unit that is supplied with the necessary key for decryption. A significant business problem can arise, however, with the distribution of this key. If the key is presented to the subscriber in the clear, then there is nothing to prevent one subscriber from passing the key on to other subscribers, but without them having to pay any type of fee for the television service. However, by locking the key away within a smart card, it was possible to define a protocol of use for the key that would allow it to be accessed only after the subscription fee was paid and then only by a specific reception station. Thus, the smart card success in this case was due to the provision of a secure means of decryption key distribution.

Trust, as we've seen, is the necessary ingredient to validate content and even make its processing by the human brain or the computer possible. So, one wonders, "What creates trust?" That is what we are now going to investigate.

6   The Shrine of Content

# 7 In His Own Image

*With earth's first clay they did the last man knead,*
*There of the last harvest sowed the seed,*
*And what the first morning of creation wrote,*
*The last dawn of reckoning shall read.*

Edward Fitzgerald
*The Rubayat of Omar Khayyam*

## Trust through Causality

Causality is the rock on which the bottom turtle stands.

"It's turtles, all the way down," said the little old lady of Chapter 4 as she explained the world's support system. To understand where the turtles stopped and something else started, we alluded to the need for establishing a basic foundation on which all else rests. This foundation we term *causality*. The story is a metaphorical reference to recursion; turtle upon turtle upon turtle. Causality then is the terminus of recursion. Within the model of social systems that we have suggested, causality is the seminal point on which a trust infrastructure can be based and from which trust may be conveyed throughout the infrastructure. We suggest that any trust infrastructure is grounded in causality; even that governed by the well defined laws of our physical ecosystem.

Various forms of celestial calendars passed down to us from antiquity demonstrate that humans have for millennia made detailed observations of the motions of the sun, moon and stars. Causality of the observed movements has long been the source of myth and mystery. Over the centuries, astronomers from many civilizations accumulated ever increasingly detailed observations of the paths of these celestial bodies. Through the ages, the movements of the heavenly spheres were endowed with supernatural justification. Indeed, it was not until the XVII[th] Century scientist Sir Isaac Newton proposed a relationship between the mass of bodies and an interaction force termed gravitational attraction that the myths surrounding them were slowly and grudgingly replaced by more quantitative causality. Newton's equations of motion predicted the observed paths within the accuracy of the measurements of the day. However, over time the accuracy of the measurements was continually enhanced to the end that the causal explanation no longer fit the observations.

One of the more obtuse such measurements was the precession of the perihelion of the orbit of the planet Mercury. The orbits of all the planets around the Sun take the form of ellipses, with the Sun located at one of the foci of the ellipse while each planet's orbit traces out the ellipse itself. The equations applied to systems of masses in motion and subject to gravitational attraction suggest that the major axis of a planet's orbital ellipse should rotate under their influence. As the closest planet to the Sun and hence the planet with the highest orbital speed, the precession of Mercury's orbit is most easily measured. When Newton's equations of motion were used to explain this precession, theory did not match experimental measurement; the established causality did not hold. It was not until Albert Einstein developed his theory of relativity that a new causal mechanism was established which did match empirical observations. This new basis for explaining planetary motion also brought with it a wealth of non-intuitive causality. Perhaps most profound was the malleable nature of time and space itself; time was found to be related to the motion of bodies and the form of space was found to be altered by their mass. Were we not in an era now tempered with scientific acceptance of even more seemingly mystical effects such as quantum mechanics giving rise to quantum computing, we would certainly have fodder for new myths to explain the mysteries. Indeed, in the consideration of the singularity that apparently gave birth to the Big Bang, we still find the threads of supernatural causality. Within the human mind, profound acceptance of seminal points of causality forms the basis of trust on which the stimuli for subsequent interactions are based.

Ecstasy is that place where the mind goes to establish trust. Where causality stops, ecstasy begins. The ultimate form of trust, it imbues the brain with certainty, the "All things here do work out very well on their own" of James Austin in *Zen and the Brain*. Unimpeded by the constant reference to lower forms of trust that would otherwise block such transformations, the brain can adjust its wiring to bring necessary changes to neural circuitry. In a ritualistic environment, those changes can be consistent across a social group. When we have a shared perception of the causality of things or processes we can make collective predictions or extrapolations regarding these things and the effect or results of these processes. Within the context of establishing social ecosystems, religions can weave causality in supernatural sources. We humans look through a lens of altered states of consciousness that we have identified as ecstasy and we establish trust in forms and mechanisms that are beyond our purely cognitive assessment of the physical ecosystem. As our understanding of the physical ecosystem has grown over the ages, the realms in which we seek causality from supernatural sources have tended to become more focused. Some would say our need for such causality is diminished, if not removed entirely. Others would say that our focus simply falls on the higher order needs which are wound throughout the more coarsely understood operations of the human mind. For computer systems, our concerns are a bit more mundane, but nonetheless critical to the operation of social ecosystems as they are extended to encompass computers and computer networks.

Historically, in an effort to establish security within computer systems, we have also sought a basis for trust through causality. However, in this case we have grounded our trust in the causality that the physical creation of our tools, that is our computer systems, provides us. Also, we seek trust in the causality that derives from our understanding of the processes that our computer tools effect. Once established, we then seek to maintain trust through an ability to determine whether any subversive modifications have been made to the systems since the time of their creation. We would like for such modifications to be difficult, if not impossible. Moreover, we would like for any such modifications, once made, to be obvious in their detection. The ultimate goal of security within computer systems is for them to be *tamper-proof*; for it to be impossible for an unwanted modification to be made to the system's operating characteristics. At the very least, we seek to avoid or prevent changes without proper credentials. Moreover, for a system to be truly tamper-proof, we would expect that even in the face of destructive disassembly, confidential information contained within the system would not be compromised. While these are goals worth seeking, to establish in a provable fashion that any system meets these goals is a daunting if not impossible task. Consequently, what we typically accept, following from an understanding of the causality of a system, is *tamper-resistant* and *tamper-evident* behavior on the part of the system.

This approach to security through causality in mechanisms dates from the earliest records and artifacts of the operation of social orders. Our rather immediate and specific objective is the use of causality as a means to establishing trust within computer systems in general, and in secure core systems specifically. We will begin our discussions by extracting something of the architectural characteristics of this approach. We'll then consider the methodology through which relevant architectures are applied to actual mechanisms for establishing trust. By first examining in some detail the intricacies of current personal electronic devices, particularly those that encompass secure core elements, we'll then seek to extract a more abstract understanding for such systems. We'll then attempt to apply this understanding to real world situations. If we cut to the chase for this discussion, in the end we'll find that relative to computer systems, trust through causality is a necessary, but not sufficient approach to achieve the desire levels of trust in our systems. This will then provide us the impetus and a bit better footing when we seek to extend the discussion in the next chapter to the concept of establishing trust through process.

Given some seminal point of causality, to convey trust from this point requires a system whose *architecture* encompasses the tamper-resistant and tamper-evident characteristics that we noted above. We expect this architecture to yield in its implementation the characteristics of security that we previously discussed in Chapter 3. Over the history of social ecosystems, such architectures have been established in a variety of forms. First, and foremost, are architectures that make use of *secrets* to convey trust from a point of ultimate causality to some other location within the ecosystem. The thing, be it artifact or process, that is kept secret is not trust in and of itself, but rather it typically establishes the identity of some entity and subsequently allows any trust imbued within that entity to be conveyed across time or space, or both. Consider in a bit more detail the bulla that we previously mentioned in earlier chapters.

From exhibits at the Louvre and other museums throughout the world, specific relics show us that as early as five millennia ago, the civilizations of Mesopotamia made use of writing on clay tablets to keep records of quantities of goods exchanged. In order to convey such accounting information in a trusted fashion, small clay tablets were enclosed in a sealed clay pocket, called bulla, about the size of a small fist. The bulla evolved over time until becoming a quite complex object with its very evolution that we see in the Louvre exhibits giving us a good understanding of the significance of its constituent components. We'll consider here its most elaborate, and final form as far as the archeological record is concerned. On the surface of the clay pocket was a *seal* indicating the identity of the source of the contained information, together with sacred symbols. The seal was intricate and difficult to construct in the first place, and hence it was difficult to replace when broken. This mechanism provided a means to convey the information found inside the bulla along with some degree of trust imbued in the originator of the information; that is, the person represented by the seal, validated by the protection afforded by the religious symbols. The owner of flocks might send some number of sheep to market to be sold. The sheep were driven to market by shepherds to whom either the temporary custodianship of the sheep, or the money received from their sale returning from market, might constitute an overwhelming temptation to sell a sheep or two on the side and tell the owner the price received for the full complement was less than anticipated. The shepherds in this situation represent a non-secure communication channel. The bulla was introduced as a counter-measure against just this type of threat. A bulla sent by the flock owner could convey to the purchaser just how many sheep were expected. A returned bulla sent by the purchaser could tell the owner what price was paid. The bulla could be conveyed by the shepherd, even though he might be of suspect trustworthiness; an example of secure trusted communication through an unsecured channel.

As Ross Anderson noted in *Security Engineering*, the use of the bulla in the manner we've just described embodies several of the characteristics of security that we discussed in Chapter 3. Specifically, it entails the characteristics of privacy, authentication, information integrity and non-repudiation. Privacy is achieved in conveying the contents of the bulla from the flock owner to the buyer without the shepherd, who is the courier, being specifically aware of the contents. More important, he is unable to alter the contents without the buyer being made aware of it because the bulla is a tamper-resistant and tamper-evident mechanism. Authentication of the identity of the flock owner is conveyed to the buyer through the seal imprinted on the bulla. The sacred symbols establish a source for confidence in the authentication, and a threat against tampering, which might unleash the wrath of gods. The integrity of the information contained in the bulla is established through the unbroken form of the clay pocket. The seal on the bulla also acts as an indicator of non-repudiation that the bulla came from the flock owner. Since ostensibly only the flock owner can produce this seal, he cannot claim that he was not the sender; again, under the threat of sacred intervention. The only one of the security characteristics that we discussed in Chapter 3 that is not established by the bulla is that of authorization. In essence, anyone who came in possession of the bulla could open it. Consequently, the mechanism can not be said to encompass any technique to keep the incorrect person from receiving the message. The assertion of authority to open the bulla is conveyed through social convention external to the mechanism itself. Thus, if a person other than the addressee of the bulla opens it, then that person may be subject to the condemnation of the social (religious) system, and subject to sanctions from that system. The protocol could have actually been more elaborate. Perhaps the receiver was required to send another bulla in return, thereby validating both identity and the amount paid. In any case, we should note that the whole mechanism comprises a vehicle of trust conveyance. Thus, it is an implementation of a trust conveying architecture.

As illustrated in the use of the bulla, but also of paramount importance in other trust architectures, secrets are indelibly linked to the establishment and conveyance of trust. From the earliest times, the establishment of guarded walls to cities or camps has made use of secret passwords to gain passage through the perimeter. In Chapter 5, we discussed in some detail the concept of authentication protocols used to verify the asserted identity of one party, a supplicant, to another party, a sentinel. The model for such interactions is exactly that of provision of a password to a sentry guarding an entry portal to a city or camp. If two parties share a secret, then one can provide the secret to the other in order to establish identity; in this case, the fact that the two parties are in fact friends. However, what happens when there are many persons on patrol outside the perimeter? Does not the fact that each of them must approach the sentinel and provide the password provide significant opportunity for a threat to overhear the password and thereby pass for a friend? This is the problem with establishing and conveying trust through shared secrets; the creation and distribution of the secrets in a trusted fashion in the first place. There are mechanisms for dealing with this dissemination problem, and we'll get to them later. For the moment, let us consider another significant architecture of trust within large scale systems.

The bulla that we noted above makes use of the conveyance of information in secret as a means of also conveying trust. The clay enclosure, while establishing secrecy of the contained information, also presents an environment of trust through the physical security of the enclosed tokens. This concept of physical security can be taken to much greater extremes and provide us with the safe or vault as a means of establishing trust. A bank, for instance, is a trusted place for storing valuables; money, jewels and the like. A safe or vault is an enclosure that is difficult to access due to its physical construction. Perhaps its walls are made of thick steel or reinforced concrete and its door is impervious steel with a locking mechanism. Thus, when something is placed within the enclosure, we have a clear understanding of the necessary causality for a change to occur in that thing. Either the thing must change due to an internal process, or it must be accessed by an external mechanism through the entry to the safe or vault. This ability to keep some entity immutable, and perhaps secret, offers a seminal source of trust when used in certain protocols.

# Science is the Religion of Disbelief

In *Religion Explained*, Pascal Boyer notes, "Persons can be represented as having counterintuitive physical properties (e.g., ghosts or gods), counterintuitive biology (gods who neither grow nor die) or counterintuitive psychological properties (unblocked perception or prescience). Animals too can have all these properties. Tools and other artifacts can be represented as having biological properties (some statues bleed) or psychological ones (they hear what you say)."

He also notices that a god, as an eternal person who never dies, is nevertheless in other respects a carrier of the normal properties of a person (listening, caring, demanding, etc). In technical terms, that god presents most of the properties of a person but supplants at least one of them; specifically, the god doesn't die. This, we would represent as follows (we simplify and take liberty with the formalism here, but this doesn't affect the message we intend to convey):

```
<person>
    <property> listens </property>
    <property> cares </property>
    <property> demands </property>
    <property> dies </property>
</person>
```

together with:

```
<person>
    <name> god </name>
    <property> never dies </property>
</person>
```

So, in a formal sense, what we've done is taken an ordinary person and made that person into a god by just changing one property from the value usually associated with a person. We've turned that property into one that we would associate with a god. To fully implement the transformation, faith is required in granting a status of existence to the new entity. Faith, as we have suggested previously, is a level of the continuum that is trust. Carrying on then, this new entity can now be involved in interactions with others, either people born out of hard sensory experience, or perhaps also created through the same mechanism as our god. If the result of those interactions brings accepted results then the initial faith is validated and repetitive observation of those results reinforces the faith involved. Conversely, rejected results either diminish that faith or are cause to seek further explanations. While we are aware that such an interpretation has been rejected outright by such respected authors as Émile Durkheim in *The Elementary Forms of the Religious Life*, we observe that this rejection was essentially reduced to a sleight of hand in a footnote (our translation): "We will not stop and discuss such an unsustainable conception, which in fact, has never been sustained in a systematic fashion by minds somewhat acquainted with the history of religions." We prefer to be called "ignorant of the history of religions" rather than relinquish a natural explanation of the personal and social interactions involved.

While we've suggested how a god can be formally created from an otherwise unaltered entity, the initial reaction of the scientist to a perturbation in accumulated experience would be symmetrically opposed to the one we have just illustrated. This reaction is part of the practice of science, but is in no way restricted to scientists. However, for convenience, we will consider for the moment the behavior of the scientist. Confronted with an unexpected event, the scientist will deny any extra, changed property to the object observed. Rather, she will attempt first to fit the experience within existing models based on unaltered sensory experience, or to derive properties from that experience only through methodologies recognized and accepted in that particular science, the body of which constitutes what is called *epistemology*.

In technical terms, let's assume that the scientist discovers the following:

```
<person>
    <name> Jesus </name>
    <property> walks on water </ property>
</person>
```

A new property is observed not previously known of a person. In such a situation, the scientist will work unrelentingly to find if that property is actually new or an artifact of other, established properties; in this case:

```
<person>
    <name> Jesus </name>
    <property> stands on glass </property>
</person>
```

We are overly simplifying here for the sake of presentation, but we assume the argument is transparent and can be readily comprehended by the reader. In correcting the formal specification, the scientist applied all the inference rules available to recast the anomalous property to an accepted one. At this point we observe that any naturally skeptical person would probably react like our scientist.

Now let's consider another situation, that of objects falling to the ground, and define the concept of force:

```
<force>
    <property> action of an object upon another </property>
</force>
```

As we saw in Chapter 3, there are four basic forces in nature, i.e. strong nuclear force, the weak force, electro-magnetic force and gravity. So we have:

```
<force>
    <name> strong  nuclear force </name>
    <property> atomic nucleus distance</property>
</force>
<force>
    <name> weak force </name>
    <property> inter-atomic distance </property>
</force>
<force>
    <name> electro-magnetic force </name>
    <property> familiar distance </property>
</force>
<force>
    <name> gravity </name>
    <property> intergalactic distances </property>
</force>
```

In these examples, we have objects whose properties are not directly observable. They are inferred from the successful applications of theories that use them to explain and predict phenomena of nature, themselves directly observable, such as, for gravity the falling of an apple from a tree to the earth. This is not formally different from positing a god with an unobserved property ("never dies"). In each case, a property finds its presence justified by accepted results. The main difference appears to be in the trust attributed to the result. Science, physics in particular, has been particularly aggressive at positing such hypothetic entities as immanent, calling them the source of laws (the law of gravity), even though such laws are periodically changed as new knowledge accumulates. For example, consider the potential changes such as we find in the current discussions in quantum physics related to the formulation of the gravitational force; the quest is incessant in the pursuit of higher laws. Such laws, while initially established with a lower level of trust, may well succeed in subsuming older laws as observed evidence mounts. In religion, one finds a different approach. There, a higher trust may be ascribed to more abstract and arcane constructs based on ecstatic considerations. Subsequently, more detailed hypotheses may be developed while modifying interpretations, or even principles, depending on the existing religious theologies involved.

From the two examples, we see that both religion and science bring with them explanatory mechanisms. Religion starts from higher hypotheses and draws conclusions from them, using actual events in an attempt to validate the hypotheses. Science starts from lower hypotheses and builds a chain of reason transforming them into substantial conclusions. Both approaches provide guidance to subsequent actions. Effectiveness is dictated by empirical environmental factors. As a bit of anecdotal emphasis on this point, we draw your attention to the 1979 movie of Peter Sellers titled Being There.

In the movie, Peter Sellers plays a rather enigmatic character known only by his first name, Chance. For years, Chance, a very slow-witted, some might say simpleton individual, has lived in a cloistered home in Washington, D.C. owned by The Old Man who has allowed Chance to live in the home and to tend the small, walled garden in the back of the house. When The Old Man dies, Chance is turned out onto the street by the attorney overseeing the liquidation of the estate. As he wanders the streets of Washington, a limousine bumps into him, belonging to the wife of an extremely wealthy industrialist and political power broker. To avoid legal entanglements, she suggests that Chance return to her home to allow her husband Ben's physician to check his minor injury. In the process, Chance rather mangles his name when asked, and for the rest of the movie he becomes "Chauncey Gardner" as opposed to his intended "Chance, the gardener." The remainder of the movie is a recurring series of Chauncey's apparently simple-minded remarks being interpreted by various members of the power elite, to whom he is introduced through his virtually instantaneous friendship with Ben, as being statements of profound import. This rather farcical comedy of misinterpretations and misconceptions culminates in the possibility that Chauncey might be suggested for the presidency at the next election. While all of this makes for entertaining theater, the most enticing point of the movie is the final scene; that is, the very final moment in which observable action is happening in the background while the end-of-the-movie credits are rolling in the foreground.

Here, following the funeral of Ben, Chauncey walks across the grounds of the grand estate. At the edge of a pond, something out in the water attracts his attention. Without hesitation, Chauncey proceeds to walk out into (onto) the pond. Perhaps 20 meters from the shore, he peers down at the water and then proceeds to insert his umbrella into the pond. He's able to push the umbrella a good meter or more into the water, apparently indicating that the water he's standing on has significant depth. At this point the movie ends and the interpretation of the final scene, for those who actually noticed it, begins.

On reading a variety of compilations of moviegoer reviews of Being There, it would appear that this final scene is generally interpreted in one of two ways. First, in what we might characterize as the scientific and pragmatic interpretation, the view is that this a bit of almost slapstick comedy in which Chauncey is obviously walking out on some very slightly submerged pier in the water. That is, it is just another instance, physical this time, in which a rather simple minded gesture on the part of Chauncey is misinterpreted as having profound significance. The other interpretation is that, for all his appearances of a simple person, in fact Chauncey could walk on water. This would give credence to the interpretation that his apparently simple-minded actions and comments throughout the movie truly did have profound significance. This provides us with an interesting illustration of the two approaches (scientific and religious) to explaining unusual situations that we've been discussing. The scientific approach, when it encounters a situation that contradicts known interaction constraints, seeks to refine the understanding of the parameters surrounding the interaction in an effort to find a set of conditions that will allow the interaction to fall within the rules. The religious approach, particularly in extraordinary circumstances, is willing to entertain, as an act of faith, the possibility that an interaction can be interpreted precisely as it appears. This may mean that it is based in beyond natural means; that it is, in fact a supernatural occurrence.

It is then worth noticing again that the religious approach to problem solving is not altogether foreign to the scientist. In chemistry, a standard way to compute a property (the pH) of a solution of two constituents (base and acid) is to make an assumption of where the range of the pH should fall, which then allows one to carry out the hand computation of the result by simplifying the equations involved. If the pH indeed falls into the presumed range, the solution is deemed valid. Other examples go to the root of mathematics, such as *reductio ad absurdum*, where a hypothesis is posited which is then eliminated as it leads to a contradiction in the system under consideration; and *inductive reasoning*, where a recurring phenomenon is assumed to follow a regular law. In both these cases, an unobserved object is created, involving an act of faith. Accepting the result validates the hypothesis, similarly to the thinking involved in religious conclusions.

# Creating Trust

The title as well as the theme of this chapter, "In His Own Image" can be construed as establishing trust through the creation of standard forms. "I am like God. If other people are like God, then they are like me. Therefore, I can confer a level of trust upon them because of our inherent divinity." Consider the golden rule as a statement of policy based on this type of trust: "Do unto others as you would have them do unto you." We have suggested that within the human mind trust is an integral aspect of the operation of the sensori-motor system. Further, we suggest that humans have formed groups as an evolution derived mechanism to enhance the natural selection prospects of the species. The establishment of shared trust within the group is a primary requisite of any successful grouping mechanism. In our parallel evaluation of human and computer systems, we have now recognized that our knowledge of one or the other may be more advanced, depending on the characteristics sought. In evaluating trust, we have associated the degree to which it was conferred to the certainty of causality chains. For example, if it is always observed that the apple falls from the tree to the earth, the level of trust in gravity will be quite high. If it is merely often observed that celebration of common rites leads to a stronger presence in battle, would it be in sport, war or other communal undertaking, trust will be granted to those rites. Actually, the level of trust imbued in gravity is more immediately assessed than the trust imbued in ritual. With that in mind, we will now turn our attention to computer networks, and particularly to personal electronic devices.

In computer systems, causality can be traced from the most elementary forms to the most elaborate. We know, and hence trust this statement, because we have actually collectively built these various elements in recent history and all the steps that lead to today's computers have been thoroughly documented and analyzed. While with humans, we are a long way from dissecting the causality links occurring in the brain, with computers we essentially know them all. Therefore, we can discuss them in some detail, and we'll use that knowledge later to see if it sheds light on aspects of human networks that would otherwise be more difficult to comprehend. We use this as an approximate means to finally reach our goal, which is to use that additional understanding to predict how computer networks will evolve.

At the sensori-motor level, trust in computer operations is, just as for humans, linked with the certainty of causality effects. If something happens somewhere in my computer or in the network, how certain am I that expected consequences will follow? As it happens, there are three mitigating factors to answering this question: quality, security and statistics. The first, quality measures the relationship between the original intent put forth in the implementation of the computer system versus the actual results obtained. The second, security measures the extent to which that implementation may have been compromised, thereby altering the causality chain. The third is related to the use of statistical evaluation in the determination of computers' actions, for example in the domains of network responses and of cryptographic measures. Before we look specifically at actual computers, let us consider the way modern systems in general are evaluated regarding quality and security.

Social ecosystems encompass the characteristic of subjective evaluation, which by its very nature allows interim assessments of evolutionary changes to be incorrect relative to the ultimate judgment of natural selection. We refer to these as interim in that, in the final analysis, the objective rule of natural selection will prevail. That said, it is useful to consider one such subjective mechanism that has emerged as a significant factor in the provision of access to content, that of *standards*.

The provision of standards is an approach through which mutational changes are removed, or at least severely constrained within a social ecosystem. Standards primarily address an interface or a process within a specific ecosystem element and they are typically established in one of two distinct forms; through a standards document agreed to by a *standards organization* or through a specification, possibly accompanied by a conformance test, issued by an organization which seeks to impact the manner of implementation of a system; most typically, a *consortium* of some type. While there are many standards associated with quality and security, we will chose two to briefly review in order to illustrate their role in establishing trust based on the rituals they are associated with; rituals known as *certification*.

The most prevalent quality standard is the family of *ISO 9000*, developed by the International Standard Organization. The approach followed by ISO 9000 is to provide means to evaluate the maturity of organizations in following set processes in their implementation of product and services. For example, in building a computer a series of steps must be followed: purchasing parts, assembling them, testing them, packaging the product, advertising, selling and distributing the computer to the customer. Trust is needed in all elements of this chain. If non-functioning parts are purchased, badly assembled, insufficiently tested, weakly packaged, fraudulently advertised, sold on promises and distributed to the wrong place, the resulting computer will not be expected to satisfy expectations. Even if only one of the steps is compromised the result is problematic. ISO 9000 requires that all processes involved in the manufacturing of the product are documented, monitored, analyzed and continuously improved. Properly done, certification will allow associating a level of trust in the computer produced following such processes.

Similarly, a fundamental security standard is *Common Criteria*; also a standard stamped by the International Standard Organization. The idea of Common Criteria is easily illustrated in reference to a familiar security situation; for example, that of one's home. When thinking of one's home protection, it is immediately apparent that security levels are relative. We will not all live in a Fort Knox kind of house. Depending on our environment and needs, we will seek specific levels of protection. For example, in our neighborhood we may consider that making sure that our doors and windows are closed when we are absent will provide us with an acceptable level of security. Alternatively, our neighborhood environment may be such that we need to install an electronic alarm system coupled with bars on all openings. Thus, we see that security is not an absolute. This observation applies to computer systems as well, and it is the basis of Common Criteria. What Common Criteria seeks to accomplish, much like ISO 9000, is the provision of means for asserting which levels of security are needed, and then to make sure that the proper processes are followed to achieve them. This allows the establishment of trust in the assertion that security is present where we need and thus want it. Certification will provide this trust by making sure that what is promised is actually done.

We've alluded to the derivation of trust from an understanding of causality. If however, one is not intimately conversant with the intricacies of a specific causal relationship, either in construction or process, then how can we derive trust from it? Well, a variation on the theme of standards provides us a useful approach, that of the establishment of certification organizations. Such bodies are common in the area of computer system quality and security. Certification organizations typically allow the establishment of a level of trust, using much the same definition for trust that we have discussed previously. Remember that our working definition for trust is *an expectation (of an outcome) with some degree of assurance.* A certification standard is aimed at quantifying the *degree of assurance.*

Certification organizations are independent companies or government agencies whose function is to gather information regarding the processes addressed by the quality and security practices under certification. Typically, after studying the information provided, certification companies or agencies perform an audit based on a comprehensive questionnaire accompanied by set and random interviews. Almost invariably, they find deviations in the execution of the processes defined, and their job is to classify those deviations, essentially as minor or major exceptions. Typically, minor exceptions may be pardoned until the next audit but major exceptions need to be fixed for the certificate to be issued.

The whole concept of certification is thus grounded in trust conveyance through a third party in which a known level of trust is imbued by various parties. The manner in which trust is established within this third party is actually a topic of the next chapter; it involves trust derived from a well known process. So, for the moment we'll simply assume the existence of a defined level of trust and then we'll consider in the next chapter how this is established. As we've seen, the compliance standards and their associated certifications are generally about processes. They are often not actually about the content being investigated. A set level of trust is imbued in the processes, which provides an understood guarantee that whatever the intent of the authors of an artifact was, they implemented the artifact in a way that is traceable in quality, putting in place security measures that are precisely defined. What this doesn't do is measure the adequacy of the artifact to the task that they are expected to perform, this being a matter of content, which we will now turn to.

Let's come back to our house example, where we will decide that our doors and windows shall always be closed while we are away. If we document that fact by following quality and security standards and that we subsequently obtain certification that we are indeed following the practices we have defined, then we should be quite sure that the proper security is in place, shouldn't we? Actually, the only thing we can trust so far is that the security mechanisms we have put in place are indeed functioning. For example, if our process is that before leaving the house we walk through it to make sure that all openings are closed and that we do this without exception each time we prepare to leave the house, then at best our certification company can measure our conformance to this process. When our process is checked, then we can have some level of confidence in our making sure that the security we're seeking is in place. Of course, what happens if in our neighborhood, thieves come and just break the windows? Obviously, the security measures we have in place are not sufficient to prevent that. Just as obviously, this problem still exists because we did no evaluate the *threats* properly before we put our securities procedures in place. So even if quality and security standards are followed making sure that our processes are set and followed, it doesn't help if those processes are based on the wrong appreciation of threats and capabilities to answer them. For computers as for houses, we need to understand the content we are trying to protect, the potential threats to that content and the measures that are available to alleviate the threats. Then we must define the quality and security processes accordingly. So, let us consider a bit how we accomplish that. Particularly as this all pertains to the establishment of trust through causality in computers or personal electronic devices.

As an anecdotal introduction, we call your attention to the construction of the new United States Embassy in Moscow. A highly sanitized version of this rather intriguing story is found on the United States Department of State Web site. A few additional wrinkles in our recounting of the story derived from various news accounts. The overture for this interaction between the United States and the Soviet Union began back in 1934. The United States sought an accommodation with the Stalin Government to build a new embassy complex in Moscow. The initial overture was rebuffed and the American Embassy occupied essentially temporary facilities for several decades thereafter. In the 1960's, a reciprocal request for new facilities from the Soviet Government finally allowed an arrangement to be consummated. Unfortunately, at least for the security concerns of the United States, the arrangement entailed the acquisition of construction materials and support from Soviet sources. This is the interesting point from the perspective of trust through causality. As it became apparent, it was difficult to certify the sanctity of wet concrete and preformed building materials. In particular, it was possible for the Soviets to secret a huge number of clandestine listening devices into such materials. Thus, once completed, the embassy building was essentially a large microphone connected directly into the Soviet intelligence agencies. Some decades later, an arrangement was finally reached to demolish the upper levels of the building and rebuild those using American companies with appropriate security clearance. In general, boundaries between security components can be the most vulnerable aspects of such systems. The boundary between successive floors of a building is a surprising point of consideration.

As we've seen previously, personal electronic devices are typically composed of two parts: a general facility and a secure core. Sometimes, a personal electronic device can be reduced to a secure core. Since trust is our subject of inquiry here, we will consider in some detail secure cores. Our consideration will look in turn at their anatomy, their physiology, their embryology and then their sociology. As we do so, we will highlight the threats to be considered as well as possible responses. Once this is done, we will be able to set the proper processes, which in turn will be candidate for evaluation following the quality and security standards we discussed previously, and their corresponding certifications. In the following, our point of view will be that of developing trust in networks. We will provide a panorama of security threats and counter measures, and their associated trust level. This will not be a detailed technical discussion, for two reasons. The first one is that we would probably bore our reader. For the interested, more specialized literature is available, a sample of which is listed in the bibliography. The second reason is that, as insiders of the security industry we choose to limit our disclosure of security since it is typically true that insiders know more than is ever presented in public at any point in time. After all, the insiders build the products. This is, of course a bit of hyperbole and is actually illustrative of perhaps the current dominant form of security within the corporate world; that is, *security through obscurity*. However, it is true that within the computer world, just as within the secular and religious worlds, neither wizard nor witch (nor, apparently, public servants) ever divulge all of their secrets! That notwithstanding, let us resume the consideration of the secure cores of personal electronic devices.

The first high-volume trusted computers were in fact not computers at all, but rather specialized electronic circuits with very limited functions. They were simple counters that were set to a predefined level at the factory, and then were decremented each time a person made a call on a public telephone. When the units of communication indicated by such a counter were depleted, the card containing the circuitry was discarded, and a new one purchased. This was in the 1980's, before cellular phones. Public telephones were found throughout the world. Over time, phone cards would number in the billions. As we noted, the original card was a simple circuit coupled with electrical contacts. Through these contacts, power was provided to the card once it was inserted in the public phone reader apparatus. The contacts also allowed information interchange with the public telephone's card reader. Power activated the circuitry at regular intervals during the phone call, causing the card to retire units accordingly from the counter implemented by the circuitry. Naturally, some people soon wanted to defeat the system. Initially, they simply tried to either duplicate the card mechanism, or to find ways to reset the counter. The latter was somewhat difficult, but the former was quite easy, since earlier communication sessions between the card and the public phone were easily recorded and replayed. More complex circuitry was subsequently built to defeat this threat, and so started the race that is still on-going between secure core security measures and counter-attacks. As far as phone cards are concerned, fraud would eventually diminish, not because of lack of inventiveness, but because the incentive for fraud disappeared as public phones were replaced by cellular phones.

The electronic phone card was invented by the French, who naturally thought of such cards when they helped design the GSM cellular phones that would eventually conquer the world. A challenge with cellular phones was to avoid repeating the initial experience of public phone card fraud. Fortunately, a great advance in secure core design intervened at about the same time as the GSM cellular phones were designed; that of the microprocessor card. By embedding a microprocessor, which is an electronic component providing computer capabilities, the cellular phone card was suddenly capable of complex operations that would make the information emanating from this secure core of the cellular phone very difficult, if not impossible, to crack. Since the SIM card would contain the information identifying the caller to the cellular phone network, the only way for the hacker to steal communication time was to defeat the card itself. The idea was to somehow dismantle the card so as to pick its inside, or perhaps to find ways to externally probe the circuitry such that it revealed the secrets it contained.

Attacks to a secure core can be *non-destructive* or *destructive*, and also *external* or *internal*. An example of a non-destructive external attack is to change the electric power feeding the card and see how the circuitry responds. If the secure core is not protected against such attack, its circuitry may react in ways that provide critical information to a would-be cyberburglar. Another non-destructive external attack involved measuring the response time of the secure computer when different data were entered. Consider that the hacker wanted to find the Personal Identification Number (PIN) that gives access to the card's information. Each time the personal identification number was sent to the card, one could measure the response time. Depending on the correctness of the personal identification number's digits, the circuitry inside the card would take certain paths, if some digits are not correct, it would take other paths. If the paths are of different lengths, it shows in the response time. In order to counter such an attack, the designers of the card's inner working must make sure that the length of the circuitry is the same whether the digits are correct or not. While this is a cumbersome task, it is absolutely needed if the user of the cellular phone is to trust that no one can find out what the card contains and thus be able to make fraudulent calls that would eventually be found on the subscriber's phone bill.

With these simple examples, we see how much the trust that is imbued to the secure core of a personal electronic device is dependent on security, which is the capability of the secure core to not reveal its secrets. An example of a non-destructive internal attack consists in disturbing the electric circuitry with an appropriate laser beam. This creates perturbations in the functioning of the secure core that affect how the flow of information inside the card is directed toward providing an answer to specific data probes. To the careful eye, this can provide telltale information that can help decode and find information hidden in the card. This is not necessarily a sport for amateurs, but experts know how to interpret virtually any form of information they can get from a disturbed electronic circuit. If the circuitry inside is not designed with such attacks in mind, it is not beyond possibility to see the card simply spew out its most intimate secrets directly. However, with modern trusted cores, the perturbations are typically much harder to decode and require considerable expertise. Still, there are those who may want to spend the money for the machinery and for hiring top experts if the information inside is of high enough value. It is possible to protect against light-beam attacks with proper coatings on the circuit chips, but it is much more difficult to defend against another natural perturbation of electronic circuits, that caused by cosmic rays. These can disturb the functioning of the trusted core either temporarily or permanently. Certain defenses are themselves destructive, as the circuitry can detect the malfunctioning and decide to just shut down. More sophisticated defenses involve having enough redundancy in the circuitry to detect an anomaly and attempt to remedy it. When trust depends on a response to cosmic rays, we certainly reach a significant, if not ultimate boundary.

Let's consider an example of a destructive, external attack. It consists in imaging particular elements of the circuitry inside after peeling the inner layers of electronics, which is a destructive operation. If the hacker has for example, several secure cores to experiment with so that damaged ones can be replaced, then it is possible to use the information on those various secure cores to decrypt internal information. That's why trusted cores can be coated with protective armor making it very difficult to peel them off without breaking at the same time the circuitry so protected.

So we have reviewed two kinds of attacks; one that relies on perturbing circuitry, the other on imaging it. The defenses are of multiple kinds, from the design of the circuitry to using special coatings with several properties of interest. This illustrates that trust can come from multiple, reinforcing, sources, and we can readily understand that the security of electronic components is a complex field of technology.

We see that destructive external attacks can be very treacherous, and obviously expensive to counter. This allows us to illustrate an important aspect of trust derived from causality through security. Before one engages in defending circuitry against attacks, one must be well-aware of the value of the information being protected because the cost of protection can easily exceed the value of that information. Trust has a price. More trust is more expensive, and one needs to know where in the trust spectrum one wants to be, depending on the costs and associated value of the trust granted. Finally, let's consider destructive internal attacks. Those consist in dismantling the card but not its contained computer chip. The secure core is now open, and it is possible to directly probe the circuitry. One way to protect against such threats is to make it very likely that as the card is dismantled, it is irreparable damaged, for example by causing the component to burn or to shatter. However, it is easy to see that one who is determined enough may be able to assemble (or disassemble) the puzzle anyway, albeit at considerable effort. Here then, we see yet another principle of security in action, that involving time. If we can make it hard enough to get to the secret, it may take so much time that it is no longer relevant if and when it is revealed. In this case, security is based on the consideration that the secrets are temporarily safe, which brings a time component to the concept of trust.

So far we've talked in general terms of the appearance of the secure core and its interior circuitry. Now, let us be a bit more specific, starting with the physical enclosure. We've already seen that the *form factor*, as is said in the trade, is a card for phone applications. Actually, the public phone cards are typically the size of standard credit cards, while a SIM card for a cellular phone is smaller. There are even smaller cards now being considered for cellular phones that are getting continuously more miniaturized. The card form factor is very convenient for embedding a secure core in a personal electronic device, as it creates a natural frontier between the untrusted part of the device and its trusted part. The natural question at this point is whether the untrusted part actually somehow taints the trusted part. The answer to that is yes and no. As long as the secure part is using the unsecure part only as a channel to talk to another secure component somewhere on the network, there is little the unsecure part can do to alter the integrity of the secure core. Of course, it can close the channel of communication or flood it with meaningless garbage; therefore it can affect the trust placed in the secure core to function properly. Also, if the secure core relies on the unsecure part for obtaining input information, such as a personal identification number, then the situation is more delicate since the unsecure part can feed bogus data to the secure component. More to the point, the unsecure part can make a copy of the information and perhaps reuse it at a later time. We must then consider that if the input itself cannot be trusted can anything be done to at least have some tamper-evident aspect to the information? As we'll see, some measures can indeed be taken.

Thus far, our discussion illustrates the fact that it is difficult to limit trust to isolated components of the network, while ignoring other components that may not be themselves trusted. We will come back later to this issue when we explore the sensori-motor environment of the secure core of personal electronic devices. Indeed, in Chapter 9 we will suggest some mutational changes in such devices for just this purpose. For the moment, let us observe that the card form factor is not the only way to physically embed trusted cores. A very common form factor outside of the computer world is that of a key. A number of emergent computer world components, such as the USB (Universal Serial Bus) memory-sticks that readers are probably familiar with, take on very similar characteristics to standard keys. Another form factor is that of an RFID (Radio-Frequency Identification) tag. Yet another is that of an identity document such as a passport in which the trusted core is found inserted in the cover of the document. In all these cases, the form is dictated by the function, but does not necessarily provide additional security properties compared to the card form factor. However, this too can happen. For example, the trusted core embedded in a passport is protected by an electrical shield that prevents reading the passport information contained in the secure chip from a distance. This chip can only be read from close proximity with specialized reading equipment, while the passport is open. In this particular case, we see clearly that trust extends to the physical environment of the secure core.

We have considered the form factor characteristics of the secure core. Now let us review the facilities of the secure core processor itself. The central part of the secure core is, as for any computer, the processor or processors. In some cases there may actually be several processors present. While a general processor might be enough in principle to provide secure operations, for reasons of efficiency, specialization is most often found in secure processors with a sharing of tasks among dedicated modules. The most typical such configuration, almost a signature of secure cores, is a *cryptographic* co-processor. This is a processor that is specialized in the particular mathematics required by cryptographic operations. Fast processing of special computations requiring long-integer arithmetic can be obtained by dedicated circuitry, coupled with particular security measures necessitated by the very nature of the operations performed. These extra protections are needed because if one wants to attack operations of a secure core the cryptographic processor is an obvious target because it does not just encrypt and decrypt information direct to or from the external world. It can also protect information inside the secure core or information related to the secure core's relationship with its peripherals. We will look into this a bit later.

Another module associated with the processor is the controller that manages the relationship of the processor with its memory. This is also a very critical element in terms of security, because the path between the processor and memory is a natural point of attack. Specific measures have to be taken to protect information going along this path. Cryptographic measures may be one of several tools used for such protection. Finally, we need to mention yet another important specialized module which enables protected ways to use the processor. This is a bit technical so we'll ask the reader to excuse us if we sound cryptic: language-specific components can define a sandbox limiting the processor functions that are accessible through generic programming. We felt we had to note it, but you probably know now why we took some oratory precautions. Actually, we'll get into a discussion about sandboxes in the next chapter, which may help clarify the point.

While the processor needs to be trusted because it is the most active part of the secure core, it does not itself contain any data that are directly linked to the owner of the personal electronic device. Such data are stored in memory. A secure core typically includes two kinds of memory: fast but short-term memory for intermediate results and slower but long-term memory for keeping data. It is possible to identify the two memories with that of humans, who can remember more of one day's activities during that day than they'll remember a week later. The brain sorts out which temporary memories should be made into long-term ones using a process of synapse consolidation described by Eric R. Kandel in his book *In Search of Memory*. Similarly, the processor uses its short-term memory to do computations whose results will be stored in long-term memory if needed. Since short-term memory, called RAM (Random Access Memory) is first of all required to be very fast, it is typically not strongly encrypted. While this is considered acceptable in general, it cannot be tolerated for very critical data such as the keys used to decipher secret information. That is why short-term memory may be accompanied by a very specialized sub-form of it, which is constructed to avoid disclosure of cryptographic information at the cost naturally of being somewhat slower. This specific memory is called *transient*. There are three forms of long-term memory, each of which fulfills specific needed functions. There is ROM (Read-Only Memory), a form of memory which cannot be changed once it has been written. This is particularly important in terms of security because it guarantees that the information that has been written at the factory will not be modified. Operations that are critical to the general well being of the secure core will often be found in such memory. In this situation, trust is related to the preservation of original information.

A different kind of memory is modifiable, and is used to store the data of the owner of the personal electronic device, together with other sensitive data; for example, of the institutions important to the personal electronic device, perhaps a bank or a cellular phone operator, and other data that may be needed to perform operations of interest. Whether it's called EEPROM (Electrically Erasable Programmable Read-Only Memory) or Flash this form of memory has long-term retention. Ten years is considered a good, average duration. While such long-term memories are good at keeping data for a long time, they are not particularly good at being too frequently changed. After a time, they wear out. That is why secure cores are very careful at selecting where they write data. They keep track of how often a particular section of memory has been written and they change the place of storage accordingly if needed. Long-term memory is typically both scrambled and encrypted since this is where the most important information of the personal electronic device resides. The central element of trust in the personal electronic device is there, at the core of the core, where our most private data resides. In a way, we can say that other elements of trust are related to entering and reading data from that central vault. To make a comparison with how a bank functions, consider that there is the central vault that contains our cherished goods. We want to trust that vault. Then, added to that are all the procedures surrounding taking goods out of the vault or of placing them inside the vault in the first place. In the case of the secure core, the vault derives rather little trust from its physical stature. Most of the trust emanates from the secure core being willing to die for the cause and its tenacity at regulating the access to its most sensitive contents.

Finally, we need to mention that in some situations an alternative element of trust is the assurance that even if some part of the memory is destroyed, the information contained therein may be recoverable, if it is of sufficient importance. This is achieved by using several mechanisms to check the integrity of the memory at all time and by employing enough redundancies so that information can be reconstructed from pieces that have not been altered. This, or course, flies in the face of our desire in many instances to see the data destroyed rather than ever be compromised. Even stronger measures are possible to insure that original data have not been modified. The process to achieve that is called a *digital signature*. The idea is that when the data, perhaps those of the owner of the personal electronic device, are written, a mathematical function is applied to them that summarizes them in what's called the signature. The mathematics is such that it is extremely difficult to find ways to change the data while keeping the signature intact. Consequently, if someone attempts to surreptitiously change the data they will be detected when the new data is compared with the existing signature. It will not match and the data will be flagged as fraudulent. Here, the trust that the data are intact is based on the trust in the underlying mathematics.

A rather routine way to find memory corrupted is what's called *tearing* in the trade. Tearing arises from the act of interrupting suddenly the functioning of a secure core processor. The term comes from the initial form-factor of secure cores, that of a card. When the card was inserted into the public phone, power was provided by the phone. If somebody suddenly removed the card, i.e. tear it out of the phone, then the current would be interrupted and with the interruption the operation of the card would cease. Whatever was in persistent memory at this point would stay there and the card would possibly be in an unstable state. This unstable state might actually stop it from functioning, or worse from a security point of view, it might let the secure core divulge confidential data when powered-up again. Today, secure cores have sophisticated anti-tearing mechanisms built in, based around the concept of a *transaction*, a concept that we've discussed at some length with respect to interactions in general. Using this concept, data are only written in long-term memory when the processor is sure that even if tearing occurs the memory will be in a stable state. Here again, trust derives from the integrity of the data of the personal electronic device. Trust is conveyed via confidence that the programmer who has defined the functions of the card has designed the programs with the precautions required for tearing protection. Actually, this requires specialized programmers, dedicated to the production of secure cores. There are few such programmers in the world and the authors have had the privilege to meet and work with many of the top specialists.

In order to offer protection against dynamic operational processes, secure cores often use *internal* and *external sensors*. Internal sensors include detectors that warn against a surge in current, whether it is accidental or intentional. Light sensors can detect the light-attacks that we have previously described. While such internal sensors provide a degree of trust, since by their presence they can protect against attacks it is worth mentioning that any protection can become a threat in itself. Specifically, the sensor can be used for promulgating an attack. In fact, this has happened with surge detectors, which then had to be themselves protected. It is not unlike hiring a body guard. The body guard provides security, but at the same time we find ourselves accompanied by an armed person that may turn against us. Any new mechanism can provide at the same time a new source of trust and a new source of distrust.

Some sensors are integrated within the circuitry they protect; other internal sensors are more remote from the processor of the secure core. Whatever the length of the link between the processor and the sensor, the link itself is an element to be protected, as well as the sensor itself. Since internal sensors are within the physical protection enclosure of the secure core, some measures of protection apply to them as to any other component of the core. An example of an internal sensor performing an external function would be an on/off toggle that would be present at the surface of the secure core and used for simple interactions, such as that of authorizing a purchase, or even more simply, to turn the secure core on and off. Another example is a microphone. If it is tightly integrated with the secure core then the physical integrity of the transducer can be protected in part by means similar to the rest of the secure core. We say "in part" because with each sensor comes new threats; for example, audio attacks on a microphone.

Internal sensors provide the most secure way to provide sensory capabilities to a secure core. A strong element of trust can be associated with the sensor's integrity. However, we must note again that the integrity of the sensor provides no guarantee as to the validity of the signal it receives. If the wrong person pushes the yes/no button or if an impostor speaks to the microphone, there may be no way for the sensor itself to know this. Trust goes only as far as the physics of the sensor itself. In order to assert further trust, additional processing must be added; for example, voice recognition for the microphone. In addition, it is possible to use multiple sensors and compute correlations. While this will never provide a total guarantee, it will increase the level of trust. Typically, however, this requires the use of external sensors.

External sensors are not part of the protection enclosure of the secure core. Moreover, they can be near to it or far away. A fingerprint scanner on the same substrate as the secure core is local. A remote camera reached through the connection of the card to the overall network can be located in any part of the world; hence, it is remote. As we are now familiar with, two security weak points are thus created: the sensor itself and its link to the processor. As with any link that is open to physical intrusion, an important defense is cryptography. This means that the sensor itself needs to be capable of cryptographic operations, a characteristic that we've found closely associated with secure cores. In other words, the sensor must itself contain a secure core if trust needs to be independently established in the integrity of the sensor. Therefore, we are back to the situation of creating an internal sensor embedded within a secure core. Unfortunately, this is an expensive proposition and it is typically not done with high-volume secure cores. Today, most external sensors sold in high volume don't have their own specialized secure core; many don't even have cryptographic means. Information is captured by the sensor and sent as such to the secure core. If we consider for example a fingerprint scanner, it is possible for an interloper to read the data flowing from the scanner to the secure core. It is also possible to modify the scanner itself to alter its properties. That's why the trust in any external sensor must be limited and precautions taken to increase that trust, again by specialized processing and by multiplying the sensori experience. If the fingerprint matches the voice signature then the likelihood is higher that the right person is there. In fact, that's how the most secure government operations in the world work: they multiply the sensors. Unfortunately, they can never be sure whether or not someone is pointing a gun at the person being finger printed? We see that we can multiply *ad infinitum* the ways to defeat the system. That is why there are so many thrillers being written. Trust in the causality of operation of physical systems seems never quite complete.

*Actuators* are the reverse of sensors. They are used by the secure core to perform actions on its environment. Displays, loudspeakers and even perfume distributors are all actuators. Much as with sensors, they can be internal or external. Moreover, they are subject to the same attacks; just in reverse. However, the trust equation is different since the owner of the personal device, or whoever is benefiting from the actuator output, is the ultimate judge of trust due to being the end recipient of the information. From the trusted core perspective, all that is needed is trust in the integrity of the actuator and its link to the core. As we have seen, more trust is put in internal systems. High-volume external systems typically don't have security mechanisms built-in. Therefore, the trust placed by the secure core in the actuators must be limited. In so far as trusting that the recipient is the intended one, there is nothing the secure core can do short of using sensors to complement the actuators. From the recipient's perspective, trust in the system may be higher than the trust the secure core has for itself. This condition arises because, while the recipient's trust in the actuators can be similar to that of the trusted core, the recipient carries in addition its own trust; trust that the trusted core doesn't have access to. So we see that with actuators, trust between a secure component (the trusted core) and an unsecured component (the combination of sensor/actuator and the owner of the personal electronic device) are not symmetrical. The trust of the secure core is limited to its physical extent.

The sensors and actuators we've seen are mostly used for communication between a secure core and a human. However, sensors and actuators can also be used to interact with the environment; for example, a temperature sensor or a light emitting diode for signaling. Significantly different however, are communication channels. These provide means of transmitting information destined to other computers that may or may not have secure cores themselves. If the other computer does not have a secure core, the security situation is similar to that of sensors and actuators that are unprotected. Trust is necessarily limited and is in fact a function of the likelihood of attacks on the other computer, knowing that those attacks are not mitigated with the same level of security as that provided by a secure core. If the other computer has a secure core, communications can be established between the two secure cores. Since both have powerful cryptographic capabilities, it is possible to render the channel between them extremely secure, even if it is physically unprotected. An exception of course, is defense against attacks that render the channel inoperable by interrupting it, or perhaps by flooding it with bogus information effecting what are called *Denial of Service* (DoS) attacks. With that proviso, the trust in the physical system constituted by the two communicating secure core is essentially predicated on the secure core technology itself.

Communication channels are of two kinds, *contact* and *contactless*. In general, contact secure cores are found today in the billions in the form of *smart cards*. Contactless secure cores, found today in the hundred of millions, are called *RFID* (for Radio-Frequency Identification) tokens. There also exists an intermediate form, called a *contactless smart card*, which marries the security features of smart cards with some of the capabilities of RFID tokens. Smart cards have a physical link with their environment thru electrical contacts whose number, positioning and functions are strictly specified by international standards. Historically, smart cards started their life as security devices and they have always assumed that function. This suggests that they have evolved considerably in response to changing threats and subsequent development of counter-responses. Smart cards are the most ubiquitous computers and are among the more sophisticated security products available. However, we must mention that another security product is likely to also number in the hundreds of millions soon; the *Trusted Platform Module* (TPM). This is a processor that is meant to be attached to a larger computer, perhaps a laptop, in order to effect security for that machine. In other words, the trusted platform module is to the general computer what the trusted core of the personal electronic device is to the owner of that device. Information in the trusted platform module relates to the computer's important information, whereas information in the trusted core of the personal electronic device relates to the owner's important information. If we have not made things too confusing, you may have guessed that the personal electronic device, being a computer, may have its own trusted platform module to store the device's important information, such as cryptographic keys used to guarantee that communication with the device is indeed coming from it. Considering a personal electronic device with both a trusted platform module and a smart card, we see that we have two sources of trust; one in the integrity of the device's identity and one in the integrity of the owner's identity.

To promulgate an attack against wired communications, an intervention in place is required. This is typically much more difficult than with wireless communications, where radio equipment can be set up at a distance. Consequently, attacking an RFID token is easier than attacking a smart card with contacts. The signal of the token can be intercepted by any device in the vicinity, the distance being dependent on the type. Moreover, as it happens, the RFID token has a very different filiation than smart cards in terms of security.

Originally, an RFID token was not a security product. The primary intent of the token was to transmit set information within applications that were not thought of as security applications; for example, the tracking of goods in a supermarket or of parts in a factory. Now-familiar applications such as the radio tag used to pass the toll booth on the highway or the employee tags used to open doors of facilities came later. These latter applications are obviously related to security. Even so, the security is largely limited to the novelty of the device when it is first introduced. It takes some time for hackers to become familiar with new technology. Even today, there is very little security in the highway RFID tag and many employee RFID tags. The tracking of goods and parts may not have been considered as security applications initially. However, it turns out that they are related to privacy, and privacy is in turn related to security because security is required to protect privacy. The recent eruption in the market of RFID tokens in hundreds of million of units has created something of a social backlash related to privacy. A typical book on the subject is *The Spychips Threat: Why Christians should Resist RFID and Electronic Surveillance*, by Katherine Albrecht and Liz McIntyre. The objection to RFID tokens comes from privacy advocates who see RFID token tracking accompanied by vast databases as a means to spy on goods. Since goods (content) can be related to people, this can eventually lead to spying on people. As a result, RFID tokens will likely be forced to evolve in the direction of enhanced security, which means coupling the radio part of the RFID token with a secure core. This is the most likely way to restore trust in the RFID token itself. Of course, as with any secure core, the security and privacy of a new secure core RFID token can only be extended to the general environment if their trusted cores talk to other trusted cores following rules conducive to trust in a global process accepted by all parties. Today, there are few databases protected by secure cores, so the issues of RFID token privacy and security will be with us for some time to come. We will come back to that discussion in Chapter 9.

Let us come back to the quintessential secure core, the contact smart card. As we've discussed already, smart cards have followed an evolution towards using radio waves for communication that has brought them closer to RFID. This happened when smart cards were coupled with antennas for secure applications requiring both high levels of privacy and radio communication; for example, in electronic passports. In such passports, the secure core is a contactless smart card, not an RFID token. However, the world of marketing being what it is, RFID advocates have claimed passports chips as their own in order to boost the security image of RFID. This is perhaps good marketing intent, but it appears that the effect has been to lower the perception of the security of contactless smart cards rather than boost the perception of RFID. In any case, as with all communication channels, it creates noise that certainly makes our book harder to follow. In an effort to be clearer, whether we're talking about contactless smart cards or RFID tokens, the radio communication components are essentially the same, assuming that we disregard issues of standards that would be too unwieldy to present here. Transmissions are easy to intercept, and in the current state of the technology, it is easy to flood the air with radio waves and make the devices inoperable, whether they are secure cores or not. This is what we described earlier as denial of service attacks. Notwithstanding those attacks, contactless smart cards have on board security processors and they can encrypt information on the radio channel, such that interception of the communication with radio equipment does not necessarily constitute a security breach.

We should mention here that most current contactless smart cards are powered though the air by the reception device. Energy is actually transmitted from the reception device to the contactless smart card via electrical induction, which means that a current is created inside the secure core by a magnetic field produced by for example, the electronic passport reading equipment. This significantly limits the amount of power that the card can use for cryptography. Additionally, one reason why contactless cards are used instead of contact cards is often to allow more convenient physical protocols to be used. Specifically, the act of inserting the contact card into a reader receptacle is avoided. This does have the added impact of making the length of time that the card is in contact with the reader an artifact of the actions of the cardholder. The card might be pressed against the reader, or it might be waved past the reader. Consequently, contactless card not only have less power to bring to the task of cryptography, they may also need to process faster. This has led to continued research into more efficient cryptographic algorithms. Without delving into the mathematics, we'll simply mention that this can entail the use of elliptic curves, a branch of number theory, to protect the communication channel. As we have suggested, a relatively high level of trust can be derived from contactless cores; however, this requires advanced circuitry that can be quite expensive. This is perhaps acceptable for a passport, but not for a tag affixed to a banana. Therefore, we see again here how cost impacts both trust and privacy.

# From Physiology to Sociology

Personal electronic devices are powered by batteries. To be practical, their consumption of electricity must be carefully monitored. In addition to powering themselves, personal electronic devices have to power their secure core. Therefore, the electricity budget extended to secure cores is limited and constantly challenged. This creates limits on what secure cores can do, and therefore careful choices have to be made in what needs to be trusted and what not. Banking accounts and the like are obvious candidates for the secure core of the personal electronic device. What about human interface functions; those operations that enable the interaction of the owner of the personal electronic device with the machine? These can involve relatively heavy graphical operations and consequently require powerful computational capabilities, accompanied with fast transmission of information to the screen. These are all characteristics that are resource intensive to put on a secure core, particularly if one considers that the processing needs to be made secure. In this case, secure generally means much more complex and threat averse. Otherwise, why put it on a secure core to start with? As it happens, since the human interface component of the personal electronic device governs the exchange of information between the machine and the person, it is an ideal place for an impostor to capture information at the source, before there is a chance to encrypt it. So, we are in a situation where we can make a security argument for having human interface functions in the secure core but an efficiency argument for having it in the untrusted part of the personal electronic device. Trust arbitrages of this kind are inevitable. Prioritization is needed, and consequences of prioritization have to be recognized and known. This is very similar to what happens with the house security model we talked about earlier. We may be willing to put a lock and key on the door, but not an alarm system. In technical systems, we also prioritize trust.

Most personal electronic devices entail wireless communication. A cellular phone can reach a communication tower several kilometers distant. This is an expensive operation in terms of electrical consumption, but it is not an operation that requires the secure core. However, we see more and more applications where the cellular phone is used to effect payment. For example, as a means to pay for public transport, when getting to the turnstile the cellular phone can be placed close to a sensor on the vehicle door. An exchange then takes place between that equipment and the personal electronic device, payment is made and the door opens. This is not done with the same communications means as those used by the phone to reach the communication tower, but rather by a much weaker radio frequency channel that can reach only a few centimeters. Since we are effecting payment, this function is obviously one for the secure core. Actually, the standard configuration for this operation is to put the secure core in charge of the financial transaction itself and of the coding of the information to transmit. The antenna and its controller can be located in the personal electronic device, external to the secure core.

When the secure core is not attached to a personal electronic device, but to a passport, it is directly attached to an antenna embedded with the secure chip inside the cover of the passport. In this case, as we have previously noted, the secure core is powered by electro-magnetic induction. Similar to the case of using a cellular phone for payment of transport, the passport's communication capabilities are very short-range; also a few centimeters. While dictated by the small amount of energy available, the limited distance is a factor of trust; the same that make us speak softer when we confide a secret to someone.

As we've seen, secure cores need to be protected in order to limit as much as possible access to their electronics. Therefore, secure core have two pieces: the body and the chip. The substrate of the body is typically a plastic frame with some generic printing. A receptacle is carved in the plastic to receive the chip and its contacts. Inside the plastic, it is also possible to have an antenna for contactless communications directly from the secure core. The size of the antenna can vary depending on the type of transmission used. As we have noted, the chip can be treated in various manners for protection against intrusion. Finally, once the chip completes the basic set up then various markings can be added to the card body to *personalize* the card. Each assembly of plastic plus chip is made unique by marking the plastic in ways that can be very difficult to alter; for example by a combination of embossing, indenting, laser and thermal marking, holograms and other means to identify the secure core with its owner and institutions vouching for the owner. An obvious example of such is the issuer logo and hologram on a credit card. This effectively says, "Trust that I, the bank, will pay you, the merchant, if the owner, whose name is also on the card, will sign in front of you." In parallel, the same operation of personalization is done with the chip. Inside the chip are digital certificates for the banking institution vouching for payment, along with coded information giving the references of the owner. So, we see that the source of trust is two-fold: it comes from the physical markings on the secure core body and from the corresponding digital marking on the secure core chip. Henceforth, the trust in the physical and digital domains follows a similar path. There is no better way to illustrate that human and computer networks use the same mechanisms. We are not seeing anthropomorphism at work here. We are seeing an actual identity exchange between human and computer trust foundations, which is in retrospect not surprising, since the computer is acting on the behalf of the human.

As with inter-human comparisons, a most important difference between run-of-the-mill computers and secure cores is their upbringing. Secure cores must be both inexpensive and secure. Additionally, they need to be personalized. This puts important constraints on their manufacturing and distribution. To give an idea of how important this is to the trust imbued to the secure core, consider that it is common for large purchasers of secure cores to request a tour of manufacturing facilities, and having them certified by third parties before issuing an order. If we realize that trusted cores, during the personalization phase, can be loaded with money, as is the case with prepaid tokens, then no wonder the manufacturing plants look like fortresses. They typically have no windows, and they have armored doors, secure enclosures within secure enclosures and the like. As one can see, it is not quite the usual computer plant.

Speed of production and yield are obvious success factors, as well as flexibility in procurement, i.e. multi-sourcing, and the capability to affect the same supplies to various purposes. For example, the move to flash memory in trusted cores is in part due to the fact that contrary to the read-only memory it replaces, flash can be changed during the manufacturing cycle to adapt to new demands. Of course, this raises the security concern of whether it can be made as immutable as ROM. To give an idea of how those various elements of manufacturing affect trust, let us consider the requirement for speed of production.

As we've discussed, in today's model of secure core systems, a necessary step is mass personalization. This means that each trusted core has to be filled with confidential information specific to the application and to the future owner. For example, for payment systems the trusted core must receive confidential information regarding the digital authentication of the payment organization. One way to do accomplish this is first to create a complete trusted core, then use the trusted core mechanisms to enter data piece by piece. The benefit to this approach is that it is reusing security mechanisms already in place. However, in a mass production mode it takes too much time to be economical. A way to do it fast is to write all the data at once into the trusted core. However, to retain trust this requires defining additional security mechanisms, which also have to be audited, certified and tested, just like other trusted core mechanisms. As we can see, the speed requirement affects directly the trust mechanism, i.e. it makes trust assertions much more expensive, even if at the end the total cost of production is lower. Finally, we should mention briefly the issue of distribution.

When the trusted core leaves the manufacturing plant, it is very important to protect it until it reaches the final distribution center. In actuality, the distribution looks less like a regular computer shipping operation than a bank transfer operation. This is because at this point, the trusted core may contain critical information related to further personalization, and must reach its destination intact. Hence, trust has to derive from the transport mechanism and associated processes.

# Modeling Trust

Trust is recursive. Trust applies to trust and trust derives from trust. In fact, any mechanism put in place to warrant trust is itself subject to trust. So trust is never complete. A good illustration is trust prioritization. We have seen that trust comes at a cost, and that we can't trust everything less we be paralyzed. In some cases, cost simply overrides any trust concern. So, if we need to establish trust in an implement, we'd better know why this implement is important. Since trust is recursive, prioritization itself needs to be trusted, as do the mechanism of trust prioritization, and so on. However, there needs to be an end to the process, otherwise no action could occur. As an aside, we might note that within human cognition, this is the place were emotion enters the trust equation. Within computer systems there must be an ultimate point of trust. In the abstract, this situation is barely distinguishable from randomness, assuming that we trust that randomness exists. This is, of course, something of a debatable proposition in itself, particularly in information and quantum theory circles, as detailed in *Science and Ultimate Reality: Quantum Theory,*

*Cosmology and Complexity*, edited by John Barrow, Paul Davies and Charles Harper Jr. A telling illustration is our discussion of cosmic rays and their influence on physical implements.

Trust in a given physical implement can be modulated without the physical implement changing. Trust can be reinforced by both multiplying its sources, and by solidifying its foundation via cross-references. For example, when elements of trust are built on mathematics, the same mathematics used for a physical implement can be reused for another, and convergent results consolidate the overall trust mechanism involved. Trust can also be diminished if the channel of trust conveyance is either damaged, or if the message it conveys is garbled. Time can lower trust as it gives more opportunities for elements of trust to erode. Sometimes that very mechanism can be reversed, with time bringing new elements of trust. As we see, in all these cases the original physical implement is constant and therefore not itself the source of change. Its illumination varies, and its trust level changes accordingly.

Conversely, the conveyance of trust might be impeccable, while the physical implement does not itself warrant trust. If the information is bad to start with, a good conduit won't make it better or worse. Trust in the physical implement is typically limited to its boundary and possibly that of its extensions. It also extends to its fabrication, its distribution and its usage. Together with the physical implement itself, this forms a *gestalt* that diverges from the rest of the environment. However, the environment also affects trust in the implement, temperature being a case in point. While trust can be decomposed into pieces, in a very deep sense it always involves all parts of the universe at its limit, for the very reason that it is, as we mentioned, recursive.

We find the technical foundation of trust in processes, such as Common Criteria; in logic and mathematics, for information management; in craft, by guarding against certain intrusion; in principles, such as that of establishing that only communication between secure cores can create higher levels of trust; and in conservation: if a situation doesn't change, its evaluation may be facilitated. Moreover, we have seen that layers of technical evaluation can create additional trust, as they essentially bring to bear higher concepts to the sensori-motor experience. To the extent that these higher concepts are themselves trusted, they can convey trust in otherwise suspect sensori-motor representations.

Trust can apply to physical goods and it can apply to processes. As far as human artifacts are concerned, processes take an additional weight because trust in the physical goods derives from the trust in the process of their assembly. Because these processes have their origin in humans, it is all about humans, the origin of the implements. Trust in physical implements ends up being based largely on trust in humans. For natural goods, trust would seem to be based on human-independent foundations. However, this would be ignoring that our interface with natural goods is entirely constructed on our sensori-motor experience, itself subject to various levels of trust. So we still end up basing our trust on human considerations. Today, computers have very little of a trust mechanism built in, so it's not possible to do an immediate comparison between their establishing trust and humans establishing trust. Certainly, the difference in the sensori-motor experiences is bound to make a difference, and we'll investigate that more later.

Now that we have the means of a more structured approach to the understanding of the secure core place in the trust infrastructure, or at least in constitutive components of the trust infrastructure, we are ready to look at the trusted core from an evolutionary perspective.

# Trust in the Real World

Money is built on trust. If I don't believe that I can get some new goods in exchange for the piece of paper that you give me in exchange for my services, then I will probably choose not to work for you. While societies have made some peace with such paper, thanks in a large part to governments attempting to establish trust in currency with all the force of law, its limitations led to new forms of commerce. The new forms faced new trust issues as well, in many cases because they were born of private initiatives. In Chapter 6, we reprised the anecdote of The First Supper. The credit card associations have subsequently provided a variant of currency that drives commerce in general, and commerce on the Web specifically. It is interesting to note that the most recent television commercials for credit cards actually disparage the use of actual cash because it makes a transaction too slow. But, such was not always the case.

In the early days, while local credit card use could keep trust in the new form of money under control, it was immediately clear to both clients and merchants that fraud could very easily affect them. A thief duplicating a card and using it to make a purchase would result in a situation where the merchant would eventually ask the wrong person for payment. Depending on settlement modalities, this situation would directly affect the client, the merchant or both. Clearly, the banks issuing the cards needed to solve the problem, which they did by offering various guarantees of compensation to both clients and merchants in cases of fraud. That moved the liability for fraudulent transactions into the banking camp, which was then confronted with mounting fraud. This rather naturally followed from the precept that unanswered fraud leads to more of the same. That's where the United States and Europe took two different paths, for reasons that were totally unrelated to the payment universe, as they had to do with the billing for telephone networks.

In the United States, the fees for telephone service were paid on a monthly basis, independent of usage as long as calls remained local. In France, which would take the lead in the management of fraud with the new form of money, local calls were metered and therefore telephone fees were based on usage, just as long distance calls are in the United States. This had the effect of discouraging merchants to make a call to verify the validity of the credit cards they were presented with. This in turn created opportunities for fraud. Conversely, in the United States, if the banks could offer merchants a local number to call for verification, they would have means to double-check the validity of a card prior to a transaction. Detecting and countering fraud in this manner became something of an art form for banks that were particularly good at it.

As the volume of payments by credit card increased, manual verification of transactions became impossible and therefore computers were brought to the party. The first thing that a computer can do very effectively is to check the card data against a *revocation list* that contains information about cards stolen or otherwise invalid. That's why we are asked to report a lost credit card rapidly; the card issuer can enter that information in the database, and subsequent checks will return a warning. In the United States, virtually as soon as new information is obtained on invalid cards, it is available for double-checking thanks to the immediacy provided by the free local call. In France, in order to save money, merchants would typically wait until a certain number of transactions were completed before sending the bundle for processing via the phone line. Obviously, this left some opportunity for additional fraud, since merchants would not get immediate information on the validity of the card. To mitigate this threat, card issuers began to send out periodic revocation lists to the merchant. However, the manual processing of verification was still too cumbersome and new means of fighting fraud were sorely needed.

The next initiative that banks would take in the United States would be to design special computer programs, called *expert systems*, which would double-check credit cards in a much more sophisticated way. Using information on the cardholders as well as by recording systematically the credit card usage, those programs could detect patterns in the shopping habits of individuals. For example, if somebody had never traveled abroad, a charge showing up from a foreign hotel might be suspicious. In the same manner, if someone only spent small amounts, a sudden big-ticket expense would raise a flag. This system turned out to lower the fraud to an acceptable rate; that is, a rate that led to an amount of global loss inferior to the cost of a potential new system that would lower that loss perhaps even further. So, the United States did not, and still has not moved beyond the magnetic stripe based credit card and card issuers have only improved their fraud detection mechanisms incrementally. For example, rather recently calling centers have been created for human operators to call the client in case the expert system flags an anomaly. This allows the tightening of the rules of expert systems, since now the human call can compensate in case the expert system is too strict, flagging as fraudulent actual expenses by the client that are perfectly legitimate. For example, the person who has never traveled may decide to start going abroad. After all, we all have to start some day.

In France, the story played very differently. Since the French were using cards with a secure core to pay for public phone usage, it was natural for them to consider that secure cores might also be used to mitigate credit card fraud at the merchant's store. Actually, both United States and French credit cards were first equipped with magnetic stripes to fight fraud. The magnetic stripe contains the card number and other information, and a swipe of the card in special equipment allows the fast and accurate reading of that number for further processing. In time of course, hackers figured out how to duplicate a magnetic stripe, and the measure's efficacy faltered. However, there was an idea in this process that could be used for migrating to a secure core to fight fraud. If the secure core itself contains not only the card number and associated information, but also secret information that can be seen nowhere on the body of the card, and if the point of sale terminal is able to read all these data confidentially, then a big step is taken toward eliminating fraud. If on top of that, the card is only allowed to disclose its data when the client enters a personal identification number only known to her or him, thus authenticating the transaction as starting from the owner of the card, then fraud should go down considerably. In fact it did; going from being measured in digits towards being measured in fractions. Fraud was essentially eliminated for credit cards equipped with a chip. To avoid fraud from the merchant, the point of sales terminals were also equipped with cards, so that the client trusted core talked to the merchant trusted core. In turn, that trusted core could talk to the bank's trusted core, or rather to an intermediary institution that would in turn talk to the bank.

What we've seen is a detailed illustration of the concept that we saw earlier of the erosion of trust. As the security mechanisms underlying trust are understood and emulated, new fraud mechanisms come in to play to lower that level of trust until it is restored via new mechanisms. This interplay between trust and fraud illustrates how trust is put into question. We saw that the French squelched fraud with the bank chip card; wasn't that the end of the story? Actually, it wasn't. Two things happened. The first is the Web; the second is a new need.

One aspect of credit card transactions over the Web is that the client and the merchant are not in each other's direct, physical presence. While the act of signing the invoice at the actual point of sale has legal value as well as psychological value, there is no *de visu* verification when signing occurs at a distance. Therefore, a new level of fraud could be expected on the Web, and in fact it happened exactly as expected. As fraud increased, the first action was to again assign liability. The first reaction of the banks was to assign liability to the merchant. The argument was that as the merchant had accepted payment without witnessing a signature, the bank could deny responsibility. While this created a reasonable legal argument, in fact merchants are clients of the banks. For the supplier or a service to shift liability to the client can only go so far in commerce. Something had to happen. A way was needed to authenticate on the Web in such a manner that the authentication was *non-repudiable*; for example, when we manually sign, we cannot reasonable refute from having done so. We need an equivalent mechanism in the digital world. Actually, this mechanism exists, it is called a *digital signature*, and it is recognized as a legal signature by several governments.

We have previously discussed various aspects of cryptography used to enable a digital signature. So, we'll only provide a cursory overview here. The basic concept behind a digital signature is for a computer to provide the proof that it knows a privileged piece of information. The digital signature itself is a string of numbers that can only be created by a computer containing a special key. As the digital signature is sent from one computer to another one, the second computer can determine that the signature of the first computer is correct, provided it trusts that only the first computer has the key. Well, as one might be able to guess by now, this means that the first computer must have a secure core. So again, we find ourselves needing a secure core to establish trust in a transaction. For that reason, several schemes have been proposed that involve secure cores for Web commerce. At this point, none has been successful on a large scale, primarily because the fraud level has not been high enough yet for banks to consider investing in this particular counter-measure. However, some intermediate steps have been taken, in particular with a derivative of secure core technology called the One-Time Password (OTP). In this scheme, the secure core generates the one time password in synchrony with the institution to be reached, limiting the possibility of tampering with it.

The second pressure for change on bank cards came from the need for efficiency; transactions that were faster and with less overhead costs involved. While it seems that presenting a credit card or a chip card at the supermarket leads to a quite efficient response, the process did not satisfy merchants. To enhance productivity, they are always in search of faster and less expensive payment mechanisms. In fact, there have been instances of merchants refusing to accept credit cards because of either or both characteristics. Among the sticking points have been fast food restaurants, where food is not the only thing that must be fast nor the only thing that must be inexpensive; the payment mechanism must be fast and cheap too. If it were possible to wave a credit card at the payment terminal resulting in a transaction that was actually faster than cash, then the restaurants would be on the road to a winning proposition. If the transaction fee charged to the merchant were not too much and it was reinforced by the security afforded from not having to store lots of bills and coins then the result would be a definite winner. What is needed is a radio wave card, in short an RFID (Radio-Frequency Identification) token, or its sibling, a contactless smart card, a radio-enabled version if the traditional smart card. Actually, contactless smart cards have been selected for this function and are currently being tested around the world. Since they represent yet another new form of payment with a chip card, they introduce new opportunities for fraud. Consider the hacker who could for example hide point of sale equipment on their body, come close to a client with a contactless card in their wallet, and debit the card, unbeknownst to the client. Of course, there are subsequent counter-measures to ameliorate this threat.

We see that the forces of change affecting trust can be negative, as in fraud, or positive, as in the answer to new needs. The search for trust is unending, and trust itself is, at any moment, the product of a long chain of causes and responses.

Another property of trust is leverage. Trust produces trust. One place where it can be seen very clearly is in the evolution of the trusted core of cellular phones. As we indicated earlier, the original idea was to tightly associate the phone with its owner in order to insure proper billing by the phone operator. The Subscriber Identity Module contained information that would allow the phone owner to be properly authenticated, with the SIM acting as a proxy. First, the owner provides a Personal Identification Number (PIN) to the SIM, and then the SIM authenticates with the operator of the digital network. By providing the proper information to the phone operator via radio waves, the cellular phone gets authorization to enter into communication with other phones, since the operator trusts that the person talking is also the person paying the bills.

Many phone operators started as regional companies that would cover a territory with enough antennas to allow their phone subscribers to communicate locally. As cellular phones became more common, people started to need to connect their phones through several operators, depending on the region they were calling from. This led to cross-agreements between operators, who agreed to service each other's customers as long as those customers could prove that they were backed up by the operator they signed up with. Naturally, the roaming operator wanted such proof so that they could be paid by the original operator for their help in making the phone connection work. But what would this proof be? As it turns out, the answer was immediate. Since the phone owner could authenticate with the roaming operator in the same way as with the original operator, it was just a matter for the roaming operator to present the credentials of the caller to the original operator to prove the veracity of the transaction. This way, the trust between one company and a person extended to a trust between several companies and that person, without the need of extra mechanisms.

But, the extension of trust didn't stop here. Since the owner was authenticated securely (or shall we say, securely enough, because Subscriber Identity Module authentication would in time become threatened, and required revisions, following the pattern of attacks and counter-measures that we illustrated earlier in this chapter), could that trust relationship be extended to other potential needs of the owner or the operator? In fact it could, and we will give a couple of examples.

A nice property of Subscriber Identity Modules is that they are removable. We can take our SIM out of our current cellular phone, buy another phone, put the module back in it, and immediately the new phone becomes our phone. From the phone operator perspective, it's just as good as the old one. Since the SIM would allow one to move from one personal electronic device to another, wouldn't it be nice if it also contained other important personal information which would then be kept current wherever the cellular phone was used? An obvious example of such personal information is the private phone book of the owner. This is the list of often called numbers, or less often called but important numbers. When we change cellular phone, we don't want to reenter all those numbers by hand. Keeping them on the SIM makes them immediately transferable from one phone to the next. However, something else may happen. We may lose our cellular phone with its SIM, or we may lose our SIM alone. In both cases, we find ourselves losing not only our capability to call, but also our cherished phone book. To mollify this situation, phone operators introduced back up services. The phone book would be regularly backed up on the phone operator's computers, and restored whenever the user needed it. This way, it is possible to buy another SIM and to restore the phone book on it. Again, the phone owner has the phone book at hand wherever in the world it is needed. However, it is obvious that the phone operator wouldn't let anybody restore a phone book without getting the proper credentials. So, here we go again. The same mechanism that was used to identify callers could be used to validate the request for a phone book restoration. Again, trust in one function was used to provide a new function.

Satisfying the phone owner with the trust in her or his ability to keep the phone book active, even in bad circumstances, was a good selling argument for operators. But other functions would also be of interest, this time to operators themselves. One issue that operators have to contend with is the multiplicity of personal electronic devices used by their subscribers. While Subscriber Identity Modules are governed by strict standards, personal electronic devices can be extremely varied. There are simple phones, smart phones, personal assistant with calling capabilities and the list keeps growing. There is no way for operators to inquire all of those multiple devices about their nature and capabilities. However, such information can be very useful. It allows operators not only to know their customers better, but also in some cases to exchange information with the personal electronic devices once they know their type. So, operators went to their central standard organization, the European Telecommunications Standards Institute, and established information standards that any personal electronic device wishing to use cellular communications should communicate to the Subscriber Identity Module. This way, the phone operators could simply ask the SIM about the type of personal electronic device used. Once again, the trust they have in the SIM extends to trusting further information than was originally thought about. Incidentally, this example illustrates again the fact that the trust in a secure core is bounded, since there is no way for the Subscriber Identity Module to know if the information that the personal electronic device communicated is indeed correct. Fortunately, the phone operator is able to put some trust in that information if it is used to communicate with the personal electronic device; either it can answer or not.

These two examples are only two of many applications that can extend the trust put in the Subscriber Identity Module even further. In many countries, cellular phones can be used for gaming, the lottery, betting and many other activities involving fiduciary value. The operator trusts the SIM enough to vouch to the racetrack that the bet will be paid. Causality is a vector of trust extension. And, as trust networks grow, they build their own dynamics so that going outside of the network becomes difficult. For example, we gave the example of the phone book. The trust between the operator and the client provides good service to the owner of the phone. However, it also makes it more painful for the phone owner to switch operators. This is a vivid example of how trust cements networks.

Unfortunately, causality also applies to a flawed assertion of trust. Let us consider a personal electronic device that does not have a trusted core, but might still attempt to provide a digital signature to obtain goods on the Web. To spare the reader flipping back a few pages, we'll repeat here how a digital signature works. Essentially, if follows the vault model. If only you and I have the key of the vault, any information I put in it, you trust comes from me, since no one else could have deposited it. In the same way, if only my personal electronic device has a key to encrypt my signature, you know that it indeed comes from me. Unfortunately, if my device doesn't have a secure core, there is no way to strongly trust such an assertion. The way a personal electronic device encodes a digital signature is by loading the key in its memory together with signature information, and by mixing them up mathematically using a cryptographic algorithm. The critical attack point in this process is the period during which the processor of the personal electronic device accesses the key. The reason for this is that there are ways to get to the value of the key in a computer without a trusted core. For example, the memory is typically accessible to more computing entities than the processor. In order to be able to move data between the short-term memory used by the processor and the long-term memory of the device, there is typically a mechanism that allows doing that without needing to ask the processor. This allows increased efficiency of the overall system, but it presents a threat to the signature operation. Another way to access the key information is to trick the processor into revealing data it is currently handling.

This is done by inserting into the normal instructions the processor should be receiving, bogus instructions that lead to the processor erroneously spewing out information it should not.

Why doesn't that all happen with a trusted core? Actually, it could, and that's why there are several layers of defense inside a secure core. They are all based on establishing trust in both the processes of building the secure core and in its physical integrity. The programs that are loaded in a secure core at the factory have been validated and verified using standards of security. When there is a need to load a program that has not been so validated and verified, it is not allowed to directly instruct the processor. It can only talk to an intermediate interpreter that checks that each instruction is acceptable, and not one that threatens the integrity of processing. Since the trusted core is physically protected, once all this apparatus in on board, there is no easy way to physically affect it. By controlling with equal strength the sensori-motor elements of the secure core, the critical keys are protected and the digital signature can be trusted as being unique to the personal electronic device containing the trusted core.

Now comes the deception. If my personal electronic device does not have a secure core, and consequently its secret key is stolen by another computer as we have seen is possible, then this other computer can masquerade as my device, which as we also know is supposed to represent me on the network. When the digital signature of my personal electronic device is copied, it is, in the very legal sense, my signature which is compromised. When the offending computer now starts to use my digital signature to purchase goods or to sign tax documents, or to perform any other electronic transaction of importance, the level of trust assigned by the institution receiving the information is very high if that institution believes that the key used for the signature was protected. Trust extends by causality; it conveys deception as well as it conveys honest credentials. What went wrong? As we suggested earlier, trust applies recursively in the full causality chain. This means it applies also to causality itself. The receiving computer should question if causality is warranted, which means it should question whether the original trust is warranted.

Subsequently, the proper way for an institution to accept a digital signature is to first get assurance that it comes from a trusted core. This is done by first checking the digital signature of the trusted core itself. Or course, to enable this, there must be a trusted core in my personal electronic device. As you may be wondering how we'd know that the digital signature of a trusted core is not itself compromised, we need to explain that part of the intricate security procedures of the trusted core is the way to load an identification key. The proper way to do it is to let the secure core itself generate its own keys, so that they never appear anywhere outside of the secure core. The way it is done is a little bit too involved for this discussion, but we can observe that it has to do with the mathematics of large prime number generation. Now, while trust can be imbued to secure cores, it can not be imbued to a personal electronic device without a secure core. So trusting a non protected personal electronic device without checking that it has a secure core is more threatening than would initially be considered. Once trust is assigned to the wrong device, it can extend in many directions, thus propagating the deception to great length. If we trust the priest, then the priest can abuse that trust. So we have to be sure that we select our priests carefully. It's the same for personal electronic devices.

As we have said, trust is recursive. Trust applies to trust, and therefore we would expect deception to apply to deception. For example, let us consider a personal electronic device with a secure core, regularly doing transactions on the Web using its digital signature facility. We can consider someone who, observing so many successful transactions might make the natural assumption that commercial and other entities trust the personal electronic device because it has a secure core.

This seemingly innocuous observation turns out to be the source of a *reversal* of trust. For example, if I manage to make my personal electronic device interact seemingly successfully with trusted institutions while an observer takes notes, I may convince the observer that my personal electronic device can be trusted. I might then be able to engage the observer into a fraudulent transaction. Well, "That's way too complicated for a computer, isn't it?" Actually, it is not, and we have today a spectacular example of such a reversal of trust with the Google search engine. The way Google ranks its pages is such that its users can trust that the most important pages are going to be presented, which means pages bearing less risk of being disingenuous. For example, when asking about a bank, it would be very disconcerting if the first page presented by Google were a fake bank page, such as we see quite often referenced in spam e-mail, designed to fraudulently capture usernames and passwords and to later use those on the real bank page. Since Google constantly tunes its algorithms to avoid such catastrophe, we imbue trust in it and typically consider that its top page ranks are synonyms of quality. For those of us who download software, we similarly trust the top pages not to offer suspect software for download. We do that because we assume that the top download pages are used by multitudes, and therefore any fraud would have a good chance to be reliably and quickly detected.

Consequently, Google is a source of trust. However, by knowing that, the potential for a reversal of trust now exists. If a hacker could somehow reverse engineer the algorithm used by Google to rank pages, then they could perhaps get their pages on top of Google's ranking; albeit, perhaps for only a short time. Users would then go to these pages based on their trust in Google, but would be then at the mercy of whatever scheme the page has in store for them, like getting their banking information or downloading software with viruses. Obviously, search engine facilities such as Google put great effort into thwarting such misuse. However, it perhaps makes one wonder, what about search engines ranking their query returns based on who has paid them the most money? So, we see that not only can trust be abused, it can also be used for abuse. As the French say, "the dress a monk makes."

How does a computer protect against trust reversal? At a rather mechanical level, the typical way is to make sure that the institutions authenticate themselves in a trusted fashion when a personal electronic device interacts with them. As we have noted, there is only one safe way to do that. Institutional systems must have a trusted core that enters into an exchange of information with the trusted core of the personal electronic device, thus making sure that the two parties are mutually trustworthy before engaging in any transaction. There is no need to emphasize that we are a far cry from finding this situation prevalent, and therefore trust, extension of trust, deception and reversal of trust are here for the long term.

# The Physical Underbelly of Trust

By examining in detail the physical properties of secure cores, we've seen that physical entities embody trust inasmuch as their production and functioning is trusted. Further, we saw that when they are indeed trusted, that trust extends to several functions of the entities. Following the methodology that we've adopted for this book, we should at this point ask ourselves whether such trust properties are only attached to physical embodiments, or whether they give us potential insights into human concepts of trust. Remember, we started with personal electronic devices and we have seen clearly that the role of the trusted core is first to serve as a means to guarantee that the personal electronic device does faithfully represent its owner. The personal electronic device is indeed the representative of the owner in the digital network. Actually, the personal electronic device has a body with a thinking part attached to a sensori-motor system, together with communication capabilities that are so close to human ones in some cases that they are actually the conduit to human capabilities, as with phones and cameras. So it would seem to be an interesting hypothesis to see what in the physical trust system maps to the human trust system, and where there would be differences. This would allow us, of course, to close the loop, since we could in turn then look at those extra human mechanisms and see if there are traces of them in personal electronic devices, in their current or future form. We will delve into considerations of the future forms in Chapter 9. The theme of this chapter was an historical perspective of trust, and hence, security through causality relationships in physical implements. With respect to computers, this translates directly into computer hardware architectures along with the design, manufacture and servicing of computer systems. With that in mind, we can now turn our attention to procedure and process. This will take us directly into consideration of computer software and its contribution to the mind of the machine.

7  In His Own Image

# 8 In Search of Enlightenment

*Science arose from poetry,*
*when times change*
*the two can meet again on higher levels*
*as friends.*

Johann Wolfgang von Goethe

## Trust through Process

Siddhartha Gautama was born into affluence. His family and surroundings promised a life of luxury and comfort that most would envy. Nevertheless, dissatisfied, he searched for spiritual meaning. He renounced his worldly possessions and left his home to wander as an ascetic monk, searching for the fulfillment that would allow him to declare this incarnation to be his final life. In his journey, he came to realize that a life of deprivation did not bring him the fulfillment that he sought. His musings suggested that a life of service did not bring it either. Finally, he sat beneath the Bodhi Tree, promising not to arise until he reached enlightenment. There, his quest finally ended. He had reached the state of perfect enlightenment and he transcended to the Supreme Buddha. Where, we might ask, did he finally come to realize was the source of enlightenment?

It is all in your head.

"It's all in your head!" That has been a pejorative phrase for as long as most of us can remember. When we felt our stomach ache on the day of an important examination, perhaps the most positive comment that our mother might make was, "It's all in your head!" This was merely preface to a stern admonition to "Get dressed and go to school!" However, in fact, our suggestion is not quite of this ilk. Rather, we suggest that the processes of our minds have a dominant effect towards determining our levels of trust. They influence our levels of trust in things to be sure. However, perhaps even more important is the establishment of our level of trust in processes and procedures, including these very same processes of our minds. This obviously suggests that recursion is once again at work. We think, and we think of thinking; right now in fact, we are thinking of thinking of thinking.

Thus far, we have tended to discuss processes in terms of how we convey trust, not how we establish it. However, there are significant areas where processes are at the heart of establishing trust. We started this chapter with a brief, paraphrased story related to the emergence of Buddhism. The words we used are perhaps a bit vague. They are certainly metaphorical, and in some sense allegorical. In an attempt to be a bit clearer, we can expand on them very slightly based on our layman's perspective of the religion.

Buddhism is a non-theistic religion. Westerners often make the mistake of equating the Buddha with a deity. In reality, the figure represents the highly venerated but mortal person who originated many of the basic tenets of the religion as now practiced by vast numbers of people around the world. In asserting the mortality of the Buddha, the religion grounds trust in the processes he symbolizes. If we characterize Buddhism using the social ecosystem model that we discussed in Chapter 5, we would suggest that it incorporates congruent trust and policy infrastructures. In essence, trust derives from a process that, having first established trust, can then be engaged for the derivation of policy grounded in that trust. The process involved is one of contemplation based in meditation. Given our prior discussions of physiology and cognitive functions, we recognize contemplation as being the ritualistic exploration of the contexts derived from our sensori-motor system. From this exploration comes the metaphorical understanding found within these contexts. In turn, we view meditation as the establishment of an altered, or as some would say, enhanced state of consciousness through which trust can be derived from the contemplative process. The term *ritualistic* emphasizes that contemplation is a form of deep thought that is highly structured. It has something of the characteristics of a protocol to it, and hence we view it as an almost formally defined process. Considering various aspects of its ritual practice, we note that meditation may occur repetitively at a fixed time of day; perhaps in the early morning shortly after arising from sleep. It might, in concert be routinely performed at a fixed location, perhaps in a garden or a set room of the home. Contemplation can often be enhanced by assuming a set position of the body; perhaps a relaxed position that induces a feeling of tranquility. Its practice can entail the use of other sensory input; perhaps the scent from burning incense or the sound of ritual music or chants. Through these various mechanisms, the meditative process induces a state of ecstasy within the mind. We believe that within this state of ecstasy, the mind imbues the resulting thought with an enhanced level of trust and hence a willingness to utilize these thoughts as a basis for future action or interaction. Thus, we see derivation of policy as well as the establishment of trust regarding the subsequent implementation of that policy.

This is all, of course, at best but a crude caricature of Buddhist practices or of any process-oriented trust and policy infrastructures. Our goal at this point is simply to illustrate the distinction between deriving trust from the causality of creation that typifies theistic religions, and instead deriving trust through the considerations of a ritualistic process that tends toward a purely philosophical basis. In essence, "I derive trust in the concept of a personal moral code and then I derive the individual tenets of that trusted moral code." We view the former mechanism as related to deriving trust relative to computer-enabled interactions from the hardware architecture of computer systems. Likewise, we view the latter mechanism as related to deriving trust relative to computer-based interactions from the trust we place in the functioning of the software that controls the processing of computers. In the former case, trust has a seminal point of creation that may be significantly distinct from any policy infrastructures that derive from it. In the latter case, trust and policy are essentially derived recursively through the same process. In the abstract, Buddhism provides us with a guiding example of trust derived through process. Current social systems, however, suggest a considerably more pragmatic approach to trust through process. This example involves the derivation of trust from a confluence of information. Let us consider an example from a typical social ecosystem in which trust derives in this manner. The process is one widely used in current social order, and is particularly used in Web-based interaction systems.

The basic premise of the mechanism is that over a long period of time, people who act in a consistent and legal manner as they are involved in various interactions within their social ecosystem build up a transaction history that can subsequently be used to validate their involvement in future interactions. The approach presupposes that duplicitous individuals will in general tend to act in the short term, thus making it highly unlikely that they will build up a fraudulent series of ostensibly legal transaction records over a long period. The types of transactions that we refer to are those that generate credentials attesting to a personal history. Such credentials can often be linked into a chain. The most typical starting point for such a chain is a *birth certificate*. While the details of the laws may vary from state to state, a general requirement mandates the birth of a child be recorded with a state's Bureau of Vital Statistics. At the completion of this act of enrollment, a birth certificate is issued. This credential lists the time and location of birth along with the names of the parents as well as that of the infant. A certified authority, typically the physician or midwife that aided in the birth, signs it. An attestation by a distinguished authority, distinguished through a registration or certification process through the state, elicits a high level of trust because it entails a transaction that is an official signature operation, for which the consequences of fraud are greater than might be the case for a more common individual. The parents must subsequently register the birth of an infant born outside of a hospital or other official setting. As part of this registration, a third-party witness must attest to the birth of the child. This attestation must be done in front of a Notary Public in order, again, to apply the force of law to the act of affirmation.

Since its inception, the act of registering a birth and of subsequently obtaining a birth certificate has been viewed as a rather innocuous act. This was at least partially due to the fact that the birth of a child typically occurred within some type of social context. This is simply recognition of the evolutionary status of the family. When there are witnesses to the expectation of a birth and its subsequent occurrence, there is an undercurrent of policy mechanisms that are subsequently fulfilled through societal action, and these mechanisms tend toward the establishment of identity for the infant growing to the child who subsequently attains adulthood. Historically, there was no mechanism routinely used to provide a trusted linkage between a person and the birth certificate credential; the linkage was usually done simply by the name on the certificate. Within a relatively small social group, a name is a moderately effective way to establish identity. Through prolonged association, the members of a small group form effective, albeit ill-defined biometric authentication procedures based at least to some extent on facial recognition, voice recognition and physical mannerisms. Within such a group, it is difficult for a person's identity to be fraudulently adopted by another person. In this type of environment, if a person consistently uses the same name throughout the progression of life, then the birth certificate forms a moderately reliable credential attesting to the start of that life. Subsequent credentials gain some level of trustworthiness by tracking back to a valid birth certificate. Perhaps one of the more profound such credentials that has gained increasing relevance over the last few decades is the social security number.

A significant aspect of the dominant policy infrastructure in the United States is that of taxation. As the Supreme Court decision in McCulloch versus Maryland alluded, "the power to tax involves the power to destroy." The current policy purveyors for this infrastructure, that is the United States Congress and the President, generally seek to support certain aspects of family grouping. Consequently, considerations related to having and rearing children find their way into the tax codes. For the purposes of taxation, a child might be viewed as both a liability and an asset, and as such must be duly reported on a family's tax return. Relatively recent changes to the tax codes require a more trustworthy authentication of the existence, and hence identity of children than is accomplished by simply listing their names on the tax return. Therefore, there is now a requirement that a child be identified by a social security number. Obtaining this number is generally dependent on the proper registration of the child's birth; hence, a birth certificate is critical to obtaining a number. With the issuance of a social security number, a person now has two credentials of some substance that can be used to authenticate identity in future transactions. If one considers the subsequent attainment of school graduation diplomas, military service records and perhaps the existence of records of legal sanctions, that is, a criminal record, then it is clear that this chain of documents related to identity can grow. Therefore, in many instances simply being able to recite or produce copies of some significant subset of these credentials is sufficient to authenticate the assertion of identity on the part of a person. "After all," the reasoning goes, "who else but the person in question could lay hands on all this personal information?" "Who, indeed?"

Rarely within this chain is there any strong, objectively verifiable connection between any credential and the actual, biophysical person. This, then, is the root of a growing systemic problem within our social ecosystems; a problem we refer to as *identity theft*. The term, identity theft, is something of a misnomer since the actual problem is one that involves the granting of privileges related to identity without satisfactorily authenticating that identity. The wrong person is allowed to spend the money in a personal checking account, for example. The real problem is not that someone else stole the account owner's identity. The problem is that the bank granted the privileges of the account owner's identity to someone else. In other words, the bank did not satisfactorily authenticate the identity of the account owner prior to allowing a debit transaction against their bank account. Hence, the process is not trustworthy and, in fact, constitutes a threat to the social ecosystem.

To this point, we have considered two pragmatic examples of trust derived through process. In fact, the trust imbued by one process attested to by a birth certificate then conveys to the second process in which a social security number is obtained. The two credentials that derive from the processes are elements of what we will discuss in the next chapter as *experiential identity*. Interestingly enough, without rigorous connection of the credentials to the person, both processes display characteristics of religious structures in that both involve trust derived from subjective evaluation; in essence, both derived trust as an act of faith. In each case, faith is derived first through logical consideration of the environment surrounding the interactions involved and then considering the details of the process of interactions within that environment. We might want to start associating process with *ritual* in these circumstances. The predictability of set processes brings them close to the formality of rituals, which we would suggest brings confidence in a community's commitment through repeated affirmation of determined synchronized action. While our examples were rather simplistic, the whole solidity of ritualized processes has been explored in depth in Victor Turner's groundbreaking *The Anthropology of Performance*.

The discussion for the remainder of this chapter will be aimed at better understanding these concepts within the context of human social structure and then relating these concepts to the software used in computer systems. In the course of this consideration, we will draw parallels between the operations of the mind and such software. In so doing, we hope to express some rudimentary thoughts on the feedback loop that seems to be at work in this provisioning process. We suggest that this consideration will illustrate how trust derives from both environments through rather similar processes.

Expanding prowess of the brain evokes a good summary of the evolutionary uniqueness of *Homo sapiens*. The physical structure of vertebrate species is remarkably similar. A turtle or a fish displays anthropomorphic characteristics. Little wonder that we can readily believe the tales of mermaids or that the Teenage Mutant Ninja Turtles could gain wide acceptance in adolescent circles. The world's great religions take the same tack; human striving for truth and beauty is more an activity of the mind than other actions of the body. Buddhism teaches the search for enlightenment as a cognitive process driven by faith in the end goal, which is the attainment of the state of pure enlightenment. Faith provides a degree of trust, which from our perspective appears as one level of the ranging emotional state that culminates in ecstasy. Protestant Christianity teaches that the right to enter the gates of heaven cannot be earned by good deeds. Rather, they can only be opened by the grace of God; and, God is approached only through faith. The performance of good deeds is to be pursued, but as an act of faith in the deity rather than as the payment of dues.

As we have seen in previous chapters, the development of the human brain in concert with the human mind has been a long, evolutionary process. It has required mutational events to modify the structure of the brain and feedback through the process of natural selection to influence its descriptors. With the development of each new person from infancy to adulthood, we can retrace many of the evolutionary steps of the species. In complement, the needs hierarchy creates a feedback mechanism that vets social groupings.

# The Mind from Antiquity

Emerging in the far distant past as collections of endoskeleton based creatures, the vertebrates share the common characteristic of a central spine that connects the head to the tail and through which passes a central nerve that facilitates the sensori-motor faculties of the individual. Vertebrate species show a propensity for four appendages, some well developed while some are vestigial in nature. On many species, the appendages are equipped with separated phalangeal extensions; for humans, hands with fingers and feet with toes. For a whale or dolphin, the appendages become fins and flukes. For lions and tigers and bears, they become paws with claws.

The central nerve is attached to an enlarged mass of nervous tissue referred to as the *brain stem*. Through a series of evolutionary stages, this central nerve, terminating in the brain stem and associated with ever more sophisticated structural components, emerged as a relatively enhanced control center for the external sensori-motor system of the individual, and the internal *autonomic system* regulating internal organs. Particularly in the case of hominid species, this evolution associated with a series of more sophisticated brains. As a systems advance over earlier species, one of the more innovative characteristics of vertebrates was likely the development of a fine grained sensori-motor system. One can at least make this argument by noting the progression, and particularly the specialization, of the sensori-motor system through the incremental development of the various vertebrate species. Consider the five senses that we humans are familiar with: sight, sound, touch, taste and smell. Each of these sensory systems can be found in other vertebrate species and the characteristics of each sense have evolved at differing rates and to different levels of capability. The hominids, with their connection of sophisticated sensori-motor facilities to the enhanced command and control capabilities of their more powerful brains offered up a superior combination.

The timetable of the evolutionary progression of hominids is still in a state of some disagreement, but their emergence from their precursor species occurred perhaps as early as six or seven million years ago. Since that time, the species has continued to evolve. While fossil records indicate some change in the physical stature of people over that period, the evidence of the greatest change has been in the record of human achievements, in the enhancement of the products of the human mind. This growth is attributed to the development of both size and mental capabilities of the brain, resulting in a tremendous improvement in the cognitive functions of mind. We would like to consider this development of the mind in an attempt to relate the resulting concepts to the facilities of computer systems and computer networks. We will base our consideration on the formative work of three pioneers in the structure, organization and operational development of the human mind: Paul MacLean (*The Triune Brain in Evolution*), Merlin Donald (*Origins of the Modern Mind*) and Jean Piaget (*The Psychology of Intelligence*).

The work of these three, while certainly augmented by many others, suggests an interesting model for the progressive establishment of the human mind as an operating unit. MacLean offers a model of brain structure that suggests a formative process for the evolutionary development of the physiological facilities of the brain. It posits an embodiment of subsystem based architecture that has many of the characteristics of human designed systems, including that of computers. Overlaid on this physiological structure, Donald's work can be interpreted to suggest an information storage structure and processing model that facilitates the manner in which the human mind acquires and stores knowledge derived from the human sensori-motor and autonomic systems. If we adopt this combination conceptual model, Piaget's work can then be interpreted to express how humans systematically provision this storage structure and processing paradigm. In essence, this provisioning operation includes what we might think of in mechanical systems as setup and calibration operations that are effected through *heuristic* processes which consist in trials where success brings validation and failure prompts another trial. In all three cases, extremely similar models are observed in virtually all ostensibly normal individuals. Thus, we observe the apparent operation of a feedback loop that encompasses more than just physiological characteristics, that one might assume are the sole targets of DNA conveyance, and instead evokes the recurring form, including content, of cognition.

Therefore, with that model in mind, including our questions regarding the feedback loop mechanisms whose operations we seem to observe, let us consider in just a bit more detail the suggestions and observations of these respective models.

# The Matter of Mind

Paul MacLean proposed that the current structure of the human brain has developed from three distinct phases of the long evolution of the vertebrates. Further to this phylogenetic perspective, he has taken the perspective of anatomy, chemistry, neurology, surgery, and other measures to identify the descent of these three constituents of the human brain. He has termed the resulting modern structure the *triune* brain, meaning the brain with three parts. His proposition is not that humans actually function with three distinct brains, but rather that those three components of the brain operate in an integrated fashion with a different focus of function within each part. From a computer perspective, this appears very much like a major system functioning through the interactive activities of three subsystems. None of these subsystems is entirely independent, but all three do exhibit aspects of autonomy in certain situations and in certain areas. Here, as throughout this book, we will be faithful to our reference material, in this case *The Triune Brain in Evolution*. We make no independent pronouncement in the domain of neurophysiology. Rather, we follow MacLean in his reviewing the measured steps of cumulative development of the brain as a progressively enhanced system achieved through the evolution of vertebrate species. During embryonic growth in particular, the ontogenetic development of the individual human provides striking illustration of these three subsystems. Further advances in the understanding of the ontogenetic development of the individual, along the lines of Sean Carrol's presentation of evolutionary developmental biology in *Endless Forms Most Beautiful*, are likely to help refine MacLean's model.

From our perspective, the triune brain is an excellent metaphorical match to the structure of a wide variety of computer systems. It is a brain comprised of subsystems, forming the interactive architecture of the complete brain system, each providing specialized facilities in distinct areas. As we will discuss in more detail just a bit later, computer systems typically have a low-level subsystem that deals with the interface between real-time actions, activities driven mostly by extra-computer stimuli, and procedural activities providing complex cognitive processing of combinations of stimuli. A background clock then provides a repetitive trigger for activity within the computer in the absence of other external stimuli. On top of the real-time subsystem, computers often have *task queues*, lists of activities that are scheduled by various subsystems in the form of a priority ordered list. At the top of computer subsystems, applications interface the computer's functional capabilities to human end-user defined services. As we will note below, these very general subsystem definitions suggest qualitative comparison to the triune brain.

In computer systems, the software that sits between the basic sensori-motor functions of the computer and the higher cognitive levels of software, which we typically call *applications*, is termed the *operating system*. The first half-century or so of the evolutionary development of computers has seen a wealth of operating system architectures and implementations. To a certain extent, we might view these as somewhat analogous to the differing brain structures that have evolved among the vertebrates. We will review some of the more salient examples of operating systems, but we are hard pressed to pick any particular one as the analogue of the basis of the brain of *Homo sapiens*. However, at least they give a flavor of the ongoing search for the best foundation for much higher cognitive levels of software.

What we consider as those higher cognitive levels of software are the applications through which the needs hierarchy of the human users of computers is specifically addressed. An indirect illustration of such applications is found within the various computer languages that have evolved in an attempt to address the needs of the application providers. As we suggested back in Chapter 4, "A good programmer can think like a computer; a good computer language sounds like a person talking to another person." Well, in fact a good programmer generally has to think like a computer operating system, because the actual computer is hidden behind a variety of *application programming interfaces* that the operating system provides. While natural languages are similar in their capability of expression, computer languages are more variable, a property that can be attributed in part to their short history compared to human languages. So, we will provide a bit of discussion about the two areas, operating systems and languages. Then, as overview to this chapter's theme of trust through process we will consider the problem of *provisioning*; the process of preparing both humans as well as computer systems to meet the real world.

So, let us first consider the progressive structure of the human brain before we delve into some of the general characteristics of computer software systems that seem to offer at least the hint of a qualitative parallel.

# The Neural Chassis

Vertebrates have a spinal cord running from tail to head, connected to the lower brainstem at the base of the brain. Two extensions of this *neural chassis* are the peripheral *autonomic* nervous system, which regulates the organism, and the peripheral *somatic* nervous system that enables the sensori-motor apparatus. For example, the autonomic nervous system addresses stimulation of the heart, breathing, and movement of the intestines to move digesting food. This subsystem of the total brain is primarily concerned with the physiological needs of the body. In terms of the sensori-motor experience, an important characteristic that we typically associate with the somatic nervous system is the initial facilities for reflexive actions that serve to help us quickly avoid danger. The most basic protection mechanism, from a physiological standpoint, is the reflex action facility of the nervous system. These processes are not routinely accessible from the higher cognitive levels of human brain activity. It is difficult if not impossible for the average person to cause the heart to palpitate through conscious thought.

It is easy to relate the neural chassis to computer architectures. Through its connection to the various reactive motor facilities located throughout the body, this facility functions very much as an independent, self-contained input/output channel. That is, certain stimuli, when detected by peripheral sensors connected to the human distributed nervous system, elicit immediate reactions, such as that of the muscle system causing a foot to jerk or the whole body to jump. The pathway of the signal from the receptor to a point of control and then back to the appropriate muscle can be of different length. A computer component analogous to the autonomic components of the body is a fan that moderates the temperature of internal circuitry, or a surge protector that automatically filters spurious electrical events. A component analogous to external sensori-motor elements is the apparatus that eliminates offensive network packets of information at the source in case of computer attacks that attempt to flood an input channel of a secure core to deny its processing of otherwise valid information.

# The Reptilian Brain

In the evolution tree, reptiles precede mammals. A contrasting study between reptiles and mammals allows studying differential properties of the organism attached to particular characteristics of the brain. The upper neural apparatus of reptiles accounts for behaviors like territoriality, courtship, and submissive displays, as well as hunting, grooming and mating activities. By comparing those behaviors across reptiles, as well as across other non-mammalian vertebrates, it is possible to recognize patterns of behaviors associated with aspects of the brain of reptiles. Through anatomical, chemical, neurological and surgical work, as well as phylogenetic and ontogenetic considerations, it is possible to define a prototypical model for the upper brain of reptiles. From there, it is possible to practice further experiments exploring the functional properties of the brain, in reptiles as well as in other species. MacLean calls this proto-reptilian brain formation the *striatal complex*, but many, including him, refer to it also as the *reptilian brain*, and we will follow that practice.

The next step, obviously, is to refine the model of the reptilian brain by comparing its formation with similar constructs in mammals, and eventually in humans. It is from identifying in reptiles and mammals similar constructs that MacLean comes to consider the reptilian brain as one of the three components of the triune brain. A natural hypothesis is that behaviors associated with the reptilian brain would be forming a pattern extending from reptiles to the full range of mammals. While this can be readily verified in some mammals through intrusive operations, it is more difficult in upper mammals and humans. A combination of medical observations, physiological and psychological experiments, and new non-invasive techniques like functional magnetic resonance imaging allow investigating the hypothesis in greater length. The reptilian denomination obviously does not mean that we are all running around with the brain of a lizard in our heads, despite our predilections towards associating people with reptiles in a very pejorative manner. Rather it is simply an observation that the human brain is an artifact of an evolutionary process, and evolutionary processes tend to build upon successful traits rather than discarding such traits and starting over again. This said, we are ready to consider mammals, an important step because it allows us to enter the realm of emotions, that we have already identified as a central element in the evaluation of trust infrastructures of computer networks.

# The Mammalian Brain

A common physiological trait of mammals, successors of reptiles in the evolutionary tree, is the ability to produce milk. This facility makes the mother essential to the early survival of an infant, but for this to really work there must be a corresponding need that entices the mother to incur the liability accrued from directly feeding her young. In fact, the young of virtually all mammals require greater support than is the case for earlier vertebrates. The emotions provide for a bonding between adults and their young, and among adults as well, that gives rise to continued support for the young following their birth. The point is not that such bonding is totally lacking in other non-mammalian species, but rather that it presents in a stronger fashion within mammalian species. The second major element in the development of the human brain is the *limbic system*, a region of the brain that surrounds and caps the brain stem of the reptilian brain. It is also termed the *mammalian brain*, recognizing the evolutionary process that got us as a species where we are today. In a way similar to his study of the reptilian brain, MacLean investigates the neurophysiology of the brain of various mammalian species to identify its components with behaviors that distinguish them from earlier vertebrates.

For example, grooming, nursing, maternal, separation and sexual behaviors can be associated with parts of the limbic system that work in association or separation. Since mammalian behaviors are much more complex than the already complex behavior of reptiles, there is still much to understand in the functioning of the limbic system. When combined with the advanced capabilities of the augmented brain of humans, the difficulty compounds, and the association of particular human behaviors with the mammalian brain is even more opaque to investigation. However, the emotional limbic subsystem does provide a bridge in the relationship between the cognitive functions of the brain and the autonomic nervous system. If driven into a state of anxiety, for example, the body might respond through heart palpitation, and similarly, a state of anger can cause blushing. In Chapter 4, we did a cursory overview of human emotions. In that discussion, the imagery implied by Scherer in suggesting that emotions lie between sensory stimuli and upper cognition based motor responses fits well with the anatomical relationships outlined by MacLean. The limbic system that gives rise to emotions is a central feature of the emergence of the mammals from their precursor species.

In humans at least, a salient state is *ecstasy*, induced by a chemical release providing a deep sensation of pleasure or importance. There are at least three distinct avenues through which the human mind can enter the state of ecstasy: (a) communal rhythmical rituals, (b) external stimulation by appropriate drugs (natural or artificial), and (c) personal experience (through meditation, or on specific medical conditions). All those avenues may be combined. Ecstasy is manifested by a disconnection of the sensori-motor system from the higher brain functions. In computers, ecstasy is the ultimate state of system change. Small system changes involve modifying one part of the operating system. Only the applications that use that part need to be changed for the computer to continue to function normally. However, if the system is changed extensively, the applications all need to be changed, or reloaded. For a time, applications are disconnected from the operating system that feeds their sensori-motor experience. We can identify a full system change with ecstasy, whereas smaller changes can be identified with more local brain rewiring, as in daily modifications occurring during sleep.

In Chapter 5, we expanded upon the concept of trust. We suggested that trust derives from the assessment that an interaction, or some aspect of an interaction, has a probable outcome that we can quantify in some fashion; an assessment of high probability that we know or can predict the results of the interaction we term high trust while an assessment of low probability we term low trust. Born in the limbic system, trust originally emanated from the involvement of the emotions of the mind, not from what would be commonly termed a logical assessment. Even with modern humans, trust sometimes seems to derive more from gut instinct than from rational thought. However in complex situations, emotions might be viewed as suspect by analytical observers, but they are nevertheless still a powerful force within the mind when performing some action. It was the next evolutionary step of the mind that offered an enhancement in personal interaction mechanisms. Specifically, this evolutionary step involved the melding of cognitive assessment with emotional reaction in establishing trust. We can illustrate this shift by considering some of the aspects of flying an airplane, particularly a small airplane.

An airplane provides a marvelous platform for the human body to be suspended within three-dimensional space. By placing the body in an enclosure that is then set into motion within an airframe whose primary purpose is to counteract the natural forces on the human body, a result is achieved in which the sensory input of the body to the mind can be suspect. The mind is used to receiving sensations of sight, sound and equilibrium to establish an understanding of orientation and direction. In an airplane subject to certain conditions, for example an overcast, hazy day, perhaps towards twilight, the visual inputs through which an understanding of equilibrium is established become very suspect. In fact, they can become erroneous; the airplane can be inverted and the pilot may not recognize it. The results can be disastrous unless a pilot is able, because of training, to disregard the trust that would normally be placed in the physiologically derived sense of equilibrium and instead rely completely on the instrumentation of the airplane. The message of the training is to become essentially counter-intuitive. Do not trust what you think you feel or what you think you see outside the plane. Instead, trust the instruments to tell you about your orientation, your altitude, your airspeed and your direction of flight. Trust the instruments to tell you whether you are climbing or descending, or whether you are turning or in straight, level flight. Then, base your decisions on what your instruments are telling you, not what your elementary senses are telling you. In essence, we learn through proper provisioning of the mind to offset the derivation of trust through primarily emotional reaction with a stronger portion of cognitive assessment.

# The Human Brain

The mind within the brain provides protection to the individual through a multi-layered collection of processes, honed through evolutionary selection to give a person an edge up in warding off danger in its many guises. The third subsystem of MacLean's triune brain paradigm is the *neocortex*, the most recently evolved portion of the human brain. It comprises a sheet of organic material perhaps one square meter in area and about 3 millimeters thick that forms the outer layer of the cerebrum. This part of the brain includes a variety of lobes that we briefly discussed in Chapter 4. For the less technical observer, the distinguishing features of these lobes are the gyri and sulci, the pronounced ridges and furrows that allow the packing of this layer of material into the confined space of the skull. It is these features that we associate with images of the brain. The neocortex can be explored through reference to cranial accidents, diseases and surgery; in particular, the lobotomies performed in the middle of the last century. More recently, new technologies enabling advanced imaging as well as the comparative studies regarding humans and animals have significantly augmented this exploration.

Cognition is the collective result of the mechanisms and processes through which the brain learns about itself, its surrounding environment and how it manifests this information in the form of comprehension and action that it derives from activities of the brain. The neocortex associates with capabilities that obviously separate us in degree of function or form of function from our mammalian predecessors, would it be art, mathematics, religion or science. It is natural to look for capabilities underlying those forms of expression in the mechanisms of the neocortex. Various types of symbolic manipulation associated with their expression in speech and other human-specific communications are part of the neocortex contribution to human cognition. We will later consider more fully the question of how this contribution relates to that of the other parts of the triune brain.

Causation is the establishment of symbolic intermediaries in the observation of correlation. Observable early in infancy, causality is sought for, which is equivalent to saying that a satisfying chemical balance in the brain accompanies the establishment of cause. One of the evolutionary advantages of causality is *planning*. Causality can be recognized directly ("He fell because someone pushed him.") or indirectly ("He fell, and I assume that someone pushed him."). Causes can also be unobservable ("He fell, and I didn't observe anyone, so a spirit may have pushed him."). As for other functions, the establishment of unobservable causes is of survival benefit if it leads to better fitness ("I avoid the spirit, and I don't fall."). The build-up of a causal chain can lead humans to gods, and then to God. If the causal chain is invalid, it can take us over the precipice.

Just as elementary causes (spirits) may offer a better theory for survival, more elaborate, unobservable causes can lead to yet other theories that are more complex. Some would consider, in resonance with the thesis of René Girard developed in several books starting with *Violence and the Sacred*, that monotheistic theories, judged by their historical expansion, have expressed a particular fitness in allowing societies to build and expand in our most recent history. The build-up of causation is based on imitation, itself apparently implemented with mirror neurons, as described by Giacomo Rizzolati, Leonardo Fogassi and Vittorio Gallese *Mirrors in the Mind* Scientific American article. Computers use state machines for communication in the same way. State machines are shared by two communicating computers. A state machine makes predictions based on historical performance, which is saying that it represents a causal model or develops a theory on the behavior of the state machine with which it is communicating. This forms a component of the causal chain, complemented by metaphoric capabilities that we review in some detail later in this chapter.

# Operating Systems

The evolutionary progression of computers over the first half-century or so of their electronic incarnation has been replete with competitive interplay among a variety of software architectures. We have made the point that identifying the analogue of computer systems relative to the human mind is not quite as simple as differentiating computer hardware from software. When the model of social ecosystems is mapped onto computer systems and their networks, the trust and policy infrastructures cross the boundaries between hardware and software. A somewhat similar effect is noted within the brain, where higher cognitive functions are spread across broad regions. That said, an interesting decomposition to recognize and attempt to understand, at least in overview, is that of the dichotomy within computer software between operating systems and applications.

Historically, computers have tended to be general-purpose tools. A specific computer platform might be expected to support work on a number of problems, perhaps sequentially or perhaps in parallel. It might be expected to work on these problems for a single person, or it might be expected to work on behalf of many different people. Moreover, it might be expected to work on behalf of many different people and on many different problems simultaneously. We tend to characterize the ability to work on behalf of many different people as a multi-user capability of a computer and we tend to characterize the ability to work on many different problems as a multi-tasking capability of a computer. A central facility of operating systems is to provide a coarse-grained establishment of context along these two axes, for multiple users and for multiple problems. Contrasting this back to the brain, multi-tasking seems a rather standard capability of a normal brain. A multi-user facility within the brain is slightly more abstractly plausible if we consider that we tend to live our lives within more than one social construct and we may present a different persona in each. We might be mothers or fathers within a family. We might be workers within a company. We might be part of the congregation of a church. Each of these invites a different establishment of context within the mind. How often have we seen someone in the wrong context and been unable to apply a name to the face? Of course, in the most literal interpretation of multi-user we might recognize the relatively unusual situation in which the mind gives rise to a multiple personality disorder.

Within most current computer architectures, operating system software is very tightly bound to the hardware platforms on which it resides. Perhaps it best finds its human analogue in the reflexive and cognitive features of the more primitive components of the central and autonomic nervous systems. Operating system software strives to provide a consistent interface to applications software that presents a uniform view of the computer sensori-motor system of the platform on which it is running. Application software, on the other hand, tends towards presenting a consistent appearance across the full range of the human sensori-motor system, independent of the operating system on which it is run at any particular time. The end result is that computer systems encompassing both operating system and application software sit astride the connection between the human sensori-motor system and technology based extensions to that system.

We noted in Chapter 4 that the sensori-motor environment of a generic computer was essentially an ordered set of memory locations, each filled with a set of switches that could be used to indicate the binary quantities, zero and one. Beyond just the vestigial components of such a generic computer, over time a large variety of peripheral devices has been incorporated into computer architectures. This has been done largely for conveying the sensori-motor environment of humans into or out of that of the computer. Hence, we see writing devices through which a computer can print characters, plot figures and graphs and project images. On the input side, we have keyboards, microphones and digital scanners. All of these elements are represented internally within the computer system as an ordered collection of words filled with bits. Through the establishment of context within the computer system, it is possible to relate through translation and conversion by the peripheral devices this collection of binary information into the forms that can be assimilated by the human sensori-motor system. In a like fashion, the physical environment to which the human senses can respond can also be conveyed into the computer system. Audio transducers in the form of microphones can transform the acoustic vibrations constituting sound into continuously varying levels of electrical currents and voltages. By sampling the levels of current or voltage at precise time intervals, the electrical signal can be represented as a continuous string of binary values. Thus, sound can be brought into a contextual domain within a computer such that it can be manipulated by stored programs that effect state changes of the computer's central processing unit.

Other peripheral devices connected to computers are able to store the sensori-motor experiences of the computer for subsequent examination and processing. A variety of memory types ranging from solid-state representations to magnetic domains on physically rotating media give the computer a tremendous spectrum of storage capacity versus access time variability. All of this is effected within the computer through stored sets of instructions called *programs.*

In the previous chapter, we suggested that threats to computer systems could be mitigated by hardware. If the architecture and construction of computer systems are well understood, then trust can be derived from that level of causality. However, this presupposes that software running on the hardware can be understood in a similar fashion. Experience has shown us that establishing this understanding requires significant procedural integrity during the software programming and installation processes. In the following sections, we will consider a very cursory overview of some of the salient developments along the paths of operating system evolution. Our purpose is certainly not to offer a history of these developments; our survey is much too terse and spotty for that. Rather, we simply want to give some contextual flavor to software development in general, and operating system development specifically, to support our consideration of computers and computer networks as extensions of social ecosystems.

# Primitive Baby Steps

The earliest commercial computers such as the IBM 650 or IBM 1620 were very much single user tools, on the order of a table saw or a lathe. Developing and running software on these machines generally required complete control over the system on the part of the programmer, who served also as the computer operator. The languages used to define some series of processing steps tended to be very close to the sensori-motor environment of the computer itself. On the IBM 1620, usually the first indication that a program had a problem was when the large, red Check Stop light came on. It was hard to miss, positioned as it was on the main control panel of the machine. It indicated in the strongest terms that either the computer was not able to do what it had been instructed to do, or it did not know where to go for its next instruction.

Since evolutionary processes have a tendency to build through enhancements to existing mechanisms, rather than replacing them whole clothe with a better approach, it might be useful to walk through the early steps of making a stored program run on the earliest computers. The point being that our most advanced systems today generally perform many of the same operations. These instructions have just been ground into the structure of the newer systems and we only see the more profound results of lots of these primitive baby steps. One might think of this as the computer equivalent of the biogenetic law: ontogeny recapitulates phylogeny. We mentioned in Chapter 4 that this law is actually not fully true for biological systems, and it is not universal for computer systems as well; but there is enough validity in the concept to warrant the comparison. Relative to biological systems, the initial thought is that the law applies to the embryonic development of an individual of a species while, in the case of computers, the observation applies to the powering up of a modern computer system. So, let us consider some of these baby steps.

Input of information to the IBM 1620 was typically through punched cards. One punched in the desired programming steps into a series of these cards, creating a *card deck.* As cattle graze in herds and whales swim in pods, so cards live in decks. The language used to convey these programming steps was generally an *assembly language.* This form of language is barely one-step removed from the pure bit patterns that defined the command structures in the most basic form of a computer's binary representation; its *machine language.* The term assembly language is not terribly colorful. Not that other terms in the computer world are particularly exciting or illuminating from an aesthetic viewpoint, but assembly language just sits there. It seems somewhat mechanical, and that is actually what it entails; a mechanical translation of a straightforward mnemonic rendition of basic machine language into pure binary strings.

Starting from the point of power up of a machine, an initial *bootstrap loader* program needed to be given control of the computer. This could be done by entering it directly into computer memory through switches on the control console. Alternatively, in a great evolutionary advance, a machine language variant of such a program could be punched into a single card that could then be entered into computer memory directly from the card reader. The evolutionary advance in this case was hardware wiring, presented in the form of a switch on the console control panel that directed a card to be read into a specific starting location in computer memory. After the card was read, control of the computer was transferred to that specific starting location. With only a modest amount of ingenuity, a single card could be created that contained a program that knew how to read many cards from the card reader, store the information from them into successive locations in computer memory and then give operational control to a specific memory location indicated on the last card of the deck.

Thus, when the computer was powered up, the bootstrap loader program was used to first load an existing program called an *assembler* into the computer. The assembler was a program found on its own deck of punched cards, but presented in the form of pure machine language. After loading by the bootstrap loader, the assembler program was given control of the computer. Its first processing step was to go into an idling loop waiting for a card to be read from the card reader. So, now comes the time to run a user program. Assuming that it was written in assembly language on a card deck, one could put this deck in the card reader hopper and press the start button. The assembler program would then read in this assembly language program, convert it into a set of machine language instructions and punch these out to a new card deck. One could then take this binary card deck, invoke the bootstrap loader and then load and run the user program.

On the early IBM 1620s, the only output channel that a program had was to punch cards. There were not any line printers yet, and no console. However, you could punch out a deck of cards. There was, then, a rather interesting device called an IBM 407 Accounting Machine. This was actually something of a computer in its own right that was programmed through jumper wires placed on a control board that was then inserted into the machine. The purpose of this device was to read punched cards and print out information on a cursory line printer. The type of programming that one could do with this system were things like adding or subtracting numbers punched into various fields on a deck of punched cards. It could also add numbers on successive cards together and then print out the sum total of a column of numbers. With a bit of ingenuity in wiring the control panel, one could generate and print out moderately complex reports from a deck of punched cards. If one's user program was computing a set of numbers from some complex mathematical algorithm, then the answers had to be punched out on cards and the cards then printed out through an IBM 407; *et voila*, one might have the output of a function. Such was the world of the earliest computers.

During the late 1950's and early 1960's, large-scale computers evolved beyond the IBM 650 and IBM 1620 in two distinct families of machines: business computers and scientific computers. From IBM came a line of business computers beginning with the IBM 1401 and then followed by the IBM 1410. These machines were among the first to make use of an actual operating system that was charged with keeping the machine busy. A modest IBM 1410 configuration would have a central processing unit with 20,000 characters of memory, four magnetic tape drives, a line printer and a combination card reader and punch. The operating system was a variant of IBM's first significant commercial system that was referred to as IBSYS. It was a single-user operating system, allowing the execution of programs in sequence in what is called a batch operation. Individual programs were entered on a card-deck that had pre- and post- control cards placed before and after the deck. A number of such decks were stacked into the card reader hopper and the operating system would read a start job card and process the following deck according to control parameters in the prefacing control card. The post-deck control card gave instructions on the conduct of the program after its deck was read. The operating system could make use of magnetic tape for intermediate storage, so it was not actually a requirement to punch out card decks. One could start from assembly language, compose machine language that was then written to magnetic tape and then execute the machine language image from magnetic tape. Programs could make use of magnetic tape for intermediate data storage. An IBM 1410 could invert a 400 by 400 matrix by tossing off intermediate stages of the inversion operation to intermediate magnetic tape storage, rewinding the tape and performing another pass of the algorithm. The task could often take several hours to run to completion, but it was a quantum leap in computational ability compared to any other approach of large-scale statistical analysis.

Again, from IBM the scientific computer family was represented by the IBM 70xx series of systems. These were 32-bit word length binary machines, and a machine with 32,768 words of memory was pretty much state of the art in the mid-1960's. This series of machines saw the significant evolutionary progression of the addition of rotating disk drives for large-scale intermediate storage. Such drives were much faster than magnetic tape and offered random access of information rather than the purely sequential access offered by magnetic tape. As we suggested back in Chapter 2, one could hazard a guess that most of the electronic computational effort within NASA to send men to the moon made use of IBM 70xx class machines, with perhaps a few IBM 360 class machines also in the mix. One can further hazard a guess that one fully configured laptop computer circa 2007 could surpass all of the computation facilities available to NASA worldwide for the Apollo missions through 1969. Well actually, since it takes about six hundred 2400 foot reels of 800 bytes-per-inch, 9-track magnetic tape to store one gigabyte, the NASA warehouses full of telemetry data might require a few extra boxes besides the laptop. Figure that today we can get a terabyte of disk capacity in a container the size of a small book and we see that the required configuration is still not too big.

So, why do we recount these rather trivial details about the days of primitive computers? Well, it may just be that the authors are old guys that don't get out enough. However, perhaps more to the point, many of these same operational procedures are used on that fully configured laptop computer circa 2007; they are just done a whole lot faster and can make use of a lot more resources. Perhaps it brings some focus to the comparison of the brains of *Sahelanthropus tchadensis*, considered to be the earliest hominid species versus that of *Homo sapiens*; a comparison of cranial cavities of approximately 350 cc versus 1500 cc.

As the computer world grew past the primitive baby steps stage, progressively more cognitively enabled systems came to the fore. The IBM 360 was a mutational advance in computer systems, from a standpoint of hardware as well as software. We touched on the evolving hardware features back in Chapter 4. Of more interest to us now is the form of operating system software that showed up on the IBM 360. The OS/360 was among the earliest large commercial-grade operating systems; it subsequently evolved to support multiple simultaneous users, multi-tasking and multiple processors. Moreover, it gave rise to a succession of operating systems that emerged much as new species in and of themselves. IBM tended to follow a policy of incorporating emulators for old computers in the new versions of computers that it brought out. This was something of a technical rendition of the idea that ontogeny recapitulates phylogeny. Through this mechanism, programs that were developed and run under the OS/360 operating system can still run on many, if not all of today's IBM systems. Actually, this philosophy held true even for the older systems before the IBM 360.

During about the same period that the IBM 360 mainframes were emerging, Digital Equipment Corporation was starting to bring out the first variants of minicomputers, primarily 8-bit machines. Not until the late 1960's and early 1970's did DEC introduce its 16-bit PDP-11 series. Shortly thereafter, they brought out their family of 32-bit computers, starting with VAX 780 systems. DEC also developed multi-user, multi-tasking operating systems for both series; the RSX system for the PDP-11 machines and VMS for the VAX machines. Both the RSX and the VMS families evolved into true multi-user, multi-tasking operating systems. By virtue of being effective multi-user systems, they had significant security infrastructures in place; both used an account and password approach to identity authentication of users.

The DEC systems also saw the introduction of one of the more powerful networking systems up to that time; a general architecture called DECnet. DECnet was proprietary to DEC; it encompassed a series of hardware based protocol line controllers that supported encrypted data transmission at up to 56,000 bits per second over telephone lines and 10,000,000 bits per second over Ethernet-based local area networks. DECnet-based networking coupled with RSX and VMS operating systems provided relatively secure, wide-area networking for the application programs of the day.

UNIX was an operating system developed by a small group at Bell Laboratories during the late 1960's through the early 1970's. Led by Dennis Ritchie and Ken Thompson, the development team focused on a full blown operating system capable of running first on the early generations of mini-computers from Digital Equipment Corporation; specifically, the various PDP series machines. It was then ported to a variety of other computer systems. UNIX was perhaps the first operating system developed from a philosophical basis. The philosophy was essentially that small is good, and many good but small programs can be aggregated into larger, more powerful programs. In that way, the tendency is to do one small thing well, and then use that rendition in every place where it is necessary to do that thing. It has been well recognized over the years that UNIX has a distinct Buddhist flair to it.

The development of UNIX went hand-in-hand with a powerful programming language called simply "C". The initial versions of UNIX were written in C, which meant that porting to new hardware systems only required the development of a C-language to machine-language compiler for each new hardware platform. This development philosophy holds even today, although the tendency is to form an abstract hardware platform through the definition of a *virtual machine*. We will consider that concept just a bit later.

One of the more minor, yet still significant mutational events that occurred concurrently with the development and deployment of UNIX, was what we might term the theorization of computer programming as a cognitive activity. Brian W. Kernighan and P.J. Plauger contributed significantly to this transformation through their publication of a small book entitled *The Elements of Programming Style*. Within its approximately 170 pages, it offered a wide range of tips for developing computer software that was more compact, reliable and robust than anything the field had seen previously. The emergence of this cognition based approach to programming contributed in no small part to the ability to develop large-scale software systems that could actually be made to work.

UNIX was one of the first operating systems developed around a collection of core software that was developed with secure operations in mind. Building secure systems on top of this *kernel* could then be done in relatively small, incremental steps, almost a mutation in the approach to systems development. In addition, as we have previously mentioned, at least one new species of operating system emerged from UNIX based on an open source philosophy; this was the Linux system.

Personal computers emerged as a rather natural result of the progression of miniaturization of electronic components and circuitry. The development of large-scale integrated circuits allowed a fully competent central processing unit to be implemented on a single chip; memory and various interface units were similarly available. Surprisingly enough however, the development and deployment of personal computers also exhibited an almost purely social aspect. The fact that small computers could apparently do things that previously only big computers could do, and could do them with smaller machines that cost a lot less money, was apparently not a sufficient justification in the marketplace for such machines to take off. The earliest personal computers were the products of a variety of start-up companies, and the modest successes that they had involved mostly the establishment of niche markets. Finally, the entire genre was legitimized when IBM offered their first personal computer line in the late 1970's. It was most interesting that in offering this basic computer platform, IBM, the developer of the most powerful operating systems then known for large and mid-range computers, chose to go to an outside vendor for the operating system of the personal computer. This unknown quantity was Microsoft and the operating system was the Disk Operating System, generally known by its acronym MS-DOS.

If one were going to design an operating system that was the antithesis of the mainframe operating system, MS-DOS might have been the natural result. Perhaps this was the prescient decision of IBM; it's hard for a mammal to build a cockroach. MS-DOS was an operating system devoid of security but offering extremely efficient propagation characteristics. One could almost think of it as a virus turned loose in a world of large, well-developed organic life forms. The technical expertise required for managing the installation and support of this software component was minimal. Therefore, the system had a natural characteristic that made it a trivial target for malicious software; it had a standard boot procedure that allowed the personal computer user to invoke specific executable programs automatically when the computer was powered up. This batch control file, or BAT file, allowed the invocation of any number of executable images. Consequently, all a piece of malicious software had to do was get its name listed within the BAT file. The earliest computer viruses, once placed into execution on a system, merely wrote their invocation sequence into the BAT file and then proceeded to propagate themselves to various places on the hard drive or floppy disks of the personal computer. From a computer security standpoint, it was as if a large bull's-eye and the words "Attack Me Here!" marked the most vulnerable parts of the system! However, the propagation characteristics of these systems were indeed akin to cockroaches; they quickly overran the domiciles of mainframes and even mini-computers.

In a startling degree of synchronicity with the explosive deployment of personal computers came the emergence of the communication protocols called TCP/IP from the development nooks and crannies of the Arpanet. When these protocols were included as standard components of personal computer operating systems, the explosion of the Internet began.

Then, seemingly out of the blue came another mutation event. As the anecdotal version of Isaac Newton's discovery of gravity was stimulated by an apple falling on his head, so was the case of the computer world. Apple dropped on its collective head. Among the early start-up companies, offering their own variants of personal computers was Apple. The early Apple machines developed a strong following of pioneers in the use of personal computers. The real mutational event that was propagated by Apple was the introduction of the first low-end systems with graphical user interfaces. Where IBM-compatible personal computers' console terminals were text oriented, Apple, beginning first with the Lisa machines and then the Macintosh machines, provided a graphical display screen coupled first to a keyboard for user-program information interchange. Then, with the inclusion of a *mouse*, it introduced the first widely distributed truly point-and-click interaction style between users and computer programs. In fact, it was a mutation implementing earlier ideas developed at Xerox that resulted in all computers growing profound extensions to the sensori-motor experience through which they interacted with people. Of course, just as in any evolutionary mix, existent species had to react to the changed environment or perish.

MS-DOS, the primary initial offering on IBM compatible personal computers was almost a throwback to what we discussed above as the primitive operating systems of the earliest large-scale computers. It assumed complete control of the computer platform on behalf of a single user who had access to all the input/output facilities of the computer; actually, access to the entire sensori-motor system of the computer. Given how far this concept was from the operating systems of the mainframe and minicomputer lines of the times, it is not surprising that IBM and Microsoft set out to collaborate on a more powerful operating system for personal computers. The target development was called OS/2.

This collaborative effort between IBM and Microsoft sought to provide a multi-tasking operating system for IBM personal computers; in effect, a replacement operating system for MS-DOS. While the system was completed and introduced after some fits and starts, in an interesting marketing end-run, Microsoft preempted the deployment of OS/2 with the introduction of its own, proprietary personal computer operating system that it called Windows. Windows was a close relative to MS-DOS while OS/2 claimed closer relationship to the mainframe operating systems. The similarly timed release of both Windows and OS/2 was one of the more startling episodes in the intermingling of market driven versus technology driven forces thus far seen in the world of computers. Both systems were, in effect, responses to the mutational advances made by Apple in the form and style of man-machine interactions.

Based on both mainframes with largely IBM operating systems and mini-computers running UNIX or UNIX-like operating systems, the late 1980's and the 1990's saw the development of Internet-based computing. This largely took the form of client-server architectures with the afore-mentioned mainframes and mini-computers forming the server components, and Windows or Mac based personal computers forming the client components. Windows continued to stress ease of propagation over security and consequently continued to suffer a wide range of attacks, some of which were disastrous to large segments of the computer network environment worldwide. Obviously, this presented a market opportunity for the right type of software.

Developed during the early 1990's by Sun Microsystems, Java was introduced as a portable computing environment with applicability ranging from distributed Web applications to individual, hand-held devices. Its true claim to fame, however, was its provision of a high degree of security for software that was intended to operate on arbitrary platforms across the full range of the Internet. Java provided this high security capability by offering a highly constrained sensori-motor system.

Following the historical perspective that we noted previously, the architectural picture for large-scale computer systems that we have thus far painted presents a view of multi-user and multi-application systems that may be found on a variety of computer platforms. Such systems offer the power and convenience of varying contexts allowing for extremely wide-ranging interactions between human users and sensori-motor extensions. Information across the full spectrum of human experiences can be addressed by different applications, allowing users to interact with each in a manner most conducive to that particular context. An alternative view makes use of a single architecture, perhaps encompassing a number of platforms, to present an extremely complete and often fine-grained representation of a particular context. Such systems are often comprised of many subsystems that present detailed interactions between one or more users and a single, often large-scale data model context. Among these subsystems may be components that have real-time constraints on the processes that they contain. An excellent example of this model is found in the avionics systems used to control aircraft.

Avionics systems on modern commercial jet airliners are capable of flying the plane from takeoff to landing in a purely hands-off mode. In most instances, they are not used this way but rather they provide the capability to pilots of fully monitoring all aircraft systems and of effecting control through a highly intuitive user interface. Moreover, these systems allow the integration of ancillary systems such as those for monitoring weather conditions that might affect aircraft operations. On military combat aircraft, such ancillary systems might also include weapons systems monitoring and control along with integration into wide-ranging threat assessment and targeting systems. Such complex environments are typically designed from the aspect of the applications that the platform must support within a single context. Major computer system components such as operating system support, database systems, graphic display and motor control are relegated to *embedded components* of larger scale dedicated systems. Therefore, we might think of an avionics system as a dedicated system that compartmentalizes along the application axis; a system dedicated to a single problem. In the next chapter, we will suggest a dedicated system that compartmentalizes along the user axis; specifically, a dedicated system providing an enhanced single user capability.

Historically, the deployment of secure cores involved the development and installation of all software on the computer platform during its manufacturing process. This had the characteristic that such software could be installed in read-only memory, making it essentially immutable. This is a very attractive characteristic from a security, and hence trust, viewpoint. Of course, a very unattractive aspect of this characteristic is that the software on a secure core is immutable and this is often, if not always, problematic with software in general. If software is determined to have errors in it, then it is useful to be able to fix it. Fixing software generally involves either removing the errant software and replacing it with good software, or altering the current software in place with a software patch, a concept perhaps borrowed from repairing an automobile tire that has a hole in it. If both the hardware platform as well as its contained software is immutable, then fixing becomes difficult if not impossible. It is a bit like fixing a wagon wheel on a covered wagon.

A solution to this general deficiency arose through the concept of introducing a *virtual machine* into secure cores. A virtual machine is essentially a pseudo-computer that exists purely within a software implementation. Thus, one can write software to run on a real computer platform that will then support the operation of a pseudo-computer within it. This provides a level of indirection in the software operation process that allows one to add new software onto a secure core.

First, the software that implements the virtual machine is installed on the secure core during the manufacturing process. This software is rather generically referred to as a *virtual machine interpreter*. Then, new software that is desired on the secure core platform is written as generic data to the secure core. Now this data can be input into the virtual machine interpreter *et voila*, new software has been loaded onto the secure core. As long as the appropriate protocols are followed, such software can be securely loaded onto a secure core even after it has been issued to a bearer of a wider system that encompasses the secure core; a personal electronic device.

Two major initiatives to exploit the virtual machine concept on secure cores were undertaken first by National Westminster Bank in the development of their Multos System and then by Schlumberger in the development of Java Card. We rather fully recounted the story of the development of Java Card back in Chapter 2, but to reiterate, Java Card is a subset of Java that is suitable for implementation and use on secure cores. It is particularly useful in that it provides a good means for adding software onto a secure core even after it has been placed in operational use. Java Card has security characteristics that allow code to be deployed on secure cores in a trustworthy fashion. The Multos System actually predated Java Card. Multos was based on a virtual machine definition that is different from Java, but it addresses essentially the same set of goals and implementation constraints. The full Multos System encompasses the complete infrastructure for developing and deploying software on secure core platforms.

# Memories of the Way We Were

Merlin Donald is a leading influence in the understanding of the evolution of human cognition. In *Origins of the Modern Mind*, he paints a clear and concise picture of *Homo sapiens'* development of cognitive abilities far beyond those of other primates. Donald has suggested that the evolution of human cognitive abilities extended beyond that of earlier primates as the result of three distinct transitions of representational systems available to the human mind, representational systems that encompass distinct forms of information storage. There are interesting parallels between these information processing and memory systems and the processing and memory mechanisms found in general purpose-computer systems. In regards to human cognitive systems, the following sections draw from the work of Donald, completed by Steven Mithen's *The Prehistory of the Mind*.

From our perspective, the human search for enlightenment follows the progression of needs identified by Maslow. The ability of the species to ascend this ladder of interaction stimuli has derived from the expanding brain and its subsequent support of the maturing mind. Structurally, the brain can be viewed as having developed as a construct of three major subsystems that MacLean denominated the triune brain. Donald then suggests an augmentation to this structure through the development of organizational characteristics of the mind. From our perspective, these two views are orthogonal; the organizational characteristics rather naturally layer upon the structural form. Indeed, it seems to us that the composite of these two facilities blends quite well to facilitate the emergence of the needs hierarchy.

The blending of structural and organizational facilities offers a potential mechanism through which the needs hierarchy becomes a part of human design. DNA provides the conveyance of structure from one generation to the next. The organizational characteristics of the resulting brain then produce requirements on the necessary and appropriate provisioning of the mind of the new generation. In response to continuous sensory input, these requirements manifest as stimuli that map to the hierarchy of needs. We are not born with minds intact; they must be appropriately provisioned within the brain. The focus of the relevant needs progresses with the successive fulfillment of the necessary provisioning. Essentially, as we grow and mature we surface appetites that reflect the sustenance that our particular stage of provisioning requires. That we do this in a consistent manner, across generations and across collections of individual humans was the epiphany of Jean Piaget. We will get to that in a bit. First, let us consider in somewhat more detail the organizational characteristics themselves.

Genetic encoding enables the basic form of cognition of all primates, including humans. It manifests itself in the form and structure of the brain. Essentially, there appear to be a variety of *procedural* thought mechanisms that are hard-wired within certain structures of the brain. Although there is plasticity in the organization of the brain, as summarized clearly by Sharon Begley's *Train Your Mind, Change Your Brain*, the various sensory input facilities are preferentially connected to certain areas or structures within the brain; likewise for motor output control. For example, the reflexive actions that the body takes in response to certain stimuli are genetically inherited. They do not have to be learned in one generation from the behavior of previous generations, nor through the results of trial and action training. This matches quite well qualitatively with the brain structures suggested by MacLean whose organization we summarized in a previous section. The most ancient of the brain mechanisms, characterized as the reptilian brain, is viewed as the source of such behavior. This brain structure is common to all vertebrates, and appears qualitatively similar in all mammals. Here we can draw a rather interesting parallel with computer structure and organization.

As with living organisms, computer implementations can take a variety of forms, a fact that has been well illustrated over the last few decades. The profound aspect of the current incarnation of computers is the concept of a stored control program that effects the cognitive facilities of the machinery. This is the *procedural* memory of the computer. A spectrum of implementation strategies exists, ranging from function specific circuits to hierarchies of mechanisms implemented in the form of stored programs that allow very basic language relationships between the stored program and its implementation hardware to be redefined at will. In essence, these strategies allow one to bring into being, intermediate metaphorical environments ranging from the basic (i.e. genetic) level of the computer to the higher (i.e. cognitive) levels.

Continuing with the theme presented by Donald, the brain of precursor species to modern humans such as *Australopithecus* and *Homo habilis* was dominated by an *episodic* form of memory coupled to its sensori-motor environment. Episodic memory involves the hippocampus, which is an element of the limbic system. This would seem to match well with our understanding of the progression of human evolution in that the limbic system is one of the earliest manifestations of the mammals. Hence, episodic memory, as a step beyond, could reasonably constitute the oldest variant of memory, distinct from the precursor species, within modern humans.

When episodic memory is the prevailing form of memory within the brain it places rather severe constraints on the manner in which members of the species learn and, perhaps even more important, how they associate with each other. In other words, it has a significant impact on the grouping mechanisms available to the species. Sensory input and motor response are connected and stored within the brain as a very literal rendition of actual events. This means that the act of learning, which is an elemental basis of cognition, requires each individual person to acquire an actual experience. Thus, one learns by doing. This would seem to place significant limitations on the ability of the members of this species in extending the horizons of their interactions with other members of the species and with the physical world around them. When a successful process or mechanism is established in reaction to a given stimulus context, there is no significant impetus to seek better processes or response mechanisms or to establish a more expansive processes or response mechanism that encompasses the specific stimulus context as well as others. This limitation is supported through the observation that across the million or more year tenure of *Australopithecus* and *Homo habilis* the tool systems of the species show little enhancement. The fossil record suggests that this situation changed with the emergence of *Homo erectus*. To go beyond this limited capability for adaptation and advancement a mutational event related to cognitive ability was required. Donald suggests that such an event occurred with the physiological development of a different variant of memory in the brain, that of *mimetic* memory.

The evolutionary advance brought by mimetic memory is an advance toward metaphoric understanding, which seems to be the doorway to significantly higher levels of cognitive ability. Mimetic memory follows from the mind becoming capable of *mimesis*. Mimesis essentially refers to the process of imitation. Mimetic learning refers to the process through which one learns by observing someone else doing. Having observed and remembered, and assuming that both the sensory input as well as the motor output from the observation is remembered, then one can evoke a motor response from the memory of having observed someone else perform an action in response to a stimulus. The memory created from observing someone else react to sensory stimuli allows us individually to form a model of the process associated. We should note once again that in Chapter 5 we associated the process of mimesis with the need of belonging. Our assumption was and is that mimetic learning leads to the establishment of trust and subsequently to the creation of groups beyond the core family.

Mimesis is a step toward higher cognitive function, but it is not the final step. Donald suggests that a second mutational event occurred when the mind became capable of *mythic* comprehension. In our considerations in Chapter 5, we viewed mythic comprehension as an enabler of establishing social groups that were not substantially grounded in the physiological facilities that gave rise to the nuclear family. When the mind became capable of supporting the mythic themes of understanding of otherwise incomprehensible actions, it provided a means of establishing trust infrastructures that could form the basis of large policy infrastructures. Mythic comprehension is an early component in the establishment of causality.

Donald suggests that the most recent, if not final, evolutionary transition of the mind was the enabling of *theoretic* cognitive processes. As the cognitive facilities of the mind have been enhanced through the evolutionary process, the search for causality in myth has been slowly replaced with the logic-based establishment of causality in theoretic constructs that are grounded upon a more systematic understanding of the physical ecosystem. In essence, mythic comprehension is a seminal quality in the establishment of trust through causality. On the other hand, theoretic processes are foundational to the establishment of trust through process.

Qualitatively similar constructs to these five variants of memory can be identified within computer systems. Realize of course, that qualitative similarity is very different from operational equivalence. While brain anatomy and the corresponding memory facilities are functions of organic development guided by DNA within living species, basic computer hardware simply provides a good paperweight until the necessary programs are added to it. It should be useful, then, for us to consider how we start to meld mind with brain in the case of computers. Please note that we are not going to suggest that the specialized forms of computer memory that we are going to discuss are direct analogues to the indicated characteristics of human memory. The observation we make is that the path to cognitive function, whether pursued organically or mechanically, involves some at least metaphorically similar facilities.

# Melding Cognition with Hardware

The set of instructions that tell a computer how to perform specific actions is generally termed a *program*. The individual instructions, or small sets of these instructions, are sometimes referred to as *code*. When we define a series of instructions, each to be performed following the one preceding, we sometimes refer to this as a *procedure* or as *procedural code*. The act of creating this set of instructions is typically called *programming*. When we install a program into a computer, we may then choose to refer to is as a *stored program*. The programming of secure cores involves an extra activity called *formal* proof, using advanced logic reasoning to validate the program. Otherwise or in addition, the act of determining that a particular program functions as expected, that it is in fact comprised of a correct set of instructions regarding the desired set of actions, is termed *testing*. If testing determines that a program is not behaving correctly, then the subsequent act of finding and correcting the problem or problems is termed *debugging*. The people who write computer programs are usually called *programmers*. The people who test programs are called *testers*, or perhaps more formally they are referred to as *quality control* personnel and the people who fix the programs are called *debuggers*. In most instances, particularly during the initial creation of a program, all of these functions can be performed by the same person and the combined process is simply referred to as *programming*. While these points are certainly basic, if not completely trivial, they do convey an important characteristic of the way that computers are prepared to address and solve problems. While there is not a clear or complete delineation, it is interesting to compare and contrast this preparatory process with the construction of a building.

We tend to anthropomorphize the act of programming a computer. While programming has a number of similarities to a construction process, it actually takes on more the appearance of *teaching* than of *building*. If we consider the construction of a building, we find that specific operations tend to be performed by *specialists*. Certain *workers excavate* the building site in preparation of laying a foundation. The foundation itself is constructed by *specialists in the pouring and finishing of concrete*. Once the foundation is in place, a superstructure of the building is put in place; for large buildings, this is done by the *steelworkers* and for small buildings or homes by the *framers*. *Finishers* prepare the internal walls and doors of the buildings. Plumbing is put in place by *plumbers* and electrical circuits are put in place by *electricians*. Finally, *painters*, *carpet layers* and *interior decorators* complete the construction. Depending on the structure, many other specialties might well be involved. On the other hand, the preparation of programs for computers, when they are of a small size, tends to be the activity of *generalists* more than that of specialists. When a building is completed, it is brought to life or commissioned by turning on the water and power and then populating it with people. When a computer program is completed, it is *provisioned* by loading in to it all the information that it will require for operation, and then it is placed into operation. Sometimes we refer to starting up a program as *executing* it; an interesting metaphorical contrast to people. Indeed, just a bit later we will consider in more detail the acts of provisioning, as they relate to people as well as computers.

The building of a large-scale program or system of programs does take on more similarities to large-scale construction. *System architects* evaluate requirements and establish the design for the systems and subsystems. More experienced programmers, sometimes referred to as *systems analysts*, define the data structures, interfaces and process flow characteristics of the system. *Coders* write code and perform preliminary debugging operations while *quality control personnel* confirm that the detailed operation of the system across its full breadth of required capabilities is conformant with the original specifications. Specialists in different areas are called to help when needed. One very specific area of specialization, much in keeping with the variants of human memory discussed by Merlin Donald, are extensions to the pure storing of ones and zeros that we usually think of when we refer to computer memory. These extensions take us into the realm of data storage; specifically leading toward databases and knowledge bases. These are the precursors in the computer world that may lead us to context sensitive memory of sensory input coupled to trust enabled motor action responses; in other words, to cognitive functions much closer to what are effected by the human mind.

In our overview of concepts presented by Donald, we have had a cursory look at five distinct memory facilities within the human mind: procedural, episodic, mimetic, mythic and theoretic memories. It is important to note that within the human brain, the elemental unit of information storage has yet to be identified. Computer memory stores strings of bits. For the moment, we do not know the equivalent to a bit in human memory, if the question makes sense. Within human memory there is a significant degree of cognitive capacity that seems inexorably intertwined with the concept of pure memory. The form and processes that these different memory mechanisms support have direct bearing on the cognitive facilities of the human mind. The same situation holds for computer systems, albeit making use of memory mechanisms of different form but with similar application. Many of the end requirements of the cognitive systems are the same in both environments.

Within the human mind, context appears to be an integral aspect of memory. However, at the most basic sensori-motor level of computer systems there exists a need to explicitly establish context. The steps of a stored computer program effect transitions between well-defined states. The interpretation of these states requires a well-defined context; it must be well defined for the central processing unit to execute successive instructions in a meaningful way. At a primitive level within a program, this context tends to be established in one of two ways: either through a set of registers that are loaded with information that defines the context in which an instruction is interpreted and executed, or through a *stack*. A stack is a sequential series of memory locations into which context information can be loaded. If a specific location within the stack is known, then context information can be positioned relative to this known location. While true, this is context at a much finer level of granularity than we are seeking. In order to draw parallels to human memory, we are interested in establishing the level of context that would allow us to differentiate among mending the wing of our pet parrot, mending the wing of our model airplane or mending the wing of our latest flight of fancy.

To begin to draw the parallels, we can recognize a similar progression in the connection of memory with the facilities of procedural computation in computer systems. These computer mechanisms derived through an evolutionary progression enabled by technological advance and market guidance. In the very earliest machines, there was little external memory associated with the central processing unit of the computer. It had what is often termed *main memory* in which the controlling stored program was contained and on which this stored program impressed the results of minute state transitions. However, the only means of entering or delivering a large volume of information was through punched cards or punched paper tape. As we have noted previously, these were mechanism more worthy of automated looms than of what we now think of as computers. The point is that the available main memory of the earliest computers had extremely limited space for just storing information.

A stored program might contain a section in which it represents a collection of numbers as something called an *array*. With a bit of ingenuity, the stored program can be made to efficiently access one particular number in the array by creating an index into the array. Building on this facility, stored programs then evolved to create arrays that could be logically interpreted as doubly indexed collections of numbers. Thus, two dimension arrays and subsequently tables came into being. It is relatively straightforward to relate these mechanisms to the purely procedural memory facilities of the brain considered by Donald. Note that before arrays or tables are of much use within an operational stored program, actual information must somehow be placed into them. That is, they must be properly provisioned. Once provisioned, these particular variants of memory are indistinguishable from the procedural elements of a program. The memory is just a means of direct support for the procedural code. Context is established by the procedural code and the contents of memory may have no meaning outside of this context.

When technology advanced to the point of providing extensive external computer memory in the form of disk drives and magnetic tapes, the facilities for representing and accessing large volumes of information continued apace. Initially, it became possible to construct sets or tables of information, each perhaps establishing a distinct context for execution within the stored program, and to maintain these tables in external memory; that is, in files on disk drives. This, we suggest, is qualitatively similar to episodic memory. Tables stored in files correlate well to the memories of specific episodes of state transitions within the stored program.

Continuing the progression toward more cognition aware forms of computer memory, we come to databases. These facilities can store large volumes of information in a form that allows for a variety of contexts to be established after the information is actually stored. In particular, databases invite the creation of data models that provide a definition of relationships among individual pieces of information. This allows us, through the mechanism of the data model, to extract the details of a context that the stored program may not have actually encountered. This seems qualitatively akin to the concept of mimesis within the mind of a human.

Thus far, in our considerations any stimulus response to stored information is completely effected through the procedural code of the stored program. Context may be established according to stored information, but motor responses are a generic facility of the program. Throughout the course of this book, we have noted a number of times the development of object-oriented mechanisms within computer systems. Such mechanisms offer the early meanderings toward the metaphoric comprehension of the human mind. In computer parlance, objects entail the hiding of information behind a set of methods that may be invoked on or through a particular object. Objects typically encompass a set of methods through which they are created, provisioned with information, stimulated to evoke some response based on that information and potentially destroyed when their utility is at an end. Such mechanisms have qualitatively similar characteristics to mythic comprehension. A single object may well entail a complete spectrum from the causality of its creation, through its provisioning and on to its subsequent use to evoke context-guided responses to sensory (information) input. It is provided sensory input, but there is no way to look inside the object to see how that sensory information is interpreted or stored. Moreover, objects offer the prospect of extracting aspects of comprehension that can be applied to other contexts.

At the current apex of computer memory facilities are *knowledge bases*. These are constructs comprised of collections of distinct objects that can influence each other's form and function. It is in this arena that the application of ontologies becomes particularly applicable. In this guise, an ontology becomes something of a metaphoric data model encompassing information, actions and interactions. Consequently, we perceive knowledge bases as qualitatively related to the theoretic memory suggested by Donald. They offer the prospect of guiding their own provisioning. Indeed, knowledge bases often comprise the central element of data warehousing and data mining operations. Within a knowledge base, when objects are constructed with a facility for reasoning about the form and function of other objects, then we conceptually see the earliest stages of independent cognitive behavior. From such endeavors, one finds systems that can systematically seek out context, that is information and actions intertwined, that offers at least some flavor of the development processes of humans as they move from infancy to adulthood. We will consider this parallel in more detail just a bit further on.

# Programming Languages

We have been considering human and computer memory. We have expressed memory as a representation of the sensori-motor system that we can reference over time. We use memory to establish context and within that context, we can store and then correctly interpret the recollection of the experiential stimuli and the motor action responses of our mind and body. As we have noted, we do not yet fully understand the basic unit of memory storage within the mind. Moreover, humans apparently do not have an instinctive facility for conveying such units, that is, our memory recollections, between individuals. Thus, it was certainly a mutational event when the species developed the means of such conveyance. In essence, an additional facet was added to the concept of memory. We represent certain contextual interpretation of sensory input and motor action response through *language* and we are then able to convey this interpretation among individuals. We discussed some of the basic characteristics of language in Chapter 4. Along the way, we have alluded to computer programming by referring to formal languages. It might be useful at this point to take at least a cursory look at the concepts and characteristics of these programming languages as an illustration of the bridge between human and computer approaches to cognition.

The march of computers from the time of their emergence until the present follows a path well marked by the progression of languages that have been used to effect their inner workings. All of these languages have been formal languages, but there has been a constant striving to match the natural language facilities of computers' creators. In so doing, there has been a corresponding effort to expand the sensori-motor framework for the metaphorical understanding that accompanies language. With the emergence of secure cores as a derivative but highly specialized form of computer, the spectrum of languages was revisited, with all of the same considerations behind the march and with all the same results in the passing.

Given the small size and relatively slow processor speeds of the earliest secure cores, their initial languages were tightly coupled to the processor foundation of the integrated circuit chip that is the heart and soul of the token. Any processing unit has its basic instruction set grounded in the sensori-motor world that forms its metaphorical base. In the case of secure core systems, this encompasses a vision constrained by very slow and simple input/output to the external environment and an ability to manipulate binary bit patterns in small and slowly accessed memory units. This said, we would now expand on general computer languages.

The basic sensori-motor environment of a general-purpose computer is that of a string of bits, zeroes and ones that can be addressed, accessed and manipulated. The basic instructions required to perform computer-level cognitive functions are bit-manipulation, bit-test and transfer to specific address for the next instruction; different computer processors will make use of a variety of these basic operations. Through these basic operations, the computer must build up a symbolic repertoire of objects and operations on those objects that it knows how to deal with. So, let's consider some of the panoply of programming languages, not to learn any significant number of details about specific languages, but rather to understand some of the very broad characteristics of each that made it useful for addressing certain types of problems.

*Machine language* in a computer is the means through which a central processing unit is instructed how to pursue a series of operations in the sensori-motor environment of the central processing unit. Any machine language presumes a very specific architecture of processor, memory and sometimes extensional elements, all of which determine this basic sensori-motor environment; indeed, machine language is the closest discourse mode that one can enter into with a computer. The general interpretation of machine language instructions is accomplished through a central processing unit that uses a program instruction counter to indicate the instruction to be interpreted (executed) by the central processing unit. A typical architecture will call for the instruction indicated by the program instruction counter to be interpreted and then the program instruction counter is updated so that it points at the next instruction; the full set of instructions is known as a program.

The sensori-motor experience of a central processing unit can be reduced to the manipulation of switched binary elements. That is, the computer's world is comprised of ones and zeros, and its sensory system is oriented toward differentiating a one from a zero and subsequently manipulating strings of ones and zeros. What, one might ask, can be accomplished with such a restrictive environment? Well, pretty much anything within the realm of human interactions, because their complete environment can be represented through the metaphorical manipulation of objects that can in turn be represented by strings of ones and zeros. In short, a computer must be able to locate the position of a binary object; tell if it's a one or a zero; switch to different sets of instructions based on what the test determines; and, change a one to a zero or a zero to a one. With this instruction set as the basic lever, one can move the world. While this seems an ambitious statement, it has been indeed proven that all computer programs resolve to such a humble origin, called a *Turing machine*, as we've discussed in Chapter 4.

One of the first epiphanies for just about anyone that learns computer programming is that of metaphorical representation and extension. This generally takes the form of a rather common experience. Mid-way through their first basic programming course, many people seek to define a number of sub-programs that provide a metaphorical context for the common programming problems thus far encountered. In other words, they begin to extract a number of common threads within the problems that they see and they seek to provide a common programming solution to these problems. The rather natural assumption is then to believe that these common solutions will have general utility to others working on the same problems. Unfortunately, at this stage of their development, most programmers tend to imbue these solutions to common problems with their own specific way of thinking; the solutions embody more of the individual person's cognitive processes than a common view towards many different problems.

Working in machine language requires the programmer to identify procedural operations through binary numeric codes. The addresses of memory locations that contain information to be accessed and processed by these procedural operations must also be identified through binary codes. This type of language is fraught with opportunities for error; it is easy to give the wrong instruction and it is easy to give the wrong memory address. Consequently, a shift in language structure towards that of human natural languages is a positive step, even if it is only a very tiny shift. Such a translation is provided by assembly languages.

*Assembly language* is a slightly higher-level language than machine language. Different assembly languages are typically found for different computer platforms. Generally, an assembly language is very tightly coupled to the machine language for a particular processor. It uses slightly more readable grammar than basic machine language, typically incorporating mnemonics in place of numeric codes for instructions or parameters. Consequently, it is significantly easier to be read by a person than is the corresponding machine language. This enhanced readability tends to decrease the number of programming errors found in any given segment of code.

Since assembly language is so close in form to machine language it is relatively easy to translate it into machine language. In particular, the translation operation can be accomplished in a single scanning pass through the assembly language representation. This makes for very efficient processing on computers that do not have large-scale forms of intermediate memory, as was the case on the earliest computers. Assembly language, however, is still very tightly associated with the sensori-motor environment of the computer. To address problems from the human domain of experience, it is extremely useful to have programming languages that are significantly closer to natural languages. This brings us to the *high-level programming languages.*

As computers grew more powerful, they offered sufficient capabilities to support the use of programming languages that were much closer in form and semantic content to the problems they were used to solve than were either machine languages or assembly languages. These languages are rather generically referred to as high-level languages. While they were close in form to the problems, they were still significantly less capable than the natural languages of human users of computers. We noted above that the earliest mainframe computers tended to be grouped into business-oriented and scientific-oriented systems. Consequently, the earliest high-level languages followed this same decomposition.

FORTRAN, which is an acronym that stands for FORmula TRANslation, has become a well-recognized name in its own right. It refers to a programming language that is very similar to mathematical formulas. FORTRAN has instructions that allow for procedural control of parametric information interspersed with the evaluation of various formulas that incorporate these same parameters. It has found widespread use within the scientific community as a means of dealing with problems that can be well expressed algorithmically. So, what does this really mean? Simply that many scientific oriented problems can be represented through algebraic formulas: one variable connected through an equal sign to a collection of variables related with arithmetic operations. With this type of representation, one seeks to address problems in which the variables in such a formula can be given values and then evaluated to an answer. In many instances, it is necessary to vary the values and parameters in a systematic way and to reevaluate the answer; a process sometimes called *iteration.*

A related, but also significantly different way to express certain problems is through *recursion.* A recursive formulation is typically a formula for a dependent variable that is expressed in terms of itself. Thus, to evaluate the formula, it is necessary to begin with some set of initial conditions, evaluate the dependent variable, and then plug that value back into the formula and evaluate the dependent variable again. This process is repeated until some related characteristic of the relationship indicates that the recursive process is to terminate. Historically FORTRAN had a serious deficiency in not being able to provide recursion in its operations. Although corrected in more recent versions, FORTRAN is nevertheless slowly being supplanted by other languages that have been found superior in dealing with more complex problems that are not exclusively within the scientific realm. As we have noted relative to a number of characteristics, including that of trust, recursion is an important concept relative to real-life problems.

Another early high-level language is COBOL. This acronym stands for COmmon Business Oriented Language, and it was (and still is) used as a mechanism to deal with business problems. We use the term business problems to rather specifically refer to problems couched in the context of finance; for example, working with equations dealing in currency and developing reports through well defined accounting procedures. COBOL is naturally suited by design to express such problems. Among the total number of computer cycles expended today on computational problems of all varieties, a very significant fraction derives from COBOL based programs. However, COBOL is a rather verbose language and it is rather awkward in its formulation of scientific, particularly logic based problems.

Many of the problem areas addressed by programming languages used for creating application level software deal with extremely large amounts of data. Consequently, very powerful subsystems have evolved for efficiently storing such large amounts of information; subsystems termed *databases*. The efficient but comprehensive storage and retrieval of information in databases gave rise to a rather special purpose language termed the *Structured Query Language*, or SQL. This language is quite adept at locating and formatting various sets of data out of an extremely large data store, but it is somewhat lacking in the ability to provide procedural processing on that data.

The C Programming Language is a product of the design methodology that gave rise to the UNIX operating system. C provides many of the mechanisms found in FORTRAN for the expression of algebraic formulas. Moreover, it offers many of the characteristics of assembly languages in allowing the programming to get much closer to the sensori-motor environment of the central processing unit in the formulation of application-level programs. As it happens, some of the mechanisms provided by C are so powerful that they allow the programmer inadvertently to create very subtle problems. Because of this, C is often viewed to be an extremely sharp-edged tool. One can carve beautiful sculptures with it, but one risks cutting off a useful appendage along the way. C offers very powerful constructs for representing complex data structures. In so doing, it came perhaps closer than other prior mainstream languages to establishing a strong context facility; but it does not yet go far enough to approach the capabilities of the brain in supporting metaphorical understanding, which is the desired derivative of effective context. That is perhaps achieved through *object-oriented languages*.

In Chapter 4, we noted the development of the Simula language as perhaps the earliest example of an object-oriented programming language. Object-oriented languages provide for contextual encapsulation of data together with procedural actions to be applied to that data. Such languages take us much closer to the metaphorical understanding facilities of the human brain. Over the course of development of high-level programming languages, significant efforts have been made to morph these into object-oriented varieties. Two of the more popular such variants are the C++ and the Java languages.

C++ is a derivative of the C language. It was initially developed by Bjarne Stroustrup. While C++ encompasses the C language for purely procedural aspects, it provides for the creation and use of encapsulated data plus procedural elements that we can then think of as metaphorical constructs called *objects*. As a direct illustration of evolutionary construction, the data map to C language structures and the methods that can act on this data map to C language sub-programs. Object-oriented languages provide a limited degree of metaphorical abstraction by enabling capabilities termed *inheritance* and *specialization*. Specialization allows one to create a new object that is substantially like a previously established object and inheritance allows actions established for that previously defined object to be applied to the new object. The two capabilities provide a first approximation to a metaphorical context, a step toward the cognitive languages we will present next in this chapter.

Java is a product of Sun Microsystems with its principal creator being James Gosling. If one talks to Sun, that is if one reaches for the general corporate message about Java, one is told that Java is much more than a programming language. It is portrayed as a comprehensive environment for allowing software to be written and to operate in a network environment. In fact, Java does encompass many of these far-reaching characteristics. But, from our perspective, the most interesting characteristics are those that would portray Java as a language; in particular, a powerful object-oriented language. As with the C language, Java adopts the algebraic formula constructs first popularized in FORTRAN. But, it is in the formulation of its object-orientedness that Java offers some significant enhancements to the metaphorical abstraction process that object-oriented programming brings to the table.

Java was originally written to be moved around various computer platforms of a wide-area network and to run wherever it found temporary or permanent residence. To enable this capability, a Java program had to be well insulated from the environment in which it found itself; it had to operate within a highly restricted sensori-motor environment. The greater the sensori-motor facilities required by a program, the greater was the surrounding support environment. In the extreme, the support environment could be so comprehensive that it was likely to be found on only a small portion of the platforms in a wide-area network. However, as Java was thrust forward to compete with the entrenched operating systems of the day, with Windows or UNIX, it had to adopt many of the heavy-weighted facilities of those systems. But, where Java could be viewed in its more focused context as a programming language, it offered some truly mutational characteristics. Principal among these is security.

A Java program was envisioned as an instruction set for a virtual computer. This has proven a valuable trait for other languages and other environments. Perhaps the most innovative aspect of Java was the provision of a protected context for that virtual computer; this context was termed a *sandbox*. It is a very telling metaphor. Many of us remember a sandbox as a playtime environment from our formative years. It was an environment in which we could construct a variety of make-believe worlds, products of our own innovation guided by our own perceptions of the world around us as evidenced by our sensori-motor experiences. Indeed, as we will see just a bit later, sandboxes tend to be relished during the cognitive development stage in which fantasy is a significant aspect of the way that we think. If sandboxes were well constructed, each child's area was distinctly separate from others. If more than one was to play in a sandbox at one time, it was truly necessary for us to play nicely together. If we could not accomplish this, then the experience was probably going to turn out badly. Within one sandbox, it was just too easy to destroy the adjacent imaginary worlds. This is perhaps a bit more of a buildup than is necessary to talk about Java, but it is central to the metaphorical constructs that Java enables.

In its earliest incarnations, Java enabled its sandbox through the characteristics of the language itself. The language provided constructs that allowed a programmer to exploit fully the extent of the sandbox, but the language would not allow a program even to refer to the areas outside of the sandbox. As we have previously noted, if a high-level language does not encompass certain abstractions, it can be very difficult or even impossible to carry on a discourse about these abstractions. For example, Java allowed a programmer to establish a data domain in the form of objects. If the Java compiler then followed the rules of Java, the program could not even refer to objects that were not of its own creation. One could simply not express the thought to "read data from an object outside the sandbox."

Because of market pressures, Java has evolved in the direction of a more traditional language and computer-programming environment. The earlier purity of its methodology was extremely well suited to the secure core facilities that we have discussed throughout the course of this book. Specifically, to address more fully the arena of larger scale problems, it was necessary to evolve Java to allow cross sandbox communication. This, unfortunately, had the tendency to abrogate the strengths presented by sandboxes in the first place. Perhaps more detrimental however was the lack of system level establishment of inter-sandbox trust mechanisms. In other words, the evolved Java presented much the same set of problems that computer networks in general have in supporting human social ecosystem facilities related to identity and belonging.

# Languages of Cognition

The programming languages that we have briefly considered up to this point have the consistent aim of defining procedural flows through which distinct states of a computer, including its various sensori-motor components, are transitioned from one state to the next. In the course of these transitions, human level sensori-motor information is translated to and from the computer sensori-motor environment. Any reasoning that we can do about this information is constrained to the procedural flows that we define through these programming languages. In order for computers to aim towards functioning at what we might think of as a higher cognitive level, it would be useful to have at our disposal language constructs that facilitate reasoning about such information through the procedural flows created with the more classical programming languages. We might think of such languages as cognition languages. The primary evolutionary path for such languages has been a succession of what are termed markup languages. In Chapter 5 we presented the role of the Extended Markup Language, or XML, in the evolution of computer content. Before we see the role of XML beyond content, i.e. as a conveyor of cognition, let's look at a brief history of this breakthrough language.

Markup languages began with the creation of the Generalized Markup Language at IBM during the 1960's. The idea came from something that is now very familiar to any user of Microsoft Word, and surely, most of our readers are in this category. When writing in Word, we point to a specific piece of text in our document, and we label it as "Title", "Paragraph", "Footnote", and the like. Nowadays, we do that using a pull-down menu on our screen, but in the 1960's and 1970's, this was done by introducing labels in the text itself. For example, with the Generalized Markup Language, we would put in our text something like:

```
:title. Computer Theology
```

When this was printed in its final form, we would not see the ":title." part. What we would see is "Computer Theology" at the proper place in the document, say centered, at the top of the first page, in large fonts. Now, you are going to ask, how did the computer know what to do with that ":title." tag? Well, this was specified separately, so that many documents could share the same definition for a title, ensuring uniformity in all documents produced by, say, a company or an individual.

While the idea is simple enough, we will see that it would eventually contribute to the revolution of the World Wide Web. However, before getting there, we pass through the 1980's. By that time, there was a proliferation of text annotation languages similar to the Generalized Markup Language. It was time to put some order in the mayhem, and the International Standards Organization eventually published a comprehensive standard called, appropriately, the Standard Generalized Markup Language (ISO 8879). Using SGML, we would define the title as follows:

```
| <title> Computer Theology </title>
```

The idea of course is that we can readily see where the end of the title is, allowing us to have the title expand on several lines if needed. While that is some progress, what we would like to emphasize is the angle brackets around "title". While seemingly innocuous, this is very significant in a way that we will try to explain, because it is the source of the cognition capabilities of successors to the language. Bear with us, because we will go a bit technical here in hopes of doing justice to the importance of the subject. We have not been able to trace who had the idea of using the angle bracket notation; perhaps it is an anonymous genius within the working groups of the International Standards Organization (ISO), or perhaps our research has not been thorough enough. In any case, we believe that we can interpret the thinking of the person who did it, because the angle brackets are exactly the same brackets that are used for what is called the Backus-Naur notation. Why is that important, you might ask? Well, this notation is used to describe computer languages. For example, we can say in the Backus-Naur notation, simplifying a little:

```
| <document-title> ::= <title> <title-text> </title>
```

We realize this line is perhaps awkward to read, as the "::=" notation is rather arcane. However, please bear with us for just a bit longer. What the Backus-Naur notation has done for us is allowing further expression of the structure of our document. What we previously said informally, namely "Here is the title of my document," now we have expressed formally. The difference is that while a computer has difficulty understanding "Here is the title of my document," for reasons we will not explore at this point, it has no problem understanding <document-title> ::= <title> <title-text> </title>. For the computer, it means that a document title is what is found between the <title> and </title> elements. What has thus been accomplished is teaching the computer to think a little more like we do (lest we be misunderstood, we need to emphasize here for the cognoscenti that we are purposely avoiding the word meta-language to eschew debating its relationship to classification, and that we are purposely attributing a morphological nature to angle brackets to load them semantically). In other words, we elevated slightly the cognitive level of the computer. However, we are not yet finished. Now, we can explain the light of genius of our unknown inventor. What the Backus-Naur translates is in fact what is called a *grammar*. Yes, essentially the same grammar we have all learned at school, but the formal version that computers understand. Now for example, using the same notation that we have used for our document, we can describe grammatical elements (our linguist readers will pardon us for the simplification):

```
| <sentence> ::= <subject><verb><object>
```

With that description at hand, we can parse sentences such as "John loves Mary," or "The bridge crosses the river." Hopefully, now you see clearly that by using the seemingly innocuous angle brackets, the International Standards Organization committee has imparted the Standardized Generalized Markup Language with a theoretical heritage. This will allow us, in time, to use the same language for people (that is the grammatical heritage, dating back thousand of years) and computers (that is the document markup heritage, dating back a few decades). Before we go further, we cannot help noticing that our anonymous genius was certainly aware of the publication of the seminal 1963 paper by Noam Chomsky and Marcel-Paul Schützenberger, *The algebraic theory of context free languages*. This paper, for the first time, united the traditional field of linguistics (Noam) with the new field of computer science (Marcel-Paul); which is exactly what the commonality of the angle brackets in the two domains expresses. To close the loop of connections, one of the authors (Bertrand) published an article in *Linguistic Inquiry* just after one by Noam Chomsky in 1978, and he had Marcel-Paul Schützenberger as his PhD jury president in 1977. Perhaps, in truth, that was the origin of this book.

To build up cognition languages from the strong basis of the Standardized Generalized Markup Language, another genius, well recognized this time, needed to intervene. Tim Berners-Lee, inventor of the World Wide Web, rooted the Web in that language. Most of the Web pages we read everyday on our computers are written in a simplified version of the Standardized Generalized Markup Language, called HTML, for HyperText Markup Language. What Berners-Lee did was marry markup languages with the Internet, hereby opening the opportunity for another step in the cognition climb of computers. Moreover, within a relatively short time came XML, the eXtended Markup Language. As we have seen in Chapter 5, it was then possible for computers to communicate via a language that was finally offering, thanks to its filiation, the possibility for them to enter the era of enhanced cognitive performance. However, enough theory; let us see how this is done through an example.

# The Structure of Metaphors

A significant leap on the evolutionary ladder in the development of cognitive abilities within the human species was taken when the mind became able to consider objects in an abstract way through metaphorical associations. For example, the ability of a person to manipulate objects through the fine motor skills of the hands can be a foundation for development. Some operations on numbers emanate from the same area of the brain that deals with the manipulation of objects, as presented by George Lakoff and Rafael Núñez in *Where Mathematics Comes From*. This corroborates the concept of the sensori-motor experience providing the basis for metaphorical understanding and thought at a higher cognitive level. Here, we are interested in the expression in a formal language of the metaphorical meanings of abstract concepts. If we succeed in doing so, we will have illustrated some of the cognitive power of modern computer languages.

The variety of metaphoric phenomena has been recognized for a long time, and an early modern description was done by Christine Brooke-Rose in *A Grammar of Metaphor*. More broadly, metaphors belong to a more general category of symbolic expressions, as presented by James Fernandez, editor of *Beyond Metaphor, The Theory of Tropes in Anthropology*. More modestly, in the following, we will consider a metaphoric construction inspired from the seminal *Metaphors We Live By*, by George Lakoff and Mark Johnson:

"We have a warm relationship. It works well. We are very close. "

These three sentences are called metaphors because at first consideration they seem grounded in physical phenomena unrelated to their actual expression. Warmth is first associated with physical implements elevating temperature, say fire or weather, work is associated with the physical experience of creating structure, and closeness is associated with the immediate perception of distance. To consider the latter, there is a difference between "We are very close" in the expression of a relationship, meaning, say "We love each other dearly," and the same sentence in the expression of a small physical distance, meaning, say, "We are sitting two feet apart." Similarly, there is a difference between a relationship that works well, as in "We like each other," and machinery, say a car or an electric saw, that works well, as in (another set of metaphors) "It runs like a charm."

While we can see a difference between a warm oven, or a warm motor, and a warm relationship, this example will in fact open the door to a more sophisticated understanding of metaphors. While, in all three sentences, the difference may be characterized as one of abstract (metaphoric) and concrete (real) implements, one should review in detail that difference, and we will start with the concept of warmth as related to relationship. At least in certain circumstances, a good relationship is actually related to a direct elevation of body temperature: we have all experienced the rush associated with courtship, and the coldness we feel when indifference sinks in. Therefore, there is a bridge between the experience of warmth traceable to direct heat transfer from inanimate objects and that resulting from personal interaction. However, can we model that? What we would propose here, in XML, would be:

```
<Body>
   <Temperature> High </Temperature>
</Body>
```

We have defined a formula that is independent of the context in expressing our body's reaction to external events with an actual, or perceived, elevation of temperature. However, we can readily identify different causes, depending on the situation, that we can now formalize. In both formulations below, we are just using the power of our formal language to describe cause and effect. In the case of fire:

```
<Determination>
   <Cause> Fire </Cause>
   <Effect>
      <Body>
         <Temperature> High </Temperature>
      </Body>
   </Effect>
</Determination>
```

In the case of relationship:

```
<Determination>
   <Cause> Relationship </Cause>
   <Effect>
      <Body>
         <Temperature> High </Temperature>
      </Body>
   </Effect>
</Determination>
```

Now let us consider the hypothetical situation of two persons separated by two languages, say one speaking English and the other one French, neither of whom speaks the other's language. In front of a fire, it is easy for one of the protagonists to point to a fire and make a sign expressing comfort. Going one-step further, the two can point again to the fire and say, "warm" in English, and "chaud" in French. They can thereafter agree on a name for the situation. This way, a direct physical experience has been translated into a symbolic expression, and that yields to, in English:

```
<Fire>
   <Property> Warm </Property>
</Fire>
```

The difference between the concrete, readily shared experience of the fire, and the abstract, subjective experience of a relationship, is the lack, or frailty, of direct observation of the latter. I may feel a warm relationship with you, but that may leave you cold. Unlike the situation with the fire, we cannot point directly to the artifact at hand. We need an intermediate representation. How am I then to express my sentiment? Coming back to our protagonists, an obvious way is for one to make a sign relating the two persons, and saying "warm." While in the presence of fire, that would mostly be understood as "We are both warm." In the absence of any particular source of heat, that might be understood as "Let's find a fire to get warm."

Alternatively, and we have now passed the threshold of metaphoric understanding, it might be understood as "Our relationship is giving me a comfort similar to the fire." Clearly, that requires a formidable advance in cognitive capabilities. Fortunately, we have just seen in excruciating detail where this advance lies: in the capability to elaborate on a symbol that can be used in a situation different from the original usage. The build-up of symbolism has been studied in some detail by Terrence Deacon in *The Symbolic Species*. Whether we express the relationship with the word "warm", or, as in certain cultures, by rubbing both our indexes against each other, we have introduced an intermediate symbol. Now let us come back to our subject, and formally express the metaphor, a step beyond Deacon's elaboration. This part of our formal description is a little cumbersome, but it is a necessary step. The directly observable artifact on which the metaphor is based is called *source*, the abstract construct that the metaphor builds is called *target*:

```
<Metaphor>
   <Source>
      <Determination>
         <Cause> Fire </Cause>
         <Effect>
            <Body>
               <Temperature> High </Temperature>
            </Body>
         </Effect>
         <Property> Warm </Property>
      </Determination>
   </Source>
   <Target>
      <Determination>
         <Cause> Relationship </Cause>
         <Effect>
            <Body>
               <Temperature> High </Temperature>
            </Body>
         </Effect>
         <Property> Warm </Property>
      </Determination>
   </Target>
<Metaphor>
```

Here is the final step, which will in fact, use the metaphoric capabilities of the reader. We can define the rule that allows building a metaphor such as the one above. As this is quite technical, the casual reader may want to avert their eyes for a moment. Suffice it to say that the rule looks at a pattern, specified with the introduction of filler variables such as "A", "X" and "P", below, and expresses the pattern change created by the metaphor. As complicated as it looks, the reader needs to be aware that we have considerable simplified the presentation. However, we still hope that the idea goes through. The rule is as follows, where the *premise* specifies the pattern to be matched, and the *conclusion* creates the associated metaphor:

```
<Rule>
    <Premise>
        <Union>
            <Determination>
                <Cause> A </Cause>
                <Effect> X </Effect>
                <Property> P </Property>
            </Determination>
            <Determination>
                <Cause> B </Cause>
                <Effect> X </Effect>
            </Determination>
    <Conclusion>
        <Determination>
            <Cause> B </Cause>
            <Effect> X </Effect>
            <Property> P </Property>
        </Determination>
</Rule>
```

What we have just expressed is indeed the rule used in building the earlier metaphor. We have left many details aside, but what remains to be done is to test the validity of the rule with the other parts of our example. Let us consider "Our relationship works well." Application of the rule yields the following, as the filler variables have been replaced in the rule by A = machine, X = orderly process, P = works, and B = relationship. The property "works", initially attached to the machine, conveys to the relationship:

```
<Metaphor>
    <Source>
        <Determination>
            <Cause> Machine </Cause>
            <Effect>
                <Process>
                    <Progress> Orderly </Progress>
                </Process>
            </Effect>
            <Property> Works </Property>
        </Determination>
    </Source>
    <Target>
        <Determination>
            <Cause> Relationship </Cause>
            <Effect>
                <Process>
                    <Progress> Orderly </Progress>
                <Process>
            </Effect>
            <Property> Works </Property>
        </Determination>
    </Target>
<Metaphor>
```

All this says is that the orderly progress of a process, derived from its realization in a machine, is akin to a similar progress expressed by a relationship. Both "work," even as the former may be more directly observable than the latter. Actually, it is easy to imagine, nowadays, machines that are more difficult to understand than a relationship. That would put into question the actual order in which metaphors may be derived, but it is beyond the scope of this discussion to venture into that territory. We will content ourselves with letting the reader try the rule on the last sentence of our example, "We are very close."

At this point, we have seen how a formal language, XML, can be used to model quintessential human capabilities like the expression of metaphor. While we have simplified the demonstration, we will refer the reader to *Generics and Metaphors Unified under a Four-Layer Semantic Theory of Concepts*, which one of the authors (Bertrand) has published with Yi Mao at the Third Conference on Experience and Truth in 2006. While the paper is less accessible than the presentation herein (imagine that!), it follows the canons of publication in the field of logic (using Richard Montague's *Formal Philosophy*) for the phenomena that we just described.

Thanks to cognitive languages, computers have now means to venture into areas previously reserved to humans. We are getting ready to come back to the processes of religion and sciences that we discussed earlier. However, we will first look at the beginning of it all, the provisioning of the capabilities that we now recognize in both human and computers.

# Evolution of Secure Core Software

With the emergence of secure core components in the late 1970's and early 1980's, a common software paradigm was followed for the development of secure systems. Within this paradigm, the secure core was envisioned as a component of a larger system, a component that could be used to establish the presence of a person at a point of interaction with some degree of assurance as to the integrity of this presence. In other words, the secure core was a mechanism to enhance the level of trust in the ensuing interaction.

The secure core could be made part of a token, for example a card that was carried on the person. The software found on the token was designed in specific relation to the larger system. The information stored on the token and the operations performed on the token were part of the context of the larger system. The token was typically given a physical interface through which it could then be accessed at a specific interaction point. The details of this physical interface might well vary from system to system. This approach tended to minimize, if not completely eliminate the possibility of using a specific token in multiple systems. The earliest incarnations of such a mechanism were obviously similar in characteristics to a door key, given that this is the model on which the token is based. One can have a system of arbitrary size and complexity locked away in a room behind a door. If the key to the door is presented, then the door can be opened and the full system exposed. Without the key, the system remains inaccessible.

In the course of deploying a number of systems in this manner, many similar problems were identified as characteristic of the use of tokens, independent of the larger scale system that they were used in. Rather obviously, one of the first recognized areas of commonality was the need for consistent physical interfaces between system interaction points and tokens. This led to the development of standards for interface that were used to connect tokens to general-purpose systems that provided the services enabled by the tokens. Many purely software level commonality issues were identified as well. For example, the need to establish some sort of authentication linkage between the token and token bearer was necessary in order to prevent a token that was lost from being easily used by a different person. A major goal of the use of a token was enhanced security of interactions, so such a linkage was important no matter the details of the specific system in question. The mechanism that evolved to meet this need was that of *bearer verification*. When the token was connected to some interface device at an interaction point, the token bearer was asked to enter a personal identification number. This number was then conveyed to the token and compared with a stored value that was, in fact, a secret number that had been placed there by the token bearer when the token was first issued. The number was ostensibly known only by the token bearer and the software on the token, so it could be used to authenticate the identity of the token bearer *to the token*. While the general theme of this operation might be similar from one system to the next, the details of the operation were quite system specific.

Standardization of a number of such common operations was one of the first consolidating events in the evolutionary progression of secure core software.

This effort began in the late 1980's within the International Standards Organization to establish a series of international standards related to secure core technology. This effort was driven largely by the financial industry but it garnered the development support from a variety of both manufacturers and large-scale issuers of tokens, like mobile phone operators. The result was the establishment of a family of standards related to tokens based on integrated circuit chips, the foundation of which define basic physical interfaces between integrated circuit chips and interface devices, communication protocols used by tokens and inter-industry services provided by compliant tokens. Through the years, this ISO/IEC 7816 family of standards has continued to evolve.

Using these standards, the software to be resident on the token was designed, developed and installed on the token prior to its issuance to the token bearer. In the early 1990's began the development of what became the Multos system, as we discussed earlier. This new paradigm involved the installation of a virtual machine interpreter on the token, allowing subsequent trusted installation of new software, even after the token had been issued. In the late 1990's, this was followed by a similar effort that made use of the Java language as the basis for the on-token virtual machine. By the end of the millennium, these efforts had resulted in a significant transformation of the secure core software environment. As we have previously noted, a major driver in this transformation came through the standardization efforts of the European Telecommunications Standards Institute in the form of standards for the use of such tokens as Subscriber Identity Modules in GSM cellular phones worldwide.

Essentially, in parallel with the development of so-called *post-issuance programmable* tokens, an evolution was also occurring in the form of enhanced cryptographic capabilities on tokens. The addition of a cryptographic co-processor allowed for the efficient utilization of complex algorithms. An example is the famous RSA algorithm. Named after its inventors, Ron Rivest, Adi Shamir and Leonard Adleman, this algorithm forms the basis of asymmetric key cryptography. This facilitated the deployment of public key infrastructures, thus laying the groundwork for tokens to become the ubiquitous purveyors of identification services. When coupled with efforts from the financial community to specify common protection mechanisms for the applications in the token, in a new organization called GlobalPlatform, tokens came to much greater utility within wide area computer networks.

Indeed, the first decade of the new millennium has seen the evolution of token systems centered upon their integration into more comprehensive computer platforms. Essentially, moves are afoot to integrate seamless secure core support into the operating systems of general computer platforms. This presents something of an evolutionary quandary. Tokens may become easier to incorporate into widespread application systems or they may be supplanted with competing mechanisms within these general computer systems. We will be considering this in more detail in the remaining chapters of this book. For the moment though, let us step back just a bit and see if we can identify some parallels between the manner in which secure core tokens are made operational and the way that people are made operational.

# Provisioning the Mind

Jean Piaget, who died in 1980 at the age of 84 was an eminent developmental psychologist and was noted, among other achievements, for developing a theory of cognitive development that offers rather profound insight into the progression of the human mind from infancy into adulthood. His far-reaching epiphany was that at different ages, the mind of a developing person is driven by different requirements and consequently the cognitive process actually changes over time. This observation might well suggest that the needs hierarchy that Maslow suggested for adult humans might have a different structure and perhaps even different elements if viewed in some age related manner. That goes well beyond our current considerations. Rather, we want to examine the developmental processes observed by Piaget in terms of the human mind being prepared for its fully capable functionality that we associate with the adult person. Our observation is that this set of processes is akin to the activity of provisioning a computer system such that it is fully capable of engaging in one or more application-level processes. What Piaget discovered, and what offers an interesting parallel to preparation of software systems for computer platforms, is that there is a well-defined process engaged in the preparation of the fully functional mind.

In conducting psychological interviews with children, Piaget noted that their responses tended to differ from those of adults, but they differed in consistent ways. Thus, children at equivalent development levels tended to think alike, albeit differently from the way that adults think. It was not that children had a different, more limited set of knowledge at their disposal compared to adults; that would be expected. It was that children appeared to reason about the questions that they were asked in a manner consistently different from the way adults reasoned about those same questions. He ultimately identified four distinct stages of human cognitive development: (a) sensori-motor, (b) symbolic, (c) concrete and (d) formal.

Our discussion in this and the following sections relates to *The Psychology of the Child* by Jean Piaget and Bärbel Inhelder. While we will stay quite close to this work as we pursue our subject, we are aware that our description should be updated and nuanced with reference to subsequent studies. However, while this would provide a more modern version of the subject, it would not alter the fundamental premise that provisioning of the human mind occurs, and the subsequent observation that similar operations are found in computer networks. Therefore, we will be content with this simplified version of the science in the domain.

It is particularly pertinent for us to recognize the two mechanisms that Piaget identifies in describing actual learning during the development stages: assimilation and accommodation. We will consider the telltale phrase "... the equilibrium between assimilation of things to the subject's action and accommodation of subjective schemes to modifications of things" (our translation) on page 152 of Piaget's *La psychologie de l'intelligence*. Assimilation is the immediate process of using the environment in a manner that allows it to be incorporated into existing cognitive constructs within the mind. This process seems akin to the mimetic learning discussed by Donald. Accommodation is the contrasting approach of modifying existing cognitive constructs to fit with the observed environment. This seems akin to Donald's mythic process. The point to these observations is simply that there appears to be corollary activities between the physiological processes supported by the brain and the resulting social activities undertaken by the individual person in bringing the resulting mind up to an operational timber. In this, the cognitive development process appears a close parallel to the provisioning activities of computer software, where the subsequent layers of software correspond to different network protocol levels of interaction.

The *sensori-motor stage* lasts from infancy until a child is approximately two years old. During this period, the infant is enabling its sensori-motor system. Indeed, the iconic image of the normal birth of a child is that of the physician or midwife swatting the baby's buttocks as a means to help clear the airways of fluid and to induce the baby to inhale and thereby fill its lungs with air. From a computer perspective, we cannot help but only slightly facetiously relate this to a reset operation on a computer system. The biophysical structure is largely in place at birth, although certainly neurological and anatomical developments do occur after birth; in fact, it takes several years before an infant becomes a fully functional adult human. That distinction aside, however, the infant does have the necessary muscles, structural support, nerves and brain in place to make effective use of its sensori-motor system. However, it requires experiential development before that effective use can actually occur. So, in the first stage of human development the infant must learn about its connection to the world around it.

As we observed in Chapter 4, one aspect of this stage is the calibration of the emotional response system. While certain very basic emotional levels seem pre-disposed from genetic development, the nuanced features of emotions seem to require a learning process. It is during this stage that the infant comes to realize that it is distinct from the world around it, and that the foundations of metaphorical understanding are laid. This entails acquiring the understanding of permanence of external things and events, the understanding that things can still exist even through they are outside the direct purview of the infant's sensori-motor system.

The learning process on the part of the infant is heavily dependent on the sensori-motor system at this level. The feedback mechanisms utilized proceed through the senses in order to effect the elemental emotional states that are being learned, not through the higher cognitive functions of the mind. Lessons learned through direct experience are recorded in an episodic manner. The real pain of touching a hot iron or the perceived pain derived from a warning sound or gesture from its mother are the effective mechanisms for teaching the infant about safely interacting with the surrounding environment. This is definitely not the time to give an infant lessons in the safe use of household implements. It is just not going to be effective to do so. Rather, we tend toward the ubiquitous admonition; "Don't touch that!" During this stage of development, generalizations are not particularly effective; the rules of engagement must be learned essentially one experience at a time.

The learning process begins with the use of non-language mechanisms; facial expressions, hand and body gestures, tactile sensation and rudimentary sounds suffice in place of natural language. Nevertheless, it is during this stage that the basic groundwork is laid for the subsequent mastery of language, as illustrated by Michael Tomasello in two complementary books, *The Cultural Origins of Human Cognition* and *Constructing a Language*. Probably nothing is more amazing to the parent than seeing the transition of a burbling, randomly gesturing infant into the defiant two-plus who is certainly capable of saying "No!" and then backing it up with moderately complete sentences.

In concert with a child mastering the underpinnings of language, a transition occurs into a new developmental stage; the *symbolic stage* (also called semiotic by Piaget and Inhelder). This lasts from about the age of two until about the age of seven years. During this stage, the child establishes in particular some facility for the manipulation of objects; fine motor skills from a physical perspective and basic arithmetic operations from a cognitive perspective. Indeed, it is during this stage that a child is introduced to the concept of counting. While it is jumping the gun just a bit, we will note that in the next chapter we will suggest a correlation between the concept of counting and the concept of identity and identification. This will be instrumental in addressing the need of belonging, beyond the physiological and safety needs that we began to see addressed in the initial sensori-motor stage. Thus, we observe that the progression through the developmental stages continues to take us up the ascending needs hierarchy. In essence, as part of our development from infancy toward adulthood, we acquire physical and cognitive mechanisms that will be instrumental in our ultimately being able to respond to the stimuli engendered through needs based appetites.

During the symbolic stage, a child learns to use symbols as representative of objects or groups of objects. Children initially consider all objects from their own perspective. In a process he calls *decentration*, Piaget presents in *The Psychology of Intelligence* the steps leading children to perceive themselves as agents in an independently autonomous world. A simple example of centration is the initial perception by the child of the mountain getting higher as the walk progresses. A more intricate one is that of the child viewing pearls transferred from one vase to another and considering that, depending on the form of the second vase, there are more or fewer pearls in it than in the first. It can take up to the age of seven or eight years for the child to associate certain rotated or inverted representations of objects with the correct corresponding objects. Eventually, the process of decentration leads us to acknowledge the world as the world acknowledges us. We suggest that its progression indicates the early stages of satisfying the need for esteem. This is accomplished through reflection on one's position in the world. We would also observe that this takes the child down the path toward metaphorical understanding and reasoning. Within this stage, the child is able to conceptualize existence, both of objects through symbolic representation and of action responses (events) through establishment of context.

During this stage, fantasy has a strong influence on the understanding and belief system of the child. This would seem to relate to the willingness to search for causality in the supernatural when one's understanding of the physical ecosystem is limited. Indeed, given the propensity for evolutionary based development to reflect phylogenetic processes in ontogenetic characteristics, this stage suggests some parallels with the mythic cultural phase of human memory development as described by Merlin Donald.

In addition, during this stage the fact that cognitive processes are still primarily egocentric suggests that development has not yet reached the level of fully relating to the higher levels of the needs hierarchy. In particular, the individual is not yet fully capable of responding to cognitive needs at or above esteem. Full logical thought is not yet supported, which leads us to think that process-based trust lags the causality-based trust mechanisms that we discussed in the previous chapter.

Around the age of seven, a child transitions into the *concrete operations* stage of development. This stage lasts from about seven to about eleven years of age and is characterized by the onset of logical thought, particularly as it relates to concrete objects. One facet of this basis in logic is the ability of the mind to quantify in a number of ways, such as numbers, space, time, speed, causality and randomness. This capability of recognizing conservation represents a calibration of the mind's involvement with the symbolic representations grounded in the sensori-motor environment of the body. Accommodation as a learning process tends to increase during this stage. Essentially, the individual's mind becomes engaged in developing truly personal rules of interaction, with such concepts of socialization as duty, heteronomy, moral realism and autonomy. We haven't used the term policy for a while, but this stage of development certainly invites interpretation as one in which personal preferences are developed that will guide participation in formally defined social ecosystems. During this stage, the individual's level of egocentric cognition diminishes, with an increasing propensity for immersion in the constraints of externally defined social ecosystems.

The final stage of cognitive development involves the transition to learning and thinking through structured and formal abstract processes primarily derived from scholarly education, for example regarding combinatorics and statistics. During this *formal stage*, the mind tends to engage in the consideration of hypothetical situations and reasoning about these situations. In other words, the mind fully engages the facilities of formal logic. Once entered, the formal operations stage lasts from about the age of twelve through the remainder of the individual's life. This stage of development seems most capable of giving support to the highest levels of the needs hierarchy; specifically, self-actualization and transcendence.

# Provisioning of Software

The developmental stages identified by Piaget and Inhelder can be viewed as a series of provisioning operations for the human mind. While the physiological structure of the brain and its subsequent facilities for information acquisition, storage and retrieval are systematically defined by biological processes, the actual acquisition of information, the process of learning, is a dynamic process that must be engaged by every individual. Piaget suggested that these dynamic processes proceed according to what he called *schemes* in *The Psychology of Intelligence*. He suggested that the initial scheme that guided the development of the infant from birth was what he called reflexes. As the infant progresses in its development, the reflexive schemes are supplanted by schemes developed within the cognitive processes of the infant's mind. We observe that, from at least a qualitative viewpoint, one can see an analog with the progression up the needs hierarchy reflected in the successive cognitively developed schemes that guide the child's developmental stages identified by Piaget.

The provisioning process appears to follow a very systematic progression, a progression that is replicated among most individuals. It would seem to us that the manner of this provisioning, specifically its ordering, has impact on the trust that can be derived from its subsequent use. The same holds true for computer systems. In essence, for the individual person or computer to develop a solid basis for the determination of trust relative to interactions, then the mind in one case, and the software systems in the other, must be provisioned through a process that is itself trusted. Once again, it would seem that the needs hierarchy provides an excellent guide as to what this ordering should be, synchronized by ritual passages of life, formal releases and handovers.

Physiological processes are strongly related to structural facilities. In organic systems, biological mechanisms hold sway over the architecture of physiological processes. Safety and security, while involving higher cognitive and hence more variable processes, are grounded in that architecture as well. Belonging, however, introduces the concept of identity and identification; in computer systems, this relates to the causality involved in protocol design and in the procedures through which are determined the keys or other markers of individual identity. Subsequent to the development and deployment of software on a trusted platform such as the secure cores that we have considered from time to time, it is necessary to provide information related to the specific bearer of the secure core system. This act typically entails the gathering of information keyed to the identity of the token bearer. To assure the ultimate trustworthiness of the computer system it is mandatory that all this provisioning be accomplished in a trustworthy manner.

The higher level needs, while grounded in the causality of architectures and processes, are heavily based on acquired information content. In other words, the higher level needs stimulate both the acquisition of information and the use of that information to sate the needs-induced appetites. Thus, we see the progression starting with the provision of trusted platforms, followed by the provision of trusted software, followed by the provision of trust mechanisms including identity and then followed by provision of support for higher cognitive activities.

# Consequences

Perhaps the most difficult aspect of social ecosystem interactions to model, whether computer based or purely human to human without computer intervention, are the consequences of an interaction. If interactions are well defined and well structured, and if the interaction stimuli of the various participants are well aligned, then the primary purpose of an interaction can be the arrival at an intended consequence as defined by all the participant parties; this much is fairly well understood. Indeed, most interactions arrive at a conclusion that is accepted by the parties involved. Problems with social ecosystem interactions arise when they need to involve subjective determination of interaction status and results. In other words, social ecosystem interactions are often based on a *political* decision process. This sometimes portends difficulty in actually bringing final closure to the interaction. This process is made all the more difficult if the interaction stimuli for the various parties originate from different levels of the needs hierarchy. In essence, a particular interaction may have a far different level of urgency for one party than for the other party, and, as a result, a far greater anticipation of the consequences of the interaction. This may make the assessment as to whether the interaction has been properly conducted and the result appropriately arrived at very different for one party versus the other.

Within a policy infrastructure, interactions proceed according to the rules established within that infrastructure. For interactions involving people, either directly or indirectly, the stimulus for interaction is recursive application of the needs hierarchy. Recursion in this case implies the net consideration of the full range of needs relative to a specific interaction. An overarching consideration in the conduct of the interaction is that of the intermediate and ultimate consequences. Across a spectrum of policy infrastructures, ranging from the physical ecosystem to a succession of applicable social ecosystems, we see that the interaction mechanism can itself range from the direct, objective application of physical laws to the recursive, subjective application of the rules of competing social systems. This subjective application of opportunistically defined rules is an example of what has come to be known as *politics*.

The formal definition of the concept and term politics is often couched in the structured interactions of secular governance, the process of creation and application of law, as opposed to the more informal interactions that we all engage in on a continuing basis. However, popular usage of the term recognizes it as an interaction process that influences the full range of our social ecosystems. "The Boss selected Mary rather than James to be the new Department Head because of office politics." While used in this context, the term politics has a pejorative connotation, we suggest that it is merely an indicator of a recursive application of needs, and that the stimulus impact of the human needs hierarchy varies from person to person. Therefore, we might view the outcome of an interaction pejoratively because it constitutes an application of a different needs hierarchy from our own. Therein lays the difficulty.

If the outcome is subjective, then at least one of the participants to the interaction may disagree with that outcome and seek redress within the policy infrastructure. The highest level policy infrastructure in the United States, that established by the Constitution, provides a judicial approach that makes all forms of interaction, be it criminal, civil or administrative, subject to post-interaction judicial review. Basically, it can be determined after the fact whether you broke the law, what the law actually was or whether the law in any case was appropriately applied.

Likewise, one can always sue someone else, except as we noted in Chapter 1, government and God. Discounting these exception cases, this approach to consequences brings recursion to a high art form.

Therefore, with these many trust-inducing mechanisms in mind, in the following chapter we will consider some of the characteristics of a hypothetical mutational event that might provide an inherently trusted platform from which humans could project their presence into the world of computer-enabled interactions; a world that is often referred to as *cyberspace*. While the mechanism would not eliminate untoward consequences in interactions, it might well make their resolution more objective.

# 9 Mutation

*I know who I was when I got up this morning,*
*but I think I must have been changed several times since then.*

Alice in *Alice in Wonderland*
by Lewis Carroll

## The Uncertainty Principle of Faith

Predicting the end point or even assessing the way stations of human evolutionary progression is something of a religious exercise. It entails the search for trust through both causality and process in an environment shaped by unknown concepts of social ecosystem formation and interaction. It's not that we don't understand them. The point is that we don't have an appreciation of their possibility or their importance until they arrive on our doorstep. As we noted back in our first chapter, such was the situation the Incas found themselves in when the Spanish arrived. An unknown social order, superior technology and devastating physiological manifestations struck at the very basis in trust of the Inca Civilization. In relatively short order, the central features of the civilization were supplanted.

When the entities contained within an ecosystem can significantly shape the structure of the ecosystem itself, one is at least two levels of indirection away from a stable platform from which to assess, let alone to act. First, driven by stimuli derived from the human needs hierarchy the social order seeks the means to sate the collective appetite. This requires an evaluation of trust at the first level of indirection. Does the collective societal stimulus point toward content that satisfies the collective need? The second level of indirection is more subtle. It derives from a characteristic fundamental to the physical ecosystem that was given rigorous expression by Werner Heisenberg. Known as the *Heisenberg Uncertainty Principle*, this maxim suggests that we cannot know exactly both the position and the momentum of a particle because there is always at least a minimal level of uncertainty in the product of the two. Thus, the act of measuring either momentum or position affects the level of our understanding of the other. To exactly determine position we must abrogate momentum. To exactly measure momentum we have to sacrifice position. If we measure both simultaneously then there must be a degree of uncertainty in the product of the two. Applied to social orders as examples of dynamic systems, the corollary suggests that we cannot know exactly both the direction of societal change (momentum) and the effective policy (position) of the social order. Put more succinctly, when through our social systems we unleash the technological engines of change, it is purely through an act of faith that we attempt to assess where those engines will take us and, in fact, exactly where we are at any point along the way.

Such is the case with anticipating the future development of computer systems and their networks within the realm of human social orders. The social order impacts the network which in turn influences the social order. To illustrate this concept, let us consider the impact wrought from the introduction of three mutations of society-wide communication systems during the relatively brief history of the United States. Specifically, we refer to the social order instigation of new transportation systems that in turn altered the very fabric of the social order itself. In the nation's history, there have been three distinct paradigm shifts regarding transportation on a national scale: the intercontinental railroads, the interstate highway system and commercial aviation. Each of these transitions, while grounded in technology, forced or enabled major shifts in the social orders of the day.

The introduction of new technology on a broad scale often encompasses a problem of *infrastructure*. While an element of the technology may be individual or personal in size and scope, the technology itself may require a significant infrastructure in order to achieve its full utility. Such was the situation with credit cards that we discussed in previous chapters. To achieve ubiquity of application, it was necessary to standardize and then deploy the infrastructure through which credit cards function. Likewise, in the deployment of telephone payment cards, France Telecom had to stimulate development of virtually the entire supporting industry. Our point here is that to address certain classes of infrastructure deployment, nothing less than stimulus from the prevailing social order will suffice. Such was certainly the case with the relevant transportation systems. Each offers a metaphorical illustration of the current computer network situation.

At the beginning of the Civil War in 1861, the United States was essentially comprised of two nations separated by a broad landscape populated by indigenous peoples. These Native Americans presented quite advanced civilizations organized along tribal boundaries. However, their technological capabilities were significantly inferior to that of the United States that existed along the west coast and the eastern reaches of the North American Continent. In the early days of the Civil War, two major railroad companies were given incentives by the federal government to build railroads linking the eastern United States to the west coast. These incentives included land, in the form of broad right-of-ways for the railroad tracks, and direct financial payments to offset the cost of laying track. The societal goal for these incentives was largely driven by commerce. Content production in the east sought markets in the west. Populating the ostensibly "available" lands with immigrant populations required large scale transportation facilities from each coast of the country. Moreover, capital needs in the east sought the wealth of the west; wealth in the form of raw materials to fuel industrial production. Again, massively enhanced transportation facilities were needed. In the end, of course, the societal outcome was significantly greater than the original goals.

In the most basic terms, the completed railroads turned the two distinct regions of the country into a contiguous nation. Resolution on the battlegrounds of the Civil War in turn affirmed the primacy of The Union over the individual states. Even more profound, this unification of both physical and social structure of the United States dealt a death knell to any hope of independence of the Native American tribes. Frederick Jackson Turner offers an overview of the conquest of the frontier and its resulting impact on American society in his writings published under the title *History, Frontier, and Section: Three Essays*. The end result was a truly united set of states that were individually encompassed by many distinct cultural sections of country all tied together by the railroads. At the beginning of the Civil War, travel from the east coast to Europe was quicker and easier than was travel to the west coast. Likewise, commerce between the west coast and Mexico and countries in Asia was more common than that with the eastern reaches of the country. By the early XX[th] Century, with the completion of the transcontinental railroad system and the ensuing conquest of The West, the United States comprised an interconnected social order that spanned the breadth of the continent.

By the middle of the XX$^{th}$ Century, following World War II, the United States was a world power. While from across the seas it might have appeared as a gigantic monolith of commerce and culture, within the United States proper the nation was still a collection of distinct sections. There was great variance within the social orders of these various sections: New England, The Midwest, The Old South, The Great Southwest, The Plains, The Pacific Northwest and California. Within these major divisions, there were major subdivisions as well. Social structures varied significantly within each, largely driven by distinct racial groupings of immigrant populations. The earliest colonists from England, Ireland and Europe predominated in New England. The descendants of the slave population were a major influence in The Old South. Hispanics and Native Americans formed much of the social landscape in The Great Southwest while large immigrant populations from the Scandinavian countries and those of Northern and Eastern Europe influenced The Plains and The Midwest. Hispanic populations were plentiful in California along with an influx of Asian laborers into both California and The Pacific Northwest. Each section encompassed its own set of tensions wrought by the intermingling of social orders. Recalling the protocol stacks through which we have examined interactions in general, the situation following World War II was one in which the high level stimuli were emerging, lacking only the low order protocol layers of the stack to instigate mutational interactions of the prevailing social orders. At this point, enter the Interstate Highway System.

A widely recounted but ill-referenced homily related to warfare suggests that "Amateurs study tactics, armchair generals study strategy, true military leaders study logistics and those that win wars study intelligence." As with most such sayings, there is a bit of truth and a bit of wishful thinking to be found therein. World War II did, however, illustrate the importance of logistics in the conduct of warfare on a global scale. A similar homily suggests that "Armies are trained to fight the last war." The aftermath of World War II lends some credence to this observation as well. Keying on the effectiveness of the great autobahn roadway system in Germany that allowed rapid movement of military forces and materiel between the two fronts on which Germany fought the war, in 1956 under the leadership of President Dwight Eisenhower who led the Allied Armies in Europe in World War II, the United States undertook the construction of the Interstate Highway System. The underlying benefit of this gigantic effort was to ensure the rapid movement of goods and services throughout the country. While ostensibly aimed at improving commerce, it had a significant contributory effect in transforming the distinct sections of United States' social structure into a relatively homogenous blend. As we noted in the case of Martin Luther's instigation of what became the Protestant Reformation, with the correct superposition of stimulus and environment an anecdotal trial balloon can become a societal mutation of the first order. In this case, the seeds of social change unleashed by the United States Supreme Court ruling in the case of Brown versus Board of Education fell into the fertile ground offered by seamless transport connectivity among all parts of the United States. The result is a continuing extension of the federal policy infrastructure into all subordinate social orders.

Brown versus Board of Education was a landmark ruling of the Supreme Court issued on May 17, 1954. The ruling overturned the doctrine of "separate but equal" facilities that was used as the rationale for segregation along racial lines in the provision of public education. The ruling required enforcement from the federal government, in some cases involving military troops, to dismantle segregated school systems around the country. The underpinnings in law on which this ruling was based were subsequently used to dismantle both *de jure* segregated facilities in areas of social discourse beyond public education as well as practices that led to *de facto* segregation. The social aspect of the ruling provided legal mobility for individuals of all races to seek equality of treatment throughout the United States. The parallel development of the Interstate Highway System provided physical mobility for those aspiring to such equality. The confluence of social and technological change enabled a mutational transformation of the social order of the United States.

The third transportation related paradigm shift occurred with the advent of commercial aviation. Beginning in the early decades of the XXth Century, commercial aviation in the United States was essentially the creation of the United States Postal Service. Mail hauling contracts were the dominant source of operating revenue for fledgling airline services until World War II. The carriage of passengers was limited due to basic infrastructure problems: the lack of planes that were big enough and safe enough to carry large numbers of people and the lack of airport and in-flight coordination facilities to handle a large number of planes. As wars are want to do, World War II injected a large dose of new flight technology and consumer demand into the mix. Following the war, aircraft became available that were able to carry an economically significant number of passengers. Moreover, the transition of the national economy from a wartime footing back to one aimed at personal goods and services created a large demand for high speed transportation that only aircraft could provide across the breadth of the entire country. So, aviation expanded. However, it did not enter the truly mutational stage until the late 1970's.

As commercial aviation expanded following World War II, it was highly regulated by the federal government. This was much in keeping with the practice in most countries of establishing national airline companies to show the respective flags around the world. Within the United States, it was not in keeping with the social order to have an actual national airline. Rather, by heavily regulating all of the airlines, competition was strictly controlled in order to give everyone at least a piece of the pie. It was a very standards oriented approach, which had the effect of keeping airline expansion stifled and the resulting fare structure rather intimidating to the ordinary traveler. In the late 1970's, as an act of the prevailing social order, the federal government deregulated the airline industry.

When deregulation came, it allowed a much more unfettered form of competition among the airlines. As competition is intended to do, it enticed a variety of product offerings from the airlines. The offerings were judged by the market, with many airlines merging and some going bankrupt. The result to the ordinary traveler, however, was the enhanced availability of high speed transportation throughout the nation, and the world for that matter, at remarkably low fares. The social result was the intermingling of the social orders of all nations at a level that had never been seen before. This is the process that the world is still engaged in, and the end game has yet to be played. As with the railroads and the interstate highways precedents, the impact of the technological advance is being strongly reflected in its impact on the social order. At the time of this writing, somewhat like the Internet, a social impact seems to be emanating outward from the United States. Also, as with the Internet, some social pushback seems certainly in the offing.

One of this book's authors (Tim) was born and raised in a small town in an obscure section of western Oklahoma; itself something of a latecomer to the United States. This small town of Sayre was intriguingly situated at essentially the geographic *schwerpunkt* of the three transportation paradigms that we have been considering. Sayre is only a few hundred miles from the actual geographic center of the lower 48 United States. At quite literally the center of town, U.S. Route 66 and the Chicago, Rock Island and Pacific Railroad intersected. With the advent of the interstate system, the mid-point of Interstate-40 was not far removed as it carried traffic from the east coast to the west coast. While the author was yet a boy, located within a concentric circle of less than 150 km radius was a collection of at least five Strategic Air Command bases, several Atlas missile silos containing intercontinental ballistic missiles tipped with thermonuclear warheads and, lest we forget, the Pantex facility at which were assembled many if not all of the tens of thousands of nuclear and thermonuclear devices in the United States arsenal. As a personal historical anecdote, we recall few if any instances of practicing *fallout drills* during the early days of the cold war. Such drills were the fodder of a number of Civil Defense films, illustrating how students in school might take defensive positions under their desks as a shield against the flash of an exploding nuclear bomb. The general assumption in Sayre was that, should the Cold War transform into a *hot war*, our school would fall within the margin of targeting error of so many incoming intercontinental missiles that hiding under a school desk or ducking into a fallout shelter was going to offer little solace to the near instantaneous vaporization resulting from literally tens or hundreds of megatons of explosive capacity unleashed on or near us. We mention these points merely to note, as we have said quite often, that understanding is based on context. Moreover, we suggest that one can garner very interesting context in unexpected places. Our collective context tended to reach somewhat beyond the local cotton patch.

Thus, with this bit of presentation of context, we arrive at our consideration of the prospects of the evolutionary progression of computer networks into the future. As we have also often noted, computers comprise the most complex set of tools yet constructed by any species. More important, among the tools of humans, computers are the most capable of supporting processes across the full range of individual appetites. They facilitate satisfying the needs of the mind as well as of the body. Existing variants of computers provide significant support for and enhancements to the human sensori-motor system. They enable people to interact across time and space with other people and with the computers and ancillary tools of other people. However, a methodical examination of existent systems suggests that something is amiss in this magnificent repertoire. In particular, we note significant deficiencies in the support across the full range of human cognitive facilities; at least, compared to the capabilities enabled through evolution-derived direct interaction processes. Very specifically, computers in general are lacking in the mechanisms through which trusted groups are formed and maintained. These mechanisms have proven to be extremely beneficial to the species across the ages. Rather, in their current incarnations, computer networks serve to diminish the threat detection and aversion facilities that groups have historically provided. In particular, when we pursue interactions across the Internet wide-area network, the result is often to establish in us an altered state of consciousness, due to distortions induced in the human sensori-motor system and in the cognitive facilities through which the connection between sensory input and motor output is effected. As currently instantiated, computers and computer networks tend to allow the predators of and on the human species to bypass our defenses where we are at our most vulnerable, in our privacy and our physical isolation. We suggest that in order to address these deficiencies and to more fully exploit the beneficial capabilities that computers provide, there may yet occur an evolutionary extension of the computer species; or, perhaps more correctly, there may yet emerge a new species of computer. This new species would serve to facilitate the traits of human social ecosystems; to amplify without distortion the capabilities of our individual sensori-motor systems and to more fully project the facilities necessary to fulfill our individual and collective needs. To accomplish these goals, we might ask, "What is missing in current networks?" In a word, trust!

In Chapter 5, we observed that social ecosystems are grounded first in the establishment, conveyance and application of trust. Successively larger and more successful groups were founded on phylogenetically derived facilities enabled by human evolution. Only within a viable trust infrastructure does it become feasible to create an effective policy infrastructure. Furthermore, the multiple policy infrastructures that we find ourselves having to navigate, some of them exceedingly complex, could certainly be better addressed with cognitive tools especially designed for the purpose. This, it would seem, best describes the evolutionary nexus that we anticipate; a species of computer that is grounded first in the establishment of trust and then in the cognitive support of complex policy for the individual for whom it provides a societal prosthetic extension into the policy infrastructures of modern life.

During the course of this book, in anticipation of this need, we have alluded to a large contingent of computers, computer related devices or system components that exhibit a nascent image of this new variant of computer. Among these examples is the full range of personal electronic devices, particularly those that encompass secure cores. The secure core, perhaps more than any other current computer component, is grounded in the concept of trust. Its *raison d'être* is to provide a trusted vehicle for storing information and a trusted platform for performing computational procedures directly in support of its containing superstructure and thereby in support of an individual person. It is positioned in the marketplace to be the ubiquitous device *of* and *for* the person; always conveyed *by* the person and owing its allegiance *to* the person that carries it. From an operational viewpoint, the secure core takes the first small steps toward enabling a projection of the person's physical and social being beyond their direct, physical presence; a projection to support interactions with other people at a distance, a projection to support interactions with other computer systems across both distance and time as well as combinations of the two. Difficulties arise, however, in the coherent integration of these facilities into the full range of human needs based physical and social ecosystems. In such situations, computers, even personal electronic devices with secure cores, seem akin to clubs and spears, while in fact a more modern weapons system is called for.

While the architecture of secure cores is indeed grounded in trust, the relevant physiology of current personal electronic devices leaves a number of gaps in their social ecosystem support. The linkage of the personal electronic device to the individual person that carries it is tenuous, and the dependence of the secure core for power and sensory input from the very system that it must engage on behalf of its bearer places it in a position of inferiority as it engages the adversary. This results in subsequent policy machinations that involve a greater degree of risk than is desirable or necessary and woefully deficient capabilities with regards to effecting complex policy based interactions. Moreover, its defensive mechanisms, while formidable, can certainly benefit from enhancement. In short, the current secure cores do not represent a nearly sufficient enough instance of a trusted agent. To meet the desired goals, some might suggest the use of secure computing boxes that are located in locked rooms with dedicated power sources that are monitored by trained security and operational personnel; boxes that, save for excessive size, cost, complexity and immobility have some of the characteristics that we seek. At least, the secure core of the personal electronic device does represent a major stride away from such systems in the direction of portability and security versus cost. So, the goal is to further improve its social ecosystem facilities without sacrificing its current advantages. How to do this? Perhaps the answer is to use the same phylogenetically derived facilities that worked for the human species. These are facilities that derive directly from the needs hierarchy and that engender action stimuli on the part of the individual members of the species.

Let us speculate on at least some of the mutational changes that can significantly enhance the characteristic of this new species of computer to involve itself effectively and securely in the complex policy environment of a person. First, it may help to set the tone if we begin to speak of the *trusted core agent* rather than the secure core. Physical appearance, better known as *form factor* in the world of computers, will likely need to shift from that of today to support additional and different physical interactions. In this chapter we will look at the improved capability set for a new species of computer, of which today's secure core is but a precursor. In the following chapter, we'll consider the enhancements in cognitive facilities within this new species of computer that is required to fully exploit these capabilities.

# Punctuated Equilibrium

The mechanics of speciation, the derivation of new species from old, has long been a subject of research and discussion among evolutionary scientists. A pioneer in the consideration of such issues was Ernst Mayr. In his *Systematics and the Origin of Species*, Mayr developed the idea that when communities within a species become disjoint from the main population body of the species, perhaps due to geographical isolation over a long period of time, then there is a larger likelihood that these communities will develop divergent traits relative to the original main population body. This means that over time, there is a stronger possibility for subsequent changes to build through mutations or genetic adaptation, which leads to an ever larger gap from the main body of the original species. The changes compound and ultimately the members of the disjoint communities and the original main body of the species may no longer be able to interbreed; a new species has hence developed. This mechanism can at least qualitatively explain results derived from geological studies of fossil records.

These fossil records for many families of organisms seem to indicate that a given species may continue in a stable form for long periods of time, but at some point (from a geological time frame perspective) a number of new, derivative species may emerge. It is unclear whether this presentation of evolutionary progression is a statistical artifact of the fossil record itself, or a true representation of evolutionary mechanics. Certainly, the formation of fossils requires a myriad of special circumstances in order to occur in the first place. Once formed, fossils must survive the deterioration caused by physical forces applied over geological time periods. So, for humans to build an interpretation of the process of evolution, a coherent set of fossils must actually be found and properly categorized as representing distinct evolutionary pathways. One interpretation of this fossil record suggests that mutational events require special circumstances for their initiation, and these circumstances might well evoke a variety of distinct mutations. If sufficiently diverse, these different mutations lead to a single species giving rise to several derivative species within a relatively short time period (within a geological time frame) through the mechanisms described by Mayr's work. The term *punctuated equilibrium* was given to this process by Niles Eldridge and Stephen J. Gould in their 1972 paper *Punctuated equilibria: an alternative to phyletic gradualism.* The gist of their proposal is that the structure of species is likely to remain static over long periods of time, due to the sparse nature of the mechanisms through which changes can be made in individual members of a species and the time and process required for any such changes to be substantially represented within a significant number of members and thus form a new species. When speciation does occur, because of the mechanics of fossil formation noted above, it is likely that the record will show a fully formed new species; that intermediate steps in the path from one species to another may not be captured in a fossil record that is found for study.

Computers appear to evolve according to mechanisms that often present in the form of punctuated equilibrium as well. Indeed, here we are using the term computer to encompass personal electronic devices that can trace significant aspects of their lineage back to the original big iron machines of the 1950's and 1960's. Today however, as a society we really do not think of these utility tools (cellular telephones, Apple's iPod and digital cameras come to mind) as computers. As suggested by Mayr's model, these are devices that grew up in populations somewhat disjoint from the main body of computer technology development. They intended to be different animals, but they drug along a good bit of the computer genome with them. There were many fits and starts along the way, but in the end they emerged as significant species in their own rights. We observed in Chapter 2 that the primary epochs of computer systems over the last half century or so were characterized by aggregate changes that resulted in very approximately 100 times as many machines being sold at also very approximately 100 times less in cost than the previous species of computer at each mutational point. This evolution typically involved new systems being brought into the market to address uses around the periphery of the mainstream of computer systems. The new machines then tended to establish a shift in the mainstream toward these new uses. The major enabler of this evolutionary progression has been the dramatic enhancements to processors, memory and peripheral mass storage devices which for decades have followed the general progression of Moore's Law, the idea that electronic circuit capabilities double every eighteen months.

The impetus of this evolutionary progression has been the development of new tools to address more, and more fully, the individual and cumulative needs of the ascending needs hierarchy. Such evolutionary forces continue today, and we note that the highest order needs are now coming into the focus of the prospects of enhanced tool systems.

# Evolutionary forces

The physical ecosystem is seldom in a state of quiescence; biological entities evolve, mechanical systems are modified and the environment changes. Within this developmental turbulence, the nature of the fittest *vis-à-vis* natural selection seems always in a state of flux. The same is true of social ecosystems. This is certainly the case with computers and computer networks; specifically with respect to the Internet and its derivative Web. As we noted earlier, in a time of great flux, it is difficult to assess the direction of change simultaneously with a determination of current effective policies of the social order. However, what we can do is reflect on the forces that drive change because within social ecosystems these forces derive largely from the human needs hierarchy. Consequently, we think it to be an interesting exercise to consider the stimuli at work in the current evolutionary mix which provides impetus for change to existing network structures and mechanisms. The Internet derived from the societal deficiency needs of physiological support coupled to safety and security. The major driver of Internet architecture was redundancy in physical connectivity and switching in the face of war or natural disaster. The extension of the Internet through the facilities of the Web provided additional mechanisms to sate the appetites of the higher order stimuli of the needs hierarchy. This extension is incomplete as it relates to fully replicating the mechanisms of human social orders. These deficiencies form the guideposts of our considerations.

We've previously considered the three most significant entities in the location and conveyance of content on the Web: the consumer whose appetites must be sated, the content provider that offers sustenance and the broker (middleman) that is typically positioned between the two and enables their subsequent interactions, for a small fee of course. Each of these parties has a personal or institutional interest in facilitating business models with certain characteristics. The consumer is driven by needs based stimuli, which on an instantaneous basis might present very asymmetric cost benefit assessments: "I need it, and I need it now! Price is no object!" Or, "That content should be a commodity that I can obtain for free!" The provider may have a different priority assessment, also needs based: "I must get this much for my product or I can't afford to stay in business!" Or, "My work is unique, it can't be had from anywhere else, so I should be compensated accordingly." Finally, the middleman is in the position to put the two together. In fact, the middleman is often the infrastructure initiator; the developer of mechanisms to bring consumer and provider together. As a consequence, the middleman may feel it only just to charge a "small fee" that is a significant fraction of the total value equation. These business models translate into operational and technical tugs of war that impact heavily on new systems.

In Chapter 6, we discussed the components of content, specifically discussing the value equations for information accessed via the Web. Information control translates into market control. Consequently, a variety of players want to position themselves as central to the interaction facilities of the Web. Network equipment and operating system vendors seek to establish themselves as the ultimate trust brokers of the Web, and thereby derive significant impact on the interaction environment. Connectivity vendors such as cable operators and telecommunication companies seek to extend their domains into that of content provision, beyond pure connectivity. And, large content providers are involved in the game as well, seeking ever greater control over not only the provision of content but in its use by the individual. It is interesting to note that many of these entities are providers and consumers of each other's products and services. Within a dynamic marketplace, it seems often tempting to pursue the customers of one's customers in an attempt to optimize one's competitive position. It seems to make for highly recursive "food chains." Consider an episode involving Sony BMG Music Entertainment.

On November 19, 2005, Dan Mitchell of the New York Times reported that Mark Russinovich, a security expert, had discovered on his computer a new *rootkit*. This is a form of software modification that allows operating a computer at its most protected level, while being possibly extremely hard to detect. After investigation, he was able to discern that modifications had been made in several software components involved with accessing Compact Discs (CD's). Finally, he was able to establish that the source of the rootkit was a Sony compact disk that he had recently played on his computer. The mere act of accessing the compact disk in order to extract a music file from it had caused new software to be loaded onto his personal computer; software that comprised a secret modification to his computer's base operating system. This new software was now in the operational path of any compact disk played on this computer; moreover, any attempt to remove the new software would leave the compact disk unusable. Finally, the rootkit was such that it could be host for computer attacks. All in all, this reflected a rather unexpected course of events for simply trying to play a legitimately purchased compact disk.

The overt purpose of the rootkit was an apparent attempt on the part of Sony to prevent the copying and distribution of the music files from their compact disk without having it actually present. In essence, the compact disk became a credential that conveyed authority for the possessor to play its music. Without the compact disk present, the music wouldn't play. Moreover, creating a music file on the computer to store the music from the compact disk became encumbered. This anecdote illustrates a couple of points.

First, the operating system on virtually any computer is complex and encompasses a lot of software. The lineage of this software at any given point in time on a specific computer is not always well established unless great care in the administration of the operating system software is maintained. In fact, the prevalent personal computer operating system, Windows, is specifically engineered so as to allow frequent, automatic updates to virtually any part of the system. There are security controls in some places, but obviously very significant elements of the operating system can be replaced with impunity and the replacement is definitely not always of the tamper-evident variety. A second major point illustrated by this episode is the apparent degree of legal ambiguity that exists with regard to who controls a given computer, and even more ambiguous, on whose behalf does a specific computer operate? It would seem highly unlikely that any of corporation would intentionally abrogate legal restraints, and in this particular case, Sony apparently felt entitled to surreptitiously install their own software on customer's computer, without the owner's knowledge, in an attempt to enforce copyright protection for the music on a Sony manufactured compact disk. Holding this view would seem to suggest that one does not perceive that a personal computer is specifically intended to act in a fiduciary capacity for the owner of that computer. We will suggest a bit later that removing any ambiguity in this assessment, as a point of law, is a necessary ingredient for the evolution of computer systems in general and personal electronic devices specifically if they're to have any chance at all of enabling a strong trust infrastructure on behalf of the computer owner and bearer.

At the seminal point of trust establishment for extended social systems in general and for widespread computer networks specifically, a variety of players have now entered the game. Not least among these are the various governmental entities that have been charged with establishing identity systems of varying extent and purpose; state driver license bureaus and the U.S. Department of Commerce are specifically driving standardization efforts aimed at establishing trusted identity mechanisms. The impetus for such activities is the increase in attacks on the benefits derived from social ecosystems; attacks that are enabled by deficiencies in our computer systems through which the fabric of our society is extended into cyberspace. Identity theft is proving an ever increasing threat to our species across the full range of the needs hierarchy. Financial facilities such as checking accounts or credit card accounts are being improperly impacted because establishing the true identity of the account holders requires mechanisms found readily in our personal cognitive capabilities but lacking in our computer systems. Attempts are being made to address these deficiencies on a piecemeal basis. An example is the formation of Internet-oriented industrial groups, perhaps best exemplified by the Liberty Alliance Project, that are seeking to establish operational standards for personal identification within the Web.

Concerns about the trust ascribed to software vendors and operators have recently become significant issues in other areas as well. The Web search engine portal Google.com provides general broker connectivity between consumers and providers of content based on search engine value. However, Clive Thompson of the New York Times reported on April 23, 2006 that Google had entered into agreements with the Chinese government to limit certain service offerings and to restrict the return of certain search results that were deemed sensitive within the People's Republic of China. The end result is that answers to search queries from Google.com would now appear to be location dependent; one could see certain information from some parts of the world but perhaps not from others. This certainly represents a perturbation in the level of trust that one can derive from this particular service. Similar restrictions are under consideration within the United States and other countries, with an impetus driven by financial considerations. The issue is termed *net neutrality*.

At the present time, the most general business model of Internet access evokes payment for speed and volume of access to the network proper but not for the specifics of traffic generated or used. The end users that constitute the bulk of consumers of Web services will typically connect to an Internet Service Provider (ISP) through dialup telephone lines, Digital Subscriber Loop (DSL) lines or cable television connections. The transmission speeds provided by these various channel mechanisms range from thousands of bits per second up to millions of bits per second, and volumes reach billions of bits. Web portals and services might use connections which provide yet higher channel speeds and volumes. However, the price of these connection channels is not currently geared to the content generated or consumed. Whether the connected system is continuously blasting bits into the Internet, or whether it is sending vast quantities of bits in spurts and idling the rest of the time, is immaterial to the cost structure of the channel. It becomes then something of a balancing act on the part of the channel providers to support a market priced purely on connectivity and yet provide adequate total capacity when the traffic (total number of bits circulating the network) might vary by orders of magnitude. So, ostensibly in an effort to provide a more equitable cost structure among different users, the providers of network infrastructure have sought a change, effected through legal means, in the pricing model for

Internet access. A potential problem of course arises if a cost structure based on content is implemented. The problem is that priority of service is likely to follow the amount of revenue; it may become more likely that your speed of response to Web queries will become dependent on the traffic generated by the middleman or content provider being accessed. Some Internet carriers would then apparently take their control prerogatives to more intrusive levels.

In an October 19, 2007 wire from Associated Press, Peter Svensson reported that Comcast, a cable television and Internet access provider was limiting the volume of traffic that could be delivered between certain Web services sites and their customers. The news report suggested that the manner in which this limitation was accomplished was with Comcast software insinuating itself into the protocol stack. Some traffic was slowed down while other was kept normal. Svensson commented that this is akin to a telephone operator intervening in conversations. As we have noted previously, in a voice-based conversation between two people, trust related to the conversation itself is partially enabled through biometric voice recognition between the two conversing parties. In a digital exchange, the fact that the mechanism attributed to Comcast can actually be used suggests a problem in the network protocols' abilities to authenticate the identities of the conversing parties. This is obviously a deficiency to be addressed in the mutational progression of the network and its derivative mechanisms.

Another driving factor in the evolutionary development of the Web is the applicability of social ecosystem consequences to Web transactions. The relative anonymity or ambiguity of the identity of the various parties to such transactions makes it difficult if not impossible to apply normal rules of engagement. The application of time based, age based or location based constraints is extremely problematic, and this same identity ambiguity makes the application of after the fact sanctions difficult as well. Consider the fact that a significant fraction of e-mail traffic on the Web today is spam; totally unsolicited, highly suspect messages from not just anonymous, but often fraudulent senders. In a similar vein, consider the fact that stolen merchandise can be more readily traded across the Web than through previously used illegal distribution channels. If one throws in the threat posed by sexual predators soliciting contact through the myriad interaction facilities offered by the Web, then we see that the scope of the problem ranges across the full spectrum of our needs hierarchy. So, we would have to assess that if the migration of business models is a driving force for evolutionary change, then enhanced safety and security needs should be considered as well, while catering to the rights of privacy and freedom of speech. As we noted in our Prologue, one of our species' most general admonitions of social interaction is "Don't talk to strangers!" This rule is hard to apply when we invite strangers directly into our homes through our network connections.

Finally, a large variety of personal electronic devices are currently engaged in something of a maelstrom of market selection. Over the past few decades, a number of facilities have come into increasingly common use; facilities which speak to much of the range of the human needs hierarchy. As this collection of devices has engaged the market evaluation process, no specific combination of form and capabilities has yet resulted in a clear winner in the race for species supremacy. We can, however, observe many of the specific enhancements that offer the prospect of blending into a true mutational advance of the genre. The question then arises, "What provides the superior stimulus for mutational success?" We suggest that the answer lies with the replication of the social mechanisms that enable human-to-human interaction. Current network connectivity affords an artificial extension of the human sensori-motor experience, but only a partial extension. Central to the full enabling of social systems is the incorporation of mechanisms to facilitate the formation and functioning of groups that allow an equivalent evocation of trust to that found within direct, personal interactions. Based on this capability, an ontology of the relevant social order should allow a mutation-class device to more fully participate on behalf of the human bearer of the device. To this end, we need to examine at least a cursory overview of the salient mechanisms.

# Identity

The human impetus to form groups springs from the full spectrum of the needs hierarchy; from physiological requirements to the drive for transcendence. It has been through groups that the species has thrived. Abraham Maslow indicated as much in *Toward a Psychology of Being* when he noted that most needs require the support of others. When considered across the full range of needs, a number of foundational concepts of group establishment and maintenance can be recognized. To be a member of a group is to be part of a collection to which others belong as well. Being the only member of a group is not conducive to satisfying the broad range of needs that require others. Having multiple members in any group, however, implies that we might well seek to tell them apart. The characteristics of being lumped into a group and then of being unique within that group are somewhat obtuse and hence the mechanisms used to differentiate among the collectives, and the individuals within them, give rise to the multi-faceted concept called *identity*.

Identity is a concept that is known to all of us but understood by few of us. This is not a statement that most people are dumb and a few are smart. Rather, it is a realization that we all have an understanding of identity, but we have many different perceptions of what that understanding is. The very term suggests so many nuances that it is difficult to speak analytically about it with the words we typically use. While thus far we have referred to identity as if it had a single, well-defined meaning, this is in fact rather illusory. Consequently, some of the other concepts we have previously introduced may need to be re-examined in light of a more detailed understanding of the full concept of identity. To this end, we need a more rigorous vocabulary in order to systematically understand or design systems that involve services related to identity in all its guises.

Within the model of social ecosystems that we have suggested, identity is a mechanism through which policy can be specifically ascribed to the entities that participate in interactions. Explicit within the model is the seminal provision of a trust infrastructure that defines the extent of a specific ecosystem. In order to effect trusted policy within this infrastructure, one must be able to establish trust in identity. However, the single word identity encompasses many facets and it is often difficult to focus on any one facet in a manner orthogonal to the other facets and hence to derive trust from either causality or process. We suggest that a necessary step toward alleviating these difficulties is to arrive at new terms with more precise definitions for characteristics that too often are all simply lumped under the single heading. We will pursue this expanded vocabulary by considering the facets of identity through distinct perspectives ranging from the physical ecosystem through current social orders.

In Chapter 3, we noted that within the physical ecosystem among-species interactions tend to fall into five categories: coexistence, competitive coexistence, symbiotic, parasitic and predatory. We can see in certain of these categories the beginning of species based identity and then subsequently of individual identity within a single species. The most benign of interaction types, that of coexistence, already assumes the differentiation of entities or of groups comprised of similar entities. Competitive coexistence suggests that the differentiation among individuals or groups is grounded in the reality of natural selection. The entities that are in competition, whether individuals or groups, can be classified according to interaction consequences, perhaps to the extreme that one group might emerge from the competition in such a superior position that the other becomes extinct. Symbiotic and parasitic interactions entail the differentiation of symbiotes on the one hand and parasite from host on the other. It is in the guise of predatory interactions that we best see the full gamut of identity's facets.

Perhaps the way to begin an overview of identity is to consider the lack of it; a concept that we refer to as *anonymity*. Consider the interaction of predator and prey in the physical ecosystem. An interaction technique used by both is that of *stealth*. The predator may use stealth as it approaches its potential prey, while the prey in turn may use stealth as a means to avoid detection by the predator. As a facet of identity within social ecosystems, stealth is metaphorically consistent with anonymity. However, the equivalence breaks down when we consider not just the prelude to an interaction, and perhaps the interaction itself, but also the consequences of an interaction. We noted in Chapter 3 the ability of animals like the arctic hare to disguise or to eliminate their forensic wakes within the physical ecosystem. In other words, they are able to minimize the consequences of interactions that leave evidence of the interaction for others to find; however, further interactions could leave traces. Within a social ecosystem, we suggest a definition of anonymity as the complete lack of characteristics through which a member of a group can be distinguished. To achieve true anonymity, an interaction in which an anonymous person participates must have no forensic characteristics that can point to the specific person. As a side effect of this definition, it would seem obvious that no level of identity-derived trust can be ascribed to an anonymous entity.

Anonymity is central to the confluence of the concepts of identity and privacy, also a multi-faceted concept. In particular, we apply the term to both freedom-of-action as well as control-of-information. Within social ecosystems, there is a natural tendency to conclude that anonymity is an effective agent of privacy. The tendency derives from our experiences with social ecosystems in the small and with our observations of physical ecosystem interactions. However, we observe that within the existing social orders, achieving true anonymity is difficult if not impossible. Consequently, suggesting it as a foundation of privacy is perhaps a bit of wishful thinking. Rather, we suggest the consideration of additional facets of identity that might be of better use in obtaining the privacy that we seek. We will try to draw out these opportunities as we consider some rather simple examples.

With respect to social ecosystems, identity is about grouping people together according to some criteria and then distinguishing each person found in a specific group. At least two distinct approaches can be considered in providing these mechanisms. One method is to specify a group, add people into it and provide some mechanism to establish uniqueness of each individual within that group. This is the approach we use when we create the Social Security System, the Texas Driver License or your favorite airline frequent flyer program. Each group operates independently of the others and hence each is responsible for distinguishing its individual members, usually by assigning some unique identifier to each person within that group. The net result of this approach is that a person may belong to lots of groups and consequently have many unique identifiers; essentially, one from each group. We will ascribe the term *experiential identity* to this form of identification. We arrive at the term by observing that historically, within the realm of small social ecosystems such as the family, clan or tribe we tend to make use of this facet of identity to denote the life experiences of a person. Note that in this setting we don't suggest that this mechanism is used to establish the uniqueness of the individual within the family, clan or tribe grouping. This is actually accomplished through a different mechanism that we'll consider below. Rather, experiential identity is strongly related to the concept of *reputation* and hence to the association of trust to identity. The concept of reputation derives from the concept of trust established through causality and process that we discussed in Chapters 7 and 8. The examples we have suggested are mundane, but there are a lot of groups with their individual identifiers that are administered in this same fashion: those who have been born (birth certificate), those who have been inoculated against childhood diseases (vaccination record), those who have graduated from high school (diploma), those who have graduated from college (another diploma), those who belong to a labor union (union card), those who have served in the armed forces (honorable or dishonorable discharge), those who have been accused of or convicted of a crime (criminal record), those who have permanent resident status (green card), and the list can go on and on. Such is the record of our life's experiences and from this record we can derive some level of trust that goes toward the anticipation of outcome of future interactions. An issue arises when we consider how these various experiences are associated with an actual biophysical person. In other words, how is trust in experiential identity established?

The answer to this question lies with an alternative facet of identity. It derives from the approach used within the family, clan or tribe that can be extended to the entire species. Specifically, this facet of identity establishes the uniqueness of each person relative to all other members of the family, clan, tribe or the entire species. In fact, when considered in the abstract, we can indeed consider uniqueness of a single person relative to all persons who have ever lived or who will live in the future. This facet of identity we will call *differential identity*. A very basic definition of differential identity is: *that characteristic of the members of a group of entities that allows them to be distinguished, one from the other, such that they can be counted.* We suggest that this is the most basic facet of the concept of identity. To understand the seminal nature of this facet, let's consider the pre-kindergarten mathematics curriculum as it describes the manner in which a child is taught to count. We first have the child establish the set of things that need to be counted. Then, we teach the child the need to do two things: first, establish a one-to-one correspondence between each member of the set and the individual members of the set of numbers, and second, define a mechanism through which one can determine whether a particular member of the set has been counted or not. So, let's look at an extremely simple example of what this means.

The positive integers comprise a set of entities that have inherent unique differential identities. Moreover, if we simply speak their names in sequence, we count them. Each name (number) we speak establishes the cardinality of the set, up to that point. Hence, we know how many names (numbers) we have thus far counted. We also know that numbers larger than that haven't been counted yet. Now, if we want to count some other set of entities that don't already have unique, sequential numeric identities built in to their very being, perhaps a box of apples, we must first establish a one-to-one correspondence between each member of the set and the members of the set of positive integers. So, we can begin to count a bunch of apples. This apple we'll call *one*; the next apple is *two*; and, so on. Now, to actually establish the count of the complete box of apples, we have to define some mechanism through which we determine that a particular apple has been counted, and that finally all of the apples have been counted.

Let us initially assume we do not want to preserve the order in which we count the apples as a consequence of the counting interaction. That would constitute a forensic wake and our concerns with privacy suggest we don't want to leave that interaction trail. Nor do we want to revisit a particular apple for more detailed analysis after we've completed the count. For example, we might have noted in passing that apple *23* looked like Thomas Jefferson when held up to the light. We might facetiously suggest that if it had appeared to be an image of a religious icon, then there might have been more interest in preserving the association or *identification*. However, the image of Thomas Jefferson we just consider to be a fleeting curiosity. In any case, under these conditions we can proceed with our count by just moving each apple from one box to another box as we count. The latter box has the apples already counted while the first box has the apples yet to be counted. In this manner, for a brief instant while each apple is between boxes and while we have a unique number associated with it, we have established that apple's differential identity within the set comprised of the original box of apples. When the first box is empty, we're through counting the apples and we know how many apples were in it. We do not, however, know the differential identity of any of the apples in the second box. Thus, we have established the most basic facet of identity and we have preserved it only long enough to use it for its intended purpose, to count. Unfortunately, in social ecosystems, we rarely want to establish any facet of identity for such a tenuous purpose. The form and structure of interactions, including their consequences, often demand a more enduring approach. However, we can at least be aware of when we have gone beyond the original concept of differential identity and in designing identification systems we can attempt to minimize this extension if we wish.

Now, suppose that we did want to preserve the differential identities of all the apples in the second box. We could do so by simply writing the number of the count (the one-to-one correspondence between each apple and a positive integer) on each apple as we put it into the *already counted* box. Then, after we have completed our counting, we could re-examine specific apples; we could even duplicate the process of our count exactly if we wanted to. We just find the apple with a *1* on it, then the apple with a *2* and so on. We could even locate apple *23* and hold it up to the light. In this example, these numbers that we write on the apples we will call *markers* through which we can authenticate the differential identity of each individual apple. These markers are quite interesting because they are unique within the box of apples that we're counting, and each marker is indelibly attached to the entity that it represents. Thus, to authenticate the fact that I'm holding apple 17, I merely need to look at the number 17 written on the apple. This all seems rather trivial, but we're establishing concepts that we want to subsequently extend to larger groups than just a box of apples. In particular, we're creating a record of the counting operation, a transaction log if you will that we can subsequently use to enhance our trust regarding an assessment that the count is correct.

It should be noted that even in this very simple illustration, we've already bumped into the very distinct demarcation line between establishing the differential identity of an entity and using that differential identity to track information about that entity. That is, we've taken the differential identity marker of an apple (e.g. the number *23*) and we've indexed some potentially private information with that marker. That's what we did when we noted that apple *23* looks like Thomas Jefferson. So, we have now intertwined the concepts of identity and privacy. Since we are not ordinarily concerned with privacy considerations relative to apples, let's consider a different simple example dealing with people. Let's divine an approach to counting the children in an elementary school. After all, it is rather common for a state to provide some level of financial support for local schools and it typically does so by providing some fixed amount of money for each child in the school. So, it is useful to count the number of children in a school because that will translate into actual money for the school.

Let us posit an example in which we have a school with five grades and we have three classes in each grade. So, in total we have 15 classrooms in our school, each with a collection of students. The Grade 1 students are in classrooms 1, 2 and 3. The Grade 2 students are in classrooms 4, 5 and 6 and so on for all the grades located in classrooms through number 15. We want to allow the teacher in each of these fifteen classrooms to perform the count, and at the end we want to be able to confirm that every student has been counted. We will perform the count by asking each teacher to prepare a class roll, or as we will refer to it, an *identity registry* for each classroom. In each room, the teacher counts each student, making a list with the student's name followed by a number comprised of the room number, a dash and the count of the student; a number that might look like 11 – 14 for the 14<sup>th</sup> student counted in Room 11. This structure for the number has the nice characteristic that it is unique across the entire school. In other words, during the count we have ascribed a *unique identifier* to each student. Based on the concepts we've thus far established, we would perhaps like to say that this unique identifier is a marker for that student. In fact, this is not the case; or, at least it is not a solid marker. We'll look into what constitutes a solid marker just a bit later, but for the moment we can note that this number is not directly connected to the biophysical person. For example, we don't write this number on the forehead of the child or tattoo it on their arm. Consequently, we have not established a strong basis for trust that we can use the number to establish that the specific child is actually participating in an interaction. However, as a component of the identity registry of the school, the list from each room can be gathered and formed into a single list. Thus we have a student identity registry for the entire school. Moreover, if we put a trustworthy process in place through which we can add new students that join the school at some later date or through which we can delete students that permanently leave the school, then we can confirm the count of students at any time by just counting the entries in the school's identity registry.

At this point, one might question why we've gone to such elaborate measures to simply count the number of students in a school. The primary reason derives from the reason we suggested for the count in the first place. That is, the state government is to provide money to the school based on the number of students in the school. Such support will likely require an ability for the government to actually audit the count to confirm that it is accurate. In other words, we need a *transaction log* of the count and the counting process. This is the primary function of the identity registry. Through this registry we can determine that a particular student has been included in the count. Moreover, if one student moves away and four more students enter the school, the registry can be updated to provide an accurate, dynamic count of the students in the school. In general, financial payments from the state government will be made on a monthly basis, using the student count for that specific month to determine the amount of the payment. Of course, it is necessary that there be a significant level of trust in the accuracy of the identity registry. Hence, as we noted we must put in place a trusted process through which the identity registry is kept current.

There is actually a fairly good foundation of trust to be found in such a registry. The foundation derives from the physical structure of the school, the reputation of the teachers, the process use in creating the list and perhaps most important, the mechanisms used by humans in establishing unique identity within more basic groups. First, each class has its own classroom. This establishes a well defined context for a small group. Each class has a teacher that administers the context established by the classroom. As an employee of the school, the teacher can be ascribed some level of trust because of the hiring practices of the school and through the ongoing reputation established by each teacher within the school. The manner in which the identity registry was initially formed is a well defined process, designed with the idea of creating a trustworthy identity registry. Finally, a teacher can be trusted to recognize a particular student. Thus, within a class, if the teacher asks Sally Green to stand, he can determine that in fact Sally Green is standing and not Kathy Brown. So, we have a unique identifier assigned to each student that is validated by a biometric authentication protocol; that is, the teacher being able to associate each student with their name through physical recognition. Or course, we have yet to determine how one would authenticate the presence of Sally Green outside of the classroom where an association of her name with her appearance might not be well established. In addition, there are other rather obvious shortcomings that speak to the trust that we can derive from the process. We'll try to address those as we extend the examples.

The association of a name to a person is itself an interesting concept. A name is actually a metaphor (admittedly with a wider application of this term than usual) for a person intended to present an assertion of differential identity across a social ecosystem. It is, of course, not necessarily unique. In a large social ecosystem, there are actually lots of people with identical names. So, if one goes outside of the context within which their name is fairly well defined, it is likely that much of the context specific information associated with the name will not convey. Of course, in small groups that exist over a long period of time, a name becomes associated with the physical and social characteristics of an individual person. Within a social group, such as within the domain of the school, it can become well established that Sally Green is the tall (for her age), red haired girl with freckles that is in the third grade. Moreover, Sally Green is good at math, poor at social studies and likes to eat peanut butter and jelly sandwiches for lunch. Now, we have greatly expanded the metaphor suggested by the name. This expansion we call a *persona*. Another way to characterize a persona is to view it as a subset of a person's total experiential identity. We suggest the term *anchored persona* to indicate this most intimate association of a person's differential identity with their total experiential identity. Of course, it is also useful to be able to establish a subset of experiential identity that can be used to establish an identity-related context. Thus, within social ecosystems one might project the persona of a mother or father, of an employee of a company, of a good athlete and so on. We suggest the term *floating persona* in such cases. An interesting application of a floating persona is the establishment of discrete information contexts for a person as a means of achieving privacy. An unfortunate application of the concept of persona may occur when someone else seeks to define a persona for another person. This is the way that *stereotypes* are formed and hence of preferential or prejudicial application of policy based on the stereotype persona rather than on the specific experiential identity of the person.

A persona to be presented by a person is a matter of choice by the person. This is simply a restatement of the concept of privacy as meaning control of information. A name, as an assertion of a persona, is a matter of choice as well. This is a central reason why a name is a very poor marker for differential identity. The name presented by a person can change, in many cases seemingly on a whim. Within the United States, the prevailing social orders typically place few limits on a person's changing their name. In fact, during the course of their lives, most people present a variety of names. Sometimes the change is merely emphasis of a middle name that is preferred to the first name. Sometimes the change adopts a nickname as preferable to a given name. Women may take the last name of their husband when they marry. In some cases the last names of husband and wife may be combined, forming a hyphenated name. In certain contexts, for example in Internet chat rooms, people may present themselves through a *handle*; a more illustrative means of indicating a persona. From the virtually official city logo of the city of Las Vegas, Nevada that says, "What happens in Vegas, stays in Vegas!" we discern that in some cases a persona is intended to be completely arbitrary and thus effectively disjoint from the experiential identity of the person in question. We suggest the term *situational persona* for this particular application.

To explore the concept of persona in just a bit more depth, let's return to the identity registry that we established when we counted the students in our example school. A rather standard feature of schools is the offering of some level of health insurance for the students. If a particular student's parents pay for the insurance, a record of that fact is maintained at the school. Perhaps during the morning recess period, Sally Green is struck in the head by a hard ball thrown by a classmate. Seeing a large bump on Sally's head, and fearing the possibility of a concussion, the teacher calls an ambulance and Sally is taken to the hospital. At the hospital, as part of the registration procedure, Sally's *student identification number* is taken down. This number is just the counting index that we saw associated with Sally's name at school. Of course, it is now a very useful number for a variety of purposes because it is a unique indicator of one specific student. Obviously, one of its potential uses is to indicate that Sally Green has student health insurance. In the course of Sally's medical treatment in the emergency room, perhaps a sample of her blood is taken to assist in the diagnosis or treatment of her head trauma. The blood tests are subsequently indexed with Sally's student identification number. Two different contexts related to Sally are now related to each other in a rather public, transparent way; her school persona and her health persona. The privacy concerns of Sally and her parents might be very different for these two domains.

The problem we perceive here is not one that derives from the establishment of a good indicator of differential identity. In fact, both of these domains have a strong expectation of being able to establish in a trustworthy fashion Sally Green's differential identity. Rather, it is useful if people can project different persona into different domains and ground those different persona in the differential identity strongly connected to the biophysical person. One approach to accomplishing this is to use a different indicator, an *identity-index*, for associating some attribute to differential identity. Suppose, for example that when performing the blood tests on Sally Green it was found that she had leukemia or at least the strong possibility of having leukemia. This might well be a health condition that Sally Green's parents did not want associated with her school record. Certainly, any disclosure of these facts should be the parent's decision. When she visits a new doctor, they may want her to be known only as a person who has leukemia. If she is older, when she goes to the voting booth, she certainly wants to be known only as a person who is legally entitled to vote. The voting booth volunteers have no business knowing that a voter has leukemia and if the voting system is well designed, they don't even need to know the name of the voter. The key to all of these situations, and maintaining privacy relative to each, is to establish an identity index that is strongly tied to Sally Green's differential identity but which is used to attribute information to her in only selected contexts. We can use such techniques to actually make the privacy constraints stronger than would be possible through attempts at anonymity. Of course, this is all contingent on being able at some point in the process to determine a person's differential identity.

As we've noted, there can be profound distinctions between counting large populations of people and counting a box of apples. If we want to count the people sitting on an airplane prior to departure from the gate, then the counting problem is quite similar to our example. We go from the front to the back of the plane while counting the people occupying the seats, and everybody behind us has already been counted; they are in the already counted box. This can even work on an Airbus 380 or a Boeing 747, both multi-deck aircraft. We just have a different flight attendant count each deck of the plane while more flight attendants monitor the stairways so a person can't change decks during the count. Our consideration of a means to count the students in a school is a more elaborate approach to this situation. Now, let's consider a more complex problem; that of counting the people in a large, diverse population while that population is in a state of considerable flux.

The people within the United States constitute just such a large population. At the time of this writing, it is estimated that there are over 300,000,000 people in the United States. A new person is born about every ten seconds and someone dies about every fifteen seconds. People enter the country from abroad each year by the millions and they depart as well in similar numbers. Some of these people are allowed to become citizens while others are primarily allowed to work and pay taxes. The seminal trust purveyor of the primary social order, that is the Constitution of the United States, mandates that this population is to be counted and a variety of subgroups identified during the count. Further, this population is to be counted at least once every ten years. The Constitution is quite clear; the population is to be enumerated, not estimated. So, it generally takes about a year to perform the count. It costs billions of dollars and the count requires the services of about a million people for some portion of that year. Alas, the count is wrong every time! The basic reason it is wrong is because the process used for the count doesn't do the two things that our pre-kindergarten curriculum says we have to do to count a bunch of things. Specifically, the process doesn't include a good way to establish a differential identity marker that we can associate with each person so that we can in the future determine whether they've been counted or not. In addition, the counting process used is comparable to our example method for counting apples, except that we're hard pressed to get the entire population of the country to stand in their appropriate boxes.

With a large population that is continuously in a state of flux, we suggest that the best count that one can do is to asymptotically approach the correct answer; that is, to determine the actual number of people in the sets to be counted. Therefore, a case can be made that if accuracy is the goal, then with the same amount of work, we would be better off maintaining a continuous count for which we can constantly improve the accuracy and precision, rather than restarting the count from scratch every ten years to reacquire information we should already have. However, to so accurately count the population of the United States, we would need a permanent personal differential identity system that could maintain a continuous count of the population. One might argue that this is the correct mandate for the Bureau of the Census. Perhaps that's a topic best left to a different discussion. However, such a system would allow us, relative to any single person, to accurately determine whether they've been counted or not and it is certainly germane to our current discussion to consider the methodology of such a system. It is, in fact, central to the concept of extending the mechanisms of human social orders into cyberspace.

While the United States Census presents a moderately difficult case, virtually any situation in which we want to be able to establish the differential identity of individuals presents the same set of issues. Moreover, we have yet to consider the problem of linking experiential identity to differential identity in a trusted manner. So, to address these issues in more detail, let's consider the issues associated with *differential identity markers*.

When faced with counting a large, constantly changing population, care must be given to the manner in which we make a correspondence between the individual person and a set of numbers that have counting as part of their being. In particular, if we're going to actually trust the final tally that we arrive at, we need to make sure this correspondence isn't easily counterfeited or misinterpreted. Historically, the approach used in establishing such a marker has been to issue a *credential* to the person that asserts the differential identity of that person relative to other persons within the set from which the credential derives. Such credentials are typically issued within some group, so each credential is aimed at distinguishing a specific person within that group. This, of course, harkens back to the examples we noted earlier under the guise of experiential identity. In fact, a credential is actually a formal record of a discrete experience of experiential identity. A major difficulty with the attempt to use credentials for establishing differential identity is that the credential is typically only ambiguously associated with the person, perhaps through physical possession or perhaps through societal convention. We have already discussed at some length an example of a credential that is associated with an actual person through societal convention; their name. As we also noted, a name is a moderately reasonable credential to be used in the authentication of differential identity in a small group. A credential might also be associated with a person through physical possession. Thus, a person might hold a credential in the form of a *token*, for example a signet ring. Using a more modern example, a useful credential might actually be a hybrid of the two, such as a card with the name printed on it (let's say that there is no picture for the time being). In the simplest of cases, possession of the credential establishes the differential identity of the credential bearer (presenter) in the eyes of the credential receiver. Of course, when physical possession is all that connects the credential token to the bearer it means that when the token passes to a new person, that person assumes the differential identity of the person that the token actually represents. To avoid this, we need more sophisticated methods of tying the token to the token bearer. So, while possession of a token with a name on it is a fairly straightforward paradigm, unfortunately its use requires that we answer the question "How do I know that the correct person is in possession of the token?"

Before we answer this question, let it be said again that probably the foremost challenge of any identification system is to properly separate the differential identity, which is a counting mechanism, from the experiential identity, which is an information mechanism. A differential identity without experiential identity does not carry private information in and of itself. Any experiential identity, on the contrary, is subject to privacy concerns. We have tried to be most careful on this. Also, the center of privacy lies in the link that can be made between experiential identities and a single differential identity. To emphasize the importance of this point, let's consider again the example of the number carved on the apple. We discussed the fact that we don't want to use this number as an identity index. We explained why by presenting the possible privacy issues of a person with leukemia; we showed that by using discrete identity indexes, the person could selectively disclose her private information according to the situations she was considering. We want to emphasize a point that we made earlier. While there are many ways to actually carve numbers or other indicators on a person, the most obvious one is the tattoo; obviously, such approaches always incur concerns about privacy. For example, using a tattoo as a differential identity marker is a total invasion of privacy since it would typically also be used as an identity index, and the indexed information about the individual could be traced back immediately to that individual. That's why we react in horror to the physical marking of prisoners. Commingling identity indexes and differential identity markers destroys the notion of privacy.

Many more socially acceptable mechanisms have evolved for divining markers that are closely associated with a person. Among these are signatures, pictures or perhaps secret passwords or Personal Identification Numbers (PINs). All of these approaches are variants of identity establishing credentials. Each is plagued with significant trust deficiencies. For example, signatures are rather easily forged and they can be affected by the emotional state of the writer. Pictures are often ambiguous and with current digital photography facilities they can be fraudulently modified. There are lots of scams in play to capture personal identification numbers. Thus, it is the case that differential identity authentication based purely on credential systems is fraught with opportunities for counterfeiting, fraud or other forms of identity theft. What then is the most effective means of establishing a differential identity marker? Well, to guide us in answering that question, let's consider some characteristics that we would like to find in a solid marker.

It is absolutely essential that the marker be unique for every individual. This suggests that we must be able to define unique markers for the six or seven billion people on the earth at the present time, and for many billions more that will exist in the relatively near future. So, to be somewhat safe, let's assume that we need at least one hundred billion markers. Put another way, a marker must be unique to one part in one hundred billion. Next, given that we want to establish the differential identity of a person over their entire lifetime, we expect a marker to be immutable for that period. It will be necessary for the marker to be very closely associated with a person. In fact, the marker may actually already be part of a person. In this case, any equipment necessary to capture the marker or the value of the marker must be non-invasive to the human body. To give a counter-example, the blood vessel pattern on the surface of a kidney, while perhaps unique to each person, would probably require invasive techniques to measure. In addition to being non-invasive, any measurement equipment should be relatively inexpensive and highly reliable. It should be possible to certify a level of trustworthiness of the equipment.

When a person enters an identification system, a copy of their differential identity marker is captured and stored in the identity registry for the system. This process is termed *enrollment*. At the time a person enrolls, the marker can be compared to all existing markers in the registry to confirm that the person is only entered into the system once. This process is termed *identification*. The process of capturing the marker from the person and comparing that to a copy of the marker that was stored away when the person enrolled in the identification system in question is termed either *verification* or *authentication*. The marker should be of such a form that a highly reliable comparison of captured versus stored markers can be made. The probability should be low that markers that should match don't, and the probability should be high that markers that should not match indeed do not match. The comparison process should be relatively quick, which means not really more than a second or so. If it takes two hours to perform the comparison process then the authentication operation will be useless for most interactions.

We can also suggest a couple of characteristics that would allow us to keep differential identity teased apart from privacy. First, the marker should convey no information about the individual other than the differential identity of that person. Moreover, the marker should offer minimal or non-existent forensic evidence. In other words, it is desirable that the marker not be amenable to unintended indication of physical presence, which is an example of forensic evidence, except through an intentionally activated authentication protocol.

Following this rather lengthy prologue, we will now cut to the chase and assert that at the present time, the most reliable differential identity marker mechanism that possesses these characteristics is one or more of the biometric traits of the human body. Principal among these are fingerprints, handprints, facial characteristics, retinal patterns, iris patterns and DNA. Further, it should be noted that we're suggesting that an actual biometric characteristic forms the differential identity marker, not some card or other token that encompasses the biometric characteristic.

The last two marker requirements that we noted illustrate our concern for the demarcation between establishing pure differential identity and using differential identity as an index for other information that we often want to relate to identity. As an example, if we want to adhere to our set of stated marker requirements, we will be more inclined to use a fingerprint or an iris scan versus using a DNA pattern because DNA conveys much more health related information that an individual may well want to hold private. Moreover, because we can derive DNA from blood or other bodily fluids, the presence of DNA is an ambiguous indicator of physical presence. That is, since blood can be taken from an individual and then placed at some location where that individual has not actually been, it is a potentially erroneous forensic indicator. We will be more inclined to use an iris scan versus a fingerprint because the iris scan offers significantly less forensic value than does a fingerprint. When we handle things, we often leave behind our fingerprints. When we look at things, we rarely leave behind our iris patterns. However, iris patterns contain more health related information than fingerprints.

# Big Brother and the Mark of the Beast

During the course of this book, while we have considered in some detail the concepts of theology and philosophy as they pertain to the form and function of human social systems, we have steered away from discussing topics of specific theology or philosophy. However, we might be perceived as lacking in some degree of intellectual honesty if we avoid specific consideration of two iconic works relative to our consideration of the concept of identity. These works are the George Orwell book *1984* and the *Book of Revelation* in the *Christian Bible*. Both are illustrative examples of apocalyptic literature and each offers prophecies for two of the social orders that we have identified; *1984* with respect to égalité and the *Book of Revelation* with respect to the religious congregation.

Orwell's masterpiece introduces us to Big Brother while *Revelation* focuses our attention on the Antichrist and his derivative mark of the beast. Both works are superb examples of the concept of metaphorical understanding. Indeed, both extend the concept of metaphor into that of allegory. Allegory, in turn, is a mechanism completely dependent upon context. Thus, more advanced scholars in their respective fields will likely see nuances in both works that will less stringently appear to us. Nonetheless, in any extended discussion of the concept of identity and its constituent facets, issues of concern will commonly be raised in reference to, and typically through immediate levels of interpretation of these two works. It is to these issues that we feel some necessity to suggest our own interpretation. We will come back to additional discussions relative to metaphoric understanding in our final chapter, which we titled in deference to the *Book of Revelation*.

When one mentions the concepts of identity and governance in the same breath, a virtually autonomic response from many is the concern that a governmental big brother will soon be looking over their shoulders. From the Christian suppliant, an equally reflexive concern is the incursion of the mark of the beast. Such is the power of art and aesthetic projection that a strong evocation of trust is imbued by this simple reference to *1984* and *Revelation*. To allay some degree of the concerns so raised, we suggest that one must interpret both works through the vocabulary that we considered in the previous section. While both raise quite valid issues, if one interprets them through the appropriate facets of the concept of identity, we suggest that one can derive a meaningful prophetic alternative as well as a more reflective response than that which their mention often engenders in a discussion about identity. To that end, let's consider the works in just a bit more detail.

Focusing on the three central characters, *1984* portrays a social order replete with references to the facets of identity that we have previously discussed. Winston Smith is the central protagonist of the story who, supported by his girlfriend Julia, engages in an ongoing struggle against an ill-recognized adversary named O'Brien. Smith is the iconic representative of the individual person found within a larger set of people. In the vocabulary we have suggested, he is the metaphor for differential identity. The plot of the book centers on his attempts to maintain some semblance of privacy, specifically as it pertains to freedom of action, within an authoritarian government regime controlled by "The Party." Through a variety of technologically enabled communication channels, The Party is able to observe and subsequently control the actions of everyone in the nation; that is, within the primary social order. An interesting mechanism used for this control, in other words a central aspect of the policy infrastructure, is that of *newspeak*; a social discourse filter based upon the premise of redefining the basic metaphors of language through which people interact, making for example a single blend of peace and war. This is perhaps one of the more profound revelations of the book, as this concept is foundational to the evolution of social systems.

In his book *The White Goddess: A Historical Grammar of Poetic Myth*, Robert Graves offers the theory that poetry emerged from ancient times representing original religious discourse, later on followed by a recurring theme of societies reshaping the metaphors by which they express themselves through their art forms and subsequently their common language. Thus, newspeak forms a hyperbolic notation of this very mechanism. It is interesting to speculate on the association of this mechanism to the concept of the "living Constitution" which gained its precursor musings from Woodrow Wilson, and more specifically from the dissent of Supreme Court Justice Louis Brandeis in the case of Olmstead versus United States. This case is interesting from a technical communications perspective because, through Brandeis' dissent, the concept of a dynamic Constitution was introduced as a means to extend the application of law as applied to the age-old mail service, which is a direct association of the original language of the Constitution, to the very new technology of voice telephony. This dissenting opinion was among the first to recognize an effective right of privacy that derived from the penumbra of more explicitly stated rights, a central legal fixture of the Roe versus Wade decision.

Returning to the consideration of *1984*, the social order itself was one in which the trust and policy infrastructures are apparently congruent. It was in fact represented by an abstract floating persona asserted through the name of Big Brother. We consider this an abstract entity because it is unclear from the book whether the individual portrayed as Big Brother actually existed. Based on the premise of the book, we can extend our consideration of identity facets by suggesting that Big Brother is actually a mechanism through which to derive *institutional anonymity*. This is a characteristic of social orders in which authority is ascribed to a persona; a persona sometimes denoted as a *role*. By assuming a designated role, a variety of people can actually assert the authority ascribed to that role; in essence, the individual person, or *actor*, achieves a state of anonymity relative to their specific differential identity. In this situation, a relatively successful state of anonymity is achieved since the forensic wake that denotes the occurrence of interactions cannot be attributed to an individual person, but rather it accrues only to the role. Thus, in the book, O'Brien, who is surreptitiously a member of the inner circle of The Party can feign to appear as a friend to Smith. Similarly, others within The Party can, while camouflaged by a communication channel, reflect a persona that can not be traced back to their differential identity. On the other hand, Smith, for all his efforts to achieve some degree of privacy by appearing anonymous, fails utterly at the process. Therefore, we can now see the popular misconception about the book.

When presented with the prospect of an identification system that allows for the strong authentication of identity of a person, many people will interpret this as a bad thing on the assumption that it negates the ability to achieve anonymity and thus privacy. In fact, anonymity of a private individual, that is one operating outside of a large, institutional framework, is difficult if not impossible to achieve in any case; their interactions in the real world just leave behind too many tracks. However, individuals who are able to assert some role within a large institution can achieve a significant degree of anonymity. The internal operations of the institution are quite private, leading to an extremely asymmetric interaction framework between individuals inside the institution and those who are outside of it. We would suggest that if strongly authenticated differential identity were available for all parties, coupled to policy based privacy rules requiring interaction records based on this same strong authentication, then privacy for the individual would be more likely to be attained as well as possibly establishing greater visibility into institutional activities. Moreover, if the system is aimed at the establishment of differential identity, rather than experiential identity, then the leaking of privacy sensitive information is greatly minimized. As this might sound paradoxical, maybe we should mention here that there are technical mechanisms to strongly authenticate differential identity without providing any means to actually trace back that identity: one mechanism is that of *differentiated keys*, i.e. keys that are derived and different from a master differential identity key, allowing asserting identity without disclosing it. In that context, we would interpret the book *1984* as offering a rather compelling case for a strong differential identity system as a means to achieve effective privacy as opposed to suggesting a repulsive reaction to such a system.

The *Book of Revelation* tells a story of an apocalyptic "end of days." Most interpretations suggest it is a story of the final battle of the forces of Satan, led by the Antichrist, against God and the "chosen elect." We note that the book never actually mentions the designation of Antichrist. Rather, it makes reference to two great beasts that are generally viewed as allegorical references to Satan and to his emissary on the Earth called the Antichrist. Embedded within the book is a reference to the mark of the beast; an identifying marker metaphorically associated with the Antichrist and the followers of the Antichrist. From our perspective, *Revelation*, much like *1984*, elicits a somewhat distorted view derived from popular misconceptions regarding the various facets of identity. The issue, relative to identification mechanisms, extends from *Revelation 13:16-18*:

> And he causeth all, the small and the great, and the rich and the poor, and the free and the bond, that there be given them a mark on their right hand, or upon their forehead; and that no man should be able to buy or to sell, save he that hath the mark, even the name of the beast or the number of his name. Here is wisdom. He that hath understanding, let him count the number of the beast; for it is the number of a man: and his number is Six hundred and sixty and six.

While sometimes interpreted that the mark of the beast so indicated is intended to establish the identity of the followers of the Antichrist, we would note that it does so through a credential of authority, not through establishment of differential identity. In other words, the mark of the beast is an indicator of a specific set of people, not of the identification of individual people within that set. The distinction is profound. The purpose of the mark is the establishment of a stereotype persona that is the same for every person within the specific group; that is, those who have mistakenly followed the Antichrist. The mark in fact is an identity index derived from the Antichrist, not the differential identity of the individual person. Interestingly enough, Graves speaks to this point in direct reference to the establishment of the specific metaphor of the mark of the beast in *The White Goddess*. He suggests that the reference to the mark of the beast was a number derived from a *titulus* (an inscription) designating the identity of the Antichrist. He considers that the number 666 is represented by the Roman numerals: D.C.L.X.V.I., abbreviating DOMITIUS CAESAR LEGATOS XTI VIOLENTER INTERFECIT. The translation is that Domitius Caesar sacrilegiously killed the envoys of Christ, an interpretation keeping with at least one path of understanding of the *Book of Revelation*.

That school of interpretation of *Revelation* is called *preterism*. It suggests that the prophecies revealed in *Revelation* were actually fulfilled in the century following the crucifixion of Jesus. In other words, the references to the Antichrist were actually references to the Roman Emperors responsible for the persecution of the early Christians. Of course, this is not the only school of interpretation. Others suggest that the prophesies are yet unfulfilled. As we will consider in somewhat more detail in our last chapter, the metaphorical presentation of *Revelation* is such that many in virtually every generation of Christians for the last two millennia have found current relevance in the book. However, no matter the specific interpretations of the identity (specifically, the differential identity) of the Antichrist, the relevant scriptures indicate that the mark of the beast is a direct reference to the Antichrist's differential identity or an identity index derived from that single differential identity. Thus, we would suggest that the mark is a credential: it has the characteristics of a generic theater ticket, not of an identification card. While not a ticket that a devout Christian would seek to hold, in fact it has relatively little in common with a secure core or with a transcendent personal device for that matter. As a Radio-Frequency Identification (RFID) Token, the only information that it would convey is "Admit One to the Lake of Fire."

In *The SpyChips Threat*, Katherine Albrecht and Liz McIntyre consider RFID tokens attached to goods on one hand, and RFID tokens potentially (in a few cases so far) inserted under the skin of humans. They warn that RFID tokens attached to goods, say in a supermarket, may stay attached to those goods when the purchase is completed, therefore allowing to trace the customer thereafter, an obvious invasion of privacy. Concerning RFID inserted under the skin, they warn, equally correctly, of the possibility to make them equivalent to tattooing an identity number on prisoners; again, an obvious invasion of privacy. Furthermore, the authors equate RFID to the mark of the beast of the *Book of Revelation*, henceforth their subtitle in: *The SpyChips Threat: Why Christian Should Resist RFID and Electronic Surveillance*. We do not think that this association with the mark of the beast is warranted, as we explained earlier that the latter is not a differential identity index of the marquee. However, it should be clear to our readers that we consider that the use of RFID outside of their purview, e.g. outside of the inventory system of a supermarket, is not acceptable. In particular, using and implanted RFID, if it allows associating a differential identity with an experiential identity, is even more condemnable. Every technology contains a possibility of misuse, but the transcendent personal device is actually intended to correct and prevent abuses of that sort, and in fact provides means to implement the very privacy that is otherwise threatened, as we will now see in more details.

# Transcendence Affected

Our perspective suggests that the human species' efforts toward transcendence consist primarily of effecting a systematic and coherent environment for group and personal interactions. With respect to computer systems and networks this need encompasses the extension of the facilities of existing social ecosystems into cyberspace in order for individuals to have the same possibilities for affecting the behavior of that environment. In the extreme, this translates into the instigation of social mutational events that serve to shape the social ecosystems in which we as humans live. At the beginning of this chapter, we noted three such mutational events with the inference that these paradigm transitions were the result of this societal stimulus for transcendence. However, we must remember that the needs of transcendence are found not just at a societal level, but in all persons, great and small. Moreover, we suggest that these needs provide impetus through our most complex, cognitive tools. They are profound in the degree to which they impact the individual. It is arguable that it is through the need of transcendence that groups evoke devotional behavior on the part of the individual. Our rather modest goal is to suggest that we can collectively provide similar capabilities within our computer networks and that to do so we require a new species of computer; a species to which we ascribe the name *transcendent personal device*.

The sating of the appetites of the individual within existing social ecosystems might be thought of as the sandbox of the transcendent personal device. As a consequence, we suggest a potential mutational shift in the manner in which individual persons interacts with their environment from a policy perspective. We can derive from current implementations of personal electronic devices some of the more basic capabilities through which such a new species of systems would offer the basis for computers and computer networks to meet this general need of the individual person. The full set of potential capabilities of the transcendent personal device is more properly derived from the needs hierarchy as reflected in the composition and utility of the Internet and the Web. One assumes that the progression of needs hierarchy stimuli progresses from the deficiency needs through the growth needs. We suggest that in considering the transcendent personal device the impetus actually begins with the highest of the growth needs; that of transcendence itself. Thus, we will consider the potential capabilities of the device beginning with the goal of affecting the transcendence facilities provided by computer networks through the device to its individual bearer.

# The Transcendent Personal Device

Transcendence builds upon the cognitive abilities of the mind coupled with its communication capabilities that are enabled through the human mastery of language. As we've noted previously, fulfilling the higher order needs in Maslow's hierarchy mandates a social structure. These are not needs that can readily be fulfilled for a person in total isolation. Indeed, this requirement for a supporting social ecosystem might be a significant, contributing factor to the observation that complete isolation of a person affects their cognitive functions. So, our interpretation of transcendence is a need aimed at actually bringing the required social ecosystems into existence. In a rather counter-intuitive twist, we suggest that this prospect can perhaps be illustrated by reflecting on the bottom left elements of the pretergenesis table of Chapter 5 and through them considering the rather complex behavior of the beaver (*Castor canadensis*).

The beaver is a large rodent that prior to 1700 lived throughout most of the lands of North America north of what is today the border between the United States and Mexico. Beavers are social animals, grouping together in multi-generational family units through which they pursue a variety of group-centric behaviors. Their natural habitat is comprised of small, meandering streams. Beavers are well suited to an aquatic environment, having a lush fur that provides insulation and excellent streamlining properties that allow them to move easily through water. They have webbed hind feet that provide strong propulsion and they have a large, flat tail. Like most rodents, they possess two pronounced upper front teeth that grow at an accelerated rate and allow heavy use that in turn keeps them worn down. These teeth are supported in an oversized jaw bone structure that gives them great power as the beavers pursue one of their prevalent activities, cutting down trees along the banks of the streams in which they live. They use the bark and leaves from such trees for food, and they use the main bodies of the trees and their branches to construct dams within their resident streams. Their teeth, paws and tail are well suited to the cutting down of trees, the movement of branches and the use of mud to bind materials together to form their structures. The dams they construct form pools or ponds of water, some of which may be relatively large, encompassing thousands of square meters. Such pools provide constant water sources for the growth of trees and shrubs along the banks, thus providing a continuing source of food for the beavers.

Beavers also use the ponds that result from the dams that they build as a means of safety and security for themselves and for their young. Within the ponds and along the banks, the beavers construct nests; in some instances, they create small floating islands on which to build their nests. These nests are completely enclosed and typically have only two entry points, one being a hole in the floor inside the nest that leads directly into the water. Through this hole, the beavers have ingress and egress to the nest by swimming underwater and coming up into the nest through the hole. For any predator that seeks to attack the nest in this fashion, it immediately places the beavers inside the nest on the high ground and in a position to use the formidable close combat weapon presented by their teeth. If predators use the other door, then the beavers have a readymade escape route that non-aquatic species might well be uncomfortable in using. The beaver has evolved a successful set of behaviors, as judged by natural selection, which require a specialized and somewhat complex environment. They need rather stable bodies of water in which to live, to find food and to construct their nests. Such environments are not naturally occurring in large numbers across wide ranges of geography. By developing a facility for constructing the necessary environment, beavers have created a means to control their physical ecosystem. One can certainly argue that the beaver dam, and its resulting facilities, constitutes one of the more complex systems encountered outside the human species' control of its environment. Considering the behaviors necessary to construct and maintain this complex physical and social environment, we see a significant precursor to the human need for, and pursuit of, transcendence.

In the case of the human species, if we consider the extension of the social fabric that is projected by computers and computer networks, then it would seem that our needs, being higher in the ontogenetic and phylogenetic scales, would provide impetus for a tool or system that better conveys human cognitive functions into this extension of human social ecosystems. So, our interpretation of the concept for this tool or system is that of a computational entity that enables humans to sate their full range of needs through interactions within various sizes of groups as effected through widespread computer networks. As instantiated within cyberspace, we suggest the need for a computer through which humans can project themselves into and through cyberspace just as their physical presence can be projected into and through the social ecosystems that have enabled the species to achieve eminence. Our model for such a tool, the manifestation of this new species of computer, derives from a blending of current systems with new capabilities and with additional characteristics that facilitate the cognitive connection of the computer to the person. This model is grounded in the form and function of current personal electronic devices, although technological advances might well transcend these currently envisioned forms and functions. As must always be noted in such situations, where the evaluation through market forces may take a different path than we envision, "Your mileage may vary."

For purposes of our discussion, we have termed this new species the transcendent personal device to reflect the highest level of need considered in the pretergenesis table. What then is our model for the transcendent personal device? What new characteristics should it possess and how will it relate to the human cognition system in order to constructively augment or reinforce that system, particular insofar as it facilitates an extension of human social ecosystems to encompass cyberspace? In essence, this brings us to the heart and soul of our examination of human and computer characteristics.

In the pretergenesis table, we mapped the association between evolutionary characteristics of the human species to the needs hierarchy that provides the stimulus for human interactions. Through the expanding characteristics provided by the evolution of the body and mind of the individual human, the needs of that individual expanded apace. We suggest that in a like fashion, the desired characteristics of the transcendent personal device should be migrating toward better support for the human species in meeting its full range of needs and specifically should facilitate the social grouping mechanisms that have proven so important to human preeminence.

Following the progression of the growth of the human needs hierarchy that we considered in Chapter 5, suggest that a reasonable way to consider the characteristics of the transcendent personal device is to elaborate about them in a parallel to human needs. As we develop the capabilities desired to support the higher level needs, they will in turn reflect on increasingly specific technological facilities elaborated in response to the lower level needs. We note that Maslow presented human needs as a *hierarchy*, not just a *list*. The computer system analogue to this might well be to portray the sating of appetites as a hierarchical set of related preemptable task queues, with a queue established for each level of the hierarchy. The sating of particular appetites can then be expressed as applications invoked through these various task queues.

The point being that the acquisition of content or perhaps more appropriately stated, the sating of appetites, is a function of the net impact of needs across the full hierarchy. Being hungry for food is virtually always satisfied according to conventions established at a higher level; social conditioning is so effective that only in the most extraordinary circumstances will humans resort to cannibalism to avoid death by starvation. So, with that rather graphic image as background, let's begin our consideration of the enhancements necessary to realize a truly effective transcendent personal device as determined by the needs of both species; that is, the human species as well as the transcendent personal device species. As prelude, we will consider the architecture of the mutationally derived device.

# Architecture

The essence of the required enhancements is to position the transcendent personal device as a fully capable electronic extension of the person; to be owned by the person, to be carried by and operated by the person and to function purely on behalf of the person. This defines not only a set of anatomical and physiological characteristics for the transcendent personal device itself, characteristics that we'll consolidate under the term *architecture*, but also a set of policy characteristics that must be established within the salient social ecosystems in which we want the device to function. In today's typical deployment for example, a secure core is viewed under most policy specifications as the property of its issuer. However, the marketing message that conveys from the issuer to the user generally stresses the utility and security benefits that will accrue to the bearer of the personal device thanks to the secure core. For example, bank chip cards are token based credentials through which trust emanating from the issuer can be conveyed through the token, on behalf of the bearer, to other entities such as content providers. An issue arises with current architectures, however, in that the connection between the token and its rightful bearer is typically rather tenuous. Further, it is usually the prerogative of the service to which the device connects to determine whether this connection has been established to a satisfactory degree; this, we suggest, is a root contributor to the epidemic of identity theft that is sweeping the Internet and other social ecosystems today. Not because such services required too great a level of trust in the authentication of the bearer, but rather because they will accept too little.

From our perspective, to fully realize the utility of the transcendent personal device, a shift in emphasis relative to current personal electronic devices within existent human social ecosystems must occur. The preeminent such system, of course, is the governmental policy infrastructure formed under the auspices of trust established by the Constitution. Consequently, to effect the required policy shift, the transcendent personal device must be considered in operation, *under the relevant law*, to be a *fiduciary* agent acting on behalf of the bearer. This shift requires that the complete fiduciary responsibility of the transcendent personal device be to the bearer and not to the seller, provider or any other party. The result of this shift is to directly link the trust infrastructure of the transcendent personal device, as a subordinate trust infrastructure, to the trust infrastructure of the preeminent social ecosystem. This will, in turn precipitate a shift in orientation within the relevant policy infrastructures that will have to be established through law. It will entail modifications to the very fabric of society that we discussed a few chapters ago, particularly as it impacts extensions of this fabric into cyberspace. As this shift occurs, we can then begin to envision these evolutionary descendents of today's personal electronic devices as truly the purveyors of complex policy on behalf of the individual person. Such use and orientation of responsibility are really not feasible with today's high security computing platforms. They are too big, too expensive and too complex for the ubiquitous personal prosthesis role. Once such systems are required to service the policy requirements, including personal security characteristics, of more than one person, their very nature becomes suspect.

Our recurring example of an iconic personal electronic device in use today is the mobile cellular telephone. The GSM variant of mobile phones is comprised of a dual anatomy: the handset and the *Subscriber Identity Module* (SIM). The Subscriber Identity Module is a secure core that provides a degree of intrinsic security through its tamper-resistant and tamper-evident construction. The handset, on the other hand, encompasses a much more powerful but complex, and hence more vulnerable, set of capabilities; a powerful processor, lots of memory and a preferably intuitive and powerful user interface. Unlike the SIM, the handset has the more general characteristics we might expect from a personal computer, including its vulnerabilities to attack from malicious hackers. In the article *Malware Goes Mobile* in the November, 2006 issue of Scientific American, Mikko Hypponen indicated that malicious software akin to the viruses that have proven such a bane to personal computer systems was beginning to show up on mobile phone handsets. Given the much more structured and protected facilities for software modification on SIMs, the same types of attacks have not proven generally successful there. Another incarnation of a personal electronic device is the Blackberry, a device that enables the user to send and receive e-mail, along with performing a variety of other personal convenience functions. Both the mobile phone and the Blackberry make use of radio frequency channels to allow the user to connect to ubiquitous communication networks. Indeed, the latest incarnations of the latter include a variant of the former. All types of such devices make use of rechargeable batteries to effect portable, local power. The devices are small, aimed at being carried on the person of their user and effecting interactions between the user and other entities through radio frequency based connections. Both use a secure core for extended communications though GSM networks. Such wireless connectivity offers enhanced convenience, as the device does not have to leave the bearer's direct, physical possession to be used. This greatly facilitates enhanced security and thereby enhanced trust characteristics. Consequently, we will assume a two-element architecture through which to consider the enhanced capabilities of the transcendent personal device; a sensori-motor body coupled to a protected, trusted core agent; a cognitive element that allows for some degree of trust establishment for the transcendent personal device as a whole. In drawing a parallel to evolutionary development leading to the human species, this suggests that current personal electronic devices are comparable to the hominids in general, if not to more specific precursors to *Homo sapiens*. But all this now leads us to perhaps the greatest departure from current architectures; a mutational leap in the vein of the emergence of modern humans some 50,000 years ago or more.

# Self-Actualization

In most systems today, a personal electronic device secure core functions as a server to the system to which it connects. More strongly stated, the secure core is a slave to the external system's mastery. When used as an admittance token, an employee card embedding a secure core may be inserted into or brought close to a turnstile, which is the interface point for a physical entry control system. When this system wants a bit of information from the employee card, it issues a command to retrieve it from the card. For some operations, the card bearer is asked to enter some identifying information, for example a Personal Identification Number (PIN) directly into the interface point for the control system. This system then conveys this personal identification number over to the employee card as a means of unlocking privileged information contained on the card. When the control system has obtained the information it wants, generally to authenticate the identity of the card bearer to its satisfaction, the employee removes the card. For the transcendent personal device to function as an effective fiduciary on behalf of its bearer, this communication exchange between such a control system and the transcendent personal device must be of a *peer-to-peer* variety. The transcendent personal device must be able to initiate interactions with external systems on its own terms. It cannot merely respond to requests or commands if it is to truly effect complex policy operations on behalf of its bearer. Today, some secure cores have already started on the path to liberation. A Subscriber Identity Module in a GSM mobile phone is able to piggyback a note on a normal command response that says in effect, "Now, ask me what to do next." Further, if the phone also has contactless payment via a wireless protocol called Near-Field Communication (NFC), the phone can get involved in a peer-to-peer payment transaction. As the current evolution progresses further, transcendent personal devices will therefore be autonomous agents, in that they will be able to start a communication exchange just as the humans they represent do.

Subordinate only to the need of transcendence, self-actualization drives individuals to assert eminence over their personal situations. Maslow characterized self-actualizing individuals in terms of a number of traits that collectively give rise to this interpretation. Again, extracting concepts from his *Toward a Psychology of Being*, we can include among these traits that of assessing the situation presented by the direct environment in objective rather than subjective terms and interpreting the presentation of issues as opportunities for solutions as opposed to threats to be avoided at all costs. Maslow further suggested that self-actualized individuals perceive the world as a pursuit of *peak experiences* rather than ongoing acceptance of the mundane. When viewed from the perspective of the transcendent personal device, we see the direct manifestation of our more generally stated requirement that the device must function as a fiduciary for its bearer, not for some other external entity. Moreover, this need requires the ability of the device to initiate an interaction environment with other parties as opposed to simply responding to them. Through its sensori-motor facilities, the transcendent personal device should actively engage the dynamic world that it finds itself in. The fulfillment of this need will evoke a variety of subordinate needs that will in turn evoke specific requirements for technical capabilities to satisfy the appetites derived from these needs. Indeed, many of these capabilities will present as extremely innovative departures from the capabilities of current personal electronic devices.

According to Maslow's original discussions regarding the human hierarchy of needs, creativity is another manifestation of self-actualization. He makes the observation that the display of creativity is not necessarily an indicator of either physical or psychological health, using as illustrations of this fact a number of writers and artists known to stray rather far afield from what was perceived to be "normal" conditions during their lifetimes. Within the transcendent personal device, we would anticipate that it is a function of cognitive needs to monitor and maintain the normalcy of health of the system and its connections to the outside world, including to its bearer. Self-actualization needs of the transcendent personal device will address the capabilities of the system to determine and apply policy in creative ways in the face of threats of either an anticipated or an unanticipated nature. This suggests that perhaps the most far reaching facility required of the transcendent personal device is the capability for it to act not just on behalf of its bearer, but to act in seamless concert with that bearer. More basic needs should address the necessity for cognitive facilities of the transcendent personal device to be in optimum synchronization with the sensori-motor system of the computer as well as with the human bearer of the computer. The facilities of self-actualization must make use of that synchrony to effect policy on behalf of the bearer.

What this rather obtusely stated need really translates into is a requirement that the transcendent personal device have a complete, well defined model of the external world in which it and its bearer exist. Moreover, it must have adequate visibility into this world via is sensori-motor translation abilities, have adequate processing capacity and have adequate short and long term memory so as to be able to proactively address its interactions with that external world. The transcendent personal device needs to be able to recognize and function in at least two distinctive modes: a mode in which it defines policy or policy preferences and a mode in which those preferences are actually applied. Manipulation of rules while they're in use is a rather tricky business; to do so effectively is an activity of some creativity. From a technical perspective, this translates into a need for the general *social ecosystem ontology* that we have alluded to at various points within this book. When we have talked about the ability to *reason* about policy, it has been in direct preparation to support this need of self-actualization on the part of the transcendent personal device.

In concluding our consideration of the need of self-actualization on the part of the transcendent personal device, we must consider the means of this reasoning facility. We noted at the very beginning of Chapter 2 the concerns voiced by Gerald Edelman regarding whether the expression of degeneracy was a facility of which computers in general are capable. During the course of this book we have observed the means of establishing trust and from this basis to engage in interactions with some anticipation of a predicted outcome. In considering mathematical contexts, we have noted two distinct such mechanisms: *reductio ad absurdum*, which we relate to causality, and inductive reasoning, which we relate to process. Through *reductio ad absurdum*, we establish a hypothetical situation counter to our assumption of trust. If we conclude that this hypothetical situation is inherently false (absurd), then we assume confirmation of the validity of our original assumption and our causality basis is reinforced. Alternatively, we establish trust through induction by assuming that the result of a process is true as long as the same process is repeated. We suggest that either approach, the capability to establish causes and compute their consequences or to establish processes and assume their repeatability, can be derived from deterministic algorithms if we have a reference ontology from which to draw causes and processes and a mechanism to effect this drawing, which is what metaphors are for. The interpretation of metaphors is sensitive to the context of an interaction. Thus, we suggest that there are ample opportunities to arrive at specific comparable interaction outcomes through a variety of computational pathways. This seems fully consistent with the concept of degeneracy. Hence, the facility of degeneracy can be viewed as a property of the transcendent personal device necessary to meet the need of self-actualization of both the device and its bearer.

# Aesthetic Needs

Central to the formation of a trust infrastructure is the altered state of consciousness that we have discussed at various points during the course of this book. It is the manipulation of this state that lies at heart of the aesthetic facilities of the human mind. Often presented as a search for, or a sense of beauty derived from emotion and sensation, we suggest that with respect to the needs hierarchy, the concept of *aesthetics* also encompasses the establishment of context through which internal interpretation and external communication occurs. This of course then establishes the basis of interactions. Aesthetics is concerned with the internal mechanisms of trust establishment and in the external mechanisms of trust conveyance. It seems significant that aesthetic needs are presented quite high within the hierarchy, essentially forming the direct foundation for self-actualization and transcendence. Thus, aesthetics encompasses both emotional assessment and response to sensory stimuli as well as cognitive assessment and response. In her book *Homo*

*Aestheticus*, Ellen Dissanayake calls *making special* the ecstatic lift brought by art. It is this apex that forms the foundation of the trust required to actually allow the stimulation of a motor response. Hence, we observe that aesthetic facilities are intimately related to the actual conveyance of trust between individual people.

One might now wonder how aesthetic needs translate into some technical manifestation that will actually impact the transcendent personal device. Surely we are talking about something a bit more profound than whether the device is red or blue or whether it uses a set of wire connected headphones or a Bluetooth earphone. Indeed, we suggest that this particular need goes a bit deeper than such superficial characteristics. In fact, aesthetic needs form the base stimuli for engaging in external interactions. We will elaborate this point in greater detail in our last chapter, but at this point it will help if we inject a direct association with an aesthetic genre; that of theatre. On the way to the theatre, let's take the trail that leads by the flight school.

As an art form, theatre encompasses the full range of human interactions. We might characterize theatre as a *flight simulator* for interactions. A flight simulator allows a pilot or a pilot in training, to engage in seemingly real-world interactions. The simulator presents a very close approximation to the full sensori-motor experience of a person in an airplane. Information is provided to the pilot through all the same facilities found in an actual airplane in flight and the pilot in turn can affect the performance of the simulated airplane through the same controls found in a real airplane. With a good hydraulic system underlying the simulator, physical manifestations of airplane motion can be closely simulated. Thus, a slight simulator allows a pilot in training to learn how to fly an airplane. It allows an experienced pilot to gain additional experience without enduring the risks of actual flight. It is certainly better to attempt to learn how to compensate for all the engines of an airplane ceasing to work in a simulator than in an actual airplane in flight. Surviving multiple crash landings in a simulator is routine while walking away from a single crash landing in the real world is problematic. Of course, one can then ask, "How does one know the difference between a simulator and the real thing?"

We draw the attention of the reader to the classic science fiction book *Ender's Game* by Orson Scott Card. Through the course of the book, a young boy known as Ender Wiggin is identified as a prospective military commander to engage in an ongoing war with an insect-like race known as the Formics. Through many years of training at Battle School and subsequently at Command School, Ender displays an aptitude for battle strategy and tactics. In a series of final examination mock battles engaged through a simulator, Ender prevails in the face of overwhelming odds. After the last such mock battle, Ender finds that in fact he was in command of an army of humans engaged in an actual battle near the Formics home world. To win the ostensibly mock battle, Ender had engaged in asymmetric practices, outside the accepted norms of combat. In essence, by breaking out of the mold of physical ecosystem interaction in what he perceived to be a simulation, he was able to prevail in an actual battle. The lesson we draw from this anecdote is the tenuous nature of reality when the complete sensori-motor experience can be manipulated. This, we suggest, is the realm of aesthetic appetites in the transcendent personal device, which in turn brings us back to our original reference to theatre.

Theatre as an art form is directly aimed at manipulation of the sensori-motor experience of the observer with the expressed intent of effecting highly structured interaction environments. From our experiences derived from the interactions that we observe, we learn about the mechanics of interaction and the assessment of potential outcomes. In essence, we learn about the evaluation of what we have previously called the *trust equation* of interactions. Hence, we suggest that in addressing the aesthetic needs of the individual, the aesthetic facilities of the transcendent personal device must learn from the conditioning mechanisms of theatre. This is truly the bleeding edge of system development. We can allude to the desired results, but the specific mechanisms are certainly fuzzy in their conceptualization. Perhaps we can provide slightly more solid ground by considering a more concrete and current example.

Consider one aspect of the interaction environments that people encounter throughout their daily activities, that of *advertising*. Advertising is one of the most dynamic art forms found in the modern world. Its purpose in all of its many guises is to impact the state of consciousness of the receiver; more specifically, to induce an altered state of consciousness that is conducive to the conveyance of trust. Through this facility, advertising seeks to elicit action stimuli from across the full range of the needs hierarchy. Interestingly enough, the more basic the need evoked, the stronger the impetus for action. Hence, we can see the rationale behind the homily that says, "Sex sells!" If a stimulus for action at the level of physiological needs can be externally induced within a person, then the content related to sating the appetite presented by that particular need becomes of higher value to the person. Hence, beautiful women and strong, virile men make excellent advocates for the acquisition of everything from toothpaste to automobiles. So, what does this have to do with the transcendent personal device?

In the establishment of individual interaction opportunities, the device must be able to offer objective assessment in the establishment of trust. Thus, we perceive a need for the device to participate in the identification, evaluation and reaction to aspects of interactions that constitute advertising. The suggestion is not for an advertising filter, because in some instances advertising can be a useful information source to the individual. What we view as a useful service on the part of the device is to recognize and, where possible, to negotiate some aspects of the *de facto* transaction that advertising comprises. Indeed, much of the current content on the Web is acquired through a *consideration offered for consideration received* transaction. "I will show you the current and forecasted weather conditions in exchange for you watching or reading this automobile advertisement." The forms of significant amounts of media based interactions have been totally transformed by the asymmetric nature of this transaction. The transcendent personal device offers the prospect of establishing both individual as well as group based responses to shift this balance. Thus, the aesthetic facilities of the transcendent personal device can be anticipated to participate directly in the operation of the trust infrastructures of cyberspace.

The anticipated functions of the transcendent personal device could certainly be added to existing personal electronic devices, but its operational orientation would be somewhat different from current systems. If we anticipate that the transcendent personal device will function continuously over long periods of time, then the architecture, design and implementation of its contained *software systems* will be systematically different from many of today's personal electronic devices.

Current personal electronic devices offer a rather thorough illustration of choices available for external form factors of the transcendent personal device. An area that's a bit less clear is the form factor choices for the trusted core agent of the transcendent personal device. Does it actually need to look like today's secure cores, for example a card, a key fob or a token? From an ergonomics perspective, it might be interesting to think of the trusted core agent as an arming device for the transcendent personal device. As such, it might be attractive to more easily attach the trusted core agent to the body, and perhaps to allow an interlock of some type that allows the body to coordinate the removal of the trusted core. We can readily understand the utility of such a capability in that it would act to control the tearing that we discussed a couple of chapters back.

# Cognitive Needs

While the consideration of aesthetic needs is delicate, the consideration of cognitive needs relative to the transcendent personal device is relatively straightforward. The primary concerns are parallel computing capability, language capability and memory. In considering the derivation of human needs in Chapter 5, we suggested that a precursor to the development of cognitive needs was the establishment of context. This facility within the human brain would seem to occur as a characteristic of the multiple processing pathways enabled by neural networks connecting sensory input with motor control output. Sensory input such as signals from the myriad of sensors in the eyes feed into multiple, parallel neural network structures. Similar signal processing activities are performed on the raw input and a refined image is transferred downstream within each network. Ultimately, it would appear that these images arrive at a variety of neuron constructs where some particular contextual situation is recognized as preeminent among all the various choices. Various, perhaps subtle, indicators are identified through cognitive pre-processors so as to establish that an image of another person drawing back an arm is, for example, a pitcher in a baseball game rather than an attacker with a knife. Once constrained within the appropriate context, cognitive functions can metaphorically interpret the sensory input and then more efficiently guide appropriate motor responses. In order for the transcendent personal device to facilitate support for the cognitive needs of the human mind of its bearer, it would be most useful if it could better establish appropriate context for the situations that it becomes aware of through its sensory input from the outside world.

The human mind is capable of multiple, simultaneous cognitive activities. Some are reflexive, some are the products of unconscious or subconscious processing, and some are functions of conscious activity. A single threaded computer, if clocked at a high enough rate and with significant interrupt facilities can approximate such multiple streams of processing. However, true replication of this facility will be greatly enhanced by actual *multi-processor architectures*. We suggest that multi-processor configurations can be effectively utilized both within the device body as well as in its trusted core agent.

In concert with memory enhancements, the evolved trusted core agents can certainly use the benefit of these multi-processor configurations. Current secure cores that provide cryptographic services already include a peripheral processor in addition to the main processor. This peripheral processor is capable of performing long integer multiply operations at a very high speed, a computation that is essential for public key cryptography. A true multi-processor facility would allow the token to further enhance its security characteristics as well as be better able to involve itself in multiple, simultaneous transactions. As we noted in the first chapter, the ability to deal with the programming and provisioning of parallel processing threads is something of an art form, related in style to the composition of music in chords. As a consequence, a derivative requirement from cognitive needs is that of programming language support. Moreover, language capabilities to support logical reasoning are mandated by the self-actualization need related to social system ontologies.

Memory enhancements derive from the discussions in the last chapter in which context was presented as an integral aspect of memory. In this case, we suggest that the device memory should encompass knowledge base facilities that allow a tight integration between information and its relevant processing.

# Esteem Needs

Esteem is about reputation. It is a foundational concept in the establishment of trust through experiential identity. Within small, stable groups we ascribe reputation to others based on our observations of their interactions. In so doing, we compile an experiential identity archive for others within our mind. In some instances, we augment our personal observations with the reputation imputed to others. In particular, if we don't have direct observations, we may adopt reputations for others as attested to by trusted third parties. Thus we arrive at an internal assessment of reputation as well as an external assessment. With respect to the much broader, technical manifestation of social orders that we are now considering, we approach the determination of reputation in much the same way. With respect to the transcendent personal device itself, we must consider an internal component and an external component. The internal component is based on causality and process; causality of the device, beginning with its design and manufacture, and process through which the device is provisioned and operated. The external component is based on experiential identity; of the device, of the device's bearer as presented through the conduct and results of interactions, and of other entities as attested to by trusted third parties. Previously, in considering the need of or for esteem, we have observed that it is related to the human mind's development of the facility of empathy; that within any given environment, we assess the situations of others based on an assessment of our own position within that environment. This internal yardstick of reputation, that we call self-esteem, forms a basis for assessing the reputation of other entities, either directly manifested or mediated by trusted third parties; for example, if we have low self-esteem, we may overestimate others, and conversely, high self-esteem may lead us to ignore possible help. So, how do these characteristics of esteem translate into required facilities of the transcendent personal device?

The first order requirement is that the transcendent personal device be accurately confident of itself. It must have an established level of trust that it is functioning correctly, not within some altered state of consciousness. A corollary to this level of trust is the need to be able to enter such an altered state of consciousness in a trustworthy manner. This manner will most typically be through an appropriate ritual as defined, for the device, by trusted protocols through which the trust infrastructure can be altered. To establish these levels of trust, the transcendent personal device must be assured of its own physical security and be confident in the security of the processes that it effects. It must, therefore, have ongoing trust in the physical integrity of both the body and trusted core agent, it must have trust in the software that is running on both and it must have trust in the relationship and interactions with its bearer.

A growing threat of personal electronic devices is their subversion during the design and manufacturing phase. The risk is that computer viruses or other forms of malevolent software be installed on the devices prior to their final provisioning and personalization on behalf of their bearers. Then, once placed into operation, they serve to intercept information and to surreptitiously provide it through network connections to attackers. This threat potential reinforces the need to establish the basis of trust in the causality of the device's design and manufacture. Fully provisioning the need for esteem requires the chain of trust to be congruent with the device itself.

For large scale purchases of any product, the consumer can make use of special protocols through which to establish trust. We've noted that within the current environment of secure core acquisitions, it is not uncommon for an issuer (a large-scale consumer of secure cores) to perform detailed audits of the secure core manufacturing facilities. This entails tracing the chain of trust all the way back to the seminal design activities of both the body and secure core agent. From this seminal point, trust must then be recursively established through auditing (visiting and inspecting) the facilities for fabrication, manufacturing, provisioning and issuance of the secure core to the owner of the personal electronic device. It typically also entails auditing of the software that is loaded into the secure core. In the case of the more advanced transcendent personal device, some modifications will be necessary in this process for it to truly be an agent of the bearer.

While the owner of the transcendent personal device will be fully in control, it will be impossible for all bearers of such devices to go through the same type of audit procedures that large scale secure core consumers go through. So, it will be necessary to fall back on certification standards; standards such as Common Criteria for the overall security level of the device, FIPS 140-2 for cryptographic operations, FIPS 201 for provisioning and ISO/IEC 24727 for operational standardization.

Additional standards will be required to cover the facilities of software loaded into both the body and the trusted core agent of the transcendent personal device. This is likely to be a more heavyweight system than is currently found in personal electronic devices, so it will require facilities for performing software updates while at the same time assuring that the transcendent personal device is truly functioning as a fiduciary agent on behalf of the bearer. Standards will be required to assure that the software systems, in addition to functioning correctly from a technical standpoint, also function correctly from a policy standpoint.

It is an interesting aspect of computer systems that the movement to what we now know as the personal computer was actually a move toward greater susceptibility to a variety of threats that were far more difficult to exploit with earlier variants of computer systems. Specifically, early architectures for mainframe computers circa 1968 made use of *multi-level memory management* systems and security oriented software architectures.

Multi-level memory management means that access to memory by the processor occurs at multiple hierarchically layered levels. Thus, a program accessed from the superior level is always able to wrest control of the computer system from programs running in subordinate levels of memory. Moreover, with such a system, it is possible for the superior level of memory to require its own involvement in certain operations performed by the inferior level of memory. This enables the superior memory to perform continuous watchdog checks on software running out of the inferior memory segment. The computer system is brought into an operational status by a process termed *booting* or *bootstrapping*, and the first program brought into operation is termed the *kernel* operating system. For subordinate programs to be brought into operation, they are subject to constraints defined by, and enforced by the kernel. When the first personal computer systems were deployed, as a means to simplify both the hardware and software architectures of the systems to make them less expensive, multi-layer memory management was discarded. The result was that such computers were then open to a wide range of attacks. Resorting to an anthropomorphic approach, such threats were given the name of mechanisms closely associated with human physiology or social structures: viruses, Trojan Horse, worms (internal parasites) and the like. The whole set of threat software is sometimes termed *malware*.

Miniaturization is advancing to the point where order of magnitude increases in the memory of secure cores are becoming possible. Now, in order to enhance the trust infrastructure, the form of memory must reflect more secure architecture possibilities; for example, multi-layer memory can allow for highly privileged secure operating system components. This offers the prospect that in dealing with ever more complex policy environments, the trusted core agents will not be subject to the limitations of the dinosaurs as they faced a rapidly changing ecosystem armed with a brain the size of a walnut.

Finally, at least with respect to the need of esteem, the concept of reputation derived from experiential identity comes to the fore. Within the computer world, experiential identity is thoroughly intertwined with archival memory; being able to establish and subsequently recall the experiences in the passing of interactions. Reputation then builds upon the memory of such experiences as reflected or reported by third parties. Thus, for the transcendent personal device to properly establish and evaluate reputation, of its own bearer and also of the other parties to interactions, it must possess or have access to a means of establishing trust in such other parties. As we have noted in previous discussions, this is a manifestation of the recursive evaluation of the trust equation of interactions. So, from an esteem need standpoint, the requirement is for a trusted means to identify and interact with other parties. The actual mechanisms needed, specifically an identification system and a method for secure interactions across time and space, build upon responses to the lower level needs of belonging and safety.

# Belonging Needs

Belonging is very much about differential identity. Computers can certainly function in groups as the wide variety of networks currently in play today reminds us. Computers however are tools of humans. They function on behalf of humans. The issue becomes, of course, on behalf of which humans do they function? In today's dichotomy of client-server computing, a secure core functions primarily as a tool of the server community as opposed to being prosthesis for the bearer, who is after all, the end-user and consumer within the content system.

In fact, differential identity is a central issue in the current state of network infrastructures. Mechanisms in use are typically insufficient to provide an adequate level of trust in the asserted differential identities of transaction participants. Consequently, mistaken identity or improper authentication of identity perceived as "identity theft" are significant problems. Perhaps even more important than solving the problems inherent in current systems, is the enabling of important new areas of policy application that highly trusted differential identity would provide. In a complementary fashion, highly trusted differential identity also provides enhancement opportunities for personal privacy.

The transcendent personal device is a central element in establishing the differential identity of a person. Only by being able to do this can one then develop a reliable credential system on which experiential identity can be based. This is primarily a social ecosystem issue, much like the establishment of the transcendent personal device as a fiduciary acting on behalf of the bearer. While the transcendent personal device itself, if done well technically, can make significant strides in extending the benefits of social grouping mechanisms into the Web, a coherent policy infrastructure will make the effort significantly more trustworthy.

As we've considered previously, one of the mechanisms used to convey trust is the use of secrets. We can use a shared secret between two entities to establish a common domain of trust that encompasses the two, as long as we're confident that no other entity shares the secret. The more entities that share a secret, the less is the degree of trust that we can convey through the knowledge or possession of the secret. If only two entities share a secret and if I am one of the entities, then when another entity can tell me the secret I know precisely the identity of that entity. However, if I want to include many other entities in my own, personal domain of trust, then I have to know and share many secrets: one with each of the other entities. Actually, all of us could share only one secret, but then I can't differentiate the other entities; they all look alike as far as the single secret allows me to determine. So, one is faced with the problem of sharing lots of secrets, which entails a big administrative problem to keep them all straight; or, we share a single secret, which entails the high risk that someone will let that secret become known to someone outside our desired circle of trust.

If I want to avoid remembering all the secret keys of all the participants in my circle of trust, what I would like is simply being able to ask each participant for evidence that they are indeed in my circle of trust. But isn't that the same as asking them for their secret key? Obviously they will not give me their secret key if they don't know who I am, will they? So I need to give them my secret key first? Is there a way to get out of this conundrum?

In fact there is one, inspired from how banknotes are made. When I look at a dollar bill, I notice that it is made of special paper, with intricate inscriptions, that are difficult to reproduce. It has a picture of a president, to make sure that I understand that the power of the state is behind this paper; don't I dare to question its value. And if I have not understood yet, there are some religions symbols, including the famous "In God we trust." So we see here a typical chain of trust. Similarly, if anybody in my circle of trust, instead of presenting me with a secret key, could present me with the equivalent of a dollar bill that could be trusted because it has the full power of the state and religion behind it, then that should be enough. However, the state is not going to print dollar bills especially for my own circle of trust, so is there some equivalent of that I could use?

It turns out there is, and it is based on some relatively complex arithmetic that we will not expand into here, and you can skip the remainder of this paragraph is you are mathematically adverse. We will just say that it is possible for a participant (let's call him John) in my chain of trust to publish a number. This number is called John's *public key*. I can use John's public key, mix it up a little with some data of my own, and ask John to untangle what I have done. In order to do that, John has to know another number, this one secret, so it's called the *secret key* corresponding to the public key. With this private key, John can untangle what I gave him, and therefore I know that he owns the proper secret key. This method is known as *public key cryptography*, sometimes also called *asymmetric key cryptography*. Now I don't need to know nor remember John's secret key anymore. I just need to ask him for his public key, and make sure that he has the corresponding private key by sending him a tangled message. But I you've followed so far, you're going to ask "Fine, but how is this public key of John related to my circle of trust?" Well, that's where it becomes a little more involved. What we need here is to all agree in our circle of trust on somebody to be the guarantor of public keys. This person will have a master public key, and will be the one distributing individual public keys when required. To come back to our dollar bill analogy, the person having the master public key has the role of the state in distributing individualized dollar bills to each participant (that's the participant's public key), who can in turn present that dollar bill to prove that they are part of the circle of trust. But who's playing God in this analogy? We'll come back to that later. The reader has certainly noticed already that the privileged participant to the circle of trust looks much like a shaman.

# Safety and Security Needs

Living organisms seek safety and security within their environments by making use of the physiological capabilities that they possess; their sensori-motor systems and their cognitive facilities. For the transcendent personal device we have identified a number of enhancements derived from the higher levels of the needs hierarchy. It is given that the device should only seek to sate the appetites derived from those needs if it can at the same time attend to its own needs of safety and security and those of its bearer. All of these higher level needs will in turn place requirements on its physiological basis. The two basic functions of the transcendent personal device are first to protect itself from compromise and second to improve the abilities of its human bearer to guard directly against threats that might arise in that person's physical and social ecosystems. In addition, by functioning as an extension of its human bearer into cyberspace, the transcendent personal device should bring these safety and security characteristics into the computer networking world that is the foundation of this cyberspace.

The pretergenesis model that we considered in Chapter 5 suggests a series of stages through which the safety and security needs of humans were addressed in successive levels of social ecosystems; stages that ranged from tools to administration. These levels, which are discerned when one considers the phylogenetic development of grouping mechanism, are also indicative of how safety and security needs are actually addressed in various ways throughout the ontogenetically derived needs hierarchy. This spectrum of stages is actually rather illustrative of the current state of the art of security within computer networks; a spectrum that, identified as a single concept, is termed *security in depth*. Rather than a single point of protection, a castle wall if you will, security in depth suggests a layered approach to security, including taking architectural and organizational steps to ameliorate anticipated threats. Consider a couple of examples that illustrate foundational aspects of this concept.

At a purely physiological level, when immediate threats are identified, they are dealt with through autonomic reaction. The tactile sensation of hot, searing pain is felt within a finger when it touches a hot iron and a rapid motor response to jerk the finger away from the iron is evoked. Cognitive processes subsequently program the emotional response system regarding reaction to burning. Direct fire or hot, burning material is avoided if it is close enough to evoke an emotional response of fear. Fire is also recognized as a necessity for keeping warm, preparing food and in some instances, a source of aesthetic pleasure. However, higher needs based stimuli elicit anticipatory actions to mitigate the danger of fire; insulated stoves for cooking, fire alarms to warn against unwanted outbreaks, and stone fireplaces or perhaps candles for aesthetic pleasure. Thus, we see that within the individual, the concern for safety and security based on the threat or danger from fire is addressed through the full range of needs. From a social ecosystem standpoint, our development of grouping mechanisms has finally brought us to support fire departments. In fact, the social conditioning relative to such institutions can evoke extreme altruistic behavior on the part of firefighters.

Assuming the two component architecture of the transcendent personal device, an obvious architectural approach to total system security is to orient the body, in response to lower level needs, towards defensive postures, and to orient the trusted core agent, in response to higher level needs, towards proactive anticipation of known and as yet unknown threats. Basic sensory input derives from physiological capabilities. Various aspects of cognitive based motor responses build upon successive levels of the needs hierarchy stimuli.

Ron Rivest, one of the inventors of the field of study known as public key cryptography, has suggested (for example in *http://theory.lcs.mit.edu/~rivest/ducttape.txt*) that cryptography in general is about "communication in the presence of adversaries." The capability to perform *cryptographic operations* in a fast, efficient manner is central to the provision of safety and security to any computer. Indeed, the various characteristics of security that we discussed in

Chapter 3 (privacy, authentication, authorization, integrity, and non-repudiation) can all be derived through cryptography based mechanisms. Interestingly enough, one can also relate the bulla that we discussed in Chapter 7 to the provision of most of these same characteristics, but using tokens and containers rather than cryptographic processes. These characteristics and processes were covered briefly back in Chapter 6, but let's expand just a bit on them here. We may be overly technical here, so the reader may want to skip over the mathematical part of our description.

Privacy is provided through encryption operations. Using the processes from a sub-field of cryptography termed *symmetric key cryptography* a number known as a *key* is applied through an algorithm to a string of bits. The algorithm scrambles the representation of the string of bits into a different, seemingly random string of bits. By passing the scrambled string back through the algorithm with the same key, the original string of bits is recreated. So, if one performs the encryption operation on a trusted platform, the scrambled bits can be conveyed across a channel that can be read by adversaries. However, unless they have the key, they're not able to discern the original string of bits. Hence, one achieves privacy on the channel. If, at the other end of the channel, is another trusted platform, and the key is known on that platform (how it got there is unimportant for the moment) then the original string of bits can be recreated. Hence, we have established communication in the presence of adversaries. Code to perform cryptographic operations is a necessary ingredient of the transcendent personal device that is driven by its safety and security needs and those of its bearer. Using the mechanisms of symmetric key cryptography, the characteristics of authentication and non-repudiation are also achieved using the same encryption and decryption operations. Symmetric key operations tend to be computationally light-weight, but they incur a tremendous liability (as a general systems approach) because of the difficulty of distributing keys in a trustworthy manner such that a different key can be used to establish the identities of different people. We'll review a potential system-level solution to this problem in aspects of *public key infrastructures* that we'll discuss just a bit later.

The characteristic of information integrity is achieved through *one-way functions*. This process makes use of a key and an algorithm somewhat like a symmetric key encryption algorithm. However, in this case, rather than creating a bit-wise translation of the original string of bits (in other words, just as many bits come out of the algorithm as go into it), instead a relatively small, fixed number of bits is generated; perhaps something like 160 bits out for any sized string going in. In essence, the algorithm is used to create a unique index for the input bit string; an index sometimes referred to as a *digital digest*. Now, one can rather quickly recognize that it is impossible to compress potentially millions of bits of information into a unique string of 160 bits. The saving grace of this technique is that it is very hard to manipulate an input string to produce a given digest. So, this technique is actually a good way to tell whether any of the bits in the input string have been modified. If the same digest is created through the one-way algorithm, then the input bit string has not changed; hence, the integrity of the original bit string is guaranteed, and the original information is known to be intact.

Because it makes validation more difficult, complexity can play against security; and, trust derives from security. Hence, one generally will take special precautions to establish trustworthiness in more complex systems than might be the case in less complex systems. In the case of a two component transcendent personal device comprised of a body and a trusted core agent, these special precautions include an ongoing requirement for the two components to retain a secure and hence trustworthy relationship with each other. One way this is achieved is for the two to *authenticate* each other. This is done through the use of protocols (remember our discussions in the Preface). In this case, protocols that allow two parties to communicate about identity in the presence of adversaries. We're going to go into considerably more detail about the concept of identity in the next section, but for the moment let's just assume that if two parties share a secret, then if they can convey proof to the other party of the fact that they possess the secret then they've effectively identified themselves to the other party. So, what does a protocol look like that can accomplish this?

Well, in fact there are a plethora of protocols available through which two or more parties can authenticate their identities to each other over channels monitored by adversaries. In their book, *Protocols for Authentication and Key Establishment*, Colin Boyd and Anish Mathuria provide detailed specifications for a large collection of such procedures. Most have a common theme to them. One assumes that a secret shared between two parties is actually a key to an encryption algorithm. One party can send an arbitrary message to the other party and say "encrypt this." It doesn't matter if an adversary can see the message because the original sending party is going to take the response message and pass it through the known encryption algorithm with its copy of the secret key. If the original message comes out of the algorithm processing then the first party knows that the second party has the same key. The first party has identified the second party. If the two parties now do this same set of operations in reverse, then the second party can identify the first party. All this is known as a mutual authentication protocol. The knowledge of such protocols, that is the software to effect them on a transcendent personal device, is an artifact of its safety and security needs and those of its bearer.

Humans have five basic senses, and their entire cognitive perception of the world around them is defined by the input from those five classes of sensors. The sensors themselves are an aspect of the basic anatomy and physiology of the human body. The interpretation of the sensor signals occurs at many levels within the mind; levels that we tend to classify according the hierarchy of needs. A sudden, sharp pain in the foot might trigger a virtually instantaneous reaction when the autonomic nervous system seeks to simply move the foot away from the perceived source of the pain. If that pain has a more gradual onset, when finally noticed it might trigger a more thoughtful response involving taking off one's shoe to remove the nail in its sole. If the pain is similar, but perhaps more chronic than acute, we might actually make an aesthetic based decision to live with it because it's caused by a fashionable, although new and unbroken-in pair of shoes. So it is with the *sensors* present within the body and trusted core of the transcendent personal device.

We discussed a variety of such sensors in Chapter 7. Applications at the safety and security tasking level should seek to identify known threats based on the signature responses from the sensors. This would include interrogation of sensors to determine whether changes have occurred in the anatomical makeup of the transcendent personal device body. It includes analysis of power filters within the trusted core agent to confirm that power levels and frequencies have not been altered in an attempt to manipulate processing within the trusted core agent.

# Physiological Needs

Driven by the biophysical structure of living organisms, the most basic needs of the individual are characterized by the elements or facilities necessary to support physiological processes. In the case of the human species and using the emergence of the vertebrates as a starting point, the evolution of such processes ultimately gave rise to the hierarchy of needs. In our emergent description of the transcendent personal device, we have thus far considered a variety of characteristics that derive from the higher order needs of the individual person as well as of the device itself. Forming the base level of the needs hierarchy, we must finally consider extensions to physiological characteristics of the device through which it facilitates its own processes as well as extensions of those processes aimed at supporting the full range of human needs. We will assume as a baseline for these enhanced physiological characteristics the secure cores that we find in current personal electronic devices. We will further assume as the impetus for development of new facilities the evolutionary forces that we discussed earlier which in turn evoked new appetites within the higher levels of the needs hierarchy. Satisfying these higher level appetites requires capability enhancements at the lower levels.

The most prevalent current instances of secure cores for personal electronic devices are smart cards and Trusted Platform Modules (TPMs). Their physiological facilities are rather limited. Probably their greatest deficiency is the lack of an internal power source. They receive power from the interface devices through which they connect to the outside world. Moreover, the extensions that enhance the mapping of the human sensori-motor system to their sensori-motor system are extremely limited. Of particular issue in this regard is the rather primitive input and output channel through which they communicate with the outside world. Of course, we must remember that we earlier suggested that the very simple nature of this channel was one of the characteristics from which trust could derive. In general, a simple channel is easier to protect than is a complex channel. In addition, it is easier to determine when we have actually protected a simple channel versus the situation for a complex channel. Nonetheless, in order to enhance the stature of personal electronic devices in the future, to actually build transcendent personal devices and allow them to function fully as extensions of the human mind into the world encompassed by computer networks, the mutational changes will have to encompass these base capabilities of the device such that the enhanced facilities can enable all the support for higher level needs satisfaction.

The *energy* to enable the processes of life is the preeminent need of all living things. Correspondingly, a reliable power source dedicated to the continuous operation of the transcendent personal device and its contained trusted core agent will significantly impact its basic physiology, subsequently altering the paradigm of security for the trusted core agent from "periods of total darkness followed by an abrupt introduction into the light," a process similar to ecstasy, to one of continuous vigilance, perhaps interspersed with periods of meditation on the state that the token finds itself in. Will ecstasy still be a relevant state for the invocation of new policy? Yes, but what is desired is the true ecstasy of the prophet rather than the temporary euphoria of the proselyte; the firm revelation of the law rather than the more tenuous illumination of instantaneous, faith based reaction. While this description may well represent a bit of metaphoric overkill, it is certainly the case that with a continuous power source, the transcendent personal device is in a much better position to establish and maintain its own trustworthiness, and to project this trustworthiness on behalf of its bearer.

Access to a power source that is dedicated to the trusted core agent rather than derived from its external world interface point completely changes the perspective of the agent's security posture. Of course, within the architecture that we have thus far suggested, power for the trusted core agent is likely to derive from the body of the device proper. However, if we consider the two parts of the full transcendent personal device as a symbiotic pair, then the trust basis of the agent is greatly enhanced over that of current secure cores. Much as is found with the human reflex and motor mechanisms, dedicated and secure power will allow the agent to effect security in depth rather than security by rote instinct. The agent will be allowed the luxury of more judicious thought before it is asked to make the ultimate sacrifice when it perceives an irresistible threat. The question becomes then, what is the source of this new facility? The answer comes from among at least three possible directions: enhancements to existing portable power mechanisms (e.g.

batteries), new portable power mechanisms (e.g. fuel cells and supercapacitors), and significant improvements in the efficiency of integrated circuit chip technology relative to power consumption and heat dissipation. In the two-component architecture that we described above, power provision can be assumed to derive from the containing body of the transcendent personal device and subsequently provided to the trusted core agent. Existing families of power quality sensors within the trusted core agent then allow it to determine that power has been continuously applied. Consequently, the trusted core agent is expected to continuously monitor the security state of the body, allowing trust in the operation of the transcendent personal device to build over long periods of effective behavior; in essence, trust is derived from reputation. Indeed, current battery technology allows for the recharging of batteries within the body while operation of the transcendent personal device continues unabated. The inclusion of enhanced supercapacitors offers the prospect of a much longer latency between the complete dissipation of battery power and the availability of recharging facilities.

If power is continuously available, then the trusted core agent can reasonably perform the tasks of securely monitoring time and location. A secure time-stamp emanating from the trusted core agent and a secure location stamp will allow the transcendent personal device to more completely form a deictic center for the person within the external, physical and electronic worlds. This capability will change the form of the language through which policy is conveyed, allowing something closer to natural communication through deictic conversation on the part of the bearer rather than a brief from the bearer's attorney. In other words, the device offers the prospect of encompassing the role of shaman in purely human social orders.

Unlike the human mind, computers are not typically driven entirely by what we might think of as sensory stimuli. Even real-time, sometimes called *process control* computers have some significant level of background tasking that they perform whenever all other sensory input is quiet. In general in computer systems, the continuous flow of awareness on the part of the computer is driven by a continuous, temporally repetitive stimulus; in other words, a *clock*. At repetitive intervals, a clock stimulus is emitted that drives a succession of recursive task queues; every 17 milliseconds perform a task off of this queue, every 34 milliseconds perform a task off of this queue, and so on. In this way, a computer prevents a single task from completely monopolizing the machine. In Chapter 6, we considered what would happen if the human mind were to dedicate itself to consideration of the statement "This sentence is false." We suggested that the mind is able to limit the degree to which it might dwell on such a thought. In the case of computers, the basic underlying mechanism that would allow one to build software that might mimic selectiveness of the human mind would be a clock driven, hierarchical series of task queues that determine what a processor is thinking about at any instant. Even with a periodic clock stimulus, of course, one still must be careful to enforce preemptive scheduling of task queues. Otherwise, a task that is going to consider the statement "This sentence is false." might get control of the processor and never relinquish it. That way madness lies.

As a purely recurrent indicator of the passage of time, a clock signal can be derived by applying power to an oscillator circuit; when power is halted, the clock signal stops. Within a transcendent personal device, a continuous clock, even if emitted from the body of the transcendent personal device, allows both the body and the trusted core agent to maintain continuous vigilance over themselves and their connection to the outside world. Recall that back in Chapter 4 we discussed a view put forward by Klaus Scherer that emotions provide for cognitive consideration that lies between sensory input and motor system response, and that the level of emotional response establishes the effective time interval within which to effect a motor response to sensory input.

Thus, we might argue that within a computer system, a clock provides a basic support mechanism for emulating the emotional mechanisms of the human mind.

An additional useful concept derived from a clock, from a trustworthiness standpoint, is the maintenance of a continuous time-stamp; an absolute timing indicator that can be coordinated with the world outside the transcendent personal device. Through this mechanism, the time of occurrence of transactions can be linked to the passage of time in that outside world. On large scale systems, clocks are often synchronized to standard time indicators transmitted by the U.S. Naval Observatory. In extreme cases, clock facilities that are synchronized to vibrational models of specific atoms provide extremely accurate interval timing. Obviously, any synchronization with the external world would require both the internal and external domains to be encompassed by a common trust infrastructure.

Communication from the outside world into today's secure cores benefits, from a security standpoint, from being simple. In actuality, the relatively low speed channel into current secure cores is attractive from the standpoint of insuring the internal security of the device. Unfortunately, this single, low speed channel greatly diminishes the effectiveness of the device in projecting the presence of the transcendent personal device bearer into the variety of policy environments in which it could be most effective in enhancing the capabilities of the bearer to meet her or his individual needs. Consequently, we see great advantage in a two phase facility for input and output within the transcendent personal device; a multi-sensory system facility with the outside world and the device body and a more direct descendant of the current, simple channel between the body and the trusted core agent.

As we've previously noted, the physical basis for communication channels within and among computers always derives from signals sent via the electromagnetic spectrum. Some channels utilize electrical signals sent along solid conductors such as copper or gold wire (we call these *contact* channels) while other channels are effected through radio frequency signals transmitted between one computer and another (we call these *contactless* channels). Contact channels typically have the characteristic of allowing higher data rate transmission to be established with a minimum of equipment relative to radio frequency based channels. Contact channels also tend to be easier to sequester in some fashion so as to prevent, or at least strongly limit, eavesdropping of the channel. Contactless channels have the characteristic of allowing effective communication without requiring physical collocation. This means that the transcendent personal device can remain firmly in the possession of its bearer at all times, thus establishing a guard against many types of attack. Of course, such radio frequency based channels are difficult, if not impossible, to shield from eavesdroppers unless they are simply shut down. Consequently, cryptographic protocols are required to render the channels *private* in the face of such eavesdroppers. The transcendent personal device would benefit from having both classes of connectivity to the outside world. Such a variety of input and output facilities would allow the transcendent personal device to interconnect with virtually any policy infrastructure that its bearer would be likely to encounter during daily life. Perhaps, this is an appropriate point to interject a more speculative technological development.

Neural research is making tremendous inroads into the capability to monitor and in some instance affect the operational characteristics of neural network structures within the brain. Micro connectors provide facilities to establish direct electro-chemical connectivity to collections of neurons. One might anticipate that in the future, perhaps even the relatively near future, nanotechnological components might allow connection to very small collections of neurons; perhaps even to individual neurons. Moreover, should this connectivity come to pass it would likely be enabled through wireless RF channels rather than wired connections. If this capability were to be blended with an enhanced understanding of the brain's memory mechanisms, then it might well be possible to establish a direct communication channel between the transcendent personal device and discrete brain functions. One might speculate that this would represent the definitive interconnection mechanism. Moreover, should it become possible, it would seem that the establishment of a trust infrastructure encompassing both the brain and the external device would be a distinct possibility.

Widespread computer networks such as the Internet present something of an altered sensori-motor experience for the human users of computer tools. Specifically, the characteristics of spatial and temporal locality are more difficult to establish than is the case in the purely physical ecosystem. Despite the admonition of the AT&T advertising campaign to "reach out and touch someone," tactile response is not readily available through a telephonic connection. The establishment of a policy infrastructure, however, quite often requires the detailed location of any transaction participants in order to fully define the rules of the transaction. For example, in transactions through which a sale of content is concluded, the governing social ecosystem may well establish a tax on the amount of the transaction based on location. Consider that in Texas, sales taxes are applied on transactions by at least three distinct taxing authorities in each county: the county itself, the applicable school district, and the applicable city. Each of these is a taxing authority delineated by geography; hence, by *physical location*. While sales taxes are not required on all Internet purchases at the present time, there is a very strong likelihood that this will become the norm within a few years. So, applying the correct rules for a transaction may require a determination of physical location. Perhaps a more pressing need, however, is the determination of physical location as a means to ward off threats.

At the 16th USENIX Security Symposium in September, 2007, Saar Drimer and Steven Murdoch of the Cambridge University Computer Laboratory presented the specification of a "man-in-the-middle" type computer attack that they claim can succeed against certain financial transaction systems based on bank chip cards and point-of-sale terminals. Their paper was entitled *Keep your enemies close: Distance bounding against smartcard relay attacks*. This attack makes use of malevolent equipment to intercept the protocols involved in one transaction and to apply those to a second, fraudulent transaction at some associated location. The end result of the attack is that a person assumes they're paying one amount for an item purchased in one store when in fact they end up providing payment for a different item at a different store. One means suggested for countering such an attack is to measure the delay time associated with various steps in the protocols in order to confirm that both ends of the transaction are within a known distance of each other. This approach is a very indirect approach to determination of both time and location. The direct establishment of both time and location as a trusted characteristic of the transaction would be a significant enhancement to the transcendent personal device.

Perhaps the most significant long term benefit to be gained from a capability on the part of the transcendent personal device to determine its physical location is the support it will then provide in the use of deictic discourse in the communication of policy. Such discourse is a very natural aspect of languages used by humans in their interactions with each other. The term refers to the ability on the part of distinct parties within a given interaction to determine relationships and hence to use language constructs that are based on these relationships. Consider the request that could be used to initiate a transaction between two people; "Please sell me this book and send it here." This statement uses a number of words, called *deictic* words, which can only be correctly interpreted through contextual relationships implicit in the statement, but necessary to the ensuing transaction. The word "please" infers a second party in the transaction, a bookseller of some type in this particular case. The word "me" refers to the speaking party. If such a statement were issued from a transcendent personal device in order to initiate an Internet supported transaction, then the speaking party would be interpreted as the bearer of the transcendent personal device. The word "this" refers to a spatial designation of a specific book. Should the utterance be made between two people, then "this" may refer to the book held in the hand of the speaker. If the utterance is issued by a transcendent personal device on behalf of its bearer, then the word might well refer to a specific Web location that references a contextual summary of the book and its physical availability, cost etc. Implied by the entire statement is the requirement to deliver the book "here," which is to the current physical location of the bearer of the transcendent personal device. Thus, to use such natural language in discourse regarding policy, it is necessary for the transcendent personal device to be able to establish the necessary contextual relationships, and therefore to become a *deictic center* for the bearer.

The determination of location for a transcendent personal device can be accomplished in at least a couple of different ways. Of course, the most general such approach is the provision of a Global Positioning Satellite (GPS) transponder within the body of the transcendent personal device. Depending on the resolution effected by the GPS, the location of the transcendent personal device could be determined to within a meter or so, if not to within a small number of centimeters. Certainly, this level of resolution is sufficient for all but the most stringent needs for the determination of locality within a transaction. An additional approach is to use the fine resolution timing of the reception of radio frequency signals from transmitters at known locations, which allows positioning according to an internalized map, which is more closely related to how we humans locate ourselves.

Most of the discussion applied to the accurate and trusted determination of location of a transcendent personal device is also applicable to the trusted determination of *date and time*. Measurement of the passage of time is somewhat more straightforward, but it offers some special problems in its own right if the numbers are actually to instill trust. As we've noted previously, if continuous power is available, then extremely accurate time periods can be established using oscillator circuits. Such circuits can be locked into external loops with highly accurate time sources (e.g. atomic clocks) such that they can maintain synchronized accuracy over long periods. The trick to accomplishing this in a trusted manner is to have the timing circuitry be part of a transcendent personal device body that can be made extremely tamper-resistant through continuous monitoring by its trusted core agent.

A significant need on the part of the transcendent personal device, since it must function as a fiduciary for its bearer, is to have some mechanism to very tightly bind to the person. In essence, there must be a strong authentication of identities between the bearer and the transcendent personal device. When this is accomplished, the bearer can expect the transcendent personal device to engage in policy machinations on the bearer's behalf and to be assured that the policy specifications that it adheres to are those given it by the bearer. Within the scope of currently available technology, the most appropriate mechanism for this tight binding, specifically of the bearer to the transcendent personal device, is the use of one or more of the *biometric characteristics* of the human body. The human body is replete with such characteristics. We recognize that our physical appearance and our very physiological being is an artifact of our DNA, so DNA is one possible biometric characteristic. Interestingly enough, DNA actually breaks down as a unique marker in at least a couple of cases: identical siblings and clones. Moreover, for some technical and societal reasons that we discussed earlier when we considered the concept of identity, DNA isn't our first choice for a biometric differential identity marker. Fortunately, due to a biophysical process called *random morphogenesis*, there are actually a number of biophysical characteristics that are quite random in their development and their subsequent randomness is adequately influenced by the statistics of extremely large numbers such that we can establish a very low probability that the characteristic will develop identically in two different individuals in a population sample the size of the population of the earth (and then some).

To engage in a trusted authentication protocol, the transcendent personal device must be able to request a biometric entry on the part of the bearer. To do this, it must incorporate the necessary sensors to capture the proffered biometric image or images. Given the capabilities of currently available technology, probably the most plausible architecture is for such biometric sensors to be incorporated into the transcendent personal device body. While this may be slightly less attractive from a security standpoint, the form factor impact of requiring biometric sensors on or within the trusted core agent is a severe limitation on the construction of this element. However, this is also a possibility given that fingerprint sensors (a fingerprint is the iconic biometric characteristic) are already available that can be included directly onto a secure core.

We've observed that a human biometric characteristic is a good mechanism through which to bind the human bearer to her or his transcendent personal device. It would be extremely useful if similar characteristics were available for equipment assemblies such as the transcendent personal device itself. Well, in fact, such characteristics are available in limited areas and the technology offers the prospect of enhanced utility within a wide range of equipment. Scott Guthery, a long time colleague of the authors and a founder of Mobile-Mind, Inc., has done a review of this area and has suggested the name *mechanimetrics* for a characteristic of machines based on electromagnetic processes that parallels that of biometrics for living organisms. This characteristic potentially allows for tamper-evident behavior of a token and its auxiliary attachments through the measurement of the aggregate differential identity of the mechanism. Central to the ability to effect a policy infrastructure is the ability to identify the players within that infrastructure to whom policy can be ascribed. Trust in a secure core derives from the immutable nature of the computer hardware and subsequently its software. The integrated circuit chip provides a relative self-contained computer system that is difficult, if not impossible to change. Its software is stored in read-only memory which is also difficult if not impossible to change. Mechanimetrics extends these trust mechanisms to more general device architectures.

# Transcendence Effected

We can recapitulate the primary requirements of the transcendent personal device as we've derived them from the needs hierarchy of people as reflected in the anticipated needs of computer networks. The need of transcendence itself mandates the connection of the primary trust infrastructure of the human social order with the primary trust infrastructure of the network. To meet this need within the device will require mutational changes within the human social order as well as within the technical facilities of the device.

Given a comprehensive environment, the capabilities of the device to function on behalf of the bearer derive from the need of self-actualization. The device must function through peer-level interactions with the external world that it encounters through its basic physiological capabilities. This functionality is guided by an ontology of the relevant social orders and network architectures. Specific interactions are engaged through processing capabilities derived through aesthetic needs on the part of the device and the device bearer. Through such aesthetic means, the actual trust equations of pending interactions are determined. Cognitive needs provide a basis through processing capability, language facilities and memory mechanisms to support these higher level needs.

Underlying the cognitive facilities is a hierarchical credentialing facility through which trust is established by way of the experiential identity of individuals. Trust in experiential identity, expressed as reputation, may be associated with the trusted establishment of differential identity. Differential identity is grounded in the mechanisms that respond to the safety and security needs of the device and of the bearer. Among these mechanisms is the linkage of the device to the individual through biometric sensors effected in response to physiological needs. With the added physiological capabilities of self-contained power, time determination and location determination, the transcendent personal device truly establishes a deictic center for the device bearer within cyberspace.

In the following chapter, we will delve a bit more deeply into the relationship between the trust infrastructure and associated interaction mechanisms through which the device will actually function. We will base this consideration of what we perceive to be the most ancient means of establishing trust in human interactions; prayer.

9 Mutation

# 10 Power of Prayer

*Prayer is not an old woman's idle amusement.*
*Properly understood and applied,*
*it is the most potent instrument of action.*

Mahatma Gandhi

## Prayer as Process

*Salah*, the ritual prayer that forms one of the Five Pillars of Islam, is offered by the faithful five times a day. *Mani wheels* incorporate repetitive renditions of the prayer mantra *Om Mani Padme Hum* and are used by Tibetan Buddhists to evoke the blessings of Chenrezig, the embodiment of compassion. For over 5,000 years, prayer has been a foundational element of the Vedic faith system that has become Hinduism, its form ranging from ritual utterances to philosophical musings. *Tefillot* are the communal prayer recitations offered in the observance of Judaism. Christians were taught by Jesus to pray according to the manner of *The Lord's Prayer*. Obviously a central feature of religious social systems, prayer encompasses a very special and in many instances highly structured form of social interaction. As such, it seems to us an extremely interesting element to be reflected in a model of social ecosystems.

Prayer comes in a variety of forms: mystical, praise, meditation, confession, and perhaps the most readily recognized form, *petitionary prayer*. All of the mechanisms represented in these various forms of prayer are present throughout the social ecosystems that we've thus far discussed. Mystical prayer maintains communication with the supernatural that we have associated in Chapter 7 with causality. Communal prayers of praise comprise an example of group ritual encompassing a state of ecstasy reinforcing shared trust in supernatural causes. Meditation, as we considered in some detail in Chapter 8, is a means for establishing trust through and with a process. Confession is a trust-based contributory mechanism to the handling of consequences in interactions. Finally, we consider perhaps the most intricate form of prayer: petitionary prayer. The particularity of petitionary prayer is that it presents itself in the form of an exchange transaction; consideration offered for consideration received. If such prayer entails an interaction with a deity, then it might be construed as placing a price tag on any ensuing actions by the deity. This depicts deities that form the prime source of causality as capable of being bought, so we clearly need to try to understand this form of prayer a bit better.

As we have come to understand it, a significant defining characteristic of all forms of prayer is that they are interactions that occur within the context of a covenant relationship. A covenant is an agreement or contract among two or more parties. Covenants come in two varieties: unconditional and conditional. In an unconditional covenant, one party makes a promise that offers consideration to another party with no reciprocal requirement for consideration from that party. A conditional covenant offers consideration from one party to another in exchange for some consideration in return. Within the context of a theistic social ecosystem, a covenant places a deity and some collection of suppliants of that deity in a structured relationship. In such a relationship, an unconditional covenant might entail the conveyance of some form of grace from the deity to the suppliants, while a conditional covenant might provide a specification of an edict to be adhered to by the suppliants in exchange for the blessings of the deity that are provided as a result of the relationship.

In Chapter 5, when we first discussed the concept of agreements or contracts, we recognized that under our current legal system only conditional covenants typically warrant enforcement under law. An unconditional covenant is generally viewed as a gratuitous promise and would likely not elicit enforcement under law should the promising party fail to provide the indicated consideration. But the recognition that a covenant between deity and suppliants is unconditional takes full significance if the deity does not fulfill the promise of the covenant. In this case, the trust established in the deity by the suppliant is lost, and with it the basis of the entire social ecosystem. Therefore, an unconditional covenant does not warrant enforcement unless it actually forms the keystone of the entire trust infrastructure, where it meets the ultimate retribution.

If the covenant is conditional, then the suppliant trusts that the deity will keep the promise made as long as the suppliant provides the indicated consideration. If the suppliant provides consideration to the deity, and the covenant promise is not kept by the deity, then trust is compromised, and consequences ensue. The rituals associated with both the maintenance of trust and the management of consequences to violations are an essential part of the trust infrastructure. With its unconditional and conditional components, the trust infrastructure forms the basis for establishment of the policy infrastructure of the social ecosystem. In turn, prayer allows suppliants to call for redress of the policy infrastructure via a natural recursive path, first towards a conditional covenant that readily contains mechanisms of arbitrage, and second to the ultimate unconditional covenant that can only provide remiss in the most intimate of redress, ecstasy, or apostasy.

Christianity, Islam and Judaism trace their theological lineage back to a common event; the establishment of a covenant between God and Abraham. While this is ostensibly viewed as an unconditional covenant, one can discern the elements of a conditional covenant as well. The Book of Genesis in the *Christian Bible* contains the declarations of, depending on how one interprets them, one or more distinct promises. *Genesis 12:2* presents God saying to Abraham "I will make you into a great nation and I will bless you; I will make your name great, and you will be a blessing." One can view this initial promise as an unconditional covenant that establishes a deity to suppliant relationship between God and Abraham and his descendants. If, however, one considers the entire Book of Genesis as establishing either a single covenant or a set of interconnected covenants, then *Genesis 22:18* "and in your descendants all the nations of the earth shall find blessing -- all this because you obeyed my command" would seem to rather clearly establish a conditional covenant.

A subsequent covenant is recognized in Christianity and Judaism in the form of the Ten Commandments given to Moses. This is a conditional covenant that is something of a template for *social compacts*. Social compact is the general term for the establishment of a governance relationship. It generally calls for a group to forfeit some aspect of the freedoms that they might enjoy operating under the policy machinations of the physical ecosystem in exchange for the establishment of a social ecosystem that can offer protection and other benefits from the threats posed by any containing ecosystems.

In establishing a covenant through Moses, the "children of Israel" were given the Ten Commandments which then formed the basis of law for a social grouping that would accrue to the benefit of the people. In return, the people, through their congregation, subsequently owed their allegiance to God who would judge their individual adherence to the laws provided. The basic tenets of Islam also surmise injunctions with the provision of a mechanism through which each person's obeisance of the law is rendered. Thus, we see the foundation of a religious trust infrastructure and a basic policy infrastructure. It is within this environment that prayer has true meaning. The laws of the policy infrastructure establish the manner in which members of the social system are allowed to interact with each other and the base covenant relationship provides a framework of trust within which the individuals can interact with the deity. Certainly, within the foundation elements of the United States government we can identify all of these same characteristics, albeit with the primary purveyor of trust, the Constitution, being purposely distanced from deity through the establishment of freedom of religion. However, we will later consider this positioning within an encompassing higher ecosystem.

Well, by this point, we've immersed ourselves a bit in the specific theologies of Christianity, Islam and Judaism. Hopefully, this still very cursory view is moderately accurate with respect to a layman's understanding of the basis of these religious structures. However, the real intent of this discussion is to reinforce the idea that prayer forms a structured interaction mechanism among the members of a covenant relationship; further among people and their god or, in associated forms, as with a call to the President for clemency, among people and their government or other trust infrastructure. What is interesting about this is that the covenant in question then defines an infrastructure of rules within which interactions occur; interactions which include their own specific rules. Thus, many rules, considerations and consequences flow from this infrastructure as opposed to solely from the specific interaction in question. This, then, becomes a recursive mechanism through which hierarchical trust and policy infrastructures can themselves interact.

Prayer seems to serve at least two common functions. At its most basic, prayer constitutes a ritual process that reinforces the trust infrastructure of the social system. Beyond this basic construct, the act of prayer also forms an individual or collective, highly structured interaction mechanism that encompasses interactions with a deity. While the mechanism reaches a level of almost formal specification with more recent religions, this extended facility may have evolved from forms of animism in which various spirits (minor deities) were ascribed to most of the common objects encountered by people in their everyday lives. Within such a context, virtually any interaction involved some association with such a deity and hence was related to prayer. This perhaps belies the observation that modern prayer, at least in some religions, often seems to adopt a near-conversational style.

As we said, trust and policy infrastructures are organized recursively, which means that there are trust and policy infrastructures that are included in and subordinate to other trust and policy infrastructures. When we use the term trust infrastructure in singular and without qualification, we mean in general the top trust infrastructure of the social ecosystem as well as subordinate trust infrastructures within that ecosystem; and similarly with the term policy infrastructure. We say that a trust infrastructure governs a policy infrastructure to formally express that policy infrastructures are subsumed by trust infrastructures.

We then consider prayer to be an interaction of persons within a group that involves the trust infrastructure of the social ecosystem within which that group exists. This description encompasses religions such as Buddhism that do not involve deities. Prayer follows the rules of the social ecosystem's trust and policy infrastructures to create an interaction involving both the policy infrastructure and its governing trust infrastructure. In that context, prayer relates to the rules of interactions of the social ecosystem. It comprises an attempt to interact directly with the trust infrastructure, and by doing so to indirectly affect policy in order to either affirm an understanding of policy rules, seek desired changes in them, or to request some special consideration under them. In essence, it's an effort to affect the trust equation of an interaction.

Prayer can be mundane:

*"Hi God, it's me. I'm still here."*

Or, it can be sublimely profound and urgent (*Christian Bible, Matthew 26:39*):

"My Father, if it is possible, let this cup pass from me; nevertheless, not as I will, but as you will."

We noted above that petitionary prayers are perhaps most intricate because they often seems at odds with our theologies. Such prayers appear to suggest that we expect to be able to barter with the deities, or in some fashion to entice them to take extraordinary measures in return for what we have to offer. At the extreme, we have already seen that prayer presents an entreaty to change the rules of an interaction in an extraordinary fashion, thus forming a mechanism to effect policy change in a manner that falls outside the policy domain.

Prayer has something in common with the characterization of the human emotion system in that the urgency of the prayer seems directly linked to our emotional response to a situation. We've observed that the level of the emotional reaction to some sensory stimulus sets the timeframe for a motor response. So it is with prayer; the direr the situation the more heartfelt is our prayer, corresponding to the strength of our emotional response to the situation and our degree of faith in the subsuming trust infrastructure.

Prayer may seek the intercession of intermediate trust arbiters in establishing communication with a deity or in gaining a desired result from the interaction. Thus, prayer may proceed through spiritual lobbyists if you will. Within the Roman Catholic religion, for example, a requirement for sainthood is a post-mortem demonstration that the candidate has successfully interceded with God on behalf of a supplicant. In the movie *Patton*, reprising what is said to be a true story, General George Patton is shown during the Battle of the Bulge demanding that one of his chaplains prepare a prayer seeking good weather for battle. His primary objective was to obtain good flying weather in order to bring the might of the Allied Air Forces to bear on the ongoing battle. After the weather actually did take a turn for the better, at least for the Allied Forces, the general was then shown telling one of his aides, "Bring that chaplain in here. I want to decorate him. He's in good standing with the Lord!" From the viewpoint of a trust and policy architecture model, this anecdote presents the trust invocation at the beginning of the battle, necessary for the warriors to transcend their individual emotions, and the return to policy at the end of the battle, where the habitual rules come back to play.

But we shouldn't leave our examples here as we need to contend with the facts that for a successful prayer to be a requirement from the part of saints indicates its paucity, and that the jocular aspect of Patton's remark shows that he had little expectation that the chaplain could actually influence the weather. Since it is actually acknowledged that petitionary prayers have little chance to be literally answered, why indulge in them at all? The most natural explanation is that while there may be little chance, the extraordinary nature of success is enough of an incentive; we play the lottery, don't we? However, that explanation cannot stand on its own. It has to be completed by our prior observation that just bringing the chaplain in with prayer allows transitioning from the policy infrastructure to the trust infrastructure, where the reliance on others is enhanced and brings the group to a better survival position. Finally, we wouldn't want to stop our investigation before introducing again the idea that prayer must be providing positive chemical releases in the brain on the road to ecstasy, which is both a reward in itself and a necessary ingredient in the trust ritual that we just discussed.

Now, we're not really seeking to delve into the specific effectiveness of prayer within any religion. That would take us full tilt into the tumult of trying to determine how best to evaluate a process, through anecdote or through statistics. From a societal perspective, we're all familiar with the anecdotal recounting of the power of prayer; and, the fact that prayer seems to have been with us, as a species, for as long as religion, would seem to lend some credence to a statistically significant belief in, if not objective observation of, the power of prayer. Certainly, we should note that prayer really does seem to be a common denominator among religions. But, our purpose is to consider the concept of prayer as a springboard to establishing the conceptualization of a social ecosystem from which can be derived the more detailed aspects of a generic ontology, or, in simpler words, a formal model of society. We would expect to be able to place trust and policy infrastructures in this ontology, which we will proceed to do further down in this chapter.

It is illuminating to note that prayer offers an excellent model of the appellate process of the United States judicial system. The Congress and the President ostensibly form the ultimate policy purveyors of this social ecosystem. The Supreme Court, as the highest court involved in policy adjudication, comprises the ultimate policy arbiter of the social ecosystem. However, through its preeminent right to interpret the Constitution, the Supreme Court also comprises the ultimate trust arbiter of the system. The illustration gets even more compelling. In certain instances, the Supreme Court can also effect profound changes in the policy infrastructure; in essence, it becomes in such cases the ultimate policy purveyor as well. The closing admonition of Supreme Court decisions is obviously telling in this regards: "It is so ordered." The fact that there is no redress, short of an Amendment to the Constitution, for such a pronouncement from the Supreme Court also suggests that it can function as the ultimate purveyor of trust within this social ecosystem. Such would be the act of God within a monotheistic religion. To illustrate this point, it is interesting to consider one of the predominant issues of our times regarding governance within the United States' primary policy infrastructure, the Supreme Court opinion in the case of Roe versus Wade.

This opinion was the end result of an appellate process concerning a case of a woman's access to abortion services. We would suggest that the initial class action suit from which was promulgated the ultimate ruling could be properly construed as petitionary prayer. While precipitated within the policy infrastructure, its clear goal was the ultimate trust arbiters of the entire social ecosystem; that is, an interpretation by the Supreme Court of the United States' Constitution. An opinion was issued by the Supreme Court on January 22, 1973. While volumes have been written regarding this case and the resulting decision, from our perspective two points emerged that are central to a model of social ecosystems. First, the opinion confirmed the primacy of the United States Constitution and its interpretation by the Supreme Court as the ultimate trust authority inasmuch as the result was to overturn a decision based on law under the State of Texas Constitution. Second, through the mechanism of this opinion, a new basic tenet was recognized as being contained within the Constitution, a *Right to Privacy* that had not been previously recognized in an explicit fashion. The majority on the court would likely suggest that the right was always there; it simply required the actions of someone able to read it. The fact that the decision was a seven to two decision lends credence to this interpretation. The fact that the decision was not unanimous suggests the variable nature of metaphorical understanding.

Prior to the decision, the law of the land allowed government to arbitrarily limit a woman's access to abortion services. People were sanctioned under the precepts of such law and individuals suffered life altering consequences from either following or not following these precepts. After the ruling, such access was deemed a right of women under the Constitution; and, this access could be limited in only extenuating situations. New precepts followed the installation of a new law of the land. People were sanctioned under these new precepts and individuals suffered life altering consequences from either following or not following them. Neither the precepts nor the consequences required further involvement from the Congress or the President. Hence, it seems fair to say that the rules of the policy infrastructure were changed in an extraordinary way. Petitionary prayer is an excellent model for this sequence of events viewed as a social ecosystem interaction. So, perhaps it is worthwhile to consider some of the processes that prayer suggests to us as we consider the evolutionary progression of computer based social ecosystems. It is also worthwhile to consider why it is worthwhile: we're always looking for ways to handicap the trust equation of transactions. We create social ecosystems in order to even out the very sharp edges of the physical ecosystem. We build structure within the interactions of our social ecosystems for much the same reason. Prayer offers agency in the search for that structure.

Within Christianity, the prayer shown below, termed the Lord's Prayer, is offered by Jesus as a model of the genre. It is, according to the *Christian Bible*, Jesus' response to the question of "How should we pray?" It is a mild form of petitionary prayer; it voices requests from the supplicant that God might actually be inclined to grant. We must note that we are using a version of the prayer from a King James translation from ancient manuscripts from which the *Christian Bible* derives. There are many such translations across the ages, each with its own subtle nuances and distinctions that make one slightly or significantly different from the others. Hopefully the meaning that we draw from the prayer is not adversely impacted by the specific rendition that we select for our cursory analysis.

We will now study this prayer from the perspective of the computer scientist, which in this case means that we are going to study it as a multi-step protocol through which is effected a transaction. From a computer perspective then, we might refer in technical jargon to this prayer as a template or perhaps even a specification. Saint Augustine, in his letter CXXX, translated as follows in volume I of *A Select Library of the Nicene and Post-Nicene Fathers of the Christian Church*, has actually offered that very suggestion: "For whatever other words we may say, — whether the desire of the person praying go before the words, and employ them in order to give definite form to its requests, or come after them, and concentrate attention upon them, that it may increase in fervor, — if we pray rightly, and as becomes our wants, we say nothing but what is already contained in the Lord's Prayer." Viewed in even more detail from a technical standpoint, this template proffers a moderately complete specification of a transaction protocol. Consider some of its elements (*Christian Bible, Matthew 6: 9-13*):

Our Father which art in heaven,
Hallowed be thy name.
Thy kingdom come.
Thy will be done in earth, as it is in heaven.
Give us this day our daily bread.
And forgive us our debts, as we forgive our debtors.
And lead us not into temptation,
but deliver us from evil.
For thine is the kingdom, and the power,
and the glory forever.
Amen.

First, the prayer establishes the participants in the transaction. It does this through the form of a *deictic expression*; an expression that implies spatial, temporal or personal orientation based on the context of the utterance. Consequently, it suggests that the language of prayer, and the infrastructure through which it is conducted, be capable of establishing deictic context. The *supplicant* who initiates the conversation is one party, or, more appropriately in this particular case, a representative member of one party consisting of some inferred but formally unspecified group. This must be inferred through the use of the plural possessive pronoun. The supplicant is the inferior party to a transaction where the act of authentication is establishing the identity of the supplicant in the eyes of the other party without reciprocity. The other party that the supplicant approaches, we will generically refer to as the *sentinel*. The sentinel recognized by the supplicant as "Our Father which art in heaven," establishes the other party: the Christian God. In *Sermons by Hugh Latimer*, edited by George Elwes Corrie, the sermon of June 9, 1536 afternoon, spells out: "It is either all one thing, or else not much different, to say, children of the world, and children of the devil; according to that that Christ said to the Jews [John viii], 'Ye are of your father the devil:' where as undoubtedly he spake to children of this world. Now seeing the devil is both author and ruler of the darkness, in the which the children of this world walk, or, to say better, wander; they mortally hate both the light, and also the children of light." Sentinel, are you awake?

The subsequent use of this prayer as a standard element in most Christian worship services forms a ritual reminder of the social ecosystem participants' ultimate source of trust. The subject of the discourse is the establishment or affirmation of a compact with God. In this case, the compact forms an attempt to achieve a desired outcome based on the perception that God can elicit this desired result; thus, the plea to affirm the rules and recognition of who the final arbiter of the transaction is. We might view this as a degenerate case of arbitration between two parties as to the rules that will govern the ensuing transaction and the arbiter who will make the final determination, because the supplicant is saying, "We'll do it your way." Once we've agreed to that, it's time to enter into the desired exchanges. The considerations due each party are relatively clear cut. The supplicant seeks material and procedural content. The sentinel will receive in return procedural content. Metaphorical bread and forgiveness comprise the consideration given to the supplicant and veneration is the consideration given to God. The conclusion of the transaction is also a degenerate case involving only one party, the supplicant essentially saying, "I'm satisfied with the results so I'm finished."

In true and earnest prayer, a supplicant generally voices most heartfelt needs, devoid of ambiguous language and obtuse meaning. As a consequence, the form and content can be extremely succinct, but with perhaps just a bit of imagination we can still discern the steps of a formal transaction. Consider the short prayers that we noted earlier in this chapter. The first ("I'm still here") corresponds to a simple recognition of presence; in computer networking parlance we might call this a *ping*. Its purpose is to periodically confirm that the lines of communication are still open. The second ("Let this cup pass from me") is very definitely a petitioner's request. The request (consideration sought) is specific while the exchange offer (consideration offered) is vague, but open-ended. It is clear, however, that the goal of the transaction is *consideration requested for consideration offered*. So, we can discern from each a well defined framework for a transaction. It is clear who the parties to the transaction are, what the subject of concern is, the desired outcome, the consideration due to the various parties, and the implied consequences of honorably, or even dishonorably, concluding the transaction.

A familiar homily suggests that "There are no atheists in fox-holes." When external stimuli are applied at the level of our most basic needs, at the level of safety or physiological requirements, we are apt to address ourselves to the highest trust authority of our primordial social ecosystem. A rather cold, calculating way to say it is that when we're scared out of our wits, we turn for protection to the god that we might well have ignored up to now. It is at such a time that we tend to recognize the source of last resort to our most desperate need of safety and protection, or more appropriately, of actions of redemption that we urgently require. It is reinforcing here that our prayers are directed at the ultimate trust purveyor in our social ecosystem (say God), not the ultimate policy arbiter (say the Pope).

Remember back in the first chapter, that this was one of the theses posted by Martin Luther. The Pope, who was the ultimate policy arbiter within the policy infrastructure in question, could only deal with supplicants to the point of their death, not beyond. Death forms a hard boundary of the observable physical ecosystem. Prayer, however, is a transaction specifically aimed beyond the boundary of the policy infrastructure. It is a direct appeal to a deity to "please forget about the physical laws." If it requires repealing the natural force of gravity to keep our plane from crashing, that's perfectly all right in this instance. Again, our point here is not to delve too deeply into the theological implications of prayer, and certainly not to disparage the earnest pleas for help that we may make when faced with dire situations, or even just the general events of our normal lives for that matter. But, from a social ecosystem perspective, it might be construed as a differentiating factor between the formal definitions of religion based social systems and égalité oriented, secular social systems. However, we also recognize that in reality such interactions do occur within secular systems, we just don't generally consider their existence in a formal definition of the system. As we've seen with our earlier discussion of Roe versus Wade, within the United States legal system, the applicability of law can occur at some post-transaction time, and new law can actually be created, outside the normal policy infrastructure, in the same fashion. We then suggest that religions in general actually provide more elaborate representative illustrations of a realistic model of social ecosystems and we would do well, as part of a scientific discourse on such systems, to seek understanding from these illustrations.

So, concerning members of the human species, can we discern a more formal specification of the mechanism that we recognize as *prayer* and why it forms a typical interaction method in the most critical of situations? It seems to us that it is the logical outcome of the trust and policy infrastructures that we humans use to establish and operate our grouping mechanisms. In times of ultimate need, when we present the ultimate stimulus for interaction, we seek redress from the highest arbiters of trust in our experience. For those in whom the threshold of religion grounded trust is continuously high, for the true believers, prayer is both a routine mechanism as well as a routinely satisfying one. Whether it's a function of how one prays, the semantics of the language that is used to pray, the policy that is the subject of prayer, or the potential recourse of prayer, this most intimate of religious activities would seem worthy of study and formalization within the context of interactions among the human species. Prayer brings into play the concepts of ritual and repetition as mechanisms well understood to entice the mind into a state of ecstasy; ecstasy then being the foundation within the mind for the concept of trust that forms the subsuming infrastructure for the social ecosystems that we, humans, have sought to achieve through the ages at progressively larger scales. Other interactions, as incantations at the beginning of team sports matches, or anthems preceding political rallies, may be studied through this prism.

At a considerably more mechanical level, within the model that we have evolved through the course of this book, prayer is a term we can apply to a transaction protocol. More specifically, it is an application layer protocol within the context of the network reference model that we presented in Chapter 3. Of course, prayer is about much more than simple communication; it embodies the very essence of complex interaction. As such, it is an application protocol that derives stimulus from the hierarchy of needs. It is an appeal that bumps at the boundaries of policy mechanisms by potentially seeking a modification of policy to address or redress our most profound needs. The boundary condition cases are generally the most telling about interactions, whether physical or social.

Throughout the course of this book, we have made a number of allusions to the concept of complex interaction. In this chapter we seek to explore the integration of an emergent species of computers, the *transcendent personal device*, into a social ecosystem infrastructure as fully capable as religious orders in establishing a framework for complex interaction. In essence, we're expecting the creation of an electronic, cyberspace analogue to the prevalent historical human interaction mechanism, religion. In this realm, the transcendent personal device will be the person. Through the establishment of identity, it will effect trust and policy considerations on behalf of the person, thereby allowing more effective control of the environment.

# The Domain of Trust

The transcendent personal device is emerging from a mutation of a personal electronic device that is based on a standard, highly mobile appliance such as a cellular telephone plus a secure core, an evolution of today's mobile phone plus its Subscriber Identity Module. Its function is the establishment and conveyance of trust coupled to active participation in the application of policy on behalf of its bearer. As we suggested in Chapter 9, the mechanisms that it uses for these purposes are a powerful connection to the sensori-motor environment of the bearer formed through a reliable processor connected to a user interface that engages all of the human senses along with a trusted container in which to store information and a trusted computer platform on which to perform sensitive computations. As we've discussed throughout the book, we view trust as a measure of the probability of predicting specific outcomes of interactions or various aspects of interactions. To be effective in this role, the transcendent personal device must serve to determine that trust is well understood prior to engaging in the interaction. It is indeed important to emphasize that trust implies a probability, not a certainty. We trust the authentication process used to establish the identities of the parties, subsequent to trusting the process used to establish and convey that identity. We recognize that the authentication may be false, but with there being a well understood path to that happening. Accordingly, we expect that within a well structured social ecosystem, this probability of failure can be anticipated properly and subsequent consequences appropriately applied.

The boundaries of a general identification system within a particular social ecosystem are defined by the mechanisms used to establish and project trust to the various components of the system. This essentially defines the scope of the reference model that we're outlining. A variety of mechanisms have been created through which trust based identity can be established and conveyed. These mechanisms tend to fall into three distinct categories:

1. Physical infrastructures – the actors, components and processes are constrained by a physical ecosystem.

2. Biometric infrastructures – the identities of actors are determined using markers comprised of physical characteristics of each person.

3. Digital infrastructures – an environment based on digital exchange of encrypted information, using private or public mechanisms.

As with any social ecosystem, the trust infrastructure for an identification system and its processes must be defined first. Its existence is specifically necessary to enable the creation of elements of the policy infrastructure which form the interaction basis for the system. Further, it should be noticed that the containing trust infrastructure cannot be modified from within the policy infrastructure; that is, the root of the trust infrastructure governs and subsumes the entire policy infrastructure. A policy infrastructure may contain subordinate trust infrastructures, thereby allowing policy controlled change of those trust infrastructures, however at the top of the conceptualization is a trust infrastructure that is essentially unchangeable, once created.

Socially, we're used to dealing or living in physical trust infrastructures. Indeed, some computer systems and networks make use of physical trust infrastructures in the form of locked rooms to protect systems against physical access, and firewalled, private circuit networks to insulate network connections against electronic access. Biometric infrastructures add to physical trust infrastructures by providing means to recognize identity based on physical properties of a person. As we discussed in Chapter 6, there are many biometric indicators, such as fingerprints, hand geometry, and face features. However, while biometric indicators are good at matching a person with a computer record of that person's characteristics, they are not meant to answer questions like: can you vouch for that person? For this, digital infrastructures have been created that can use third parties to convey trust to actors of computer networks.

Digital trust infrastructures are based on *keys*. We've discussed this more than once in previous chapters, but perhaps it will help to refresh the illustration. So, for example let us say that my friend and I both have a key for a box that nobody else can open. Then it's safe for me to put a secret message in the box, give it to a messenger, and have my friend get delivery of the box and open it to read the message. This can also be done in the digital world, using mathematics instead of physical boxes. This is called a private key system because, for it to work the keys must all remain private to each of the participants. While this is a robust way of enforcing security on computer networks, it is nevertheless cumbersome in that great care must be given to the distribution of keys, which is an impediment to the scalability of the scheme. Today, private key security is used extensively, albeit in small to medium size networks. A better architecture is needed for extensive networks.

So the idea was to split the operation of transmitting a secret message. In the private key example above, my friend and I are using a single mechanism to communicate. Whether I send a message to her or she sends a message to me, we are using the same box and the same key. This is why it's called *symmetric key cryptography*, where cryptography is the mathematical technique equivalent of opening a box in the digital world. Is there an asymmetrical version of the scheme, where my friend would have her own key, and I would have mine, and all we'd have to do would be to keep our keys protected, and there would be no key distribution problem?

Surprisingly, it can be done. As it relies on sophisticated mathematics, it's not easy to find an equivalent to this digital world operation in our day-to-day physical world, but we can try, so please bear with us. Suppose that instead of sending keys to my friends, I send them an open box that I alone can open once closed. When my friend wants to send a message to me, all she has to do is to put the message in that box, close it, and give it to a messenger. When I get the box, I know that nobody has been able to read the message but my friend and I. But wait a minute, how can I be sure that this is actually my friend who sent me the message? Well, my friend also sends me an open box that she alone can open once closed. I take her box, I put a message in it showing that I have read her message, for example by repeating part of it, and I send her back the box, closed. She alone can open her box, and voila, we have exchanged a secret message without having to share keys.

We just distribute boxes, and we don't need a complex distribution system of shared keys. Of course, in order for this to work, it must be impossible to dismantle the boxes. In our day-to-day physical world, it is very hard to build such boxes, or very expensive, or both. That scheme wouldn't work on a big scale. But in the electronic world, that's another story. Instead of boxes, we send a piece of mathematics, a number, over the network. And a key is just another number that we mix with the first one. We won't spell out the mathematics, large numbers factorization, elliptic curves, and the like. We'll just mention that the box scheme is called *asymmetric key cryptography*, as participants to the system all have different keys. Actually, we need to introduce two more concepts, that are unfortunately a little confusing: in asymmetric key cryptography, the key that I keep private is very naturally called my *private key*, whereas the box I send out, which is public, is not called public box, which would have made things simple, but instead *public key*, that really makes things hard to understand, but such is life; it's not just the religious that are obscure from time to time.

As one might imagine, as clever as the box scheme is, it still requires sending boxes around, and at some scale, that becomes cumbersome; if everybody sends boxes to everybody, even digitally, that's too much to bear. We need box distribution centers, where anybody in need of one can find it. For example, let's say that I want to send a secret message to somebody I have never met before, say a banker in Mongolia. I'm going to contact the Mongolia distribution center, and ask them for the banker's box. But then, you are saying, how do I trust that Mongolia distribution center? Is there anybody who can vouch for them? In fact there is: around the world, there are a few distribution centers that are so much used that everybody knows them. Their public key is published everywhere on the network, it's embedded in our computers when they are sold to us, they form the *root certificates* that make the whole system work. We'll refer you back to Chapter 8 for a more detailed discussion of just what a *certificate* is. Anyway, as we said earlier, there is always a top trust infrastructure: it is one of those top distribution centers. A famous one is the Verisign top (root) certificate authority, named after the company that pioneered the use of asymmetric key cryptography for distributing public keys. I can ask Verisign for the box of the Mongolia distribution center to make sure if I need to.

Keeping with our box analogy, a certificate is not a bland box that we would send around, but rather a box that has written on it information on who sent it, together with indications on how serious is the sender, and also associated data like, for example, how long the box can be used before it is considered too old to be reliable. While that information may be written in clear on the box, it is easy to check that it is genuine information, since it is possible to also put inside the box a secret message that verifies what's on it. So now we are ready to understand how a digital trust infrastructure works. At the beginning, there is a top authority, which is so well-known that their boxes are available to everybody without any doubt as to whom it belongs to. Then this top authority enables lower authorities, who now use the top authority to vouch for them, by distributing boxes that contain information that can be verified with the top authority. As you can imagine, lower authorities can have even lower authorities, and so on, until the world is covered with distribution centers that allow scaling down the trust system from the top authorities to all the levels of authorities needed for the full network to be covered. That's an elegant system, which has now taken the name of *public key infrastructure*. The similarity with trust infrastructures of religious systems should be readily apparent.

Well, we now understand how trust can be conveyed by a third party. If I want to know about this stranger in Ulan Bator, Mongolia that I need to do business with, I can ask her for a certificate. I can then check with the certificate authority of Mongolia, and I furthermore check that this latter authority is itself certified by the root authority, let's say, Verisign. So now I should be contented, since a reputable institution, the certificate authority of Mongolia, has told me that my banker from Ulan Bator is a recognized person, and presumably reputable. However, I would certainly want to know something more first. That is, how did the certificate authority of Mongolia double-check the identity of the banker? Moreover, if I am the truly suspicious sort, how did Verisign double-check the reputation of the certificate authority of Mongolia? Well, we are now back to the question of identity, of a person or of an institution. Suffice it for the moment to say that certificates typically include an indicator of the thoroughness with which an identity search is performed, starting with simply accepting the word of the person to using the most advanced biometric measures.

At this point, the reader should have a good idea of what a formal trust infrastructure looks like in the computer world today. We should emphasize its two main characteristics, which are trust conveyance and identity assertion. We will now look in details into policy, but let's not forget that trust infrastructures need to address aspects of trust way beyond those basic elements. Even if I know with good assurance that I am talking with a recognized banker of Mongolia, I still don't know if that person is going to help me in all our interactions: where is the additional trust? This is the subject that we will now develop.

# Purveyors of Interaction Rules

We have alluded to the actual formulation of social ecosystems. It might be useful to identify two of the principal mechanisms for such formulation found in the dominant social structures of today, those of organized religion and of secular governments. The build-up of the trust and policy infrastructures is a distinguishing characteristic between religions and secular governments. Trust and law within a theistic religion ostensibly emanate from a deity. Trust and law within secular government emanate specifically from people acting either individually or collectively. Let's very briefly note the primary purveyors of each: *prophets* and *solons*.

As Mircea Eliade illustrated thoroughly in *Shamanism: Archaic Techniques of Ecstasy*, religions are characterized by the presence of the shaman: an individual who can enlist a state of altered consciousness through which enhanced trust is established. Within deity based religions, the shaman is trusted to convey the message of the deity into the physical and social ecosystems that encompass peoples' lives. In this way, law is established as ostensibly a direct dictate from the deity. In Islam, the Angel Gabriel conveyed the laws of God to Muhammad who enumerated them within the Qur'an. In both Christianity and Judaism, a variety of prophets created the various manuscripts from which the Christian Bible Old Testament and the Jewish Torah were derived. Also in Christianity, Jesus served a similar purpose in conveying the new covenant that served as the basis for the Christian Bible New Testament, which was actually compiled by a different set of prophets.

An interesting characteristic of religious organizations emanated from the Protestant Reformation; secular mechanisms were instituted to deal with what we might term the more mundane aspects of religious congregation governance. In some instances, the entire congregation of a local church may act on certain issues such as the selection of a new pastor for that church. For issues such as keeping physical facilities in good repair and making sure all the bills get paid, an elected body is often selected by the congregation. For some religious organizations, a hierarchy of such elected bodies serves to coordinate the more secular policy considerations for a large collection of churches. Thus, within protestant Christianity we see the mechanism of both religious and secular governance social systems.

Solon was a Greek philosopher, statesman and politician who lived around 600 B.C. Due to his widespread popularity among all the social ranks of the city-state of Athens, he was tasked with revising the political system of the day. He did this by writing a well-defined constitution and then adapting the laws to this constitutional framework. His system replaced heredity as the basis for being or selecting the leadership with a social structure where, according to *Encyclopedia Britannica* (1910 edition), "Solon made property the measure of political power, and confined the higher offices of state to the wealthiest citizens; but election to these offices was to be made by the whole body of the people, the tenure of office was limited as to time, and an account had to be rendered publicly as to its exercise." Naturally, as he developed the first tenets of democracy, there was still a long way to universal suffrage from citizens with equal rights. However, while the constitutional government that he established was ultimately overthrown, much of the set of civil laws that he established survived. Today, we tend to refer to the legislators that we elect to our various policy making bodies as "solons." Moreover, the name of the Athenian public assembly, "Ecclesia," has come to mean church ("Église" in French), a matter not without importance for ontological discussions later in this chapter.

Within a democratic domain, the source of policy is the collective action of the solons representing some assembly of people. A variety of mechanisms are found around the world for elected representatives to effect policy. In the United States, unicameral and bicameral federal and state legislative systems encompass both a law making body as well as a parallel administrative function. In the United Kingdom, the parliamentary system has both legislative and administrative functions. In the United States, state institutions have their own trust and policy infrastructures, with parallel administrative functions, and those institutions are subject to policies established by the federal government. Additionally, non governmental entities like public companies also come with their trust and policy infrastructures, in the form of board and management, subject to state and federal policies.

# Arbiters of Interaction Rules

The governance of consequences is central to any social ecosystem. Beyond a purely objective identification and enforcement of consequences, a social ecosystem has at the pinnacle of its controlling architecture an arbiter with ultimate authority for the application of consequences. There are three distinct variants of such arbiters found within the primary social ecosystems of the United States. Within religious systems are found the clergy, often organized within some ascending hierarchy that culminates in a controlling figure or group within respective religious denominations. There is no all encompassing trust infrastructure for all religions, nor is there a single set of rules that encompasses all religious. In the United States, there is however a supreme trust infrastructure that encompasses a supreme policy infrastructure. Within this legal environment, both civil and criminal, are found the judiciary, also hierarchically structured and culminating in a court of last resort, the Supreme Court. Finally, within administrative infrastructures are found the administrators of such groups. Administrative organizations, while comprised of persons with varying degrees of authority, essentially exert their control of policy in the name of the highest level administrator, for example the President.

The *clergy* found within different religious organizations show a wide variance in both the authority required to place them in the positions that they occupy within their respective congregations and the authority that they can elicit as arbiters within these same congregations. At one extreme of the congregations are the religious groups that are pejoratively called cults; for example, the Branch Davidians of Waco fame (or infamy). These are typically small, highly focused groups that break off from the central body of a religious organization. In most instances, this schism is due to some disagreement with theological tenets of the core religion, but it is sometimes derived from a very strong personality that leads the small group away from the large. Within social ecosystems, cults encompass an evolutionary mechanism quite similar to that described in *Systematics and the Origin of Species* by Ernst Mayr for organic species; a mechanism that can result in speciation through the further process termed punctuated equilibrium. Should a cult gain wider acceptance, it might evolve into a sect; a similar organizational construct but one not nearly so harshly regarded by mainstream organizations. At the other extreme lay what we might call mainstream, organized religions. If we consider Roman Catholicism as an example, the church encompasses a well defined, hierarchical structure within which the clergy is established and through which it operates. The culmination of this hierarchy is the Pope, the person in whom resides the authority as the ultimate policy arbiter of this particular religion.

Within most religious structures, the members of the clergy are viewed as better versed in the tenets of the particular religious order than are the typical members, a group sometimes referred to as the *laity* to differentiate them from the clergy.

Within secular social ecosystems, the ultimate arbiters of consequences are typically the *judiciary*. Depending on hierarchy, the judiciary tends to either be directly elected by the people or appointed by a government's administrative arm and confirmed by an elected body. Members of the judiciary are typically chosen from a precursor group that is ostensibly trained in the intricacies of policy interpretation and application; that is, attorneys. The judiciary effects its interpretation of policy through a variety of courts. As part of the base level of the court system, sometimes referred to as *trial courts*, an additional mechanism is added to allow for the differentiation of the interpretation of policy from the assessment of whether or not a particular interaction conforms to stated policy. This mechanism is the *jury*. A jury is comprised of some collection of ostensibly unbiased observers. Details of interactions for which policy infractions are claimed are presented to the jury under the auspices of the specific court. The jury is then charged with making a *determination of fact* as to the details of the interaction. Again, under the auspices of the court a determination can then be made as to whether the interaction did, in fact, infringe the policy in question.

The federal judiciary comprise a hierarchical grouping whose members are all life tenured. At the highest level, the Supreme Court of the United States functions as the ultimate arbiter of the trust infrastructure. As we have noted, in some instances the Supreme Court appears able to function as the ultimate purveyor of policy as well.

354                                    10   Power of Prayer

*Administrative systems* have the general capability to enforce the consequences of interactions prior to the occurrence of the interaction proper. Such systems typically make use of credentials issued to persons that attest to their having achieved some status allowing them to participate in certain types of interactions. Probably the simplest example is the driver license, a credential issued by the state that attests to a person having demonstrated an acceptable level of competence to operate a motor vehicle. More complex examples entail the issuance of credentials that allow their bearers to practice law, practice medicine, or to be a certified engineer trusted in the construction of buildings, bridges and the like. The operators of heavy trucks require a credential as do the pilots of commercial and private aircraft. In all of these administrative systems, an infrastructure is put in place allowing a person to be tested for competence in some area and to have a credential issued when this faculty is demonstrated.

Lest administrators be underestimated, we should make at least passing reference to perhaps the most powerful single administrative facility within the United States Government, the Internal Revenue Service. This agency has extraordinary power to deal with the enforcement of tax law. The Supreme Court has generally held that this unique power is well grounded within the Constitution. The general interpretation is that a state has the ultimate right to survive, an interesting example of multi-level selection. The ability to levy and collect taxes is a central feature of survival. Consequently, this ability on the part of the federal government will actually trump many conflicting rights held by individuals.

# Evolution of a Basic Social Ecosystem

A simple metaphor allowed the emergence of the salient characteristics of the World Wide Web. Based on our earlier consideration of petitionary prayer, we suggest that the metaphor is well illustrated by the statement:

*Grant me this.*

Interpreted either as a humble supplication or as a command imperative, this sentence forms an iconic example of deictic discourse. It appears deceptively simple and hence acceptably supported by the current incarnation of the Web. However, its interpretation becomes considerably more involved when at least some of the additional inferred elements are made explicit:

*(You) (please)* **grant** *(to)* **me this** *(content) (here or where) (now or when) (since I need it because...) (and I am allowed to have it because...) (and you are allowed to give it to me because...) (and we will exchange consideration according to our negotiated basis of commerce) (and conclude our interaction according to the covenant relationship under which it is conducted).*

When considered in its full semantic guise as a formally posed transaction, the seemingly simple supplication or imperative gives way to a complex interaction within a well-defined social ecosystem. We suggest that its full derivation arises from the concept of prayer, pursued through a structured protocol with a recursive reference to an overarching covenant relationship. Delving just a bit into a more detailed parsing, consider the expansion of the personal pronouns. "You" can refer to another person, an inanimate individual entity, a group or even a deity. "Me" refers to the speaker, but this could take any of the forms that "you" might take. "This" is a direct, metaphorical indicator establishing reference to some content whose identity can be established within the social ecosystem. It is resolved through a selection vector which leads from the speaker to the indicated content. Thus, each of these pronouns requires interpretation or specification within the full context of the interaction.

Once the discrete entities noted within the imperative are identified, or more appropriately, authenticated, then the logic suggested by the remainder of the construct can be addressed. Its inferred elements complete the deictic description by establishing time and location for the impending transaction. As we have noted previously, application of policy directives can be made contingent on either. The urgency of application of policy within the transaction relates to the needs. Reference to authority to have and to provide the indicated content dictates the connection of differential identity and experiential identity within the context of the interaction. Moreover, when presented in extended form, the transaction entails the exchange of consideration with all the required facilities of a content system that we discussed in Chapter 6. Taken in total then, this ostensibly simple statement illustrates the context of a full-blown social ecosystem. Given that the current incarnation of the Web does not inherently facilitate all of the characteristics of this social ecosystem, it becomes an interesting conjecture to consider how we might evolve our current social order into such a cyberspace enabled system.

The foundation of the prevailing social ecosystem of the United States of America is formed by the Constitution and the law derived according to the policy constructs mandated there. Can we then find a basis for extending this social ecosystem into cyberspace? Certainly! We note that one of the basic elements of a social ecosystem, as suggested by the imperative with which we started this section, can be established through a straightforward trust and policy infrastructure presented in the form of an *identification system*. As we suggested when we discussed the facets of identity, the constitutional mandate to conduct a census forms a seminal justification for the identification of all the individuals found within the trust infrastructure. The facilities of such a system effectively establish an extremely useful, albeit rather simple trust and policy environment in a stand-alone fashion. From this simple foundation, the legal doctrine of a living Constitution readily supports the extension into cyberspace of concepts established through social orders based on physical interactions. Indeed, with an identification system to build upon, more wide-ranging infrastructures can then be constructed through the progressive addition of other trust and policy mechanisms. The point being that an identification system is perhaps the most basic social ecosystem. It is then of further interest to consider how one blends an identification system based on formal electronic and physiological means with the more recondite systems on which our current social orders are founded. So, let's pursue that thread a bit further.

The primary boundary of a social ecosystem is formed by its trust infrastructure. For an identification system, we are particularly concerned with the establishment and conveyance of *trust* in at least two ways. If a person presents herself to a sentinel with the assertion that "I am Jane Doe!" then first, it should be possible to affirm that this biophysical person is uniquely represented within the trust infrastructure of the identification system. Second, it must be possible to determine in a trustworthy manner that the biophysical person currently in contact with the sentinel is in fact the person uniquely represented within the identification system. In other words, it is necessary to trust the fact that the person is enrolled in the identification system once and only once, and that the authentication process is able to discern that a specific person is indeed the person enrolled in the system. The requirement for unique enrollment demands ongoing affirmation that the markers being used within the identification system are actually able to differentiate between people to a sufficiently high level of selectivity. The requirement for a trusted authentication process derives from the need to repetitively discern the differential identity of the same person in multiple interactions. Thus, we suggest that enrollment and authentication of differential identity comprise the most basic services required of an identification system.

The extension of a pure identification system to provide the more general transaction basis of a widespread social ecosystem requires implementation of the concept of reputation derived from experiential identity and that of authority granted to differential identity. Authentication of differential identity gives some level of assurance that this is Jane Doe. Reputation born of experiential identity then tells us that this would then be THE Jane Doe that owns the checking account #4179456. Authority granted to differential identity in deference to experiential identity tells us that Jane Doe can write a check for $37.44 against this account because she has previously deposited at least that amount of currency into the account. Thus, we see the connection between two episodes of experiential identity; depositing currency into an account and withdrawing currency from that account.

While the trust establishment components of the human mind are yet merely qualitatively understood, in the digital world, there are more quantitative models of evaluation of uncertain situations. One expects the transcendent personal device to embody such probabilistic networks to assign a level of trust to both the uniqueness of an identity and the strength of the authentication process that established it. These evaluation networks can be based on quantifiable data, for example the number of biometric measures being applied, and the discriminatory nature of the identity features being established. Additionally, much like a safe or an armored vehicle, a secure core is designed to prevent entry by an attacker. Entry, in this case, is the ability of an external agent to gain access to the computer that forms the heart of the secure core. The trust in the secure core itself should be well established through the causality of design and the trusted process of manufacture.

We can build the desired differential identification system using the transcendent personal device. As a basis for conceptual illustration, consider its hypothetical incarnation to be a device much like a standard GSM cellular telephone. Such phones already encompass the two sub-systems architecture described in Chapter 9, namely a device body and a secure core agent. We will assume that the device includes a high-resolution digital camera, as many cellular phones do, and we'll assume a sensory extension through the addition of a fingerprint pad. Thus, the device can be used to establish differential identity of an individual person through the detection of an iris pattern and one or more fingerprints. This is virtually congruent with the current biometry requirements for many state driver licenses. For example, the State of Texas requires a facial photograph and two thumbprints.

For identification systems on which we base historical grouping mechanisms, within the mind of the individual person the differential identity enrollment process essentially begins at birth, as we discussed in Chapter 8. Physiologically based information and subsequent authentication mechanisms that make use of this information comprise the early bonding between infant and parent, most typically the mother, or with some other primary caregiver in the absence of one or more parents. At the earliest age, the markers for differential identity are biometric characteristics of a person; facial features, characteristics of a voice, odors, tactile presentation and combinations of all of these. For a time as infants, we only make the association of marker with person as an internal cognitive function. We can identity a person and perhaps make known our act of authentication through externally visible emotional responses, but we don't yet have a way to reference our internally derived marker with some symbolic reference that we can convey externally. In our earliest stage of infancy, we might recognize our mother, and smile accordingly, but we don't yet have a symbolic reference through which we can convey our association to another person. It is always a noteworthy event when a baby first learns to say "Mama!"

Following this cognitive transition, an infant or child becomes able to establish symbolic references to other people; they begin to learn names and with this facility comes the further ability to associate other salient information with that name. In other words, we begin to establish our own assessment of the experiential identity of persons we encounter within our lives. This forms a second enrollment process; that for experiential identity. The two forms of identity work hand in hand as a basis for trust within the informal or formal policy infrastructures in which we live our lives. Most such infrastructures have some passage event that signifies the completion of the act of enrollment. Within some social groups, there may be a physiological basis for such an event; for example, the achievement of puberty. At this point, boys become men and girls become women. A variety of associated policies may well come into play at this point. We view these as modifications to the authorization states associated with specific differential identities and we'll discuss these in greater detail in the following sections.

So, within the realm of the transcendent personal device, how do we begin the enrollment process for the general population to be encompassed by the trust infrastructure? Since our initial system is predicated upon conducting a census, we might speculate on a process that begins with a large number of census takers, each equipped with a transcendent personal device. Each device could be tightly bound to its bearer through issuance within a secure facility. For example, within the confines of a few, central census offices the individual devices could be imprinted with the biometrics of their specific census taker by simply having the bearer take a picture of her or his own iris patterns and enter two thumbprints into the device while it is in a trusted *issuance state* under the control of a census office supervisor. While in this state, the bearer's biometrics could be entered into the device's secure core agent as part of an authority credential that controls subsequent operation of the device and limits it to actions enabled by the specific census taker. Only by subsequently providing the correct bearer biometrics can the device be placed in an operational state. Otherwise, the device is essentially a high-tech paperweight.

Now, we have a collection of census takers, each in possession of a transcendent personal device trusted by the census system. The primary purpose of these particular devices is to acquire the biometric markers of people for the purpose of counting them. Obviously, these transcendent personal devices may be useful for much more than this simple task, but it's important to note that they allow this relatively simple task to be imbued with a great deal of trust. This process of counting is highly resilient in the face of superfluous entry of redundant biometrics. So, it is perfectly all right for census takers to attempt to count the same person more than once. The transcendent personal device simply accepts the entry of one or more biometrics and transmits them to the census database that comprises an identity registry for the population. As part of this enrollment operation, the census database performs an identification process as we have previously defined it. It performs a comparison of the new biometric images to all the biometric image sets currently contained in the database. If there is no match, then the biometric images are added to the database and the count of the total number of people in the census is incremented by one. It then becomes the purpose of census takers to encounter as many people as possible and to count them. The capture of biometric images such as iris patterns or fingerprints is non-invasive. Hence, the counting process itself requires no more than a few seconds to perform and privacy can be protected, as there is no legal mandate at this time to associate each person's name with their biometric images. As the primary facility for the count, the census database needs to ascertain that the enrollment transcendent personal device is operating within the proper physical confines of the census by obtaining an indication of physical location; perhaps through a trusted GPS signal from the device. It can then tag each biometric marker with a time-stamp and a location-stamp in order to establish the seminal trust point of each differential identity. The differential identity registry is now a repository of biometric markers that can establish differential identities within the social ecosystem. It is perhaps as close as we can get to a pure identity system in which there is no place for theft of identity to occur and for privacy to be abrogated.

In the interest of presenting a moderately succinct description of a basic system, we've swept under the rug several issues. For example, within a population of several hundred million individuals, some number of people will not be able to present either an iris pattern or a fingerprint. In such cases, an ultimate fallback position of using DNA patterns as a differential identity marker would likely be required. Moreover, if we consider that being born and dying are the only significant state transitions for personal differential identity, then perhaps a DNA pattern should always be maintained as an auxiliary marker, along with iris patterns and fingerprints. In some instances, as we've just noted, this may be the only effective biometric that an individual can present. In a similar vein, in some instances it is only through forensic DNA evidence that it can be determined that a person has died. This obviously has significance if our differential identity registry is intended to present a count only of living individuals. So, this illuminates the need for trusted processes to be put in place to deal with the progression of a person's experiential identity. While it is important to remember that people are not required by current constitutional mandates to use this registry for the subsequent establishment of experiential identity for purposes other than the census, we note that the registry offers the prospect of enabling the establishment of trust through reputation to the contained individuals through such extended use on a voluntary basis. This brings us to the consideration of extending the basic differential identity system to encompass experiential identity as well. In so doing, we also must consider how to meld the historical methods of identification with this more rigorously constructed system.

If one can establish a differential identity system first, then building experiential identity in addition to it is relatively straightforward. However, the current situation is one in which we have one or more *de facto* experiential identity systems already in place. In general, these systems are not based on a rigorous differential identity marker. Thus, these systems warrant significantly less trust than can be achieved with biometry based differential identification systems. However, there is not a realistic option of discarding our current systems and starting over again. Thus, one must understand and bring to bear a number of trust evoking processes to blend the old systems into the new. We'll begin by considering the melding of a new, biometry based enrollment facility with an existing, more arcane identification system based on *confluence of information*.

Most identity systems today derive their trust in establishing differential identity through the enrollee's ability to produce one or more documents from a list of acceptable identity source documents. In essence, they establish differential identity through a recurrent process of reference to experiential identity. Consider for example the list of acceptable source documents in applying to the District of Columbia for a driver license, which can then be used subsequently as an identification card for a variety of purposes:

- State-issued United States birth certificate or birth certification card.
- DC driver's license, learner's permit, or identification card, not expired for more than 180 days.
- Unexpired United States passport.
- Certificate of Naturalization (N-550, N-570, or N-578).
- Certificate of US Citizenship (N-560 or N561).
- Letter with picture from Court Services and Offender Supervision Agency (CSOSA) or DC Department of Corrections certifying name and date of birth.

- Unexpired Foreign Passport with un-expired visa issued for six or more months and I-94 stamp (Arrival and Departure Record).

- Unexpired Refugee Travel Document (I-571).

- Form I-94 (Arrival and Departure Record) stamped Asylee, Refugee, or INS Asylum Approval Letter.

- Unexpired Employment Authorization Card (I-688A, I-688B, I-766).

- Unexpired Resident Alien Card (I-551) (also known as Green Card).

- Unexpired United States Citizen Identification Card (I-197, I-179).

- Unexpired Diploma Certificate with Diplomat Identification Card issued by the United States Department of State.

These various forms of identification documentation are usually connected to the distinct person only through a name. Thus it is impossible to achieve a very high level of trust in the differential identity of a person as established by these documents. The primary reason for this is that there is no strong binding between the biophysical person and the document. For example, while a passport contains a picture, the document can still be of questionable trustworthiness because it may have been obtained by presenting a birth certificate, which doesn't contain a picture. So the documents fail to fully meet the quantitative requirements that we stated in Chapter 9 for differential identity markers able to establish that a person is not an impostor. The reason that such systems work at all with some level of efficacy is because most people are not in the business of beating the system, and they have established moderately verifiable forensic trails during the course of their lives. However, for the serious adversary, creating an identity through the forgery of source documents is relatively straightforward.

Before going further in our discussion, we want to emphasize that in some situations, this adversary stance may in fact be our friend. For the French Resistance in World War II, forged identity was the way of survival. This, of course, is the ongoing dilemma with identification systems; they can be used for good but also perverted for ill. In the following, we will illustrate clearly the technical underpinning of a formal identification system. We will ascertain that our description brings clarity to the evaluation of the positives and negatives associated with the use of such a system in a given social order. However, the choices made following this evaluation are dependent on further elements of trust associated with such an order. As we will now see, these choices are not binary, but rather a matter of selection amongst various tools and possibilities.

Since the most common denominator in existing, credential based experiential identification is a name, the first step to associate an experiential identification system with a biometry based differential identification system is to attach a name to the biometric markers in the differential identity registry. The name then forms the seminal point of experiential identity for a person. In Chapter 9, when we discussed the concept of identity in some detail, we ascribed the term *anchored persona* to this connection point between differential identity and experiential identity. This is similar to existing systems in which a name is specified on a birth certificate. So, we would like to consider how to bring into being a "birth certificate equivalent" based on the trust infrastructure of a biometry based differential identification system. Now, the use of any identity credential, including a birth certificate, requires a significant vetting and issuance process by a *trusted third party* if any significant level of trust is to be ascribed to it. So, a rather interesting question is "What trusted third party can be used to connect a name to a differential identity?" Moreover, "What technical means make the connection of a name to a differential identity such that during repetitive interactions it can be affirmed, to a high degree of trust, that the person asserting a specific name is always the same biophysical person?" If we reflect on the discussion about identity in Chapter 9, what we're really considering is the mechanism through which to establish an anchored persona.

Given the differential identity registry established through the census, a necessary addition to provide for experiential identity is a policy infrastructure allowing for the creation and operation of trusted third parties. Today's best technological approach to this infrastructure is the establishment of a public key infrastructure such as we discussed in some detail in Chapter 8 and in Chapter 9. This entails the creation of a means to build a hierarchy of trusted third parties that emanates from a root organization that forms the base of the hierarchy. In practice, it is plausible to consider a collection of independent hierarchies, each with its own root organization. To simplify our current discussion, however, let's consider a single hierarchy that is grounded in some federal agency that parallels the Bureau of the Census. We suggest a federal agency because, given the critical nature of the public key infrastructure and its constituent transcendent personal devices, the consequences of abrogation of the policy under which the infrastructure and devices are provided should be correspondingly profound. Such consequences may constitute an overwhelming level of risk for any organization that doesn't benefit from the concept of sovereign immunity. So, for the moment, let's assume that the device is derived from a government agency, perhaps akin to a driver license. For example, we might consider establishing it in a context similar to the Centers for Disease Control and Prevention. They are charged with storage, protection and study of the most virulent disease manifestations on the planet. Some of their methods may also be trusted to store the root keys of a public key infrastructure.

Whatever organizational niche it shows up in, once the root key of a public key infrastructure is in place, we're in a position to establish subsequent identification of trusted third parties. We might suggest creation of the first such trusted third party as the "Book of Life." While it's highly unlikely that this particular entity would ever actually be fielded under this name, given the hallowed position the name holds within the traditions of Christianity, it in fact conveys the desired concept with iconic purity. To establish a high degree of trust through reputation, we need a reliable means of associating differential identity with experiential identity, including a reliable archive of experiences. Hence, we will use the term as an attempt at clarity within this discussion.

So, let's think of the registration of an anchored persona associated with a differential identity. This digital persona will allow the third party to assert a name on the Web while the digital differential identity marker lets us mutually authenticate our interaction to that name in a highly trusted manner. In addition, trusted records of transactions engaged through this anchored persona can be preserved. This requires a few steps to accomplish.

To first establish a digital persona and differential identity marker, we ask the Book of Life to grant us a public and private key pair that is associated with our biometric differential identity. Remembering our earlier consideration of public key cryptography, we know that our digital name (that is, the public key from the key pair) can be freely disseminated. This now forms a digital metaphorical reference to us on the Web. The private key, however, is then our digital differential identity marker. If someone else besides us has this private key, then they can masquerade as us on the Web. So, the truly trusted way for the Book of Life to deliver our digital identity to us is within the secure form of our own transcendent personal device. How does it do this?

Well, within the confines of the Book of Life physical location there can be unassigned transcendent personal devices. To provision (remember the discussion in Chapter 8) this device for a specific person, the public and private key pair can be generated within the secure core agent of the transcendent personal device. Next, biometric markers from the census differential identity database can be loaded into the secure core agent such that only when this biometric marker is entered can the device actually function. *Et voila!*, we now have a transcendent personal device that can only be operated by the intended bearer, and it can be used to project the differential identity of that bearer across the Web.

The transcendent personal device is provisioned within the secure confines of the Book of Life facility. Once provisioned, it can actually be shipped to the correct bearer through an unsecure communication channel such as the U.S. Postal Service. Moreover, it can maintain its trustworthiness once it reaches the hands of its intended bearer. This has many of the characteristics of a bulla such as we discussed in Chapter 7. It does have the very important additional characteristic that it can only be "opened" (that is, operated) by a single, specific person. Now, this transcendent personal device can be carried by the individual as a means of trusted participation in policy interactions. Since it is predicated upon the differential identity registry that we saw established as part of the census process, this device looks similar to a national identity card. However, it's quite different. As we discussed in Chapter 5, the historical identity card is one of a credential issued by some authority which then retains some right to demand its presentation by the bearer. The transcendent personal device carried by the individual, if predicated upon the comprehensive foundations of Chapter 9, provides for a peer-level interaction mechanism established under an overarching covenant relationship. In other words, *on behalf of its bearer* it is able to negotiate the rules of interactions with well-identified individuals also enrolled in the differential identity system. During and following the transaction, it can maintain trusted records regarding the full breadth of the interaction. This facility forms a formidable bulwark for enforcing personal privacy in the face of otherwise unfettered institutional anonymity. For example, a useful transaction would now be to obtain from the appropriate trusted third party, for storage within the transcendent personal device, a copy of an official birth certificate.

In order to connect a birth certificate to a differential identity, the most obvious potential trusted third party would be a Bureau of Vital Statistics. In general, such an office exists in each state and through this office one can obtain a copy of a birth certificate. In fact, the National Center for Health Statistics, an office within the Centers for Disease Control and Prevention, already provides a clearinghouse through which such vital statistics offices can be located within each state. So, all that is really necessary from a technical standpoint is a transcendent personal device that can engage in a transaction with such an office. What one needs to supply, via the transcendent personal device, is indexing information for a birth certificate and an authenticated digital differential identity. If the authentication process is supported by the transcendent personal device which in turn is limited to operating only when the correct biometric marker for the bearer is entered, then the vital statistics office has a highly trusted identification of the requestor.

The index information can be used by the vital statistics office to ostensibly determine the right of the requestor to obtain a copy of a specific birth certificate. The effect of this transaction is at least two-fold. It allows an experiential identity credential to be issued by the vital statistics office; that is, a digitally signed copy of a birth certificate. In addition, if the request is deemed to come from an anchored persona of the person actually named in the birth certificate, then it can create a signed credential that links this anchored persona of the requestor to that specific birth certificate. If a cross reference is maintained within the vital statistics office, then a birth certificate can be shown to be reliably associated with a persona anchored in the biometric differential identity registry.

Of course, one might well wonder whether such a history is of benefit to a person and to the social order, or is it in fact a threat. On the benefit side of this consideration, under such a comprehensive identification system the contained information has a high probability of being correct, and therefore worthy of trust. In addition, within a system grounded in strong authentication of differential identity, it becomes trivial to require an anchored persona for anyone who seeks to access this record. It is technically possible to forbid all anonymous access to the Book of Life. Indeed, within such an environment, anonymity on the part of any requestor becomes a threat, whether by hacker or by authority. Globally, there are obviously details of experiential identity on the part of an individual that are the proper concern of the full social order; records of criminal conviction for example. Individually, we often seek interaction benefits based on our reputation, and the Book of Life provides this. However, in the quest for privacy, sometimes we would like to compartmentalize our reputation just a bit. Two other facets of identity that we discussed in Chapter 9 allow us to do this: the *floating persona* and the *situational persona*.

Since the public key infrastructure allows for the creation of a hierarchy of trusted third parties, we have the capability to establish subordinate archives of experiential identity. We could, for example, establish a Book of Aliases. With this facility, through our personal transcendent personal device we can establish a digital persona associated with a floating persona, in other words a name of our own choosing. The Book of Aliases could then invoke within our transcendent personal device the creation of a key pair, with the private key protected by our differential identity marker and the public key exported to the Book of Aliases. Within the Book of Aliases, a digital certificate could be issued that would associate the name we had selected with the public key from our transcendent personal device. A copy of this digital certificate could then be loaded onto our device. Now, through our transcendent personal device, we are able to engage in a transaction with some other entity through a floating persona. The other party can thus know the limitations on experiential identity acquired through this facet of identity of an individual. In essence, the record of experiential identity established in the Book of Aliases is highly trusted to refer to the same biophysical person, but there is not a direct connection to the differential identity of that person. This looks like our credit history as currently maintained by various credit bureaus, with a couple of new wrinkles. First, the information contained in the Book of Aliases is much more likely to be correct than the information found within a person's credit history. Moreover, the information in the Book of Aliases is much more likely to all refer to the same biophysical person than is the information within a person's credit history. Finally, a level of privacy is formally enforced, as the information is not indexed on the actual name of the person.

Now, in certain situations, we would like to engage in interactions where the only record maintained is what is remembered by ourselves or the other party. Moreover, we may not choose to disclose our "true identity" in such situations. This is the interaction of the *situational persona*; the "What happens in Vegas, stays in Vegas!" style of interaction. However, if one engages in an interaction with a red chameleon, it is only fair that all parties know that chameleons are involved and that chameleons can change colors with great alacrity. So, to engage in such interactions on the Web, it would be most useful if our transcendent personal device can establish a situational persona for us. In fact, this is rather straightforward since it does not involve a trusted third party at all. In this case, the device simply generates a digital persona; a name and a public and private key pair. The device then creates a digital certificate that associates the name with the public key, and then signs it with the private key. When this digital certificate is given to some other party in advance of an interaction, that party can authenticate the digital differential identity across the Web. Hence, an ongoing interaction can be maintained if desired. However, the other party knows from the form of the digital certificate that this is a situational persona it is interacting with.

So, we've now illustrated how to establish three levels of personal identity. In addition, we've seen how to blend our historical identification systems with a digital system based on biometrics. We can engage in interactions under the guise of any of these levels of identity. By clearly specifying the levels, all parties to an interaction have the same expectations of interpretation. Perhaps more important, with these well-defined levels, our transcendent personal devices can be expected to better act on our behalves. Finally, no matter the level of personal identity used, the interaction process is the same. Let's briefly review the steps of the interaction.

# Drawing the Party Line

The first step we will term the *overture*. As with a play, this step is prelude to the main action. It entails bringing the supplicant and the sentinel in contact such that they both decide that they wish to enter into the authentication protocol proper. The actions that occur during the overture suggest that either side can first take the initiative in the process. The sentinel may first notice the approach of the supplicant and issue a preliminary challenge: "Halt, who goes there?" Alternatively, the supplicant can take the initiative: "Hello the house!" Following this very preliminary exchange, the sentinel can then begin the formal authentication procedure: "Advance and be recognized!" The supplicant then responds with an initial assertion of identity: "I'm Jane Doe." Within the cyberspace interaction, we would actually like to give the somewhat stilted assertion: "I am the anchored persona, Jane Doe."

In essence, we've codified an exchange that might occur between two strangers meeting in an isolated location where the intentions of either can range from benign to threatening. For the etiquette of a transcendent personal device, this corresponds to the range of actions from a person plugging an identification token into an apparently dormant system versus an application reaching a point where it needs token services and issuing an order to "Insert Your Token." We've gone a bit overboard in discussing the overture stage because this is an area where operational models of different systems can diverge rather significantly; so, it is useful to model this well such that the two parties can land on their feet no matter how they get started.

The remaining stages are typically understood in a generic sense, but they can vary a great deal in the details. Once a supplicant name is asserted during the overture then the next step is that of *marker acquisition*. This step is aimed at gathering a marker from the supplicant and providing it to the sentinel. The only real new wrinkle here, from a conceptualization viewpoint, is recognizing that these successive stages may be pursued recursively in order to achieve an adequate trust level among all the elements of the two systems. For example, the two sides might first seek to recognize that each is presenting or using trusted equipment and then subsequently seek to establish trust in the differential identity of the supplicant as well as that of the sentinel. This is particularly important because, for most current token based systems, the token needs to trust the sensors on the sentinel through which the marker is acquired.

The marker to be acquired can run the full gamut of approaches to uniquely authenticate differential identity. It might consist of having the marked party select a series of objects from a list, providing a graphical password. Or, it might entail actually entering a text password or a personal identification number. On a more complex plane, it might entail capturing a facial image of the supplicant or perhaps an image of their iris pattern or one or more fingerprints. In the extreme, it might entail capturing a swab of bodily fluids from which DNA can be obtained. Once the marker is acquired, it can be compared by the sentinel to a marker template that was gathered from the supplicant on enrollment.

Following this *verification* operation of the acquired marker, the sentinel establishes the *state* of the authentication operation (for example "accepted" or "rejected"). Once this state is established, the authentication operation is over. The *departure* stage allows for shutting down this procedure and gracefully moving to the next one. We now need to consider what uses we want to make of identity once we rigorously established it.

Differential identity of the potential participants in a transaction is a central characteristic of policy; that is, policy may be ascribed to identities as well as to transactions. In particular, provision of policy as an aspect of both parties of a transaction, requiring negotiation between the two prior to a transaction is absent from most, if not all identification systems today. In the application of identity concepts and identification systems, it is typically the case that the use of identity is more the purview of the receiver of identity rather than the provider of identity. Consequently, there is diminished concern regarding whether identifiers through which the identity of people is ostensibly authenticated are compromised, and hence can be used by other people to impersonate the identity of the true target of the identifiers. Through this theft of identity, an attacker can perform any action or make any claim that the impersonated person could perform or make if they were physically present and participating in the transaction in question. This obviously points out a huge problem with such identification systems and leads one to consider at least partially alleviating this problem through the provision of user controlled policy definition mechanisms.

Specifically, the policy through which the use of identity is established must be expanded in law and then provided for within identification systems. That is, the ultimate source of the policy should either be general law or it should be the result of a negotiation between the provider and the receiver of identity on a transaction by transaction basis. There are a wide range of issues from which policy could be defined under the personal control of each individual with the definition of policy itself being related to the strength of the authentication mechanism used to establish the differential identity of a person. Authentication protocols can range from high trust variants, perhaps requiring a person to go to an office equipped with very secure and accurate biometric sensors, to low trust variants, perhaps only requiring a person to present a contactless token at a turnstile. Policy allowing for making use of varying levels of security for entry of authentication parameters (biometrics, personal identification numbers, etc.) allows for a variety of performance levels when an identity token is presented as well as a variety of trust levels in the resulting authentication.

Through policy definition, it can be specified what trust can the receiver place in materials or services attested to by a specific authenticated identity. For example, a person may want to disavow any trust being placed in casual e-mail messages. Today, the perception in some circles may be that an e-mail message is akin to a highly trusted, absolutely truthful document to which the signer attests, under pain of liability. Other people, however, may consider e-mail to be a highly informal mode of communication, worthy at one extreme of simply passing along gossip. So, it should be possible for a person to establish a policy regarding the trustworthiness of specific messages and allow the sending and received to negotiate a well-defined policy for the sending and receiving of messages. If one side attests only to passing along unsubstantiated gossip, and the other side doesn't want to hear any such gossip, then no exchange takes place.

The processes through which the interactions supported by a policy infrastructure proceed can take on a variety of forms aimed at a variety of purposes. We have just spent some effort looking at the most general of the interaction protocols, that of authentication of the entities which will engage in the interaction. After authentication, we are able to ascribe specific aspects of policy to these identities. Perhaps the most generic of these dependent aspects of policy is that of *authority* and *authorization*. Remember that a necessary facility to be provided within a social ecosystem is the establishment and conveyance of trust. Authentication of identity is one major facet of the trust infrastructure of the system; authorization is a major facet of the policy infrastructure of the system.

Authorization protocols are the mechanisms through which a differential identity, once authenticated, is approved by a sentinel to access through a portal the general interface to content. An interface typically provides a collection of actions that can be applied to the relevant content. A permission to access each action is established for one or more differential identities. There are two distinct facets of authorization processes: first is the establishment of authorization policy, and second is the application of this policy at the point of interaction between the supplicant and content.

# Manifestations of Interactions

Successful interactions within social ecosystems typically follow similar processes grouped into informal yet consistent protocols. When interactions go awry, it is often because some aspect of these processes or their grouping protocols is not adhered to with sufficient rigor relative to the interaction's potential consequences. "I left my keys in the car while I went into the convenience store and someone stole the car!" "The candidate said she was your friend and that you'd vouch for her, so I gave her my recommendation!" "The customer handed me your credit card and said he was you, so I let him charge for a new camera!" Each of these interactions illustrates some rather obvious failings in the application of well understood, albeit ill-defined protocols of human social interactions. The basic problem in such instances derives from this ill-defined nature of the relevant protocols. So, perhaps it would be useful to identify at least some of the more basic elements of interaction mechanics as the opening step in providing a better definition of them.

The first requirement for the conduct of an interaction is the establishment of the framework or the environment for the interaction. This entails establishing between the various parties to the interaction a communication channel that has well defined security characteristics. This is the step that we're taking when we walk up to the sales clerk in the store and say "I'm ready to purchase these items." In this environment, we assess the security characteristics of the channel based on personal observation coupled to probable threats. We convey our account number by passing the credit card to the sales clerk. We shouldn't leave it lying on the counter in view of anyone else standing around. We should be cautious in displaying our checkbook lest someone see it and decide that we're a good target. Rarely do we think consciously about these steps; they're just conventions of social processes that we develop over time. And, our establishment of interaction environments extends well beyond the checkout counter of a store. We're also involved in this activity when we dial a telephone number, or when we walk up to someone on the street and say "Excuse me, can I ask you a question?"

However we begin the process, there's probably a bit of activity that goes on before we get down to the more serious aspects of the interaction. For example, the other party to the interaction might be currently engaged in other interactions. The sales clerk might say "I'm sorry. I'm still helping another customer. I'll be with you in a moment." When we dial the phone, it may be that no one answers at the other end. And, when we approach someone on the street, they may turn and run the moment we say the first word to them. Such is the admonition from our formative years: "Beware of strangers!"

Once the interaction framework is in place, we are in a position to establish the participants in the interaction. We typically accomplish this through a series of authentication protocols. We convince ourselves that the person we're talking to is a sales clerk, because she is behind the counter in the store where she has access to the cash register, and she's wearing a name tag with her name and the store's logo on it. Bear in mind that this is an informal protocol, and we've all engaged it only to have it fail. For example, most of us have inadvertently asked assistance of someone in a crowded store only to find that they are not actually a store employee; they just happen to have "that look" about them. The authentication operation is often multi-directional. A typical response when we approach the sales clerk at the checkout counter is for her to ask, "My I have your credit card and see a photo ID please?"

As we complete the authentication of identities, we're ready to negotiate the rules of the interaction. "I believe that these items are on sale and there will be an additional 25% deducted from the marked price; is that correct?" And, the negotiation is multi-directional as well; "Well these three items are on sale, but this one is not so, it is priced as marked." And, the negotiation may be iterative as well: "Oh, I must have picked it up from the wrong table. Let me exchange it for one from the For Sale table." At some point, the rules of engagement, that is the applicable policy has been established, and an actual exchange transaction can now take place; consideration offered for consideration gained.

The exchange transaction in this case might entail clipping the price tag off of the items, scanning them into the cash register, adding the applicable sales tax and arriving at the total sales amount. The credit card is then engaged, a valid charge is made and a receipt is presented for signature by the buyer. The signed receipt forms a transaction log with some characteristics of non-repudiation: the signature ostensibly affirms that the buyer did actually participate in this transaction. At this point, this transaction is completed and the end-game of the interaction is entered. "Is that all, or can I help you with something else today?" "No, that's all. Thanks for your help." The interaction framework is then terminated when the buyer walks away from the sales counter. If you're next in line, this is the point where the sales clerk might put up an "Out to Lunch" sign on the counter. But, that's an interaction of a different color.

Perhaps whimsically stated, but this model derived from personal interaction experience has been implemented in many Web-based store operations. In this case, each of the steps that we've noted in the purely human interaction environment is mimicked to the extent possible in the interaction facility of a Web browser connected across the Internet to a Web server. However, we recognize that there are significant differences in the conduct of a transaction through personal contact at the sales counter of a retail store versus an attempt to conduct the same transaction through a Web browser talking to a Web server across the Internet. In particular, because the Web environment does not naturally provide the social ecosystem mechanisms that we take for granted in purely human interaction environments the levels of trust that can be naturally established in transaction processes is greatly diminished.

The authentication of identities that occurred between purchaser and sales agent as virtually a reflexive action in a retail store requires significantly more attention in the Web environment. Even then, the trust implicit in the environment is diminished. Finding a salesperson physically located in a place behind the counter and identified through a credential allows one to imbue a level of trust in the environment that does not naturally occur when we access a Web server from our Web browser. Unless additional mechanisms are brought into play, we have no reason to believe the asserted identity of the Web server and we certainly have no way of knowing its exact physical location. Conversely, the Web server has no reason to believe the subsequently asserted identity of the person behind the Web browser. The same lack of trust establishment mechanisms can be identified at virtually every step of the Web-based interaction. Consequently, we can expect as we go forward the development of a more general interaction model that encompasses both human and computer environments with equal facility, along with the many other interactions that we engage in on a daily basis; and, through this model we can quantitatively assess the levels of trust that we will reasonably expect from the various facets of the interaction environment.

Any consideration of policy, particularly within a comprehensive policy infrastructure, must take into account the ubiquitous concerns about *personal privacy* if it is to have any measure of popular acceptance. Somewhat like identity, privacy is a complicated concept in its own right. Within the social ecosystems of the United States, privacy presents itself in at least three rather distinct guises: "I am free to do what I want." "What I do is my business and therefore the fact and results of my actions belong to me." and "What I do is private; it's no one else's concern!" We might paraphrase these aspects as freedom of action, ownership of transactions and opaqueness of interactions.

We have observed that one of the first aspects of establishing a framework for interactions is to arrive at an agreement on the applicable rules of engagement. Paramount among such considerations is the determination that the parties have no prohibitions against participation in the specific transaction. In fact, we live and operate within an environment of such complex and overlapping policy infrastructures that we rarely have complete freedom of action. As we have alluded more than once previously, we often have a problem knowing what policy constraints may be in effect within any given situation.

The ownership of the fact of transactions and of the information involved in transactions is typically a matter of the specific body of law that comprises the foundation of the policy infrastructure within which the interaction occurs. In some instances, these points are subject to negotiation among the respective parties but in many cases they are established by law, subject to the proper consideration of the rights of personal privacy.

We've alluded to the concept of *negotiation* as prelude to interactions. Obviously, this negotiation is only appropriate for certain interactions. When we drive our automobile into the toll booth on a turnpike, the fee we have to pay is non-negotiable. On the other hand, when we walk into an automobile dealership to purchase a new car, the price to be paid for that car is certainly negotiable. Where appropriate, the purpose of negotiation is to seek more detailed agreement by the parties involved as to the conditions and expected results of a specific interaction. The goal of this approach is to minimize post-interaction disagreements due to subjective evaluation of the outcome. This in turn minimizes the need to resort to a consequence infrastructure to sort out interactions gone bad. Pre-interaction negotiation using well-defined terms and actions offers a mechanism through which to achieve this goal. Consider a few areas where current interactions often present problems.

Most obvious is the authentication of the identities of the parties to an interaction. This provides credibility to any negotiation of policy that subsequently occurs. By using both differential identity and experiential identity mechanisms, constraints established by law can be readily addressed. "If you live in Texas, when you buy this product from the Web you must pay this rate of sales tax." "You must be at least 18 years old to access this material." "You have two hours to complete this examination." All of these are relatively routine occurrences for network based interactions as well as purely personal interactions. We would like to handle both human and computer variants with similar ease and effectiveness.

As we considered in some detail in Chapter 6, the Web offers a powerful mechanism for the delivery of content. A question that we noted with this capability is the limitation of further distribution of content obtained through exchange transactions. We pay for a file containing a popular movie that we want, but how would the provider guard against our turning around and giving the file to all our friends? Conversely, of course, when we buy a file containing a movie we may feel entitled to play it on various computers or personal electronic devices that we might possess. On a more technical level, we sometimes seek to gain legitimate access to information that another person or company views as proprietary to their business. Consequently, they want assurance that we will safeguard that information. Historically, we provide such assurances by signing Non-Disclosure Agreements. While such agreements have significant commonality, companies often have specific assurances that they want included in the language of the document. Moreover, it is generally a requirement of a non-disclosure agreement to explicitly list the information being shared. All of these requirements are well suited to systematic negotiation through computer based systems.

Other areas where per-transaction policy negotiation is quite amenable to computer based systems are the implied or specific warranties on content obtained through exchange transactions. It is straightforward to set a personal policy directive that I want at least one-year parts and labor warranties on all computer systems that I buy. In some transactions, this might be included in the purchase price while in others it might cost extra. One might also be concerned about the return policy for purchases. And, elemental to most transactions is agreement of what laws apply to the transaction and what the recourse for disputed results is. While pre-interaction negotiation won't solve all problems, it might help make clear what each party's recourse is when something goes awry. These are all transaction details that a transcendent personal device could address.

Computer enabled *applications* typically entail the definition of their own contextual environment. They define actions that they'll perform and parameters to describe those actions in detail. This results in such applications sometimes providing the definition of entirely new sensori-motor concepts to the human experience. Their actions and defining parameters constitute the specification of a vocabulary through which a person interacts with the application, or through which one application interacts with other applications. Most of the time, this new vocabulary seems centered on new nouns, adjectives and adverbs. The extensions to the language center on the objects of our actions or in the more subtle nuances defined for actions themselves. On more rare occasions, new verbs are brought to light. In such cases, the applications themselves suggest new sensori-motor responses to new stimuli that actually expand the paradigm for human activity. In some instances, the end result is the transformation of nouns into verbs. Consider that just 15 years ago, most people would not have understood the sentence "Text me when you get home;" at least not in the same way that we would interpret it today.

This evolution of language brought about by expansion of the sensori-motor environment is certainly not new. It is the way that languages are extended to encompass a changing environment. It is a great power of the recognition of context and metaphorical understanding that comprise at least some aspect of the physiological evolution that gave rise to *Homo sapiens*. It is much easier to integrate nuance into our existing metaphors than to develop entirely new metaphors; in essence, that's something of an alternative definition of metaphor.

Within the agreed upon policy specifications that result from the negotiation phase of a transaction, one aspect of the transaction that may have significant impact on future interactions is the maintenance and control of information related to the transaction itself. It is the development and control of this information that most affects the privacy of all the parties of any given transaction. Perhaps the most basic such information is the record of participation in the transaction itself, followed closely by the positions taken by the various parties to the transaction.

In many if not most instances, the occurrence of a transaction is indeed a matter of record within the particular policy infrastructure and as such a registration of the transaction is mandated. In particular, if a transaction involves a "consideration offered for consideration received" exchange then a detailed record of the transaction may well be required by all parties to the transaction in order to properly document their tax liability. Within the United States, even pure barter transactions are subject to income tax liability. Consequently, a trusted record of a transaction may well be a requirement that conflicts with privacy claims on the part of the individual participants. Such a record would likely need to include evidence of the authenticated identities of the participants, trusted time, date and location indicators as well as the financial details of the transaction itself. Mechanisms available within public key infrastructures make such records quite plausible, assuming that a computing entity such as the transcendent personal device is available to provide the cryptographic processing and key storage required for these operations.

Part of the trust infrastructure is the treatment of *consequences* of interactions. This covers as broad a range as do the interactions themselves. The purpose of an effective policy infrastructure is to allow the parties to an interaction to agree beforehand what the consequences will be given the different possible outcomes of the interaction proper. The most generic form of interaction is what we have described as "consideration offered for consideration received." In general, within such an interaction if the consideration due each party is acceptable, as determined during the conduct of the interaction, then the main purpose of the determination of consequences is to confirm that the agreed upon consideration is actually delivered. As with many other aspects of the transaction, this determination may actually require recursion in its application. For most effective social ecosystems, there is an overriding policy infrastructure that encompasses the conduct of interactions in subordinate policy infrastructures. The most general such infrastructure is that of the law but direr consequences reach into the trust infrastructure.

# Conceptualization of a Social Ecosystem

The boundary of a social ecosystem is defined by the extent of the *trust infrastructure* on which it is based. Different systems may utilize different mechanisms through which trust is established and through which it is conveyed, perhaps ranging from physical constraints and boundaries to logical mechanisms such as those we discussed earlier for computer networks. Consequently, a social ecosystem can be of piece-wise extent with different origins and levels of trust. It may consist of non-contiguous enclaves surrounded by untrustworthy areas. Its protected trust conveyance mechanisms allow the extension of trust through untrustworthy communication channels. Co-existent within the trust infrastructure, but governed by it is the *policy infrastructure*. Just as the extent of the trust infrastructure may be non-contiguous, so may the policy infrastructure, as it may leave undefined behavioral areas inside the social ecosystem.

Within the trust infrastructure is found the *identity registry*, an accessible compilation of the identities of the social ecosystem. A central feature of a policy infrastructure is an applicable identification system through which the identities of all entities of the social ecosystem can be authenticated.

The trust infrastructure has for root an *unconditional covenant*, and it includes *seminal edicts* that establish the governance of the policy infrastructure. The Ten Commandments, the United States Declaration of Independence, the Constitution, are examples of such edicts. *Rituals* form the backbone of the trust infrastructure, conveying a uniting understanding and promulgation of the trust evaluation system. Also, the policy infrastructure includes a *consequences* sub-system that is the domain of exception conditions relative to the application of policy within the governance of the trust infrastructure. As far as policy is concerned, there is no law without punition; as far as trust is concerned, there is no trust without consequences.

The policy infrastructure is the realm within which policy definitions can be made that will subsequently constrain the use of the mechanisms and processes through which policy is administered. Also, contained within the policy infrastructure is the *policy registry* which is a formal specification of the policies that govern any transaction, including the specification of negotiable characteristics of transactions. Throughout the policy infrastructure are found *transaction points* at which policy specific processes can be applied. Two of the critical processes always provided within a policy infrastructure are *authentication* and *authorization* operations. Both of the processes in turn depend on the seminal process of *enrollment*. A *transaction point* is a locus of the processes that are provided by a policy infrastructure through which an exchange between two entities can occur. A transaction point is bounded by the spatial and temporal locations of the specific processes that it incorporates. These locations may further characterize the specific policies applicable to a specific transaction. A transaction point includes a *portal* through which access to *content* can be gained. Content is the general concept that we discussed in Chapter 6. It might be an end point in itself, in the form of goods and services, or it might comprise access to a second transaction point through which multi-point transactions can be conducted. Access to a portal is guarded by a *sentinel*, which is an entity identifiably distinct from a portal, but generally viewed as a facet of a portal.

A *supplicant* is an entity that seeks access to the content guarded by a portal. In the most basic form of a transaction, a supplicant will approach a sentinel and enter into an authentication protocol with it. We characterize the general definition of a transaction as the ability of a supplicant to access the content available through a portal, as limited according to the policies defined for that content. *Applications* of the *application registry* define subsequent interactions. A transaction can succeed, fail or abort. A successful transaction entails subsequent access to content according to the policy provisions of the transaction. A failed transaction entails a denial of access to content due to a failure to meet the necessary policy provisions. An aborted transaction entails an abrogation of the policy provisions of the transactions. An aborted transaction will engage the facilities of the consequences system of the trust infrastructure.

So, we suggest that a social ecosystem is comprised of at least the following general components:

1. Trust Infrastructure - an evaluation system based on identification, edicts, rituals, whose purpose is to assess the integrity of entities and processes.

    a. Covenant – unconditional covenant and conditional compact based on seminal edicts.

    b. Rituals - implementation of the trust infrastructure, including consequences to policy violations.

    c. Registry - a compilation of identity markers.

2. Policy Infrastructure - an interaction system based on established rules for processes of authentication, authorization, negotiation and transaction.

    a. Registry - a compilation of interaction rules.

    b. Supplicant - a person or a token acting on behalf of a person, seeking identity verification.

    c. Sentinel - a reception and judgment entity for authentication of a supplicant, and for authorization of content access.

    d. Portal - an access barrier to the source of content.

    e. Authentication - identification and verification of asserted identity

    f. Authorization - permission to access a portal according to policy rules.

    g. Application Infrastructure - common models of negotiation and transactions.

    h. Application Registry - a collection of entities and processes used with a common theme or purpose.

Within social ecosystems that are not specifically computer aided or based, these components may exist as structured formal elements such as the United States Code, or they may exist as informal yet substantial knowledge shared by the social group in question; for example, the identity registry of the members of an extended family. Likewise, the processes engaged in such systems may be informally defined and applied. However, we can draw a number of observations from the interactions within such systems that can form the basis for more formal definitions of similar processes within computer based social ecosystems.

The structure of modern democracies is patterned after the XVIII[th] Century's *The Spirit of the Laws* by Montesquieu, who reformulated principles first established by the Greeks and Romans, adding equality ("égalité") and a worldwide review of policy practices to their view of the world. It goes to the credit of XVIII[th] Century philosophers that in the XXI[st] Century, the political discourse, if now different from shedding away some of the racist and supremacist theories of the time, is not essentially different in its constitution. Montesquieu would be as comfortable reading modern political writings as we are reading his original words. However, in the new world of computer networks, such a theory needs to be formalized to be accessible to computers. This is what we will now do, hoping, as usual, that such formalization will in return allow us to better understand the original concepts as formulated by Montesquieu and more than two centuries of subsequent writing.

Within a collection of hierarchical social ecosystems that encompass a broad geographical area and are intended to function over a long period of time, it is necessary to specify the elements of trust and policy in a manner that can be disbursed across both time and space. For purely human interactions, as our species evolved this facility required the use of language, both spoken and written. The same is true for the specification and implementation of policy infrastructures that encompass widespread computer networks. To fully exploit the benefits that computer systems can bring to such an environment, the language used for this expression must be capable of supporting significant computer utilization of it. Specifically, computer systems should be able to reason about the information prescribed by the language, a point that we considered in some detail in Chapter 8.

Within the current digital trust infrastructures, the set of languages through which policy is communicated is still to emerge. Essentially every application system defines its own language, usually in the form of extremely context sensitive parameter definitions. Consider the set of applications that one might routinely utilize on one's personal computer; a word processing system, a presentation tool, an e-mail tool, a calendar system, a Web browser, perhaps a spreadsheet application and sometimes a variety of databases containing context sensitive information. Even when they're obtained from a single vendor, each of these applications typically has control facilities that are unique. If obtained from different vendors, the likelihood that they will utilize similar control mappings to the human sensori-motor system is minimal. Rarely do the controlling parameter sets have well thought-out grammars or semantic definitions. The result is that interactions within different application infrastructures make use of these highly specialized languages, and this use tends to limit, if not completely prohibit the systematic negotiation and application of effective policy to be applied among all parties to a transaction. Moreover, these ad hoc mechanisms provide little coherence among different application infrastructures and rarely facilitate effective semantic transfer between people and the computers they interact with, including their identification tokens. So, a central need for a comprehensive policy infrastructure is a reference model that defines the semantics to be expressed by a commonly understood language. As we discussed in some detail in Chapter 8, cognition languages can express sensori-motor metaphors in such a fashion as to allow computers to reason about them. They are based on a comprehensive semantic data model that defines the elements of the metaphoric information in question. This model is an ontology, the representation that we discussed in Chapters 5 and 6.

The most wide ranging activity engaged in the construction of a general-purpose ontology is that of the *Semantic Web*. This a derivative of the World Wide Web proposed by Tim Berners-Lee as part of his early architectural work on the Web itself. While we will attempt to provide the right flavor of how a formal model of a social ecosystem looks like, we will again emphasize that we are simplifying drastically the formalism of the description for reasons of readability. Also, we need to say that while we are comfortable in the simplifications regarding the formalization itself, as it is within our domain of core competence, we want to consider the examples as more tentative, as the social evaluation of political system is less of our specialty, and we'll need to leave to others the tasks of confirming or infirming our analysis. In order to minimize our chances of error though, we have followed very closely the model of Montesquieu in *The Spirit of The Laws*, in particular Books XXIV and XXV on the rapport of laws and religion. Our point here is to highlight the digital representation of social ecosystems; we certainly hope that the model we are presenting is strong enough in its general line so that further elaboration will bring even more strength to the presentation.

The top architecture looks as follows:

```
<social_ecosystem>
   <trust_infrastructure/>
   <policy_infrastructure/>
</social_ecosystem>
```

For example, we can choose to describe Islam's theocratic state organizations as:

```
<social_ecosystem>
   <name> Islam </name>
   <trust_infrastructure> Sharia </trust_infrastructure>
   <policy_infrastructure> Shura </policy_infrastructure>
</social_ecosystem>
```

The United States systems of government would look first as:

```
<social_ecosystem>
   <name> United States </name>
   <trust_infrastructure> Constitution </trust_infrastructure>
   <policy_infrastructure> Laws </policy_infrastructure>
</social_ecosystem>
```

However, this would ignore the 1776 Declaration of Independence ("We hold these truths to be self-evident, that all men are created equal, that they are endowed by their Creator with certain unalienable Rights, that among these are Life, Liberty and the pursuit of Happiness"), which would argue more for the following:

```
<social_ecosystem>
   <name> United States </name>
   <trust_infrastructure>
      <name> Declaration of Independence </name>
      <social_ecosystem>
         <trust_infrastructure> Constitution </trust_infrastructure>
         <policy_infrastructure> Laws </policy_infrastructure>
      </social_ecosystem>
   </trust_infrastructure>
</social_ecosystem>
```

Similarly, the French system would have the 1789 Declaration of Human Rights ("In consequence, the National Assembly recognizes and declares, in presence of and under the auspices of the Supreme Being, the following rights of Men and Citizens" [our translation]) as its top trust infrastructure:

```
<social_ecosystem>
   <name> France </name>
   <trust_infrastructure>
      <name> Declaration of Human Rights </name>
      <social_ecosystem>
         <trust_infrastructure> Constitution </trust_infrastructure>
         <policy_infrastructure> Laws </policy_infrastructure>
      </social_ecosystem>
   </trust_infrastructure>
</social_ecosystem>
```

Or perhaps it would have the more modern 1948 version of the Universal Declaration of Human Rights ("Whereas the peoples of the United Nations have in the Charter reaffirmed their faith in fundamental human rights, in the dignity and worth of the human person and in the equal rights of men and women and have determined to promote social progress and better standards of life in larger freedom"), where the "Supreme Being" is no more referenced, while the source of "faith" is unsaid, religion being referenced only in relation to the freedom to exercise it.

While we've illustrated above the hierarchical, recursive organization of the trust infrastructure, we can further expand downwards the policy infrastructure of the United States to account for individual states. We'll limit ourselves to Texas for the sake of clarity:

```
<social_ecosystem>
   <name> United States </name>
   <trust_infrastructure>
      <name> Declaration of Independence </name>
      <social_ecosystem>
         <trust_infrastructure> Constitution </trust_infrastructure>
         <policy_infrastructure>
            Laws
            <social_ecosystem>
               <name> Texas </name>
               <trust_infrastructure> Constitution </trust_infrastructure>
               <policy_infrastructure> Laws </trust_infrastructure>
            </social_ecosystem>
         </policy_infrastructure>
      </social_ecosystem>
   </trust_infrastructure>
</social_ecosystem>
```

At this point, we'll reiterate how much we've simplified the model, but we certainly hope that the reader will have seen how an actual conceptualization can be carried out embodying complex concepts such as trust and policy infrastructures, their embedding into religious systems, their applicability at different scales, all in a form which is palatable to computer understanding. While an actual model of computer networks anywhere close to the complexity of human activity will take time to emerge, we may now turn to a form that is germane to computers; synthetic social ecosystems.

# Synthetic Social Ecosystems

In considering the environments in which members of various species interact, we have considered first the physical ecosystem and then the social ecosystems that exist within it. The rules that govern interactions within the physical ecosystem are, or derive from, physical laws and the rules that govern interactions within social ecosystems are defined in the context of trust and policy infrastructures. Now, for completeness given developments within wide area computer networks, we should briefly consider yet a third form of ecosystem, the synthetic social ecosystem. Consider an essay provided to us by Scott Guthery, a colleague of ours author of multiple books, some with one of us (Tim). This is printed with his authorization.

---

### Synthetic Social Ecosystems

The first widely-used multi-player, computer-mediated virtual world was a Multi-User Dungeon (MUD) written in MACRO-10 assembly language for a DecSystem-10 mainframe computer at Essex University in England. This first virtual world went on-line and began enrolling inhabitants in the fall of 1978. The MUD was the creation of and was written by Rob Trubshaw, an undergraduate computer science major at Essex. [1, 2]

The first MUD exactly like the 100's of MUDs, MOOs, MUCKs and MUSHes that have come on-line over the next thirty years [3] was purely text-based. You typed in what you wanted to say to somebody else in the virtual world and you read on your screen or your Teletype printout what they said to you. All at 1,200 bits per second. Not megabits. Not kilobits. Bits.

---

This sounds a lot like today's instant messaging but a MUD differs from instant messaging in two ways that are directly relevant to our examination of the rapidly evolving nature of identity.

First, the person-to-person interactions in a MUD take place in a computer-generated context – a virtual world. A MUD is conceptually presented to the player as a collection of rooms. Each room contains doors through which you move to get to other rooms. A room might have writing or pictures on the walls. And it might contain furniture and a jar of cookies. A room might be outdoors and be a garden. Or a room could be inside a radio or a can of soup. When you moved from one room to another the MUD program would describe to you what the room you moved into looked like, in 1,200 bit per second text, of course.

In some MUDs the text descriptions creating the virtual world were static and built into the MUD software. In other MUDs players could add new decorations and artifacts to existing rooms and in some MUDs they could create whole new rooms. As an aside, the notion of user-provider content that is so hot today originated with a computer game called Lost in the Caves written by Dave Kaufman and published in 1973. Yes, open source was alive and well back then too.

The second difference between a MUD and instant messaging is that unlike instant messaging where you use your real name and sometimes post a picture of yourself, in a MUD everybody is a fictitious, constructed identity – an avatar. The players in a MUD are just as conceptual as the rooms and the gardens and the soup cans.

Being or more properly presenting oneself as an avatar (we really don't have agreed upon word constructs to describe the relationship between a human being and their avatars) is not to be confused with being anonymous.

Indeed, being an avatar is all about being identified and identifiable albeit within a well-defined context. In virtual worlds – in the MUDs of 30 years ago as well as the Massive Multiplayer Online Role-Playing Games (MMORPG) of today – players are heavily vested in creating an identity that is distinctly and explicitly not anonymous.

To convince yourself that on-line identities are very real and that people are very serious about them, you need only go to eBay and type in the name of any of the larger MMORPGs. As I write this I see that a Level 70 Alchemist Rogue is going for $400 – that's 400 U.S. dollars, not some funny in-world money.

The avatars wandering the MUDdy rooms of 30 years ago came slowly and painfully to the understanding that there were large number of subtleties of on-line societies that had not been at all apparent when the MUD was turned on and everybody dialed-in for the first time. Interactions between avatars were just as intense, just as complex, and, yes, just as real as interactions between real, live human beings.

What is more, feelings and emotions and understandings and wonderings generated in-world did not instantly go away when you hung up. There was a much stronger bond between real-world identities and in-world identities than anybody imagined there'd be. The in-world identities were perhaps too real.

The nature and social operation of a virtual world populated by virtual identities proved surprisingly hard to analyze, characterize and write down. Julian Dibbell [4] and Sherry Turkle [5] were early reporters on this scene. They wrote with intensity and insight about how the avatars tried heroically to define and agree upon social norms for these new societies.

Now fast forward to the 21$^{st}$ century. Megabit broadband connections to anywhere in the world. $5,000 gaming machines with $1,000 super high-speed graphics boards and physics engines.

Early in 2007 Blizzard Entertainment announced that The World of Warcraft, one of their on-line games, had just passed 8 million subscribers worldwide. At peak times 250,000 of these subscribers were on-line and in the game. Yulgang, a virtual reality that is available only in China, claims over 9 million subscribers, with a similar number of simultaneously connected players. These are two of the biggest direct descendents of the DecSystem-10 MUD at Essex University, but there are hundreds and maybe thousands of other MMORPGs out there. The number of avatars roaming the land is approaching the population of France.

In [7] Edward Castronova argues that while these worlds may be virtual, they are still very real. He coins the phase "synthetic world" to refer to this emerging form of society. In one of the recently constructed synthetic worlds, Second Life [8, 9], player avatars can buy and sell in-world land.

They can manufacture and sell products. And they can offer and charge for services. All of these transactions are conducted in Lindens, the Second Life currency that can be exchanged at any number of money exchanges for U.S. dollars. It is Castronova's view that Second Life is just as much an economy as any first life economy you might mention.

What is and is not an identity gets harder and harder to fathom. If avatars aren't identities then why do my emotions react to them as if they were? In what sense is the patch of pixels on my screen with whom I conduct financial transactions and with whom I exchange sweet nothings as the synthetic sun goes down not an identity? It sure feels like one after I've logged off and I long to see the pixel patch again tomorrow evening.

It may be that as we strive to harden up the notion of real-world identity we are starting to glimpse complexities of what it is to be an identity that are hauntingly similar to what the inhabitants of the DecSystem-10 wrestled with over thirty years ago. Perhaps there is something that could be learned from the struggles of these early forms of synthetic being.

Bibliography

[1] R. A. Bartel, *Designing Virtual Worlds*, New Riders, 2003.

[2] *http://www.ludd.luth.se/mud/aber/mud-history.html*

[3] *http://en.wikipedia.org/wiki/Category:MU%2A_games*

[4] J. Dibbell, *My Tiny Life: Crime and Passion in a Virtual World*, Owl Books, 1999. First published as "Rape in Cyberspace: How an Evil Clown, a Haitian Trickster Spirit, Two Wizards, and a Cast of Dozens Turned a Database Into a Society, *The Village Voice*, December 1993.)

[5] S. Turkle, *Life on the Screen: Identity in the Age of the Internet*, Simon and Schuster, 1995. (Also cataloged as *Beyond Dreams and Beasts*).

[6] *http://en.wikipedia.org/wiki/List_of_MMORPGs*

[7] E. Castronova, *Synthetic Worlds: The Business and Culture of Online Games*, The University of Chicago Press, 2005.

[8] *http://www.secondlife.com/*

[9] M. Rymaszewski, W. J. Au, M. Wallace and C. Winters, *Second Life: The Official Guide*, Sybex, 200

The social ecosystems considered in Guthery's essay derived from computer games and game playing. These in turn are derivative environments of non-computer interactions. Such systems have progressed to the level of displaying a rather seamless interface with other social ecosystems. We find the term "synthetic" as suggested by Edward Castonova to be an interesting recognition of this seamless interface. The term seems particularly appropriate given that these social systems actually encompass their own virtual physical ecosystems. This tends to set them apart, albeit perhaps only slightly from the other social ecosystems that we've considered through the course of this book. It would appear, or course, that just as with the semantic Web, the interaction model that we've considered seems entirely appropriate.

# Recursion

We began this chapter with a brief consideration of prayer as a model for social interaction. The characteristic of prayer that makes for such an interesting model is the concept of the interaction existing and occurring within a social ecosystem. At a higher level, constraints can be specified that apply to interactions, from a trust infrastructure in a governance relationship to a policy infrastructure. This extends a recursive application of trust and policy. This seems rather common to us today, but tracing the characteristic back some thousand years to early instances of its use is perhaps not so well appreciated

So, we come to a pausing point, if not the end of our consideration of the parallels of human evolutionary development with that of computer systems. In the course of these considerations, we have noted the importance of recursion in a variety of mechanisms associated with the evolutionary development of the human species; in truth, with all living species.

One can find recursion in the evolutionary process itself; in the feedback loop comprised of the introduction of change into the basic structural blueprint of a living organism and the natural selection that keeps score as to the efficacy of the change. One finds recursion in the establishment of groups and their corresponding grouping mechanisms. This recursion then leads to hierarchical infrastructures of trust and policy through which human social organizations are formed and exist. So, it is not inappropriate that our considerations have been somewhat recursive in nature.

We have considered the mechanisms of interactions from a variety of viewpoints. We correspondingly considered the mapping of such mechanisms derived from human to human interactions to those of human to computer and computer to computer interactions. As the penultimate activity of our considerations we have suggested a mutational step for a personal device derived from a specific class of computing platforms and we have augmented this with a consideration of the mechanisms of social systems derived from, or at least exemplified by, religious organizations.

In the following, last chapter we will try to glean some observations of evolutionary effect that are plausible given these mutational changes and interaction models. We can already observe that our recursive journey has taken us across a much wider range of interrelated mechanisms than was our perspective at the beginning of the trek.

# 11 Revelation

*All the world's a stage,*
*And all the men and women merely players:*
*They have their exits and their entrances;*
*And one man in his time plays many parts,*
*His acts being seven ages:*
*infant, school-boy, lover, soldier, justice, old-age, senility and death*

William Shakespeare
from *As You Like It*

## Sigh of the Oppressed

Karl Marx remarked in a manner seemingly pejorative that "Religion ... is the opium of the people." In the fullness of his complete observation, extracted from his *Critique of Hegel's Philosophy of Right*, the comment is perhaps less than pejorative and, in fact, offers a prescient interpretation on many levels. At a basic physiological level, the state of ecstasy that is foundational to the formation and continuance of religious social structures is comparable to the state induced by a variety of opiates, including those used for medical treatment, specifically the treatment of severe pain. Conversely, religion itself is often viewed as a treatment for both psychological as well as physical pain; a point that would seem to be more in line with Marx' full meaning. Consider some of the additional context regarding his oft repeated quote noted above: "Religion is the sigh of the oppressed creature, the heart of a heartless world, and the soul of soulless conditions. It is the opium of the people." Clearly, he recognized that religion is a force to be reckoned with. However, from his perspective the benefits of religion were illusory and hence detracted from the "real" solution to the problems faced by "the workers" in existent social settings. To Marx, religion was the drug that soothes the symptomatic pain, but it did not address the underlying disease. This perception of the illusory nature of religious manifestations is rather typical of scientific discourse. It is perhaps also illuminating that with this seeming denigration of the effectiveness of religion, Marx, and his associate Friedrich Engels, laid the groundwork for a social framework to be pursued through essentially religious means. Perhaps therein lay the greater truth in Marx' observations on religion. Religion presented a powerful competitive social ecosystem to communism; and vice-versa.

We observe that the mechanisms inherent in religions' apparent effectiveness, witnessing its ubiquity, seem to be consistently ignored within the scientific community. Certainly, there is a perception that one's personal religious preferences are not a subject of polite, scientific conversation; rather like having a painfully obvious deformity of one's person. This detachment is understandable when the intent is to distance the seemingly subjective aspects of religious endeavors from the equally seemingly objective consideration of natural effects. However, one can entertain the possibility that in the United States we have elevated the concept of separation of church and state to one of also separation of church and science. Indeed, the current discourse between religion and science is one of considerable asymmetry, a characteristic of interactions that we have mentioned from time to time and which we will consider in a bit more detail below. In this case, the asymmetry manifests from significant acrimony on the part of some religious devotees and studied dismissal on the part of many in the scientific community. Yet, given the evolutionary success that religion has wrought in the ages-long struggle for supremacy of the human species, to ignore its concepts and mechanisms is tantamount to ignoring the impact of bipedal versus quadrupedal locomotion in primates or excluding consideration of the electromagnetic spectrum in the millimeter range when we attempt to observe the world around us.

In the subtitle for this book, we allude to the concept of intelligent design in relation to the World Wide Web. So, one might wonder whether we are trying to assert the necessity of discourse between the concepts of intelligent design and evolution? Well, our answer is, "certainly not..." at least, not as intelligent design is currently portrayed. At the moment, the asymmetry present in the conversation is perhaps too great to allow for an interaction with any type of resolution. Rather, what we've attempted to do in the course of this book is to suggest a model rooted in human physiological characteristics that encompasses social ecosystems of interactions in both human and computer networks. Concordantly, we've noted that the design process of a complex technical system such as the World Wide Web displays many of the same characteristics as the evolutionary processes that have given rise to the human species. This approach, it would seem, has the tendency to place the concepts of intelligent design and evolution on a more common footing. Perhaps from there, one might actually have a discourse should one be so inclined.

When viewed as systems that derived from evolutionary principles, it seems clear that we are still in the midst of the emergence of the Internet and the World Wide Web as social collectives of a variety of computer based species. If we view these technical entities according to their parallels with biological entities, then we would presume that we are actually in the initial evolutionary evaluation which will most surely result in further adaptation of both the Internet and the Web. Further, we can readily discern a number of differences between the currently availed mechanisms within the technical systems versus those of the social systems derived from biological entities. So, we've tried to consider the likely direction of technical development if a consistent parallel with social systems is to be observed. If similar human-borne market and social pressures apply on biological and technical systems, then what are some of the resulting technical adaptations we'd expect to see?

The ascendance of *Homo sapiens* to dominance within the physical ecosystem was largely based on the human mind's ability to deal extensively with symbols rather than concrete objects, while manipulating these symbols through metaphoric reasoning rather than relying purely on episodic comprehension. The emergence of these capabilities gave rise to language and to the transcendent extension of the species through social ecosystems. Through the ages, religion has been a consistent manifestation of this ability to manipulate symbols and to reason through metaphoric constructs. In the first Paleolithic era paintings we find on the walls of ancient caves, we see religious imagery, following in that the powerful demonstration of David Lewis-Williams in *The Mind in the Cave*, where he compares parietal art found in 30,000 years old European caves to similar Southern African San rock art of the XIX[th] century, in association with contemporary live testimony of corresponding religious events. When humans discovered new materials, it led them to create artifacts whose religious signification is both unavoidable and related to the paradigm illustrated by Davis Lewis-William. In *El Diseño Indigena Argentino* (Argentinean Indigenous Design), South-American pots, whose symbolism Alejandro Fiadone analyzes in regards to historical progression and contemporary recordings, are shown to present shamanistic displays that mirror those painted in the caves of Africa, Europe and, for that matter, North America. So, we have related our inquiries into the grouping mechanisms of the human species to the symbolism that forms the foundation for our very thought processes.

What we believe we've learned from studying the works, each quoted in the bibliography, of a variety of fields, including among others anthropology, archeology, evolutionary biology, neurology, physiology, and developmental psychology, is a sequence of enabling events that have occurred roughly according to the following progression. Biological organisms were founded on self-contained instructions embedded in a language that provides for maintenance of a history of past construction and a blueprint for future construction of the organisms themselves. These instructions are susceptible to changes that allow for profound shifts in functional capabilities as well as fine grained adaptation to environmental conditions. An objective evaluation mechanism enables the preferential progression of successive collections of entities, each with incrementally different and adapted facilities for dealing with their physical ecosystem. These change and evaluation mechanisms ultimately gave rise to the vertebrates, and hence to mammals, and ultimately to hominids. A characteristic of mammals is a system of emotion that provides more nuanced response stimuli to sensory input and consequently facilitates more effective grouping mechanisms than were found in previous species. When physiological capabilities in the hominid brain allowed expanded exploitation of, among other facilities, mirror neuron complexes, the mind was provided at least one, but perhaps more mechanisms to form, store and easily recall specific contexts for the sensori-motor experiences that it encountered and subsequently represented through symbolic expression. This gave rise to the ability to evaluate and manipulate these symbols through large-scale metaphoric reasoning which in turn formed the basis of the higher level cognitive processes that support the ascendance of the species, ultimately giving rise to the sub-species of modern humans termed *Homo sapiens sapiens*. Humans are guided in their interactions with each other and with their physical ecosystem by a hierarchy of needs. Across generations of individuals, these needs manifest within the mind based on sensory input processing driven by brain structure and memory mechanisms. The needs hierarchy guides the provisioning of the individual mind from infancy through adulthood. Enabled by physiological and cognitive processes that encompass a combined emotion and cognition based response, these needs evoke appetites that subsequently give rise to motor action stimuli. Within this sub-species, religious systems appear to be consistently recurring examples of the exploitation of these cognitive mechanisms. Religion in general functions through the exploitation of a trust infrastructure grounded in a physiological facility of the human mind that allows for the establishment of an ecstatic altered state of consciousness. This trust facility in turn enables the development and application of effective governance mechanisms expressed through language, which we term theologies (a term that one may consider abusive in the case of non-theistic religions), upon which are established communities of common interest and shared action. This allows the assertion of codes of moral and ethical conduct giving rise to groups whose members interact with some level of efficiency with each other and with other groups. Members of a group are expected to base their participation in interactions on these codes to the extent that adequate infrastructures can establish a personal level of trust sufficient to elicit the appropriate stimulus for the required actions. When the codes are abrogated, trust is affected, yielding consequences with potentially deep rooted impacts on the various levels of the hierarchy of a person's individual needs.

As with biological systems operating purely in the physical ecosystem, social ecosystems encompass a variety of threats to the resident species as well as to the contained social orders. With respect to religion, certainly there are charlatans, predators even, that have learned all too well the nuances of religions; of religious practice and religious mechanisms. Some would argue that organized religion itself is the fertile playground of the disingenuous if not the malevolent. But, the evolutionary successes of religious systems offer lessons that we would all be better off to learn explicitly. We well know from experience that any method or mechanism derived from scientific pursuits can be misused, and yet we thrive on them in the face of this prospect. The social methods and mechanisms that have been honed through older evolutionary processes are no less double edged. It is better that we fully understand the risk and benefit equation as opposed to confusing the field of discourse through ignorance or simple indifference.

During the course of this book, we have attempted to do a bottom up survey of people and computers, encompassing a bit of how each works and a bit more about the mechanisms each has developed over the course of their evolutionary progression. We started this endeavor with the suspicion that religion figured into the mix in a central fashion; certainly with respect to people, but also with respect to computers. In particular, we were impressed with what we perceived to be a connection between the mechanisms of religion and the mechanisms used in our particular field of computing; to wit, secure systems grounded in secure cores, the base of personal electronic devices and their next mutation, the transcendent personal device. In this final chapter, we'd like to offer our assessment of at least some of the lessons that we think we've learned in the course of this journey. We set out with the intent of trying to better understand where we thought computer systems would tend to go given the evolutionary pressures that got them to where they are today. We've gone somewhat beyond this original goal by offering some considerations on not just these mechanisms, but on the social interaction systems within which these mechanisms function. That said, perhaps we should start this beginning of the end by relating the somewhat eccentric ponderings that set us off in the first place.

# Stalking the Wily Metaphor

In our first chapter, we discussed the concept of contextual communication. We now recognize that this is an endowment of the mind's ability to conduct metaphorical reasoning. We will borrow from Christine Brooke-Rose's *A Grammar of Metaphor* the following example by the XVI[th] Century poet Edmund Spenser:

> Yet hope I well, that when this storm is past
> Helice the lodestar of my life
> shine again, and look on me at last
> lovely light to clear my cloudy grief.

The lodestar is a metaphor that reads on two levels, at first as the guiding star of the protagonist's life, and then as the saving grace in the storm that is love. For the second level to work, the first level metaphor must be reversed in order to reach the broader context of the storm, which then brings a global metaphoric context to this extract of the poem. Our journey that produced the book began with imagery that suggested metaphorical context and here at the end we will again make use of such imagery and context in a parallel presentation of religious and computer systems. Similarly, the final book of the *Christian Bible, Revelation,* makes extensive use of imagery and metaphorical understanding. We have therefore adopted this as the title of our final chapter. A writing that has become a virtual icon for the field of apocalyptic literature, *Revelation* exemplifies many of the characteristics of social ecosystems that we have discussed in the pages of this current book. It is often an excellent illustration of the systems we've discussed as well as an example of the power found in them. It is a masterpiece of contextual communication. It offers a projection of the future in terms of metaphors based on past history. However, among the difficulties that it illustrates is the force as well as the ambiguity of metaphoric understanding. A single appropriate context within which the author of *Revelation* was immersed while writing the manuscript has never been universally agreed upon. Moreover, where we have suggested that a primary feature of religious systems is the systematic identification of its adherents, this author of *Revelation* is still, even after perhaps 2,000 years, open to conjecture. Of course, the recurrent power of metaphorical understanding is illustrated by the fact that *Revelation* has been adopted as having current day relevance by virtually every generation of Christians for the last two millennia.

So, let's consider a bit the journey that comprises this book. The original impetus for our embarkation was an observation by one of us (Bertrand) that highlighted a connection between ancient imagery and modern technology. Rachel Levy, in *Religious Conceptions of the Stone Age and Their Influence upon European Thought*, mentions the inscription of hands in the cave of Gargas, in the southwest of France. Hand inscriptions are found in caves dating back to 30,000 years ago all around the world; some made in the positive, with the hand dipped in pigment and pressed against the cave wall, and some in the negative, with pigment blown against the hand to leave its outline. In the Cueva de las Manos rock formation of the middle of Patagonia, a picture of which graces the cover of this book, the hand inscriptions are actually outside the cave. While this practice may also have been common, it obviously subjects the display to deterioration from the weather and other conditions. That assessment aside, what is particularly fascinating about Rachel Levy's hands of Gargas is that many hands have one or more fingers missing.

While this might be a curious feature to many, it was virtually predestined to attract the attention of a specialist of computer security, because the time at which he read Levy's book happened to coincide with new technological developments in computing. Thanks to advances in electronics, the circuitry of some biometry systems could be reduced to a size small enough to think of associating biometry sensors with a secure core in a tamper-resistant electronic packaging. One such biometry component was a fingerprint sensor presented either as a small square where a person would place a finger, or alternatively, a small bar on which the finger would be moved uniformly for the fingerprint to be scanned. The question, of course, was how to protect the integrity of the secure core if the system was attacked by, say, intercepting the connecting circuitry between the sensor itself and the secure core. The first idea was naturally to do what secure cores do when they are under an attack that they can't manage, which is to shut off the cause of the attack by blowing up the circuitry involved, in this case the connection. For a security specialist, that act meant cutting off the fingerprint.

A finger missing from a body, or a fingerprint sensor missing from a computer, the similarity was striking. As the reason for the fingerprint sensor elimination was to answer a threat on the sensor, could it be possible that the missing fingers would also be answering a threat? To better consider that proposition, it is useful for us to delve a bit more deeply into the meaning and nature of threats.

# Asymmetry

If anyone were ever to formalize the concept of threat, it seems it would likely be the military. In true form, the U.S. Department of Defense published the following transcripts of a conference call dated February 12, 2002, by Donald H. Rumsfeld, then Secretary of Defense: "Reports that say that something hasn't happened are always interesting to me, because as we know, there are known knowns; there are things we know we know. We also know there are known unknowns;

that is to say we know there are some things we do not know. But, there are also unknown unknowns -- the ones we don't know we don't know. And if one looks throughout the history of our country and other free countries, it is the latter categories that tend to be the difficult ones." What Rumsfeld was expressing in a way that was perhaps somewhat cryptic to the public was in fact a new military understanding of threats, presented for example by Rod Thornton in *Asymmetric Warfare: Threat and Response in the 21st Century*. Known threats are readily confronted. Unknown threats of a known origin can be prepared for. But, threats that are not even known to exist present a bigger danger: Thornton presents a series of events that changed the nature of war, such as the battle of Agincourt and the attacks of September 11, 2001.

As far as the known knowns are concerned, we can follow our now customary approach and look at the computer understanding of threats. Such works as *Threat Modeling*, by Frank Swiderski and Window Snyder, provide a systematic approach. The authors classify known computer threats and define processes adept at addressing them. Trust levels afforded interaction agents, entry points of interaction, and possible targets of attacks are evaluated against vulnerabilities to create an overall assessment of precautions and answers. Possible scenarios are accordingly specified to elaborate corresponding approaches to threat mitigation. As with everything regarding computer security, the goal is to identify risks and rewards. Every counter-measure has a cost that needs to be compared to possible losses. The resulting threat model makes trade-offs explicit, and allows putting in place relevant developments and operational practices that are eventually validated by testing and on-going evaluations. One such trade-off is borne of the study of asymmetries.

Asymmetry in the conduct of interactions presents itself in the physical ecosystem where it forms an unstated theme of the evaluation process survival of the fittest. If there are relatively few parameters that define a particular interaction, then a parameter by parameter comparison will likely suggest the outcome if there is a significant asymmetry in the facilities of the interacting parties. If one constrains a rabbit to a cage with a hungry python, then the subsequent interaction outcome is relatively easy to project. Likewise, if one constrains an antelope in a cage with a single, hungry lion, the lion is probably going to feed on the antelope. However, if one places a single lion on the veldt with a single antelope, the outcome is far less certain. In this case, the trust equations for the various components of the interaction become much more balanced and often more complex. In many instances, an antelope will be able to outrun a lone lion. Hence, lions generally hunt in groups in order to stack the odds in their favor. This social grouping mechanism is an evolutionary trait of lions as well as other predators that has given rise to their hunting in groups or packs. Thus, at a very basic level, we view the occurrence of asymmetry in the various aspects of an interaction as indicative of a potential threat in or to the interaction.

Interaction asymmetry carries through to social ecosystems as well. Indeed, various functions of social systems serve to both offset as well as exploit asymmetries in the characteristics of individuals. On the one hand, social structures aim to protect the weak from the tyranny of the strong, but on the other they seek to garner the capabilities of the strong to augment those of the weak. A common thread for both theistic and non-theistic religions is the concept of accommodation of the weak by the strong. Among the beatitudes listed in the *Book of Matthew* in the *Christian Bible*, there is no special blessing for the strong, but rather for, among others, the meek and the merciful. Hence, the moral tenets of the religious order demand an altruistic behavior on the part of the strong in favor of those that are weaker. This is a behavior that, in general, runs counter to the individual behavior that one might otherwise expect to see rewarded by natural selection at the individual level.

Within the social ecosystem of the United States, we see stark asymmetries in the demands of the state, as representative of the social grouping, for taxation on the one hand and national service on the other. The tax codes at the national level are progressive in nature; those who have more in the way of resources pay more in the way of taxes. The same holds true for national service in the form of staffing the military; the few who volunteer serve at the pleasure of the many through their elected representatives. While democracy ostensibly provides for equality for all, forming a congregation that we have termed égalité, in fact it provides asymmetries in the demands it makes for altruistic behavior. The Social Security System offers another example.

Social Security was originally specified according to actuarial statistics. Hence, it should offer a relatively objective approach to the distribution of financial assistance to persons of retirement age. When originally specified, this was indeed the case. All workers paid a portion of their income into a trust fund. Persons of retirement age of 65 years were paid a stipend from this trust fund. Initially, the retirement age fell later than the average life span of a person within the system. So, the average expectation was that a person who paid into the system would die before receiving much back from the system and hence would probably not get back as much as had been paid in, if anything at all. Thus, the overall system was financially solvent. A problem occurred as people began to live longer. This skewed the relationship between those who paid into the system versus those who received aid from the system as measured by actuarial statistics. As time marched on, the general population has gotten older and some projections are that in the near future the system will become insolvent.

As the system progressed in such a manner as to require change, the feedback mechanisms provided within the social ecosystem proved ineffective. For example, the age of retirement, the amount of assistance and the amount paid in have not been altered so as to make the system sound from an actuarial viewpoint. One interpretation of this situation is the existence of significant asymmetries throughout this system, both in terms of how it performs and also in terms of the feedback loop that should control its operations. The asymmetry in operations derives from the fact that large numbers of people must pay into the system in order to fund the assistance payments for those that live long enough to collect. This assumed asymmetry was built into the definition of the system. As standards of living have improved, people are tending to live longer which means that more people collect benefits and they do so for a longer period of time. Thus the required asymmetry between those who pay and those who receive is becoming smaller. The other asymmetry is in the feedback loop. The policy purveyors who should make the necessary adjustments to keep the system solvent are elected officials. A preponderance of their electorate is comprised either of people who pay into the system or people who receive from the system. To fix the potential insolvency, most likely either the one group will need to pay more or the other group will need to receive less. Neither group, in the aggregate, appears inclined to elect policy purveyors who will potentially enact either corrective measure. What appears to exacerbate this disconnect within the feedback mechanism is that there is a tremendous time lag built into this interaction model. If a correction is not made on the revenue income side in the near term then the insolvency cannot be corrected without very onerous consequences for those who pay into the system. If no correction is made at all, then the similarly onerous insolvency consequences for those who receive from the system will not occur until some years down the road. This vividly illustrates the role of asymmetries in the determination of the well-being of many, or in reverse, in the establishment of threats to that well-being.

Personal interactions among individuals within a social ecosystem may exhibit significant asymmetries as well. In such cases, the asymmetries may derive from the level of stimulus for each party participating in an interaction. We've suggested that the stimulus for action on the part of the person is a product of the needs hierarchy and that the degree of stimulation is related to the level of emotional response to any given situation. If two parties engage in a common interaction and they are not each driven by the same level of need, then the emotional response of each may vary. If we're gauging the level of involvement on the part of two different participants in a sporting event interaction then we might say "The one who wants to win more will actually win." In this case, "want to" is a form of shorthand for the individual level of stimulation. Voicing a more fundamental observation, we must be aware that trust derived from a state of ecstasy can give rise to those willing to die for their cause; perhaps illustrating the ultimate level of stimulus response. Such stimuli make for extreme asymmetries in interactions and as a consequence exemplify threats to be addressed in the mechanics of interactions. Consider that a person whose family is starving for food may be driven by a very different level of stimulus than are the persons who want to be paid a fair price for the loaf of bread that they have produced. Thus, a useful and sometimes necessary aspect of establishing the rules of engagement for an interaction is the determination of the specific stimulus for each party. If it cannot be ascertained to some level of trust just what is driving the participants to an interaction, then it may actually represent a threat factor to the interaction itself.

Asymmetry can lead a social ecosystem beyond its state of equilibrium. As the uncertainty increases, so does the threat of disruption. For example, if even modest asymmetries in the effectiveness of a trust infrastructure are found to exist, it can result in severe dislocation, if not destruction, of the entire social system. Consider the effectiveness of terror tactics within our modern social order; the extreme actions of the few influence the trust of the many in their social systems. The attacks on the World Trade Center and the Pentagon on September 11, 2001 evoked extreme response measures as a result. One could argue that certain of the responsive measures in essence abrogated various constraints defined by the Constitution, the seminal trust point within this social ecosystem. The challenge of answering threats becomes one of identifying potential asymmetries and providing corrective feedback mechanisms. We now notice that asymmetries reflect an effective evaluation discrepancy between the *competence* and the *performance* of a particular aspect of the interaction system. So, on that basis let's consider the results of our interaction model in just a bit more detail.

# Freedom

We've identified asymmetries as sources of threats, ranging from the repertory of the known, to the unknown, and on to the unknown unknown. In evaluating the capability of organisms to answer threats, we must evaluate both the competence and the performance of the participants to interactions. Competence refers to the innate capabilities of a system, while performance refers to how well those capabilities are utilized to realize some end goal of the system. A worm comes equipped with a set material to face the world, where the full functioning of the animal is expressed by a finite number of neuronal connections set for life. We expect all leeches (of the family Erpobdellidae) to answer threats in the same manner; competence and performance in this case match, a situation that we can associate to a system without any degree of freedom. In a computer model, we'll say that the model of a leech is that of a set ontology, a fixed competence.

A fish, however, exhibits more variability. It does not come equipped with all the neuronal connections it'll ever use for its lifetime. Game fishes called northern pike (Esox lucius) builds nest from which they hunt prey. They do not come with neuronal connections that point to a specific hole in the river's bank. However, while they all can discover and dig a hole, they each associate with a particular hole under specific environmental conditions. As neural circuitry goes, no two pikes will have the same, as each neural network is capable of referring to the memory of conditions complex enough that the same situation is very unlikely to be identical in two geographical locations. This will obligatorily be reflected in different, albeit perhaps subtly so, answers to threats. One would expect fishes to respond differently to threats, and indeed, that's what any fisherman would confirm: some fishes are harder to catch than others. In the case of the pike, the performance is variable, if in a restricted register. The ontology is still set in a fixed competence, but accumulated history in memory provides for different behaviors, and henceforth different performance.

Mammals add to that freedom. Thanks to their emotional system, the degree of variability between individuals is greatly enhanced due to the prolonged circumstances of the newborn's education (provisioning). Accordingly, the number of possible answers to threats is also extended, and one would expect the answers to hunting to be possibly very sophisticated, a fact that can be confirmed for example in the patterns of deception exhibited by stags in venery. The distance between competence and performance in mammals is in relation to the variations in their upbringing and subsequent experiences. The capability of the animal to learn from having escaped past threats in order to protect itself against further attack is well documented in hunting annals. This we would readily characterize as an example of adaptation to the unknown, a subject we will come back to soon. Learning affects competence, providing a modified ontology that adds to variations of performance and henceforth the evolutionary capability to answer threats.

Judging by their evolutionary success so far, it can be readily asserted that humans have established a superior system to recognize asymmetries and associated threats. Our organization of social ecosystems is a mitigating factor in dealing with asymmetries in the physical realm. By annihilating or confining superiorly performing animals, humans have developed an environment in which physical threats are modeled in an increasingly precise and set way, which however doesn't exclude asymmetries in the performance of social ecosystems in new physical situations like global warming. In the social ecosystems themselves, it is necessary to note that the capability to answer threats is balanced with the capability to create them. It is ironic that the same freedom that affords reaction to unknown situations of increased complexity is also capable of creating them. This is the conundrum that necessarily demands a model of trust capping the infinite possibility of measures and counter-measures, so that decisions can be made. This evolution of the human trust system is a further elaboration of the mammalian ontological capabilities that adds further performance variability and associated capabilities to the amelioration of threats.

Computers started as leeches, and, to stay with secure cores, whose primary purpose is in fact to recognize asymmetries and answer threats, the first secure computers were set circuits that would predictably answer any form of attack, but would not be able to alter behavior depending on contextual circumstances beyond the immediate recognition of the threat. For example, an original secure computer was the ubiquitous telephone card used throughout the world in the now rapidly extinguishing fixed telephone booth. That card was a single circuit that had the single capability of decreasing a counter each time a fixed length of time had been expanded talking on the phone. Just as with the leech, the performance and the competence of the computer were equal, all cards reacting similarly to threats.

Slightly more elaborated are the Subscriber Identity Modules of mobile phones. Those cards are far more sophisticated than the fixed telephony ones, as batches of them are born with the same competence, but rapidly endowed with performance capabilities that vary, depending on the level of service afforded the phone owner. More strikingly even, cards with the same level of service can show some adaptability to threats, for example by modulating their answer to invalid personal identification number entries. Typically, a card would mute itself after three invalid attempts, at which stage a new identification number, called an unblocking identification number, could be used to recover. If that unblocking number itself would be invalid, then the card would shut off for good. So we find in usage cards with different states of answers to a particular threat, that of an invalid entry. That variability added to service levels is a source of asymmetry, itself offering a rich environment for threats and counter-measures.

Threat modeling allows computers to assess with great finesse approaches to known asymmetries. The domain of the unknown is today beyond the capabilities of secure computers; however, we will now see how answering the known unknown is already in the purview of today's technology, and how we can study humans' approach to unknown unknowns and anticipate future computer responses to ever evolving asymmetries. That, we will see, is where myths and religions will bring us to the brink of seeing computers self-actualize.

# Deus ex Machina

Among the highest order needs revealed by the person is that of aesthetics as reflected by an appetite for beauty rendered through sensation and emotion. As is often said, "Beauty is in the eye of the beholder." The various genres of expression that we know as the *arts* form a collection of manifestations of the sating of such appetites. As a reflection of these needs, within most endeavors we tend to seek to identify and hopefully understand, at least to some degree, the artistic aspects of them. One can construct a building with the expectation that the building will satisfy the functional requirements for which it was constructed. However, we tend to separate the function of *design* from that of *architecture*. A building designer is to a large extent an engineer while an architect is to an even larger extent an artist. The artist is able to illuminate that altered state of consciousness that is often the basis of our internal trust mechanism. This is not to denigrate the need for the designer, but rather to emphasize the role of the artist in enabling us to fully appreciate an endeavor.

The arts comprise a broad range of mechanisms through which a state of ecstasy might be evoked within the minds of the observers. Among these various mechanisms, that of *theatre* provides a most interesting reflection of the trust and policy infrastructures that we have described as the basis for social systems. Indeed, theatrical performances offer dynamic simulations of the very social systems in which we all actually live our lives. It is essentially an art form directed at the interaction process itself. Among all the branches of theatre, a significant aspect of the impact of performance is realized through altered states of consciousness created by and resulting from the acting, establishing an alternate version of reality, symbolized by artifacts and practices specific to the art. As with all such endeavors, the degree of ecstasy derives as a product of the performance and of the receptivity of the persons involved. With this basis in mind, we will attempt to illustrate our observations about the evolutionary progression of the interrelation of computer systems and social ecosystems through metaphorical allusion to three distinct forms of theatre: the scripted play, commedia dell'arte, and repertory improvisation.

Correspondingly, we want to explore three distinct phases of the use or participation of computer systems, particularly secure core based platforms and ultimately transcendent personal devices, in the conduct of complex policy based interactions. These phases constitute our perception of the progression of computer systems as social ecosystems expand into the realm of the Internet. As we've attempted to illustrate, the function of social ecosystems is to moderate the extremes of the physical ecosystem; to add an element of mediated conduct of interactions in place of the direct impact of the physical ecosystem. A significant aspect of social ecosystems is the amelioration of threats to the social order of groups of people and to the individuals within the social groups. In a like manner, a central aspect of the extrapolation of these social systems in computers and their networks is the amelioration of threats within these expanded environments. Thus, the primary themes of the phases we want to consider are the means by which threats are identified and addressed while at the same time providing effective participation in all the interactions that present themselves.

The three phases present our assessment of the chronological progression of the capabilities of secure core computer systems from their earliest inception into the relatively near future. This covers a time period that ranges from perhaps two decades in the past to perhaps three decades into the future; a half-century more or less. The first phase is comprised of the ability of computer systems to manage known attacks, and covers today's state of the art in secure cores. The second phase provides for answering unknown attacks through established means of defense. This is the phase that we're just entering and encompasses the transition of secure core systems from auxiliary components of computer applications to peer level computing platforms that can begin to function on behalf of human bearers of the secure core. Finally, the third phase anticipates the creation of new answers to unknown attacks, or, in asymmetric language, defense from the unknown unknowns. This is our extrapolation or projection of the direction that transcendent computing systems might take us if they truly follow parallels to human social evolution. At their most capable, they should function as the fully functional interface of the human into the cyberspace of the Internet; interacting with a variety of systems and guarding against threats, both known and unknown, that might be encountered there. The Internet itself seems on a deployment path that will involve ubiquitous interaction facilities with virtually every system that we encounter on a daily basis ranging from every device in our homes to those in our various transportation systems and everything thereby accessible. Moreover, we will be involved in such interactions from the time of our birth and our societal provisioning via education to our ultimate death.

As should be clear by now, our understanding of the evolution of the cognitive facilities of the species is tightly intertwined with the concepts of symbols and metaphors. Consequently, we will make use of metaphorical allusion as we attempt to offer some insights to future directions. Thus, we will relate each of the three phases to a distinct metaphorical interpretation based on the three forms of theatre noted earlier. However, we need to provide a bit of expanded context; it's hard to understand the play without a quick perusal of the program. First then, we must consider the title of this section. A theatrical mechanism first popularized in Greek drama, *deus ex machina* provides the artist with a means to extricate a story from total collapse when it is ultimately painted into too constrained a corner. This extreme form of artistic license allows a Gordian knot of plot contrivances to be slashed with a bold stroke. Notwithstanding aesthetic debates surrounding the use of the practice, the words themselves are just too inviting in the context of our current discussions for us to ignore the opportunity they suggest. As we look toward the evolved future of the computer, are we not seeking to extract something of the deities that we derive from or that form the basis of religion? More specifically, we seek to establish something of the trust that we find within religious systems that is ultimately grounded in the ecstasy of faith.

# Setting the Stage

A play is a metaphorical expression of the social ecosystems that we have discussed at some length in the previous chapters. The operational objective of the "play" is to be "performed" within a "theatre" for an "audience", where each of the quoted terms is capable of metaphorical extension. Performing the play manifests a subordinate social ecosystem created in a trust infrastructure grounded in distantiation between the actors' creation and the audience's mirror participation. Furthermore, to produce and perform a play requires policy definition; the rules of engagement, the form of interactions and the potential consequences. A number of theatrical elements go into the makeup of this policy definition. The *dramatis personae* constitute, at the most basic, a listing of the characters in a play. The *mise en scene* specifies the stage setting and environment within which action occurs. The *script* of the play defines the dialogue among the characters; essentially the interactions within the play, including the appropriate stimuli or motivation of the various actors during the various interactions. Finally, a play typically has a *director*; the person responsible for determining the details of a specific performance. As we have discussed in some detail, these elements are all found within the trust and policy infrastructures of social ecosystems of the world enlightened by theatre performance.

Metaphorical constructs of theatre are projected onto the physical or other social ecosystems, and match their characteristics. A central feature of a trust infrastructure is the registry of identities of entities that are known within the infrastructure. By known we mean that the identities found within the registry can be asserted and that assertion or identity can be subsequently proven to some level of accuracy through an authentication protocol, a process singularly exemplified by the use of masks and other guise and disguise. The environment of interaction must be defined, also an important aspect of setting the stage, which encompasses the specification of the boundaries of interactions. This specification will typically take the form of identification of the entities to be involved and the processes that these entities will use in the conduct of the play. Finally, we come to the script itself. Through the course of the three phases that we want to consider, it is the form, content and placement of the script that will undergo the greatest change. This will range from an application being the purveyor of the script to having the script be dynamically established through negotiation among the participating parties to the interaction.

# Plots and Sub-plots

The *plot* is the storyline of a play. It is, in fact, the *raison d'être* for the play. It is the extraction of metaphorical understanding from the action of the play. It is largely the presence, allusion to or ambiguity of a plot that carries us through the three phases of evolutionary progression that we'll consider below. As we progress through those phases, we'll note that the plots become more complex and the sub-plots more numerous. With complexity come more interaction types, and therefore increased risk from threats. Hence, we will see more twists within the plots and sub-plots as we seek to ameliorate the threats. As we consider the three phases, we'll consider in more detail the plots relevant to each.

But first, we need to return to the observation that with increasing capabilities to answer and create threats comes more distance between the competence of participants to interaction and their performance as afforded by previous experience. Consider in the previous chapter where we suggested prayer as a model for interactions involving both trust and policy infrastructures. Note that prayer considers the limits of the policy infrastructure, what happens when we want to change the rules during a transaction? Before examining how theater provides a model of such climb towards ultimate change, let's consider shortly how computers themselves have built their competence over time, perhaps helping understand better in return our very human capabilities.

In earlier secure cores, the central machinery of the system, that which defines its competence, its operating system, was contained in read-only memory. It is a form of electronic circuitry that is imprinted only once with the operating system, and never changeable thereafter. In other words, the competence is defined once and for all. The performance of the secure core is established through the use of applications, which are means of instructing the computer. Applications need to retain states of their operations, and therefore require memory that can be written more than once. Actually, this memory can be used for storing the applications themselves, which can subsequently be modified at will, providing means to actually vary the performance of the secure core, still within the limits of the competence of the machine. If a threat is discovered that affects an application, it can be addressed by changing this application. However, if a threat is discovered that affects the competence of the machine, that is a defect in the operating system, that threat may deny any usefulness to the secure core, and this can lead to a full series of secure cores needing to be replaced.

While the read-only memory static properties are a problem when there are defects in the operating system, it is, on a contrary, a benefit when there are none, as the fact that the operating system cannot be modified increases the trust in the secure core. For that reason, plus the economic reality that read-only memory was far cheaper than forms of memories that can be modified, it is only around year 2000 that new forms of secure core rewritable memories could be at the same time sufficiently trusted to carry an operating system and inexpensive enough to satisfy the needs of volume production. When that happened, an important change had occurred, because suddenly not only the performance of a secure core, but also its competence, could be changed, albeit, of course, within the limit of the physical capabilities of the electronics involved: if the secure core doesn't have a fingerprint sensor, no change in the operating system will provide one.

The performance of a computer is effected through *applications*. Applications are sets of instructions to the operating system that affect the sensori-motor part of the secure core. For example, an application may decide to activate the fingerprint sensor. For this, it will simply instruct the operating system to do so. How the operating system does it, the application doesn't know. It just trusts the operating system to do what it's told. (Similarly, when we decide to move our finger, the actual operations leading to our finger actually moving are not part of our conscious experience: in computer parlance, our application has ordered the finger to move, our operating system has performed the moving.) This separation of functions is a necessary feature of complex systems, as we cannot imagine each application having to spell out again and again all the elementary operations, which easily number in the million, that lead to any action. By issuing higher orders, tremendous gains are made in the capability of the machine to effect its work. But now, this creates the very situation that we wanted to illustrate here.

Let's say that we want an application to change its behavior, let's say by only activating the fingerprint sensor at the explicit request of the user instead of doing it systematically at each use of the secure core We can effectuate this change in the application without modifying any other part of the secure core. The application still instructs the operating system to activate the fingerprint sensor; simply, it now waits for an order to do so instead of doing it all the time. However, let's now consider that we need to change the operating system itself because we discovered that its handling of the fingerprint sensor activation is faulty. To take an illustrative example, let's consider that the problem comes from the fact that the fingerprint sensor draws so much electricity that another sensor, say an antenna, needs to be shut down first. To solve that problem, the operating system, which knows about power consumption, needs to shut down the antenna each time the fingerprint sensor is required, and conversely, needs to shut down the fingerprint sensor each time the antenna is in use. However, when that happens, it obviously affects both the fingerprint sensor operation and the antenna operation. For example, the current antenna application cannot trust the operating system to allow it to operate continuously anymore.

In other words, the change we need to make affects not only the initial application, but also the operating system and other applications that depend on it. They need all to be revised.

So when the competence of the machine is changed, its performance can be dramatically altered, to the point of not being able to function. At the least, there is a moment where performance is hampered until applications are changed to adapt to the new competence. That moment allowing to go for a level of competence to another one, and ultimately to a higher level of performance, results in a temporary deprivation of sensori-motor capabilities while the full circuitry of the system is modified. As it is strikingly similar to out-of-body experiences described in ultimate stages of ecstasy, we have considered that it is in fact a good model of ecstasy. When human beings, who rely on unconscious mechanisms to affect their sensori-motor system, actually evolve their competence by altering those mechanisms, they go through stages that map features inherent to the functioning of complex computer systems.

With that said, let the show begin.

# Drama

In *The Attic Theater: Description of the Stage and Theatre of the Athenians, and of the Dramatic Performances at Athens*, Arthur Elam Haigh quotes Plato to mention that in the IV[th] Century B.C., "It was enacted that a public copy should be made of the works of Aeschylus, Sophocles, and Euripides, and deposited in the state archives; and that the actors, in their performances, should not be allowed to deviate from the text of the copy." The concept of a scripted play couldn't be expressed more clearly. Greek productions of the antiquity featured both tragedies and comedies, and the mechanics of their presentations featured a number of techniques still found in the modern theatre. Within the scripted play, a fixed set of characters present a fixed plot. We refer to them as fixed because they're the same for every instance of a presentation of the play. It is the function of the director of the play to map the script to the actors chosen to play the various roles and to define the details of the setting of the play. The response of the audience to a particular presentation is due not only to the content and the form of the play itself as they have been defined by the writer and interpreted by the director, but also of the degree to which the actors are able to exploit a shared capability for metaphoric experience. A well acted play often elicits a similar reaction from us each time we see a performance. A superbly acted play might well evoke nuances in our interpretation that we had not previously appreciated.

In the theater of secure cores, the typical plot of a performance is that of authentication and authorization within the very limited context of a specific application. In fact, the script is defined by the application and cues for the lines spoken by the token are provided by the application to the token as needed. For example, one application might entail the use of a chip based credit card to pay for a meal at a restaurant. There are essentially five roles in this particular play: the credit card, the cardholder, the point-of-sale terminal of the restaurant, the waiter and the bank managing the account to which a charge is to be made on behalf of the cardholder. When it comes time to pay for the meal, the scripted action is rather straightforward. Trust for this particular script comes primarily from causality; knowing the lineage of the secure core based credit card and the other equipment involved. However, trust in this script also derives from the process through which the credit card and the terminal are provisioned with keys through which identities are authenticated. It is imperative to the trustworthy function of the system represented by this script that the various keys be truly secret within the constraints of their use.

As the play unfolds, the diner is coming to an end:

```
DINER: L'addition, s'il vous plait!
WAITER: May I have your credit card?
```

The diner cardholder presents her card to the waiter who has the point-of-sale terminal in hand. The waiter inserts the card into the terminal. The terminal authenticates the identity of the chip card and the chip card authenticates the identity of the terminal as well. After all, "Don't talk to strangers" holds for cards and terminals just as it does for people. So, once the two devices have established a sufficient level of trust to continue, they do. In the course of the authentication operations, the credit card and terminal may have agreed upon the necessary keys to establish a private, trusted channel between the two, because even though the credit card is inserted into the terminal, it's still possible that someone is eavesdropping on the conversation. Hence, this constitutes one of the threats (plot twists) in this story. So, assuming that the communication channel is private, the terminal now asks for the account number of the cardholder that is stored on the card. This account number is then validated by the point-of-sale terminal. An amount to be charged to this number is displayed on the screen of the point-of-sale terminal.

```
WAITER: Would you mind entering your personal identification number in the
terminal?
```

Now, the cardholder is asked to enter her Personal Identification Number (PIN) into the terminal. A point-of-sale terminal is certified, by the vendor that provides it, to guarantee secure personal identification number entry. If the correct personal identification number is entered, then an authorization operation is conveyed from the card to the terminal indicating that the cardholder allows the amount indicated on the point-of-sale terminal screen to be charged to the indicated account number. Because of the certification processes that the credit card and the terminal went through before being commissioned, the cardholder cannot repudiate the transaction, which means that it bears legal and fiduciary value. Once this is done, a receipt is printed by the terminal that can be given to the cardholder for confirmation of the transaction.

```
WAITER: Here is your receipt, and here is your card.
DINER: Thank you.
```

So, all in all this comprises a rather standard script. It is followed by a myriad of terminals acting on behalf of a plethora of restaurants around the world dealing with a multitude of diners using credit cards with embedded secure cores. So, what are some of the twists to the plot, the threats that the card and terminal are wary of?

Well, within the context of a script like this, the most common threats are the fraudulent expression of identity on the part of the terminal, the card or the cardholder. Depending on which of these identities is actually counterfeited, the end result can be a problem for any of the parties involved. For that reason, several layers of security measures are present, each presenting an answer to a possible attack. For example, the card will refuse to divulge information to the terminal before it has obtained from it proper credentials of the kind we discussed earlier when we presented private and public key infrastructures. Reciprocally, a terminal will refuse to communicate with a card that itself does not present proper credentials. Therefore, any threat that the card is not an accredited card, or that the terminal is fraudulent, is eliminated as far as transmission of information between the two is concerned. As this information is needed for the bank to provide credit, the threat of an improper financial transaction is covered. However, the next level of threat is if the credit card and the restaurant terminal are both genuine, but the credit card doesn't actually belong to the diner. The mechanism to guard against that is the personal identification number, working on the assumption that if the card has been found or stolen, it is unlikely that the fraudster also obtained the access personal identification number. Therefore, the terminal asks for the personal identification number of the card before effectuating the transaction to answer the threat of a diner presenting somebody else's card. So we see that a battery of known answers to potential problems have been embedded into the scripted play.

However, in the world of security, there is always a new threat. We will now look at how scripted plays are modified and evolved as security improves. As we just say, stealing a chip card without stealing the personal identification number is of limited value. Therefore, elaborate schemes have been developed to uncover the personal identification number of a card, and actually, this has been so much of a threat that it is already guarded against in some respect in the way we will now explain. Actually, when the diner enters her personal identification number in the restaurant banking terminal, the entry is very different from entering a personal identification number in a regular computer, as opposed to a secure core device. In a regular computer, a person enters a personal identification number at the keyboard, the computer reads the personal identification number from there, and then sends it wherever is needed. However, this creates a security hole. The computer can decide to store the personal identification number somewhere before sending it, and then, it can reuse it at will later on. To guard against this, certified banking terminals have a personal identification number entry mechanism that does not transit by the terminal before being presented to the card. There is actually a direct physical link between the personal identification number entry and the card, so that only the card can see the personal identification number. Entry of the personal identification number is therefore protected from onlookers, and yet another threat has been answered and is included in the scripted play.

But now, we'll look at the next step the fraudster may take, and what we'll describe has actually occurred, and is still occurring today. By tampering with the terminal, it's possible to steal the personal identification number. This has been done in various ways, from the simple idea of spying the personal identification number entry with, say, a tiny camera, to elaborate ways involving superimposing the keyboard with a fake one, and even more pernicious ways consisting in designing a bogus terminal embedding the first one. We will not detail those here; suffice it to say that the personal identification number is secure only to a point in attaching a card to a person. When we're talking about paying the restaurant, the fraud might be tolerable. When we're talking about using similar technology in higher security situations, we may be talking about threats that cannot be accepted. That's why the next idea has been to include a fingerprint sensor in the card itself. As we described it earlier, a tiny sensor is used either as an array where the finger is placed, or a bar against which the finger is scanned. To come back to our restaurant, with a fingerprint sensor on the card the banking terminal would never be involved in the capture of the link between the card and the cardholder, and that link would therefore be much more trustworthy than the personal identification number; actually, in situations of higher security, the two can be combined. With this new measure then, yet another set of threats are addressed, and the scripted play can change.

Using the traditional form of theater inherited from the Greeks as a metaphor for interactions in a social ecosystem, we see that the competence of the system (the script in this case) is fixed and predetermined, and the performance (the actual play) maps very closely the competence. This model of interaction defines a set way to answer possible threats, and is capable to guide us in many of our activities. It is very close to the way computers know how to do things today: instruct them in advance of all threats and answers, and they'll faithfully perform the play, albeit with different levels of performance depending on their other strengths and capabilities, like their inherent speed or communication bandwidth.

# Commedia dell'Arte

In the XVI<sup>th</sup> Century, a new style a theater flourished in Italy. In *The Commedia dell'Arte: A Study in Italian Popular Comedy*, Winifred Smith says: "A *commedia dell'arte* was always in part the transitory creation of the individual actors who played it; the plot was known to each member of the troupe, so well-known, indeed, that an entrance or an exit was never missed, but the dialog was chiefly left to be struck out by the suggestion of the moment." The art then comes in the flexible presentation of the play and it takes a level of improvisation by the actors to tell the story while at the same time remaining in character and also remaining true to the plot. In *A Short History of the Drama*, Martha Fletcher Bellinger notes about the commedia dell'arte: "The actors had to find the proper words to make the tears flow or the laughter ring; they had to catch the sallies of their fellow-actors on the wing, and return them with prompt repartee. The dialogue must go like a merry game of ball or spirited sword-play, with ease and without a pause." Compared to the scripted play, interactions contain the increased threat that comes with the need for the actors to find inspiration. To lower their anxiety, Smith notes that "each player possessed a book which he filled with compositions either original or borrowed, suitable for his rôle." The unknown of impromptu interactions is widespread, and the actors' approach to it in the commedia dell'arte is also very common. To come back to the military's preparedness to threat confrontation, the sweat expensed at the training field is said to be the blood saved at the battlefield. Similarly, athletes in group sports rehearse extensively all sorts of plays to be ready with alternatives when the big game comes. Each of us has discovered how studying for exams gets one ready for the curved balls to come. So we see a common thread of preparing from the unknown by building a set of ready answers to use as the threats come by.

In the computer world, threats of impromptu interactions are named *exceptions*. An elaborate formal framework allows exceptions to be specified at several levels, where each exception can raise one of more generality. For example, a computer program may regularly access a file, perhaps a spreadsheet for content needed for processing. Under normal operations, the computer just finds the file in its hard drive and opens it to read its data, just as we might fetch a file from our cabinet in the office. However, there can be situations, for the computer just as for us humans, where the file is not there. Did somebody borrow it? Am I looking in the right cabinet? Do I remember incorrectly the name of the file? The number of possible reasons can be quite large, and we can't in advance try to list all the possibilities for error. First, these exceptions are unlikely, and second, there are always some errors that we will not anticipate. Therefore, before reading the file, the application just signals the system that it is ready for an interaction that contains the threat of not performing as expected, by setting an exception. If the threat materializes, say the file is not found, the raised exception is said to be *caught* and the computer attempts to fix the problem with whatever solutions it has in its arsenal; for example, it may decide to try substituting a new file for the one that has disappeared, or it can prompt the user for information. If none of these solutions work (there is no new file, or the user is not answering), then it may decide that the task is too hard, and it may *throw* a higher exception. The higher exception is then caught by a supervisory part of the program that may decide to try more drastic solutions, like just shutting down operations. In the same way, if the clerk doesn't find a file in the cabinet, then perhaps it is time to call the manager to present the situation.

If we consider now our secure core reinforced with a fingerprint sensor, it should be anticipated that the sensor could be attacked, for example by presenting a fake finger, or by tampering electronically with the sensor, or by trying to modify the signal between the sensor and the secure core processing unit. Again, the possibilities are many, and therefore the secure core will set an exception which will react with a set of tried solutions, like just ignoring the entry if a fake finger is suspected, or more drastically, shutting down the sensor altogether if electronic tampering is detected. The approach is the same as above: try known solutions, and, if they don't work, go for more drastic measures. On a wider scale, we can consider as another example the new driving permits that are now under study in some states. A driving permit containing a secure core presents the credentials of the driver directly to digital systems, allowing a quick review of the permit and the rights associated. For example, in the case of infraction, the policeman would just insert our driving license into a terminal connected with the overall police network. Now, as this technology develops somewhat independently in many states and countries, we will see areas of commonalities in the various driving permits, and we'll see differences. For each state checking another state's driving license, the differences might be viewed as so many threats. Each state's network will have to decide for itself how it wants to manage these differences, again, using set solutions or taking more drastic solutions, like for example deciding to check by phone with the original state instead of relying on the digital network, which is a way to actually cut the licensee, in her or his digital representation, from the network. Here we see again that humans, computers, and computers representing humans on the network can, like the actors of the commedia dell'arte, manage unknown situations, relying of a set of pre-staged and relief actions.

# Improvisation

Throughout this book, we have investigated fields far removed from our core domains of expertise. Any domain of knowledge is a constantly evolving field of surprises, inventions, arguments and discovery. The only way for us to avoid technical arguments that we would be unable to defend has always been to attempt to be faithful to the seminal writings that those well versed in the field take for granted, whether they agree or disagree with, or want to disprove or improve, the premises. Therefore, we will leave the unavoidable and healthy critique of our interpretation to the experts, and we choose Constantin Stanislavski as our $XX^{th}$ Century teacher of acting. In *An Actor Prepares*, Stanislavski wants actors to get ready for the interactions of the scene by relaxing to prepare their sensori-motor system to the stimuli of interactions; to study the play in details and do what-if scenarios to prime their emotional system with the projected characteristics of the role; to master the script so that the objectives and sub-objectives stay in constant perspective; to establish faith, communion, and adaptation to keep the scene flowing so the audience empathizes with the characters of the plot. The lesson is "unconscious creativeness through conscious technique," the threat is breaking the flow of sensations, sentiments, actions and events that establish the alternate reality allowing to develop the feelings and metaphors that the spectators build up into their own psychology and understanding.

Following on Stanislavski theory, theater can be turned on its head as the actor's role can now become its own rationale, by performing in front of an audience in the absence of predefined plot or script, In *Impro: Improvisation and the Theatre*, Keith Johnstone condenses the performance to its fundamentals: the status rapport of the actors, the creativity developed in the interaction and their flow, and decoration, epitomized by the mask. For him, rapid changes in the relative status of the actors match the essence of conversation, and we can only relate this to Roland Dunbar's *Grooming, Gossip, and the Evolution of Language*. With an explicit or implicit plot, plays on status form the backbone of the improvised script, whose sustenance keeps the audience involved: interaction must be spontaneous, which means that there is little time for the brain to process the immediate emotional reaction; much of the success of the improvisation is related to the audience relating to the state of mind that led the actor to a particular reaction. To sustain the narrative, actors need to consciously break routines, creating the very threats that lead to resolution and comic relief. In our terms, the creation of asymmetries yields intriguing interactions via the immediacy of emotional reactions. Finally, the use of masks allows changing the very perception that actors have of themselves, thereby altering their sensori-motor environment, as well as that of the audience, shortening even more the alternate nature of the emotional reaction time. Johnstone associates the use of masks in the threatening environment of improvisation with *trance*, an ecstatic state derived from the combination of the alteration of the sensori-motor experience with the immediacy of the emotional circuitry.

We see then that Stanislavski and Johnstone have expressed a model which is as close as can be to trust-based interactions. The actors must trust their reactions as well as that as their co-actors and the audience, and the policies that support this trust are implemented in a ready manner thanks to appropriate training. The impromptu plot that frames the improvisation allows the dynamic development of a script that conveys a message of communion that the director, the actors, and other participants carry to the audience. If theater performance is indeed a metaphor of our everyday interaction experience, this argues for searching for the unifying scripts, or myths, that serve to convey the message of the group to another group in a shared version of alternate consciousness based on the trust that the actors and the audience develop to sustain the rhythm of the lesson. The study of the constitution of such modern myths has been developed in Roland Barthes' *Mythologies*. The improvisation model of theatrical performance allows to more generally look at performance as a group experience formed around a common myth that can be deconstructed and understood as a model of community building, an exercise that we have already alluded to regarding Victor Turner's work in *The Anthropology of Performance*.

In this book, Turner borrows from the French folklorist Arnold van Gennep the term *liminality*, which characterizes the passage from one identity to another, for the actor from the here and now of one deictic state to the here and now of another one, that of the masked character. The term would apply in the trust infrastructure of networks where identities may represent different persons, or different personalities of a person. When we pay with our credit card, we appear to the network as clients of a bank; when we access our workplace with a badge waved at a sensor at the door, we are an employee; and when we call with our cellular phone, we are one subscriber to a telephone operator. In the same way the wearing of the mask and body ornaments changes the sensori-motor experience of the mask wearer and brings an external stimulus to liminality, the presentation of digital identity associates a new presence interfaced through its own sensori-motor capabilities, with a personality embodied in its hardware and software. Each such identity allow us to change role in our daily plays, and liminality appears as a concept illustrating that transcendent personal devices represent us in various sensori-motor capabilities with representations that are images of subsets, and sometimes supersets, of our own capabilities. In the same way as we have a different persona in personal, professional, public or other aspects of our life, we have different personae in each of our digital network presentations. It is immediately apparent that the acting that we request from our transcendent personal devices should tend towards providing the same capabilities as that observed in the theater. From our perspective, at every level of our interaction with the network, we are driven by a plot that the transcendent personal device needs to convey in the scene that is our window into the society of computers and other humans behind them. We have seen that secure cores and transcendent personal device understand trust, can implement policies, and have sensori-motor experiences that can be mediated by reactions based on their hierarchy of needs. Are they ready for improvisation?

# Laying-on of Hands

During the journey of this book, we have considered wide scale changes among living organisms brought by evolution coupled with natural selection. With respect to such changes, while the mechanics of observation might suggest schism, the actual mechanics of change suggest significant continuity. In particular, some evidence of change derives from a fossil record which is anecdotal in nature. Anecdote forms the dots of the picture. When it comes time to connect the dots, they must be carefully evaluated if the picture is to be faithfully rendered. We suggest that this holds true for understanding the groups within social ecosystems just as it does for the species that inhabit the physical ecosystem. To reinforce this understanding, we might consider in just a bit more depth the current state of observation of the hominids, exemplified by *The Speciation of Modern Homo sapiens*, edited by Tim Crow.

We can begin by paraphrasing the concept of punctuated equilibrium that we considered in Chapter 9. The available fossil record gives evidence suggesting many discrete species. However, modification of DNA through mutation and genetic recombination creates change primarily through minute steps. When the DNA of successive generations is examined, which has been done "in the small" for the evolutionary progression of simpler organisms, genomic alterations allow for a continuous development of new capabilities based mostly on the reuse of older ones. Over long enough periods of times, relative to any collection of species the difference between the early species and the late ones may show stark contrasts. However, the differences between one species and the next that evolved from it may be less profound. Indeed, among the hominids as characterized by the fossil record, it is becoming less clear where the actual species boundaries are. If one adheres to the rather strict definition that a species boundary delimits an ability to interbreed, then some of the more recent distinctions among subsets of the genus *Homo* likely differentiate what could perhaps be called *ethnic groups* as opposed to distinct species. Similar continuity holds for social systems. Indeed, when different grouping mechanisms are examined the overlap of adjacent "species" seems even greater. In fact, today there still exist plentiful examples of iconic forms of human groups.

Thus, it was something of a revelation to us as we came to understand that since the emergence of modern man, the progression of social order has been one of remarkable continuity as well. Of course, the fact that we could observe and suggest a possible model under which all human social orders could be interpreted is indicative of this continuity. This progression is marked by the recursive application of the same metaphors; metaphors that are seminally grounded in the human sensori-motor system. As we've previously noted, we were drawn down this path by the imagery of parietal art that forms one of the earliest illustrations of modern man as a social animal. Among such imagery are often found pictures of human hands. Hands are found imprinted in pigments on walls of rock throughout the world and across the horizon of the human dispersion from Africa. This common form was central to our earliest musings that subsequently gained form in the pages of this book. Among those illustrations are reproductions from caves in the south of France.

In 1985, Henri Cosquer, a professional diver from Cassis, a small seaside village next to Marseille, France, found at a depth more than 100 feet under water the entrance to a cave which 27,000 years ago was on dry land. It was yet another cave showing human hands, but several had apparently amputated fingers, in a form quite similar to images found in Gargas and a few more caves in the south of France and the north of Spain. Jean Clottes, the author, with David Lewis-Williams, whom we met earlier in this chapter, of *Shamans of Prehistory*, learned to dive, and visited the cave with Cosquer. He then wrote with Jean Courting *The Cave Beneath the Sea* in which are reviewed theories of the hands and of cut fingers, a quite complicated story that includes studying the rationale for the hand imprints, and the sub-story of whether the fingers were actually missing when applied to the wall. Perhaps, were they simply folded?

In a subsequent book entitled *A Cosmos in Stone*, David Lewis-Williams offered an expanded interpretation of the timeliness and meaning of the handprints found among varied instances of parietal art. The timelines that he considers show that hand imprints were present from the earliest instances of such imagery. However, he suggests that a reinforcement of the genre came from the common reaction of the human nervous system to states of altered consciousness associated to the presence of shamans who served as facilitators of the myths that illuminated religious thought. The central role of myth in the creation and subsequent utility of grouping mechanisms has been an underlying constituent of this book.

While we cannot prove that the creation of myths has been constitutional to the expansion of mankind beyond the scale of the tribe's proximity, we can certainly observe that their universality may find an explanation in the teaching through which the young are provisioned by the old and the experiences of the trusted ones are passed to the uninitiated. So, before we return to some final thoughts on the relationship of social order to computers and their networks, let's consider that the mechanisms leading from the observation of direct causes to the constitution of myths are readily bound up in the images of hands and fingers.

The human hand is a central feature of the human sensori-motor system. As we noted in Chapter 4, few naturally occurring organic structures offer the nuance of sensory input or the finesse of motor action as the human hand with its fingers and opposing thumb. Thus, the hand is central in the establishment of metaphors of higher level communication ("Did you catch that?"). Moreover, the loss of the hand or fingers constitutes a serious blow to the sensori-motor system. Hence, the conscious removal of a hand or finger, whether actual or symbolic, would constitute a serious actual or symbolic illustration of loss to the body of the individual. Now, in some situations a person might cut a finger in the face of possible higher physical threat such as further infection of the limbs, in a way parallel to groups of humans forcing the ostracism of a person threatening its integrity and survival prospects. In the extreme, the group might demand the death of the individual, a ritual still observed in some states and countries. Conversely, the preeminence of the group, perhaps even its survival, may well demand altruistic sacrifice on the part of individuals within the group. Thus, in the same way that cutting a finger can be symbolically associated with the broader concept of sacrifice and separation in mourning and other life events, the ritual sacrificial killing of humans in societies around the world can be associated with a higher expression of societies being ready to separate from some of their own in exchange for protection for the greater number.

In *Mythes et dieux des indo-européens* (Myth and Gods of Indo-Europeans), George Dumézil shows on the wide scale of Central Asia and Europe the consolidation of myths under common threads of religious aggregations. For myths to form a learning basis of innovative conquest of new territories of the mind there must be shared trust in them, would it come from process or causality. For example, the shared ecstasy enforced by rituals can be reflexive of fundamental mythology rooted in religious revelation. For Dumézil, the common Indo-European heritage is the tri-partite organization of society in clergy, warriors and producers. We immediately recognize a trust-enabled policy infrastructure similar to those our study of computer organizations has generated. Whereas computers today are barely capable of associating symbolism to the treatment of threats in computer networks beyond their mechanism of exceptions, their future management of myths associated by common trust is to be expected. We have seen that the necessary mechanisms of stimuli via need hierarchies, association via metaphors, and the building of ontologies are all available today to computer networks, albeit sometimes at the frontier of knowledge.

A worldwide study of myths and religion of the depth of Dumézil's is still to be made. Dumézil himself establishes the parallel between his studies and comparative Indo-European linguistics of the XIX[th] and XX[th] Centuries. If we consider that broader linguistic studies of the same depth, exemplified by Joseph Greenberg's *Indo-European and its Closest Relatives: The Eurasiatic Language Family*, are advances that had to wait until the XXI[st] Century, we see that a global understanding of the religious roots at the center of global myths is still somewhat distant. However, some works like *Maya Cosmos: Three Thousand Years on the Shaman's Path*, by David Friedel, Linda Schele and Joy Parker, already map the same advances in methodology that allowed the decipherment of Maya writing, i.e. its decipherment in the context of modern Maya language, to an understanding of antique Maya religious practices in the context of modern Maya shamanistic practices. The similarity of the underground, earth and sky trilogy, accompanied by its derivation of time and cardinal points, between European, Middle-Eastern and Maya practices is hard to ignore; but future inquirers will have to go through the research. The quest is on for the roots of the social realization of religious beliefs. Since computer networks are indeed global in nature, their shared beliefs have correspondingly yet to find bases, starting with those of the human mind.

As networks of computers grow and pass human organizations in size and complexity, they'll build their own myths, following their needs hierarchies, empowered by their sensori-motor capabilities, and accumulating memories constantly reorganized by time and experience. Their trust infrastructures will reflect their evolutionary interests, and will collide along the boundaries of their theologies. Policies arbitraged by their trust infrastructures will change as trust clouds will merge and disassociate, eventually defining broad communities of worldwide computer networks. As long as humans will remain the originators of the networks and their prime benefactors, they will instill their will through their digital representatives, the transcendent personal devices that will summarize the human needs, myths and religions to affect the dynamic behavior of all the actors of that augmented theater of life.

So, we return to our specific consideration of hands and fingers. Extending the significance of the handprints, Lewis-Williams suggests that they comprise objects of interest in their own right, not simply as the image of a hand. He suggests that handprints found in the Western Cape Province of today's South Africa and worn smooth by ages of being touched by actual human hands indicates a ritual conveyance from handprint to the hand of the supplicant who touches it. While the object so conveyed is unknown, even as to whether it reflected physical or spiritual concepts, the ritual itself offers interesting parallels to practices expressed in the writings that form the basis of Judeo-Christian religious thought. Specifically, beginning within the earliest renditions of the *Book of Genesis* are found instances of the ritual known even in the current day as the *laying-on of hands*.

We have no more evidence to divine a connection of parietal handprints to the ritual laying-on of hands than the observation that such a connection could explain the similarity of the handprints' environments and displays between North and South America along proven migration routes; the ritual would provide for the continuity of practice, in either physical or symbolic form. In any event, we can note the central theme of the hand in each practice; a theme that offers consistent presentation over millennia of social interaction. The ritual laying-on of hands, recorded in historical literature at least three or four millennia ago, offers a well traveled path from then to now. Throughout the history of its explicit expression, the ritual has formed the basis for conveyance of trust and authority among groups and individuals. Within the model for social ecosystems that we have suggested, it appears as a ritual through which trust is directly conveyed and hence forms the mechanism for extension of the social ecosystem across space, across time, or both. In that guise, it offers a response to the aesthetic needs of the species.

As practiced within modern churches, the laying-on of hands represents yet another variant of prayer; that of the benediction. Within various forms of worship, it is a typical closing prayer offered by the shaman to the supplicants. Its purpose is one of fulfillment to the faithful. It offers assurance that their acts of supplication will be reflected through the benefits of the group going forward. We suggest that in this guise, it forms a complementary response to the metaphorical illustration that we recognized as representative of the World Wide Web in Chapter 10. The benediction symbolized by the ritual laying-of hands makes the statement:

*I grant you this.*

In both the literal as well as abstract sense, it is the response of the sentinel, or the ultimate source of content behind the sentinel, to the supplicant. Through gesture and speech, generally by the shaman, it forms a conveyance of blessings to the supplicant on behalf of the deity; essentially bestowing on the supplicant the purest form of content within the social ecosystem. The transaction framework of this prayer is bi-directional as well as recursive. The laying-on of hands illustrates the continuity of social order across the full lifetime of the species of modern man. Of course, if the ritual of the hand symbolizes trust and its conveyance, what then of the cut fingers?

In the 1990's, expeditions lead by Luc-Henri Fage discovered 10,000 year-old painted caves in Indonesia with numerous hand imprints (*National Geographic*, August 2005). In one of them, Ilas Kenceng, an imprinted hand has cut fingers. Without needing to demonstrate a link, it is interesting to note that not far away, in Irian Jaya, today there live tribes where women still have fingers cut in ritual remembrance of a lost husband or other close relative. A picture of such can be found in Armando Favázza's *Bodies Under Siege*, together with a list of recorded rites associating amputations with religious rituals. It seems quite plausible that if the plot represented by the ritual of the hand was trust, then the sub-plot of finger cutting was sacrifice, and 30,000 years ago our forebears performed the play for posterity under the direction of the shaman. The set of that story may have been a cave. The continuity of social order as an integral aspect of the species of modern man would thus be well illustrated. So, we come back to the nexus of computers and social systems.

The continuity that we observe suggests that as members of the species we're much the same as our forebears who lived long millennia ago. Significant change is found primarily in the manner and content of the provisioning that we incur in our growth from infancy to become fully functional adult members of the species. Our brains are likely the same and our sensori-motor systems are likely the same. Perhaps our diet and daily activity has changed our form and size a bit; a by-product of our need of transcendence. However, we likely differ mostly in the mind that develops within the brain through our provisioning. With continuity in our sensori-motor system, the base metaphors through which we interact with the world around us and on which we base our social orders are much the same. As our tools have changed, we have modified the metaphors to keep pace. In relatively small ways we have altered our social orders. However, the painters of the handprints on the walls of the caves of antiquity would likely fit seamlessly into a NASA spaceship if given the same provisioning as was Neil Armstrong. Trust and authority are still conveyed through variants of the ritual laying-on of hands. Indeed, within a social grouping of the type we label as égalité, the President of the United States assumes office by laying a hand upon a symbol of personal trust and expressing an oath of sacrifice to the basis of trust for the social order. Thus, over the long ages as a species we have merely changed the context.

A transcendent personal device uses its sensori-motor apparatus and reasoning capabilities on behalf of its bearer to effect policy through interactions with other agents within the same trust infrastructure. Transcendent personal devices present to the network different aspects of our person, be it that of financial agent, a contributor to the work force, or other roles associated with specific identity credentials. With our conventional life thus extended to computer networks, we sit at the intersection of the physical and digital ecosystems we participate in. We've seen how biometry can be associated with transcendent personal devices to link them more closely to our physical selves. With advances in biological and other digital circuitry, we can expect to become an even more integrated part of the digital network ourselves, becoming in a sense our own transcendent personal devices. This will increase the integration of our physical, social and digital ecosystems and will also create new opportunities for asymmetries.

As the Internet and the Web thus grow in power through their connectivity and capabilities, we can expect an ever increasing clamor from existing social ecosystems to exert greater control over Internet and Web facilities. The Internet as it originally emerged constituted an extension of the physical ecosystem into the digital realm. Social ecosystems seek to establish some level of subjective influence over the physical ecosystem. So, it is not surprising that existing social orders seek to put their imprint on the facilities of the Internet. Some rail against unfettered access without any societal controls on either access or content. Others are concerned with protecting the individual against communal intrusions. Evolutionary processes will determine whether these threats to the existing Internet bring good or ill. One asymmetry we perceive with the concerns involved is the attempt to deal with these issues through existing social ecosystems' mechanisms, all of which exist within their own independently derived trust infrastructures. In that perspective, the only way such attempts can succeed is by attacking the efficacy of the Internet itself. In other words, the rules of engagement then revert to the physical ecosystem; if the Internet cannot be controlled, it must be destroyed. An alternative is the establishment of new trust infrastructures fit for the expanded social ecosystems of integrated physical and digital worlds. We hope that this book will help in the intelligent design of such a computer theology.

As we said at the very beginning, we will continue our journey until we come to the end. Then, we will stop.

11 Revelation

# Bibliography

The bibliography is divided in two parts, general and computer-related. During the course of writing this book, we have read or consulted in some detail each of the works; we made a point to actually own almost all the books of the bibliography. While they are not all directly referenced in our text, they are all part of what made us write Computer Theology, and their influence will be felt throughout our writing.

## Books (general)

This part of the bibliography is by essence eclectic, and specialists in one matter may cringe at our choice of references in certain domains. We are of course much more comfortable with those areas of knowledge in which we have formal education. We apologize in advance for misrepresenting an expert's point of view if and when we've adventured too far in foreign territory. This is the price we've been ready to pay for our cross-disciplinary undertaking.

Bruce Ackerman. We The People: Foundations, The Belknap Press of Harvard University Press, Cambridge, MA, 1991

Henri Alford. The Works of John Donne, John W. Parker, London, 1839, digitized by Google at Stanford University

Christopher Alexander. The Nature of Order: An Essay on the Art of Building and The Nature of the Universe, CES Publishing, Berkeley, CA, 2006

Ahmid Ali, translator. Al-Qur'an: A Contemporary Translation, Princeton University Press, Princeton, NJ, 1999

Matthew Alper. The "God" Part of the Brain: A Scientific Interpretation of Human Spirituality and God, Rogue Press, New York, NY, 2000

Emmanuel Anati. La religion des origines, Bayard, Paris, 1999

Eugene d'Aquili and Andrew B. Newberg. The Mystical Mind: Probing the Biology of Religious Experience, Fortress Press, Minneapolis, MN, 1999

Mark Aronoff and Kirsten Fudeman. What is Morphology? Blackwell Publishing, Malden, MA, 2007

Nicolas Asher and Alex Lascarides. Logics of Conversation, Cambridge University Press, Cambridge, UK, 2003

Scott Atran. In Gods We Trust: The Evolutionary Landscape of Religion, Oxford University Press, New York, NY, 2002

James H. Austin. Zen and the Brain, MIT Press, Cambridge, MA, 1999

Louise Barrett, Robin Dunbar and John Lycett. Human Evolutionary Psychology, Princeton University Press, Princeton, NJ, 2002

John D. Barrow, Paul C. W. Davies Jr and Charles L. Harper, Jr , editors. Science and Ultimate Reality: Quantum Theory, Cosmology, and Complexity, Cambridge University Press, Cambridge, UK, 2004

Roland Barthes. Mythologies, Vintage, New York, NY, 1993

Frank R. Baumgartner and Bryan D. Jones, editors. Policy Dynamics, The University of Chicago Press, Chicago, IL, 2002

Spencer Baynes and W. Robertson Smith, editors. Encyclopaedia Britannica, Ninth Edition, Werner, Akron, OH, 1907, digitized by Google at the University of Virginia

Sharon Begley. Train Your Mind, Change Your Brain, Ballantine Books, NewYork, NY, 2007

The Holy Bible: Standard Edition, Thomas Nelson & Sons, New York, 1901 (referred to in the text as the Christian Bible)

Derek Bickerton. Language and Species, The University of Chicago Press, Chicago, MI, 1990

Howard Bloom. The Lucifer Principle: A Scientific Expedition into the Forces of History, Atlantic Monthly Press, New York, NY, 1995

Geert Booij. The Grammar of Words, Oxford University Press, Oxford, UK, 2005

Book of Order, Presbyterian Church USA, Louisville, KY, 1988-89

Daniel J. Boorstin. The Creators: A History of Heroes of the Imagination, Vintage Press, New York, NY, 1992

Daniel J. Boorstin. The Discoverers: A History of Man's Search to Know His World and Himself, Vintage Press, New York, NY, 1985

Denis Bouchard. The Semantics of Syntax: A Minimalist Approach to Grammar, The University of Chicago Press, Chicago, MI, 1995

Pascal Boyer. Religion Explained: The Evolutionary Origins of Religious Thought, Basic Books, New York, NY, 2001

Christine Brooke-Rose. A Grammar of Metaphor, Secker and Warburg, London, 1958

Walter Burkert. Creation of the Sacred: Tracks of Biology in Early Religions, Harvard University Press, Cambridge, MA, 1996

Chris R. Calladine, Horace R. Drew, Ben F. Luisi and Andrew A. Travers. Understanding DNA: The Molecule and How It Works, Elsevier Academic Press, London, UK, 2004

Louis-Jean Calvet. Histoire de l'écriture, Hachette, Paris, France, 1996

Orson Scott Card. Ender's Game, Tom Doherty Associates, New York, NY, 1991

Sean B. Carroll. Endless Forms Most Beautiful: The New Science of EVO DEVO, W.W. Norton and Company, New York, NY, 2005

Rita Carter. Mapping the Mind, University of California Press, Berkeley, CA, 1998

Luigi Luca Cavalli-Sforza. Genes, Peoples, and Languages, University of California Press, Berkeley, CA, 2001

John Chadwick. The Decipherment of Linear B, Cambridge University Press, Cambridge, UK, 1958

Jorge Fernandez Chiti. La simbólica en la cerámica indígena argentina, Condorhuasi, Buenos Aires, Argentina, 1998

Clayton M. Christensen. The Innovator's Dilemma, Harper, New-York, NY, 2000

Noam Chomsky. Aspects of the Theory of Syntax, MIT Press, Cambridge, MA, 1970

Grahame Clark. World Prehistory in New Perspective, Cambridge University Press, Cambridge, England, Third Edition, 1977

Jean Clottes and Jean Courting. The Cave Beneath the Sea: Paleolithic Images at Cosquer, Harry N. Abrams, New York, NY, 1996

Jean Clottes et David Lewis-Williams. Les chamanes de la préhistoire: Transe et magie dans les grottes ornées, Seuil, Paris, France, 1996

George Elwes Corrie, editor. Sermons by Hugh Latimer, Cambridge University Press, Cambridge, England, 1844, digitized by Google at the New York Public Library

Tim J. Crow, editor. The Speciation of Modern Homo sapiens, Oxford University Press, Oxford, UK, 2002

Antonio Damasio. Descartes' Error: Emotion, Reason, and the Human Brain, Penguin Books, New York, NY, 1994

Charles Darwin. The Origin of Species, Gramercy Books, 1979

Richard Dawkins. The Selfish Gene, Oxford University Press, New York, NY, 1989

Richard Dawkins. The God Delusion, Transworld Publishers, London, England, 2006

Terrence W. Deacon. The Symbolic Species: The Co-evolution of Language and the Brain, W.W. Norton and Company, New York, NY, 1997

Daniel C. Dennett. Kinds of Minds: Toward an Understanding of Consciousness, Basic Books, New York, NY, 1996

Jared Diamond. Collapse: How Societies Choose to Fail or Succeed, Viking Penguin, New York, NY, 2005

Jared Diamond. Guns, Germs, and Steel: The Fates of Human Societies, W.W. Norton and Company, New York, NY, 1999

Jared Diamond. The Third Chimpanzee: The Evolution and Future of the Human Animal, Harper Perennial, New York, NY, 1993

Ellen Dissanayake. Homo Aestheticus: Where Art Comes From and Why, University of Washington Press, Seattle, 1992

Merlin Donald. A Mind So Rare: The Evolution of Human Consciousness, W.W. Norton and Company, New York, NY, 2001

Merlin Donald. Origin of the Modern Mind: Three Stages in the Evolution of Culture and Cognition, Harvard University Press, Cambridge, MA, 1991

S. N. Dorogovtsev and J.F.F. Mendes. Evolution of Networks: From Biological Nets to the Internet and WWW, Oxford University Press, New York, NY, 2002

Robin Dunbar. Grooming, Gossip, and the Evolution of Language, Harvard University Press, Cambridge, MA, 1996

Will Durant. The Story of Civilization; Volume 6 - The Reformation, MJF Books, New York, 1957

Will and Ariel Durant. The Story of Civilization: Volume 7 - The Age of Reason Begins, MJF Books, New York, 1961

Émile Durkheim. Les formes élémentaires de la vie religieuse: Le système totémique en Australie, Quadrige/PUF, Paris, France, 1960

Gerald Edelman. Wider than the Sky: The Phenomenal Gift of Consciousness, Donnelley & Sons, New York, NY, 2004

Paul Ekman and Richard J. Davidson. The Nature of Emotion: Fundamental Questions, Oxford University Press, Oxford, 1994

Mircea Eliade. Shamanism: Archaic Techniques of Ecstasy, Princeton University Press, Princeton, NJ, 1964

Walter Farquhar Hook. Church Dictionary, John Murray, London, England, 1859, digitized by Google at Oxford University

Karen Farrington. The History of Religion, Barnes & Noble, Inc. by arrangement with Octopus Publishing Group Limited, China, 1998

Gilles Fauconnier. Mental Spaces: Aspects of Meaning Construction in Natural Language, MIT Press, Cambridge, MA, 1985

Gilles Fauconnier and Mark Turner. The Way We Think: Conceptual Blending and the Mind's Hidden Complexities, Basic Books, New York, NY, 2002

Armando R. Favazza. Bodies Under Siege: Self-mutilation and Body Modification in Culture and Psychiatry, Johns Hopkins University Press, Baltimore, MD, 1987

James W. Fernandez, editor. Beyond Metaphor: The Theory of Tropes in Anthropology, Stanford University Press, Stanford, CA, 1991

Alejandro Eduardo Fiadone. El Diseño indígena argentino: Una aproximación estética a la iconografía precolombina, la marca editora, Buenos Aires, Argentina, 2006

Martha Fletcher Bellinger. A Short History of the Drama, Henry Holt, New York, NY, 1939

David Friedel, Linda Schele and Joy Parker. Maya Cosmos: Three Thousand Years on the Shaman's Path, Quill, New-York, NY, 1993

Anne Foerst. God in the Machine: What Robots Teach Us About Humanity and God, Dutton, New York, NY, 2004

René Girard. La violence et le sacré, Grasset, Paris, France, 1972 [Translation by P. Gregory. Violence and the Sacred, The Johns Hopkins University Press, Baltimore, MA, 1977]

René Girard. Les origines de la culture, Desclée de Brouwer, Paris, France, 2004

Kurt Gödel. Collected Works, Oxford University Press, New York, NY, 1995

Temple Grandin and Catherine Johnson. Animals in Translation: Using the Mysteries of Autism to Decode Animal Behavior, Scribner, New York, NY, 2005

Robert Graves. The White Goddess: A historical grammar of poetic myth, Farrar, Straus and Giroux, New York, 1948

Joseph H. Greenberg. Indo-European and its Closest Relatives: The Eurasiatic Language Family, Stanford University Press, Stanford, CA

Pierre Guiraud. Structures étymologiques du lexique français, Payot, Paris, 1986

Arthur Elam Haigh. The Attic Theater: A Description of the Stage and Theatre of the Athenians, and of the Dramatic Performances at Athens, Clarendon Press, Oxford, England, 1889, digitized by Google at Stanford University

Edward T. Hall. The Hidden Dimension, Anchor Books, Doubleday, Garden City, NY, 1969

Dean Hamer. The God Gene: How Faith Is Hardwired into Our Genes, Doubleday, New-York, NY, 2004

E. Brooks Holifield. Theology in America: Christian Thought from the Age of the Puritans to the Civil War, Yale University Press, New Haven, CT, 2003

Hélène Huot. Morphologie: Forme et sens des mots du français, Armand Colin, Paris, France, 2001

Keith Johnstone. Improvisation and the Theatre, Routledge, NY, 1992

Eric R. Kandel. In Search of Memory: The Emergence of a New Science of Mind, W.W. Norton, New-York, NY, 2006

Hans Kamp and Uwe Reyle. From Discourse to Logic: Introduction to Modeltheoretic Semantics of Natural Language, Formal Logic and Discourse Representation Theory, Kluwer Academic Publishers, Dordrecht, The Netherlands, 1993

Stuart A. Kauffman. The Origins of Order: Self-Organization and Selection in Evolution, Oxford University Press, New York, NY, 1993

Barbara J. King. Evolving God, Doubleday, New-York, NY, 2007

Donald E. Knuth. Things a Computer Scientist Rarely Talks About, CSLI Publications, Stanford, California, 2001

Arthur Kornberg and Tania A. Baker. DNA Replication, University Science Books, Sausalito, CA, 2005

George Lakoff and Mark Johnson. Metaphors We Live By, University of Chicago Press, Chicago, MI, 1980

George Lakoff and Mark Johnson. Philosophy in The Flesh: The Embodied Mind and Its Challenge to Western Thought, Basic Books, New York, NY, 1999.

George Lakoff and Rafael Núñez. Where Mathematics Come From: How the Embodied Mind Brings Mathematics into Being, Basic Books, New York, NY, 2000

Jean-Baptiste Lamarck. Philosophie zoologique, GF-Flammarion, Paris, France, 1994

Ronald W. Langacker. Foundations of Cognitive Grammar, Stanford University Press, Stanford, CA, 1987 (vol I) and 1991 (vol II)

Richard Leakey and Roger Lewin. Origins Reconsidered: In Search of What Makes Us Human, Anchor Books, Doubleday, New York, NY, 1992

André Leroi-Gourhan. Le fil du temps, Ethnologie et préhistoire, Librairie Arthème Fayard, Paris, France, 1983

G. Rachel Levy. Religious Conceptions of the Stone Age and Their Influence Upon European Thought, Harper and Row, New York, NY, 1963

Michael Lewis and Jeannette M. Haviland-Jones. Handbook of Emotions, The Guilford Press, New York, 2000

J. David Lewis-Williams. A Cosmos in Stone, AltaMira Press, Walnut Creek, CA, 2002

David Lewis-Williams. The Mind in the Cave: Consciousness and the Origins of Art, Thames and Hudson, London, 2002

Douglas Lockwood. I, the Aboriginal, Rigby, Adelaide, Australia, 1962

Marcel Locquin (avec Vahé Zartarian). Quelle langue parlaient nos ancêtres préhistoriques? Albin Michel, Paris, France, 2002

Earl R. Mac Cormac. A Cognitive Theory of Metaphor, MIT Press, Cambridge, MA, 1985

Paul D. MacLean. The Triune Brain in Evolution: Role in Paleocerebral Functions, Plenum Press, New York, NY, 1990

JP Mallory. In Search of the Indo-Europeans: Language, Archaeology and Myth, Thames and Hudson, London, 1989

William Manchester. A World Lit Only By Fire: The Medieval Mind and the Renaissance, Little, Brown and Company, London, 1992

Abraham H. Maslow. The Farther Reaches of Human Nature, Viking Press, New York, NY, 1972

Abraham H. Maslow. Toward a Psychology of Being, Van Nostrand Reinhold Company, New York, NY, 1968

Ernst Mayr. Systematics and the Origin of Species from the Viewpoint of a Zoologist, Columbia University Press, New York, NY 1947

Alister McGrath. Dawkins' God: Genes, Memes, and the Meaning of Life, Blackwell Publishing, Malden, MA, 2005

Terence McKenna. Food of the Gods: The Search for the Original Tree of Knowledge, Bantam Book, 1992

David McNeil. Hand and Mind: What Gestures Reveal About Thought, University of Chicago Press, Chicago, IL, 1992

Patrick Michel, éditeur. Religion et Démocraties, Albin Michel, Paris, France, 1997

Steven Mithen. The Prehistory of the Mind: The Cognitive Origins of Art and Science, Thames and Hudson, London, 1996

Steven Mithen. The Singing Neanderthals: The Origins of Music, Language, Mind, and Body, Harvard University Press, Cambridge, MA, 2006

Richard Montague. Formal Philosophy, Yale University Press, London, England, 1974

Montesquieu. Oeuvres Complètes, La Pléiade, Gallimard, Paris, France, 1949

Pierre-Louis Moreau de Maupertuis. Essai de cosmologie, Oeuvres de Mr. de Maupertuis, Tome premier, Jean-Marie Bruyset, Libraire, Lyon, France, 1761, digitized by Google at Oxford University

Pierre-Louis Moreau de Maupertuis. Vénus physique, Oeuvres de Maupertuis, Tome second, Jean-Marie Bruyset, Imprimeur-Libraire, Lyon, France, 1768, digitized by Google at Oxford University

Madhusree Mukerjee. The Land of Naked People: Encounters with Stone Age Islanders, Houghton Mifflin, New York, NY, 2003

Larry Niven and Jerry Pournelle. Oath of Fealty, Simon & Schuster, New York, NY, 1981

George Orwell. Nineteen Eighty Four, Penguin Books Ltd., London, 1970

Roger Penrose. The Emperor's New Mind, Oxford University Press, New York, NY, 1989

Michael A. Persinger. Neuropsychological Bases of God Belief, Praeger Publishers, New York, NY, 1987

Jean Piaget. La psychologie de l'intelligence, Armand Colin, Paris, France, 1967 (The Psychology of Intelligence, Routledge, London, UK, 2001)

Jean Piaget et Bärbel Inhelder. La psychologie de l'enfant, Presses Universitaires de France, 2004 (Psychology of the Child, Basic Books, New-York, NY, 1969)

Jérôme Pierrat et Alexandre Sargos. Yakusa, Enquête au coeur de la mafia japonaise, Flammarion, Paris, France, 2005

Steven Pinker. The Language Instinct: How the Mind Creates Language, HarperCollins, New York, NY, 1994

Alfred-Louis de Prémare. Les fondations de l'Islam: Entre écriture et histoire, Éditions du Seuil, Paris, France, 2002

V.S. Ramachandran and Sandra Blakeslee. Phantoms in the Brain: Probing the Mysteries of the Human Mind, HarperCollins, New York, NY, 1998

Colin Renfrew. Archaelogy and Language: The Puzzle of Indo-European Origins, Cambridge University Press, New York, NY, 1990

Peter J. Richerson and Robert Boyd. Not by Genes Alone: How Culture Transformed Human Evolution, The University of Chicago Press, Chicago, MI, 2005

Andrew Robinson. Lost Languages: The Enigma of the World's Undeciphered Scripts, McGraw-Hill, New York, NY, 2002

Robert John Russel, William R. Stoeger, S.J. and Francisco J. Ayala, editors. Evolutionary and Molecular Biology: Scientific Perspective on Divine Action, The University of Notre-Dame Press, Notre Dame, IN, 1998

H.W.F. Saggs. Civilization before Greece and Rome, Yale University Press, New Haven and London, 1989

Sue Savage-Rumbaugh, Stuart G. Shanker and Talbot J. Taylor. Apes, Language, and the Human Mind, Oxford University Press, New York, NY, 2001

Philippe Schaff, editor. A Select Library of the Nicene and Post-Nicene Fathers of the Christian Church, Volume I, The Confessions and Letters of St Augustin, The Christian Literature Company, Buffalo, NY, 1886, digitized by Google at the Stanford University Library

Adam Smith. The Wealth of Nations, Bantam Dell, New York, NY, 2003

Winifred Smith. The Commedia Dell'Arte: A Study in Italian Popular Comedy, Columbia University Press, New York, NY, 1912, scanned by Google at the New York Public Library

Constantin Stanislavski. An Actor Prepares, Routledge, New York, NY, 1989

Publius Cornelius Tacitus. The Annals of Imperial Rome, translated by Michael Grant, Penguin Books, London, 1996

Charles Taylor. A Secular Age, Harvard University Press, Cambridge, MA, 2007

John R. Taylor. Cognitive Grammar, Oxford University Press, New York, NY, 2002

Rod Thornton. Asymmetric Warfare: Threat and Response in the 21st Century, Polity Press, Cambridge, UK, 2007

Michael Tomasello. Constructing a Language: A Usage-Based Theory of Language Acquisition, Harvard University Press, Cambridge, MA, 2003

Michael Tomasello. The Cultural Origins of Human Cognition, Harvard University Press, Cambridge, MA, 1999

Frederick Jackson Turner. History, Frontier, and Section: Three Essays, The University of New Mexico Press, 1993

Victor Turner. The Anthropology of Performance, PAJ Publications, New York, NY, 1988

Frans de Waal. The Ape and the Sushi Master: Cultural Reflections of a Primatologist, Basic Books, New York, NY, 2001

Frans de Waal. Chimpanzee Politics: Power and Sex among Apes, Johns Hopkins, Baltimore, MD, 1998

Frans de Waal & Frans Lanting. Bonobo: The Forgotten Ape, University of California Press, Berkeley, CA, 1997

Frans de Waal and Peter Tyack. Animal Social Complexity: Intelligence, Culture, and Individualized Societies, Harvard University Press, Cambridge, Massachusetts, 2003

Duncan J. Watts. Six Degrees: The Science of A Connected Age, W.W. Norton and Company, New York, NY, 2004

Duncan J. Watts. Small Worlds: The Dynamics of Networks between Order and Randomness, Princeton University Press, Princeton, NJ, 1999

Anne Wells Branscomb. Who Owns Information? Basic Books, New York, NY, 1994

H.G. Wells. The War of the Worlds, Ann Arbor Media, Ann Arbor, MI, 2006

David Sloan Wilson. Darwin's Cathedral: Evolution, Religion, and the Nature of Society, The University of Chicago Press, Chicago, MI, 2002

Terry Winograd. Understanding Natural Language, Academic Press, New York, NY, 1972

Stephen Wolfram. A New Kind of Science, Wolfram Media, Champaign, IL, 2002

# Books (computers)

As with any technical domain, books in Computer Science come in various shape and form. Some of the books here are seminal books, some are reference books, and others are just interesting from an historical perspective. They all shaped our understanding and practice of the art.

Harold Abelson and Gerald Jay Sussman with Julie Sussman. Structure and Interpretation of Computer Programs, MIT Press, Cambridge, MA, 1985

Katherine Albrecht and Liz McIntyre. The Spychips Threat, Why Christians should Resist RFID and Electronic Surveillance, Nelson Current, Nashville, TN, 2006

Ross Anderson, Security Engineering. A Guide to Building Dependable Distributed Systems, John Wiley and Sons, New York, NY, 2001

Grigoris Antoniou and Frank Van Harmelen. A Semantic Web Primer, MIT Press, Cambridge, MA, 2004

Ryan Asleson and Nathaniel T. Schutta. Foundations of Ajax, Springer-Verlag, New York, NY, 2006

Franz Baader, Diego Calvanese, Deborah McGuinness, Danielle Nardi and Peter Patel-Schneider, editors. The Description Logic Handbook: Theory, Implementation and Applications, Cambridge University Press, Cambridge, UK, 2003

Maurice J. Back. The Design of the UNIX Operating System, Prentice-Hall, Englewood Cliffs, NJ, 1986

Stewart A. Baker and Paul R. Hurst. The Limits of Trust: Cryptography, Governments, and Electronic Commerce, Kluwer Law International, The Hague, The Netherlands, 1998

Albert-László Barabási. Linked: The New Science of Networks, Perseus Books, Cambridge, MA, 2002

Kent Beck. Extreme Programming Explained: Embrace Change, Addison-Wesley, Upper Saddle River, NJ, 2000

Ted J. Biggerstaff and Alan J. Perlis. Software Reusability, Addison-Wesley, Reading, MA, 1989

Margaret Boden. Artificial Intelligence and Natural Man, Basic Books, New York, NY, 1977

Daniel P. Bovet and Marco Cesati. Understanding the Linux Kernel, O'Reilly, Sebastopol, CA, 2001

Colin Boyd and Anish Mathuria. Protocols for Authentication and Key Establishment, Springer-Verlag, New York, NY, 2003

Ronald R. Brachman and Hector J. Levesque. Knowledge Representation and Reasoning, Morgan Kaufmann, San Francisco, CA, 2004

Per Brinch-Hansen. The Architecture of Concurrent Programs, Prentice-Hall, Englewood Cliffs, NJ, 1977

Michael Brundage. XQuery, the XML Query Language, Addison-Wesley, Boston, MA, 2004

Carl F. Cargill. Open Systems Standardization, A Business Approach, Prentice Hall, Upper Saddle River, NJ, 1997

Elizabeth Castro. XML for the World Wide Web, Peachpit Press, Berkeley, CA, 2001

Stefano Ceri and Giuseppe Pelagatti. Distributed Databases, Principles and Systems, McGraw-Hill, New-York, NY 1984

K. Mani Chandy and Jayadev Misra. Parallel Program Design: A Foundation, Addison-Wesley, Boston, MA, 1988

David A. Chappell. Enterprise Service Bus, O'Reilly, Sebastopol, CA, 2004

Zhiqun Chen. Java Card Technology for Smart Cards: Architecture and Programmer's Guide, Addison-Wesley, Boston, MA, 2000

George W. Cherry. Parallel Programming in ANSI Standard Ada, Prentice-Hall, Reston, VA

Charles A. Cianfrani, Joseph J. Tsiakals and John E. West. ISO 9001:200 Explained, ASQ Milwaukee, WI, 2001

W.F. Clocksin and C.S. Mellish. Programming in Prolog, Springer-Verlag, Berlin, 1981

O.-J. Dahl, E.E. Dijkstra and C.A.R. Hoare. Structured Programming, Academic Press, New York, NY, 1972

C.J. Date with Hugh Darwen. A Guide to the SQL Standard, Addison-Wesley, New York, NY, 1993

Randall Davis and Douglas B. Lenat. Knowledge-Based Systems in Artificial Intelligence, McGraw-Hill, New-York, NY, 1982

Dieter Fensel. Ontologies: A Silver Bullet for Knowledge Management and Electronic Commerce, Springer-Verlag, Berlin, 2004

Eric Foxley. Unix for Super-Users, Addison-Wesley, Wokingham, England, 1985

Richard P. Gabriel. Performance and Evaluation of Lisp Systems, MIT Press, Cambridge, MA, 1986

Matthew S. Gaist. 802.11 Wireless Networks, The Definitive Guide, O'Reilly, Sebastopol, CA, 2002

Georges Gardarin and Patrick Valduriez. Relational Databases and Knowledge Bases, Addison-Wesley, New York, NY, 1989

Françis Giannesini, Henry Kanoui, Robert Pasero and Michel van Caneghem. Prolog, Addison-Wesley, Wokingham, England, 1986

Robert L. Glass. Real-Time Software, Prentice-Hall, Englewood Cliffs, NJ, 1983

Asunción Gómez-Pérez, Mariano Fernández-López and Oscar Corcho. Ontological Engineering, Springer-Verlag, London, 2004

Peter D. Grünwald. The Minimum Description Length principle, MIT Press, 2007

Peter D. Grünwald, Jae Myung and Mark A. Pitt. Advances in Minimum Description Length, Theory and Applications, MIT Press, Cambridge, MA, 2005

Scott B. Guthery and Mary J. Cronin. Mobile Application Development with the SMS and the SIM Toolkit, McGraw-Hill, New York, NY, 2002

Scott B. Guthery and Timothy M. Jurgensen. Smart Card Developer's Kit, Macmillan Technical Publishing, Indianapolis, IN, 1998

David C. Hay. Data Model Patterns: Conventions of Thought, Dorset House, New-York, NY, 1996

Thomas F. Herbert. The LINUX TCP/IP Stack, Networking for Embedded Systems, Charles River Media, Hingham, MA, 2004

W. Daniel Hillis. The Connection Machine, MIT Press, Cambridge, MA, 1985

Steven Holzner. Perl Black Book, Coriolis, Scottsdale, AZ, 1999

Friedhelm Hukkebrand, editor. GSM and UMTS: The Creation of Global Mobile Communication, Wiley and Sons, New York, NY, 2002

Watts S. Humphrey. Managing the Software Process, Addison-Wesley, New York, NY, 1990

Timothy M. Jurgensen and Scott B. Guthery. Smart Cards, the Developer's Toolkit, Prentice Hall, Upper Saddle River, NJ, 2002

Michael Kay. XPATH 2.0 Programmer's Reference, Wiley, Indianapolis, IN, 2004

Michael Kay. XSLT 2.0 Programmer's Reference, Wiley, Indianapolis, IN, 2004

Brian W. Kernighan. The UNIX Programming Environment, Prentice-Hall, Englewood Cliffs, NJ, 1984

Brian W. Kernighan and P.J. Plauger. The Elements of Programming Style, McGraw-Hill, Boston, MA, 1978

Brian W. Kernighan and Dennis M. Ritchie. The C Programming Language, Prentice-Hall, Englewood Cliffs, NJ, 1978

Tarun Khanna., Foundations of Neural Networks, Addison-Wesley, Reading, MA, 1990

Benjamin Kuipers. Qualitative Reasoning, Modeling and Simulation with Incomplete Knowledge, MIT Press, Cambridge, MA, 1994

Lee W. Lacy. OWL: Representing Information Using the Web Ontology Language, Trafford, Victoria, BC, Canada

Brian A. LaMacchia, Matthew Lyons, Sebastian Lange, Rudi Martin and Kevin T. Price. .NET Framework Security, Pearson Education, Indianapolis, IN, 2002

Christopher G. Langdon, editor. Artificial Life III, Addison-Wesley, Reading, MA, 1994

Henry Ledgard. ADA An Introduction and Reference Manual (July 1980), Springer-Verlag, New York, NY, 1981

Donald Lewine. POSIX Programmer's Guide: Writing Portable UNIX Programs, O'Reilly, Sebastopol, CA, 1991

Tim Lindholm and Frank Yellin. The Java Virtual Machine Specification, Addison-Wesley, Boston, MA, 1997

Anton Meijer and Paul Peeters. Computer Network Architectures, Computer Science Press, London, UK, 1982

Alfred J. Menezes, Paul C. van Oorschot and Scott A. Vanstone. Handbook of Applied Cryptography, CRC Press, Boca Raton, FL, 1997

Eric T. Mueller. Common Sense Reasoning, Morgan Kaufmann, San Francisco, CA, 2006

Mark O'Neill, Phillip Hallam-Baker, Sean Mac Cann, Mike Shema, Ed Simon, Paul A. Watters and Andrew White, Web Services Security, Osborne, Berkeley, CA, 2003

Shelley Powers. Practical RDF, O'Reilly, Sebastopol, CA, 2003

Roger S. Pressman. Software Engineering, A Practioner's Approach, McGraw-Hill, Boston, MA, 2001

Guy Pujolle. Sécurité Wi-Fi, Eyrolles, Paris, France, 2004

W.J. Quirk, editor. Verification and Validation of Real-Time Software, Springer-Verlag, Berlin, Germany, 1985

W. Rankl and W. Effing. Smart Card Handbook, John Wiley and Sons, Chichester, England, 2001

Marc J. Rochkind. Advanced UNIX Programming, Prentice-Hall, Englewood Cliffs, NJ, 1985

Scott Seely. SOAP, Cross Platform Web Service Development using XML, Prentice Hall, Upper Saddle River, NJ, 2002

Michael Rosen and David Curtis. Integrating CORBA and COM Applications, John Wiley and Sons, New York, NY, 1998

James Rumbaugh, Ivar Jacobson and Grady Booch. The Unified Modeling Language Reference Manual, Addison Wesley, Reading, MA, 1999

Bruce Schneier. Applied Cryptography, John Wiley and Sons, New York, NY, 1996

Thomas B. Sheridan. Humans and Automation: System Design and Research Issue, John Wiley and Sons, New York, NY, 2002

Edward Hance Shortliffe. Computer-Based Medical Consultations: MYCIN, Elsevier, New York, NY, 1976

Avi Silberschatz. Peter Baer Galvin, Greg Gagne, Operating Systems Concepts, John Wiley and Sons, New York, NY, 2002

Olivier Sims. Business Objects, Delivering Cooperative Objects for Client-Server, McGraw-Hill, Cambridge, UK, 1994

Richard E. Smith. Authentication: From Passwords to Public Keys, Pearson, Upper Saddle River, NJ, 2002

Guy L. Steele Jr. Common LISP, The Language, Digital Press, Burlington, MA, 1984

Bjarne Stroustrup. The C++ Programming Language, Addison-Wesley, Reading, MA, 1991

Frank Swiderski and Window Snyder. Threat Modeling, Microsoft Press, Redmond, WA, 2004

Andrew S. Tanenbaum. Computer Networks, Englewood Cliffs, NJ, 1988

Bruce A. Tate and Curt Hibbs. Ruby on Rails, Up and Running, O'Reilly Media, Sebastopol, CA, 2006

Andrew Troelsen. C# and the .NET Platform, Springer-Verlag, New York, NY, 2001

Jeffrey D. Ullman. Principles of Database and Knowledge-Base Systems, Computer Science Press, Rockville, MA, 1988

John Warnock. PostScript Language, Addison-Wesley, Reading, MA, 1985

Peter Wegner. Programming with Ada: An Introduction by Means of Graduated Examples, Prentice-Hall, Englewood Cliffs, NJ, 1980

Andrew White. Web Services Security, Osborne, Berkeley, CA, 2003

Patrick Henry Winston. Artificial Intelligence, Addison-Wesley, Reading, MA, 1977

Nicklaus Wirth. Algorithms and Data Structures, Prentice-Hall, NJ, 1976

Nicklaus Wirth. Programming in Modula-2, Springer-Verlag, Berlin, 1982

S.J. Young. Real Time Languages, Design and Development, John Wiley and Sons, New York, NY, 1982

# Articles and Presentations

Apostol T. Vassilev, Bertrand du Castel and Asad M. Ali. Personal Brokerage of Web Service Access, IEEE Transactions on Security and Privacy, Volume 5, Number 5, September/October 2007

Tim Berners-Lee, James A. Hendler and Ora Lassila. The Semantic Web, Scientific American, May 2001

Bertrand du Castel. Form and Interpretation of Relative Clauses in English, Linguistic Inquiry Volume 9 Number 2 (Spring, 1978), 275-289 (MIT Press)

Bertrand du Castel and Yi Mao. Generics and Metaphors Unified under a Four-Layer Semantic Theory of Concepts, Acts of the Third Conference on Experience and Truth, Soochow University, Taipei, Taiwan, 2006

Bertrand du Castel. Intelligence in "Artificial" Wireless (Death of the Washing Machine), Innovative Applications of Artificial Intelligence Invited Talk, American Association of Artificial Intelligence Annual Conference, Austin, Texas, 2000

Saar Drimer and Steven Murdoch. Keep your enemies close: Distance bounding against smartcard relay attacks, 16th USENIX Security Symposium in September, 2007

Vittorio Gallese and George Lakoff. The Brain's Concepts: The Role of the Sensory-Motor System in Reason and Language, Cognitive Neuropsychology, 2005, 22:455-479

Nils Eldridge and Stephen J. Gould. Punctuated equilibria: an alternative to phyletic gradualism, from *Models in Paleobiology* edited by T.J.M. Schopf: Freeman, Cooper and Company, San Francisco, pp. 82-115, 1972

Thomas R. Gruber. A Translation Approach to Portable Ontology Specifications. Knowledge Acquisition, 5(2):199-220, 1993

Mikko Hypponen. Malware Goes Mobile, Scientific American, November 2006

Michael Kosfeld, Markus Heinrichs, Paul J. Zak, Urs Fischbacher and Ernst Fehr. Oxytocin increases trust in humans, Nature, June 2005

Giacomo Rizzolati, Leonardo Fogassi and Vittorio Gallese. Mirrors in the Mind, Scientific American, November 2006

Julian B. Rotter. A new scale for the measurement of interpersonal trust, Journal of Personality, 35 (4), 651-665, 1967

Paul J. Zak. The Neurobiology of Trust, Scientific American, June 2008

# World Wide Web

While we obviously used the World Wide Web to maximum extent, we made it a principle to go as much as possible from information on the Web to the original published sources, with a preference for book references. We are indebted to the innumerable contributors to the Web, who made this multi-disciplinary book possible by pointing us most of the time in the most fruitful direction of investigation. Actual references to the Web will be found directly in the text.

# Index

**N**

Index